Writing Through Music

Writing Through Music
Essays on Music, Culture, and Politics

Jann Pasler
WITH A FOREWORD BY GEORGE LEWIS

OXFORD
UNIVERSITY PRESS

2008

XFORD
UNIVERSITY PRESS

...sity Press, Inc., publishes works that further
Oxford University's objective of excellence
in research, scholarship, and education.

Oxford   New York
...nd   Cape Town   Dar es Salaam   Hong Kong   Karachi
...ala Lumpur   Madrid   Melbourne   Mexico City   Nairobi
New Delhi   Shanghai   Taipei   Toronto

With offices in
Argentina   Austria   Brazil   Chile   Czech Republic   France   Greece
Guatemala   Hungary   Italy   Japan   Poland   Portugal   Singapore
South Korea   Switzerland   Thailand   Turkey   Ukraine   Vietnam

Published by Oxford University Press, Inc.
198 Madison Avenue, New York, New York 10016

www.oup.com

Oxford is a registered trademark of Oxford University Press

Library of Congress Cataloging-in-Publication Data
Pasler, Jann.
Writing through music : essay on music, culture, and politics /
Jann Pasler.—1st ed.
p. cm.
ISBN 978-0-19-532489-1
1. Music—Social aspects.   2. Music—History and criticism.   I. Title.
ML3916.P37 2007
780.9—dc22   2006037220

1   3   5   7   9   8   6   4   2

Printed in the United States of America
on acid-free paper

For my mother, Josephine Pasler,

who infused my life with music and unconditional love

~

Foreword

GEORGE E. LEWIS

RINGING TOGETHER a group of the most important and influential recent essays by a major scholar whose work bridges musicology, ethnomusicology, the sociology of art, and other fields, Jann Pasler's *Writing Through Music* directly confronts one of the most perplexing anomalies in public intellectual discourse. In recent years, it has become evident that, in contrast to previous eras, the work of many of the best known public intellectuals of our time seems distanced from musical considerations, and from new and experimental music in particular. As a result, the practice of culturally and philosophically theorizing contemporary nonliterary, nonvisual texts tends to become marginalized and devalued in the public sphere—not because music scholars are not producing these works but, perhaps, simply because it is somehow assumed that music has little to teach us about the critical issues of our time.

Pasler's introduction to this book moves quickly and forthrightly to counter the effects of this lacuna, by presenting an ambitious, well-argued agenda for reasserting the centrality of music study to contemporary intellectual discourse. Implicitly accepting as given the interdisciplinary landscape in which contemporary scholars operate allows Pasler to move directly to an explanation of how her methods of theorizing music draw on music's own most basic strengths. In a very real sense, scholars in many other fields could benefit from using music as, paraphrasing Pasler, a lens that focuses the analysis.

Pasler acknowledges the debates that have animated musicological discussions in recent years, including canon formation, *Werktreue*, the role of the so-called extramusical, and so on. At the same time, her introduction is a ringing call to bring together the insights drawn from these debates in the service of a greater and more ambitious historiographical agenda. Pasler demonstrates that one crucial way of writing through music is to acknowledge that music scholars need to write "through" their own field to address others—not by simply deploying the tools and methods of other fields (the standard version of "interdisciplinarity") but by (again in Pasler's words) using music as a critical tool to analyze contemporary critical, cultural, historical, and social issues whose importance cuts across fields. Here, it is not interdisciplinarity itself that matters, but the kinds of interpretational catholicity that an interdisciplinary landscape makes possible.

This book introduces a younger generation of scholars to Pasler's work, and allows Anglophone readers access to those pieces whose primary impact has been on those able to read the work in its originally published Francophone versions. This alone would have a salutary impact on the field of music scholarship. However, this collection promises a considerably greater impact, in that in Pasler's hands, the study of music becomes a prime site for the investigation of the nature of meaning itself. By prodding music scholars toward a similarly ambitious agenda, Pasler seeks to provide intellectual leadership; by deploying contemporary critical methods in innovative and often ingenious ways, she points the way toward the new historiographies that can arise from sustained engagement with music.

Both "Narrative and Narrativity in Music" and the later "Postmodernism, Narrativity, and the Art of Memory" have exercised considerable influence among scholars since they first appeared, not least because of the way they remedy the rather tardy (and sometimes still grudging) engagement of music theory and musicology with postmodern theory. The second essay in particular continues to challenge music scholars to engage with the implications of a globalized condition of musical postmodernity, rather than simply repositioning particular works and composers as "postmodern" with an eye toward recharging their cachet.

Pasler is one of the most influential of her generation of scholars of nineteenth-century French music, and her use of this period as a platform for investigating twentieth-century postmodernity need not be seen as ironic or incongruous. Her mature theory of inquiry centers on her positing of "question-spaces" that permit a fluidity of interaction with the historicity of events and individuals. These question-spaces, in turn, open up complex networks that evince the interdependence among musical, political, social, and cultural structures. Traditional notions of "extramusicality" have no place in such a conception. Just as literary scholars have drawn new meaning from exploring the "textuality" of social practice, a similar freedom of reference should encourage scholars to develop new insights about larger-scale societal organization and interaction through a well-theorized "musicality." In this way, Pasler draws important theoretical insights from compositional methodologies such as those of Pauline Oliveros or John Cage, a fact that lends further credence to her assertion of the intrinsic centrality of music study to intellectual inquiry and human experience.

One expects that "Resituating the Spectral Revolution," which explores the intellectual and social antecedents of spectral music, will have particular resonance in the North American context, just as French spectralism is now emerging as an important musical methodology among a younger generation of composers from that part of the world. The paucity of serious Anglophone critical perspectives on spectralism is well redressed by this essay, which, in distinction even to French-language writing on the subject, includes perspectives on the cultural articulation between science and race, along with the more usually invoked scientific and philosophical perspectives in the musical-theoretical literature.

The vivid New Historicist approach taken in "Deconstructing D'Indy" finds Pasler navigating a complex network of articulations among individual ambitions, aesthetic directions, assertions of national pride and nativism, government-driven cultural policies, ethnic essentialisms, and international competition for cultural capital. Demystifying the *métier* of the composer, in Pasler's account Vincent D'Indy's founding of the Schola Cantorum appears as a crucial expression of self-fashioning—unto death and beyond.

Indeed, self-fashioning appears as a major unifying theme in this book, as the essays on D'Indy, Augusta Holmes, Jean Cocteau, and John Cage all attest. In each piece, the artist is shown to be crucially concerned with reputation; in each, the artist interacts with contemporaneous ironies of race, national identity, and gender, overarching aspects of Pasler's methods of inquiry that stand apart from much of the work on European classical music. In these pieces, Pasler's poststructuralist approach seems to me to point toward a notion of reputation as Sisyphean recursion; however carefully constructed with an eye toward both immediate political careerism and a species of historically oriented altruism, reputations seem in the end to bob with the tides of history like fragile bits of seaweed.

"New Music as Confrontation" is a signal contribution to studies of Cocteau and Stravinsky, and "The Ironies of Gender, or Virility and Politics in the Music of Augusta Holmes" finds the author at her very best in contextualizing nineteenth-century French music in ways that resonate with twentieth- and twenty-first-century histories. The thoroughness and care with which Pasler mines and sifts the archival evidence is matched by a sophisticated gender analysis that, as with the work of other contemporary scholars outside the musicological field, insists on the necessary articulation of gender analysis with race. Similarly, "Countess Greffulhe as Entrepreneur" demonstrates the crucial relevance of perspectives from fin de siecle France to contemporary gender ideologies.

"Inventing a Tradition" is one of the most important recent essays on Cage, and one that breaks with the tendency in some older Cage studies toward the avoidance of criticality where the composer, his life, and his work are concerned. The work challenges Cage scholars to engage more deeply with newer directions in American studies that oblige an informed engagement with issues of race, class, and national identity that were critical to the period in U.S. history in which Cage produced his most influential work. The same approach to historiography marks "*Pelléas* and Power," as well as the groundbreaking "Race, Orientalism, and Distinction," in which Pasler brings musicology face to face with the postcolonial in ways that are resonant with the work of a younger generation of scholars.

"The Political Economy of Composition in the American University, 1965–1985" (originally published in French as "Musique et Institution aux États-Unis") invites parallels with Pierre-Michel Menger's book *Le Paradoxe du Musicien*, a pioneering study of support infrastructures for twentieth-century French composers. However, Pasler's long and searching essay stands practically alone in the Anglophone literature for its detailed examination of the history of the university composer in the United States. Although the most evident antecedents for Pasler's work here lie in the sociology of art, historical and ethnographic techniques take their places alongside the sociological in the creation of the piece's impact. Her analysis of the impact of gender and race on support systems for American composers includes, notably, an effective presentation of data documenting the dominance of northeastern white males as grant recipients and peer-review panelists. Despite the fact that the piece ends its inquiry in the mid-1980s, its findings remain salient today.

The last two essays, "Concert Programs and their Narratives as Emblems of Ideology" and "Material Culture and Postmodern Populism," are centered on what Pasler calls "the everyday life of the past." For Pasler, interrogating the quotidian reveals the historical value that can accrue when scholars reorient their methods of archival research in the direction of material culture. Applying twentieth-century techniques of media analysis, Pasler contributes to a prehistory of the notions of popular culture and mass culture, reclaiming these for the nineteenth century. With a practiced and detailed eye, Pasler shows what these artifacts reveal about the social and economic implications of consumption patterns, a topic that has greatly interested scholars of twentieth-century popular culture.

The pieces demonstrate Pasler's unique ability to show the connections between such seemingly prosaic, leaf-level archival minutiae as the payment of a long-forgotten ancillary chorus and forest-level concerns such as the privileges of the aristocracy, ideologies of national identity, and the assertion of agency by women in the field of music production. Her inclusion of detail is never gratuitous but is always in the service of a larger theoretical agenda. Along the way, she points up the ironic contrast between nineteenth-century Paris, with its regular presentation of new music in such popular venues as the Bon Marché department store (a tradition that, as it happens, continues with alacrity in present-day Japan), and our own era, with its constructed canon of great works that, as Pasler and Lydia Goehr have pointed out, encourages the presumption that music by long-dead composers has always dominated concert life.

Few collections by a single author of which I am aware cover with trenchancy such a wide range of issues, fields, historical periods, composers, and theoretical and cultural perspectives. Even fewer scholars working today are able to combine Jann Pasler's theoretical innovations with a sophisticated cultural analysis that foregrounds a hard and unsentimental look at race, ethnicity, and national identity—still major blind spots in the musicology of the West that, in an era of globalization, work to the disadvantage of the field in terms of its currency relative to other areas of inquiry. Pasler's development of postcolonial perspectives on European music is, I believe, without parallel in the literature that has emerged from her generation of music scholars (I am including the late Edward Said's work on opera here). This book will undoubtedly provoke both younger and older scholars to rethink many of the premises that have characterized the field, while at the same time encouraging general readers to read through music in the way that she writes through it.

Contents

Part IV. PATRONS AND PATRONAGE

Part V. THE EVERYDAY LIFE OF THE PAST

Appendices

Index

Writing Through Music

INTRODUCTION

$\mathcal{M}$Y LOVE FOR MUSIC began in the white living room, where, for years, there was nothing but a Steinway and a record player. My mother had a special touch for Debussy and Chopin, and I would lie under the instrument, listening to her play for hours. My father liked to crank Russian music as loud as we could tolerate through theater-sized McIntosh speakers. I still remember dancing around the room to the *Firebird* suite and *Peter and the Wolf*. Listening was exhilarating and acutely sensual, whether the delicate arabesques of the piano or the powerful, all-enveloping universe of the orchestra. Of course, I played piano as soon as they would let me, later becoming a serious interpreter of twentieth-century repertoire. But growing up in post-*Sputnik* America, I learned to view music as secondary to more substantial pursuits, and so, in college, I majored in math.

Studying in France changed my mind. There, my junior year, I encountered people who experience music as part of culture and civilization and for whom artistic progress engenders national pride. Playing the piano works of Debussy, Ravel, and Fauré while reading French symbolist poetry introduced me to the bold artistic

The concept of "writing through music" arose in correspondence with George Lewis, who first encouraged me to assemble this volume of essays and whose brilliance and generosity of spirit have long been an inspiration to me. I am grateful to George, my doctoral students (Tildy Bayar, Guy Obrecht, and Chris Tonelli), and Nancy Perloff for reading early drafts of this introduction, to Marjorie Perloff for encouraging me to develop a more personal voice in it, and to Juliana Snapper for her editorial expertise. They each made pertinent and helpful suggestions that pushed me to me think more deeply. For stimulating discussions and their contributions to the original form in which these essays first appeared, I would also like to thank Elliott Antokoletz, Georgina Born, Hugues Dufourt, Jean Gribenski, Joseph Kerman, the late Jonathan Kramer, Roberta Marvin, Max Paddison, Marjorie Perloff, Cathy Pickar, Lewis Rowell, Manuela Schwartz, and William Weber, many of whom have become friends through our mutual musical interests. Finally, I am indebted to my editor, Suzanne Ryan, and the perceptive responses of three anonymous readers for their support and enthusiasm, which were essential in helping the project come to fruition.

visions underlying early modernism. I grew curious about correspondences among the arts. The symbolist imagination fascinated me, as did music's power to reveal the dynamism of the mind and abstractions without expressive signification.[1] Such concerns provided my generation with pleasurable escape from the chilling realities of the Cold War. They not only helped shape how we thought and listened, they also transported our attention away from the troublesome social conflicts of the 1960s and 1970s. After my experiences in France persuaded me to focus wholly on music, I turned increasingly to contemporary music. Then in the late 1980s my research in Bali and India introduced me to other value systems as well as other musics, leading me not only to make two documentaries about music in ritual contexts but also to rethink the meaning and the use of music in the West.[2] As the ideology of progress and the avant-garde itself came increasingly under question, the postmodern world reminded us that politics and sociocultural circumstances are part of the creation as well as reception of all art, and that what we know is often linked to what those in power want us to know.

The essays in this volume, spanning over twenty years, trace an intellectual journey that began with the sensuality of sound and the radical new forms composed by Debussy and Stravinsky, then evolved into a need to understand the broader contexts in which music is conceived, created, and enjoyed. Whether it interrogates our perception of time, helps us understand our past in the context of our present, or connects personal to communal identity through the dynamics of gender, sexuality, race, class, and nation, music embodies and helps us understand human experience. It nourishes the private world of individuals, imbues social and political ideals, and shapes civic consciousness, both expressing and producing community. In much of my work, then, I write not just about music but through music.

As the lens that focuses my analysis, I write "through" music in two ways. I do not stop at the notes and their structures, but investigate the questions these formal elements spark. In this sense, music can serve as a critical tool, activating and developing multiple layers of awareness. I also write through music by engaging with the activities and practices associated with music, as well as with the concepts, myths, reputations, and material culture that affect how we hear it. This means investigating elements often considered peripheral to the sound of a work in as much depth and detail as scholars usually devote to the art work itself. Acknowledging the significance of these elements allows me to examine how people negotiate relationships with music, and how musical meaning is often complex and contingent. Through this approach, I aim to ignite and expand musical meaning by

---

1. These interests culminated in my master's thesis, "Paul Valéry and His Concept of Harmony," University of Chicago, 1974.

2. The two documentaries are *Taksu: Music in the Life of Bali* (1991) and *The Great Ceremony to Straighten the World* (1994), both currently distributed by Berkeley Media.

suggesting a dialectical relationship between music and the attitudes, behaviors, and values of the people who produce or consume it.

With my writing, I invite the reader to listen for music's resonance in the world and, through music, to help us imagine our future. For too long, historians have left music out of their stories and in doing so have left out an important part of who we are as individuals and members of society. Putting music back in—not only works, but also performances—and examining the uses to which they were put give us a more integrated experience of our past, as well as a sense of what people have to negotiate in expressing themselves. Understanding the formative function of musical interactions within social identity can help us to understand how cultural artifacts interface with sociopolitical contexts. With its own multiple meanings and uses, even as it ensures the continuity of a tradition, music encourages us to see value where there are differences. In a world with populations and identities in flux, music provides a medium for voicing aspirations, whether consonant with or resistant to dominant ideologies; for cultivating and circulating taste among diverse groups; for sharing experiences and forging relationships without the necessity of being rooted to time and place; and for discovering shared values that transcend discord over the past, present, and future. By writing through this medium, we can enrich our understanding of music's capacity to illuminate meaning itself.

Writing as a Woman and Postmodernist

Over the years I've become increasingly aware of how my perspective as a woman affects the questions I ask, the materials I examine, and the methods I use. The writer Adrienne Rich has famously described "thinking like a woman in a man's world" as a mode of critical engagement that refuses to accept "the givens" and forges unexpected connections between events and ideas. "And it means," Rich writes, "that most difficult thing of all: listening . . . for the silences, the absences, the nameless, the unspoken, the encoded."[3] Thinking and indeed listening "like a woman" have led me to interrogate assumptions such as Western superiority; the story of music as a succession of heroes, and a reflection of the musical tastes and practices of elites; and the march of the canon with works by certain composers inevitably dominating musical life. Acknowledging gender, race, and class differences pulls back the curtains on much of what matters in life, what determines how we see and hear what goes on around us and even how we imagine ourselves. Investigating the forgotten as well as the memorable, the silent as well as the voiced, I have aimed both to deconstruct old stories about the well known and to construct new stories about the little known, giving voice to unspoken relations

3. Adrienne Rich, "Taking Women Students Seriously," quoted in Elizabeth Flynn, "Composing as a Woman," in *Gender in the Classroom*, ed. Susan Gabriel and Isaiah Smithson (Urbana: University of Illinois Press, 1990), 112.

between them. Very often these involve ironies and paradoxes. I have sought not only to contribute new knowledge but also to renew our curiosity and evoke our empathy—two attitudes capable of opening us to the past and present in broader ways. This approach has helped me understand how cultural artifacts of all kinds acquire value, and how values change over time.

All the essays in this book reflect a postmodernist interest in why and how people engage with music. By postmodernist, I mean looking to what the experience means in the largest sense, and what is to be gained from thinking of subjectivity as multilayered, sometimes contradictory, and inevitably performative, that is, the product of what one chooses to enact at a particular time and place. Late nineteenth-century France, a central focus of my scholarship, has much to teach us about why governments and elites might want to make art music increasingly accessible to the masses and encourage listeners to bring music into their lives through sentimental and imaginative listening. They understood its power to stimulate change as well as community, to give people experiences in beauty and harmony while teaching critical judgment. The place of music in French culture at the time helps us understand how deeply meaningful art music can be for all classes of society, especially to the extent that it speaks to one's predilections, needs, and desires. Music allows one to negotiate the complexities of personal identity and to play with an elastic sense of the self vis-à-vis others.

Western art music today is, in part, a result of modernist reaction to the uses people made of music and its increasing commodification at the end of the nineteenth century. As composers began to seek more control over how music was used and reproduced, they also sought more freedom to innovate, to push on conventions and move the boundaries of the possible. Their increasingly difficult music, sometimes an embodiment of complex concepts, encouraged audiences to listen in contemplative admiration. Underestimating the collaborative nature of musical meaning, however, these composers often failed to consider what listeners contribute to the perception of meaning. The modernist focus on composers and works ignored the fact that any musical event also involves diverse groups of listeners at specific times and places, and these dynamics cannot be entirely controlled by the composer or anyone else. Of course, the experience of music is never detachable from the composer's intentions, or merely an opportunity for listeners to "read" a performance as what Frederic Jameson has called a "text," making of it what they will. Even Pauline Oliveros and John Cage, whose music openly depends on significant audience participation, consider their pieces "works" with structural coherence. Still, we need to get beyond modernist constraints on our understanding of music and acknowledge that something valuable is lost when audiences are pushed away from intimate relationships with art music.

My attitude toward interrogating and decrypting the past has nurtured this writing through music. I'm less troubled by postmodern anxieties over facts and the possibility of truths in part because I've read too many biographies and histories that were not about verifiable truth but strategic invention. For better or worse, like music, these represent an understanding rooted in the expression of intuition. If they have narrative coherence, like language they can have symbolic power.[4] Yet what if the purpose of discourse is not to reduce the people or the music one discusses, whether to the writer's personal agenda or to general principles such as style? What if it is instead to flesh out the contingencies and rich complexity of the particular moments in which music was written, performed, and heard? This would entail acknowledging the collective as well as personal experiences music evokes and embodies. And it would include study of the culture music addresses. In order to understand these contingencies, we must focus on musical practices as much as works or ideas, people and events involving distinct or unique social relationships. The truth of contingencies neither collapses into relativism nor aspires to the certainty of principles. Instead it turns discourse into an engagement with the social ontology of music. Its contingencies make space for our contingencies and those of each successive generation.

In order to let music demonstrate how lived experience emerges from the local, the variable, and the contingent, I explore new categories of facts and materials. As with any building blocks, it is the choice of facts, together with what one does with them, that makes them salient.[5] In contemporary music, I've been drawn to how some composers bring nonaesthetic elements into their works and invite audiences to listen to and acknowledge everything they hear, including their own breath. This encourages a new kind of listening in which nonmusicians without specialized musical competency can participate. Such works become recipes for increased awareness of self and other through the medium of sound, as well as for a larger relationship beyond the "work" and the self to the social world. In studying the past, the ephemeral and spontaneous aspects of musical life interest me as much as the works. Materials that others have considered of transient value and ignored or discarded as trivial can clarify what was at stake in a composition, a performance, or a concert.

4. While it is certainly a historian's construction, to the extent that history aspires to represent the past, I agree with Paul Ricoeur in *Memory, History, Forgetting*, trans. Kathleen Blamey and David Pellauer (Chicago: University of Chicago Press, 2004), that it is not fiction (190).

5. In *Memory, History, Forgetting*, Ricoeur comments on the constructed notion of a historical fact and its difference from both empirical fact and event: "A vigilant epistemology will guard here against the illusion of believing that what we call a fact coincides with what really happened." He also warns of the "need to resist the temptation to dissolve the historical fact into narration and this latter into a literary composition indiscernible from fiction" (178–79). When it comes to the word "true," he speaks in the sense of "refutable" and "verifiable" and sees the "search for truth" in history running through "all three levels of historical discourse: at the documentary level, at the level of explanation/understanding, and at the level of the literary representation of the past" (179, 185). Such notions have influenced my use of these terms.

They argue strongly that works are not created or perceived in a vacuum, but are part of an ongoing social dialogue about taste and ideology. With such materials, I urge us to reconsider the subject of our discourse as well as the boundaries that have separated classical and popular music, musicology and ethnomusicology.

SOFT-FOCUS METHODOLOGIES

Writing through music requires a soft-focus approach to asking questions and seeking answers. Questions for me are not so much about interrogating something as engaging in a certain way. Questions give the conversation a place to start. More than answers, it is "question-spaces" that I look for. Question-spaces open up a range of issues embedded in and around music that take us beyond the sounds and the people who made them to the ways they were understood and the uses they served. Such spaces thus help us reconsider not only how we construe analysis and interpretation but also how we write biography and history.[6]

In some ways, question-spaces are an expansion on the hermeneutic method outlined by Hans-Georg Gadamer. For Gadamer, interpretation begins in the effort to understand an experience (such as an art work, performance, or concert) not only through its aesthetic qualities, which may transcend time, but also through its relationship to history and culture. The "hermeneutic universe" elicits the sense that "its world still belongs to ours," that our understanding "belongs to the being of that which is understood."[7] Gadamer frames the search for this understanding in questions more than answers, for questions recognize the "interests guiding us with respect to a given subject matter."[8] When we engage with a work of art, we

6. These concepts originated in my correspondence with the composer/theorist Ben Boretz. In my review "Some Thoughts on Susan McClary's *Feminine Endings*," *Perspectives of New Music* 30, 2 (summer 1992): 202–5, I used Boretz's expressions "question-spaces" and "discovery-spaces" to refer to what interested me in McClary's book—her questions (or "searching") more than her conclusions (or "knowledge"). I expanded on these notions in "Boretzian Discourse and History," *Perspectives of New Music* 2 (2005): 177–191, from which this material is borrowed. The idea of soft focus came from Pauline Oliveros, who, at a Deep Listening Retreat in New Mexico in the early 1990s, encouraged me to open to a more "soft-focus" relationship to the world. I am grateful to Ben and Pauline for the inspiration these ideas have engendered.

7. Hans-Georg Gadamer, "Foreword to the Second Edition of *Truth and Method*," in *After Philosophy: End or Transformation?* ed. Kenneth Baynes, James Bohlman, and Thomas McCarthy (Cambridge: Cambridge University Press, 1987), 341–43.

8. From Gadamer's perspective, "every [art work] is a response to a question and the only way to understand [it] is to get hold of the question to which [it] is an answer." What is important is both to open up "the broader contexts of meaning encompassed by the question" and to narrow the field of possibilities in which an art work situates itself. Hans-Georg Gadamer, "Hermeneutics as Practical Philosophy," in Baynes et al., *After Philosophy*, 332–33.

also add our own "interests" to those of the artist. As Gadamer explains, "without an inner tension between our anticipations of meaning and the all-pervasive opinions . . . there would be no questions at all."[9] Question-spaces take Gadamer's approach one step further by broadening our awareness of "the vague presuppositions and implications" involved in any question. Understanding that is nurtured within question-spaces, I would argue, more fully embraces the partial nature of understanding, always being "on a path whose completion is a clear impossibility." If understanding and consciousness are both characterized by what Gadamer calls a "relentless inner tension between illumination and concealment," with question-spaces they are not forced into a compromise; their complexity can just be, without being reduced to one's prejudices or otherwise distilled into some image, representation, or other narrow definition.[10]

Question-spaces can also operate somewhat differently from questions. Whereas questions, even broad ones, tend to be oriented in a given direction and at some point become teleological, that is, motivated by a linear force (as in traditional biographies and histories), question-spaces allow for what can be learned from chance, in the Cagean sense. Moreover, to the extent that the exploration of such spaces unveils interactions and networks of connection between people, practices, and art works, question-spaces allow for multiple linearities, nonlinearity, and simultaneities. In this sense, question-spaces allow for geometrical relationships as conclusions. They lead to a kind of synchronic analysis à la Saussure, involving a whole series of intersecting interests that share a certain time and place. Meaning in such contexts comes from contiguity and interaction in time and space more than from linear development or cause and effect. The pleasure of using question-spaces to write biography or history comes from holding many diverse elements in one's mind at once and from watching connections emerge and concurrent stories unfold like the jigsaw of personalities and events in Georges Perec's novel *Life: A User's Manual*. The end may not be a neatly completed puzzle as at the end of the novel, but hopefully a richer understanding than even language can provide.

Question-spaces ensure that I write through music in part because that they require me to examine an unusually wide range of data. This is not necessarily an impediment to understanding—for me, ironically, more breadth enables more depth, as if they were two interdependent coordinates on the field of knowledge. Abundant facts can be pleasurable to the extent that they loosen the grip of what Gadamer calls "prejudgment" and challenge one to process them through creative assimilation. Options for meaning can be kept open rather than being forced into prescribed molds. This presumes that understanding is not merely an extension of what one already knows, a dissolution of the unfamiliar into the recognizable, but

9. Gadamer, "Hermeneutics," 332–33.

10. Gadamer, "Hermeneutics," 330–31, 335–36; Ben Boretz, "Music, as a Music: A Multitext in Seven Fragments," *Open Space Magazine* 1 (spring 1999): 61–62.

multivalent by nature, many-layered, and not always reducible to language. The "access" this process provides seems more real to me than seeking answers or interrogating foregone conclusions because it doesn't settle into laser-beam narrowness, but rather stays wide-band and, as such, more like life. Question-spaces also leave room for my own subjectivity to meander and explore as in a landscape, to seek depth of connection or surface playfulness, and hopefully not to collapse into the pretense of mere objective observation. From this perspective, "contextuality" is part of the being at the center of the inquiry.

Antoine Prost explains that questions "construct the historical object through an original carving out from the unlimited universe of possible facts and documents."[11] However, question-spaces allow the historical object to form through a *fluid* relationship between fact and event, music and musical activity, the personal and the social. Question-spaces respect the interdependence and the correspondence of phenomena. As such, they are ideal for coming to grips with the complexities and contingencies of music and performance as well as the various attitudes, beliefs, and behaviors we bring to them. They encourage us to describe the "confusion and incoherence" of life without being overly "ascriptive" or sliding into "coercion, conviction, or manipulation." This kind of engagement with the past calls on us to be "imaginative, thoughtful, creative, intricate, acute and profound" while remaining rooted in the actuality of the past. It thus sets the context for discourse, in Ben Boretz's words, ideally to bear the imprint of "the entire residual experiential content of 'music' in our world."[12]

What one discovers in such a pursuit, like Cage's chance-determined answers, "opens the mind to the world around" by inevitably posing new questions that spin out more searching in a chain-like, multifaceted, and multidirectional manner. This possibility encourages one to savor the searching mode, to recognize the "limitless possibility of interrogation, expression, and understanding" and, just as with a work of art, never to settle on any final meaning. Such a method, then, presumes that understanding is not just the articulation, rediscovery, or ascription of meaning through thought or discourse, but is instead "*transformative, productive* of new meanings," a transformation that in its effect on the perceiver resembles what Cage sought through his music.[13] Writing in this way proposes a postmodern perspective on the nature of inquiry and the purpose of understanding. Instead of reinforcing the grand narratives, history so conceived can be a medium for expanding our experience and our creative understanding an extension of music's creativity.

11. Antoine Prost, *Douze leçons sur l'histoire*, cited in Ricoeur, *Memory, History, Forgetting*, 177.

12. Boretz, "Music, as a Music," 58.

13. In *The Hermeneutics of Postmodernity* (Bloomington: Indiana University Press, 1988), G. B. Madison points out that this idea links Gadamer's hermeneutics to deconstruction (113–14).

In leaving meaning open and vibrating, its signifiers still in endless play and projecting meaning that escapes the boundaries of individual answers, musically imbued question- and answer-spaces encourage a kind of polyphony (à la Bakhtin) situated in one time and place that includes us in our own.

TIME, NARRATIVE, AND MEMORY

In analytical writing about music, we can use question-spaces to interrogate our experience of the work for its uniqueness as well as its connections to other works we already know. Such a method emboldens us to trust our own reactions. It can also help us to retrieve and to deepen that experience. Viewed from this perspective, the work can tell us how to listen, while at the same time inviting us to examine its elements and how they function in the whole. Analysis calls on what Jean-François Lyotard calls our "know-how, knowing how to speak, knowing how to hear." But it can also test the limits of our competencies, especially if there are no written scores or if we only hear the works once. How can we trust our perceptions? How can we balance our biases and blindspots? And, as writers, how can we create a space that opens to others' views and invites them in, rather than establishes a closed space of presumed authority?

In writing through music, I seek to loosen our grip on what we think music means so that the sound and experience of music carries the potential for all kinds of engagement—from the personal, ethical, affective, perceptual, semiotic, social, and cultural to the limits of such perspectives. Any of these can affect our understanding of the world or our relationship with it. As such, music can encourage us to change, to conceive a new way of being. The openness of musical meaning also frees us to accept the world's complexities and bond with one another despite our differences, seeing ourselves as part of a larger community—specific communities as well as the community of humankind. As Cage once suggested, music can help us become "a society at one with itself," in "accord" because we have heard a metaphor or model of this in music. I see such discourse about music and the changes it can inspire as part of the "constellations of musicking behavior."[14]

The first three essays in this volume arose in response to working aside colleagues focused on contemporary music in both San Diego and Paris. In examining composers' renewed interest in opera and neo-tonality in the 1980s, postmodern

14. Boretz, "Music, as a Music," 57. The concept comes from Christopher Small, *Musicking: The Meanings of Performing and Listening* (Hanover, N.H.: Wesleyan University Press, 1998). Small defines "to music" as "to take part, in any capacity, in a musical performance" or to contribute to "the nature of the event that is a musical performance" (9). In his book, he proposes "a framework for understanding all musicking as a human activity, to understand not just *how* but *why* taking part in a musical performance acts in such complex ways on our existence as individual, social, and political beings" (12).

trends in the early 1990s, and French spectral music since the 1970s, I show how music engages the mind in distinct ways, builds structures from our memories, and sheds light on how meaning emerges through temporal processes. Whereas the first and third expand on my earlier work on Debussy, the second essay is a kind of manifesto that traces a major change in my own aesthetic sensibilities. Producing my first documentary on music in Bali and giving seminars on hermeneutics and postmodernism for young composers who were covertly writing video operas and film music, taking inspiration from 1970s popular music, and investigating pleasure in music led me to question my own assumptions about music as well as how I relate to the world. In this context, attempting to write about my recent musical experiences of Japanese dance, Boulez's music, and an Oliveros radio play gave rise to a new kind of theorizing.

"Narrative and Narrativity in Music" addresses how attention to narrative by literary theorists and philosophers in the 1980s signaled a new preoccupation with how one comprehends a succession of temporal events. When our experience of time changed in the twentieth century and when people grew frustrated with the conventions associated with stories and other belief systems, we yearned to consider more ambiguous kinds of meaning. This essay, written as a contribution to the International Society for the Study of Time, argues that music, with its unique relationship to time, has much to contribute to our understanding of narrative. It presents a theory for analyzing how in the twentieth century composers sought to avoid narrative and erase the role of memory through antinarratives, nonnarratives, and works without narrativity. With a renewed desire to engage perceivers in the aesthetic experience by calling on their own knowledge of life's processes, as painters were returning to landscapes, composers in the 1980s returned to narrative. They showed how one could embrace genres (opera) and syntaxes (tonality) associated with narrative while expressing the multiplicity of existence, fragmentary and seemingly irrational orders, and meanings that go beyond the known.

This understanding of the world as fragmentary and incoherent has led many people to feel increasingly isolated from one another, distant from their pasts, and unsure of their futures despite the apparent increases in connection through satellite simulcasts, e-mail, conference calls, and growing interdependence among nations. Meaning is now lodged in our experience of the present. In "Postmodernism, Narrativity, and the Art of Memory," the first article published on these ideas in music (chapter 2 here), I propose the notion of a *musical* memory palace, inspired by those of ancient Greece and the Renaissance, as a way to understand how certain composers help us make connections within synchronic situations and mentally organize our complex, kaleidoscopic experience of the contemporary world. Memory, something we all possess, makes communication possible. Whereas modernists such as Pierre Boulez, in their preoccupation with the past and their predecessors, have struggled with how to forget and what to forget, postmodernists such as John Adams see positive benefits in stimulating memory and encourage us to accept our pasts rather than attempting to subjugate or distort them. However, I find in the music of Cage and Oliveros an aesthetic that both embraces postmodern concerns and makes it difficult to consider modernism and postmodernism as completely exclusive and oppositional. By emancipating the realm of memory, allowing for the interpenetration of different domains, and encouraging the listener to explore relationships through his/her own memory, these works engage the listener's participation in an interactive process. At the same time, while using nontraditional forms in whose construction the listener plays an important role, they are not without structure. By calling on experience of all kinds (including the personal and the social) and suggesting links between memories recorded in different, apparently unrelated categories, these works present us with occasions to come to understand the disparate parts of our lives as fundamentally related. In this sense, music is a kind of ecosystem defined by what is connected and what effects the connections, rather than a product of what establishes and fulfills or subverts goals. Incorporating participants from various cultures, Oliveros's *Nzinga* presents an aesthetic model for intercultural cooperation. Music thus encourages us to discover our connectedness to others and through the individual shape we each give to our memory palaces, to find meaning in our lives. My responses to this music exemplify what music can stimulate in the attentive listener and articulate how music can move us beyond the modernist-postmodernist divide.

At the end of the twentieth century, a number of French philosophers and composers began to rethink the nature of temporal continuity. In "Resituating the Spectral Revolution: French Antecedents," commissioned as a response to four essays on spectral music, I examine how Henri Bergson's radical notions of time, inspired by music, have helped composers conceive of continuity as a dynamic process. In late nineteenth-century France, many, including those focused on racial differences among peoples, objected to Darwin's "mechanistic" view of evolution that involves only transitions and variations of degree rather than of kind. While scientists, photographers, and cinematographers too forced reconsideration of assumed continuities and acknowledged discontinuity in our perception of reality, Bergson looked to music as a model for a new concept of organic growth. Bergson argued that the time of the unconscious (which he called duration) was characterized by the interpenetration of heterogeneous elements, and he explained this kind of time as "a succession of qualitative changes which melt into and permeate one another like the notes of a tune." This was to distinguish time as duration from time as space that resembled the minutes of the ticking clock with its homogeneous parts. This idea of a melody may sound close to Wagner's, but Bergson confessed an "intuitive predilection" for Debussy's music. Applying Bergson's intuitive method (as understood by Gilles Deleuze) to an analysis of Debussy's *Jeux*, I suggest that it is the succession of sections more than the melodies in Debussy's music that embody the "sonorous becoming" of Bergson's duration. Through time, I argue, Debussy expects the listener to take an active role in perceiving continuity despite the music's surface discontinuity. Recalling neo-impressionists' concerns with perception and musical acoustics, French spectral composers have taken this preoccupation further. Also influenced by Bergson, they have dilated the musical instant, deconstructing sound to reconquer its continuity. With their focus on irregularities of sound rather than stable elements, their musical hybrids alter the nature of musical perception.

SELF-FASHIONING

Many histories portray the great work as the result of a struggle, and history itself as a series of perpetual conquests. The great artist/composer is a rugged individual with the courage to go where others have never gone and a spirit capable of stretching beyond conventional boundaries and imagining new horizons. As Emerson once put it, the artist has a duty "to cheer, to raise, and to guide men," in short, to serve as the "world's eye and the world's heart." Certainly these concepts elevate the work of art and its maker, using beauty, aesthetic values, and the heroic genius to inspire us. But they also have limitations, and not only because of the autonomy sometimes presumed, particularly in music. They can veil reality for a purpose.

What draws people to certain music or composers is often their reputation for greatness. Reputations signal renown, the way in which a person or work is known in public and the sum of values associated with them. But reputations also circumscribe our perceptions, affecting what we hear and how we understand. In chapters four through six (and several others that follow), I investigate various strategies artists and composers have used to create reputations. I approach this work from two perspectives. First, I take reputation to be a process that helps form an individual, a process involving actions, interactions, and associations as well as works. Second, I see it as a conscious construction based on presuppositions and purposes, whether crafted by composers themselves or by critics who write about them. Reputations can be made by anyone with a stake in preserving, enhancing, or demeaning a certain image of a composer or work. Saint-Saëns, for example, was virtually written out of French music history by his successors despite his major role in French music during the late nineteenth century, while Fauré, whose career was very limited until his 50s when he became the Conservatoire's director, was retrospectively elevated. The "trinity" of Fauré, Debussy, and Ravel that has since dominated our idea of modern French music is a concept that addressed the needs and desires of their friends and admirers rather than accurately represented the hierarchies of musical taste or achievement at the time.

Working with living composers for almost three decades has made me acutely aware of how composers construct their careers. To counter the illusion that this is an individual affair, I looked to Howard Becker's notion that art is produced by (as well as in) art worlds. Teachers, friends and enemies, social and professional contacts, institutions, patrons, jobs, awards, or critics, any of these may influence the conception and creation of art as well as its reception. Unlike Becker, however, I use the concept to mean that the work of art is a fulcrum of activities, involving both listeners and creators, in and through which both meaning and reputation take shape.[15] Such a perspective explains much better than traditional reception studies how a work's meaning and a composer's reputation can shift over time and in different contexts. It also respects the complex nature of musical taste. Building on Pierre Bourdieu's theory of the social space in which artists work, I have deconstructed the dynamic relationship between a composer's identity and the culture that supports it. Study of these forces and relationships offers a way to rethink the processes of identity formation and agency in composers' lives and makes us more aware of the ambiguities, paradoxes, and networks of relationships associated with music and its meaning.

Perhaps more than any of his contemporaries in turn-of-the-century France, the composer Vincent d'Indy fashioned an identity based on opposition. Understanding the dynamic of oppositional politics, he knew how to turn it to his advantage. With a taste for struggle, he defined himself, his music, and the music school he directed, the Schola Cantorum, through difference. This has led both his successors and his critics up through the present to associate him with defiant ultra-conservatism. However, d'Indy was also a man of alliances, alliances that served the composer and the State well. In "Deconstructing d'Indy," I throw into question the attitudes that have accumulated about him and suggest a more nuanced view of the man and his politics based on his practices. I show how he allowed government officials to use his difference to help them combat monopolies and bridge conflict with the Republic. The essay argues that in misconstruing the nature and function of political differences in France and their relationship to reputation-building strategies, we risk substituting ideology and our own projections of its meaning for a composer's identity and importance in his or her times.

Jean Cocteau, like d'Indy, was also concerned with his image and its meaning. He too understood the need for distinction. Like other French writers who have looked to music for inspiration, he wore his musical tastes as an emblem of identity. In "New Music as Confrontation," I show how, through a conscious change in his musical tastes, Cocteau distinguished himself from the conventional social circles in which he and his family moved without having to separate himself from this milieu. From Stravinsky, Satie, and jazz he learned about the effect of music on its public and came to see music as a set of situations that encouraged a certain social rapport between makers and their audiences. What he found in new music—an attitude of contradiction toward predecessors and of confrontation toward the

15. For Becker, art produced in an art world suggests a diffused identity for the work and its creator.

public—allowed him to forge much of what we think of as Cocteau. While the change in his musical tastes helped the writer build his own distinct yet socially bounded identity, these tastes also reflected and expressed the paradoxes of the artist in the social world in which he moved. Even as the poet surprises, stuns, or insults, he appeals to that which his audiences seek from him. Paradoxically, the values Cocteau assigned to music sheltered him from the fiercely political issues of the day and helped him to construct an apparently apolitical identity.

John Cage perceived himself and his work in the glow of history. To insure that future generations would understand his values, he "invented" a tradition that reflected the way he made, discovered, invented music, that is, a tradition based on the principles and methods he used in his music. Much of this is articulated in his "Composition in Retrospect," the focus of my next essay, in which he contemplates his personal history and defines his compositional rules and practices. Unlike most modernist composers, Cage was not reluctant to admit the influence of others. Just as d'Indy presented himself as heir to the ideas of his teacher, César Franck, Cage here positions himself in the lineage of Arnold Schönberg, despite their profoundly different music. But, unlike d'Indy and Cocteau, Cage does not need differences to secure his own identity. A careful study of his texts reveals that by 1981 Cage was still quoting the ideas borrowed from others, but had begun deleting the quotation marks. He was not afraid to take on others' voices as if his own, for what was important was not what distinguished him from others, but rather what he shared with them. He hoped to inculcate certain values and inspire respect in his listeners and readers, the same respect and admiration his sources of wisdom may have inspired in him. Cage's "mesostic" texts,[16] full of various kinds of source material, including newspaper citations, show how traditions function, how artists build on others' ideas as they come to represent aspects of themselves, how they use these ideas to legitimate new concerns, and how they expect listeners to join in the tradition by adopting its beliefs and doctrines. The multiple-voiced text itself exemplifies a political concept at the heart of Cage's work.

Identity and Nation

Individual works, together with the reputations that accrue to them, have always played an important role in the fashioning of national identity. To the extent that

16. Mesostic is a technique Cage used to write his poetic-like texts and a name he gave for them. After placing a word or phrase vertically on the page, he then composed or borrowed horizontal lines of text using one of its letters in each line. Unlike acrostics, the vertical word or phrase appears in the center rather than at the beginning of each line. A multiplicity of voices for the reader results from not only the two simultaneous discourses running vertically and horizontally, but also the various sources that Cage often incorporates into these texts.

a scandal erupts, as it did with the premiere of Claude Debussy's *Pelléas et Méli-sande*, critics can use a work to argue over larger issues such as the use, purpose, and nature of music. All too often even today critics suggest that certain aspects of music reveal something about the composer, as if the apparent formlessness of Debussy's music implied a life filled with smoke, if not drugs, or the boldness of his innovations implied anarchist politics. With performances as springboards for the discussion of everything from personal morality to nationalism, theatrical scandals serve as occasions in which a society confronts and works out its social, political, and cultural differences. Rightly or wrongly, extra-musical concerns not only affect how a critic formulates a message, but also determine whether a work fails or succeeds. Debates over differences can help a work survive.

In "*Pelléas* and Power," I offer a methodology for studying the reception of major works. In addressing the social, moral, and political presuppositions that can lurk behind aesthetic judgments, I show that while people's diverse responses to the same music sometimes correlate with their class, politics, or other aesthetic preferences, relationships between social class, politics, and taste are complex, rarely predictable, and need to be deconstructed to be understood. Nonetheless, intense controversy can elicit impassioned defense of a work, thereby giving rise to a taste public with a pronounced sense of the work's importance.

But what music contributes to national identity is not merely determined by the men in power and the most important composers of an era. Much can be learned from those working on the boundaries of the mainstream—women, lesser-known composers, and even amateurs. Their efforts to achieve distinction, recognition, and even prestige reveal what is important to a culture as well as what it is willing to reward.

At the end of the nineteenth century, gender and class inevitably constituted considerable barriers to women who wished to make their lives in public, despite the important strides of feminist organizations in assuring more female participation in culture and society. Yet those who fashioned their identities on addressing the needs of the nation commanded respect and admiration, especially when they combined feminine charm with "virile" power—boldness, tenacity, individuality, energy, and even innovative ideas. To the extent that they understood and expressed what the mainstream wanted to hear—love of country and other patriotic ideals—they were accepted and allowed to pursue their ambitions.

Augusta Holmès, a composer, was one such woman, for a time an "icon of the nation." In "The Ironies of Gender, or Virility and Politics in the Music of Augusta Holmès," I address the advantages and pitfalls of writing music as a woman, especially when one chooses to foreground virility instead of femininity. Holmès used music both to engage and to escape the social and musical stereotypes of her day, attracting men with her feminine exuberance and long blond hair and then engaging in gender-bending manipulation of ambiguities in her music and personal identity. In this essay, I suggest that the discourse surrounding virility at the time had political implications. Her engagement of these through her libretti and music help explain why her work was accepted, widely acclaimed, and eventually became a symbol of the ideals of the French Republic. But her reputation lasted only as long as she played the same game and the political climate remained relatively constant. Having disdained women's traditional attitudes and subverted the norms of women's music ultimately counted for little in the long run for, when the times changed, her music was forgotten and written out of history. This essay explores the ironies of writing politically useful music.

Composers also achieve distinction and reputation through carving out an identity from a relationship between self and other. After 1900, French attitudes toward the Orient (which they perceived as their quintessential other) were in flux, especially after Japan attacked the Russians at Port Arthur, threatening the white race for the first time since Genghis Khan. When the Far East proved to be a force capable of defeating the West, the discourses associating Orientalism with narratives of national identity became complicated. Composers were among those who stood to profit from the growing interconnectedness of the international economy especially to the extent that they could diffuse traditional binarisms and reinterpret them in view of coexistence. In "Race, Orientalism, and Distinction in the Wake of the Yellow Peril," I examine one of the effects of increased diplomacy among European nations and specifically the Entente Cordiale: French artists' turn to Britain's other, India, as a safer, more neutral terrain for their Orientalist fantasies. Rather than focusing on how race posits the positional superiority of the west, Albert Roussel and Maurice Delage agreed with those who saw Aryan Civilization as the cradle of European Civilization. Indian music was thus something from which they could learn. After having located these composers' sources in India, I show what elements they borrowed from Indian music to produce new musical hybrids. These offered models for a productive interdependence in the world.

PATRONS AND PATRONAGE

In choosing what to support and what to offer audiences, patrons play an important, and often overlooked, role in what a country embraces. Whether public or private, visible or invisible, institutions or individuals, patrons not only help make art happen, they also help shape its meaning by the contexts in which they place it. But, to be effective, patrons must have a deep understanding of the social networks of power and share with whomever they support both taste and values.

In France, perhaps the most important music patron of the early twentieth century was Countess Elizabeth Greffulhe, Proust's primary model for the Duchess de Guermantes. Like Augusta Holmès, Countess Greffulhe successfully negotiated the complexities of gender, class, and politics to forge an identity reflecting an accurate intuition of how music could serve the nation. Crucial was her ability to identify both a body of works ignored in France, including Wagner's operas, and a constituency for concerts of these works. Through a music society she created to enact her ambitions, she promoted concerts as a form of not only entertainment, philanthropy, and patronage, but also national pride and international diplomacy. Her ability to navigate the ambiguities inherent in aristocratic identity at the time helped assure their success. So too did making connections and alliances and building networks of cooperation and collaboration. Calling on fashion, a liminal area between private desire and public display, she attracted a new public to art music concerts. She gave elites a sense of themselves as a group with shared tastes, not just a class divided by old rivalries, and created a cultural analogue for political coalition. By inviting foreign musicians into her home and sponsoring public concerts of music her peers in other countries felt were the best and most representative, Countess Greffulhe sought to enhance mutual understanding and respect among people from different nations.

Commissioned to address the cultural identity of music in the United States for a special issue of an IRCAM journal in the mid-1980s, I turned to Americans' major patrons, the university and the National Endowment for the Arts (NEA). The editors in Paris wanted to know which musicians were most "representative" of our nation, whose music they should take seriously and perhaps perform in France. The plethora of musical styles in the United States, however, has made it difficult to grasp the sum of values underlying any "American" identity. To go beyond generalities, I felt it was absolutely critical to examine the art world in which American art music is produced, supported, and understood. Since writing, thinking about, and even performing new music has taken place predominantly in universities since World War II, these institutions became my focus.

"The Political Economy of Composition in the American University, 1965–1985," originally published as "Musique et institution aux Etats-Unis," is a two-part study exploring how modernist composers integrated themselves into the fabric of American universities in the 1950s and 1960s and then maintained their aesthetics through their monopoly on grants, fellowships, and other awards. Based on extensive interviews, it examines the influence of the university's social environment, economic resources, and function as a power base on the values embraced by university composers and their musical choices. When I was preparing the original article, my colleague, the late Robert Erickson, challenged me to investigate whether relationships and connections forged through educational institutions or university positions helped composers win grants from the NEA. Indeed, through a study of the 125 composers who won the largest or most frequent NEA grants from its inception in the 1960s through the peak of its importance in the 1980s, I show the extent to which universities, particularly on the East Coast, function as political entities whose associates protect and promote each other, helping build a composer's reputation and career and encouraging the replication of certain values. Unfortunately, as becomes clear, the university network, for the most part, did not benefit women and people of color. However, when blind judging was introduced in 1980, at least support began to flow towards lesser-known composers and those outside universities. Fleshing out a larger and more complex picture of art music in America, these composers lend some credence to an American musical identity as pluralist, synthetic, and free from any one kind of stylistic constraints.

EVERYDAY LIFE OF THE PAST

In concentrating on composers and works, music scholars have typically studied scores, composers' manuscripts, letters, and first editions. Critical reviews and other print journalism have served as the basis of most reception studies. However, research in Parisian archives over thirty years, especially the Bibliothèque Nationale, has enabled me to pour through a far wider range of materials in exploring my question- and answer-spaces, indeed to open a Pandora's universe of materials meticulously collected and catalogued for posterity, but rarely if ever consulted. Popular music magazines, music society statutes, military band transcriptions, sheet music reproduced in newspapers, and especially concert programs—this debris of the past, resonant with meaning, offers countless clues if what we wish to understand are the values a society associated with music and the uses to which it was put. Not only does it help us to reconstruct the everyday life of music-making in the past, supporting context-specific, intertextual analyses of musical meaning, this kind of material also helps us to understand the perspectives audiences brought to music and how these may have shifted over time.

Such material culture encourages us to consider history in a new way, focusing attention on performances as much as compositions, on consumers as well as producers. It allows us to approach works in the context of their resonance in the musical world and from the perspective of their multiple uses and meanings: in this sense, the reception of music is an interactive process. It helps us to understand how performances create publics and turn music into a form of sociability and an expression of taste, important aspects of any social history of culture. It also de-centers our histories by giving voice to the activities of a wide range of cultural participants, a historical precedent to the amateur musical practices being studied by sociologists today.[17] Part of what we learn in examining this diversity is that boundaries of all kinds in a musical world can be fluid. This throws into question our concepts of not only center and periphery, but also professional and amateur, public and private, serious and popular, the tastes and musical activities of elites as well as the lower classes.

Concert programs are perhaps the most useful in helping trace the history of musical taste and the changing values reflected in concert life. As links between

---

17. See, for example, Tia DeNora, *Music in Everyday Life* (Cambridge: Cambridge University Press, 2000); Antoine Hennion, *La Passion musicale* (Paris: Metaille, 1993) and Hennion et al., eds., *Figures de l'amateur* (Paris: Documentation française, 2000).

organizers, marketing managers, and the public, they not only record what audiences heard, but also what was done to construct and manipulate music's meaning, whether through explanatory notes or what works were surrounded with on concerts. They suggest the confluence of taste and ideology. In "Concert Programs and their Narratives as Emblems of Ideology," I show how, from 1890 to 1914, Parisian programs document a series of radical transformations in how music was represented to the public and, analogously, how the French thought of music. Examining not only the choice of repertoire and the program notes, but also the cover magery, print typefaces, and advertisements reveals a gradual repudiation of one form of modernism commonly associated with feminine imagery, art nouveau designs, and Beauty with a capital B, for another, more male-oriented, abstract one, valued for embodying the new. Through these means, concert programs suggest how modernism became embedded and accepted as part of French culture.

Western European art music has too often been understood as something strictly by and for elites. While its language begs a certain fluency from listeners and productions often require substantial institutional resources for its production, the connection between social class and the taste for classical music is not so simple. Scholars such as Lawrence Levine have analyzed the emergence of hierarchical distinctions between highbrow and lowbrow arts in America, associating them with rigid class-bound definitions of culture at the end of the nineteenth century.[18] But these contentions can also be seen as a metaphor for the European/American divide, or perhaps an historical insecurity about the relative value of our artistic production hiding behind a kind of pride in that difference. A close look at musical life in Paris at the turn of the century reveals that there were far fewer differences in the production and consumption of art music among the classes than we have been led to believe in part because of the political ideals of the French Republic. When working-class girls sang alongside Opéra singers for a mixed crowd of employees and their customers, such as in concerts at the Bon Marché department store, music could help mediate class and cultural differences. Not only did the lower classes have access to art music (or what we today call classical music) including opera (albeit in transcriptions), they participated in the supply as well as the demand. Some believed that to the extent that all classes developed similar tastes and tastes represent inner desires, people would come to resemble one another. In this way, concerts were perceived to play a role in promoting social change. In "Material Culture and Postmodern Positivism: Rethinking the 'Popular' in Late-Nineteenth-Century French Music," I thus refute several assumptions that popular music scholars tend to be making: namely that in the past, only elites had access or an interest in serious art music; that serious and popular domains were

18. Lawrence Levine, *Highbrow Lowbrow: The Emergence of Cultural Hierarchy in America* (Cambridge, Mass.: Harvard University Press, 1988), 255.

distinct; that commodification of musical works was necessarily bad. In insuring that music was broadly accessible in France, in part through workers' music societies that brought art music into their neighborhoods, French republicans pursued their goal of democratization and looked to music as a way of forming citizens. The gradual fusion of art and consumer culture served the national interest.

By writing through music, I hope to incite my readers to engage with music in new ways and to deepen their awareness of music's capacity for meaning. Studying music, musical practices, and musical culture can yield crucial insights into how people make sense of their lives. All musical experiences begin with works but, as I've shown, audience attitudes and participation can dramatically affect what those experiences entail. Music gives listeners as well as composers a medium for reflection, self-interrogation, personal growth, connection to the world, and identity— Cocteau being one such example in this book. The aspirations of listeners are as important as those of composers.

In presenting these essays, I wrestled with allowing such ideas alone "to make a case for music to take its place among the set of practices that must be considered central to thinkers of our time," as George Lewis puts it. At the same time I recognized that for me, as I am sure for others, ideas about music are inextricably linked with life experiences, experiences that in turn underline how meaningful music can be. As my career brought me into close contact with living composers, I became increasingly interested in not only contemporary music, but also composers' lives. Observing composers' attempt to fashion a certain identity and how this could affect the music they write raised my awareness of the social and political forces that often underlie the creation of music. Noting the way contemporary composers and critics sometimes evaluate music by women and people of color with criteria that reflect their own prejudices sensitized me to the dynamics of gender and race in the musical world and to the underbelly of musical taste. Studying the role played by patrons in the determination of what music gets played and heard taught me that national identity in music is not just the domain of composers. Through my work on music in Bali, I came to understand that culture expresses community as much as individuals. Asking new questions of music in the west, I shifted my focus from the avant-garde and analysis of canonic works to the social relevance of music. This in turn led me to digging around in material culture. It was debris of the past that provided the most powerful motivation to rethink some of our most stubborn preconceptions about Western culture.

To understand why any of this matters, we must broaden what we consider central to the musical experience and thereby what we study. I hope this volume encourages others to ponder their own question-spaces through music and expand their appreciation of the many ways music can give shape to our ideals, help craft our identities, and illuminate what is important in our lives.

Part I

Time, Narrative, and Memory

1. NARRATIVE AND NARRATIVITY IN MUSIC

Time becomes human time to the extent that it is organized after
the manner of a narrative; narrative, in turn, is meaningful to
the extent that it portrays the features of a temporal experience.

Paul Ricoeur, *Time and Narrative,* vol. 1 (1984)

*R*EVERSING DECADES OF NEGLECT and almost complete disinterest, more and more composers are writing operas again.
Beginning in the 1980s, the number of contemporary operas increased dramatically
by comparison with the rest of the twentieth century, and the diversity of styles
ranges across the entire field of musical thought. For example, with *Donnerstag aus
Licht* in 1981, Stockhausen began a series of seven operas, one for each day of the
week. Two years later Messiaen finished his first opera, *Saint François d'Assise.*
Philip Glass completed two operas, *Satyagraha* in 1980 and *Akhnaten* in 1984. In
1986 the English National Opera premiered the second of Harrison Birtwistle's
three operas, *The Mask of Orpheus.* The Frankfurt Opera mounted John Cage's first
two operas *Europera I* and *II* in 1987. Operas by many other well-known composers
followed: Jacob Druckman (1982), Bernard Rands (1985), George Rochberg (1986),
and Morton Subotnick. To celebrate their tenth anniversary in 1987, the Centre
Georges Pompidou and the musical research center IRCAM (Institut de Recherche
et Coordination Acoustique/Musique) in Paris commissioned a video opera from
the young American Tod Machover. What is behind this renewed interest in a
genre that fell into disrepute for much of this century? Is it simply opera's commercial appeal, or the fame it brings, or does opera fill a need, felt by both
composers and audiences, created by the difficulty of comprehending much contemporary music?

This essay originally appeared in *Time and Mind: Interdisciplinary Issues. The Study of
Time VI,* ed. J. T. Fraser (Madison, Conn.: International Universities Press, 1989), 232–57,
included here by permission of the International Universities Press. An earlier version was
presented at the twentieth anniversary meeting of the International Society for the Study of
Time, Dartington Hall, Totnes, Devon, England, 9 July 1986.

I would like to thank the following composers for interviews with them on narrative in
their music: John Cage, Tod Machover, Will Ogdon, Bernard Rands, Roger Reynolds, and
John Silber. Thanks also to Lewis Rowell for editing an earlier version.

Leaving aside these interesting sociological issues for separate consideration, this chapter explores that significant *aesthetic* force that has led composers to write for the theater again—a renewed concern about narrative in music. Narrative has always been one of artists' primary means of organizing and giving coherence to experiences and has certainly been the temporal gestalt most broadly used in the arts.[1] After years of structural, semiotic, and deconstructive analyses, the special attention to narrative in recent years by literary theorists (such as Roland Barthes, Seymour Chatman, Gérard Genette, and Mieke Bal), linguists (such as A. J. Greimas), and philosophers (such as Ricoeur) has signaled a new preoccupation with how meaning can be communicated through a temporal process, as opposed to structural relationships, and with how one understands a succession of temporal events. Many scholars of narrative have found the novel and film particularly enlightening, but they have generally ignored music, the quintessential art of time, perhaps because the musical world itself has rarely pondered the nature of a musical narrative. This chapter seeks both (1) to deepen our understanding of narrative and narrativity in general, and (2) to demonstrate the relevance of narrative concepts to criticism of contemporary music.

First, I will derive a definition of narrative and narrativity in music, building on the works of scholars named above while pointing out the limitations of their theories as applied to music. Just as recent analyses of narrative have extended well beyond the ancient Greek notions of epic or diegesis (i.e., the telling or indirect representation of a story), so this discussion will go beyond the conventional notions of a musical narrative as program music and even as music with a single dramatic curve.

Second, with respect to the temporal organization of twentieth-century music, I will suggest that three radical musical innovations developed in part from composers' attempts to play with, manipulate, and abort their listeners' expectation of narrative so that they might nourish understanding of other perceptions of life, which are neither unilinear nor goal oriented. I call these antinarratives, nonnarratives, and works without any narrativity.

Third, I will propose that the return by some composers in recent years to genres, such as opera, and syntaxes, such as tonality, that have traditionally been thought of as narrative can be understood only in light of these other developments. Moreover, I will show that narrative, as some contemporary composers use it, not only incorporates a multiplicity of perspectives and references, as in some contemporary novels and films, but also presents events in a kaleidoscopic manner. These two techniques have previously been associated only with works created with the intention of denying traditional narrative expectations.

---

1. The theme of this chapter has made it necessary to employ a number of concepts, more or less well known in everyday use but carrying special meanings in literary theory. Appendix 1 at the back of this book defines these terms. When they first appear in the text, they are italicized.

DEFINING NARRATIVE IN MUSIC

Story and Narrative Discourse, Signified and Signifier

For most people, including composers, narrative means story. A narrative is something that tells a story. This concept, however, is not as simple as it may appear, for much rests both on what "story" is and what "tell" may mean. Most literary theorists differentiate between narrative (*récit*) and story (*histoire*). Because the process of storytelling involves both *signification* and communication, many of them (especially the semioticians) speak of the *story* as the *signified* or the subject of a *discourse*, and the *narrative* (or what some call the narrative text) as the *signifier* or that which communicates the story to the perceiver. From this perspective, a narrative is a kind of discourse, a manifestation of some content in a given medium. Although narratologists disagree as to whether or not this concept of narrative includes the narration of a text, that is, its enunciation or performance before an audience, for present purposes, I will use *narrative* to refer only to the level of discourse and thereby consider it distinct from both story and narration and capable of entering into various relationships with them. In a later section, I will also distinguish it from *narrativity*, or what mediates between a narrative discourse and the language structures that inform its production and comprehension.

The very broad notion contemporary literary theorists have of a narrative's story opens the way to a much fuller understanding of narrative than has previously been the case, particularly in music. For Bal, Genette, and Chatman, a story is a series or chain of "events" that are logically related to one another (i.e., in a temporal and causal order) and are caused or undergone by agents, and an event is the passage from one state to another.[2] Depending on how one defines an event in music, this means that a relationship of signifier to signified may exist between a composition and a wide range of extramusical and even musical ideas.

In programmatic pieces such as Berlioz's *Symphonie fantastique*, Strauss's *Till Eulenspiegel*, and Stravinsky's *Petrushka*, what is signified by the music, its "story," can be a series of actions, a given character, or the flux of a character's emotions. The abrupt change from the very slow, frequently broken, chromatic lines and the C minor tonality to the quick, spiccato, diatonic melody and the C major tonality in the opening of the *Symphonie fantastique* musically embodies the "melancholy reverie, interrupted by a few fits of groundless joy" described in the work's program. The traditional way, especially since Wagner, for a composer to accomplish signification in a composition telling a story, however, is by allying a musical motive—a

---

2. Mieke Bal, *Narratologie* (Paris: Klincksieck, 1977); Gérard Genette, *Narrative Discours*, trans. J. E. Lewin (Ithaca, N.Y.: Cornell University Press, 1980; originally published as *Discours du récit*, 1972); and Seymour Chatman, *Story and Discourse* (Ithaca, N.Y.: Cornell University Press, 1978).

melodic pattern, harmony, rhythmic shape, and even instrumental timbre—with each character and by transforming them as the story unfolds. In the second tableau of *Petrushka*, for example, Stravinsky uses two superimposed triads in the incompatible relationship of a tritone (F-sharp–C) to depict musically the existential state of the puppet Petrushka, who is cursed with a mechanical body together with the human feelings trapped in it. These arpeggiated triads, the clarinets, piano, and then trumpets that play them, and their triplet rhythms return in the third tableau to alternate dramatically with the fierce woodwind and string chords associated with the Moor as Petrushka battles his competitor. Understanding what the "story" is in these examples is thus essential to understanding why the musical events succeed one another as they do.

The musical innovations Stravinsky developed in working with a story in *Petrushka* (1911) led him to experiment with a second kind of signified in *The Rite of Spring* (1913): stage gestures and actions not dependent on a conventional story for their meaning. In conceiving this ballet, Stravinsky considered the work's organizing principle a certain "choreographic succession" rather than any plot. He recounts in his *Autobiography* that he "had imagined the spectacular part of the performance as a series of rhythmic mass movements" (the ordered movement of large groups rather than individual dancers) and sought, as did the choreographer Nijinsky with whom he worked extensively, to create formal structures in the music and the dance that would be intimately linked.[3] In the "Games of the Rival Tribes," for example, Stravinsky juxtaposes two different sets of instruments, two motives, and two rhythmic patterns that alternate constantly throughout the dance to mirror the visual confrontation of the two tribes of dancers on stage. The signified of this kind of music is, therefore, the dance itself. Such a change by Stravinsky from depicting a story, as in *Petrushka*, to incorporating the structural relationship of another art form, as in *The Rite*, marks an important shift of interest in this century away from program music and toward visual and other analogies between the arts not based on or supported by stories.[4]

A third type of signified, used throughout history, is reference to, and perhaps elaboration of, some aspect of the musical language itself. More than the previous kinds of signifieds, quotation of a tune, a form, a genre, a style, or a performance practice depends on the listener's ability to perceive and understand the reference and its function in the context at hand. In the opening of the last movement of Beethoven's Ninth Symphony, for example, the double basses interrupt the orchestra with a melodic line that recalls eighteenth-century opera recitative. Minutes

3. Igor Stravinsky, *An Autobiography* (New York: Simon and Schuster, 1936), 48.

4. Jann Pasler, "Music and Spectacle in *Petrushka* and *The Rite of Spring*," in *Confronting Stravinsky*, ed. Pasler (Berkeley: University of California Press, 1986), 53–81.

later Beethoven confirms this allusion by giving the same melody to the baritone soloist and adding the words "O friends, not these tones; instead let us sing more pleasing and joyful ones." Furthermore, when the text is "Follow your path with joy, Brothers, like a hero marching to victory," Beethoven composes in the style of "Turkish" music (fifes, triangles, cymbals, and bass drum), which was associated with military ensembles at the time. By incorporating into this movement such unusual elements as a chorus, fragments of themes from all previous movements, and a theme-and-variations form, Beethoven played with their function as signifieds in order to stretch conventional notions of the genre and form of a symphony.

With such an open definition of story (as not just the structural support of a composition but also a parallel structure to it, a source of inspiration for new musical ideas, or merely a referent), clearly all that is necessary to bind signifier and signified is (1) a certain duality—the music and something outside it; (2) a presumed perceptibility of the two; and (3) a relationship linking them. Since the succession of the signified's events often illuminates or reinforces those of the signifier, such a concept helps explain many experimental works wherein composers, to make their meaning clearer or guide their audience to listen in new ways, link pure sound to something external.

Identifying the elements of a narrative discourse is somewhat more difficult. Russian formalists such as Tomashevsky view "the smallest particle of thematic material," the motif, as the primary element of a narrative.[5] This thematic approach is appropriate in analyzing much eighteenth- and nineteenth-century music, and, if one construes a theme as more than merely a melodic line or sequence of pitches, it may also be extended to some contemporary music. In Roger Reynolds's *Vertigo* (1986), for example, the elements treated thematically are microcompositions, not only composed but also performed in certain ways and recorded in advance. Two other theories are suggestive here. Chatman's idea of narrative as "a connected sequence of narrative statements," with the statements being the expression of either dynamic events or static existents, and Christian Metz's notion of the sentence, "or at least some segment similar in magnitude to the sentence," as the proper unit of narrative posit the complete phrase as the narrative unit of music. But they do not necessarily account for the relationship between the parts of the whole.[6] Others approach the narrative as the amplification of a verb. Thus Vladimir Propp and Barthes refer to the narrative units as functions, Claude Bremond as

---

5. Boris Tomashevsky, "Thematics" (1925), in *Russian Formalist Criticism: Four Essays,* ed. L. Lemon and M. Reis (Lincoln: University of Nebraska, 1965), 61–95.

6. Christian Metz, *Film Language,* trans. M. Taylor (New York: Oxford University Press, 1974; originally published as *Essais sur la signification au cinéma,* 1967), 25; Seymour Chatman, *Story and Discourse* (Ithaca, N.Y.: Cornell University Press, 1978).

elementary sequences, and Greimas as narrative programs.[7] In his analysis of Chopin's Polonaise-Fantasy op. 61, Eero Tarasti shows how Greimasian narrative programs (e.g., diving in and recovering; topological disengagement; the various dances; fulfillment) function to advance or to frustrate movement to a final resolution.[8] The decision to consider static entities or functional processes as the basic elements of a musical narrative should probably depend on the work at hand, whether its signified is a static entity or dynamic process, and exactly what undergoes transformation in the composition.

Given this distinction between story and narrative, then, two important interrelated issues of debate arise. First, whether—in the Aristotelian sense—the narrative describes a story through indirect means (diegesis) or presents or acts out the story dramatically (mimesis). What otherwise might differentiate the former, used in epic, from the latter, used in tragedy, is not as clear-cut in music as in literature.[9] Obviously, opera exploits mimetic devices, but in his song "Erlkönig," for example, Schubert, respecting Goethe's text, uses both diegesis for the narrator, who describes the action in the first and last stanzas, and mimesis for the three characters—father, son, and erlking—who enact it in the middle stanzas.[10] The second issue is whether or not the narrative, independent of the story, can contain meaning. Ricoeur takes a helpful stance in this regard, in that he characterizes narrative not by its "mode" but by its "object." For him, diegesis and mimesis are both subcategories of a more general Aristotelian concept called mythos, or the organization of events: "The essential thing is that the poet—whether narrator or dramatis—be a 'maker of plots.'"[11] He furthermore defines mimesis not merely as representation, but as creative imitation, involving an ordering, or reordering, of a story's elements. Unlike Bremond and Genette, for whom a narrative cannot contain but only carry meaning, Ricoeur posits meaning in the construction of the narrative itself. In discussing music, Ricoeur's interpretation is preferable, because music can both tell or convey the meaning of something extramusical (such as a program or a text) and present a strictly musical meaning all its own.

7. Roland Barthes, "Introduction to the Structural Analysis of Narratives," in *Image, Music, Text,* trans. S. Heath (New York: Hill and Wang, 1977), 88–91; A. J. Greimas and J. Courtés, *Semiotics and Language,* trans. L. Crist et al. (Bloomington: Indiana University Press, 1982; originally published as *Sémiotique,* 1979).

8. Eero Tarasti, "Pour une narratologie de Chopin," *International Review of the Aesthetics and Sociology of Music* 15 (1984): 53–75.

9. Aristotle, "Poetics," in *Introduction to Aristotle,* ed. R. McKeon (New York: Modern Library, 1947).

10. Edward Cone, *The Composer's Voice* (Berkeley: University of California Press, 1974), 1–19.

11. Paul Ricoeur, *Time and Narrative,* vol. 1, trans. K. McLaughlin and D. Pellauer (Chicago: University of Chicago Press, 1984; originally published as *Temps et récit,* vol. 1, 1984), 36, 41.

A number of relationships between narrative and story can be manipulated when both are seen as inherently meaningful. Metz and Genette discuss at length the numerous possibilities of aspect, the way the narrator perceives the story; mood, the type of discourse used by the narrator; voice, the characters or personas he assumed in the telling; and especially tense, the time of the narrative in relation to that of the story.[12] Concordances and discordances, or what Genette calls anachronies, may be constructed between the temporal order of events in the story and the pseudotemporal order of their arrangement in the discourse, the duration of events in the story and in the telling, as well as the frequency of repetition in both. If one views the standard idea of a sonata form as a work's underlying signified, then any rearrangement of parts, such as placing a final cadence at a work's beginning, can be discussed in this regard. Although these notions could be greatly elaborated, further discussion must be relegated to future articles.

Narrative Structure and Narrative Logic

A narrative is also a kind of structure. As a structure, considered by some as independent of any medium, it must have wholeness (in that its events must be related or mutually entailing), transformation, and self-regulation (i.e., self-maintenance and closure, that is, all transformations must engender only elements already within the system).[13] Most literary theorists view narrative as an object more than as a process and thereby emphasize its closed, finite nature. They point to the stability of the boundaries that separate it from the real world (and physical time) and to the order, or temporal sequence, in which its events are presented, namely, its beginning, middle, and end.[14] Ricoeur focuses instead on how the configurational dimension of narrative structures its episodic or chronological dimension. This means how the succession of events is integrated, using repetition and relying on the listener's recollection, into a significant whole. Ricoeur calls this the invention of a plot. Herein lies an explanation for the claim mentioned at the beginning of this chapter: in the narrative's organization and retelling of the events of a story, "time becomes human time." The beginning of a narrative, as Ricoeur sees it then, involves "the absence of necessity in the succession" rather than merely "the absence of some antecedent." The "sense of an ending," from his perspective, also

---

12. Metz, *Film Language,* and Genette, *Narrative Discourse.*

13. In his *Story and Discourse,* 20–21, Chatman cites Jean Piaget's conception of a structure in his *Structuralism,* trans. C. Maschler (New York: Harper and Row, 1971), 3–16.

14. All these issues have close correlations in music. See Lewis Rowell, "The Creation of Audible Time," in *The Study of Time,* vol. 4, ed. J. T. Fraser (New York: Springer-Verlag, 1981); Jonathan Kramer, "Moment Form in Twentieth-Century Music," *Musical Quarterly* 2, no. 64 (1978): 117–94, and "New Temporalities in Music," *Critical Inquiry* 3, no. 7 (spring 1981): 539–56; Thomas Clifton, *Music as Heard* (New Haven, Conn.: Yale University Press, 1983).

differs from the "openendedness of mere succession" because of the shape imposed by the plot's configuration.[15]

Only in conversation theory and in music do people speak of a very specific kind of configuration as narrative. In his studies of stories told by African-American adolescents, William Labov describes a fully formed narrative as having the following: a summary clause (abstract), an orientation of who, when, and where placed anywhere in the text, a complicating action, an evaluation of the point of the narrative, a result or resolution, and a coda, often returning the listener to the present time.[16] Barney Childs calls a similar pattern in music a "narrative curve" and describes it as an introduction (involving some question or tension), a statement, a development (possibly of relationships increasing irregularly in complexity and intensity), a climax, a resolution or relaxation or "falling action," and a concluding gesture (possibly a restatement and the renewal of cosmic order). Childs finds this curve to be the most "basic structural organization of a work of time art" and sees it as a way of representing life.[17] Other musicians have defined narrative in a like manner. Edward Cone calls it "introduction, statement, development, climax, restatement, peroration," of which the sonata allegro form is the best example in eighteenth- and nineteenth-century music.[18] In an interview, Roger Reynolds spoke of it as proposition, elaboration, and conclusion.[19] Interestingly, Childs and Jonathan Kramer (whom Childs quotes) suggest that listeners endeavor to hear such a curve in a composition even when it demonstrably does not exist. Unless some manner of this "narrative dramatism" exists, it is feared, listeners may not be able to understand the music.[20]

This concentration on the structure of a narrative and on the order of its events, however, says little about the logic of the movement from one event to another. Unfortunately, most literary theorists give little attention to this, the truly temporal aspect of a narrative. Those who do discuss a narrative's temporality, such as Metz

15. Paul Ricoeur, "Narrative Time," *Critical Inquiry* 1, no. 7 (1980): 179; Ricoeur, *Time and Narrative*, 1:3, 38, 67.

16. William Labov, *Language in the Inner City* (Philadelphia: University of Pennsylvania Press, 1972), 363–70.

17. Barney Childs, "Time and Music: A Composer's View," *Perspectives of New Music* 2, no. 15 (spring/summer 1977): 194–219.

18. Edward Cone, "Beyond Analysis," *Perspectives of New Music*, 6, no. 1 (fall/winter 1967): 37.

19. Roger Reynolds, interview with the author, 19 May 1986. In *Recent Theories of Narrative* (Ithaca, N.Y.: Cornell University Press, 1986), Wallace Martin cites a diagram of the "normal plot" (as developed by the German critic Gustav Freytag) whose inverted V shape resembles in great part the narrative curve of many musical compositions. The trouble with this diagram, as Martin points out, is that it doesn't describe most plots, except perhaps those of short stories (81–82).

20. Childs, "Time and Music," 116.

and Genette, speak of it in relationship to that of a story, which it refigures, and thus skirt the issue. The notion of a narrative curve, found in conversation theory and music, may be somewhat constricting, but it offers some insight into the most primary characteristic of a narrative's movement; that is, the inherent directedness of the succession of its events. A narrative must go somewhere. Circularity as well as stasis is disturbing to its dynamic nature. Something propels the story and the perceiver's interest, even though the answer to the question "So what?" is neither predictable nor deductible (were it so, the story might not be worth telling, that is, *narratable*). Some, such as Ricoeur, view the story's conclusion as the "pole of attraction of the entire development."[21] In his studies of oral narratives, Labov found the speaker's evaluation of the story to be the crux of the narrative, for without it, the story could be perceived as pointless.

In music, the few theorists who have analyzed narrative (Ivanka Stoianova, Childs, and Kramer) define goal-orientation as central to a musical narrative. Stoianova refers to the existence of not only an "end-goal" but also an "initial impetus."[22] The early-twentieth-century Austrian music theorist Heinrich Schenker has demonstrated the extent to which most tonal works begin in a tonality, modulate to some alternative one, usually its fifth, and return to the opening tonality at the piece's end. In her analysis of Boulez's *Rituel in Memoriam Maderna*, a nontonal work, Stoianova shows a similar kind of teleological movement. Just as in Stravinsky's *Symphonies of Wind Instruments* (from which Boulez borrows the idea), the initial impetus, E flat, is also the end-goal of the piece, the last note, as well as the center of a symmetrical system based on the tritone, A–E-flat–A. Stoianova even goes so far as to add unidirectionality to her definition of narrative—although contemporary composers and other theorists may disagree. The point being that a narrative must have a fundamental point of reference, and its events must progress, not just succeed one another.

Most people generally think of a narrative as linear, or consisting of events that are dependent on immediately preceding events and following the irreversible order of time. For Ricoeur, however, this "then and then" structure characterizes only the episodic dimension of a narrative, not the configurational one.[23] Those literary theorists who tie the temporal progression of narrative to that of a story would also argue that ellipses, summaries, flashbacks, and flashforwards interrupt any linearity a narrative might have. Chatman, moreover, believes that the author

21. Ricoeur, "Narrative Time," 174.

22. Ivanka Stoianova, "Narrativisme, téléologie et invariance dans l'oeuvre musicale," *Musique en jeu* 25 (1976): 15–31, 16. For a more recent study, see Byron Almén, *A Theory of Musical Narrative* (Bloomington: Indiana University Press, 2008).

23. Ricoeur, *Time and Narrative*, 1:67. In his "Introduction to the Structural Analysis of Narratives," Barthes posits that the "confusion between consecution and consequence, temporality and logic" is the central problem of narrative syntax (98–104).

"selects those events he feels are sufficient to elicit the necessary sense of continuum" and finds "inference-drawing," or the listener's filling in of the gaps left by these temporal condensations or reorderings, to be an important aspect of narrative and that which differentiates it from lyric, expository, and other genres.[24] In music, likewise, a work may or may not have linearity, as Kramer has shown, on a number of hierarchic levels (i.e. from one section to the next), within an individual section but not beyond it, or from one section to another "previous but not immediately adjacent" ones.[25] For a narrative to be connected, it is not necessary that the movement from one moment to the next be linear, but that linearity exist on the structural level of the piece.

Narrative Transformation

The ultimate reason narrative events are directed and connected is that they undergo or cause transformation, which is probably the narrative's most important and most illusive characteristic. Some change, or what Aristotle in his *Poetics* calls peripety, must take place in the middle of a narrative text. The narrative situation itself calls for it, as D. A. Miller points out, in that narrative arises from some disequilibrium, suspense, or general insufficiency.[26] Reynolds adds that a musical narrative must also start with something that is incomplete and enticing so that the listener is interested in its future possibilities.[27]

Most analyses of narrative largely ignore this aspect of a narrative because they emphasize structural relationships rather than their transformation in time, and static rather than dynamic relationships between the parts of a narrative. Even Piaget, who claims that all structures are "systems of transformations," adds that "transformations need not be a temporal process."[28] In defining a narrative event as a narrative program, "an utterance of doing governing an utterance of state," and narrative as a string of presupposed and presupposing narrative programs, or a narrative trajectory leading from an initial state to a final state, Greimas comes to grips with the dynamic nature of a narrative; but his use of $f(x)$, a mathematical symbol borrowed from calculus, to describe a narrative program as a function that operates in a given way on an object or state over time implies that the transformations in a narrative are continuous in the mathematical sense (that is, that there are no interruptions or points of discontinuity), that they are therefore consistent and predictable according to the formula, and that they belong to a set of

24. Chatman, *Story and Discourse*, 30–31.

25. Kramer, "New Temporalities in Music," 554.

26. D. A. Miller, *Narrative and Its Discontents* (Princeton, N.J.: Princeton University Press, 1981).

27. Interview with author, 19 May 1986.

28. Piaget, *Structuralism*, 11.

preexistent codes, none of which is necessarily the case in musical transformations.[29] As Stoianova points out, detours along the way are more the rule than the
exception in music.

Only Tzvetan Todorov proposes a typology of narrative transformations, and
for him they are the essence of narrative.[30] Those expressible as simple sentences—
changes of status (positive to negative), of mode (necessity, possibility), of intention, manner, or aspect—he calls simple transformations; those requiring a
dependent clause—changes of supposition (prediction—realization) and of knowledge (problem—solution, deformed presentation—correct presentation)—he calls
complex transformations. What is critical about these transformations in his view
is that they help explain the tension that exists in narratives between difference
and similarity. Transformation, as he explains it, represents a synthesis of differences and resemblance; that is, it links two similar things without allowing them to
be identified with one another. The exclusive presence of one or the other would
result in a discourse that is no longer narrative.

While it is difficult to translate these notions into ways of thinking about music,
they do suggest a fundamental difference between two kinds of transformation in
music. The first, thematic transformation—"the process of modifying a theme so
that in a new context it is different yet manifestly made of the same elements"—
was perhaps the most widely used developmental technique in nineteenth-
century music, especially that of Liszt, Berlioz, and Wagner.[31] It allowed a composer to suggest different programmatic intentions, such as those effected by
Todorov's simple transformations (i.e., despair into joy; aggressive into lyrical),
while ensuring a composition's unity.

A second kind of musical transformation that is characteristic of narrative does
not necessarily depend on any recurrent material, but rather on a certain kind of
relationship between events that are in themselves complex states of being. One
example is tension into resolution. Very often in tonal works, this has meant
extending a dissonance structurally through modulation into and elaboration of a
new harmony, then returning to the opening tonality. But tension and resolution
may be created by other musical means as well. In Debussy's *Jeux*, for example,
tension results at rehearsal number 16 from the superimposition of six different
rhythmic divisions of the measure and numerous melodic lines moving in different directions, the increasingly loud dynamics, and the dominant seventh harmony. The sense of resolution that follows results from not only the cadence but
also the sudden stasis and rhythmic regularity, the reduction to one melodic line,
and the *molto diminuendo*. This excerpt also exemplifies what Leonard Meyer and

29. Greimas and Courtés, *Semiotics and Language*, 207, 245.

30. Tzvetan Todorov, *Poétique de la prose* (Paris: Seuil, 1978).

31. Hugh Macdonald, "Thematic Transformation," in *The New Grove Dictionary of
Music and Musicians*, ed. S. Sadie, (London: Macmillan, 1980), 19:117–18.

Eugene Narmour call an "implication–realization model of communication," of which narratives are special cases. Like other syntactical or "script-based" implications (antecedent–consequent phrases, etc.), the dominant seventh chord inherently suggests the cadence that follows. Perhaps not prospectively but certainly retrospectively, the rhythm, timbre, and melody also call out for what follows—simplicity after extreme complexity, the reestablishment of balance and equilibrium—only in a different way. These fall into Meyer's category of statistical or "plan-based" implications, because they lead to a climax by virtue of their increasing intensity and to resolution through abating processes.[32] Narrative transformations thus depend on mutually entailing implications within the events themselves.

Transformation, particularly in music, also involves a creative manipulation and integration of the three senses of time—past, present, and future. Ricoeur calls this the "threefold present" and defines it as "distention" or "extension," borrowing the concepts from Augustine. "The soul 'distends' itself as it 'engages' itself," he explains, or alternatively, one can only really experience distention "if the mind acts, that is, expects, attends, and remembers."[33] The shape narrative gives to distention involves expectation, memory, and attention, not in isolation but in interaction with one another. To follow a narrative in music as in literature, one must develop expectations from the work's implications, use one's "accumulated memory" of its events to comprehend or, as Ricoeur puts it, "grasp together in a single mental act things which are not experienced together" and pay attention to understand what comes next.[34]

Narrativity

Narrativity is that which allows a perceiver to develop expectations, grasp together events, and comprehend their implications. Greimas describes it as the organizing principle of all discourse, whether narrative or nonnarrative. Such a concept mediates between what Ferdinand de Saussure called "langue," the semionarrative structures of the language itself, and "parole," the discursive structures in which language is manifested.[35] Narrativity governs the production of a discourse by an author as well as its reading by a perceiver, and relies on the author's and perceiver's narrative competence, or their culturally engrained ability to apprehend how such structures normally behave, as well as how they might behave in the

32. I wish to thank Leonard Meyer for providing me with a copy of his lecture, "Music and Ideology in the Nineteenth Century," presented at Stanford University, 17 and 21 May 1984, and for bringing these categories to my attention.

33. Ricoeur, *Time and Narrative*, 1:21.

34. Ricoeur, *Time and Narrative*, 1:41, 155–61. Ricoeur borrows this idea of comprehension as a "grasping together" from Louis O. Mink, "Interpretation and Narrative Understanding," *Journal of Philosophy* 9, no. 69 (1972): 735–37.

35. Ferdinand de Saussure, *Cours de linguistique générale* (Paris: Payot, 1976).

narrative at hand. Jean-François Lyotard defines this competence as threefold: "know-how, knowing how to speak, and knowing how to hear";[36] but one should add that this competence is not only prospective, but also retrospective, allowing the perceiver to understand what it means to have followed a narrative. From this definition, it is evident that narrativity is based on the temporal archetypes known and understood by a given culture, perhaps even those "presignified at the level of human acting," as Ricoeur puts it.[37] As such, it is clearly much more than the generic word for narrative, more than what Metz loosely defines as that which makes a narrative recognizable and what Ricoeur calls the referential capacity of narrative works; it is what permits a categorical understanding of a narrative's plot, its configuration, and its semantics.

The narrativity of a composition, or the presence of some organizing principle, some macrostructure and syntax characteristic of a certain period and place, presents the listener with a set of probability relationships concerning, for example, where to expect a climax, or how opposing ideas may be brought into reconciliation. The more familiar the listener is with them, the more definite will be the order he or she seeks in the work, and the more occasion the composer has to play with expectation and surprise.[38] It is in fact the "arousal and subsequent inhibition of expectant tendencies in the shaping of musical experience" (through delay, ambiguity, and improbability), as Meyer points out, that gives rise to musical meaning.[39] A work's narrativity then sets the stage for the communication of meaning.

ALTERNATIVES TO NARRATIVE

In the twentieth century, many composers have rejected the paramountcy of narrative or narrativity in music. Their attempts to thwart listeners' expectation of narrative have stimulated three significant innovations with respect to how a composition proceeds through time. The first two innovations—antinarratives and nonnarratives—both challenge important aspects of narrative, but still have narrativity (i.e., some organizing principle). The third—works without narrativity—try to eliminate completely the listeners' predilection to seek for narrativity. My discussion does not intend to reduce composers' search for deeper or less constricting ways of expressing man's relationship to sound and time to merely a

36. Jean-François Lyotard, *The Postmodern Condition: A Report on Knowledge*, trans. G. Bennington and B. Massumi (Minneapolis: University of Minnesota Press, 1984; originally published as *La Condition postmoderne: Rapport sur le savoir*, 1979), 21.

37. Ricoeur, *Time and Narrative*, 1:81.

38. Childs, "Time and Music," 117.

39. Leonard B. Meyer, *Music, the Arts, and Ideas* (Chicago: University of Chicago Press, 1967), 5–11.

rejection of narrative or narrativity. Rather, I seek to show the relationship of these widely divergent styles, whatever their other intentions might be, to narrative concepts.

Antinarrative

Antinarratives are works that rely on the listener's expectation of narrative but frustrate it through continual interruption of a work's temporal processes and proceed by change without narrative transformation. Stravinsky's (indeed even Debussy's) abrupt juxtaposition of contrasting and often unrelated ideas exhibits antinarrative tendencies in the occasional discontinuity of their music's moment-to-moment motion, although the overall structure of their works is not necessarily antinarrative. In literature, Chatman finds such forms dependent on "antistories," or stories in which all choices are equally valid. As in the definition I give to the term, they call into question the logic of narrative that "one thing leads to one and only one other, the second to a third and so on to the finale."[40] Music that leaves "open" to the performer the exact realization of a given set of notes, chords, or rhythms, without giving up some overall organizing principle, may achieve a similar effect. Whatever the definition, Stockhausen's experiments with "moment form" in the late 1950s and 1960s are perhaps the clearest example of antinarrative in music.

Explaining his *Carré* (1958–59) in the program notes for its first performance, Stockhausen first asserts, about the form he is developing, "This piece tells no story. Every moment can exist for itself."[41] In this work, he both eliminates any signification a text may have through using phonemes composed according to purely musical criteria and he defines the units of these forms as moments—quasi-independent sections that neither depend on one another nor are necessarily interrelated.

Stockhausen further explained the intent of his moment forms in an interview with the West German Radio in Cologne on 12 January 1961:

> During the last years there have been forms composed in music which are far removed from the forms of a dramatic finale; they lead up to no climax, nor do they have prepared, and thus expected, climaxes, nor the usual introductory, intensifying, transitional, and cadential stages which are related to the curve of development in a whole work.[42]

This statement reveals that the "story" Stockhausen is rejecting is the narrative curve discussed by Childs. Moment forms, he continues, "are rather immediately

---

40. Chatman, *Story and Discourse*, 56–57.
41. Composer's note, record jacket for *Gruppen* and *Carré*, Deutsche Grammophon 137 002.
42. Liner note for Stockhausen's *Kontakte*, Wergo WER 60009.

intense and—permanently present—endeavor to maintain the level of continued 'peaks' up to the end." By thus refusing to make a hierarchy of the events in such pieces, he shuns any structural configuration of his moments, narrative or otherwise. Without configuration, the precise order of events as well as the beginning and end are more arbitrary. Stockhausen also points out that "at any moment one may expect a maximum or a minimum" and "one is unable to predict with certainty the direction of the movement from any given point," thereby denying any explicit directedness from one moment to the next and any goal-orientation in the work as a whole. Such a focus on individual sections that do not rely on one's accumulated memory from one to the next aims to engage the listener in the "now," a "malleable Now" as Kramer observes,[43] that is a key to escaping our otherwise conventional concept of time as horizontal.

To create a moment form, Stockhausen turned in many of his works to the technique of juxtaposition and the use and integration of noise. In his *Stop* (1965), twenty-eight sections of notated pitches, with only general indications as to the manner in which these notes are to be played, alternate with fourteen sections of "noises," also to be played in certain tempi and with certain dynamic properties. Changes between sections can be abrupt from one of the six instrumental groups to the next, or involving some manner of overlap of either groups of instruments or individual ones. In the middle of the piece, there is even a quotation from a work Kramer considers the first moment form, Stravinsky's *Symphonies of Wind Instruments*. The noises, which, by definition, have no functional implications, "stop" the pitched sections and prevent one from anticipating what will come next.

While there might not be a story, connectedness, mutually entailing implications, or even hierarchical configuration in *Stop*, there is, however, narrativity. The piece consists of not only a continuous metamorphosis of tones and noises but also a particular organizing principle: the presentation of a twelve-tone row, the gradual interpenetration of noises with pitches, and the noises' gradual increase in dynamic intensity from being very soft to very loud. *Stop*, moreover, begins and ends with a single pitch, played *forte*, the work's highest and lowest notes and the first and last notes of the twelve-tone row.[44] The second section, the longest in the work, is in a sense the kernel of the work in that it presents all the twelve tones, "to be read upwards and downwards, several times, with different beginnings and endings," the intervals of a fifth in the tone row,[45] and all the work's dynamic levels, from the loudest to the softest, to be played irregularly and by different instruments. Each note of the row is then presented in its own sections, and at the exact middle of the work, section 21, the three middle notes of the row occur simultaneously, drawing attention to this structural point. In a typical twelve-tone

43. Kramer, "New Temporalities in Music," 194.
44. The row is B, B-flat, G, A, G-sharp, D-sharp, E, A, F, C-sharp, F-sharp, C.
45. That is, F-sharp, C-sharp; G-sharp, D-sharp.

manner, all eleven notes of the row except the last one return in the next to last section, giving a sense of arrival to the final low C when it comes at the very end.[46]

Nonnarrative

Nonnarratives are works that may use elements of narrative but without allowing them to function as they would in a narrative. Much minimal music falls into this category.[47] It consists largely of traditional tonal triads and their inversions; however, the triads are not used as structural means of establishing, departing from, and returning to a tonal center, nor are they incidental references to the tonal system. Operas composed in the minimal style may likewise employ traditional operatic means—singers, stage events, and so on—but they are usually not signifiers of some drama or the signifieds of the music. Stage activity and sound in the Glass operas, for example, are linked only in that they occur at the same time. Most singing in *Akhnaten* is by choruses that, by their nature, do not attempt any characterization.

Minimal works are usually also well-defined structures, in that their elements are mutually related and derive from one another; however, there is no tension inherent in their openings, no peripety in the middle, and the transformations these works undergo is little other than the gradual unfolding of an objective process. Many consist of the constant recycling of a limited number of notes (six in Reich's *Piano Phase* [1967] and five in Glass's *Two Pages* [1968]) whose order, combination, and accentual pattern may change, but without implying any hierarchy either between the notes of the pattern or from one pattern to the next. Lacking any tonal or thematic dialectic, they proceed continuously through repetition, addition, and subtraction of the pattern, but without conflict or interruption, direction or goals. The particular succession of patterns and the number of times one may be repeated is unpredictable. Beginning and end merely frame the processes, articulate the work's boundaries, and separate it from real time; they do not serve to unify the whole.

46. Interestingly, as in other moment forms that Kramer has analyzed in his "Moment Form in Twentieth-Century Music," Stockhausen uses the Fibonacci number series in *Stop* to determine the duration of each of his moments. Each of the sections lasts the duration of one of the Fibonacci numbers between 3 and 55: 8, 55, 5, 5, 5, 13, 5, 5, 13, 8, 8, 13, 8, 5, 13, 5, 21, 34, 3, . . . except immediately before and after the middle point, when two sections last 32 and $27 \times 2 = 54$ beats, respectively. I thank Eduardo Larin for bringing this piece to my attention.

47. Glass, in an interview with Cole Gagne and Tracy Caras, 13 November 1980, in Gagne and Caras, *Soundpieces* (Metuchen, N.J.: Scarecrow Press, 1982), specifically calls his music nonnarrative and remarks: "because it is non-narrative, we don't hear it within the usual time frame of most musical experiences . . . we don't hear the music as narrative or a model of colloquial time. What we're hearing then is music in another time system" (214).

Although several minimal pieces return to their original material at the end, such as Reich's *Clapping Music* or his *Piano Phase*, which begins and ends on a unison after a series of phase shifts, memory does not function in them as it does in narrative music.[48] As Mertens points out, one has to forget or move away from something to remember or return to it, and the repetition in this music is constant.[49] In minimal music, repetition, therefore, does not require a backward glancing, the "existential endeepening" of time; it does not require us to recollect.[50] Instead of mediating past, present, and future, it forces us to concentrate fully on an extended present. Time appears to stand still as the work turns in place. Indeed the object here is not time but eternity.

Contrary to what one might expect, nonnarrative works can have narrativity. Reich's *Music for 18 Musicians* (1974–76) has a clear organizing principle. The piece is built on a type of "cantus firmus," a series of eleven chords, first presented in the opening section and then serving as the basis of a chain of successive compositions (either in an arch form, ABCDCBA, or a phase process), one for each of the chords. The way that certain elements return in the piece from one section to another, even though often in new roles and instrumentations, gives the work an arch shape. For example, not only do the opening chords return at the end of the piece but also the women's voices and bass clarinets that play them. The musical material characterizing section 2, that is, the canon or phase relation between the two xylophones and the two pianos, also returns in section 9, although in a different harmonic context. And so forth. Wesley York has shown how the alternation between two basic processes and their integration in Glass's *Two Pages* also results in an arch form;[51] however, the exposition, development, and varied return he hears in this piece is not obvious and remains for this author inaudible.

Nonnarrativity

A third type of innovation is works without narrativity, those that shun any organizing principle, whether an overall structure or preordained syntax, and thereby try to erase the role of memory.[52] In their search for more ambiguous kinds of

48. An unpublished paper by my research assistant Toshie Kakinuma, "Minimal Music and Narrativity—Reich's *Piano Phase*," presents a penetrating analysis of *Piano Phase* as nonnarrative. I am grateful to her for help in researching this article.

49. W. Mertens, *American Minimal Music*, trans. J. Hautekie (New York: Alexander Broude, 1983; originally published in 1980 as *Amerikaanse repetitieve muziek*).

50. See Ricoeur, "Narrative Time," 183–89, for a fuller discussion of "narrative repetition."

51. Wesley York, "Form and Process," in *Contiguous Lines*, ed. T. DeLio (Lanham, Md.: University Press of America, 1985), 81–106.

52. In his *Film Language*, Christian Mertz discusses the many forms in which the "breakdown of narrativity" has been argued in modern film (185–227).

meaning they cannot or do not wish to clarify, composers of these works renounce and refuse to mediate between the sounds they produce or call for and
all inherited, specific, and codified musical signification.

John Cage has said that syntax in language is like the army in society; to rid
ourselves of it, we must demilitarize language.[53] Since the 1940s, he has turned to
chance procedures for generating his notes in order to use only "sounds free of
[his] intentions" and to ensure a complete absence of repetition, redundancy, and
patterns. Such a compositional method emphasizes not the choices a composer
makes but the questions he asks. Cage explains: "It is, in fact, my taste and my
memory that I wish to be free of."[54] In composing the *Freeman Etudes* for solo
violin (1977–80), for example, as well as the *Etudes Australes* for piano and the
Etudes Boreales for piano and cello from the same period, Cage superimposed a
transparent sheet on a map of the stars and derived his sound aggregates from a
one-centimeter-wide grid drawn on the sheet. After determining which of the
twelve tones on his grid each star was nearest, he then used chance operations to
select in which octave the note would be played, with which duration and dynamic
intensity, which microtonal inflections would be added to it, and so on. Only
bowing and fingering were left to the performer's discretion.[55] The composer refers
to this piece as "all process" and to the variety that arises from the different etudes
as being "like changes in the weather."[56] Constant dynamic changes between each
note give the work great fluidity, but perhaps the most striking effect of this music
(whose every note is determined independently of the surrounding notes) is like
that of the stars, which, on a clear night, appear singular, independent of one another, and of varying densities while at the same time nonhierarchical and undifferentiated within the larger picture of the whole.

As with viewing the stars, whatever shape the perceiver might hear in a *Freeman
Etude* derives more from what he or she is seeking in it than from the work
itself. The extreme registral leaps from virtually inaudible notes four octaves above
middle C to those in the middle register, and occasional extraordinarily long silences such as the nine-second one followed by the twenty-one-second one in the

53. Cage borrows this notion from Norman O. Brown. See his *M.* (Middletown, Conn.:
Wesleyan University Press, 1973), ii, and *Empty Words* (Middletown, Conn.: Wesleyan
University Press, 1979), 183.

54. William Shoemaker, "The Age of Cage," *Downbeat* (December 1984), 27.

55. Telephone interview with author, 21 October 1986. For more details on how Cage
used the star maps to generate his *Freeman Etudes*, see Paul Zukofsky, "John Cage's Recent
Violin Music," in *A John Cage Reader*, ed. P. Gena and J. Brent (New York: C. F. Peters,
1982), 103–5.

56. Telephone interview with author, 21 October 1986. In his *Empty Words*, Cage furthermore explains how a process is like the weather: "In the case of weather, though we
notice changes in it, we have no clear knowledge of its beginning or ending. At a given
moment, we are when we are" (178).

fifteenth etude, mitigate strongly against any narrativity being read into the work. It is a strange coincidence, then, when, in the fifth etude, the first nine notes—probably the most regular rhythmic succession of notes in the set—sound like a phrase when they end with a falling fourth and a diminuendo to ppp [*pianissimo*], and when they are followed by another quasi phrase of fifteen notes that ends with a falling fifth and a large *crescendo*.

Other composers, like Jean-Charles François and John Silber in the improvisatory group Kiva, have investigated how to get away from "collective memory" by doing away with notation systems and traditional instruments, both of which in their view severely limit the "information content" of music. Their interest has been in sound, prelinguistic sound that is essentially nonrepeatable and cannot be fully notated, and in composing with color and timbre rather than with notes, lines, or counterpoint. To free themselves of automatic reflexes and knowledge of semantic and syntactic musical systems, over a twelve-year period they developed a series of movement exercises for the body and the voice ranging from placing the body in certain positions to produce different vocal expressions to experimenting with "nasal projections very high in the head," "sounds that are chest driven," and others that are "almost abdominal in their projection."[57] In three essay-performances, Jean-Charles François described their search for a "music of no memory, yet presence" that derives from sound itself rather than any "belief systems embedded in our ears."[58]

In this music of constant change, sounds are explored rather than exploited, sometimes collectively by the performer-composers, sometimes by only one of them. Silence plays a preeminent role, shaping the sounds that move into and out of it, usually almost imperceptibly. Many of Kiva's sounds derive from mundane gestures, such as moving objects on a table or parts of an instrument, others from using the voice and playing traditional instruments—keyboard, percussion, winds, and the violin—in nontraditional, at times electronically altered ways. Their incorporation of media, ranging from dance to silent film to video, serves to increase the variety and complexity of the expression and its meaning.

New Forms of Narrative in Contemporary Music

In the late 1980s, there developed a gap between music whose organizational principles or lack thereof are used to stretch the limits of our perceptions (such as totally serialized works and some chance-determined ones) and music whose

57. Interview with author, 22 May 1986.

58. Jean-Charles François, "Music without Representation and Unreadable Notation," "Trigger-Timbre, Dynamic Timbre," and "Entanglements, Networks, and Knots," papers presented at the departmental seminar of the Music Department, University of California, San Diego, 2, 9, and 10 October 1986.

experience is easily perceptible but vaguely structured (such as some minimal music and Pauline Oliveros's meditation music). Both have risks—the intricate complexity of the former may be imperceptible, while the utter simplicity of the latter may appear without meaning. Some composers have used narrative again as an explicit form of communication in order to bridge that gap.

First, the signification process returned in art music. In the mid-1960s, George Rochberg began to quote tonal music of the past; later he composed sections of movements or whole movements in the language of tonality. The variation movement of his Third String Quartet (1971–72), for example, is not only unambiguously in A major and thematic, but in each variation the rhythmic values become increasingly quick—from eighth notes to sixteenth and triplet sixteenth notes, to thirty-second notes, to trills—as in variation movements of late Beethoven works. Penderecki's Second Symphony (1979–80) uses a tonal form, the sonata allegro, as well as a Brucknerian orchestra. In pieces such as these, tonality and other references to music of the past are as much the subjects of the discourse as operatic recitative was for Beethoven in his Ninth Symphony.

John Cage's two operas, *Europera I* and *II* (premiered at the Frankfurt Opera, November 1987), consist entirely of quotations. The ten singers in the first opera and nine in the second perform a collage of sixty-four opera arias of their choice, ranging from Gluck to Puccini, interspersed with instrumentalists playing fragments from the same arias. Chance determines the order of the arias, and both operas end when their time is up—one and one-half hours for the first and forty-five minutes for the second. Unlike most operas, there is no story, although the stories of the various operas quoted are printed in the program notes, and no relationship between the music and the costumes, lighting, singers' actions, or décor.[59]

Composers also increasingly linked their music to other art forms, using them to reinforce a composition's meaning or make it more apparent. Roger Reynolds's music and Ed Emshwiller's video for *Eclipse* (1979–81) treat images analogously to suggest an analogous content. Both communicate the idea of emerging and going beyond traditional boundaries by taking an abstract outline (whether synthesized sounds with vowel-like properties or a circle) and then continuously transforming it, first into something representational (standard speech or faces) and then into something suprareal (represented by the juxtaposition of six or eight fragmented texts and three different voices behaving in three different ways, together with the image of the face whose various aspects are in constant metamorphosis). After alternating between only sound and only image, the modes only combine when both are attempting to exceed their boundaries.

In a number of works that resemble dramatic cantatas, composers have even turned to the use of a story in the traditional sense of the word. Frederic Rzewski's

59. From interview with author, 21 October 1986.

setting of Brecht's epic poem *Antigone-Legend* (1983), for soprano and piano, is literally programmatic, using musical means such as register, rhythm, dynamics, and timbre to differentiate the personas and recount the drama. The first two times Antigone speaks, the singer uses *sprechstimme* to distinguish her from the narrator. Many descriptions and introductions of her and occasionally her vocal line are characteristically marked by syncopated rhythms, sometimes simultaneously in both the piano and the voice (such as at r. ns. 46–50, 51–52, 55, 57–59, 64, and 74). At one point (r. ns. 103–11) the singer (as narrator) describes a conversation between Kreon and his son, while the piano interrupts the tale after each sentence as if to act out their dialogue. "To avoid the risk of losing the element of action in the sterile ritual of the concert hall," the composer indicates that the music should be accompanied by either hand-held puppets that represent the play's action or by screens on which the most important scenes are painted. Harrison Birtwistle's *Nenia: the Death of Orpheus* (1970) also uses one singer in three roles (Orpheus, Eurydice, and the narrator), has each sing in a different manner, and rapidly changes from one to the next to suggest several simultaneous perspectives on the action.

Bernard Rands's two song cycles, *Canti Lunatici* (1981) and *Canti del Sol* (1983), embody four signifieds—a story, another art form (the poetry), other musical compositions, and tonality, but without representing characters or actions with specific musical material. In *Canti Lunatici*, the chosen order in which the fifteen poems appear tells a three-tiered story—a mythical one of the waxing and waning of the moon, a stellar one of the seasons, and a psychological one of humans' responses to the moon's phases. The poems of the second cycle tell a similar story of the sun's cycle. The composer ensures the accessibility of these texts to English-speaking audiences by providing translations of those sung in Italian, Spanish, German, and French and by having the lights on during performances so they can be read. He differentiates the two cycles, moreover, by setting the moon poems in a melismatic or florid manner (to suggest a kind of lunacy) and the sun poems with quickly moving syllables, particularly at the beginning, when the work gathers momentum rapidly, the way the sun rises.

In the middle of *Canti Lunatici*, wherein the composer sets the eighth poem of the set $(7 + 1 + 7)$ describing the moon at its fullest, Rands quotes Debussy's *Clair de lune* in the piano, changing it somewhat (such as the intervals of a fifth to tritones) but maintaining exactly the same rhythms, gestures, melodic contours, and registral changes. The singer, meanwhile, occasionally repeats the same notes and rhythms as the piano part but most of the time reads the text, drawing the listener's attention to the surreal images (white moons with diamond navels, with weeping black tears, etc.) of the Hans Arp poem. The instrumentalists, quiet at first, gradually overwhelm both stanzas of the poem with aggressively loud oscillating figures in the winds and xylophones, reiterating the tritone on which the piece is based, A–E-flat. At the end of *Canti del Sol*, Rands also quotes the contour and rhythms of the vocal line of Debussy's setting of Baudelaire's *Harmonie du soir* in his vocal setting of the same poem. Although quite fitting references, these quotations depend on the listener's familiarity with what is being quoted for the meaning of these sections to be truly multiple.

This extensive use of signifieds and even story in Rands's pieces raises the question of whether their structure and logic are those of a narrative. Other than the return to the opening middle-register A in the vocal part of *Canti Lunatici* at the end of the piece, and the return at the end of *Canti del Sol* to the words that began *Canti Lunatici*, "Ognuno sta solo . . . ed subito sera" (Each one stands alone . . . and in no time it's evening), thus marking the end of a twenty-four-hour cycle, there is no repetition or return in the two works. But the order in which the poems are arranged gives an arch shape to the first cycle as well as to the two cycles as a whole. And even though there are two tonal centers in *Canti Lunatici*, A and E-flat, the continual elaboration of these tonalities throughout the work gives it great coherence. The opening melisma that introduces the tritone between the A and E-flat is furthermore a classic "narrative situation," posing the musical question of how the two tonalities will be brought into a satisfying relationship.

Moreover, while the organization of *Canti Lunatici* is not that of a narrative curve, the work does generally follow the story. In addition, though each poem, surrounded by some silence, seems almost self-sufficient, the work's events do progress, not just succeed one another. They are connected by a configuration the composer calls "labyrinthine," which he compares to that of Joyce's *Ulysses*.[60] Sometimes the story is in evidence and the musical phrases develop linearly; other times, the composer digresses, and the music moves tangentially to explore myriad possibilities suggested in the musical ideas themselves, before returning to the story and picking up the thread again. Because the musical events are not primarily dependent on previous ones and are implied only ultimately, they do not occur in the traditional narrative order wherein if one leaves out one aspect of the story, then one cannot continue and is lost. Narrative in this music results instead from the kaleidoscopic presentation of elements of a story whose *cumulative* impact, rather than moment-to-moment logic, is that of a narrative.

In conclusion, I am suggesting that a new kind of narrative arose in some late twentieth-century works. These narratives borrow the most important attributes of traditional narratives—the use of signifieds, well-defined structures, configuration, unifying reference points, transformation, and memory. But they continue to respond to the modern desire for expressing the multiplicity of existence, fragmentary and seemingly irrational orders, and meanings that go beyond those that are known. They may use many signifieds—complementary ones (as in *Canti Lunatici*) or contradictory ones (as in Cage's *Europera I* and *II*)—that reinforce each other's meaning or inspire new meanings. Even if their configuration is not

---

60. From interview with author, 16 May 1986.

that of a dramatic curve, their structures generally have clearly defined beginnings and endings, and they reach closure of one sort or another. They often progress to and from what Machover calls "nodal points," points of departure and arrival provided by the story.[61] But perhaps most important, such works may incorporate more than one narrative, either successively or simultaneously. Birtwistle, for example, presents four versions of Eurydice's death in *The Mask of Orpheus* (1986), and intersperses six related myths that comment on the Orpheus myth. By contrast, in his opera *Valis* (1987) Machover develops four narrative strands at the same time—the main character's normal life, his connection to the narrator, his double, his relation to a woman trying to commit suicide, and his mental world as reflected in the journal he is writing.

The logic of these narratives is often that of the kaleidoscope. Rands says he felt no compunction about reordering the events of Van Gogh's life to present them in a kaleidoscopic manner in his opera *Le Tambourin* (1986). Such a method of composition places emphasis on the whole rather than the precise movement of one section to another. Transformation in these works thus does not depend on immediate connections from one section to the next but rather on some overall connectivity. The goal, as in *Canti Lunatici*, is to make a cumulative impact. From this perspective, then, narrative is the sense that one has of a certain kind of a whole when one has reached the end, not necessarily while one is listening to each and every part in its middle.

TIME AND MIND

As it reflects the mind's search for making sense and for order, narrative is not just a mode of perception and cognition but also a mode of thinking. With time as its material and its ultimate reference, it differs in a significant way from the mode of thinking that involves abstract logic.[62] The mental process Ricoeur calls configuration, or the "grasping together" of events that are not simultaneous into one thought he calls plot, is a critical characteristic of narrative thinking, that which makes possible the conception and construction of temporal wholes. As Ricoeur points out, "it is only in virtue of poetic composition that something counts as a beginning, middle, and end."[63] The fact that we tend to impose narrative or try to perceive it, especially when listening to music, even when it is clearly not in evidence, suggests that narrative has come to dominate the way we think of the processes of life and nature. As such, then, it provides us with a way of understanding

---

61. From interview with author, 4 June 1986.

62. As Claude Bremond points out in his *Logique du récit* (Paris: Seuil, 1973), the minimal condition for narrative's existence is that something happen to a subject between a time *t* and a time $t + n$ (99–100).

63. Ricoeur, *Time and Narrative*, 1:38.

our predecessors and of communicating not only with each other but also our successors.

However, because people's experience and understanding of time has changed in this century, artists of all kinds, particularly composers, have sought to give form to other processes that are not necessarily goal-oriented, dramatic, or organic. One cannot develop expectations about these processes or resolve their inexplicable but inherent contradictions; one cannot grasp them into one thought; one can only endure them. Antinarratives, nonnarratives, and works without narrativity, particularly in music, reveal how inadequate the idea of basing a narrative on ordinary time has become. The return to using narrative concepts, perhaps in response to the crisis over a lack of norms in this century,[64] signals a renewed desire on the part of composers to have their audiences participate in the aesthetic experience by bringing their own knowledge of life's processes to the music; however, as life has changed, the events that are signified and organized by those narratives have changed. Postmodern narratives, if one dares to call them that, do create an order—what Lyotard calls an "internal equilibrium"—but at the same time, unlike their predecessors, they "tolerate the incommensurable."[65]

---

64. Jürgen Habermas calls this the century's "legitimation crisis" in his *The Legitimation Crisis*, trans. T. McCarthy (Boston: Beach Press, 1975), 6–9. Lyotard borrows and expands on this concept.

65. Lyotard explains: "Postmodern knowledge is not simply a tool of the authorities; it refines our sensitivity to differences and reinforces our ability to tolerate the incommensurable. Its principle is not the expert's homology, but the inventor's paralogy" (*The Postmodern Condition*, xxv, 7).

2. Postmodernism, Narrativity, and the Art of Memory

O N Saburo Teshigawara's "Blue Meteorite" (Aoi Inseki), a man is caught between, on the right, an enormous wall of large glass panes representing the past and, on the left, a sheet of blue suggesting the future. His dilemma, as the Japanese dance company Karas presented it at the Los Angeles Festival in September 1990, is not unlike our own. "Standing before the huge present time, what can I do?" writes the choreographer and soloist; "I dance. . . . Dancing is the present, come out and go away in each moment. The eternal present, that's my sense of time—sense of beauty."

Is this "white dance," "pure dance," one that formulates "a bold new vocabulary for the human body," as European critics and the company in its promotion have described it? By quoting such descriptions in his program notes, Teshigawara places himself squarely in the modernist tradition. He seeks to "exponentially increase the possibilities for choreographic expression." The production itself, however, tells another story.

In front of the seductive blue screen on the left, as distant and illusive as the *azur* of a French symbolist poem, lies a field of broken glass three or four feet wide. The first sentence in the poetic program note explains: "The broken pieces of glass which are spread on the stage as shadow of the blue wall represent both crystals of light and fragments of time." As such, these transparent fragments represent shards

This essay originally appeared in the *Contemporary Music Review* 7 (1993): 3–32; it is included here by permission, copyright 1993 Harwood Academic Publishers.

I would like to thank the students in my postmodernism and hermeneutics seminars in 1990 and 1991 at the University of California, San Diego: Mark Applebaum, Eric Dries, Steve Elster, Stevan Key, Erik Knutzen, Keith Kothman, Charlie Kronengold, Tim Labor, Rafael Linan, Richard McQuillan, Dave Meckler, Margaret Murray, Mary Oliver, Frank Pecquet, Linda Swedensky, and Carol Vernallis. Their insights, commitment to the inquiry, and music were an inspiration; I dedicate this work to them.

of the past, standing guard before the future and demanding reconsideration before one can move forward.

During the hour-long, three-part work, the dancer interacts with these symbolic elements. In the first part, he exults in his own presence. Then, moving before and behind the glass wall, flirting with the distance between spirit and body, he engages with each of his three doubles ("five years old, fifteen years old, ninety-five years old"). In the second part, he approaches cautiously and then enthusiastically the glass field on the left "where as a white faun he dances." The glass shatters; dancer and audience alike wince. But as if to suggest that reliving the agony of past moments brings its own pleasure, the dancer begins to pick up the pieces and caress them. At the same time, the music modulates from electronically produced background sound to Debussy's *Prelude to the Afternoon of a Faun*.

When accompanied by Debussy's music, these caressing gestures are not "pure dance"; they recall those of Nijinsky when at the end of his 1912 choreography for *Faun* he picked up and affectionately fondled a veil one of the nymphs had left behind. As Teshigawara lies down and thrusts his body into the glass pieces, trying to make love to them, the knowledgeable viewer cannot help remembering Nijinsky's similar gesture at the end of his ballet. In the manner of Pina Bausch, the choreographer calls on such references to clarify his meaning. Like the veil, which symbolized Nijinsky's memory of the nymphs, and like the Ballets Russes production of *Faun*, which harked back to ancient Greece, the shards of glass here suggest a past the dancer is desperately trying to hold onto, despite it being in fragments.

Unlike Nijinsky, however, Teshigawara rises after his ecstasy to continue the dance, despite the piercing sound of the glass underfoot. In this, the third part of the dance, the dancer returns to center stage. From there, unable or unwilling to face the blue wall of the future, he repeats the same gesture over and over, reaching out and falling down, rising, reaching, and falling again in apparent despair. The work ends where it began.

Much of this work's choreographic vocabulary, its self-consciousness and pretense at autonomy from any specific context, its preoccupation with the past, and its final despair show modernist concerns; however, the dancer's attitude toward time amid this spatialization of the past, present, and future is somewhat different. Although the choreographer may wish to confront the frontiers of expression, the dancer does not engage with the blue wall of the future. The modernist notion of progress is absent. He is willing to confront his past, to traverse the wasteland of his memory, to make sense of it, to enjoy it. But ultimately he does not escape the present.

The dancer's despair at the end of "Blue Meteorite" invites us to reexamine our perception of time, not as an abstract Kantian category of knowledge or the flow that leads us into the future but as an interactive experience involving personal and social meaning. In the postmodern era, as Frederic Jameson has argued, spatial rather than temporal concerns dominate "our daily life, our psychic experience, our cultural languages";[1] interest is focused on the meaning lodged in our experience of the present, even the physical present, more than in our expectations about the future. In musical terms, the challenge this suggests for composers is not one of creating continuity or discontinuity within a work or a tradition, establishing and fulfilling or subverting goals, but rather one of making or suggesting connections within a synchronic situation.[2] Despite (or because of) the world of satellite simulcasts, email, conference calls, and growing interdependence among nations, many people feel increasingly isolated from one another. Connections are neither easy nor evident. An important tool for making them is memory. The past is not something to embrace or reject or something on which to build in spiraling toward the future; it is also the repository of memory. Whether private or public, intimate or collective, memory is something we all possess. It makes possible communication.

Before the written tradition became dominant, philosophers, rhetoricians, and preachers considered memory a powerful tool for reflecting on the world and turning sense impressions into understanding. In her book *The Art of Memory*, Frances Yates examines how this concept evolved over the centuries.[3] Plato believed our memories contain forms of the Ideas, the realities the soul knew before its descent. (For example, we perceive two things as equal because the Idea of equality is innate in us.) Knowledge of the truth consists in remembering, in the recollection of these Ideas. Aristotle went further. From his perspective, constructing images to help us remember is similar to selecting images about which to think; memory makes possible the higher thought processes. To explain reminiscence, or how to navigate through memory, he emphasized two principles, association and order. Using places and images arranged in some order—what was later called a memory palace[4]—one

1. Frederic Jameson, "Postmodernism, or The Cultural Logic of Late Capitalism," *New Left Review* 146 (1984), 64. As the reader will soon see, when it comes to music, I do not entirely agree with other aspects of Jameson's argument about postmodernism (the role of memory, the breakdown of the signifier, the replacement of works by texts, etc.).

2. While what I am referring to shares important aspects with Jonathan Kramer's notion of "vertical time" in his "New Temporalities in Music," *Critical Inquiry* 7, no. 3 (1981): 539–56, it is actually closer to Ken Gaburo's definition of composition as an ecosystem wherein a sense of the whole, a sense of place, is defined by what is connected and what effects the connections. Gaburo presented these ideas to my seminar on postmodernism in music at the University of California, San Diego, 12 April 1990.

3. Frances Yates, *The Art of Memory* (Chicago: University of Chicago Press, 1966), 36, 33. I am grateful to Stevan Key for pointing me to this book, which he says he has found on the bookshelves of many composers on the West Coast in recent years.

4. Yates, *The Art of Memory*, 3–4, 34–36, 46–47, 71–72. Augustine explains *loci* as "the fields and spacious palaces of memory where are the treasures of innumerable images, brought into it from things of all sorts perceived by the senses" (46). George Johnson, *In the Palaces of Memory: How We Build the Worlds Inside Our Heads* (New York: Knopf, 1991), defines a memory palace more generally as "a structure for arranging knowledge" (xiii).

can effect an artificial memory consisting of mnemonic techniques that improve one's natural memory. Cicero and Augustine expanded on these ideas. The former included memory as one of the five parts of rhetoric, the latter as one of the three powers of the soul, along with understanding and will. In the Renaissance and later, the occult movements turned memory into a science, paving the way for the development of the scientific method.

In the arts, the notion of memory relates closely to that of narrativity. Typically, scholars and critics use this term to refer to what characterizes narratives. In chapter 1 I argued somewhat differently, following the example of the French semiotician A. J. Greimas. Even antinarratives and nonnarratives can have narrativity, if this means the presence of some organizing principle, some macrostructure and syntax that permits categorical understanding of a work's configuration and its semantics.[5] Here, in response to more recent musical developments, I wish to expand the definition of a work's narrativity to that mutually agreed-on quality, normally preexisting in the culture, that allows the composer to plug into the listener's mind, to engage his or her memory. Of course, this relies on what Lyotard calls "know-how, knowing how to speak, and knowing how to hear,"[6] but it does not necessarily refer exclusively to a macrostructure or specific syntax. As for new narratives with which composers have been experimenting, this more general definition of narrativity permits discussion of multiple kinds of meaning and works that follow the logic of a kaleidoscope. Only those works that try to erase the role of memory, that refuse to mediate between the sounds they produce and any specific meaning, can be called works without narrativity. Because I have already discussed new forms of narrative in recent music, what interests me here are new forms of narrativity. How can composers engage their listeners, call on memory, and play with it without necessarily having recourse to overarching forms and syntax? What does it mean to use narrative devices such as storytelling without creating a narrative macrostructure? Answering these questions will help to define an emerging musical aesthetic that is rooted in postmodernism but beginning to go beyond conventional notions of it in important ways.

Modernist Influence Anxiety

It is one of the ironies of modernism that this aesthetic can embrace the ephemeral, the transitory, and the ever-new and at the same time as be persistently preoc-

---

5. In chapter 1, I defined antinarratives as "works that rely on the listener's expectation of narrative but frustrate it through continual interruption of a work's temporal processes and proceed by change without narrative transformation";" nonnarratives are "works that may use elements of narrative but without allowing them to function as they would in a narrative."

6. François Lyotard, *The Postmodern Condition: A Report on Knowledge*, trans. G. Bennington and B. Massumi (Minneapolis: University of Minnesota Press, 1984), 21.

cupied with tradition and the past. In his book *Remaking the Past*, Joseph Straus defines the incorporation and reinterpretation of earlier music as the "mainstream of musical modernism."[7] This practice links neoclassical composers like Stravinsky with progressive ones like Schönberg. Borrowing from Harold Bloom, Straus speaks of the relationship between these composers and their predecessors as being fraught with the "anxiety of influence." This anxiety arises because all language is always the revision of preexistent language, and analogously, "poetry lives always under the shadow of poetry."[8] Poetic strength, as Bloom defines it, involves the "usurpation" from one's predecessors and the "imposition" of one's own will on their accomplishments.[9] Straus, like Bloom, calls works creative misreadings when composers deliberately appropriate elements associated with their predecessors, ranging from specific quotations of certain pitch-class sets, textures, or sections of music to triads and conventional forms. They do this to overcome and neutralize these forerunners, or, in Bloom's terms, "to clear imaginative space for themselves."[10] From this perspective, quoting from the past is a way to assert one's own priority, power, and strength. An obsession with the past can reflect an obsession with one's own place in history, and vice versa.

Like most contemporary theorists, Straus's focus is "musical construction." To illuminate deep structure, he uses pitch-class set theory. The thrust of his argument, however, goes further as he proposes a theory of the strategies composers use to treat borrowed material. Inspired by Bloom's categories of revision, Straus explores the ways composers rework their predecessors' music often to serve different aesthetic intentions, how they compress, fragment, neutralize, immobilize, generalize, and marginalize borrowed elements. It is these strategies, he asserts, more than any specific structure that "define a twentieth-century common practice."[11] On one level, Straus thus shares the preoccupations of modernist composers with coherence; but on another he recognizes that many twentieth-century works "are relational events as much as they are self-contained organic entities"[12]— "our understanding of such pieces will be enriched if we can fully appreciate their clash of conflicting and historically distinct elements."[13]

---

7. Joseph Straus, *Remaking the Past: Musical Modernism and the Influence of the Tonal Tradition* (Cambridge, Mass.: Harvard University Press, 1990), 2.

8. Harold Bloom, *Poetry and Representation* (New Haven, Conn.: Yale University Press, 1976), 4.

9. Bloom, *Poetry and Representation*, 6.

10. Harold Bloom, *The Anxiety of Influence* (New York: Oxford University Press, 1973), 5.

11. Straus, *Remaking the Past*, 17.

12. In his *The Anxiety of Influence*, Bloom writes of poetic influence or "poetic misprision" as "necessarily the study of the life-cycle of the poet-as-poet" and the "intra-poetic relationships" as "parallels of family romance," though without the Freudian overtones (7, 8).

13. Straus, *Remaking the Past*, 16.

Boulez's first important work with text, *Le Visage nuptial* (1946–47; 1951–52; 1988–89), is a good example of this influence anxiety. Boulez began this setting of René Char's love poetry when he was twenty-one. A soprano and an alto are accompanied by a small instrumental ensemble in the 1946–47 version and by a chorus of sopranos and altos and a large orchestra in the 1951–52 one. The vocal writing encompasses microtones, one between each conventionally notated semitone, and intonations ranging from spoken to *sprechstimme* to sung. For each of these performance indications, Boulez developed a special notation. Doubtless because of the difficulty of this work, these versions were never recorded.[14]

In the orchestral score published by Heugel in 1959, and especially in the revision performed at the Festival d'Automne in Paris on 17 November 1989, one can surmise Boulez's attitude toward his predecessors: make reference in order to overcome and surpass. In many ways, the work is a direct response to a work of his teacher, Olivier Messiaen—*Trois petites liturgies de la présence divine*, written in 1943–44 and first performed on 21 April 1945. In his notes to the 1983 recording, Messiaen recounts that Boulez was in the audience for the premiere along with virtually every other composer and cultural figure in Paris.[15] The work was so successful that it was performed again almost immediately and one hundred times all over the world by 1956. Whether it was the social success that the young Boulez coveted or the power of the aesthetic innovations or both, the work left a mark on Boulez's imagination as he began *Le Visage nuptial* a year after the Messiaen premiere. As in *Trois petites liturgies*, wherein piano and Ondes Martenot play major roles, the first version of *Le Visage nuptial* features piano and two Ondes Martenot (an electronic instrument invented in 1928), in addition to percussion, a soprano and an alto. In 1951–52 Boulez deleted the piano and Ondes Martenot when he revised the work for full orchestra, soloists, and chorus.

In the orchestral version, the most obvious quotations come in the chorus, again one of only women, as in the Messiaen work. The presence of a chorus is in itself a reference to the past, the early part of the century when, in response to public taste, composers wrote many large choral works. Echoes not only of Messiaen but also of Messiaen's predecessors, Debussy and Stravinsky, pervade both the 1959 score and the 1989 revision, as if Boulez was trying to diffuse the immediate influence of his teacher by reference to the earlier composers.[16] The chorus's unison singing, for example, recalls not only Messiaen's exclusive use of this technique throughout *Trois petites liturgies* but also the texture of the women's chorus in "Sirènes" from Debussy's *Nocturnes*. But it is one section in the middle of the

14. Leduc published the 1989 revision in 1994; it is this version that Erato recorded in 1990: WE 2292–45494–2.

15. United Musicians International Productions, UM 6507.

16. I am grateful to Charlie Kronengold for urging me to give more attention to the complexities of Messiaen's influence on this work.

third poem that makes explicit reference, this time not to Messiaen but to Stravinsky. In it, the man of the poem describes the consummation of his love:

> Timbre de la devise matinale, morte-saison de l'étoile précoce,
> Je cours au terme de mon cintre, colisée fossoyé.
> Assez baisé le crin nubile des céréales;
> La cardeuse, l'opinâtre, nos confines la soumettent.
> Assez maudit le havre des simulacres nuptiaux:
> Je touche le fond d'un retour compact.

> Doorbell of the morning's motto, dead season of the precocious star,
> I come to the end of my arch, a grave-dug coliseum.
> Enough of sucking the nubile horsehair of grain:
> The carder, the obstinate carder is subject to our confines.
> Enough of cursing the haven of nuptial images:
> I am touching bottom for a compact return.[17]

Musically Boulez borrows here directly from Stravinsky's *Les Noces*, also the source for certain rhythmic vocabulary and intervallic contours in the first of the *Trois petites liturgies*, another work about ritual and love, albeit divine instead of sexual love. Like the poetry of Char, *Les Noces*, as Boulez puts it, synthesizes violence and irony.[18] It is almost as if Boulez wishes to suggest analogues for the "nuptial images" the man is cursing, not only with the reference to the nuptial preparations in the opening of *Les Noces* but also with the incorporation of Stravinsky's music, a possible emblem of Boulez's own musical preparation, of which he may have felt he had had enough.

What clues the listener in to this similarity with the Stravinsky is the descending minor ninth. Boulez uses this interval throughout the song. But when (beginning in m. 141) it is followed by numerous reiterations of the same note as the chorus syllabically declaims the text in changing meters, this "doorbell of morning's motto,"

17. For the most part, this translation comes from René Char, *Hypnos Waking: Poems and Prose by René Char*, trans. J. Mathews (New York: Random House, 1956), 74–83; it also appears in Joan Peyser, *Boulez: Composer, Conductor, Enigma* (New York: Schirmer, 1976), 268–77.

This stanza of the poem, as Kronengold pointed out to me, has a relationship to the poetic tradition that is similar to that of Boulez's music to its predecessors. The poet here borrows from the troubadours the tradition of the aubade, which M. Drabble in *The Oxford Companion to English Literature* (Oxford: Oxford University Press, 1985), 49, defines as a "dawn song, usually describing the regret of two lovers at their imminent separation." By reducing the "morning's motto," the morning star, to only a reverberation, an echo, a "doorbell," the poet divests the "precocious star" from its mythic and poetic history and its association with Lucifer. Char thus also treats the past as a "simulacrum," merely an image of what it was. I am grateful to Charlie for reading this chapter and offering many valuable suggestions.

18. Pierre Boulez, "Style ou idée: Éloge ou de l'amnésie," in *Orientations*, ed. Jean-Jacques Nattiez (Cambridge, Mass.: Harvard University Press, 1986), 351. This essay was originally published in *Musique en jeu* (1971).

EXAMPLE 2.1a. Igor Stravinsky, *Les Noces,* beginning at two measures before rehearsal number 2.

Soprano solo

Pauvre, pauv - re d'moi pauvre en - core une fois!

chorus

On tresse on tresse - re la tresse à nas - ta - sie, on tres - se - ra

EXAMPLE 2.1b. Pierre Boulez, *Le Visage nuptial,* third movement, mm. 140–41.

chorus *f* sub.

Tim - bre de la de - vi - se ma - ti - na - le

EXAMPLE 2.1c. Boulez, *Le Visage nuptial,* third movement, mm. 147–48.

chorus *mf*

As - sez bri - sé le crin nu - bi- le de cé - ré - a - les

itself an image of echo, recalls not Messiaen's use of gesture passage in the bird song played by the piano in the opening of *Trois petites liturgies* (m. 6) but rather the augmented octave at two measures before rehearsal number (r. n.) 2 and what follows in the vocal lines of *Les Noces,* that is, when the bride-to-be laments "poor me, poor me," as her hair is being bound in preparation for the wedding ceremony. The rhythmical relationships of m. 141 in the Boulez also resemble those in the first measure of r. n. 2 of the Stravinsky.[19] So, too, do many of the ensuing phrases. (Compare exs. 2.1a, b, and c.)

19. If the language sung is French, the analogy is even clearer because of the necessity for dividing one of the eighth notes into sixteenth notes in the middle of the line to accommodate an extra syllable.

Likewise, the analogous sections both begin with tempo changes and *subito forte* after a *diminuendo* at the end of the previous phrase. The soloists in m. 140 of *Le Visage nuptial* enter in the same range as those in *Les Noces* (but on E-flat rather than F-sharp); then the sopranos and altos in the chorus continue in both pieces, the only significant difference being in how the soloists and the chorus split the phrase. The responsorial alternation of soloists and chorus, and the chorus's unison singing in this section, also echo those of *Les Noces*.

In the orchestra, Boulez uses extended trills just before and during climaxes, as Messiaen does in the second song of *Trois petites liturgies* (r. n. 9 to the end); but the texture and sound of these trills, particularly when coupled with tremoli and short ostinati in other parts, recall Debussy's and especially Stravinsky's use of these gestures more than Messiaen's. As the man of the poem encourages himself to go forward in the pursuit of his love, his body trembling, Boulez creates a series of five such musical climaxes, each followed by a dramatic change of tempo, dynamics, and, especially in the piccolos, a drop in register. These mirror the sexual ebbs and flows suggested in the poem. In the first, mm. 48–50, they accompany the chorus shrieking *fortissimo* on a high E-flat as they express the man's hope soon to be realized: "J'évoque la nage sur l'ombre de sa Présence" (I dream of floating on the shade of her Presence). Another section of strident trills and short ostinati at m. 69 accompany the second climax at m. 71 and the highest notes of the piece, as the man tells himself, "Descent, do not change your mind" and then speaks of "lapidated departures." A third climax gathers momentum with the percussion's pulsating triple-sixteenth-note patterns and the two measures of trills and tremoli in the full orchestra just before the *fortissimo* chord in m. 105 as the chorus completes the phrase "Nativité, guidez les insoumis, qu'ils découvrent leur base, / L'amande croyable au lendemain neuf " (Nativity, guide the unsubmissive, let them find their foundation, / A believable kernel of fresh morrow). This intensity reaches its apex at m. 113. When the piccolos reach again up to the high E-flat at m. 148, and as the man is "cursing the haven of nuptial images" in mm. 153–55, Boulez builds his fourth climax with a very Stravinskyan block-like texture of trills and tremoli in the winds, xylophone, glockenspiel, vibraphone, harps, and strings. At he same time the singers reiterate the minor ninth borrowed from *Les Noces*, E-flat–D, to close this section as it began (see ex. 2.2).

The fifth and final climax of this song begins to build in m. 178 after the man "feels the obscure plantation awakening" and as he utters four parallel phrases in his final drive to "the plateau." Here a similar combination of harp ostinati and string and wind tremoli and trills, as in the beginning of *Petrushka*, accompanies "Je ne verrai pas tes flancs, ces essaims de faim, se dessécher, s'emplit de ronces" (I will not see your body with its swarms of hunger dry up, cluttered with thorns [mm. 178–80]) and "Je ne verrai pas l'approche des beledins inquiéter le jour renaissant" (I will not see the approach of buffoons disturb the coming dawn [in mm. 186–88]). In the latter example, there are also three different but overlapping arpeggio

EXAMPLE 2.2. Boulez, *Le Visage nuptial*, third movement, mm. 153–55.

EXAMPLE 2.3. Boulez, *Le Visage nuptial*, third movement, 186–87.

ostinati in the second violins divisi, like those in r. n. 2 of Debussy's *Sirènes*. (See ex. 2.3.) Tremoli and trills throughout the orchestra, including the percussion, then punctuate the moment the sopranos sing "Chimères, nous sommes montés au plateau" (Illusions, we have climbed to the plateau [mm. 195–96]). Such quotations of orchestral textures (which do not recur in the last two songs) thus function as musical analogues to the "illusions" that the man embraces, then abandons.

At the end of this poem, with "nothing fierce [having] survived," the woman is left "breathing [*respire*]," as if depleted, while the man is "standing erect [*se tient debout*]," his energy still vital. After a long fermata pause, Boulez likewise reasserts this virility in the last four measures of the song with another rapid crescendo to a *tutti fortissimo*. It is in the next two songs, however, that he demonstrates the strength of his imaginative power. There he eschews further quotation of Stravinsky in order to experiment with and expand on a radically new treatment of chorus and orchestra inspired by the third part of Messiaen's *Trois petites liturgies*. In the Messiaen work, the chorus alternates between speaking and singing their lines. Addressing God, they sing; describing the "time of man and of the planet" (such as in r. ns. 1 and 10) or God present in man (r. ns. 3 and 12), they speak. Messiaen reinforces these changes by alternating between triple and duple accompanimental patterns, as well as between different material in the piano and celesta. He also reserves the maracas for the spoken lines only, while having the strings provide continuity throughout the piece.

The chorus in the third song of the Boulez work also alternates between the two techniques, although for no apparent reason. In "Evadné" and "Post-Scriptum," the fourth and fifth songs of *Le Visage nuptial*, however, Boulez accentuates even more blatantly than Messiaen the juxtapositions that in the third song he had otherwise buried within a continuous texture. For these last songs, he asks that the singers be placed on a different level than that of the orchestra. In the fourth one, which recounts the consummation of their love in the past tense and expresses how their "hunger and restraint were reconciled [avidité et contrainte s'étaient réconciliées]," five altos, alternating with five sopranos, dispassionately declaim the entire poem without any determined pitches and in absolutely regular sixteenth notes, as in the spoken sections of the Messiaen. When declaimed by the sopranos, the full orchestra accompanies; when declaimed by the altos, silence or minimal percussion accompanies. The percussion is the only element that bridges the sections. In "Post-Scriptum," the juxtapositions are even more stark, as the man of the poem begins to leave the woman, "A vos pieds je suis né, mais vous m'avez perdu" (I was born at your feet, but you have lost me). The orchestra here consists of only two groups, the percussion and the strings. The strings, playing divisi with up to twelve to sixteen different lines per part, accompany the sung lines; the percussion the spoken ones.

The last line of the cycle, "Ecartez-vous de moi qui patiente sans bouche" (Leave me, let me wait unspeaking), is very significant. One can imagine Boulez himself thinking such an idea as he finally turns away from his musical predecessors. In his hands, this line becomes a refrain—what was the first and seventh line of the original poem he reiterates again in the middle and at the end of the work, just as Schumann for similar reasons added "Ich grolle nicht" to the middle and end of Heine's poem in the *Dichterliebe*. In addition, the recurrence of this line constitutes an occasion for special treatment, a display of Boulez's creative imagination. In the first appearance, the soloists and altos sing it *mezzo piano*, dividing its phrases among themselves; in the second, the altos speak it with "half-voice" in the low register; in the third, the soloists and the sopranos sing it *fortissimo* and passionately at the same time that the altos simultaneously speak it in a "broken, violent" manner. In the last instance, the five altos utter it "with their breath," "almost without articulation, without any timbre." At this point, pitch and durational changes in the orchestra also nearly freeze. For seven measures, the strings maintain a trill on one chord, *pianissimo*. The only instruments punctuating the syllables of the almost inaudible chorus at the end of the work are the percussion.

The change in the percussion's function from being part of the orchestral texture in the first three poems to becoming the sole accompaniment to the voice in parts of the last two poems marks an important development for Boulez. While the singers and orchestra are tainted with purposive references to the past, the percussion represents the exotic, the unusual, and is not used in a way that makes quotation evident.[20] Boulez's placement of this group center stage but far to the back in the 1989 performance suggests that the composer considered these instruments a central force in his work, but also one still working in the background. In some ways, one might say that the percussion represents Boulez's own voice at the time, still in its formative stage. Like him, they come forward and ask to be treated on equal terms with the more conventional forces, the strings and the voices. Viewed from this perspective, the work not only reflects a composer trying to come to terms with the music of his predecessors (which he did by incorporating some of their most original vocal, instrumental, and rhythmic innovations and then leaving them aside); more important, it also shows him beginning to "clear imaginative space" for the expression of his own individuality and the assertion of his own historical importance.

The end of *Le Visage nuptial* suggests another latent message as well. This comes from the gender connotations that become associated with the voices and percussion. Here gender refers not only to the sexuality of the man and woman of the poem but also to the masculine and feminine forces, including their manifestations within the composer himself.[21] Boulez may not have intended this association,

20. Boulez uses three kinds of percussion in this work: wood (including maracas, fouet, claves, guiro, woodblock), skin (bongos, snare drum, bass drum, tambourine, Provençal drum, military drum), and metal (cymbals, tam-tams, gongs, triangle, iron blocks). He also uses xylophone, celesta, glockenspiel, and vibraphone.

21. Stevan Key suggests that the work concerns the struggle of the composer to dominate the feminine within himself and that, as in primitive cultures, he garners power to do

even though, as Joan Peyser points out, he began the work in the midst of a passionate love affair.[22] Nevertheless, the score supports two observations.

First, as the altos and the percussion eventually take over in the last two songs, it seems that Boulez associates the male of the poem with them. Throughout these songs, Boulez treats the sopranos and altos in increasingly different ways. In "Evadné," they never sing together but rather alternate groups of lines. The sopranos declaim much longer ones than the altos, but the altos begin and end the song. In "Post-Scriptum," the altos become more important than the sopranos. Boulez makes this point by changing which group initiates phrases. Whereas the soprano soloist begins the opening refrain, followed by the five altos and then the alto soloist, the alto soloist enters first when the refrain returns in mm. 37–40, the midpoint of this song. Afterward, it is the five sopranos and soprano soloist who complete the phrase. In the end, only the alto soloist and alto chorus deliver the text, the soprano soloist having dropped out after m. 50 and the soprano chorus after m. 55. The association of the sopranos with the woman and the altos with the man begins at the end of the third poem, when the soprano sings of the "woman breathing" and the alto of the "man standing erect," and culminates in the last one, when Boulez asks the altos to sing in a "low tessitura" (mm. 18–25) and a "violent" manner (mm. 37–46). The altos, moreover, are uniquely responsible for the repetitions of the man's refrain, "Leave me," which Boulez adds to the poem and is the only spoken line in the last song.

If one can assume that in this piece Boulez intends the male to control the tempo of the lovemaking, the way he uses the percussion also suggests an association of these instruments with the male. In the third song, where its role is greatest, the percussion provides a rhythmical breathing, alternating measures of activity with those of total silence, as the sexual tension being described builds before and during each of the five climaxes. For example, from m. 32 to the first climax at mm. 48–50, the pattern of alternation is at intervals of approximately one measure percussion followed by one measure of silence, then two of both, and finally three measures of both. Later the two may alternate as rapidly as within measures or almost every measure for extended periods, as in mm. 160–76.

In the last two poems, the percussion gradually goes hand in hand with the altos. Only in the beginning of the fourth poem are the altos accompanied by more than bare silence or minimal percussion. By contrast, all the long sections of the sopranos' declamation have the accompaniment of the full orchestra. In the fifth song, the percussion plays only when the altos speak the refrain, echoing the association Messiaen built in the last part of *Trois petites liturgies* between spoken verses, percussion, and the "time of man." The sole presence of the altos and the

---

this by taking on, incorporating into his body— of which the piece is an extension—the most significant male figure in the culture: in this case, Stravinsky. I am grateful to Stevan for reading this chapter and urging me to push my feminist reading.

22. Peyser, *Boulez*, 33.

percussion at the end of the work thus not only asserts Boulez's triumph over the traditional orchestral and choral forces esteemed by his predecessors but, when read as representing male forces, also hints at notions of conquest and male superiority.

Second, one can read Boulez's reduction of the female voices to rhythmic breathing in the final measures of the work as a determination to control and even conquer the beauty of the female voices, perhaps the feminine force itself, as the man of the poem conquers the woman. In several instances earlier in the work, Boulez makes it clear he intends to control not only the notes and how the singers produce pitches and timbres but also when they breathe. In the middle of the third poem's first climax (m. 49), for example, he instructs the singers not to breathe in the middle of the phrases where certain rests are indicated. The importance he attaches to breathing may derive from the final line of the third poem that heralds and in some ways explains the work's musical conclusion. Just as the man of the poem has the woman in a submissive state, only "breathing," her energy consumed by the end of this poem, so too Boulez leaves the women singers in the work's final measures "almost inarticulate," "without the slightest timbre," their vocal power reduced to a "whisper." When Char writes, "Here is the dead sand, here is the body saved," it is arguably Boulez who feels saved, the male forces having prevailed, "the intimate undoing of the irreparable" to follow in future works.

It is no accident that this confrontation with the female/feminine forces parallels Boulez's confrontation with his predecessors. Andreas Huyssen sees it as a problem characteristic of modernism that people persistently gender as feminine that which they may wish to devalue.[23] In the case of Le Visage nuptial, Boulez treats these two representations of the other as passive forces to be used as he wished and to which he was unwilling to surrender strength. Especially in the last two songs, he asserts his authority over both by increasingly differentiating and distancing the representations of his own ego from those of the ever-different other. He opposes the voice of his own creativity to those of his predecessors; the percussion alone to the full orchestra, as ultimately represented by the strings; the altos to the sopranos, at the same time as the male and the female forces they come to signify. Both kinds of encounters are characterized by violence, domination, and irony; stated baldly, both end with the submission of the other and the resurrection/triumph of the idealized self.

Le Visage nuptial launched a challenge for Boulez: how to continue what he initiated in this work. His response, as he describes it, was to begin exploring instrumentation, about which he soon "became passionate."[24] In the early 1950s, he

23. Andreas Huyssen, After the Great Divide: Modernism, Mass Culture, Postmodernism (Bloomington: Indiana University Press, 1986), 53.

24. Pierre Boulez, Par Volonté et par hasard: Entretiens avec Célestin Deliège (Paris: Seuil, 1975), 86–87. Boulez's association with the Domaine Musical concerts beginning in 1949 brought him into close contact with performers specializing in contemporary music, and in that context he became sensitized to "all the problems and resources of instrumentation" (87).

wrote many instrumental works, including an unfinished one for percussion, and set two more cycles of Char's poetry. In the second, *Le Marteau sans maître* (1952–54; 1957), Boulez revisited the relationship of voice to ensemble, this time using the vibraphone, xylophone, and percussion in major roles. As Stockhausen's analysis of *Le Marteau* has shown,[25] the female voice in this work eventually retreats from leading the instruments with her syllabic declamation of the text to becoming part of the instrumental texture, only humming with her mouth closed, uttering no text at all. In the final section of the last piece, the flute takes the musical lead, accompanied by the gong, and the instruments thereby succeed in overcoming the voice. The female human voice, bearer of nostalgic references to the past in *Le Visage nuptial*, gives way to Boulez's authorial voice, the voice of his own future.[26]

What led Boulez to revise *Le Visage nuptial* in 1989 cannot be fully explained by his confession that he "cannot separate himself from material while it's still alive for him."[27] Although he has revised many works, his return to this one after nearly a forty-year pause seems to relate to the aesthetic conditions of the late 1980s. In recent years, as sensuous beauty has returned to being a viable aesthetic option, composers in France have shown renewed interest in the female voice, even in bel canto singing. Boulez's return to a work with female chorus should be understood in this context, especially because we now have the women's lines stripped of their original *sprechstimme*.

The work's revival, however, goes beyond responding to current public taste; in many ways, it reasserts Boulez's belief in his original achievement, deletes some of Messiaen's influence, and clarifies his message. The revisions alter the character of some of the singing, stripping it of some of its novelty, while enhancing the role of the orchestra. At the end of the third song (mm. 211–14), for example, Boulez rewrites what was unison unpitched singing as richly harmonized, slightly contrapuntal lines, thereby eliminating a technique inspired by his predecessors. (He also

25. Karlheinz Stockhausen, "Music and Speech," trans. Ruth Koenig, *Die Reihe* 6 (1960): 40–47.

26. Lest one think that Boulez's confrontation with the past ended with *Le Visage nuptial*, one need only consult the philosophy underlying the statutes and programs of the Domaine Musical, which he helped organize. This organization, known for its defense of the avant-garde in Paris in the 1950s and 1960s, was founded with the idea that old and new should coexist on all programs. They believed that new works might find "their origins, their roots, their justifications" in very old works. (See Claude Rostand, "Un jeune compositeur," *La Nef* [November 1957]: 90.) Arguing for the simultaneous presence of the old and the new in music was a powerful tool for suggesting mutual legitimacy and was a common practice in concert series in France from the late nineteenth century. I discussed this in my "Forging French Identity: the Political Significance of *la musique ancienne et moderne*" at the National Meeting of the American Musicological Society, Washington, D.C., 28 October 2005.

27. Boulez, *Par Volonté et par hasard*, 63.

harmonizes the opening solo of the fifth song and changes some of the vocal lines in this song.) Then in the section citing *Les Noces*, his conducting of the new score overwhelms the voices, so that the reference that comes in m. 140 is not audible until its reiteration in m. 147. In the fourth song, he almost completely alters the work, deleting the juxtapositions inspired by *Trois petites liturgies*. The singers now modulate their pitch, the alto accompaniment changes from silence or minimal percussion to a full orchestral texture, thereby eliminating the abrupt juxtapositions with the soprano sections characteristic of the 1959 score, and there are interludes between the texted lines. Boulez adds string and other instrumental parts to the beginning and end and lengthens the opening to mirror the ending; the result is a continuous and more apparently organic form.

Boulez also increases the force and presence of the percussion. The revised third song begins with a huge brass and percussion gesture even before the voices start, radically changing the original opening, in which the singers spoke the first line of text unaccompanied. Elsewhere too, when the singers had unaccompanied lines, such as m. 70, Boulez adds percussion. He also reinforces each of the climaxes in this song, adds several measures of interlude between sections (such as after the climax of m. 113), and completes the song with an additional measure of loud, aggressive percussion after the text in m. 210, leaving it difficult for the listener not to grasp his point.[28]

I see the work as exemplifying an approach to memory to which Boulez now wishes to draw attention. In a text written on 27 June 1988 (for a special issue, "Memory and Creation" of *Inharmoniques*, a journal on whose editorial board he sits), Boulez asks: "memory or amnesia?"

> It appears that in the middle of a period burdened with more and more memory, forgetting becomes absolutely urgent. And yet not only do we not forget, but we display all the possible libraries of all the Alexandrias: the reference should take part in the invention, serve as the source of the only innovation still possible. Now that the time of avant-gardes, of exploration, has passed for good, that of perpetual return, of the amalgam and the citation will come. The ideal or imaginary library provides us with an overabundance of models; our only problem is choice and what form to use.[29]

28. When questioned on the nature of Boulez's revisions, Boulez's colleague, Jean-Baptiste Barrière, explained that Boulez claims not to have redone the work but only to have expanded, elaborated, and developed one of its original themes; letter to author, 4 March 1991. With the 1989 score published in 1994, it is now possible to do a complete study of these changes.

29. "Il semble qu'au milieu d'un temps chargé de plus en plus de mémoire, oublier devienne l'urgence absolue. Et pourtant non seulement on n'oublie pas, mais on arbore en panoplie toutes les bibliothèques possibles de toutes les Alexandries: la référence devrait faire partie de l'invention, être la source de seul renouveau encore possible. Le temps des

Indeed, as Boulez puts it, "this is all very tiresome, whether it means permanently consulting the cultural library or taking refuge in some intangible period."[30] Then how to forget? What to forget? *Le Visage nuptial* is one answer to these questions. The work recognizes the existence of history, of predecessors who also wrote for voices and orchestra. (For the premiere of the 1989 revision, Boulez even programmed the work after works by Stravinsky and Messiaen, perhaps so that audiences would have these composers' music in their ears as they listened to his work.) But *Le Visage nuptial* is not exactly modeled on the past. Boulez uses the voice but eventually disenfranchises it, eliminating its pitch and its character as it disintegrates into breath. The memory such a work embraces is one Boulez continues to find value in today: "a deforming, faithless memory that retains from its source what is directly useful and perishable." "Absolute authenticity" is still his credo; no libraries except those that "appear only when he seeks them" or those "on fire that are perpetually reborn from their ashes in an always unpredictable, elusive form."[31]

Boulez may see his refusal to bow to the pressures of contemporary postmodernism as courageous.[32] Yet, given what he writes, the composer underestimates the positive role memory can play in a work. Approached differently, memory may serve a variety of purposes, leading composers to as-yet-unexplored ways of connecting with their listeners and creating musical meaning. Appealing to a listener's memory is not necessarily a "perpetual return," and for those whose use of memory implies primarily a return to the past, I question whether their ultimate purpose is not more properly speaking a modernist one, albeit in a new guise.

POSTMODERNIST CHALLENGES

In his introduction to the essays collected in *The Anti-Aesthetic*, Hal Foster defines two kinds of postmodernism: one of reaction and one of resistance. Although his book concentrates on the latter, his concept of the former is equally enlightening, even when it comes to musical developments in the last two decades:

---

avant-gardes, de l'exploration, étant définitivement passé, viendrait celui du perpétuel retour, de l'amalgame et de la citation. La bibliothèque idéale ou imaginaire nous fournit une pléthore de modèles, il nous reste l'embarras du choix et la forme de l'exploitation." Pierre Boulez, "La Vestale et le voleur de feu," *Inharmoniques* 4 (1988): 8.

30. Boulez, "La Vestale et le voleur de feu," 8.

31. Boulez, "La Vestale et le voleur de feu," 11.

32. For further evidence of such a feeling, Susan McClary (personal communication, May 1991) suggests that the reader consult a conversation between Michel Foucault and Pierre Boulez, "Contemporary Music and the Public," trans. John Rahn, *Perspectives of New Music* (fall/winter 1985): 6–12, wherein Boulez defends the world of high modernism and rejects postmodernist concerns as a "supermarket aesthetic."

The postmodernism of reaction is far better known: though not mono-lithic, it is singular in its repudiation of modernism. This repudiation, voiced most shrilly perhaps by neoconservatives but echoed everywhere, is strategic: as Habermas cogently argues, the neoconservatives sever the cultural from the social, then blame the practices of the one (modernism) for the ills of the other (modernization). With cause and effect thus con-founded, "adversary" culture is denounced even as the economic and po-litical status quo is affirmed—indeed, a new "affirmative" culture is proposed. . . . Modernism is reduced to a style . . . and condemned, or excised entirely as a cultural mistake; pre- and post-modernist are then elided, and the humanist tradition preserved.[33]

In music, we all know about the nostalgia that gripped composers in the late 1980s and early 1990s, resulting in neo-Romantic works, a festival dedicated to presenting such works at New York's Lincoln Center, the sudden popularity of writing operas and symphonies again, of construing one's ideas in tonal terms. Whether com-posers believe they are recovering musical "truth" or not, the time of "terminal prestige" and aesthetic distancing is ending:[34] many of those returning to Romantic sentiment, narrative curve, or simple melody wish to entice audiences back to the concert hall. To the extent that these developments are a true "about face,"[35] they represent a postmodernism of reaction, a return to premodernist musical thinking. David del Tredici might argue in terms similar to these,[36] but in most cases, the situation is more complicated.

Quotation in a modernist sense, as we have seen, often implies a desire to overcome and surpass one's predecessors through cutting off the borrowed ele-ment from its original context and containing it.[37] But when the choice is Mahler

33. Hal Foster, "Postmodernism: A Preface," in *The Anti-Aesthetic*, ed. Hal Foster (Seattle: Bay Press, 1983), xii.

34. I borrow the expression from Susan McClary, "Terminal Prestige: The Case of Avant-Garde Music Composition," *Cultural Critique* 12 (1989): 57–81.

35. I am here playing with the title of an orchestral composition, *About Face* (1988–89), in which the composer Jonathan Kramer explores not only "multiple personality" but also notions of return in his own compositional language and personal life. Unlike that of many others, his return is from a more simplified, modal style characterizing works in the 1980s to a dissonant one reflecting "nostalgia for the age of modernism" (from notes about the work by the composer, personal communication with the author).

36. See also George Rochberg, "Can the Arts Survive Modernism?" *Critical Inquiry* 11, no. 2 (1984): 317–40.

37. It can also be driven by what Leonard Meyer, *Music, the Arts, and Ideas* (Chicago: University of Chicago Press, 1967), calls "ideological nostalgia," though perhaps less so during the twentieth century (192). For the modernist, Meyer argues that the past is a "repository of countless potentially absorbing problems and possibilities," artistic and compositional problems more than ideological ones (193).

and Beethoven, as has so often been the case in recent years, something else seems to be going on. In the third movement of his *Sinfonia* (1968), for example, Luciano Berio incorporates the scherzo of Mahler's Second Symphony, super-imposed with excerpts from Beethoven, Brahms, Strauss, Ravel, Debussy, Webern, and Stockhausen. On the one hand, as Michael Hicks points out, these quotations serve to illustrate the text Berio sets, Beckett's *The Unnameable*, a story in which the writer "despairs of ever being able to decisively separate himself from [his characters] and becomes a prisoner of his art: he can do nothing but quote."[38] On the other hand, the quotations function in the music and text "as aspects of the total identity of the narrator."[39] In other words, the composer sees his predeces-sors as the various voices of his own memory, or perhaps as invocations of those memories.[40]

It is with the latter purpose in mind that many composers seem now to be quoting, even those as radical as John Cage and John Zorn. In many of his works based on mesostics, Cage incorporates long excerpts from the writings of Satie, Duchamp, and especially Joyce, predecessors with whom he most identifies. Of them, he writes, "it is possible to imagine that the artists whose work we live with constitute not a vocabulary but an alphabet by means of which we spell our lives."[41] In much of Zorn's music, the collage of jazz, swing, pop, reggae, film and television soundtracks, and a recurrent Japanese voice create a kind of musical microcosm of the composer's sound world.[42] As Jon Pareles writes, Zorn wants to "evoke

38. Michael Hicks, "Text, Music, and Meaning in the Third Movement of Luciano Berio's *Sinfonia*," *Perspectives of New Music* 20, no. 1/2 (fall/winter 1982): 209.

39. Hicks, "Text, Music, and Meaning," 223. See Raili Elovaara, *The Problem of Identity in Samuel Beckett's Prose* (Helsinki: Suomalainen, n.d.).

40. The composer David Felder has been interested in a variation of this idea: how composers can take advantage of the physical memory players can retain of works per-formed by them or otherwise written for their instruments. He wishes to call on such memory, for example, of Debussy's *Rhapsodie for Clarinet* or Paganini's *Violin Concerto* in his works for the clarinet or violin.

41. In his introduction to "James Joyce, Marcel Duchamp, Erik Satie: An Alphabet," in *X: Writings '79–'82* (Middletown, Conn.: Wesleyan University Press, 1983), John Cage goes on to say that he did not follow this idea in his text *An Alphabet*, but then on the same page he admits, "The effect for me of Duchamp's work was to so change my way of seeing that I became in my way a Duchamp unto myself. I could find as he did for himself the space and time of my own experience" (53). This mesostic was given its American premiere by Cage and fifteen of his friends at the Second Acoustica International Sound Art Festival, New York, 29 April 1990.

42. Mark Applebaum, in his seminar paper, suggests that Carl Stalling's influence on Zorn was great. Zorn himself describes the "constantly changing kaleidoscope of styles, forms, melodies, quotations, and of course the 'Mickey Mousing'" of Stalling's music as "broken into shards" (liner notes to the 1990 Warner Brothers release of *The Carl Stalling Project: Music from Warner Brothers Cartoons* [1936–1958]).

a present that is choppy and unpredictable, but not amnesiac; there are still memories, and hopes, of pleasure and romance."[43] That audiences come to performances of works built of such musical allusions to the past and present, Hicks posits, "is evidence of their own search for identity."[44]

This is not the place for a full-scale analysis of the function of quotation in modernist or postmodernist work. I would like merely to observe that many of those composers now incorporating other people's music tend not to diffuse the power of their sources or try to subjugate them through distortion or commentary; rather, they seem to accept each source in its own terms, revel in the association with this music, and delight in the coexistence they have tried to create. It is no accident in recent music we hear little of Bach, who, for many modernists, has embodied pure music free of personality. Mahler is in some ways a more ideal model—his music is eclectic, never stylistically pure, and full of musical quotations.

The choice of Beethoven as an even more popular predecessor to quote is particularly suggestive. The heroic spirit and strength of Beethoven has almost universal appeal among classical music audiences.[45] Composers may be attracted to this and wish to tap into his musical power. Those like George Rochberg, much of whose Third Quartet sounds like Beethoven (and Mahler), think they are "abandoning the notion of 'originality,' in which the personal style of the artist and his ego are the supreme values."[46] But are not such works still composer-centered, many of them still power-driven and perhaps promoting heroism of another kind, glory through association? If a postmodernism of reaction has had influence on the musical world, it may be in its encouragement of the Romantic hero (often just another version of the modernist hero).

Foster's postmodernism of resistance, by contrast, "is concerned with a critical deconstruction of tradition, not an instrumental pastiche of pop- or pseudo-historical forms, with a critique of origins rather than a return to them. In short, it seeks to question rather than exploit cultural codes, to explore rather than conceal

43. John Pareles, "There Are Eight Million Stories in John Zorn's Naked City," *New York Times* (8 April 1990).

44. Hicks, "Text, Music, and Meaning," 217. Jochen Schulte-Sasse, "The Prestige of the Artist Under Conditions of Modernity," *Cultural Critique* 12 (1989), argues that "quotations serve as signs of recognition; they mediate between our desire for identity, for containment of our ego-boundaries, and for our desire for dissolution, for transgression of our ego-boundaries" (100).

45. Today Beethoven represents our most common model of musical genius. In France, particularly, when the press wishes to praise a composer in the highest terms, it is often to Beethoven that comparison is made, whether the music resembles Beethoven's or not. William S. Newman examines the origins of this phenomenon, "The Beethoven Mystique in Romantic Art, Literature, and Music," *Musical Quarterly* 3 (1983): 354–87.

46. George Rochberg, notes to the Concord String Quartet recording of his Third Quartet, Nonesuch H71283.

social and political affiliations."[47] Susan McClary puts in this camp some minimalist composers,[48] Philip Glass more than Steve Reich or John Adams (another
composer who quotes Beethoven),[49] Laurie Anderson, and other "downtown"
composers. Their works address the "master narratives" of tonality, narrative
structure, Western hegemony, and male dominance, sometimes by making puns or
ironic commentary on them, sometimes by deconstructing their inherently contradictory meanings. Unfortunately, as McClary points out, the oppositional stance
of this kind of postmodernism has begun to wane, especially as critics find much
of it becoming sterile language games.

Both of these postmodernisms imply that presentation is more important than
representation, that the subject of a work is less important than how it is treated.[50]
The distortion of source material and extreme speed made possible by computer
manipulations, possibly expected by a generation raised on television, may indeed
contribute to the preeminence of style over subject and the disruption of the
signifier's capacity to signify in some computer music. Still, although it may be true
in certain literature, I do not see the "death of the subject" taking place in most
music, neither for composers nor audiences. To the contrary, the "subject(s)" of a
composition and its "meaning" in some ways have never been more important.
I was drawn to contemplating Boulez's Le Visage nuptial after rereading Susan
McClary's analysis of Bach's music as reflecting the struggle between Bach's need
for self-expression and his desire to reconcile various influences.[51] The striking
juxtaposition of the singers on both sides of front stage with the percussion in the
center back stage dramatized for me their musical differences, one occasionally
referencing the past, the other rigorously new and original, and led me to hear the
musical relationship between the two as the structural conflict just discussed.

For our understanding of recent music to be complete, however, we cannot
confine ourselves to the study of pieces as the embodiment of pure structure,
whether specific to that piece or reflecting universal "Ideas." We may be born with
certain intuitions about structure and the organization of surface patterns, as gestalt
theorists and contemporary scholars like Fred Lerdahl and Ray Jackendoff have
suggested. And these may reflect the inherent organization of the mind, giving it the

47. Foster, "Postmodernism," xii.

48. Susan McClary, "Music and Postmodernism," manuscript. For her recent thoughts
on this topic, see her Conventional Wisdom (Berkeley: University of California, 2000).

49. In the last movement, "On the Dominant Divide," of his Grand Pianola Music. My
thanks to Richard McQuillan for pointing this out.

50. For this reason, postmodernism as an artistic style is sometimes compared with
mannerism.

51. Susan McClary, "The Blasphemy of Talking Politics During Bach Year," in Music
and Society: The Politics of Composition, Performance, and Reception, ed. Richard Leppert
and Susan McClary (Minneapolis: University of Minnesota Press, 1987), 13–62.

capacity to comprehend large-scale narrativity. Yet even as such generative theories help composers to understand what Lerdahl and Jackendoff refer to as "the facts of hearing," they overshadow other kinds of memory that the composer may call on and the listener may bring to a work.[52] It was my memory of other recent concerts of music written for female voices by Boulez's French contemporaries that colored my hearing of Le Visage nuptial and oriented my understanding of it to begin with.

Postmodernist works of reaction or resistance, like modernist ones, depend on the "experienced" perceiver's knowledge and understanding of the "cultural libraries" to which Boulez refers, the images, gestures, and conventions of the past repertories being revived and commented on. Increasingly in the early 1990s, I find what might be called another kind of postmodernism arising in music, poetry, and the visual arts, a far less elitist one that dramatically expands the notion of post-modernist as bricoleur. To locate it, we must look beyond the concert halls, be-yond traditional media and the university, beyond what McClary calls the "boy's club of modernism."[53]

It is difficult to use one word to describe what from one perspective is a third kind of postmodernism and from another is something that projects beyond the modernist/postmodernist dialectic. What I see emerging involves an emancipation of the realm of memory, what John Cage might call an "interpenetration" of different domains, and an exploration of what Pauline Oliveros calls "relation-ships," connections the perceiver may come to understand not primarily within the work itself or through the work's relationship to a precursor work, style, or genre, but rather through his or her own memory. Like other postmodernist aesthetics, this one is based on engaging the listener's participation, often in an interactive process. It also encourages a mirroring effect that may lead to greater self-awareness and self-knowledge.[54] The works at issue here, however, are not only texts about other texts; nor is the image they reflect merely the creator's or per-ceiver's cultural knowledge or cultivated tastes. In response to their sounds, images, words, and gestures, postmodernists with this perspective expect the perceiver to recall experiences, and not only those of an aesthetic nature. Through calling on experiences of all kinds (including the personal and the social) and suggesting links between memories recorded in different, apparently unrelated categories, their works constitute occasions for us to come to understand the disparate parts of our lives as fundamentally related. In other words, those espousing this new aesthetic,

52. Fred Lerdahl and Ray Jackendoff, A Generative Theory of Tonal Music (Cambridge, Mass.: MIT Press, 1983), 301.

53. McClary, "Terminal Prestige," 72.

54. David Harvey, The Condition of Postmodernity (London: Blackwell, 1989), describes postmodernism as "the mirror of mirrors." He uses this expression to explain an attitude that "came of age in the midst of this climate of voodoo economics, of political image construction and deployment, and of new social class formation" (336).

as they enact their priestly function as artists, elicit the magical power of memory not to criticize, educate, or elevate morally, but to empower us to create our own memory palaces. Through the recognition of similar experiences, we can discover our connectedness to others and through the individual shape we each give to these memory palaces, we can find meaning in our lives.

Architecture has been the dominant art form used to discuss postmodernism. In architectural terms, the materials of the memory palaces suggested by this third kind of postmodernism resemble those used by Frank Gehry (oddly ordinary materials such as corrugated metals, raw plywood, chain-link fencing, telephone poles, and cardboard) as opposed to Robert Venturi or Michael Graves whose works suggest historical allusions or playful pretentiousness;[55] they tend to be common ones filled with signifying potential instead of idealized ones pointing to abstractions. In music, likewise, sampling elements or using sounds that are fun to identify and do not depend on elite knowledge (such as those from daily life) is an easy way to engage listeners. Because they understand these materials in relation to what they already know, listeners can entertain the meaning suggested by the order and interplay of the elements as well as what is stimulated in their own memories. Thus, if Aristotle was right, calling on memory stimulates higher thought processes. Perhaps for this reason, works exemplifying this third postmodernism proceed with sincerity rather than irony, something that distinguishes them from works by postmodernists of resistance.

In many ways, the quintessential postmodern memory palace is not a building but a certain kind of city.[56] David Harvey's book *The Condition of Postmodernity* begins with a discussion of Jonathan Raban's *Soft City*, a portrayal of London in the 1970s as a labyrinth, an encyclopedia, a theater "where fact and imagination simply *have* to fuse."

> For better of worse, [the city] invites you to remake it, to consolidate it into a shape you can live with. You, too. Decide who you are, and the city will again assume a fixed form around you. Decide what it is, and your identity will be revealed, like a map fixed around you by triangulation. . . . The

55. See Charles Jencks, *The Language of Postmodern Architecture* (New York: Rizzoli, 1977), and Frederic Jameson, *Postmodernism, or The Cultural Logic of Late Capitalism* (Durham, N.C.: Duke University Press, 1991), 107–21. Also compare Gehry's house in Santa Monica, the Santa Monica Museum he designed in Los Angeles, and the hotels designed by Graves at Disneyworld in Orlando, Florida, and La Jolla, California.

56. In *The Art of Memory*, 297–98, Yates discusses Tommaso Campanella's philosophical work *City of the Sun* (1602) as a Renaissance memory palace. The Città del Sole is a description of a utopia, an ideal city based on an astral religion. Such a city, it was thought, could be used as a way of "knowing everything 'using the world as a book.'" Louis Marin, *Utopics: Spatial Play*, trans. Robert A. Vollrath (Atlantic Highlands, N.J.: Humanities Press, 1984), also writes about a utopia as a "space organized as a text and discourse constructed as a space" (10).

city as we imagine it, the soft city of illusion, myth, aspiration, nightmare, is as real, maybe more real, than the hard city one can locate in maps and statistics.[57]

Such a city is not tightly defined, rationally ordered, the result of pre-compositional planning. Los Angeles is the geographer Edward Soja's image of the postmodern-ist city. To describe it, Soja uses Jorge Luis Borges' image of an aleph, "the only place on earth where all places are—seen from every angle, each standing clear, without confusion or blending."[58] The analogy with an aleph suggests the difficulty of trying to contain the city's globalism, extraordinary heterogeneity, and fragmentation in any one image.

The experience of such a city also resembles that of a postmodernist work. Seemingly limitless in size, constantly in motion, and traversed on crisscrossing freeways, Los Angeles contrasts markedly with more "modernist" cities like mid-town Manhattan or Washington, D.C., with their grid layouts. Not that all post-modernist works are episodic, like Los Angeles—"then and then" structures that are continually in flux—nor are all modernist ones, like New York, configurational structures that can be grasped as a whole, at least in the imagination.[59] In fact, as I have shown, many modernist works are nonlinear, episodic antinarratives.[60] Without necessarily embracing overall narrative structure, postmodern works often incorporate stories, especially those with personal or relative meaning. There tends to be a difference in the perspectives of postmodern and modern works, however, that mirrors the difference in the experiences of these two kinds of cities. Italo Calvino juxtaposes these perspectives in his novel *Invisible Cities*. Marco Polo, the explorer, recounts his travels from one city to the next as through a maze of ever-changing variety, while Kublai Khan, the emperor who listens, maintains the distance of an all-encompassing gaze and tries to "discern . . . the tracery of a pattern."[61] The postmodernist perspective more closely resembles that of Polo, because the memories evoked by postmodern works are embedded in the per-ceiver's ever-changing experiences, not the creator's control.

57. Jonathan Raban, *Soft City*, (London: Hamilton, 1974), 9–10, cited in Harvey, *The Condition of Postmodernity*, 5.

58. Borges's *The Alpeh* (1949, revised 1974) is discussed in Edward Soja, *Postmodern Geographies* (London: Verso, 1989), 222.

59. Paul Ricoeur, *Time and Narrative*, vol. 1, trans. Kathleen McLaughlin and David Pellauer (Chicago: University of Chicago Press, 1984), chaps. 2 and 3, contrasts episodic and configurational structure.

60. See chapter 1, section entitled "Antinarrative."

61. Italo Calvino, *Invisible Cities*, trans. William Weaver (San Diego: Harcourt, Brace, Jovanovich, 1974), 6. Tim Labor, in his seminar paper on this novel, argues that the level of distance the author takes from the work and the patterns traced by the chapters would make the novel in effect more modernist than postmodernist.

In his seminal article "Postmodernism, or The Cultural Logic of Late Capitalism," Frederic Jameson pushes this notion further. He uses the idea of people living in cities to explain how our minds might represent "the coordination of existential data (the empirical position of the subject) with unlived, abstract conceptions of the geographic totality." This he calls "cognitive mapping." A map is a description of what is perceived to exist, not a diagram of what could or should be.[62] If modernist work at its most alienating, like the modernist city, is "a space in which people are unable to map (in their minds) either their own positions or the urban totality in which they find themselves," then could not postmodernist work, like "disalienation in the traditional city," attempt "the practical reconquest of a sense of place, and the construction or reconstruction of an articulated ensemble which can be retained in memory and which the individual subject can map and remap along the moments of mobile, alternative trajectories"?[63] This sounds like a new kind of narrativity, and those espousing an aesthetic of emancipation, interpenetration, and relationships try to do just this: they call on us to "cognitively map" our own diverse experiences onto the ensemble of elements that make up the work, to create memory palaces therewith, and thereby to imagine an interactive relationship with this apparently "endless, formless ruin" over which Calvino's Khan despaired. Perhaps they also invite us to feel a collective identity through this relationship.

Of course, there may not be a perfect embodiment of what I am calling a new aesthetic based on the emancipation of memory, interpenetration, and relationships; nevertheless, the spirit underlying this aesthetic permeates some composers' works increasingly as memory of all kinds becomes important in the conception of recent music. For years John Cage has created artistic situations that invite listeners to bring their own meaning to his works. In his 1988–89 Norton Lectures at Harvard, he describes his work as coming "from ideas but is not about them but somehow brings them [sic] new ideas or other ideas into existence."[64] By its openness and indeterminacy, he has tried to ensure his audience's participation.

As he grew older, Cage was increasingly interested in memory. He admitted his works are "highly suggestive" and that he "want[s] that suggestion to oh be in a spirit [he] agree[s] with."[65] In the opening of "Composition in Retrospect" (1981–82), the first METHOD mesostic, he writes: "My / mEmory / of whaT / Happened /is nOt / what happeneD // i aM struck / by thE / facT / tHat what happened / is mOre conventional / than what i remembereD." Later, in the section on "IMITATION" he

---

62. In addition, Marin, *Utopics*, proposes that city maps represent "the production of discourse about the city" (211).

63. Jameson, "Postmodernism," 89–92.

64. John Cage, *I–VI* (Cambridge, Mass.: Harvard University Press, 1990), 338.

65. Cage, *I–VI*, 16.

continues: "the past must be Invented / the future Must be / revIsed / doing boTh / mAkes / whaT / the present Is / discOvery / Never stops //what questIons / will Make the past / allve / in anoTher / wAy." A treatise on his composition, this lecture suggests why memory becomes his "method" in the works that follow, and why the past is the subject of their "imitation." The text of the "DEVOTION" mesostic, which describes a piano teacher who "loves the past" and the "classics she's sO devoted to," explains the tone of reverence and sincerity that permeates his last works.[66]

Cage's goal, as expressed at the end of this lecture, is to bring "the play of intelligent anarChy / into a world Environment / that workS so well everyone lives as he needs."[67] To accomplish this, he adopts certain materials and structure. Complicated chance operations still give him a "discipline" that can "sober and quiet the minD / so that It / iS / in aCcord / wIth / what haPpens / the worLd / around It / opeN / rathEr than//closeD."[68] But besides "noises" and "empty words," he comes to incorporate explicitly signifying materials. These are elements from his own memory in works like "James Joyce, Marcel Duchamp, Erik Satie: An Alphabet" and standard opera arias in his *Europera I* and *II*. The narrative aspects of music which he once underplayed or reduced to those of "Zen stories"—specific references, the voice and rhetorical devices of story-telling, as well as clearly defined beginnings and endings—he begins to engage more overtly.[69] With these materials and techniques, Cage entices audiences to bring their own associations to the work's anarchical "play," the sometimes surprising order and manner in which the chance operations place them. There he hopes audiences will experience their coexistence. The result can be an intelligently anarchic memory palace, a "musIcircus / maNy / Things going on / at thE same time / a theatRe of differences together / not a single Plan"[70] that encourages a certain approach to life.[71] In the last

66. John Cage, "Composition in Retrospect," in *X: Writings '79–'82* (Middletown, Conn.: Wesleyan University Press, 1983), 123–24, 145, 147–48. See also chapter 6 here.

67. This is an excerpt from the "CIRCUMSTANCES" section of his mesostic text "Composition in Retrospect," 151, of which, in his introduction to *I–VI*, Cage says *Europera I* and *II* were "illustrative" (5).

68. This is the first stanza of the "DISCIPLINE" section in "Composition in Retrospect," 129.

69. Compare the short "Zen stories" Marjorie Perloff cites from Cage's *Silence* (6, 95, 271) with the long citations and imaginary stories in "James Joyce, Marcel Duchamp, Erik Satie: An Alphabet." See her *The Poetics of Indeterminacy* (Princeton, N.J.: Princeton University Press, 1981), 310–13.

70. This is the opening of the first stanza of the "INTERPENETRATION" section in "Composition in Retrospect," 141.

71. In *The Poetics of Indeterminacy*, Perloff calls this aspect of Cage a "new didacticism" (31).

line of both "Composition in Retrospect" and "James Joyce, Marcel Duchamp, Erik Satie: An Alphabet," Cage sums up the feeling to which he hopes this process will lead his readers/listeners: "I welcome whatever happenS next."

Even as Cage preached the merits of nonintention, however, "intelligent" control and choice play important roles in determining the final shape of these works. Aiming to communicate a message not only about music but also about the world and its future, he carefully selected and edited the texts that serve as source material, especially in the mesostics. Through conscious reiteration and variation of words and ideas, Cage questioned, elicited, played with, and created various musical relationships that mirrored the linguistic, philosophical, political, or cosmic implications of his materials. The result is not just texts that can be read in multiple ways but compositional shape, a playful shape that communicates both "anarchy" and "accord."[72]

A different and in some ways more representative example of this aesthetic of emancipation, interpenetration, and relationships is the work of Pauline Oliveros. To enjoy its playfulness, the audience need not possess specialized knowledge about other artists or the ability to recognize eighteenth- and nineteenth-century operas. Instead what it expects listeners to start with is knowledge and experience of the human body. Works like *Sonic Meditations* and the *Deep Listening* pieces invite audiences to listen to and acknowledge all they may hear, beginning with their own breath. They are recipes, catalysts for invention and increased awareness of self and other through the medium of sound.

In her *DreamHorseSpiel* (1990), for example, she intends "to cue listeners into their own experience" in a much broader and more socially defined sense than in the meditation pieces.[73] This work consists of a poem, prerecorded short stories, referential sounds and images, and simple tunes. The text began as an image, Dream Horse, and was conceived as a *Hörspiel* (radio play), commissioned by Westdeutscher Rundfunk Köln, one of the largest public radio stations in Europe.[74] To the names of horse-related things ("horseshoe," "saw horse," "sea horse," "horse manure") Oliveros added dreams and experiences about horses she collected from a variety of people speaking and singing in their own languages, including Ger-

---

72. See the analysis of Cage's lectures in my "Intention and Indeterminacy in John Cage's *I–VI*," *Parnassus* 16, no. 2 (1991): 359–75, and the analysis of Cage's *Roaratorio* in Marjorie Perloff, "Music for Words Perhaps: Reading/Hearing/Seeing John Cage's *Roaratorio*," in *Postmodern Genres,* ed. Perloff (Norman: University of Oklahoma Press, 1988), 210–27.

73. All references to Oliveros in these paragraphs come from my "Interview with Pauline Oliveros," *AWC News/Forum* 9 (1991): 8–14, commissioned by American Women Composers, Inc.

74. In China, 1990 was also the year of the horse, a fact acknowledged by the calligraphy for horse on the shirts of the performers at its premiere on 28 April 1990 at the Second Acoustica International Sound Art Festival in New York.

man, French, and Spanish. There are also clichés involving horses, for example, "You can lead a horse to water, but you can't make it drink," "proud as a horse," "Ride the horse in the direction it's going!" and "Why kick a dead horse?" In performance, she mixed in horse sounds (snorting, drinking water, walking, trotting, chewing).

This work is about memory and the relationship between perception and thought. For the composer, the horse calls to mind the period before the Industrial Revolution, before machines took its place, before "the change to an information society"; when the horse was a daily companion, a work animal, as well as a source of food; when the animal's presence was important. The work traces what the horse has left behind in the memories and dreams of the work's listeners. Almost no word, image, or sound is without allusion to something the listener has or could have seen or heard—visual images like "horse face," "horse tail," and "horse lips"; experiences like a "horse ride" and the film *They Shoot Horses, Don't They*; smells such as "horse shit"; associated images like "horse carriage," "horse whip"; and tunes in different languages, such as "She'll be riding six white horses when she comes." It is easy to remember and to empathize with what these evoke, as it is with the process of dreaming herein captured, the suspense of storytelling, and the earnest simple-mindedness of clichés and children's music. Listening to this work is like performing it; both involve an interactive process, calling on memory and the imagination to respond to the constantly changing material at hand.

What makes this a work consists in the relationships both performers and listeners make of it in real time. In its first performance, the trumpet call (from a prerecorded tape of the beginning of a horse race) recurred again and again, as if to announce new beginnings throughout the work. Many of the horse sounds—trotting, drinking water, and so on—also came back, interspersed in the text. One sequence, for example, consisted of the words "horse carriage," the sounds of horseshoes being thrown and of horses walking on pavement and then rhythmically trotting, and finally the expression "proud as a horse," all of which together recall a time and place in which horses played an important role in society. As material was repeated, in complete or only partial segments, it became associated with the images and sounds of its new context. This often resulted in unusual juxtapositions of tone, spirit, and meaning. Evoking sense impressions recorded in memory thus became a way of stimulating thought.

The constant changes, nonhierarchical order of events, and wide variety in modes of communication make one continually reevaluate where one is in such a piece. Yet what creates this effect is not just the materials themselves but also how the performers approach time and space in the work. Through the use of technology—digital delay, artificial reverberation, and so on—the composer ensures that performers and audiences alike will experience the past, present, and future simultaneously. As soon as sounds are uttered, the performers know they will return, transformed by the technology. At any one moment, then, what a performer experiences is something very nonlinear: that is, what the performer is doing is affected by the past, what there is already, the unexpected return of the past in the present, and the future, the knowledge that whatever one produces will have to interact with whatever comes next.

The work has a regular pulse. Text entries occur every eight seconds, in part to allow the delay processors to affect the sound. This pulse "actually regulates the breathing. The audience will unconsciously begin to breathe more slowly, more deeply," Oliveros explains. The regular pulse of text entries puts the listener in a constant state of readiness as well as wondering which performer, which speaker, what kind of mode will return next.

The digital delay process also enables the composer to create multiple spaces, to "allow the work to go into or become any space, outdoors or indoors, small, large, cavernous, cathedral, closet." In other words, by delaying the sound or extending it from a millisecond to eight full seconds, the composer can use the experience of sound to communicate different kinds of space, those associated with the memory of different kinds of places. Sometimes Oliveros also uses this technique to replicate the sound of acoustic instruments, aiming to create replicas that make it "very, very difficult to tell which was the original sound and which the delayed sound." Her ideal is "mirrors," not being aware of the technology, "getting the reflection instantaneously," and hardly being able to tell the difference between "what you just did and what is coming back to you." Echo is the key to the form of such works, "as in a Bach invention," she points out. "The shape comes in the way you use the materials and the sources you're working with"; "the form [of my music] is more statistical," "a form of consensus," or the sense one has of the whole when one has reached the end of the piece.

Pauline Oliveros's art is one of presence; "experience" has replaced "experiment" as a way of describing what recent avant-garde work like hers has become. "It's being aware in the moment and being able to reflect upon it, being able to reflect on what has happened rather than theorizing. Dealing with what is," she points out, rather than setting up a thesis in advance and projecting into the future. If there is a frontier in music, she says "it's relationships, and collaboration, and an aesthetic arena that is developed in performance."

Oliveros's *Nzinga* (1993) takes the exploration of memory and the process of collaboration one step further. Like Steve Reich in *Different Trains* (1988), commissioned for the Kronos Quartet, Oliveros explores the role music can play in stimulating collective memory.[75] Both incorporate the participation of people from other cultures, whether in taped recordings or live interaction; both use analogy to emphasize cultural differences more than similarities; both are what

---

75. I use this term in the sense developed by George Lipsitz, *Time Passages: Collective Memory and American Popular Culture* (Minneapolis: University of Minnesota Press, 1990).

Reich calls documentaries as well as musical realities. Reich's point is that his own experience of riding trains back and forth between New York and Los Angeles from 1939 to 1942 was in a certain way analogous to yet different from that of the Jews who were carried in trains across Europe to reach concentration camps during the same period. Recorded personal reminiscences and train sounds provide not only engaging subject matter but also certain speech rhythms that he incorporates into the string quartet melodies. *Nzinga*, a play with music and pageantry by Oliveros's partner, Ione, involves performers, instruments, and prerecorded material, music, ritual, and dance from three cultures—Angola, Portugal, and Salvador of Bahia, Brazil. What links them all is the character of Nzinga Mbandi, a seventeenth century androgynous Angolan queen who had to dress as a king to rule and succeeded in keeping colonial powers out of her country for the forty years of her reign. The Portuguese eventually transported her people to Brazil, where they, too, had to adapt various disguises in order to survive. Forbidden to fight, Angolan slaves developed the kicking games of the capoiera as disguised forms of self-defense. Today people still dance various forms of the capoiera and sing chants to Nzinga, invoking her protective, redemptive role. The Oliveros/Ione work reflects the three hundred years of cultural interaction in Angola, Portugal, and Salvador. The work uses video to break through the past to the present and suggest relationships between the past, present, and future.

Nzinga is an aesthetic model for intercultural cooperation. Its emphasis on cultural differences rather than similarities comes from Oliveros's belief that different cultural forms are like parts of "a map of human consciousness," with "each one emphasizing a different aspect of this map, or a variation." This work is a stunning example of the cognitive mapping Jameson longs for; an "aesthetic arena" mirrors a possible relationship between individuals and cultures, ourselves and the world we inhabit. "The fundamental thing is for me to listen," Oliveros points out, "and not go in with my idea of how things have to go." Such an aesthetic is quite different from that of another politically committed composer, Frederic Rzewski, who, in his variations entitled "The People United Will Never Be Defeated" (1975), maintains his modernist language and virtuoso technique. Moreover, *Nzinga* does not take a colonialist approach to the music of other cultures, as do recent works by Paul Simon or Jon Hassell's *Fourth World: Possible Music*. Nor is this aesthetic necessarily committed to what Susan McClary might call a space of cultural struggles, even though the spirit of *Nzinga* is one of resistance to conquest. Oliveros explains: "It has to do with interdependence, meaning interaction. Not as someone who is controlling the way things are going to go, it is cooperating to make a story or make a presentation. Each performer or collaborator has a stake in it, is aware of one another in a way that it can develop, can happen. There is an enrichment process."

With the promise of such works, it is clear that the "time of avant-gardes, of exploration" has certainly not "passed for good." What has changed is the purpose and locus of exploration. With the slowly increasing acceptance of women in the musical world has come a different message, one not so much of heroic conquest as of cooperation and community. It is no longer the pseudoscientific search for the fundamentals of the medium that interests many explorers but inquiry into what makes people connect to and through music. The composer's orientation toward the listener's experience is critical in this inquiry, as are the expectations a composer may have of listeners' interactive participation, the positive value of memory and contemplation of the past, as well as the celebration of personal and cultural diversity.

BEYOND DUALITIES

In music, it is difficult to consider modernism and postmodernism as mutually exclusive and oppositional in every way. The purposes pursued by modernists earlier in the century and the forms modernism took are no longer those to which many of today's creative artists can subscribe. Some question the extent to which music, presumably the most "abstract" and "autonomous" art, can or should help people escape their surroundings. Others argue whether difficult music can or has ever enriched anyone's moral fiber. Modernist values may now seem wanting and empty, yet most composers are reluctant to give up what lies at the very basis of the aesthetic: substantial control over the work itself.

Frederic Jameson and others have argued that there can be no more "works," only what postmodernists call "texts." The possibility of creating unique pieces that reflect one coherent, consistent voice is evaporating as it becomes clear to these postmodernists that artistic creations can only serve as pretexts for what the reader/listener may bring to the work and create of it. The belief these postmodernists have in the heterogeneity of any work's meanings has become a given, as has the idea that no work can be a closed system. What I have described as works involving an emancipation of memory, an interpenetration of different domains, and an exploration of relationships may very well sound like "texts" in this sense. Like other postmodernist works, they certainly depend on the meaning the listener brings to them. Each performance of works like Pauline Oliveros's *Sonic Meditations*, *DreamHorseSpiel*, and *Nzinga*, furthermore, is unique and very much depends on audience participation. As I have shown, however, these performances are hardly without structure; Oliveros herself thinks of her pieces as "works," often having a "statistical" form. Cage, too, uses structural devices such as repetition and variation, ideas he says he learned from Schönberg, to ensure structural coherence.[76] His intent is as visionary as that of many modernists: to teach through music and embody a way to a better future.

---

76. See Cage, "Composition in Retrospect," 124, Cage, *I–VI*, 421, and Pasler, "Intention and Indeterminacy in John Cage's *I–VI*."

My use of "memory palaces" to describe what such works evoke is an attempt to define their structure, one resembling not the idealist "spatial forms" of high modernism but a nontraditional and open kind of form in whose construction the listener plays an important role. This idea brings attention to the importance of memory and to the order and associations—the thought—composers elicit through it. It uses the past to suggest meaning in the present, a meaning that may provide models for understanding the future. This is very much lodged in the synchronic connections, the "interreferentiality," that the spatial dimension of these palaces reveal.[77] A musical memory palace, as I describe it here, places the listener not in a despairing mode, like the dancer in "Blue Meteorite," or in the alienated and distanced mode of most modernist works, but in an active one. It remains to be seen what new memory palaces composers will stimulate listeners to construct from their own experiences, and what effect these structures will have on people's lives.

77. The anthropologist Michael M. J. Fischer defines "interreferentiality" as one of the key elements of the postmodern sensibility, the others being "bifocality or reciprocity of perspectives, juxtaposition of multiple realities, intertextuality, and comparisons of family resemblances." Cited in Lipsitz, *Time Passages*, 149.

3. RESITUATING THE SPECTRAL REVOLUTION

FRENCH ANTECEDENTS

*S*ITUATING THE DIALECTIC between discontinuity and continuity in twentieth-century music primarily with Germans from Wagner through Schönberg to Darmstadt composers is an error. Certainly *Parsifal* opened new horizons with its unusual silences and its composition in blocks.[1] But so did François Joseph Gossec a hundred years earlier with his famous *Marche lugubre*, a work revived and often performed in popular contexts at the fin de siecle, and Stravinsky in many of his early works. Yes, serial and postserial music prioritized the discontinuous over the continuous.[2] However, there were also precedents to this in France, and a French response well before spectral composition of the 1970s. In this article, I place the achievements of spectral music as part of a cumulative development, but one rooted in the French interest in perception and continuous with French values, especially the philosopher Henri Bergson's notion of "duration."

EARLIER RESEARCH ON PERCEPTION, SOUND, AND TIMBRE

Roots of our current "era of timbre" and interest in the nature of sound and musical perception go back many years. Since the seventeenth century, an important

This essay, written at the request of the journal editors and in response to the first four essays in the volume, was first published in "Aspects du temps dans la création musicale," a special issue of *Musicae Scientiae*, the journal of the European Society for the Cognitive Sciences of Music, Discussion Forum 3, 2004: 125–140. It is included here by permission, copyright 2004 European Society for the Cognitive Sciences of Music.

1. Michel Imberty and Nadia Capogreco, "Repères pour une problématique du temps en musique au cours du vingtième siècle," in "Aspects du temps dans la création musicale," ed. Irene Deliège and Max Paddison, special issue, *Musicae Scientiae* 3 (2004): 71.

2. Antonio Lai, "L'Instant innovateur et l'évolution historique des langages musicaux," in Deliège and Paddison, "Aspects du temps dans la création musicale," 37–46.

current of French intellectual thought has been belief in a mechanical connection between music and the body. While Descartes argued this from a philosophical perspective, Marin Mersenne in his acoustical studies and later Joseph Louis Roger in his treatise on the effects of music on the body promoted sound as an object of research.[3] In the nineteenth century came renewed interest in perception and physiopsychology, first in the visual domain. Just as Gérard Grisey and other spectral composers have sought help from contemporary acoustic theory and computer technology in understanding the microscopic aspects of perception, impressionist and postimpressionist painters looked to positivist studies of perception begun in the 1860s. Hippolyte Taine and Emile Littré, among others, focused on sensations—the effect that objects make on sense organs—for their empirical research. They believed that impressions (a synonym for sensations) were primordial, the embryos of one's knowledge of self and the world and, significantly, a product of the interaction between subject and object. Like them, the painters dubbed "impressionists" believed that any art based on impressions had the capacity to synthesize subject and object. Impressions were not ends in themselves, but the means to new experiences of reality.

Whereas today the word "impressionism" is pejorative, perhaps associated with the desire of the middle class to share in the lifestyle of the old aristocracy, in the 1870s and 1880s the movement referred to the avant-garde artists who responded to these studies and theories.[4] Establishing a precedent for many in the twentieth century, they rejected the use of imposing forms and concentrated on the immediacy of perception, hoping to use art to reveal the deep intuitions of the unconscious. Impressionists believed that the way images and sounds are produced affects their perception. Responding to physicists' breakdown of the visual spectrum into what was assumed to be characteristic of unreflective vision, that is, the vibrations of color and light, these painters simplified their palettes by using only colors of the prism, replaced light and dark oppositions with a new concept of visual harmony, and created mosaics of distinct rather than blended colors and forms. Instead of working from line to color, artists like Cézanne conceived painting in terms of color relationships, line and form being secondary to juxtapositions of color and light. Critics considered this a "physiological revolution of the human eye," an attempt to render visual experiences more alive, more perceptive of nuances.

Visual and aural perceptions were understood to share some important elements. In 1883 Jules Laforgue compared the kind of vision elicited by impressionist

---

3. See Marin Mersenne, *Harmonie universelle* (1636), Joseph Louis Roger, *Traité des effets de la musique sur le corps humain* (1748), and Kate van Orden, "Descartes on Musical Training and the Body," in *Music, Sensation, and Sensuality*, ed. Linda Austern (New York: Routledge, 2002), chap. 1.

4. This section borrows from my "Impressionism," in *The New Grove Dictionary of Music and Musicians*, 2nd ed., ed. Stanley Sadie and John Tyrrell (London: Macmillan, 2001).

paintings to aural experiences in which "the ear easily analyzes harmonics like an auditory prism." Directly inspired by Hermann von Helmholtz's theory of harmonics, the physicist Charles Henry later proposed a color spectrum in a "chromatic circle" that directly related visual to aural perception. The goal of his analysis was to help artists intensify the viewer's sensory perception through the systematic juxtaposition of contrasting colors. Henry believed that perception would be dynamic to the extent that, responding to the tension of opposites, the eyes move back and forth rapidly between discontinuous, contrasting color fields (e.g. red and green).[5] As an interest in optics and Henry's color theory grew, the more scientifically minded neoimpressionists of the late 1880s, such as Paul Signac and Georges-Pierre Seurat, focused on the physics of colored vibrations per se. Applying principles derived from Henry's theories, they broke colors down into their constituent elements and used contrasts to create visual harmony. They were also interested in the effect of the artist's nervous system on the nature of the impressions and wished to elicit specific "correspondences" for emotional states. These preoccupations paved the way for the early experiments by postimpressionists like Matisse with antinaturalistic flat surfaces made of juxtaposed colors.

Similar issues were associated with late nineteenth-century music that was deemed impressionist. Wagner's nature music, especially his "Forest Murmurs" from the *Rheingold* and vaporous moments in *Parsifal* and *Tristan*, elicited vague references to musical impressionism, but it was Debussy who extended these ideas in a way that had a lasting impact on the future of music. His *Printemps*, an evocation of the "slow and arduous birth of things in nature," parallels not only the painters' turn to "open air" subjects but also their exploration of unusual colors and mosaic-like designs.[6] Like impressionist painters, he sought artistic equivalents for water, fountains, fog, clouds, and the night, substituting sequences of major seconds, unresolved chords, and other sound-colors for precise designs, solid, clear forms, and logical developments. In *Prelude to the Afternoon of a Faun* and subsequent pieces, Debussy increasingly emphasized distinct sound-colors, those produced by individual instruments, rather than the composite ones of chamber or orchestral ensembles.

5. See Charles Henry, *Introduction à une esthétique scientifique* (Paris, 1885); *Cercle chromatique: Présentant tous les compléments et toutes les harmonies de couleurs avec une introduction sur la théorie générale du contraste, du rythme et de la mesure* (Paris, 1888); *Harmonies de formes et de couleurs. Démonstrations pratiques avec le rapporteur esthétique et le cercle chromatique* (Paris, 1891); and also his publications on music during this period, *Wronski et l'esthétique musicale* (Paris, 1887) and *La Théorie de Rameau sur la musique* (Paris, 1887).

6. Gounod, as secretary of the Académie des Beaux-Arts, used the word "impressionism" in 1887 to attack *Printemps*, Debussy's *envoi* from Rome. Besides having an exaggerated sense of musical color, the work questioned the authority of the Académie's values. The work's "impressionism" seemed "one of the most dangerous enemies of truth in art."

In part because of the unusual sounds heard during the Paris Universal Exhibitions, an interest in primitive cultures and nature also led the French to reconsider Western notions of timbre. The various "musical promenades" published in the press, and especially Debussy's focus on the timbre of Annamite instruments, have been well studied. Far less known is a series of articles published during the final month of the 1889 Exhibition by the mystic writer and composer Edmond Bailly called "The World of Sound" and subtitled "Sound, Harmony of the Spheres, Voices of Nature."[7] The first began with an acoustician's definition of sound as "movement that becomes audible at a distance. Every sound, every noise announces a movement." Movement, in turn, also creates sound, even "the projection of light across space." Writing eighty years before John Cage, Bailly observes, "The complete absence of any sound does not exist on our planet any more than radical darkness or absolute cold." There are "microscopic ambient sounds" everywhere—ranging from the planetary ones evoked by Greek philosophers to those made by the earth, animals, even plants. Studying references to sound in essays written by travelers to Africa, Oceania, and the South Pole, Bailly was led to thinking about sound in all its variety and effect on the human listener.[8]

Just as contemporary physics informed new ideas about painting, Helmholtz's acoustics and developments in the spectral analysis of sound fed composers' interest in musical resonance and the dissolution of form by vibrations (which was compared to dreams and deep intuitions). In much of Debussy's music, as in impressionist pieces by Ravel and others, the composer arrests movement on ninth and other added-note chords not to produce dissonant tension but, as Dukas puts it, to "make multiple resonances vibrate."[9] This attention to distant overtones, particularly generated by gong-like lower bass notes, produces a new sense of musical space, in effect giving a greater sense of the acoustic reality of sound. Using a wide range of dynamic and registral sounds—a complete scale of nuances—such music can bring about subtle vibrations in the listener's nervous system. In one of his earliest essays (1899), Emile Vuillermoz reiterates Laforgue's concerns with the problems of line and fixed forms and, sounding like a neoimpressionist, suggests

7. Edmund Bailly, "Le Monde sonore," *La Musique des familles* (31 August–5 October 1889).

8. The very month his series on sound ended, Bailly formed a journal and publishing house to support occultist and symbolist work, the Librairie de l'art indépendant. The salon he held in its office attracted some of the leading symbolists of the time, including Debussy, a regular there from 1890 to 1894. During this period, Bailly distributed Debussy's *Cinq Poèmes de Baudelaire* when it was first published and published Debussy's *Damoiselle élue* in a limited luxury edition. In this context, Debussy developed a new theory about music. Connecting sensations associated with exotic music, symbolism, and the occult, he proposed that music should express "the mysterious correspondences between nature and the imagination."

9. Paul Dukas, *Ecrits sur la musique* (Paris: Société d'editions françaises, 1948).

that "the progressive refinement of our nerves [by this music] leads us to think that *this* is the path of musical progress."[10]

In many ways, the spectral composers of the 1970s have continued to explore related research trajectories. As for the impressionists, Grisey's music, Hugues Dufourt explains, "is a movement of back and forth between sensation and object." The work is meant to "intensify or sharpen our sensations by situating them on another scale" than the one we are accustomed to. Grisey does this by focusing on an instant, dilating the sound spectrum of a microsecond, in a way as Monet freezes a moment of time to decompose its light.[11] Like Seurat using a pointillist technique to build form with tiny dots of juxtaposed colors, Tristan Murail works by additive synthesis. As Dufourt explains it, he fragments the diverse elements of a process whose parts operate in opposing pairs.[12] In deconstructing paint and sound at the micro level, these artists alter the nature of aesthetic perception.

With a similar attitude toward sound and the benefit of computer analysis, spectralists have also revisited the dynamic nature of musical acoustics, the structure of musical resonance, and the use of timbre to rethink one's musical vocabulary and syntax. In 1974–85, Grisey studied acoustics with E. Leipp at the University of Paris VI and began a cycle exploring the acoustic properties of sound and human perception, "Acoustic Spaces" (1974–85).[13] Like Debussy and Bailly, Grisey did not consider musical parameters distinct. While Debussy treated quick rhythmic patterns as an element of timbre, especially the superimposed polyrhythms in "Sirens" from *Nocturnes*, Grisey conversely explored the pulse inherent in certain timbres. Both have blurred the difference between single sounds and chordal sounds (e.g. the parallel chords of *Canope*) and between vocally produced timbre and instrumental timbre (*Pelléas et Mélisande*, "Sirens," and Grisey's *Quatre chants pour franchir le seuil*), and both have sought new ways to envisage timbral succession. Both have conceived of sound as a living organism, perpetually waxing and waning, although not always in accordance with acoustic principles (i.e., Debussy liked to use short *crescendos* that break off at their zenith, while Grisey focuses on the moment of attack and subsequent demise of sound). Still, if nineteenth-century

10. Emile Vuillermoz, "L'Impressionisme en musique," *Revue jeune* 2, nos. 24–25 (10–25 July 1899): 1–6.

11. Hugues Dufourt, "Gérard Grisey: La Fonction constituante du temps," in Deliège and Paddison, "Aspects du temps dans la création musicale," 57. See also Gérard Grisey, "'Tempus ex machina': Réflexions d'un compositeur sur le temps musical," *Entretemps* 8 (1989): 103.

12. Dufourt, "Gérard Grisey," 64.

13. For a discussion of this work, see Julian Anderson, "Gérard Grisey," in *The New Grove Dictionary of Music and Musicians*, 2nd ed., ed. Stanley Sadie and John Tyrrell (London: Macmillan, 2001).

research centered on discovering the normative characteristics of sound and color perception, the spectralists, Dufourt observes, have found valuable information in the "irregularities and deviations" of sounds. For them, musical sound can include not only noises of all sorts—which fascinated Bailly and later composers of *musique concrète*—but also inharmonic sounds and filters. Using computers, spectralists have come to redefine what is primary in our perception of sound as the timbre that results from an interrelationship among several acoustic indices. Manipulating these in their compositions has resulted in what Grisey called perceptual "hybrids."

Some of today's French composers have moved beyond traditional acoustics, physics, and psychophysiology, and Grisey, along with others, has realized that the best art is not applied science. Still, perceptual research has been important to their development. The French focus on perception has kept the music made in response to it rooted in hearing and in the effect of sounds on listeners rather than in mathematical concepts or idealistic notions of how hearing might evolve, as Schönberg and his followers may have assumed in writing serial music. Incorporating the insights of computer technology, spectralists have pushed on the limits of what is possible while maintaining a connection to the physicality of sound.

BERGSON, DISCONTINUITY, AND CONTINUITY

From Grisey's perspective, even more primary than the sound spectrum in the experience of music is the process Bergson called "duration." Bergson used this concept to distinguish the time of the unconscious and dreams, characterized by the interpenetration of heterogeneous elements, from time as space, which might be illustrated by the minutes of the ticking clock, whose measurement divides time into homogeneous parts.[14] Duration is "the development of a thought that gradually changes as it take shape."[15] In music, it concerns the dynamic aspects that unfold in time, not the stabilizing ones often associated with traditional form. Whereas Bergson saw in the idea of a melody an example of the way the unconscious perceives this kind of time—"a succession of qualitative changes which melt into and permeate one another . . . like the notes of a tune"[16]—Grisey's great

14. Translating this into Hegelian terms, Imberty sees this as the difference between pure being and abstract thought. He proposes that, in music, time as duration is like the time experienced by the listener, whereas time as space is the time of the score, "rigid and rationalized by the categories of intelligence and abstract thought." See Imberty, introduction to Deliège and Paddison, "Aspects du temps dans la création musicale," 8.

15. Henri Bergson, *Oeuvres complètes* (Paris: Presses universitaires de France, 1970), 783.

16. Henri Bergson, *Time and Free Will*, trans. F. L. Pogson (New York: Allen, 1910; originally published as *Essai sur les données immédiates de la conscience*, 1889), 104.

accomplishment, as Imberty puts it, was to "dilate the moment to perceive its duration and thus reconquer continuity within the world of sound."[17]

This statement implies that a sense of duration and continuity had been lost in music. Imberty and Dufourt suggest that the postserial avant-garde was responsible for an aesthetic of absolute discontinuity, causing one of the greatest crises in the history of Western music. However, one does not have to wait until the 1950s to find motivation for exploring discontinuity in music or the 1970s for a musical response to the "intuition of dynamic continuity" conceptualized by Bergson. At the end of the nineteenth century, not only Bergson and French composers but also much of French society were becoming increasingly frustrated with Darwinian concepts of organic growth. Many objected to a "mechanistic" view of evolution that involves only transitions and variations of degree rather than kind. Republicans espoused the idea that people, through education and reason, can adapt and change, but their theories of monogenist evolution (the idea that all races descended from one) were increasingly challenged by polygenists, who espoused a separate origin for each human race. The latter thought that variations between human populations (and anything they produced) reflected distinct racial characteristics. Polygenists like Gustave Le Bon considered the nature of a people—its soul, forms of thought, logic, and character—to be fixed and homogeneous, inalterable by education or intelligence. With problems in attempting to impose French institutions in Indochina, the French were also increasingly divided over the notion of assimilation that pointed to the potential of the environment to influence people, especially those in the lower classes or the colonies. After 1900, those interested in racial, social, and political coexistence without assimilation and a colonial policy based on association, or gaining cooperation and participation by native peoples in their own government, education, and defense, had an increasing influence on French discourse.

Science, early photography, and cinematography also forced reconsideration of assumed continuities, as well as an acknowledgement of discontinuity in our perception of reality. In 1900, the German physicist Max Planck showed that even radiant energy did not proceed in a continuous flow but rather was emitted and absorbed in integral quantities, or packets, and was therefore discontinuous. This was contrary to the causal relationships of nature that had been assumed since Newton and Leibniz. The invention of photography provided a way to freeze motion and spontaneity, capturing "instantaneous" moments that passed too rapidly for the eye to see them. Cinema exposed the important role of the temporal process in one's visual perception. For Bergson, however, the cinematic way of thinking was artificial, one of the many fictions of the mind, since it conveyed what is actually changing as a series of distinct forms. In his *Creative Evolution*, Bergson

17. Imberty, introduction, 7–19.

came down hard on what he considered the cinematographic nature of perception as well as conceptual thought.

These ideas had significant implications for those working in the temporal arts and led to an interest in Bergson's philosophy and method (intuition).[18] His notion of duration helped composers reconceptualize musical continuity in ways that do not rely on the perpetual motivic development and teleological motion of nineteenth-century Romantic music. Cinematography, as discussed by Bergson, drew attention to the process of constructing form and to a formal freedom that escaped the constraints of traditional practices. This led to thinking of any motion between distinct entities as cinematic. Cinematography also helped composers reconceive discontinuity without denying or obliterating temporality, and experiment with juxtapositions that bring the perceiver closer to the abruptness of the creative process.[19] In 1913, Debussy acknowledged this when he commented on "the cinematography of instants through which the author moved while he was composing his piece."[20] In some ways, this focus on new kinds of continuity and discontinuity in music contributed to what I have argued is a reversal in the traditional relationship between structure and process at the heart of modernist music in early twentieth-century France, or, as Imberty and Capogreco put it, the perceptual shift from "categorization" to "incessant accommodation to the process of continuous transformation."[21] For Bergson's successor Vladimir Jankélévitch, Gabriel Fauré was the "true Bergsonian" composer. In works such as the "Sanctus" from his *Requiem* and the Berceuse from his *Dolly* suite, Jankélévitch finds the "continuity of becoming [devenir]" in the "melody of internal life." The musical equivalent for water in his music is a "vehicle of becoming." While he finds the temporality of Fauré's music inspiring confidence in a future, the aspects of "becoming" in Debussy's music, by contrast, seem to Jankélévitch to lead to "an

18. See Julien Benda, *Le Bergsonisme ou le philosophie de la mobilité* (Paris: Mercure de France, 1912). In this text, Benda argues that the intuitive method elevates feeling over ideas, the feminine over the virile, the musical over the plastic arts, and the spirit that seeks over that which possesses (59).

19. In *The Banquet Years* (New York: Vintage, 1955), Roger Shattuck devotes a chapter to the use and meaning of juxtaposition.

20. Claude Debussy, *Monsieur Croche et autres écrits* (Paris: Gallimard, 1971), 242. The composer Alfredo Casella, in his essay "Matière et timbre," *Revue musicale* (1 April 1921), about the "metaphysical relationships of music with our consciousness," pointed to the "close affinities" of "free, bare, and voluptuous sonorities, extra-rapid in their cinematographic mobility," with "the ultimate refinements of our civilization" (40). See also R. Charbonnel, "La Musique et la renaissance de l'inconscient," *Mercure musical* (15 Feb 1909).

21. Imberty and Capogreco, "Repères," 71–87. I develop this idea in my *Debussy Stravinsky and the Ballets Russes: The Emergence of a New Musical Logic*, Ph.D. diss., University of Chicago, 1981, part III.

impasse, a dead-end" with his melody, as in the Prelude from *Pour le piano*, often reduced to a "rhythmic formula."[22]

Why, then, in a 1910 interview, did Bergson confess he had an "intuitive predilection" for the music of Debussy and, for this reason, can one see it as a precedent for the music of Grisey? Bergson's description of Debussy's music as "a music of duration because of the use of a continuous melody that accompanies and expresses the unique and uninterrupted current of dramatic emotion" sounds like Wagner's unending melody.[23] Debussy himself once claimed: "all my music tries to be nothing but melody."[24] To understand how his music can be Bergsonian, however, we should not look to his individual melodies, for these can lead to the impasse Jankélévitch observed. Instead we should examine his musical form. Jean Barraqué has pointed out how the "sonorous becoming" of *La Mer*, especially in "From Dawn to Noon," results from a "developmental process in which the very notions of exposition and development coexist."[25] With short motives as building blocks in such works as *Jeux* (1913), I would argue, Debussy goes further, shifting attention to the movement of large segments of music. These segments succeed one another like Bergson's "musical phrase that is constantly on the point of ending and constantly altered in its totality by the addition of some new note." It is the succession of sections that "may be compared to a living being whose parts, although distinct, permeate one another" and whose "mutual penetration, an interconnection and organization of elements" resembles the process Bergson called duration.[26] In 1914, when Bergson was "the philosopher of our time" and Debussy "the musician," Debussy's friend Louis Laloy went so far as to claim that such a music could not have been produced except in the same environment as such a philosophy, and vice versa.[27]

DEBUSSY'S *JEUX*

To understand *Jeux* as an expression of Bergson's duration, the schemas of abstract thought (which, Bergson points out, "operate in the realm of the immobile") are less useful than Bergson's intuitive method. It focuses on the nature of mobility.[28]

22. Vladimir Jankélévitch, *Debussy et le mystère de l'instant* (Paris: Plon, 1976), 99, 118.

23. George Aimel, "Une Heure chez H. Bergson (*Paris-Journal*, 11 December 1910)," in Henri Bergson, *Mélanges* (Paris: Presses universitaires de France, 1972), 844.

24. In a letter to Vallas from Vienna, cited in Françoise Gervais, "La Notion d'arabesque chez Debussy," *Revue musicale* 241 (1958): 23.

25. Jean Barraqué, *Debussy* (Paris: Seuil, 1962; reprint, 1994), 182, 184.

26. Bergson, *Time and Free Will*, 104–6.

27. Louis Laloy, "La Musique chez soi: M. Henri Bergson et la musique," *Comoedia* (c. February/March 1914); copy provided to author by Vincent Laloy.

28. Bergson, *Oeuvres complètes*, 1412.

As Gilles Deleuze explains, this method involves three stages: the stating and there-fore creating of problems, the discovery of genuine differences in kind, and the apprehension of real time.[29]

Stating the Problem

Debussy was preoccupied with movement. In his youth, particularly when writing *Pelléas et Mélisande*, he expressed interest in translating into music the "lyric movements of the soul" and the "capriciousness of dreams." Moreover, inspired by the time of nature and of the universe, he did not wish his music to capture just one instant, as a painting or sculpture might. Musicians, he once wrote, have the privi-lege of being able to "capture all the poetry of night and day, of the earth and sky, and recreate their atmosphere and give rhythm to their immense pulsations."[30] These attitudes raised important questions about musical form and led him to assert in 1907, the same year Bergson published *Creative Evolution*, that "music is not, in its essence, a thing which can flow within a rigorous and traditional form. It is *de couleurs et de temps rythmés*."[31]

In my previous work on *Jeux*, I have suggested that this is not just a new definition of form in the terms of timbre and time, replacing traditional thematic development and functional harmony. If we read "rythmés" as modifying both "temps" and "couleurs," it also implies that form is the "rhythmization" of sec-tions, each with their own "color and sense of time."[32] Such a statement makes the temporal dimension primary in the creation and perception of form. In *Jeux*, I argue, the successive volleys of a tennis game and the ever-changing relationships between the three characters gave Debussy an opportunity to create the "constant becoming" of Bergson's duration on the level of form. Interestingly, both Imberty and Dufourt refer to the evolution of music in the second half of the twentieth century in remarkably similar terms: "forms entirely based on fluid relationships of textures and timbres."[33] For spectral composers, as for Debussy, there were formal consequences to this focus on sound as timbre. For Murail, this meant attempting to create an equivalence between the construction of sounds and musical form. In this context, Dufourt notes, they realized that time is that which

---

29. Gilles Deleuze, *Bergsonism*, trans. Hugh Tomlinson and Barbara Habberjam (New York: Zone, 1991; originally published as *Bergsonisme*, 1966), 14–35.

30. Claude Debussy, *Monsieur Croche et autres écrits* (Paris: Gallimard, 1971), 249. In 1901 he also commented: "Music and poetry are the only two arts that move in space" (240).

31. Claude Debussy, *Lettres à son éditeur* (Paris: Durand, 1927), 55. In his *Ecrits sur la musique*, Dukas commented similarly, "Debussy seeks to notate a series of sensations more than the deductions of a musical thought" (591).

32. Jann Pasler, "*Jeux*: Playing with Time and Form," *Nineteenth-Century Music* 6, no. 1 (summer 1982): 72.

33. Imberty, introduction; Dufourt, "Gérard Grisey."

"organizes form." The problem thus posed for Debussy and the spectralists was similar.

Creating Differences in Kind

Deleuze explains that Bergson's obsession with pure presences goes back to his call for the restoration of differences in kind and that only tendencies differ in kind. "The composite," Deleuze writes, (and any form aspiring to express the flow of duration, I propose), "must therefore be divided according to the qualitative and qualified tendencies, that is, . . . the direction of movements."[34] In his *Creative Evolution*, Bergson explains how such a creative process begins:

> From our first glance at the world, before even we discern shapes in it, we distinguish qualities. One color follows another color, one sound another sound, one tension another tension. Each of these qualities, taken separately, exists until another replaces it; each can be reduced to an enormous number of elementary movements. . . . The permanence of a perceptible quality consists in the repetition of movements. . . . The principal function of perception is condensation, in other words, the grasping of elementary changes as a quality or a simple state. . . . In short, qualities of matter are stable views we take of what is essentially unstable. . . . When the successive images do not differ from one another too much, we consider them all to be the expansion and contraction of a single mean image, or the distortion of this image in different ways. And it is to this mean that we refer when we speak of the *essence* of a thing, or the thing itself.[35]

These words could be used to explain why Debussy, before he could draw attention to a form made of differences in kind, first had to create a distinct quality of sound and directional tendency for each section of *Jeux*. He does this with a short, clearly recognizable motive that is flexible and easy to manipulate, whose quantitative aspects—its metric, melodic, and even harmonic shape—he fixes. He then plays with it in different instrumental, registral, dynamic, and rhythmic contexts. The rhythms of statements of the same motive structure and shape time. The function of each section is not to develop or transform an idea or to flesh out part of a formal scheme, but rather to use these building blocks to create a certain "essence," its quality.

If Jankélévitch was frustrated with this turning-in-place, the postwar generation admired the extent to which compositional and orchestral processes were interdependent in such works. Boulez points to the "orchestra-invention" and how Debussy's use of timbre modifies "l'écriture," even if he situates this as a logical

---

34. Deleuze, *Bergsonism*, 22.
35. Bergson, *Oeuvres complètes*, 749–50.

consequence to work done in *La Mer* and *Images*.[36] What has been less recognized is the debt owed by Steve Reich and his process pieces to this important aspect of musical Bergsonism, not to speak of the spectralists, who likewise slow down time and dilate the moment in order to open the possibility of composing a certain quality of sound and time. For the spectralists, as for Debussy, timbre refers to the distinct quality of sound characterizing an entire section of music and involves a dynamic process. In this sense, timbre helps create structure rather than merely articulating it.

The saturation of this kind of quality causes interruption by whatever follows to come as a surprise. The first two sections of *Jeux* provide ample evidence of this. Measures 1–8 have three sound-levels: descending whole-tone harmonies in the winds, a pedal in the violins and violas, and an accompaniment pattern of two rising semitones in the horns, harp, and celesta. In mm. 9–42, the chromaticism latent in the first section's accompaniment pattern comes into the foreground, replacing the whole-tone harmonies. The basses enter for the first time, and the melodic line switches from the winds to the strings.

Just as timbral differentiation between adjacent sections characterizes all of *Jeux*, so does temporal and rhythmic differentiation. Along with the sound metamorphosis between sections 1 and 2, there is a shift of tempo from slow to *scherzando*, duple to triple meter, and half notes to quick staccato sixteenth notes. Each section also develops its own vector or what Bergson might call "tendency," a force with shape and direction. By looking to the kind of tension each moment creates, either by the saturation of one quality or the eventual disintegration of its rhythmic patterns, one can begin to have a sense of the kind of music that comes next. The anticipation aroused by this music is not one of what will recur—what melody or harmony—but a sense of what quality of sound and rhythm will provide counterbalance. For example, after an insistently descending line (around r. n. 8) comes a rising one; after ambiguous motion or a turning in place (r. n. 9) comes defined movement; after the tension of being pulled in many directions at once (r. n. 14–16) comes resolution by unidirectional movement; after a static turning (r. n. 21), there follows an expansive melody; periods of whispering alternate with those with full, lavish orchestral sound, and so on. This succession of impulses and tensions— which can be conjunct or disjunct—keeps the form fluid. Balance or equilibrium is constantly being recreated. The contingency of the formal unfolding—like "the free play of sound" Debussy called "arabesque"—depends on the conditions of the moment, and these are always changing, sometimes in response to the scenario. Not conceivable, then, in the spatial terms of geometry or architecture, this form is a process in flux.

36. Pierre Boulez, "Debussy," in *Relèves d'apprenti* (Paris: Seuil, 1966), 344.

Even if its sections, as Jonathan Kramer has pointed out, are "as often in motion towards other sections as they are static," Darmstadt composers such as Stockhausen and Boulez looked to *Jeux* as a predecessor, a source of their "moment forms."[37] And because it "incites the perceiver to change his perspective continually to see the work under constantly new points of view, as an object in perpetual transformation," *Jeux* also anticipated the open forms of the 1960s.[38] In their shared focus on a qualitative approach to sound and the elasticity of time, spectralists, too, can look to *Jeux* for resonance with their concerns. Like Debussy, they consider becoming to be the nature of reality. Seeing music likewise as the organization of "tensions" moving in waves of contraction and expansion (Grisey) and involving a "network of interactions" (Dufourt), they focus on a continuum of transformations. Time converts structures into processes, and process, as Grisey explains, manages the mutation of sound figures, leading to the endless creation of new ones.

Like Grisey's explorations in the late 1980s, *Jeux* also embodies simultaneities within the flux of duration. In attempting to explain how music can express the unconscious aspects of our sensitivity, Julien Benda suggests that, as early as *Pelléas*, Debussy chose emotions that could be expressed simultaneously, for this simultaneity would involve a process distinct from the developmental processes associated with intellectual phenomena. He also notes that it is by the "combination of sounds and timbres" that Debussy's orchestra translates the "coexistence of *mouvements sensitifs.*"[39] Later in *Jeux*, Debussy works with contrasting qualities of sound and time inspired by the three characters on stage. Two types of timbre—clearly defined melodic lines in the strings and trills, tremolos and glissandi in the winds and harp—differentiate the young man from the girls, while three metric areas—3/4, 3/8, and 2/4—carefully delineate the three individuals. In the middle of the ballet, the successive contrasting qualities do not function strictly to balance one another, but rather embody in music the interactions between these characters, as each tries to persuade the other to dance, and they engage in three *pas de deux*. Abrupt shifts mirroring their dialogue cause a fascinating dissonance between what one perceives, the new quality, and what one conceives, the expected continuation of the previous quality—perhaps foreshadowing the "widening gap between what is perceived and what is conceived" in Grisey's later music. Occasionally there is

37. See Karlheinz Stockhausen, "Von Webern zu Debussy, Bemerkungen zur statistischen Form," in *Texte zur electronischen und instrumentalen Musik* (Cologne: Dumont Schauberg, 1963), 75–85; Pierre Boulez, "Debussy," *Gravesaner Blätter* 2/3 (1956): 5; and Jonathan Kramer, "Moment Form in Twentieth-Century Music," *Musical Quarterly* 64, no. 2 (April 1978): 189.

38. Umberto Eco, *L'Oeuvre ouverte* (Paris: Seuil, 1965), 20. See also the posthumous publication of Jean Barraqué, "*La Mer* de Debussy, ou la naissance des formes ouvertes," *Analyse musicale* 12 (June 1988): 15–62.

39. Julien Benda, "A propos de *Pelléas et Mélisande*," *Revue blanche* (1 July 1902).

also what Barraqué has called "alternative continuity," connections between fragments that do not immediately succeed one another.[40] In the final *pas de trois*, Debussy forges a remarkable synthesis of these opposing meters and rhythmic patterns, using duple (2/4), triple (3/8), and hemiola (3/4) patterns in ever-changing relationships from figure to ground and from successive juxtaposition to simultaneity. At the climatic "triple kiss" comes their ultimate reconciliation.

In his *Le Temps et l'écume* (1988–89), Grisey likewise works with three kinds of time—slow, compressed, and normal. As in *Jeux*, they are contrasted, involving both smooth transitions and abrupt shifts, and superimposed. In *l'Esprit des dunes* (1993–94), as Imberty and Capogreco point out, Murail also attempts a synthesis between the "absolute continuity of sound" and the discontinuity associated with discursive forms.[41] Such works thus hark back to the dialectic between discontinuity and continuity that is characteristic of Debussy's late music.

Apprehending Real Time: The "Mysterious Link"

Debussy's criticism and correspondence suggest that the composer did not consider formal mobility and underlying continuity mutually exclusive. Analyzing Mussorgsky's song cycle *The Nursery* in 1901, he praised Mussorgsky not only for using a form he found "quite multiple" but also for connecting this "succession of little strokes" by a "mysterious link."[42] Debussy returned to this idea of a link in a letter of 1914 to Gabriel Pierné, just after Pierné had conducted *Jeux* for the first time in concert: "It seems to me that the different episodes lacked homogeneity. The link that connects them may be subtle, but it exists, doesn't it? You know it as well as I."[43]

Indeed, as Imberty and Capogreco remark, duration must have continuity as well as what they, with Deleuze, call differentiation: differentiation because of the unpredictable newness of the creative process and continuity because of the nature of the inner life.[44] Continuity arises from interpenetration, which is crucial to the experience of duration, and this is the interpenetration of perception and recollection.[45] This means that qualitative change involves continuity of the past in the present.

Despite the apparent discontinuity of its sections with their differentiated qualities, in *Jeux* the past can also be said to "melt into and permeate" each present moment. Between most sections, there is some element that subtly continues from one to the next, whether a pitch or pitch-class, a motive, a rhythm, a mode,

---

40. Barraqué, *Debussy*, 214.

41. Imberty and Capogreco, "Repères," 84.

42. Debussy, *Monsieur Croche*, 29.

43. Letter to Gabriel Pierné printed in the catalogue of the exhibition, *Claude Debussy* (Paris: Bibliothèque Nationale, 1962), 67.

44. Deleuze, *Bergsonism*, 38.

45. Deleuze, *Bergsonism*, 26, 60.

a harmony, or an articulation. The discontinuity is thus often bridged. Moreover, from one section to the next, new motives spin out in a chain-like manner, recurring, dividing, and recombining, as do certain timbres, meters, and rhythmic patterns. Only one motive keeps its identity throughout the piece, even as its role vacillates throughout between figure and ground. Its return signals a process Deleuze explains as "psychic repetition," a "virtual coexistence" that takes place at moments when new ideas are engendered out of older ones.[46]

Still, Debussy's comment that the episodes of *Jeux* are homogeneous is puzzling. In 1905, Husserl argued that one perceives the homogeneity of a multitude of "temporal shadings" through the "unity of temporal apprehension."[47] From this perspective, I have argued, we should examine temporal continuity in *Jeux*. Without denying the fluctuating meter and tempo indications or the ever-changing qualities of sound and time discussed earlier, Debussy was signaling the necessity for a common pulse or eighth note throughout the piece.[48] Obviously given the amount of rubato indicated, this pulse or beat is not rigid but rather like a heartbeat, accelerating or decelerating depending on the context. This kind of temporal continuity mitigates the rhythmic tension between the triple and duple divisions at all levels of the music and holds together sections that contrast and pull apart in other ways. It is through time that Debussy implicitly expects the listener to take an active role in perceiving the continuity within the music's discontinuity.

As I noted earlier, the spectralists have long been interested in the pulse inherent in timbral change. What is new in more recent spectral music is a return of other kinds of continuity. If Grisey, until his late works, embraced the notion that consciousness of change is a continuous process not involving repetition, his younger successors have found ways to use repetition of motives, rhythms, and musical situations even within long linear processes.[49]

MATTER AND TIMBRE

Dufourt has recently posed an important question: do the polemics about timbre imply a change in the essence of art? In his article "Matter and Timbre," published in France in 1921, the Italian composer Alfredo Casella addressed this issue. Taking into account the insights of Bergson and pointing to the importance Debussy,

46. Deleuze, *Bergsonism*, 60.

47. Edmund Husserl, *The Phenomenology of Internal Time-Consciousness* (Bloomington: Indiana University Press, 1964; originally published as *Vorlesungen zur Phanomenologie des inneren Zeitbewusstseins,* from a series of lectures given in 1904–10), 119.

48. I explain this in my "*Jeux,*" 71.

49. Philippe Hurel, "Spectral Music: Long Term . . . Perspectives," notes on Gérard Grisey, *Quatre chants pour franchir le seuil,* Klangforum Wien dir. Sylvain Cambreling (Kairos 0012252KA, 2001).

Stravinsky, and Schönberg gave to timbre, Casella not only argued that a revolution in musical perception had already taken place but also proposed a "hypothesis" about the future. "From my perspective," he writes, "the musical evolution of the last decades has been dominated especially by one essential and fundamental development whose importance cannot be exaggerated: the arrival of the fourth element of sound . . . 'timbre' or 'the sense of sound color.' " Whereas this element used to serve a subsidiary role in music, it is now in a predominant position in aesthetics and contemporary technique. While the "numerical relationships" of pitch (melody and harmony) or duration (rhythm) are "merely quantitative," timbre offers the possibility for "qualitative" relationships. Casella points out that such a concept, although new in Europe, has long existed in the Far East. What is essential in Asian music is "the sense of matter."[50] More than melody or rhythm, he hears their music as "exploiting the resources of substance." Endorsing this evolution in Western musical perception from the "purely quantitative" to the "qualitative," Casella envisages composition based on matter as the primordial element. He imagines one day that "a single chord could contain in its 'simultaneity' a sum total of the sensation and emotion equal to that which unfolds today in the 'duration' of this or that other musical fragment."

> It is not fanciful to imagine, even today, a music which is free of rhythm (an element which is not in the least musical), liberated from all trace of counterpoint in which groups of sounds only obey the fantasy of the creator and the necessity to achieve "different colorations," a music that would be "melodic" not in the still primitive sense which we attribute to this word, but in the much larger sense of any coordinated succession of sonorities in time.[51]

Casella was clairvoyant. So was Edgard Varèse, who envisaged an electronic music that would allow him to write music that was not an "interplay of melodies" but rather a "melodic totality," music that "flows as a river flows."[52] As Dufourt points out, Jean-Claude Risset has now shown how sounds can be composed like chords, and in 1969 he proposed a music based on relationships of timbre rather than pitch.[53] For Grisey too, it has been critical to get away from counterpoint, to write "antipolyphonic" music. What his predecessors could not have predicted, however, was what we've learned from computer musicians and psychoacousticians

50. Already in 1872 some French believed that in Asia, music is basically "only the glorification of sound in matter and in nervous impressions." See "La Vie publique et privée des castes musicales," *Revue et gazette musicale* (25 August 1872), 267.

51. Casella, "Matière et timbre,"42.

52. Edgard Varèse, "The Liberation of Sound," *Perspectives of New Music* 5, no. 1 (fall/ winter 1966), 11, 16.

53. Dufourt, "Gérard Grisey."

about the nature of a sonority—its unstable equilibrium, the "singularity of instrumental timbres" coming from the anomalies and accidents involved in the attack and waning of the sound wave that make up its microscopic morphology. Still, from Dufourt's perspective, spectral music is not just "a kind of abandonment to the increasing domination of matter that would find its ultimate sanction in the factitious objectivity of the thing for its own sake."[54] Spectral composers have certainly redefined musical matter as an ensemble of parts with reciprocal implications. But who could have imagined the "hybrid" sounds, neither timbres nor chords, with which they are now working?

54. Dufourt, "Gérard Grisey."

Part II

SELF-FASHIONING

4. DECONSTRUCTING D'INDY, OR THE PROBLEM OF A COMPOSER'S REPUTATION

HE STORY OF A LIFE, like history, is an invention. Certainly the biographer and historian have roles in this invention, but so, too, does the composer, for whom making music necessarily entails building and maintaining a reputation. Reputation is the fruit of talents, knowledge, and achievements that attract attention. It signals renown, the way someone is known in public or the sum of values commonly associated with a person. If it does not imply public admiration, it does suggest that the public takes an interest in the person in question. The ordinary sense of the word refers to the public's notion of someone well after death—the social consensus articulated by the biographer—as well as the quasi-historical judgment that we make with the distance of time. This often produces the semblance of authority, the authority of one manifest meaning.

In reality, reputation is also the result of the steps taken during a professional life to assure one's existence as a composer, a process involving actions, interactions, and associations as well as works. This includes all efforts to earn credibility, respect, distinction, and finally prestige. As Pierre Bourdieu has pointed out, these inevitably take place in a social space, be it of teachers, friends and enemies, social and professional contacts, institutions, jobs, awards, or critics, any of whom may influence the conception, creation, or reception of art.[1] Involving individual as well

A previous version of this chapter, here expanded, appeared in French as "Déconstruire d'Indy," *Revue de musicologie* 91, no. 2 (2005): 369–400, and in *19th-Century Music* 30/3 (2007) used by permission, copyright 2007, Regents of the University of California. Earlier versions were presented at the conferences "Vincent d'Indy and His Times," Trinity College, Hartford, Connecticut, 11 May 2001, and "Vincent d'Indy et son temps," Bibliothèque Nationale, Paris, 26 September 2002, as well as l'Institut des Hautes Etudes, Brussels, 15 December 2004.

I would like to thank Gayle Hilson Woldu, Manuela Schwartz, and Henri Vanhulst for their invitations, Robert Wangermée for his comments, and especially Manuela Schwartz, Keith Chapin, and Jean Gribenski for editorial contributions.

1. For example, Pierre Bourdieu, "Espace social et pouvoir symbolique," in *Choses dites* (Paris: Minuit, 1987), 147–66.

as collective strategies, a reputation, then, is the result of the process that helps form an individual. It is also a construction based on presuppositions and purposes. The projection of aesthetic coherence in a composer's work or ideological identity in his or her life, however, tends to minimize ambiguities and paradoxes. To understand a composer better, we must unveil the ambiguities underlying his or her actions, associations, and compositional choices and consider the ironies and paradoxes in what we may have expected.

This is particularly important when a composer's renown is linked with that of a group or a certain lineage, as is true of Vincent d'Indy (1851–1931). Disciples have a stake in the preservation of difference, as do adversaries. While the former can build a composer's visibility and clarify his or her value, both can also harden a composer's position into dogma or obscure significant aspects of his or her life. When this happens, a composer's reputation is not an accurate reflection of the life or work and may actually impede us from a full comprehension of them. It is important, therefore, to examine critically a composer's attempt to project or protect a certain reputation, others' contributions to this legacy (especially those with a stake in preserving, enhancing, or demeaning it), and the different contexts that can lead us to rediscover an artist. Questioning the stability of a composer's identity and studying the dynamic relationship between composer and culture offers a way to rethink the processes of identity formation and agency in a composer's life.

The case of d'Indy provides an important example of the ways a composer's actions, disciples, and even enemies can lead to the construction of a reputation that prevents us from understanding significant aspects of his life and music. In this article, I attempt to throw new light on d'Indy's reputation before 1900 by examining what has been omitted by his disciples and their successors, including his little-known works, and by deconstructing the attitudes that have accumulated about him over time. To understand how d'Indy became a major player in the musical world of the Belle Époque, despite the limited public taste for his music, we need a more nuanced view of his politics, one that is based on his practices before and even during the Dreyfus Affair rather than on the ultraconservatism that has since become associated with him.[2]

---

2. In his "Les Chapelles musicales en France," *La Revue* (15 November 1907): 179–93, Camille Mauclair predicted a certain frustration with d'Indy as he compared d'Indy with Manet. At first, he writes, "people attack them because they bring something new for their time . . . then it is recognized that basically their works are classical and refer to a certain classicism that had been forgotten when they were starting out." As a result, they are treated as old-fashioned by their young successors. In the 1920s, perhaps because he was growing bitter about his limited success as a composer, d'Indy began to use the press to articulate increasing hostility to contemporary music. In his "Le Public et son évolution," *Comoedia* (1 October 1923), he railed against the public of his past, current listeners who think of

The principal image we have today about d'Indy comes from his reputation for opposition. A wealthy aristocrat as well as organ pupil at the Paris Conservatoire, where most enrolled students were from humble or middle-class backgrounds, undoubtedly he felt himself an outsider. Watching how his principal teacher there, César Franck, was treated, isolated as a professor of organ rather than composition, bred frustration and contempt for official circles.[3] D'Indy also had a personal taste for struggle, as if it was an emblem of credibility or a prerequisite for success, and practiced his own form of self-appointed distinction. His conception of Franckism as an oppositional current in French music, a parallel to Wagnerism, eventually fashioned him as *the* disciple of Franck by helping a group identity coalesce and a lineage begin.[4] Later, by pitting the music school he helped found—the Schola Cantorum—against the Paris Conservatoire, d'Indy was able to increase his public visibility and the distinction associated with his students.[5]

---

themselves as "modern" or "advanced" and practice a "cult of curiosity," and composers who are "slaves to fashion." Mauclair, for his part, "Matière et forme dans l'Art musical moderne," *Comoedia* (28 January and 11 February 1924), and cited in Pierre Maudru, "Où en est la musique française?" *Comoedia* (21 February 1928), attacked Schönberg as a "fool" and young French composers for supposedly adapting his procedures, forgetting French clarity and logic, and "not acquiring the necessary skills [*métier*]" before composing their music. Jean Wiener, "Réponse à M. Vincent d'Indy," *Comoedia* (25 February 1924), defended his generation, noting that they were not imitating Schönberg, and wonders why a composer "so temperate and profoundly intelligent could publicly, and without fear of appearing ridiculous, denounce the 'impotence' of a period that possessed, among other artists, Stravinsky and Picasso." See also Guy Davenel, "Vincent d'Indy contre l'Avant-garde musicale," *Le Matin d'Anvers* (20 April 1924). When d'Indy died in 1931, Emile Vuillermoz, long an ardent adversary, wrote of d'Indy's "intellectual elevation" but also of his "courageous and magnificent intolerance" and noted, "it would be an injustice to reproach his intransigence, which originated in his absolute certitude about going in the right direction." As one of d'Indy's only contemporaries to write a *Histoire de la musique* (Paris: Fayard, 1949; reprint, 1973), Vuillermoz ensured that these attitudes would cast a long shadow over d'Indy's earlier accomplishments (344–47).

3. This was especially the case after 1878, when Franck put himself up for professor of composition at the Conservatoire, only to lose to Massenet.

4. See Joël-Marie Fauquet on Franck and his son's disdain for these constructions in his *César Franck* (Paris: Fayard, 1999), chap. 1, "Au nom du père."

5. Two forces contributed to this. First, as Henry Malherbe explains in his eulogy on d'Indy's death, published in *Le Temps* (12 December 1931), "his pupils were not ordinary pupils. They formed a group of exalted disciples, novices who were preparing for proselytism. . . . The master was less a professor than a preacher and sovereign [*suzerain*]. He didn't instruct his listeners, he preached to them, indoctrinated them." Second, whatever their perspective, critics contributed to the promotion of the idea of differences between the Scholists and the Conservatoire students. These included Jean Marnold,

Theorists such as Jacques Derrida and Jonathan Culler have pointed out that difference is often produced by such differing.[6] Reality is more ambiguous. Elsewhere I have shown that while both the Debussysts and d'Indysts used a discourse of opposition, this did not tell all, for important affinities, personal alliances, and collaborations linked graduates of the Conservatoire and the Schola.[7] D'Indy's Catholic religion and his own texts, especially when filled with anti-Dreyfusard ideas, have also veiled his relationship with the secular, Dreyfusard Republic, for they allowed the composer to downplay its importance in his career. If we have not grasped this, it is in part because we have not understood the Republic of the 1880s and 1890s any more than we have d'Indy's apparent contempt for it. To further a more nuanced understanding of the composer, I deconstruct d'Indy's relationship with the state. The task is not to deny his difference but instead to examine it carefully. In many ways, he and the Republic profited from his attitude of opposition, the basis of mutually productive interactions. D'Indy was a man of alliance as much as opposition, I argue, in part because in the 1880s and 1890s, republican leaders engaged with the diversity he represented as a stimulus for progress.

"Le Conservatoire et la Schola," *Mercure de France* (July 1902): 105–15; Mauclair, "Les Chapelles musicales en France"; Louis Laloy, "Les Partis musicaux en France," *La Grande Revue* (25 December 1907): 790–99; Emile Vuillermoz, "La Schola et le Conservatoire," *Mercure de France* (16 September 1909): 234–43. In "La Schola et le Conservatoire," *Courrier musical* (15 October 1909): 575–78, the Belgian correspondent G. Urbie, a critic who got it right (perhaps because he did not live in Paris), pointed out many errors in this discourse. See also Christian Goubault, "Les Chapelles musicales françaises ou la querelle des 'gros-boutiens' et des 'petits-boutiens,'" *Revue internationale de musique française* 5 (June 1981): 99–112, and Fabien Michel, *La Querelle des d'Indystes et des Debussystes*, Université de Bourgogne (UFR Littéraires), December 2000 (unpublished). Jane Fulcher, *French Cultural Politics and Music* (New York: Oxford University Press, 1999), takes this opposition at face value in her portrayal of the musical world of Paris as characterized by ideological "battles."

6. See Jacques Derrida, *L'Écriture et la différence* (Paris: Seuil, 1967), and *Positions* (Paris: Minuit, 1972); Jonathan Culler, *On Deconstruction: Theory and Criticism After Structuralism* (Ithaca, N.Y.: Cornell University Press, 1982), 50, 150.

7. In "La Schola Cantorum et les Apaches: L'enjeu du pouvoir artistique, ou Séverac médiateur et critique," in *La Musique: Du théorique au politique*, ed. Hugues Dufourt and Joël-Marie Fauquet (Paris: Klincksieck, 1990), 313–44, I show that while they differed over the importance of Franck and the direction of French music, the Debussysts and the Scholists shared an almost religious devotion to music, the sense of having a mission and "apostles" to lead them, a distaste for commercial success, similar means of unifying their group, and similar political tactics for advancing their ideas. Moreover, the group most closely associated with the Debussysts, the Apaches, had representatives from both the Schola and the Conservatoire as members and co-collaborators.

LEARNING *LE MÉTIER* AND ACHIEVING DISTINCTION

Like most French composers, d'Indy was formed by Conservatoire professors, even if he worked privately with most of them.[8] Franck's organ class, which he audited in 1873 and attended as an enrolled student in 1874–75, functioned as an alternative composition class for many at the Conservatoire (including Debussy) and introduced d'Indy to like-minded peers and future collaborators.[9] Under Franck's tutelage, d'Indy concentrated on fugues, even as he continued to write orchestral music and conceived two opera projects. These lessons also helped to shape his taste. Before studying with Franck, for example, d'Indy considered Meyerbeer "the greatest musical genius."[10] In 1873, he came to prefer Beethoven, Weber, and Berlioz; later, after he had been to Bayreuth and found *Die Walküre* "the greatest masterpiece he'd even seen," Meyerbeer became for him a "skillful jeweler, a jeweler of genius, who had the talent to pass off false jewels as real ones."[11] D'Indy left the Conservatoire in 1875 after earning only a *premier accessit* in Franck's class (no *premier prix*). This disinclined him from competing for the Prix de Rome, the most significant of a young French composer's career.

Although he later told his own students they didn't need competitions, d'Indy went on to pursue some of the most important state-subsidized prizes and awards of his day. After leaving the Conservatoire, he immediately began a one-act *opéra comique*—what many French of the period considered "le genre français"—entitled *Attendez-moi sous l'orme.*[12] To enter the state-sponsored Concours Cressent, he

---

8. In the 1860s, d'Indy studied privately with Louis Diemer, Antoine Marmontel, and Albert Lavignac. He began private lessons with Franck in 1872.

9. Julien Tiersot audited this class in 1876, Ernest Chausson in 1879, Paul Vidal in 1880, Claude Debussy in 1880–81, and Paul Dukas c. 1885. Other enrolled peers of d'Indy included Camille Benoît (1875–77), Georges Hüe (1878), and Gabriel Pierné (1880–82). For the complete list that includes his private students, see Fauquet, *César Franck*, app. 7, 960–64.

10. In his letter of 28 February 1870, d'Indy called Meyerbeer's opera *Le Prophète* "sublime" and "the great masterpiece of all masterpieces"; in that of 5 April 1870, he praised the composer as "the greatest musical genius in modern times"; and in that of 25 March 1871, he explained that he knew "nothing as beautiful in dramatic music" as the end of its act 4. These letters are published in Vincent d'Indy, *Ma Vie*, ed. Marie d'Indy (Paris: Séguier, 2001), 103, 109, 129.

11. See his letters of 17 January 1872, 8 March 1873, 23 September 1873, 15 September 1876, and July 1877, in *Ma Vie*, 158, 193, 256, 318, 323.

12. D'Indy acquired practical knowledge of the stage by playing timpani in eight performances of Massenet's *Marie-Magdeleine* in 1874 and timpani and organ in twenty-one performances of Saint-Saëns's *Timbre d'argent* at the Théâtre-Lyrique in 1877. During this period, he also worked as choral conductor for the Concerts Pasdeloup in 1874. Beginning in 1875, he held the same position for the Concerts Colonne, where he also competed, albeit unsuccessfully, to become the assistant conductor of the orchestra in 1876. Later, in 1887, he prepared the chorus for the first French production of *Lohengrin* at the Eden-Théâtre.

hurriedly completed it in the fall of 1877, although, having made his first trip to Bayreuth the year before, he admitted, "I will finish this because I *want* to finish it, but the genre disgusts me profoundly."[13] The opera failed in competitions. At the premiere of a fragment by the Société des Auditions Lyriques (20 April 1879), juxtaposed with works with which it had little in common (see fig. 4.1), the work was reproached for being too simple and not "recherché" enough.[14] (Ex. 4.1 gives an idea of its style.) Just after its Opéra-Comique premiere in 1882, d'Indy explained, "I have tried to react against those who say that for a seventeenth-century subject [sic], one should take inspiration from Rameau or Campra." He also admitted, "I mistakenly thought I could express human feelings in a human way in spite of their powdered wigs."[15] As one might imagine, his friends told him the genre did not suit him.[16] D'Indy never returned to it, although the next year he published a piano reduction of Destouches's *Les Élémens* in Théodore Michaelis's series *Les Chefs d'oeuvres classiques de l'opéra français.*[17]

---

13. "Je le finirai parce que *je veux* le finir, mais ce genre me dégoûte profondément." Letter to Charles Langrand, 8 June 1876, *Ma Vie,* 303. Around the same time, d'Indy also began to search for a subject to enter a competition for a prize at the 1878 Exposition offering 10,000 francs, but this project did not materialize. See his letter to Langrand, November 1876, *Ma Vie,* 321.

14. Henri Moreno, "Semaine théâtrale," *Le Ménestrel* (27 April 1879): 171. On this program were *Jeanne d'Arc* by Amand Chevé, a composer more known for his contribution to musical education than his composition; *Les Trois Parques* (1860), by a little known composer, Wilhelm (he did not use a first name and should not be confused with Guillaume Louis Wilhem, pedagogue and founder of the *orphéon* movement); and *Le Bois* by Albert Cahen, one of Franck's students. Even though d'Indy directed the chorus in Cahen's *Endymion* at the Opéra-Comique in 1873, he had little respect for Cahen's music (see his letter to his cousins, the Pampelonnes, 8 January 1873, *Ma Vie,* 187). In 1880, *Le Bois* was performed at the Opéra-Comique.

15. "J'avais essayé . . . de réagir contre ceux qui disent que pour un sujet XVIIe il faut s'inspirer de Rameau et de Campra. . . . Je me suis trompé dans la tentative de vouloir exprimer humainement des sentiments humains malgré leur perruques et leur poudre"; Vincent d'Indy to Adolphe Jullien, 21 February 1882, Bibliothèque de l'Opéra, Paris (hereafter F-Pn, Opéra), l.a. [autograph letter] d'Indy 3.

16. Vincent d'Indy to Isabelle d'Indy, July 1877, *Ma Vie,* 323.

17. Vincent d'Indy to Adolphe Jullien, 28 March 1883, F-Pn, Opéra, l.a. d'Indy 5. In 1883, d'Indy also made a reconstruction of *Les Bayadères* (1810) by Charles-Simon Catel, a composer of Revolutionary hymns, marches, and military symphonies and opera in the Napoleonic empire style. This opera allowed him to put recurring musical motives in the service of dramatic continuity. Katharine Ellis, "En route to Wagner: Explaining d'Indy's Early Music Panthéon," in *Vincent d'Indy et son temps,* ed. Manuela Schwartz (Sprimont: Mardaga, 2006), shows that in the preface he wrote to this work, d'Indy saw it as a "precursor" to Wagner (113).

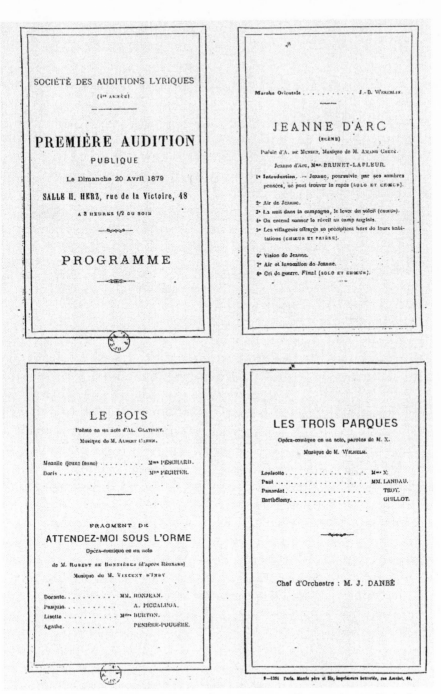

FIGURE 4.1. Vincent d'Indy, *Attendez-moi sous l'orme,* Salle Herz (20 April 1879). Courtesy of the Bibliothèque Musée de l'Opéra, Paris.

EXAMPLE 4.1. D'Indy, "Ronde poitevine," *Attendez-moi sous l'orme* (1876–82).

N.º 6.

RONDE POITEVINE

It may seem surprising, then, that for the next state-sponsored composition competition he entered, that of the City of Paris, he won first prize in 1885, and with a symphony, with soloists and chorus of extreme complexity, *Le Chant de la cloche*. To comprehend this, we must revisit the early Third Republic. In the 1870s, the government recognized the need for something that would play the role of the annual salon for painters, a prize in music that would compete with the Prix de Rome in stature and importance but escape control by members of the Académie des Beaux-Arts, one of the groups in the Institut de France. Ernest L'Epine suggested a jury modeled on the Conseil supérieur des Beaux-Arts, an organization conceived to institutionalize greater democracy in arts administration. Made up half of artists chosen to reflect aesthetic diversity and half of politicians and arts administrators, the Conseil sought to break the monopolies held by the Institut over educational policy and public awards. By encouraging the confrontation of diverse opinions, the Conseil sought to master both the inevitable ideological contradictions of the Republic's double heritage (the Revolution and the Ancien Régime) and the social antagonisms between its conservative and progressive forces.[18]

The City of Paris prize was created in this spirit. When it was finally funded in 1876, politicians decided the work should be a "symphony with soloists and chorus," a genre not taught per se at the Conservatoire. Politicians considered this "the most pure, abstract and powerful of the various expressions of musical genius." With the addition of the human voice, they hoped composers would be able to "explore new effects as in Handel's *Messiah,* Beethoven's Ninth Symphony, and Berlioz's *Enfance du Christ.*" In the tradition of Berlioz, there could be a program or story. The idea was to address "feelings of the highest order" without recourse to religion or politics. The winning composer would receive 10,000 francs, and a subsidy of 10,000 francs would be given to support a performance in a major venue.[19]

The first such prize was awarded on 7 December 1878. Six separate votes were not enough to break the tie between two composers: Théodore Dubois and Benjamin Godard. Dubois's *Le Paradis perdu,* supported by Gounod, was praised for

---

18. Since 1874 the Conseil municipal de Paris had been studying a proposal by L'Epine for a government-sponsored series of concerts featuring works by living composers. The Prix de Rome and the Prix de Salon, also called the Prix de Paris, had complementary purposes. The former, meant to put artists in touch with their origins, rewarded "Italian imitation"; the latter, focused on European trends, recognized "French originality." See Gustave Larroumet, *L'Art et l'État en France* (Paris: Hachette, 1895), 52–53, and Marie-Claude Genet-Delacroix, *Art et État sous la IIIe République* (Paris: Sorbonne, 1992), 130–31.

19. Ville de Paris, *Concours pour la composition d'une symphonie, soli, et choeur* (Paris: Chaix, 1876), and three articles in *Journal de musique:* "Nouvelles de Partout" (4 November 1876): 4, "Le Prix de 10,000 francs" (11 November 1876): 1, and "Un rapport de M. de Chennevières" (25 January 1879): 3–4.

its "pure" style, vast proportions, and clear musical construction.[20] Godard's *Le Tasse*, promoted by Jules Massenet, had lively orchestration, "picturesque" symphonic writing, effective choruses, and resemblances to Berlioz's *Damnation de Faust*, a hit in concert halls beginning in spring 1877. Godard appealed to Wagnerians as well as fans of Berlioz, though some thought his unusual harmonies "curious" if not "bizarre," his instrumentation sometimes overdone, and his ideas too conventional.[21] That the jury rewarded both works reflects the conflicting tastes of the jurists and the ongoing battle over the direction of French music.

These results—together with the poor reception given his *Attendez-moi sous l'orme* and the public enthusiasm for Jules Pasdeloup's premiere of *Lohengrin*, both on 20 April 1879—may have encouraged d'Indy to begin work on *Le Chant de la cloche* that July.[22] With its focus on the symphony, this project intersected better with d'Indy's interests. Before *La Cloche*, he had written six orchestral works, including a symphony. He long admired Berlioz's orchestration treatise and had prepared Berlioz's choruses for the Concerts Colonne. Based on Schiller's dramatic poem *Das Lied von der Glocke* (1799), which makes an analogy between the casting of a bell by a master craftsman and the possibilities of human life, *La Cloche* reflects d'Indy's enthusiasm for Germany (which he had visited three times),[23] Wagner's music, medieval times, and German Volkslieder.[24] The story of an artist misunderstood and not recognized until his death may have recalled his feelings for César Franck, to whom he dedicated the work. Conceived as "the exact expression of what I want to do in a dramatic genre, no concessions, nothing for women nor for members of the Institut," he accepted that the work would be "quite a pain in the neck for the audience about which I could care less."[25] However, *La Cloche* addressed the jury's concerns and the public's emerging taste for Berlioz and Wagner in effective ways.

Members of the jury for the City of Paris prize in 1885 again represented diverse aesthetic preferences: previous winners Godard and Dubois (1878), Augusta Holmès and Alphonse Duvernoy (1880), and Paul (or Lucien) Hillemacher

20. Reviews of *Paradis perdu* are cited in Georges Favre, *Compositeurs français méconnus* (Paris: Pensée universelle, 1983), 122–23.

21. Adolphe Jullien, in a review of *Le Tasse* (December 1878), reprinted in his *Musiciens d'aujourd'hui* (Paris: Librairie de l'art, 1894), 2:427–34.

22. See *Le Ménestrel* (27 April 1979): 175–76.

23. See Manuela Schwartz, "Die 'pèlerinage à Bayreuth' als Brennpunkt des europäischen Kulturtransfers: Französische Komponisten auf dem Weg nicht nur zu Richard Wagner," in *Le Musicien et ses voyages: Pratiques, réseaux, et représentations*, ed. Christian Meyer (Berlin: BWV, 2003), 427–52.

24. D'Indy had seen German Volkslieder at the Bibilothèque Nationale.

25. "L'expression exacte de ce que je veux faire dans le genre dramatique, pas de concessions, rien pour les femmes ni pour les membres de l'Institut . . . fort embêtant pour le public ce dont je me fiche absolument." Letter to Ernest Chausson, 2 March 1883, *Ma Vie*, 369.

(co-winners in 1882); Conservatoire professors Léo Delibes, Ernest Guiraud, Dubois, and Franck; a member of the Institut, Saint-Saëns; Charles Lefebvre; the conductors Edouard Colonne and Charles Lamoureux; plus the rest, appointed by prefect.[26] Seventeen works were submitted, including those by three Prix de Rome winners. For the first time in the competition, composers were allowed to submit their music without the veil of anonymity; only five competitors chose to remain anonymous, and d'Indy was among the twelve who indicated their names. Each of three committees examined one-third of the scores and established a short list on which the entire jury voted. Eliminated in the first round were two works by Prix de Rome winners, three that used Prix de Rome librettists (Edouard Guinand and Paul Collin), and works with patriotic subjects, *Jeanne d'Arc* and *Gloria Victis*. Massenet and Charles Lenepveu probably would have defended these had they been on the jury.[27] Whatever the criteria used to reject the scores, at this crucial stage the jury lived up to the city's expectation: they proved they were not interested in duplicating what the Prix de Rome rewarded.

For the next round, one jurist presented each of the four remaining works: *Merlin enchanté* by Georges Marty, *Rübezahl* by Georges Hüe, *Les Ancêtres* by Auguste Chapuis, and *Le Chant de la cloche* by d'Indy. Augusta Holmès was responsible for presenting, analyzing, and organizing the performance of *Le Chant de la cloche*.[28] Another Franck student, Holmès recognized the importance of this moment. Winning a close second prize in 1880 had launched her career and had led to numerous high-profile performances of her music, and, that January, to the title Officier de la Légion d'honneur. On the first vote, d'Indy tied with Hüe, nine to nine; on the second vote, d'Indy won, ten to nine. Saint-Saëns, Dubois, and Colonne's negative votes were balanced by support from Franck, Holmès, and Lamoureux, who consented to perform *La Cloche* if it were to win.

We can understand why d'Indy's work tied with that of Hüe and then prevailed if we compare the situations of the two composers. Neither represented the emerging dominance of Massenet at the Conservatoire. A student of Henri Reber,

26. F. Hattat, "Rapport au nom du jury classant des partitions," in Ville de Paris, *Concours pour la composition d'une symphonie avec soli et choeur* (Paris: Imprimerie nationale, 1885), 1–5. See also "Nouvelles diverses," *Le Ménestrel* (8 February 1885): 79, (22 February 1885): 94, and (15 March 1885): 119. Among the composers, Duvernoy was chosen by the prefect, Holmès, Colonne, and Lamoureux by the Conseil municipal, and Saint-Saëns, Guiraud, Hillemacher, Delibes, Dubois, Franck, Lefebvre, and Godard by the competitors.

27. *Gloria Victis* was by Victor-Alfred Pelletier (called Rabuteau), a winner of the Prix de Rome. Libretti by Edouard Guinand were used in Prix de Rome competitions in 1878, 1881, 1882, and 1884, and those of Paul Collin in 1898 and 1912.

28. See the archives for this competition at the Archives de Paris. An analysis of the works Holmès composed for this prize (*Lutèce* in 1878 and *Argonautes* in 1880) can be found in my "The Ironies of Gender, or Virility and Politics in the Music of Augusta Holmès," chapter 8 here.

Hüe had won the Prix de Rome in 1879, the last competition before Massenet's students began to dominate in the 1880s.[29] Hüe, like d'Indy, represented "modern tendencies" and successfully negotiated an alliance between Wagner and Berlioz, composers gaining widespread acceptance with Parisian concert audiences.[30] On 1 February, when the City of Paris prize competition announced its jury, d'Indy and Hüe had important premieres, both warmly reviewed, albeit with some mixed sentiments. Arthur Pougin called one of Hüe's works, composed in Rome and performed by Colonne, "inspired and in a grandiose style," even if another such *envoi* seemed like "the work of a good schoolboy," without any main idea and with only a vague structure."[31] Some enjoyed his sense of orchestral color and thought his *envoi* one of the best things composed in recent years, while others felt he still had a lot to learn about connecting orchestral timbres and wished for more personal distinction in his style. Similarly, reviewers praised the orchestral effects in d'Indy's *Saugefleurie*, performed by Lamoureux, with some calling them "very studied, very new," and the work composed by a "master of the genre."[32] In the final discussions about the City of Paris prize, the jury found similar differences between the two competitors. While they praised Hüe's *Rübezahl* for its "brilliant style, always easy, knowledgeable, and well-organized," they found d'Indy's *Cloche* "original," with "a clever symphonic section that shows real personality."[33]

Coming from the jury of the City of Paris prize, such words were meant to signal the Republic's encouragement of individuality and originality. Jules Ferry, who between 1880 and 1885 alternated between being ministre de l'Instruction publique et des Beaux-Arts) and Président du Conseil, was firmly opposed to the conservative Moral Order that had determined the policies of government and the arts during the 1870s. In his speeches, he insisted on "independence,"

29. In a letter of 18 May 1885, d'Indy wondered why Saint-Saëns voted against him when d'Indy had "rendered him services in the past" (see note 12) (*Ma Vie*, 326, 385). In a conversation of 26 September 2002, Yves Gérard suggested to me that Saint-Saëns had probably voted for Hüe because he was Reber's last student.

30. *Le Ménestrel* featured articles about Wagner in almost every issue of spring and summer 1885. In the 1880s, his music, as well as that of Berlioz, was played regularly in Parisian concerts. See my "Building a Public for Orchestral Music: Les Concerts Colonne," in *Le Concert et son public: Mutations de la vie musicale en Europe de 1780 à 1914*, ed. Hans Erich Bödeker, Patrice Veit, and Michael Werner (Paris: Maison des Sciences de l'Homme, 2002), 209–40, and Manuela Schwartz, *Wagner-Rezeption und französische Oper des Fin de siècle: Untersuchungen zu Vincent d'Indys Fervaal* (Sinzig: Studio, 1999), 19–25.

31. Arthur Pougin, "Audition des Envois de Prix de Rome au Conservatoire," *Le Ménestrel* (8 March 1885): 109.

32. G. M., "Concerts et soirées," *Le Ménestrel* (1 February 1885): 71.

33. Hattat, "Rapport au nom du jury classant des partitions," 5. See also reviews in *Le Ménestrel* (14 March 1886) and *Journal des débats* (28 March 1886).

"individuality," and the "revolt" of artists against conventions. As Michael Orwicz has pointed out, this permitted the state to "represent itself as the liberator of artists' professional concerns, safeguarding art and culture in the interests of the nation at large, by constructing its aesthetic values against the Academy, rhetorically produced as the symbol of a pre-republican order."[34] At the same time that he reformed national education, calling for "exciting and evoking spontaneity in the student" rather than teaching by rote, and encouraging students "to pursue their own moral development" rather than "imprisoning them in fixed rules," Ferry wished to encourage an aesthetic individualism. Rejecting the idea of any "official doctrine" or aesthetic, seeking to weaken old hierarchies, and highly attentive to equality and fraternity in French society, he was determined to help individual initiative thrive.[35] He wished to encourage aesthetic diversity as a counterbalance to academic traditions and to broaden representation on the Conseil supérieur des Beaux-Arts and the jury of the Composition Prize of the city of Paris. With its elevation of a humble bell-maker, its worker choruses, and its triumphant "people's festival" suggesting universal fraternity, d'Indy's dramatic symphony spoke to republican preoccupations.

Change, too, was in the air. In 1884, when Debussy won his Prix de Rome, some Academicians agreed with the government's openness to innovation. Just before a performance of Debussy's winning score at the Académie des Beaux-Arts, Eugène Guillaume—sculptor, member of the Institut, and director of the École des Beaux-Arts (1868–78)[36]—explained the new values permeating their chambers:

> We are aware that the conditions in which art is made have changed. We need movement, novelty, and even visionary qualities. We like to discover the artist in his work, we prefer him to his subject, and if he turns up something truly from himself, if he is original, there is much we are prepared to forgive him for. . . . Today, respect for personality [prevails] . . . individual feeling is now more recognized than it used to be.[37]

34. Michael Orwicz, "Anti-academicism and State Power in the Early Third Republic," *Art History* 14, no. 4 (December 1991): 573–74.

35. Ferry's reforms affected who ran the primary and secondary schools (including the choice of teachers, inspectors, and school directors), what was taught there, and how it was taught. In a speech given in 1880 to 250 school directors, he outlined his plan to replace memorization with the development of judgment and initiative in students and to turn instructors into educators through a more interactive teaching style. For more extended discussion, see my *Useful Music, or Why Music Mattered in Third Republic France* (Berkeley: University of California Press, forthcoming).

36. Guillaume was also the director of fine arts at the Ministry of Public Instruction and Fine Arts (1878–79, 1883) and, beginning in 1882, professor at the Collège de France.

37. "Nous ne l'ignorons pas, les conditions de l'art ont changé. . . . Nous avons besoin de mouvement, de nouveauté, et même de qualités voyantes. Nous aimons découvrir l'artiste

Increasing respect for Franck may also have helped d'Indy to win. In August 1884 Franck received the Légion d'honneur, and in February 1886 he was elected to serve as a member of the Prix de Rome jury. In addition, d'Indy's reputation was not yet threatening. He was praised for his great skill, but it was seen as commanding respect, not yet emulation.

Even if the public reception of *La Cloche* in February and March 1886 was not what d'Indy may have hoped—mixed reviews and a financial disaster[38]—winning the prize gave him his first claim at public distinction and the confidence to take several important steps. That year he returned to his opera, *Fervaal*, pursued his interest in the past with a *Suite dans le style ancien,* and initiated plans to build his chateau, Les Faugs, based on German gothic models. Winning the prize, despite Saint-Saëns's and Dubois's negative votes, also perhaps made him willing to confront Saint-Saëns on the direction of the Société Nationale in November (and later Dubois on that of the Conservatoire).[39] The City of Paris prize, therefore, set an important precedent for d'Indy. It rewarded his advocacy for reform, not despite his disagreement with what was supported by the Conservatoire or rewarded by the Institut but precisely because of it.

---

dans son œuvre . . . s'il est original, nous lui pardonnons beaucoup. Aujourd'hui le respect de notre personnalité . . . le sentiment individuel acquiert maintenant plus d'autorité." Eugène Guillaume, "Discours," *Séance publique annuelle de l'Académie des Beaux-Arts* (18 October 1884): 15.

38. The same day Henri Barbedette called *Rübezahl* "one of the best works produced in recent times," another *Ménestrel* critic thought d'Indy was only a "wonderful craftsman," not yet a composer. "Concerts et soirées," (14 March 1886): 119. In a letter to Henri Heugel reproduced in *Le Ménestrel* (16 May 1886): 193, Charles Lamoureux explained that he found the press coverage of the work unusually harsh and that for this reason it was his duty to give two performances at his own risk. Because ticket sales were not strong, he lost 10,000 francs. Lamoureux also notes that d'Indy had to contribute some of his commission to help pay the deficit not covered by the official subsidy. See also *Le Ménestrel* (9 May 1886): 186.

39. The composers and performers of this private music society had helped d'Indy to define, articulate, and develop what Bourdieu might call a taste public for Franck's music as well as his own, performing eleven of his works on fourteen of their concerts between 1871 and 1881. In 1886, as a protectionist spirit gripped the country after an economic recession, Saint-Saëns wished to continue the tradition of performing little to no foreign music, while d'Indy sought to change this. In the draft of a letter to Bussine, d'Indy says he will ask for a revision of the Société Nationale's statutes at their November 1886 meeting, noting "it seems to me the moment has come." (See Michael Strasser, *Ars Gallica: The Société Nationale de Musique and Its Role in French Musical Life, 1871–1891* [Ph.D. diss., University of Illinois, 1998], 404.) When Saint-Saëns resigned over this revision, d'Indy became secretary of the organization and took control, while Franck functioned as a sort of honorary president until he died in 1890.

COLLABORATING WITH REPUBLICANS

Whether or not it was the result of Wagner's encouragement to seek out French equivalents for what attracted him to German culture,[40] d'Indy shared with certain republicans an interest in provincial peoples. In 1887, like Louis Bourgault-Ducoudray, J. B. Weckerlin, and Julien Tiersot—a professor of music history, librarian, and administrator at the Conservatoire—d'Indy began to collect French *chansons populaires*. Like them, he heard in these songs the memory and history of the races, including those that were lost or had disappeared, even though he disagreed with them as to the origins of the songs. (Bourgault-Ducoudray pointed to what the songs owed to ancient Greek melodies, whereas d'Indy credited plain-chant.) D'Indy wished to use them to create a French basis for his compositions. With this in mind, he built his entire *Symphonie sur un chant montagnard français* (1886), otherwise known as his *Symphonie cévenole*, from the thematic transformation of a *chanson populaire* he had heard in the mountains of his ancestors.[41] For his own collecting, D'Indy turned to regions where no one had yet done extended work—the Vivarais and the Vercors.[42] This attracted the attention of republicans, including Tiersot, who became his collaborator and contributed extensive critical commentary to the edition.[43] While the Parisian-born d'Indy may have been interested in studying his ancestral origins and exploring the regional identity of music, Tiersot, like other republicans, concentrated on showing how these songs reinforced republican notions of a shared musical tradition throughout the country and could be used as part of Ferry's educational agenda to link the disparate populations of the provinces. To this end, the government funded many

40. "Se procurer un poème simple, humain, expressif, conforme avant tout au génie de votre nation. Tout un folklore, riche trésor national est à votre disposition. Sur un poème vraiment français si vous ne vous inspirez que de la vérité des mœurs vous ferez de la musique vraiment française. . . . Vous ferez pour la France ce que j'ai fait." Richard Wagner to Louis Fourcaud, cited in *Ma Vie*, 360.

41. D'Indy also wrote a *Fantaisie sur des thèmes populaires français* (1888) for oboe and orchestra.

42. The *Revue des traditions populaires*, founded in 1885 and published by the Société des traditions populaires, reproduced in 1887 some of the folk songs d'Indy had collected; in 1892 this journal published his volume of these songs, *Chansons populaires recueillies dans le Vivarais et le Vercors*, arranged and with a preface and notes by Julien Tiersot. For fuller discussion of the meaning of these songs for diverse groups in France, see my "The Chanson Populaire as Malleable Symbol in Turn-of-the-Century France," in *Tradition and Its Future in Music*, ed. Y. Tokumaru et al. (Tokyo: Mita Press, 1991), 203–10, and "Race and Nation: Musical Acclimatisation and the *Chansons Populaires* in Third Republic France," in *Western Music and Race*, ed. Julie Brown (Cambridge: Cambridge University Press, 2007), 147–67.

43. D'Indy got to know Tiersot on a trip to Bayreuth in 1886. Tiersot had just finished his *Histoire de la chanson populaire*, which won the Prix Bordin.

song-collecting missions. D'Indy received one of these in 1897 to collect songs in the Ardèche. His three versions of "La Bergère et le Monsieur" in his *Chansons populaires du Vivarais* (1900)[44] recall his interest in rural simplicity and a story similar to the one he recounted in his *Attendez-moi sous l'orme*.

In the late 1880s and early 1890s, d'Indy's interest in exploring the distant origins of France also found sympathy with state administrators. In 1888, when Gustave Larroumet became director of fine arts and in 1891, when Henry Roujon took over, the state was determined to impose changes on the Conservatoire. This time it was not personality or originality they wished to support. In official speeches at the Conservatoire, while they explained that students should "welcome and profit" from Wagner, they also asserted the importance of tradition and advocated studying the origins of French music.[45] After making d'Indy a Chevalier de la Légion d'honneur in January 1892, Léon Bourgeois, the minister of public instruction and the fine arts, in March asked d'Indy to be one of five composers (with Guiraud, Massenet, Ernest Reyer, and Ambroise Thomas) to serve on a committee to reform the Conservatoire. There were also ten politicians among the thirty-two members. D'Indy's inclusion can be seen as a result of the new politics of *ralliement* (realignment). When Pope Leo XIII encouraged Catholics to accept the Third Republic and participate in it, he made possible a conservative alliance between moderate Catholics, especially aristocratic elites, and republicans opposed to socialist gains in the government.[46] The political reconciliation had major repercussions on the musical world. During this period, contrary to the image we tend to have of him today, d'Indy was known for being a "dedicated and conscientious worker, never uncompromising or closed-minded . . . excessively modest and welcoming to all, above any kind of scheming."[47]

This committee constituted another opportunity for the composer to collaborate with the state to promote change. D'Indy profited from the occasion to propose some truly innovative notions, even if few of them were accepted. His

---

44. In his *Chansons populaires du Vivarais* (Paris: Durand, 1900), d'Indy's stated intention was to "unveil the Vivarais soul" and explore regional identity as well as to show the origin of songs such as "La Pernette" in the Gregorian musical liturgy (15–19).

45. For an analysis of these speeches, see my "State Politics and the 'French' Aesthetics of the Prix de Rome Cantatas, 1870–1900," in *Musical Education in Europe (1770–1914): Compositional, Institutional and Political Challenges*, vol. 2, ed. Michel Noiray and Michael Fend (Berlin: BWV, 2005), 585–622.

46. In his *Rerum Novarum* of 15 May 1891, Pope Leo XIII criticized workers' associations and rejected socialist demands concerning public property; in *Au milieu des solicitudes* of 16 February 1892, he instructed French Catholics to prefer peace in the country to political conflict.

47. "Un apôtre, poursuit son but en travailleur convaincu et consciencieux, sans intransigeance ni parti-pris . . . modeste à l'excès et accueillant pour tous, au dessus de tout espèce d'intrigue." Henry Eymieu, *Études et biographies musicales* (Paris: Fischbacher, 1892), 30.

idea to "divide musical instruction into two levels corresponding to technical and artistic concerns" would have brought about a "total remaking of the Conservatoire," involving an increase in teaching staff and other resources. This was voted down. With the exception of two members, the entire committee also voted against his idea to separate symphonic composition from dramatic composition. The idea went against the contemporary taste for forms that mixed symphony and theater. Nevertheless, his presence on this committee was significant. Like Larroumet, he encouraged young composers to analyze great works from the past, and he supported the committee's decision to enhance the artistic interest in counterpoint: students were to harmonize in chords, not just chorale tunes but also *chansons populaires* in four to eight parts. It is possible that these ideas originated with d'Indy. He would also have agreed with the proposal that the orchestra class should read new works by young composers, even if the committee ultimately found this unrealizable. Moreover, he probably had a strong influence on their decision to separate the teaching of counterpoint from that of the fugue, defending the argument that "free-style fugue can be regarded as the form from which symphonic development originated" and thus should be taught with composition. The committee agreed with this, even though it meant creating two new classes. With he and Larroumet in agreement on the importance of the symphony, the committee concurred unanimously that the next composer hired at the Conservatoire should be a symphonist.[48] Honoring this desire, and perhaps also d'Indy's work on this committee, when Guiraud died in May of that year, 1892, Roujon proposed that d'Indy take over Guiraud's position as professor of composition at the Conservatoire. D'Indy refused, but some thought that he had such a great influence on the minister that, if he had wanted to, he could have brought about Thomas's retirement and replaced him as director of the Conservatoire.[49]

48. In Constant Pierre, *Le Conservatoire national de musique et de déclamation: documents historiques et administratifs* (Paris: Imprimerie nationale, 1900), see Vincent d'Indy, "Projet d'organisation des études du Conservatoire national de musique, 1892," 373–76; Henry Marcel, "Rapport présenté au nom de la Sous-Commission de l'Enseignement musical, 1892," 376–83; and Bardoux, "Projets de décret et d'arrêté préparés par la Sous-Commission de la musique," 383–93.

49. Malherbe, perhaps among others, had the impression that d'Indy wanted this position. D'Indy explained his decision in a letter to his wife, Isabelle, on 18 November 1892: "comme on ne peut pas supposer qu'un Monsieur agisse autrement que par intérêt personnel, le bruit courant est que je veux forcer le Ministre à mettre à la retraite Ambroise Thomas afin de me mettre à sa place. Il y a vraiment des gens bien bêtes dans le monde artistique et il ne peut pas entrer dans ces esprits bornés qu'un individu puisse combattre pour l'art d'une façon désintéressée. . . . Je n'en suis que plus content de n'avoir pas accepté la place de professeur de Composition qui m'était offerte, outre l'embêtement de l'attache, ça aurait été leur donner en quelque sorte raison et tu vois ma position, seul au milieu de ces 74 ennemis jurés" (*Ma Vie*, 482).

Table 4.1. Works for Amateur Choruses, Civic Ceremonies, and Military Bands.

Year	Works
1885	*Sainte Marie-Madeleine*, soprano, women's chorus, and piano or harmonium
1888	*Sur la mer*, women's chorus, piano
1893	*Cantate de fête pour l'inauguration d'une statue*, baritone, mens' chorus, orchestra
1894	*L'Art et le peuple* (Victor Hugo), four-voice men's chorus
1897	*Ode à Valence* (Genest), soprano, men's chorus
1897	Mosaique on *Fervaal*, military band
1903	*Marche du 76e régiment d'infanterie*, military band

For the next decade, d'Indy articulated and enacted his belief that art's function was to serve to such an extent that in 1897, right in the middle of the Dreyfus Affair, this anti-Dreyfusard musician confessed, "I'm becoming an official musician . . . and it's disgusting."[50] Being an "official musician" had several meanings, each of them touching on music's social purpose. The very republicans who set the foundations for the Third Republic, such as Jules Ferry, Jules Simon (minister of public instruction and fine arts and later senator), and their successors, believed that musicians, at least those who received a free education at the Conservatoire, should serve their country and their music should contribute to its glory. D'Indy shared some of their beliefs. Like them, he saw art as the spirit of progress and, like them, he yearned to educate the masses, to elevate them and give them a sense of liberty through their experience of music. With these in mind, he once performed for the Cercle des Ouvriers, a workers' group on the rue Montmartre.[51] More important, he also made some of the same compositional choices as his republican peers (see table 4.1). Like Delibes, who was professor of composition at the Conservatoire until 1891, d'Indy wrote choruses for amateurs such as *Sur la Mer* (1888), even if his were more difficult than many others (see ex. 4.2).

50. "Je deviens musicien officiel . . . c'est dégoûtant." Letter to Octave Maus, 1 September 1897, *Ma Vie*, 568. This letter came after his announcement that he had been charged by the committee organizing the 1900 Exhibition to collect and organize *chants populaires in* the Ardèche. During the late 1890s, d'Indy often articulated this desire to serve. In his 1896 speech about the Schola Cantorum, "Une Ecole de musique répondant aux besoins modernes," later published in *Courrier musical* (15 November 1900): 8–9, d'Indy asserted that the goal of art was to serve. In his opera *l'Etranger* (1898–1901), the hero sings "Aider les autres, servir les autres, voilà ma seule joie, mon unique pensée."

51. D'Indy mentions this in a letter of 24 November 1973, *Ma Vie*, 262.

EXAMPLE 4.2. D'Indy, *Sur la mer*, women's chorus, piano (1888).

Sur la mer.

Chœur pour voix de femmes.

Paris, J. Hamelle, Editeur, 22 Boulevard Malesherbes. J.3022. H.

TABLE 4.2. *Orphéon* Competitions (Selection).

Date	D'Indy's participation	Type	City	Occasion
1889	Committee	Wind and brass bands	Paris	Universal Exhibition
August 1894	Vice-president	*Orphéon* competition	Lyon	
1897	Jury	*Orphéon* competition	Valence	
1898	Jury	Music competition	Roanne	
August 1899	Jury	*Orphéon* competition	Saint-Etienne	
August 1900	Committee	Wind and brass bands	Paris	Universal Exhibition
August 1902	Jury	*Orphéon* competition	Geneva	

Although he did not share their political convictions, d'Indy, like his republican colleagues, also wrote music for official ceremonies and other activities subsidized by the government and, even if he criticized them as being useless and characterized by mediocrity,[52] he, too, served on the juries of numerous *orphéon* competitions involving amateur singers, many of them workers, including those of the 1889 and 1900 Expositions (see table 4.2). In 1894 his choral setting of Victor Hugo's *L'Art et le peuple* was premiered at one such competition by the Enfants de Lutèce, one of Paris's best working-class choruses (ex. 4.3). In addition, like Lenepveu, Delibes's successor at the Conservatoire, d'Indy wrote ceremonial works for civic occasions, two of them at Valence: his *Cantate pour l'inauguration d'une statue* (1893) and *Ode à Valence* (1897), commemorating President Félix Faure's visit to Valence.[53] In 1897 d'Indy also composed his own fantasy for military band from selected excerpts of *Fervaal*, and, like Saint-Saëns, he wrote a military march for a regiment of the French infantry (1903).[54] His continued alliance with Roujon assured him not only of ongoing participation in major juries but also support for his preferences.[55] In

52. Vincent d'Indy, "A propos du Prix de Rome: Le Régionalisme musical," *Revue musicale* 2 (1902): 248.

53. He wrote to Octave Maus, "Sais-tu que j'ai été une journée *musicien officiel*! . . . à Valence, ou j'ai été chargé de recevoir le Président Félisque [Félix Faure] à coups de trombones et de cymbales." Letter of 1 September 1897, *Ma Vie*, 567.

54. *Le Petit Poucet*, a journal distributed to the public of military band concerts in Parisian parks, published a front-page article on d'Indy and his music in every issue during the last week of June 1896. By 1910, Parisian military bands were also performing a transcription of his *Le Camp de Wallenstein*.

55. According to d'Indy, it was due to the "tacit connivance of Roujon" and "against the wishes of Conservatoire and Institut composers" that he was able to obtain places for Chausson, Debussy, and Dukas in the orchestral concerts of the 1900 Exposition. Letter to Octave Maus, 22 April 1900, *Ma Vie*, 605.

EXAMPLE 4.3. D'Indy, *L'Art et le peuple*, four-voice men's chorus (1894).

1900, in despair over the organization of *orphéon* performances, he concluded that they should be eliminated; still he dreamed of an "art of the people truly worthy of the name."[56]

In portraying Théodore Dubois as d'Indy's strongest opponent, the composer, his successors, and recent scholars have given short shrift to what they shared.[57] Certainly they had different backgrounds and personalities, but both started out in the 1870s as choral conductors (Dubois for the Société des Concerts and d'Indy for various Parisian orchestras) and as organists (Dubois at Saint-Clothilde and la Madeleine, d'Indy at Saint-Leu near Montmorency); both won the City of Paris prize in composition; and besides being composers and professors of composition, both went on to direct music schools. As "integrated professionals," they could hold and express strong opinions but ultimately were good team players, able to build a consensus around their positions.[58] They also shared some musical tastes. Both were interested in Gregorian chant and in *chansons populaires* of the same region. Well before it was taught at the Schola, in 1884 Dubois published *L'Accompagnement pratique du plainchant*; and in 1895, recalling d'Indy's use of such a tune in his *Symphonie cévenole*, Dubois incorporated a *chanson cévenole* into his opera *Xavière*. Both also wrote religious and liturgical music for use in Catholic services. Dubois wrote eight masses, including one in the style of Palestrina (1900), and more than seventy motets; d'Indy wrote six Latin motets, beginning with *Deus Israel* (1896) and *Sancta Maria* (1898). In addition, the correspondence between d'Indy and Dubois from 1894 to 1909 demonstrates a much more cordial relationship that we have been led to believe. Even if d'Indy admitted that the two composers did not conceive of art in the same way, they went to concerts of one another's music, they exchanged words of appreciation, and in 1898 they recognized that their "goal remained the same," as d'Indy wrote somewhat elliptically.[59]

DECONSTRUCTING DIFFERENCES AT THE SCHOLA CANTORUM

With his role in the Schola Cantorum, the aura of difference surrounding d'Indy reached an apex. Free versus official, Catholic versus secular, private versus

56. D'Indy to Charles Malherbe, 27 December 1900, F-Pn, Opéra, l.a. d'Indy 34. See also d'Indy, "Le Régionalisme musical," 249.

57. One of the texts that vigorously opposed Dubois and d'Indy was Marnold, "Le Conservatoire et la Schola."

58. Howard Becker explains the concept of integrated professionals in his *Artworlds* (Berkeley: University of California Press, 1982), 228–33.

59. On 17 February 1909, d'Indy wrote to Dubois that he would be "happy to work on [Dubois's] motets in the vocal ensemble class" he directed (l.a. d'Indy 379, Music Division, Bibliothèque Nationale, Paris, hereafter F-Pn, Musique); see also d'Indy to Théodore Dubois, l.a. d'Indy 374–380.

public—yes, the Schola differed from the Conservatoire. Its statutes, its conditions of admission (no age limit), and the everyday life of its students contrasted with those of the Conservatoire.[60] But can we really oppose their attitudes through such binarisms as art versus skills, morals versus virtuosity, counterpoint versus harmony? Whether used to gain visibility, attract students, or enhance d'Indy's importance as its director, certain oppositions have been exaggerated.[61] Certainly d'Indy used the Schola to instigate reforms he had proposed for the Conservatoire. When he took over the direction of the Schola in 1900, he divided the classes into two sections, leaving to the first the classes of "special technique and the mechanics of writing . . . in a word, craft [métier]." He compared these to the warm-up drills of military exercises. To the second, he allocated "all that concerns interpretation, knowledge of style, study of important works . . . in sum, art."[62] In reality, however, Dubois, director of the Conservatoire from 1896 to 1905, saw musical instruction not that differently. He too believed that "all art is composed of two equally important parts, aesthetics and technique."[63] And when he took over the Conservatoire, republican administrators, such as Gustave Larroumet, expected Dubois to incorporate much of what the reform committee had proposed but been unable to enact while Thomas was still alive. Larroumet, too, felt that the Conservatoire attached "too much importance to virtuosity and not enough to art" and needed to give more attention to masterpieces of the French past and the symphony.[64]

D'Indy's first sentence in his manifesto for the new school—that the Schola would not function as a professional school because art is not a métier (that is, a profession or trade, as well as a craft)—is ironic as well as misleading. His early reputation up through Le Chant de la cloche was based on his craft more than his art: reviewers found him a "wonderful worker [merveilleux ouvrier]" but not yet "a composer," and they noted, "If his inspiration and ideas can raise to the level of his prodigious skill, France would consider him another great master."[65] With his

60. For more details on these differences, see Ladislas Rohozinski, Cinquante ans de musique française (Paris: Librairie de France, 1925), 2:220–22.

61. See notes 5 and 7 here.

62. D'Indy, "Une École de musique répondant aux besoins modernes," 8–9.

63. Vincent d'Indy, "La Schola Cantorum (1904)," and Théodore Dubois, "L'Enseignement musical," in L'Encyclopédie de la musique et dictionnaire du Conservatoire, ed. Albert Lavignac (Paris: Delagrave, 1931), 11:3623, 3437, 3439.

64. Gustave Larroumet, "La Direction du Conservatoire," Le Temps (3 March 1896). See also André Maurel, "Le nouveau Directeur et la réforme du Conservatoire," Le Figaro (7 May 1896).

65. "Vincent d'Indy est d'ores et déjà un merveilleux ouvrier. Il lui reste maintenant à devenir un compositeur. Si son inspiration et ses idées peuvent un jour monter au niveau de son faire prodigieux, la France comptera un grand maître de plus." Le Ménestrel (14 March 1886): 119.

next major success, *Fervaal* (1886–95) at the Opéra-Comique, critics again referred to his "patient and relentless labor" and continued to recognize his knowledge (*science*) and masterful skills. Yet while some saw him as a leader of the French school of composition, others found this music overly complex and difficult to listen to—one critic compared the experience to "a cerebral accident analogous to a vehicle accident [*accident de voiture*] for the body." They also stressed the almost insurmountable difficulties in performing it.[66] In the program notes for an 1897 performance in which d'Indy conducted four of his works at the Concerts Colonne, again he was praised above all for his "*science.*"

At the Schola, d'Indy stressed art over skills, in part to shift instructors' attention away from the production of virtuosi and opera composers, long the Conservatoire's focus. However, he devoted much of his own compositional efforts in the 1890s to writing dramatic music and, ironically perhaps, selected texts quite similar to those used by Conservatoire students preparing for the Prix de Rome. The opposition between love and duty in *Fervaal* was not only a recurrent theme throughout music history (as in the works of Lully and Gluck) and the basis of French classical drama (as in Corneille) but also a quintessential republican preoccupation. Composers who competed for the Prix de Rome often had to set it to music—for example, *Jeanne d'Arc* (1871), *Calypso* (1872), *Geneviève* (1881), *La Vision de Saül* (1886), *Didon* (1887), *and Velléda* (1888). In the early 1890s, the theme was also popular at the Opéra, where three works based on the Judith story were premiered—Saint-Saëns's *Samson et Dalila*, Reyer's *Salammbô*, and Bourgault-Ducoudray's *Thamara*. During the same period when d'Indy was at work on *Fervaal*, a good number of Prix de Rome libretti—from *Velléda* (1888), *L'Interdit* (1891), and *Amadis* (1892) to *Frédégonde* (1897) and *Radegonde* (1898)—also focused on medieval myths and old French history. The subjects went hand in hand with the growing public taste for Wagner and also reflected the politics of *ralliement*, which led conservative republicans and traditional aristocratic elites to look for shared values in the French past. Later, when he wrote the incidental music for Catulle Mendès's play *Médée* (1898), d'Indy returned not only to the subject his arch-rival Georges Hüe set to music for his Prix de Rome in 1879 but also to one used by Conservatoire students in their January cantata exercises in 1891 and 1893.[67] D'Indy thus had all the preparation he needed to teach dramatic music at the Schola.

66. Compare Léon Kerst's review of an excerpt from *Fervaal* in *Le Petit Journal* (18 September 1895), F. Régnier's review of the same in *Le Journal* (18 September 1895), Bruneau's review of *Fervaal* in *Le Figaro* (13 March 1897), and Kerst's review of *Médée* in *Le Petit Journal* (29 October 1898).

67. See the discussion of these cantatas in my "State Politics and the 'French' Aesthetics of the Prix de Rome Cantatas," 593, 612–13, 618.

In fact, the Schola did function as a professional school, albeit not for the production of opera composers, and it received a state subsidy as such. It promoted its traditions and values with means similar to those of the Conservatoire and taught students just as rigorously, even if these students, a certain number of whom were aristocrats like d'Indy, did not need to make a living from their art. And while the Schola did not give prizes, it gave semester exams just as at the Conservatoire, used the same terminology to evaluate students' work,[68] and awarded diplomas at the end of classes. In their hiring of professors, their teaching of fundamentals and music history, their promotion of symphonic music, and their performance of early music, the two institutions shared important elements that have too often been ignored.[69]

First, when they concentrated on composition at the Schola, d'Indy and his disciples neglected how other disciplines were taught, such as singing and instrumental performance. All students had to learn Gregorian chant and participate in the choral ensemble. Although the minister did not accept it, a proposal for mandatory universal participation in a choral ensemble was also made in 1892 at the Conservatoire.[70] Moreover, d'Indy said that all professors should try "to form not virtuosi infatuated with their talents, but artists conscious of their mission of complete devotion to the work of art that they have the honor of performing."[71] However, half the professors at the Schola were prizewinners from the Conservatoire. For example, Madeleine Jaeger (Mme Jossic), who had studied composition with Guiraud and Massenet and received first prizes at the Conservatoire in solfège, organ, harmony, piano accompaniment, and counterpoint/fugue, was hired to teach solfège at the Schola after teaching it at the Conservatoire from 1896 to 1899. The same was true of the Schola's professors of piano, woodwinds, string instruments, and voice.[72] Eléanore Blanc, the Schola's voice teacher, received her first prize at the Conservatoire in 1890 where she specialized in *opéra comique*.[73] It

68. "Très bien, bien, assez bien." Compare *Le Tribune de Saint-Gervais* (September 1903): 306, 312, with the exam notes at the Conservatoire, Archives Nationales, Paris, AJ^{37}, 234.

69. For those who might have discussed these, see Vincent d'Indy et al., *La Schola cantorum en 1925* (Paris: Bloud et Gay, 1927), and Louis Laloy, *La Musique retrouvée, 1902–27* (Paris: Plon, 1928).

70. Pierre, *Le Conservatoire national*, 373 and 385.

71. See d'Indy, "La Schola cantorum," 11:3624.

72. Woodwind teachers (Prosper Mimart, clarinet; Clément Letellier, bassoon; Louis Bleuzet, oboe) tended to come from the Conservatoire and were members of some of the major orchestras in Paris—the Opéra, Société des Concerts du Conservatoire, the orchestras of Colonne or Lamoureux. So, too, for the string teachers, for example, Henri Casadessus (viola) and Nanny (bass), as well as the piano teachers Gabriel Grovlez and Marie Prestat.

73. In a performance of the Easter Cantata in the Concerts Lamoureux (31 March 1899), Eléanore Blanc had proven she could also sing Bach.

is not clear that the methods and repertoires used by these professors were different from those used at the Conservatoire.

Second, Scholists, such as Louis Laloy, and even adversaries such as Emile Vuillermoz have asserted that harmony was not taught at the Schola, that "counterpoint was supposed to be enough for Scholists," and that d'Indy was "responsible for this position."[74] However, the Schola, like the Conservatoire, did begin students' training with harmony. D'Indy published a collection of exercises for harmony exams at the Schola, his *Cent thèmes d'harmonie* (1907–8) (see ex. 4.4), showing students how to harmonize bass lines and given melodies. The material of this volume closely resembles that of not only Franck's classes at the Conservatoire but also the harmony classes there, as documented in Dubois's *87 Leçons d'harmonie* (1891) and Lenepveu's *Cent leçons d'harmonie* (1898).

Similar misperceptions cloud our understanding of counterpoint at these two institutions. Scholists promoted the idea that they taught counterpoint while the Conservatoire taught harmony. But although it is true that, where studies at the Conservatoire began with solfège and harmony, and those at the Schola programmatically included counterpoint, counterpoint was also taught at the Conservatoire, integrated with harmony and composition.[75] In exercise number 7 from his *Cent leçons d'harmonie* (ex. 4.5), Lenepveu shows how students might use permutations of a two-bar contrapuntal model to connect one part to another. This is not too different from d'Indy's exercise number 31 from his *Cent thèmes d'harmonie* (ex. 4.6). In both cases, the pedagogues were interested in imitative and canonic procedures associated with instruction in counterpoint. That is, they wished to encourage students to study how lines combine and voices interact in functionally harmonic fields. Moreover, like d'Indy, Dubois considered counterpoint (as well as harmony) "the best exercise [*gymnastique*] for composers."[76]

---

74. Vuillermoz, "La Schola et le Conservatoire," and Laloy, *La Musique retrouvée*, 77–78. Laloy went so far as to admit that musicians who graduated from the Schola had a characteristic problem with chordal succession and modulation. He noted that he had had occasion to study Reber and Dubois's harmony treatise, used at the Conservatoire for decades, which was a "great help." In his "La Schola et le Conservatoire," Urbie attempts to correct Vuillermoz, noting specifically that harmony was taught at the Schola (577). Fulcher accepts d'Indy's reputation for "dismissing" harmony and assumes its "total exclusion from the Schola" (*French Cultural Politics and Music*, 149).

75. For a discussion of when counterpoint entered the Paris Conservatoire and how the different fields of craft were divided and taught, see Renate Groth, *Die französische Kompositionslehre des 19. Jahrhunderts* (Wiesbaden: Steiner Verlag, 1983). See also François Bazin, *Cours de contre-point théorique et pratique* (Paris: Lemoine, c. 1871), Théodore Dubois, *Traité de contrepoint et de fugue* (Paris: Heugel, 1901), and André Gédalge, "Les Rapports de l'harmonie et du contrepoint: Définitions et considérations générales," *Revue musicale* (April 1904): 326–29.

76. Dubois, "L'Enseignement musical," 3439; also in the introduction to his *Traité de contrepoint et de fugue*.

EXAMPLE 4.4. D'Indy, "Examples of elementary exercises," *Cent thèmes d'harmonie* (1907–18).

100 Thèmes d'Harmonie

Epreuves d'examens des Cours d'Harmonie de la "SCHOLA CANTORUM"

(1907-1918)

2ème LIVRE
RÉALISATIONS
les BASSES et CHANTS DONNÉS
exposés dans le premier livre

Composés et ordonnés progressivement
par **VINCENT d'INDY**
Op. 71.

I — Epreuves des Cours élémentaires

Emploi des accords *parfaits* majeurs et mineurs, de leurs renversements, et les accords de *sixte* du deuxième degré *(sixte sensible)*.

127

EXAMPLE 4.5. Charles Lenepveu, "No. 7, bass and melody in alternation," *Cent leçons d'harmonie* (1898).

PREMIÈRE PARTIE

Cinquante Leçons de M^r CH. LENEPVEU

128

Example 4.6. D'Indy, "No. 31," *Cent thèmes d'harmonie* (1907–18).

D'Indy recognized Dubois's talent as a teacher of counterpoint. In a letter of 1 June 1901, he thanked Dubois for sending him his new counterpoint and fugue treatise, in which d'Indy found "precisely the French qualities lacking in [works] of his predecessors . . . clarity and precision."[77] In addition, as at the Schola, the study of fugues was an important part of composition lessons at the Conservatoire. Fugues

77. Lettre to Théodore Dubois, 1 June 1901 (F-Pn, Musique, l.a. d'Indy 377).

were sometimes submitted by students for their exams and were always required as part of the Prix de Rome competition.[78]

Third, even if d'Indy gave more attention to pre-Revolutionary music history and integrated it into his composition classes more than was done at the Conservatoire, many of his educational policies were extensions of Conservatoire traditions, not their opposites, as has recently been suggested. This was especially true in matters of teaching music history and training conductors.[79] At the Conservatoire, Thomas saw the importance of teaching history to musicians. In 1871, he instituted a history and aesthetics class, which addressed music from its origins to the present, musical paleography, sacred as well as secular music, diverse musical systems, and the critical study of individual works. When Bourgault-Ducourday was hired as music historian in 1878, Thomas made these classes obligatory for all harmony and composition students.[80] From 1873 to 1885, Deldevez taught an orchestra class at the Conservatoire to train future conductors and to perform works by student composers. Afterward, Godard taught an instrumental ensemble class. Similar training continued in the piano accompaniment class, one of whose goals was to teach orchestral score reading, among other skills. (This is the class in which Debussy earned his first *premier prix* and the right to enter the composition class.) Ironically, despite the importance of orchestral music for d'Indy, the Schola had a hard time attracting enough string players to have an orchestra, and in 1903 this orchestra was still not yet fully functional.

Contrary to what d'Indy and others have implied, a wide array of genres was also taught to composers at the Conservatoire. They included religious and instrumental music, although not systematically. In a survey of the Conservatoire archives from 1888 to 1893, for example, I found student compositions in religious vocal genres (e.g., an *Ave Maria*, a *Bénédictus*, an *Agnus Dei* from the Catholic mass, and a good number of motets) presented in several of their exams (see table 4.3a). Student composers also had the option to present purely instrumental works

78. In the semester exam of 13 January 1891, for example, all six of Massenet's composition students presented fugues. See Archives Nationales, Paris, AJ[37], 234 (3).

Elsewhere I've shown the importance of counterpoint in works by Debussy, specifically the counterpoint of timbres. See my "Timbre, Voice-Leading, and the Musical Arabesque in Debussy's Piano Music," in *Debussy in Performance*, ed. James Briscoe (New Haven, Conn.: Yale University Press, 1999), 225–55.

79. In her *French Cultural Politics and Music*, Fulcher asserts that "the Conservatoire placed little value on music history or the performance of works from the distant past" and implies that a "class on music history" was among Gabriel Fauré's reforms in 1905. She concludes: "This would eventually change, but only in response to the Schola's challenge and to the escalating assaults on the institution in the next decade by the nationalist Right" (27–28; see also 151).

80. Pierre, *Le Conservatoire national*, 310.

TABLE 4.3a. Teaching of Composition at the Conservatoire: Religious Music Composed for Conservatoire Exams.

Composition at the Conservatoire, 1888–93	Professor	Exam date
Handel, Fugue subject	Massenet	1888
Ave maria	Guiraud	1890
Pavane	Guiraud	1890
Bénédictus	Guiraud	1891
Salva Regina	Dubois	1892
Agnus Dei	Guiraud	1893
Ave Verum	Dubois	1893

for their exams, for instance, a movement of a piano sonata, a violin solo, a quartet, or an orchestral piece.[81] What was expected of composers in preparation for the Prix de Rome competition also evolved during this period to include more orchestral music. Beginning in the late 1890s, the libretti used in the Prix de Rome competitions called for symphonic music from composers in the first significant way. It was not just a matter of functional marches or imitative music, but rather of program music meant to take full responsibility for the expression of charm in certain sections of the work.

Most important, in comparing the Schola's training of composers with the Conservatoire's, we have ignored the fact that the direction of a composer's work and its oversight by Conservatoire professors continued with the annual *envois* composed in Rome. These works, requirements for the fellowship, were submitted to the Académie des Beaux-Arts for its review and performed at the annual fall meeting of the Institut. Since most music members of the Académie were also composition teachers at the Conservatoire, these required *envois de Rome* should be considered as part of composers' institutional training.[82] As table 4.3b shows, the genres taught at the Schola follow the same sequence as that required of Prix de Rome composers if one takes these *envois* into account: after writing melodies and choruses, fugues and sonatas, they were to turn to chamber music, then symphonic

81. See Archives Nationales, AJ[37], 234 (3).

82. In the late nineteenth century, of the six members of the Académie des Beaux-Arts at any one time, Thomas (1851–96), Reber (1853–81), Félicien David (1869–76), Victor Massé (1872–84), François Bazin (1873–78), Massenet (1878–1912), Delibes (1884–91), Guiraud (1891–92), Dubois (1893–1924), and Lenepveu (1896–1910) were also composition professors at the Conservatoire. Only Gounod (1866–93), Reyer (1876–1909), Saint-Saëns (1881–1921), and Emile Paladilhe (1892–1926) were not professors.

TABLE 4.3b. Teaching of Composition at the Conservatoire: Composition Sequence after 1894 (Subjects Taught at Both the Conservatoire and the Schola).

Subject	Conservatoire (class)	Schola (year)	
Plainchant	Organ	I	(1)
Harmony exercises	Harmony	I, II: 1	
Counterpoint exercises	Counterpoint	I	
Melodies, choruses, motets	Composition	II: 1	(1)
Fugues, sonatas	Composition	II: 2	(2)
Chamber music, especially quartets	1st year, Rome	II: 3	(3)
Early music	2nd, 4th year, Rome	II: 1, 2, 4	
Motets	2nd year, Rome	II: 2	
Symphonic works	2nd, 3rd year, Rome	II: 3	(3)
Sacred or secular oratorios	3rd, 4th year, Rome	II: 4	(4)
Dramatic scenes	Composition; 2nd year, Rome	II: 4	(4)

works, and finally oratorios and dramatic scenes. Under the influence of the politics of *ralliement,* with its increased attention to the French past, by a decree of 21 July 1894, winners of the Prix de Rome were also required to work on *la musique ancienne* (early music). That is, "in French libraries among the works of the French School of the sixteenth, seventeenth, and eighteenth centuries, both vocal and instrumental," they were "to seek out an interesting work, to copy it or make a score of it, or, if need be, to translate it into modern notation." Beginning in 1903, they could choose Italian early music for their exercise, as did the composers Florent Schmitt in 1903 and André Caplet in 1904[83] (see table 4.3c).

Fourth, d'Indy, together with his biographer Léon Vallas and others, have overstated the Schola's importance in introducing early music to French audiences through assertions such as this one, made in 1903: "Bach, Rameau, Gluck . . . one never plays them in France."[84] Before it was sung at the Schola, this music had an

83. Winners of the Prix de Rome and graduates of the Conservatoire, Schmitt copied a fragment of Cavalieri's *Dialogo musicale dell'anima e del corpo* and Caplet a fragment of Monteverdi's *Orfeo* the same year d'Indy published his edition of the opera. For a thorough study of this genre, see Alexandre Dratwicki, "Les 'Envois de Rome' des compositeurs pensionnaires de La Villa Médicis (1804–1914)," *Revue de musicologie* 91/1 (2005): 99–193.

84. "Bach, Rameau, Gluck . . . le propagande par le concert est nécessaire, puisqu'on ne les joue jamais en France"; letter of 23 November 1903, published in *Les Tablettes de la Schola* (15 January 1904), and in *Ma Vie,* 650. See note 59 here. Among the works d'Indy specifically names earlier in this letter as examples of works "performed nowhere else," three of the four works by Rameau and all of those by Gluck are listed in table 4.4. See also Léon Vallas, *Vincent d'Indy* (Paris: Albin Michel, 1950), which claims that these works became known "grâce aux expériences scholistes" (2:47).

Table 4.3c. Teaching of Composition at the Conservatoire: Early Music Copied by Prix de Rome Winners in Rome.

André Bloch, *Magnificat* by Arcadet and a *Kyrie* by Claudin de Sermisy, 1896
Charles Silver, *La Naissance d'Osiris* by Rameau, 1896
Henri Rabaud, *Magnificat* by Goudimel, 1897
Henri Büsser, *Mass* by Campra, 1897
Omer Letorey, *Credo* by Magliadri, 1898
Bloch, *Mass* by Du Caurroy, 1898
Jules Mouquet, *Mass* by Alessandro Scarlatti, 1899
Rabaud, *Missa pro defunctis* by Etienne Moulinié, 1899
Max d'Olonne, madrigal with organ, *Entra di Maesta*
   by Francesco Anerio, 1900
Mouquet, *Psaume L* for two choruses and orchestra by Lully, 1901
Letorey, *Mass* by Sermisy, 1901
Charles Levadé, manuscript by Monteverdi, 1902
Florent Schmitt, *Dialogo musicale dell'anima et del corpo* by Cavalieri, 1903
Edmond Malherbe, *Salve Regina* and *Magnificat* by Charpentier, 1903
André Caplet, chorus and finale of act 5 from *Orfeo* by Monteverdi, 1904

Registres des séances de l'Académie des Beaux-Arts, 2-E-20, Institut de France, Paris. Alexandre Dratwicki and I interpret the years associated with these envois differently. Whereas he takes the year they were assigned (e.g. June 1904–June 1905), I here refer to the year they were delivered to the Institut (September–October 2005). For a thorough study of such works, see Dratwicki, "Les 'Envois de Rôme' des compositeurs pension-naires de la Villa Médicis (1804–1914)," *Revue de musicologie* 91/1 (2005): 99–193.

ongoing presence in France, and especially in Paris.[85] When d'Indy was a young composer studying in Paris, excerpts from operas by both Rameau and Gluck were in many pianists' repertoires and in manuals used in elementary schools, both

85. From different perspectives, others have also worked on early music in nineteenth-century France. Christine Wassermann, "Die Wiederentdeckung Rameaus in Frankreich im 19. Jahrhundert," *Archiv für Musikwissenschaft* 50, no. 2 (1993): 164–86, concentrates on Rameau in the 1840s and 1850s, the new Rameau edition (1895–1924), and the presence of Rameau in Schola concerts after 1900. Catrina Flint de Médecis, *The Schola Cantorum, Early Music, and French Cultural Politics from 1894 to 1914* (Ph.D. diss., McGill University, 2006), focuses on early music at the Schola. Katharine Ellis, *Interpreting the Musical Past* (New York: Oxford University Press, 2005), discusses the cultural meaning of Palestrina, Handel, and other composers for French listeners. For a perspective on Bach's popularity in nineteenth-century France, see Joël-Marie Fauquet and Antoine Hennion, *La Grandeur de Bach: l'amour de la musique en France au XIXe siècle* (Paris: Fayard, 2000). The topic is also discussed in my *Useful Music* and was addressed in my "Forging French Identity: The Political Significance of *la musique ancienne et moderne*," paper presented at the annual meeting of the American Musicological Society, Washington, D.C., 28 October 2005.

public and religious, throughout the country. During the 1880s and 1890s, scores of *la musique ancienne* and new music written *dans le style ancien* (such as Debussy's *Sarabande*, Fauré's *Pavane*, and Ravel's *Pavane*) were included in a great variety of publications destined for use by workers as well as elites. One could hear instrumental and vocal excerpts from such works in many orchestra concerts of the time—those of the Société des Concerts du Conservatoire, Pasdeloup, Colonne, Lamoureux, and Eugène d'Harcourt—as well as the Opéra and the Opéra-Comique (see table 4.4).[86] D'Indy was even involved in some of these. In 1888, the composer-run Société Nationale premiered his *Schumanniana* in a concert framed by a scene from Rameau's *Dardanus* and act 1 of Gluck's *Iphigénie en Tauride* (with Gluck's original orchestration); and in 1895 the Opéra premiered an excerpt of *Fervaal* in the same concert as a scene from Gluck's *Alceste*, a work done frequently by the Concerts Colonne at the turn of the century. Selections from Gluck's operas could also be heard at concerts by military bands between 1889 and 1899. Moreover, just as in these other venues, Schola performances presented only selected excerpts and individual acts until their production of *Dardanus* in 1907.[87]

D'Indy's assertions also ignore amateur chorus performances of cantatas by Handel and Bach, as well as airs and choruses by Rameau. Besides the Société Bourgault-Ducoudray, which sang numerous Handel cantatas in the 1870s, the Société d'Harmonie Sacrée, directed by Lamoureux, performed the *St. Matthew Passion* in 1874; the Société Chorale des Amateurs, directed by Antonin Guillot de Sainbris, performed Bach cantatas in 1875, 1881, and 1884, along with airs and choruses by Rameau. The Société chorale, la Concordia, directed by Charles-Marie Widor, professor at the Conservatoire, sang Bach in 1884 and in 1888 put on the *St. Matthew Passion*. Another choral group, L'Euterpe, sang Bach cantatas in 1896 and 1897. Finally, in February 1900 d'Indy himself conducted a chorus of amateurs in Bach's Mass in B Minor.

This taste for musical "archaeology" was also embraced in official republican circles. In 1895, a group of Conservatoire professors created the Société des Instruments Anciens. Its founder, Louis Diémer, included early music in his keyboard classes at the Conservatoire, as did teachers of the vocal classes there, some of which d'Indy accompanied in the 1880s.[88] Such cultivation of early music

86. This list is selective. I have left out Gluck's *Orphée*, performed at the Opéra-Comique, as its popularity was not in question, as well as other works not performed in the vocal classes of the Conservatoire, including those by J. S. Bach. The latter had an increasing presence in Parisian concerts halls beginning in the late 1890s.

87. I would like to thank Catrina Flint de Médecis for allowing me to compare my work on the Schola's concerts with hers.

88. D'Indy's job accompanying singing classes at the Conservatoire is pointed out in Malherbe's program notes for a Concerts Colonne performance of his works on 12 December 1897.

TABLE 4.4. Performances of *la musique ancienne* in Paris (Selection).

Works	Conservatoire, vocal exams, 1880–1903	Public concerts[a]	Schola
Gluck, *Iphigénie en Aulide*	1881, 1886 (2x), 1889 (3x), 1891 (2x), 1899	SC 1880, 1882, 1883, 1884, 1885, 1890, 1897, 1898, 1899; SN 1888; CC 1887, 1889, 1897; CL 1894, 1900	1907, ed. d'Indy 1908
Gluck, *Iphigénie en Tauride*	1888, 1899 1900 (3x)	CC 1885, 1887; SN 1888 (1 act); SGA/OC 1893; CL 1894; CC 1897, 1899; TR, mil bands 1899; OC 1900	1901, 1902, 1904
Gluck, *Armide*	1888, 1889, 1890, 1894, 1900	CP 1881, 1890; CC 1882, 1887, 1889, 1890, 1900; SN 1889; SG 1893, 1899; SC 1884, 1901; Opéra 1905	1901, 1902, 1903, 1905
Gluck, *Alceste*	1886, 1897, 1900 (3x), 1901, 1902	SC 1887; mil bands 1889; CC, 1886, 1887, 1888, 1889, 1891, 1897, 1900, 1901; CO 1895; SC 1895; CL 1897; SG 1898	1900, 1902, 1903
Sacchini, *Oedipe à Colonne*	1889		
Lully, *Alceste*	1898, 1900	SC 1886; CC 1891; CH 1893	
Cavalli, *Xerxes*	1899		
Rameau, "Le Rossignol"	1899		
Rameau, *Hippolyte et Aricie*	1899	CH 1894; CC 1899; SC 1902; Opéra 1908	ed. d'Indy 1900, 1900, 1901, 1903, 1904
Rameau, *Dardanus*	1902 (3x), 1903	CP 1881; SC 1887; SN 1887, 1889; SG 1895	1900, 1901, 1903, 1904, 1907, ed. d'Indy 1905
Rameau, *Castor et Pollux*	1902	CC 1880, 1884, 1888; SC 1883, 1888, 1889, 1900; CH 1894	1902, 1903, 1904

(continued)

TABLE 4.4. (*continued*)

Works	Conservatoire, vocal exams, 1880–1903	Public concerts[a]	Schola
Handel, *Jules César*	1889, 1899, 1900, 1903		1900, 1904
Handel, *Judas Machabée*	1899, 1902	SA 1869; HS 1874; SC 1886; CH 1894, 1896: SG 1901	1901, 1902
Handel, *Hercules*	1902 (2x)		
Handel, *Xerxes*	1902, 1903	CC 1900	
Handel, *Rinaldo*	1902		

[a]Abbreviations: CC: Concerts Colonne; CH: Concerts d'Harcourt; CL: Concerts Lamoureux; CO: Concerts de l'Opéra; CP: Concerts Pasdeloup; HS: Société chorale l'Harmonie sacrée; mil bands: military bands; OC: Opéra-Comique; SA: Société des Amateurs Guillot de Sainbris; SC: Société des Concerts du Conservatoire; SGA: Société des Grandes Auditions, SG: Chanteurs de Saint-Gervais; SN: Société Nationale; TR: Théâtre de la Renaissance

provided a precedent to the early music taught at the Schola. Table 4.4 outlines the extent to which this music was taught to singers at the Conservatoire and performed on Conservatoire exams in the 1880s and 1890s, some of it long before it was studied and performed at the Schola.[89] Instruction included the very works d'Indy mentioned as unknown in 1903: Gluck's *Iphigénie en Aulide*, *Armide*, and *Alceste,* as well as Rameau's *Hippolyte et Aricie*. Handel also found his place. Beginning in 1895, it was the republican Saint-Saëns who directed a new edition of the works of Rameau, of which d'Indy later contributed one edited volume. This music was thus studied and performed long before the Schola became an alternative to the Paris Conservatoire, and by numerous predecessors. By 1900, *la musique ancienne* was literally in fashion.[90]

D'Indy was thus much less marginal and removed from republican institutions and their ideologies than he, his disciples, and some recent scholars have led us to believe. Especially before 1900, his actions and works reveal a man who built

89. See the end-of-the-year competitions at the Conservatoire, Archives Nationales, Paris, AJ[37], 255 (3), and AJ[37], 234 (3).

90. As further evidence of this taste, consider that the music prizes sponsored by the Société des Compositeurs were for a motet in 1896 and a madrigal in 1897.

alliances, and these alliances served both the composer and the state well. Winning the City of Paris prize, despite opposition from Saint-Saëns and Dubois, taught d'Indy early in his career the power of his difference. In the 1880s and 1890s, state administrators recognized the value of this difference as a way to combat two monopolies, that of the Académie des Beaux-Arts over the most important composition prizes and that of professors at the Conservatoire over the advanced teaching of music. In other words, d'Indy helped the government confront and stand up to the Academicians and professors who controlled the conventions that were impeding progress in French music. One need only recall that *Le Chant de la cloche* introduced music of extreme complexity in a competition subsidized by the city of Paris. To reward it was, for the government, to encourage aesthetic individualism, even if that meant coming to grips with the influence of Wagnerism in French music.

D'Indy's differences also helped bridge conflicts within the Republic and contributed to growth and change in the musical world. Although he shared with republicans an appreciation for the simple and the naïve as essential aspects of the French temperament—as illustrated by Massenet in his *Scènes alsaciennes* (1882) and Saint-Saëns in his *Rapsodie d'Auvergne* (1884)—d'Indy demonstrated how a composition could integrate multiple worlds. Through his incorporation and treatment of a *chanson populaire,* his *Symphonie cévenole* (1886) symbolically mitigated the emerging conflict between regional and national identity in France and, through its leitmotif-like treatment of the *chanson*, it linked national musical material to international taste and stylistic trends. During the political *ralliement* of the early 1890s (which made possible the alliance between conservative republicans, Catholics, and traditional elites), the government turned to d'Indy as someone who understood the importance of tradition and could help it to reform pedagogy at the Conservatoire. Participating in state-sponsored activities—the Cressent competition, the City of Paris prize, juries of various *orphéon* competitions, and especially the committee to reform the Conservatoire—gave d'Indy significant inside knowledge about how such institutions functioned. At the Schola, under his direction after 1900, d'Indy turned this knowledge to his own benefit. While to all appearances he conducted a war with the Conservatoire and played down what they shared, he put into place educational reforms that he conceived while working on their committee, and, moreover, showed how these could work. It should not be surprising, then, that in 1912 he was again honored with the Légion d'honneur, and, after the minister cast the deciding vote, was soon thereafter offered a position teaching an orchestra class on the Conservatoire's faculty.[91]

---

91. According to Albert Bertelin, "M. Vincent d'Indy au Conservatoire," *Courrier musical* (15 November 1912): 613–14, d'Indy applied for this position. On the need for the minister's vote to have a majority, see *Courrier musical* (1 December 1912): 657.

Thereafter, in the opposition most associated with d'Indy today—his hostility to the avant-garde— ironically, he resembled his old adversaries, Dubois and Saint-Saëns. Just as they once defined the role of music as to "translate and transform ideas into feelings," d'Indy found the music of Stravinsky, Schönberg, and Bartok "too much for the mind and not enough for the heart, which is for me the only purpose of a work of art."[92]

In studying French composers, it is important to scrutinize any reputation that depends on an oppositional discourse. Even if many French people love to distinguish themselves through an oppositional opinion or stance—a heightened version of Bourdieu's *distinction*—the reality is that politics in France have long been a complex web of highly interconnected relationships. Many wish to dramatize their ambivalence about the state, stand apart from the masses, escape that most despicable of bourgeois sins, mediocrity, and test the limits of dissension. Opposition in France, especially since the revolution, has never been simple or easy for outsiders to grasp. At the end of the nineteenth century, it was all the more complex as the Dreyfus Affair fanned the flames of difference within the smallest family unit. In this article, I have tried to shift the discourse from focusing on the opposition d'Indy represented for the Republic to d'Indy's role in various forms of opposition within republican institutions: within the "family" of the Conservatoire (e.g., Franck vs. Massenet); between the Conservatoire under the musically conservative Ambroise Thomas and the Ministry of Public Instruction and the Fine Arts under the politically moderate Jules Ferry, who sought to support progress in all forms; then between Thomas and a ministry determined that the Conservatoire incorporate pre-Revolutionary music in its curricula; and lastly between the committee to reform the Conservatoire, appointed by the minister in the spirit of *ralliement* politics, and the minister himself, who in the end was willing to institute only a portion of the suggested reforms.

Vincent d'Indy understood this world and the dynamic of oppositional politics. He played an important role in each of these manifestations of difference, using his own to support the republican state in its efforts to effect change within its institutions. He also understood the currency of distinction produced by competition and recognized that competition was one of the Republic's most important principles. Since 1875, when France embarked on its first lasting democracy, the state held up competition as a way to further social equity and, through the struggle of difference, to build individual renown. Preferring to keep their distinction under the umbrella of the school, d'Indy told his students that they need not take part in external competitions. Yet he himself engaged in competition to gain at-

---

92. See J.-L. Croze, "La Musique à l'Académie de Médecine," *Le Soir* (21, 22 July 1895), and d'Indy's letter of 19 June 1914, *Ma Vie*, 740.

tention and notoriety throughout his professional life, beginning with the City of Paris prize. Taking control of the Schola Cantorum and turning it into an alternative to the Paris Conservatoire allowed him to situate himself and his students as a counterculture and thus to compete with the state in the realm of music education, even though, as I have shown, this institution shared much with the Conservatoire. As a sign that this oppositional discourse was successful, d'Indy won a position there while running the Schola.

To broaden our understanding of d'Indy, then, we need to situate the oppositional aspects that were essential to his reputation in the context of his achievements. With the armor of his students' devotion, in his later years d'Indy may have felt comfortable airing his private prejudices through his music and publications; but that does not mean that we should understand his life before the age of fifty or his legacy in those terms.[93] If we misconstrue the nature and function of political differences in France and their relationship to strategies by which reputations were built, we risk projecting our own ideas and ideology onto d'Indy and may miss his importance in French musical life of the *Belle Époque.*

---

93. The most egregious of these was his anti-Semitic book *Richard Wagner et son influence sur l'art musical français* (Paris: Delagrave, 1930), written the year before he died. James Ross, "D'Indy and Barrès: A Parallel Aesthetic?" paper presented at the conference "Vincent d'Indy and His Times," Trinity College, Hartford, Connecticut, 12 May 2001, argued that d'Indy was not anti-Semitic in any public way before the late 1890s. He found that neither d'Indy nor Barrès had referred to the other in their surviving correspondence and construed this lack of references to mean that d'Indy hardly knew the politically extremist Maurice Barrès. Ross also argued, "D'Indy's 'Fervaal': Reconstructing French Identity at the 'Fin de Siècle,' " *Music and Letters* 84, no. 2 (May 2003), that d'Indy was not as politically active as we have imagined—"there is scant evidence that his politics moved far from his piano stool" (224). He concluded that d'Indy's musical choices were motivated instead by idealism and practical regionalism. For an in-depth study of this problem as it relates to differences between the private and public aspects of d'Indy's anti-Semitism, see Manuela Schwartz, "Nature et évolution de la pensée antisémite chez d'Indy," in Schwartz, *Vincent d'Indy et son temps*, 37–63.

5. New Music as Confrontation

The Musical Sources of Cocteau's Identity

*J*EAN COCTEAU KNEW HE WAS DIFFERENT. Not a very good student, drawn to men more than women, admired for his "feminine soul," his physical beauty, and his incisive wit. He was the fruit of his upbringing—privileged, wealthy bourgeois suburbanites—yet not entirely so. By age twenty-nine, in writing *Le Coq et l'Arlequin*, he had figured out: "what the public reproaches in you, cultivate it, that's who you are."[1] To arrive at this clarity—a self-definition essentially based on a confrontive relationship with the public—took most of his twenties, a period during which he gradually learned to distinguish himself from yet still define himself in terms of the conventional social circles in which he and his family moved. I suggest that Cocteau achieved this distinction through a conscious change in his musical tastes, and that it was indeed what he found in and extracted from new music that allowed him to construct much of the identity we think of as Cocteau.

Cocteau was not, of course, the first French writer to look to music for direction. Charles Baudelaire took inspiration from Wagner's music and used his understanding of that music to elucidate a new aesthetic ideal in poetry—symbolism—

This essay originally appeared in *Musical Quarterly* 75, no. 3 (fall 1991): 255–78; it is included here by permission, copyright 1991 Oxford University Press. An earlier version was presented to the symposium "Jean-Cocteau and the Parisian Avant-Garde," University of California, Irvine, 19 February 1989.

I'm grateful to the Harry Ransom Humanities Research Center (HRC), University of Texas, Austin, for permission to quote from the Valentine Hugo and Erik Satie manuscripts there and to Edouard Dermit for permission to quote from Cocteau manuscripts in the HRC and in the Alain Rivière Collection, France.

All figures in this chapter are courtesy of the collection at the Severin Wunderman Museum. I am grateful to Tony Clark, executive director, for permission to photograph and reproduce these drawings.

1. Jean Cocteau, *Le Coq et L'Arlequin: Notes autour de la musique 1918* (Paris: Stock, 1979), 70. All translations are my own unless otherwise indicated.

Figure 5.1. Jean Cocteau, cubist self-portrait, ca. 1909, pencil on paper.

and a new methodology: correspondences. Stéphane Mallarmé publicly envied music's power of suggestion, of mystery. Paul Verlaine wrote, "De la musique avant toute chose." Henri Bergson looked to melody to explain the way the unconscious perceives time in his path-breaking book *Time and Free Will*. Marcel Proust made the effect on the narrator of one involuntary memory—a "petite phrase" of music— one of the cornerstones of his novel *A la recherche du temps perdu*. And Paul Valéry, perhaps the most influenced of them all, borrowed the idea of recurring rhythmic patterns and harmonic modulation as organizational principles in his poetry.

But for Cocteau (to cite the composer Ned Rorem), music "inevitably reflected *situations* rather than constructions, *social rapport* with makers and their audiences rather than the 'creative process' " (emphasis mine).[2] Cocteau focused his attention on the interdependent relationship between the artist and the public, particularly the composer and his public. Cocteau understood, furthermore, that when the French talk about music, they are talking about themselves. "The public like to recognize," he writes.[3] Recognize themselves, he might have elaborated.

In Paris at this time, musical tastes were an important barometer of one's social class and even political orientation. Performances, especially of music, served as springboards for the press to discuss everything from personal morality to nationalism, and for society thereby to work out its social and political differences. This was never more evident as in the scandal surrounding Claude Debussy's *Pelléas et Mélisande*, when, during the first two weeks of its performances in spring 1902, the monarchists, the aristocrats, the *haute bourgeoisie*, the anti-Dreyfusards, the socialites, and the conservative musical public felt threatened or antagonistic toward the new work, whereas the republicans, the businessmen, the socialists, the Dreyfusards, the professional writers, the art-lovers, and the progressive musical public tended to be more willing to give it a chance.[4] This confrontation of values fueled the numerous artistic scandals we associate with Parisian culture of the period.

Cocteau's family seems to have had some interest in music. His grandfather owned a set of Stradivarius violins and played quartets regularly in his home, often with such distinguished violinists as Pablo de Sarasate. (Hiring top professionals to perform one's music or to accompany oneself in one's home was a common privilege of the rich at the time.) His parents went regularly to the Opéra, carrying scores of Wagner's music when appropriate.[5] Given the concert series they patronized, however, it is not clear whether they went out of a passion for music or because such attendance was expected from those of their social standing.

In his *Portraits-Souvenir*, Cocteau recalls as one of his first memories visits to concerts of the Société des Concerts du Conservatoire. "My grandfather had seats for these in the third row of the main floor, on the right. There I discovered thrown together Beethoven, Liszt, Berlioz, and Wagner."[6] Proust once called this the "Senate" of Parisian concert series: its repertoire had the "mark of authority," its

---

2. Ned Rorem, "Cocteau and Music," in *Jean Cocteau and the French Scene* (New York: Abbeville, 1984), 155.

3. Cocteau, *Le Coq*, 71.

4. See *"Pelléas* and Power: Forces Behind the Reception of Debussy's Opera," chapter 7 here.

5. The practice of bringing scores to performances was not unusual. Lights were up and scores sometimes sold at performances.

6. Jean Cocteau, *Portraits-Souvenir 1900–1914* (Paris: Grasset, 1935), 23.

performances were the "most perfect," and its subscribers "considered themselves and prided themselves a little . . . as if they were invited guests."[7] These concerts, the Opéra and the Comédie-Française, to which Cocteau says his family also subscribed regularly, were the principal venues for seeing and being seen in Paris. Good aristocrats, "wealthy bourgeois families," like Cocteau's,[8] or those with such pretensions considered attendance at these series almost a social obligation. For them, the Opéra, with its huge staircase and elegant hall of mirrors modeled on those of Versailles, served as a nostalgic reminder of the days when the aristocracy flourished. The writer Octave Mirbeau describes it as an "institution of luxury, that luxury upholds, and that is made only for it," a sort of "grand banal salon divided into an infinity of small individual salons" that provided subscribers with "all the conveniences for holding fashionable receptions."[9]

Cocteau's own initial fascination with the theater came from watching his mother dress for the occasion—the "prologue to the spectacle," he called it, full of "foreshadowing resemblances." "This madonna covered with velvet, choking with diamonds," whose servant tried to create the air of "a Spanish virgin's nobility," "would go flowing like a red river and blend her velvet with the velvets of the theater, her brilliance with the brilliance of the chandeliers and stage lights."[10]

When it came to his family patronizing any of the other important musical series in Paris, Cocteau is silent. Conspicuously absent from his discussion are the Opéra-Comique, the Concerts Lamoureux or Concerts Colonne for orchestra (religiously attended by the symbolist writers including Mallarmé), and the Société Nationale (formed to encourage the performance of French music). The audiences for these were largely distinct from those of the Opéra, the Société des Concerts du Conservatoire, and the Comédie-Française. Subscription lists for the Opéra-Comique, for example, are much smaller than they are for the Opéra: in 1900, 425 people subscribed to the Opéra and 550 to the Comédie-Française (61 of whom subscribed to both), while only 70 subscribed to the Opéra-Comique (only 8 of whom also subscribed to the Opéra and 6 also to the Comédie-Française).[11] The ticket prices of the Opéra-Comique cannot be blamed in this differentiation, for they were between those of the Opéra and the Comédie-Française. Nor can the size of the hall, which is 40 percent, not 84 percent, smaller than the Opéra. Moreover, in 1905–6, the Concerts Lamoureux had a sizable list of 208 subscribers, the great majority of whom were not subscribers of any of the three major series.

7. Marcel Proust, "Un Dimanche au Conservatoire," in *Cahiers Marcel Proust*, n.s., 3: *Textes retrouvés* (Paris: Gallimard, 1971), 115.

8. Pierre Chanel, *Album Cocteau* (Monaco: Henri Veyrier-Tchou, 1979), vi.

9. Octave Mirbeau, *Des Artistes*, 2nd ser. (Paris: Flammarion, 1924), 253, 259–60.

10. Cocteau, *Portraits-Souvenir*, 39–40.

11. These numbers come from counting subscription lists published in the *Annuaire des Artistes* (1900).

The primary difference between these two kinds of subscription series lies in their organizers' attitudes toward new work. Institutions like the Opéra and the Comédie-Française maintained French traditions, an ideal many of its subscribers were perhaps more committed to than to the actual music or theater presented therein. Article number 1 of the Opéra's *Cahiers de charge* in 1879 reads: "The Opéra is not an experimental theater; it must be considered a museum of music." By edict, only two new works every other year must be performed at the Opéra: one could be a translation of a foreign opera, and one had to be by a recipient of the Prix de Rome (in other words, a young up-and-coming "official" composer). The Opéra-Comique and the two orchestral concerts series performed new works far more regularly and by a much wider variety of composers, including Vincent d'Indy, Gabriel Fauré, and Debussy. They even repeated a new work at the same concert and again a week later if the audiences liked it. The Société Nationale gave premieres at almost all of its concerts. Cocteau later vehemently criticized the work of composers like Debussy, but he never refers to their music in his autobiographical essays or portraits of friends; this absence suggests that he might not have had a regular exposure to this music when he was growing up. Moreover, in her notes for a radio program on Cocteau in 1951, Cocteau's dear friend Valentine Hugo (née Gross) points out that in the milieu in which they lived, "people made fun of *Pelléas*."[12]

Cocteau apparently had an excellent musical memory and a good tenor voice. The composer Georges Auric recounts that he could play the piano, but only pieces written in the key of F major (with its one flat).[13] Yet his tastes throughout the first decade of the century, in music as in literature, were very conventional. For the most part, they derive from and reflect his social milieu.

The composer he most often refers to is Reynaldo Hahn, another elegant young man, a student of Massenet, and ever the darling of the salons, whom Cocteau met through Proust in 1908. Hahn wrote charming melodies the ladies loved to perform, several operas, and one ballet for which Cocteau provided the scenario. After hearing his opera *La Carmélite* in December 1902—six months after the premiere of Debussy's *Pelléas*—one critic compared Hahn's score with the salons he frequented. In it, "very well-known phrases meet, their very archaic melodic contours wearing wigs pass closely by one another."[14] *La Carmélite*, based on the story of

12. Valentine Hugo, notes for "Une Heure avec Jean Cocteau," 18 November 1951, manuscript, Carleton Lake Collection, Harry Ransom Humanities Research Center University of Texas, Austin.

13. Georges Auric, "Témoignages," in *Cahiers Jean Cocteau 7: Avec les musiciens* (Paris: Gallimard, 1978), 71.

14. Louis Schneider, "Opéra-Comique: *La Carmélite*," *Revue Musicale* December 1902): 509.

a nun who was the lover of Louis XIV, could not fail to charm the Opéra public. The theater director spent a fortune on the production, and the critics pointed out: "never has the stage seen such a sumptuous evocation of the Sun King's court."[15] Although the work was supposed to be a pastiche of seventeenth-century music and dance as well as its mores, it was pure Massenet. Hahn "gives the same nice turn of phrase to God, the devil, love, and the priesthood. He makes everything from the nun's fall to her redemption into Massenet," observed the critic of *Le Soleil*.[16] When the well-regarded critic Willy (Colette's first husband, Henry Gauthier-Villars) blasted the work for its lack of originality, Hahn publicly responded in an interview published in *Le Figaro*: "Sometimes taste is the worst enemy of what the public calls originality. I admit that what I have always tried to stay away from is errors in taste."[17] Such a preoccupation with the public and its taste presages that of Cocteau and links the two in an important way.

Catulle Mendès, the librettist of *La Carmélite* and a critic at perhaps the most prominent newspaper in town, *Le Journal*, was another of Cocteau's close associates during this period. The subject of one of Cocteau's portraits in his memoirs, Mendès was his mentor for a time. They ate lunch together every Saturday for years. One wonders about the extent to which Mendès influenced Cocteau's musical tastes before he died in 1909. He was a staunch Wagnerian and not particularly sympathetic to Debussy, although Debussy once promised to set Mendès's play *Rodrigue et Chimènes* to music. In his review of *Pelléas*, Mendès said that he left the theater wanting to see the music and the play performed separately, thereby rejecting Debussy's innovative integration of music and text, and he told Debussy's symbolist supporters that they had been "deceived" in placing their hopes in Debussy.[18]

Cocteau's other well-known literary friends during the first decade of the century, Léon Daudet, Jules Lemaître, and Anna de Noailles, were staunch royalists. Lemaître, the "victim and the success" of Madame de Loynes and her salon, made it all the way into the Institut by advancing the views of his patroness. This world of aristocrats, would-be aristocrats, and the writers through whom they chose to speak revolved around the idea of glory (according to the dictionary known as the *Petit Robert*, *gloire* means "great renown spread throughout a very large public"). Cocteau writes of Madame de Noailles:

It's glory that she idolized. Glory, her *idée fixe*. "You only admire failures! she said. In vain, I tried to show her that the privilege of France is in fact

15. Gaston Carraud, *La Liberté* (18 December 1902).
16. O'Divy, *Le Soleil* (17 December 1902).
17. Robert de Flers, *Le Figaro* (18 December 1902).
18. See "*Pelléas* and Power," chapter 7 here.

FIGURE 5.2. Cocteau, Anna de Noailles, ca. 1920, black ink on paper. Cocteau's mother apparently wished him to marry Anna.

to have its secret glories, famous men whom the crowd doesn't suspect. Rimbaud a little. Verlaine just enough. Hugo! Glory is the number of squares, of streets, of avenues. His [God's] celebrity, Rome, and the number of His temples are, in the eyes of the Countess, proof of the existence of God. "Anna," I told her, "you want to be a bust, while still alive, but with legs to run everywhere!" She insulted me, I retorted. Our arguments

finished by my fleeing. . . . Tender arguments, pretexts for unending dialogues![19]

Glory in post-Revolutionary, democratic France was only possible through what
genius claimed for itself. This group wished to link the aristocracy of blood with
the aristocracy of talent. In *Le Coq et l'Arlequin*, Cocteau later wrote: "The artist,
that's the true rich man. He rides in the automobile. The public follows by bus."[20]

Cocteau knew he needed to stand out from the crowd and to achieve some sort
of "glory." But after five years of public life, in 1912 he suffered a devastating review
of his poetry in the *Nouvelle Revue Française*, one of the most forward-looking
journals of the time, warning him that premature success was ruining his talent.[21]
The same year, the prestigious Ballets Russes' production of Hahn's ballet *Le Dieu
bleu*, for which Cocteau had written the libretto, was a flop; even their impresario,
Serge Diaghilev, found it "dull and ineffective."[22] Cocteau's future was at stake.
When Diaghilev commanded him "Astonish me!" Cocteau was taken aback: "The
idea of astonishing had never come to me before. I was from a family in which one
didn't ever think of astonishing. We believed that art was an undisturbing, calm,
different kind of thing—one didn't have a choice."[23] But he listened and paid
attention, while the Ballets Russes—even as it was supported by the French and
Russian aristocracy (and the French banking establishment)—rapidly won the attention and admiration of the French public through making very different assumptions: "The troupe taught me to scorn everything that it shook up. This pho-
enix teaches that one must burn oneself alive in order to be reborn."[24]

Music, in some ways the most aristocratic of the arts because it is the most pure
(meaning highly refined) as well as the most mobile internationally, was in a good
position to teach him ways to distinguish himself without having to separate from
his social milieu. But to do so required a change in his attitude toward music and a
willingness to accept "new music."

The first stage in this transformation developed out of his response to Igor
Stravinsky's music. In his *Journals*, he writes: "*The Rite of Spring* totally upset me.
Stravinsky . . . was the first to teach me how to insult *habits*, without which
art stagnates and remains a game" (emphasis mine).[25] From his understanding
of Stravinsky—heavily influenced by the antiimpressionist argument in Jacques
Rivière's review of *The Rite* (and not necessarily how Stravinsky would have chosen

19. Cocteau, *Portraits-Souvenir*, 220–22.

20. Cocteau, *Le Coq*, 47.

21. Henri Ghéon, "Les Poèmes," *Nouvelle Revue Française* 45 (1912): 507–11.

22. S. L. Grigoriev, *The Diaghilev Ballet 1909–1929*, trans. Vera Bowen (New York:
Penguin, 1960), 78.

23. Francis Steegmuller, *Cocteau* (Paris: Buchet, 1973), 67.

24. Jean Cocteau, *Prospectus 1916* (Paris: Stock, 1924), 9.

25. Wallace Fowlie, ed., *The Journals of Jean Cocteau* (New York: Criterion, 1956), 41.

to be understood)[26]—Cocteau came to define originality as the *contradiction* of preceding expressions, and the creator as someone who contradicts his predecessors.[27] These are very simple concepts, but they have very real power. An artist who understands a set of givens may "change the rules of the game," as Cocteau puts it[28]—do something differently with the givens his public already understands and avoid the search for a new public willing to accept a new set of givens.

Clearly this revelation was only a first step. The spirit of rebellion was new for Cocteau; only two years earlier, on 23 June 1911, he had written to the composer Florent Schmitt: "People like discord. Me no, you neither."[29] But the effects of *The Rite* were not short-lived. By 1919, in a speech to Belgian musicians, Cocteau had expanded his response to the ballet into a general theory: "One could say that the spirit of the new in every period is the highest form of the spirit of contradiction." His theory, moreover, began to take on the tone of a manifesto: "The true creator *must* contradict and the next masterpiece *can only be* the violent contradiction of the preceding masterpiece" (emphasis mine).[30]

Besides this notion of contradiction, Cocteau took inspiration from the way Stravinsky "detected what lies beneath the surface, despite appearances," particularly in the ballet *Petrushka*.[31] Appearances in an art work could remain conven-

---

26. Jacques Rivière, "Le Sacre du Printemps," *Nouvelle Revue Française* 5 (1 November 1913): 706–30. In this review, Rivière contrasts Stravinsky's ballet with Debussy's music, saying it is the first masterpiece to "break away from Debussysme," to renounce impressionist "sauces": "Stravinsky "passes from the sung to the spoken, from invocation to discourse, from poetry to prose." In an unpublished letter to Rivière dated 5 November 1913, Cocteau wrote, "I haven't yet had the pleasure of meeting you, but why hold oneself back? *Never* have I read a critical article more *beautiful* than yours on *The Rite of Spring*. I admire you and feel I must let you know. The day we will meet I will tell you the intimate service that this article will render to Igor S. for whom my friendship holds you in profound recognition" (Alain Rivière Collection, France). In his admiration of Rivière's review, however, one should note that Cocteau ignores Rivière's clarification of Stravinsky's work as "not simply a negative novelty": "Stravinsky did not simply amuse himself by taking the opposite path from Debussy. If he chose instruments that don't quiver, that say nothing more than they say, of which the timbre is without expansion and which are like abstract words, it is because he wants to speak directly, expressly, by name. There is his principal preoccupation. There is his "personal innovation in contemporary music" (706–9). Moreover, both Rivière and Cocteau ignore Ravel's contribution to such notions, for example, in his *Histoires naturelles* (1906).

27. Jean Cocteau, "Présentation d'oeuvres de musiciens nouveaux," Institut des Hautes Etudes de Belgique, 19 December 1919, manuscript, Carleton Lake Collection.

28. Cocteau, *Le Coq*, 72–73.

29. Jean Cocteau, l.a. [autograph letter] 3, F-Pn, Musique.

30. Cocteau, "Présentation d'oeuvres."

31. Cocteau, letter to Stravinsky [n.d.], in *Stravinsky: Selected Correspondence*, vol. 1, ed. Robert Craft (New York: Knopf, 1982), 85–86.

tional; from Cocteau's perspective, the Ballets Russes' public accepted *Petrushka* from the start because it considered the ballet to be "an arm against the very new"[32]—the folk tunes must have lent an air of tradition to it. Yet a consciously artificial exterior, like that of the puppet in *Petrushka*, could provide an interesting means to "entreat the public to penetrate inside for the *internal spectacle*." In his next work, *David* (conceived in 1914 in the hope of collaborating with Stravinsky but never completed), Cocteau devised a masked character as the main character. Note the opening text of scene 1:

> Enter ladies and gentlemen!
> Enter inside—enter ourselves!
> To the other side! To the interior!
>
> Outside one only sees my poor friend the acrobat
> who, for the eye, is like
> an orchestral instrument is for the ear.
> . . . .
> everything—inside outside happens at the same time.[33]

Such a notion represents not only an aesthetic stance but also a relationship between the artist and his public. As Milorad observes, the scenario of *Parade*, derived in part from *David*, "already explains the drama that was taking place and would take place, between Jean Cocteau and his public"; that is, while the public could see only "the 'parade' of the poet," the poet "was trying in vain to interest it in the 'internal spectacle.' "[34] This idea from *Petrushka* later plays a major role in Cocteau's films, where characters walk through mirrors and use various other devices to bring the public with them to the other side of their consciousness.

To project a certain kind of social identity for himself, as if he was hoping for glory through association, Cocteau used his acquaintance and a feigned intimacy with Stravinsky. He advertised to his friends and in print that at 2 a.m. after the scandalous premiere of *The Rite of Spring*, he was with Stravinsky, Nijinsky, and Diaghilev in the Bois de Boulogne, a claim Stravinsky later denied. He dedicated his first book, *Potomak*, to the composer, an act Stravinsky considered "pure flattery destined to assure his collaboration for *David*."[35] In an unpublished letter of 22 July 1914 to Rivière, the author of the influential *Rite of Spring* review, Cocteau reports from Switzerland where he was visiting the composer:

32. Cocteau, *Le Coq*, 86.

33. Jean Cocteau, *David*, manuscript, Carleton Lake Collection.

34. Milorad, "Avec les musiciens," in *Cahiers Jean Cocteau* 7, 22. See also Jerrold Siegel, *Bohemian Paris* (New York: Penguin, 1986), 359–63.

35. Steegmuller, *Cocteau*, 81.

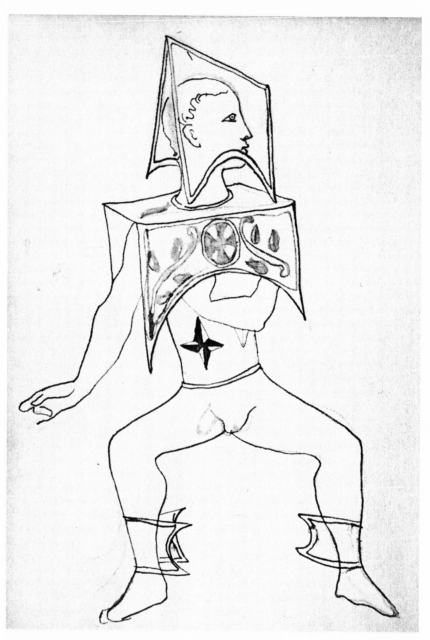

FIGURE 5.3. Cocteau, design for dancer, ballet *David*, c. 1915, pen, ink, pencil, and watercolor on paper.

Figure 5.4. Cocteau, Igor Stravinsky at the home of Coco Chanel, 1930, pen, ink, and wax with white chalk on paper. Cocteau notes on it that Coco sings in the room next door.

Igor . . . has been writing *Le Rossignol* in order to *stay alive* under a huge avalanche of telegrams from S[erge]. de D[iaghilev]. But he's been living to write *David. . . .*

He played me his work every morning the way one points out a finished fragment of a difficult puzzle and discovers an unexpected image. *Le Rossignol* was born of his insect skull, of his *binocle* [pince-nez], of his sixteen hands, of his tenacious dynamo. *His love was elsewhere.*[36]

36. Alain Rivière Collection, France.

As Cocteau's biographer Francis Steegmuller so aptly points out in his analysis of the Cocteau-Stravinsky correspondence, this assumption on Cocteau's part was pure nonsense. The composer never showed any real interest in collaborating on *David*.[37] Yet in the summer of 1916, Cocteau was still writing Stravinsky of his "veneration" for the composer, which by then, he admitted, had become "well-known. . . . You are the one I admire and respect the most."[38]

Stravinsky, however, was not altogether the perfect model. Eventually, Cocteau realized that *The Rite of Spring* presented a paradox he found increasingly troublesome, not for its aesthetic implications but for its effect on the public. In *Le Coq et l'Arlequin*, he writes, "I consider The *Rite of Spring* a masterpiece. But in the atmosphere created around its performances, I find a religious complicity among its followers, the same hypnotism as at Bayreuth."[39] And in his "Notes on Music" he concludes, "Any music that attracts a group of faithful" and that "creates a kind of religious atmosphere is suspect."[40]

In October 1915, Cocteau met Erik Satie, thanks to the efforts of their mutual friend Valentine Gross, a young painter and Ballets Russes follower. As early as March 1914, only months after meeting Satie, Gross considered him "the French equivalent of Stravinsky in music."[41] Whether it was Gross's idea to bring the two together, which is implied in Satie's letter to her of 15 October,[42] or Cocteau's, which his biographer proposes,[43] the two began to see each other regularly after this point. Satie's correspondence with Gross traces the history of their relationship, Satie's frustrations with Cocteau, and his intent to remain independent (presumably in musical matters), as well as their eventual success in attracting Diaghilev to the project in July 1916 and Picasso in August. *Parade* evolved not only as a transformation of the ill-fated *David* but also as a result of Satie's desire to write a new piece rather than make any preexisting music available to Cocteau.[44]

Satie's music helped Cocteau to go somewhat further in discovering what he truly valued. Like Stravinsky's, it was a reaction to impressionist vagueness: "without the sauce"—an expression he borrows from Rivière's review of *The Rite of Spring*.[45] It also "contradicted," for Satie knew he could not follow in the path of *Pelléas*.

37. Steegmuller, *Cocteau*, 73–84.

38. Cocteau to Stravinsky, in Steegmuller, *Cocteau*, 85–86.

39. Cocteau, *Le Coq*, 53–54.

40. Jean Cocteau, "Notes on Music," in school-type notebook, Carleton Lake Collection.

41. Valentine Gross to her mother, Zélie Gross, March 1914, Carleton Lake Collection.

42. Carleton Lake Collection.

43. Steegmuller, *Cocteau*, 102, 111. In an undated letter to Misia Sert, Cocteau writes, "Satie asked for my collaboration at the very moment when I was going to ask for his" (117).

44. Satie to Valentine Gross, 25 April 1916, Carleton Lake Collection. See also Steegmuller, *Cocteau*, 111.

45. Cocteau, *Le Coq*, 68. See Rivière, "Le Sacre du Printemps," 706.

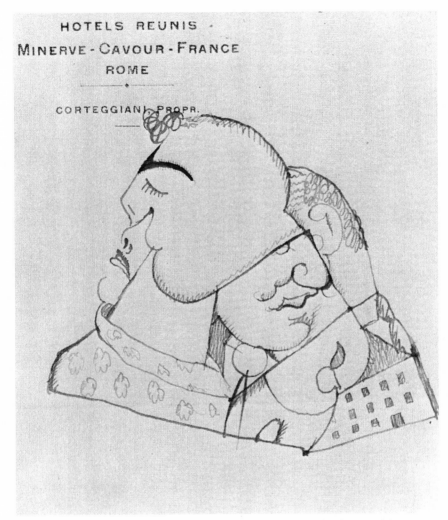

Figure 5.5. Cocteau, collaborators on *Parade*, 1917, pen and ink on writing paper.

Cocteau explains Satie's turn to writing counterpoint as "the only way to contradict harmonic refinement. . . . His friends scorn the fugue as an academic exercise, Satie works on it."[46]

The ultimate form of contradiction Cocteau found in Satie's music—his "opposition in a period of extreme refinement," his rejection of bourgeois values—was the aesthetic of simplicity, which Cocteau calls "the greatest audacity of our time. . . . Not a retreat, not a return to old simplicities, not a pastiche of the

46. Cocteau, "Présentation d'oeuvres."

harpsichordists." Satie's simplicity appeared new and "enriched" to Cocteau; in *Parade*, he thought of it as that of a mechanical toy.[47]

The reduction of materials this simplicity implies was already present in Stravinsky's music. But whereas "Stravinskysme risked pushing the young toward a riot of colors, brutalities, and cruelties that are not made for types like us," Satie's music seemed to Cocteau "white, and so delicate that in listening to it, one thinks about Nietzsche's phrase: ideas that change the face of things come from the wings of doves. . . . His music is finally a French music."[48] In his "Notes on Music," it is Satie whom Cocteau sees as capable of standing up to Wagner and who, then, becomes Cocteau's next "schoolteacher."[49]

What he learned from Satie, besides the value of simplicity, again comes from how he perceived Satie's relationship with his public. The public as a whole did not even know Satie. He had never written a major orchestra piece or an opera; and he spent much of his time in small cafés. From Cocteau's perspective, this protected Satie. "The café concert is often pure; the theater always corrupts . . . even a Stravinsky," he later wrote.[50] It was certainly not a question of the public deifying him but of Satie's attracting their interest. Listening to Satie play his *Pieces in the Form of a Pear* for piano four hands with Ricardo Viñes in 1915, Cocteau began to understand the value of humor in Satie's music, not only as tool with which to contradict people's expectations but also as a form of social power. Works such as *Airs to Make People Flee* (1897) helped Satie get people's attention. "They allowed him to stay alive . . . they protected him from hatred and from people tortured by the sublime who only judge a piece by its title." Cocteau also noticed that when Satie no longer needed humor, he no longer used it. There is none, Cocteau points out, in *Parade* (1917), *Socrate* (1918), or the *Nocturnes* (1919).[51]

When referring to Satie, Cocteau defines originality quite differently than he did when discussing Stravinsky:

> The profound originality of a Satie teaches young musicians in a way that
> doesn't imply they must abandon their own originality. Wagner, Stravinsky,

---

47. Cocteau, "Présentation d'oeuvres," *Le Coq*, 60.

48. Cocteau, "Présentation d'oeuvres." Of course, Cocteau was not alone at the time in using national identity as a way of attracting attention to a composer's work, of ascribing validity, even of hoping for a place in history through it. Debussy used the same tactic throughout. By 1915, to bolster his own identity as Rameau's successor in the realm of French composition, Debussy was willing to bury all French composers from Berlioz to his contemporaries with the claim that "since Rameau we don't have any clearly French tradition"; Claude Debussy, *Monsieur Croche et autres écrits*, ed. François Lesure (Paris: Gallimard, 1971), 260.

49. Fowlie, *Journals*, 38.

50. Cocteau, *Le Coq*, 62, 79.

51. Cocteau, "Présentation d'oeuvres"; see also *Le Coq*, 56–57.

FIGURE 5.6. Cocteau, a jazz bar, c. 1921, pen and India ink on paper over board.

and even Debussy, are beautiful octopuses. Whoever approaches them has a hard time extricating themselves from their tentacles: Satie points out an empty path where each one may freely leave his own footprints.[52]

Such a message suggests that Satie's example, more than that of others, provided Cocteau with the encouragement he needed to search out and pursue his own identity.

52. Cocteau, Le Coq, 59.

Satie's example, furthermore, succeeded in turning Cocteau's attention away from the narrowly defined milieux of the aristocrats and their obsession with glory toward the proletarian milieux and, especially, popular music. By the time he wrote *Le Coq et l'Arlequin* in 1918, Cocteau had become critical of the "exhausted public, seated on Louis XVI garlands, Venetian gondolas, soft couches, and oriental cushions. . . . On this diet, one digests in a hammock, one dozes off; one chases away what is really new like a fly; it disturbs."[53] Moreover, Cocteau began to realize that important groups in Paris were not part of such a public. With rare exceptions, the painters did not come to the Ballets Russes. "Montparnasse ignores *The Rite of Spring*."[54] At some point, Cocteau began to frequent different parts of town. In a draft of his "Why I Play Jazz," he mentions "nevermore having recourse to the old café of Verlaine and Moréas." There in "a practical part of town" he found the newest popular music of his time, jazz.[55] This "curious amalgam of the rhythm of machines and the rhythm of Negroes—of the banal cry of the poster and the advertisement of New York and the wooden idols/fetishes from the Ivory Coast" seemed to Cocteau the ultimate reaction to the "sluggishness of impressionism" and the "haziness of symbolism."[56]

What appealed to him in this music, as in that of Stravinsky and Satie, was again its effect on the public. Note his description of the "jazz band" in one of his notebooks:

> Little black orchestras where a barman, surrounded by the accessories for making resonant noises, banging, and whistling, composes cocktails to swallow . . . all this resulting in a furor of sound. Rimbaud's drunken boat that predicts the future in the travel books becomes Cendrars's drunken train (free association, Jules Verne).[57]

The two principal "advantages" of such music, he points out in another notebook, are that, first, "it makes so much noise that it suppresses any literary conversation," and second, "it prevents people from taking me seriously."[58] Given his description of the time he spent with such people as Anna de Noailles, these state-

---

53. Cocteau, *Le Coq*, 88.

54. Cocteau, *Le Coq*, 93–94.

55. Jean Cocteau, "Pourquoi je joue du jazz," "Miscellany: Drafts and Notes," manuscript, Carleton Lake Collection.

56. Jean Cocteau, "Notebook on Art, Music, and Poetry," manuscript, Carleton Lake Collection. Note that even though Cocteau saw jazz, the music halls, and the circus as totally different kinds of artistic experiences from those offered by impressionist or symbolist works, Debussy, too, looked to the same sources as fodder for his imagination, and many of his works employ popular tunes or humoristic gestures inspired by those nonelitist milieux.

57. Cocteau, "Notebook on Art, Music, and Poetry."

58. Cocteau, "Pourquoi je joue du jazz."

ments represent quite a change of attitude and values. "Interminable dialogues" about "grandeur" and "glory" were not only out of place but also physically impossible in such a context.

As Cocteau explains at the end of *Le Coq et l'Arlequin*, the period 1910–20 was for him one of "transformation": "I was maturing, I was in a growth spurt. It was only natural that after a period of being frivolous, spread very thin, and overly talkative would follow an excessive need for soberness, method, and silence."[59] In the music of Les Six, especially Auric and Poulenc, Cocteau found a similar attitude toward popular milieux, popular music, and art that is "stripped of the superfluous." Since he wrote *Le Coq* after "all kinds of conversations about music" with Satie and Auric,[60] it is not clear who had a greater influence on whom, the musicians on Cocteau or he on them. He articulates their shared aesthetic attitudes— "the brief, the gay, the sad without romance." He presages many of their interwar preoccupations: "orchestras without the caress of the strings. A rich *orphéon* of woodwinds, brass, and percussion," writing for a "mechanical organ"—the pianola, as it turns out.[61] But, as he once pointed out, "I am the friend of the group, not its mentor."[62]

His work with these musicians helped him to clarify his own aesthetic goals and to find a revolutionary banner that distinguished him from his contemporaries; yet his interaction with them seems to have been limited to formulating their commonly held aesthetics and to providing them with an outlet for their music. In other words, it does not appear that he had any direct influence on their composition per se. Milhaud, for example, regretted how Cocteau used his score in the "spectacle-concert" *Le Boeuf sur le toit* (1919).[63] Rather than constructing a scenario about a carnival celebration in Rio de Janeiro, as Milhaud intended for his already-composed music, Cocteau devised a farce set in New York during Prohibition. This "Nothing-Doing Bar," as it was called for the English public, had little to do with the Brazilian popular songs, the tangos, and the sambas in Milhaud's music.

Their next collaborative venture, *Les Mariés de la Tour Eiffel* (1921), also involved a scenario and text by Cocteau, music this time by five of the six members of the group, and costumes designed by Valentine Gross's husband, Jean Hugo. The story of a petit-bourgeois marriage at the Eiffel Tower, conceived as an eighteenth-

---

59. Cocteau, *Le Coq*, 97–98.

60. Auric, "Avec les musiciens," 62.

61. Cocteau, *Le Coq*, 64–65, 69.

62. Cocteau, "Pourquoi je joue du jazz."

63. Steegmuller quotes Milhaud from his memoirs: "Forgetting that I had written *Choéphores*, the public and the critics decided that I was a comical and entertaining composer . . . me who hated the comical and who, in composing *Le Boeuf sur le toit*, aspired only to writing a gay diversion, without pretension, in memory of the Brazilian rhythms that had so seduced me and great gods! never made me laugh" (*Cocteau*, 180).

century-style *pièce-ballet,* plays up the nostalgic, the gay, the banal, and the absurd but incorporates music only as a diversion. Cocteau saw it as "a secret marriage between ancient tragedy and the review from the end of the year, the chorus, the music-hall number"—in effect, a new genre involving theater, acrobatics, panto-mime, drama, orchestra, and speech. He thereby considered it not only "my most beautiful toy" but also "the first work in which I owe nothing to no one, which is unlike any other work and in which I found my code."[64]

For the participating composers, however, *Les Mariés* represented a far less radical gesture. Of the nine short compositions, the only piece that functions as more than incidental music is by Arthur Honegger, the composer least sympathetic to Cocteau. During his "Funeral March of the General"—a farce incorporating both a theme from Milhaud's previously heard "Nuptial March," only much slower and in a minor key, and, at its climax, a waltz tune from *Faust*—someone in the play cries out "Finally! there's some music."[65] The other musical interludes make little if any musical commentary on the scenario. The score remained in oblivion until the 1960s, and the group never worked together again.

The exchange with Auric, Cocteau's favorite Les Six composer and the person to whom he dedicated *Le Coq,* was of a different nature from his exchange with these other composers, yet still not truly significant from a musical perspective. Satie and Picasso did not allow *Parade* to turn out the way Cocteau had envisaged it, with the music serving merely as background to "suggestive noises" such as sirens, type-writers, and dynamos. Although these sounds do appear in the work, Cocteau claims that *Parade* was "so far from what I would have wanted that I wouldn't go see it in the hall."[66] Stravinsky did not actually work with Cocteau until *Oedipus Rex* in 1926–27, when, according to Stravinsky in a 1965 film, Stravinsky apparently dictated both story and tone to the poet and rejected Cocteau's first two versions until he got what he wanted. In Auric, Cocteau found a composer willing to accommodate his desires, but there was still very little interaction between the two. As Auric recalls, "He told me simply, evidently: in such-and-such a passage, I imagine a music with this kind of character. It ended there. When I played my music, when he heard my music, there was no discussion of any sort between us. He was happy with what I had done."[67] For *La Belle et la Bête* (1946), Cocteau did not even want to hear what music Auric wrote until it was being recorded after the

64. Cocteau's discussion of the work as a "spectacle" first appeared in *La Danse* 9; see Jacques Pradère, "*Les Mariès de la Tour Eiffel* du group des Six," note to Darius Milhaud, *Les Mariès de la Tour Eiffel,* Orchestre de l'O.R.T.F., dir. Milhaud, Ades 14.146-2 (compact disc), reissue of 1966 recording. Steegmuller, *Cocteau,* 204; Fowlie, *Journals,* 38.

65. Darius Milhaud, "L'Enregistrement des '*Mariès,* '" program note (compact disc), Ades 14.146-2.

66. Cocteau, *Le Coq,* 66–67.

67. Auric, "Avec les musiciens," 68

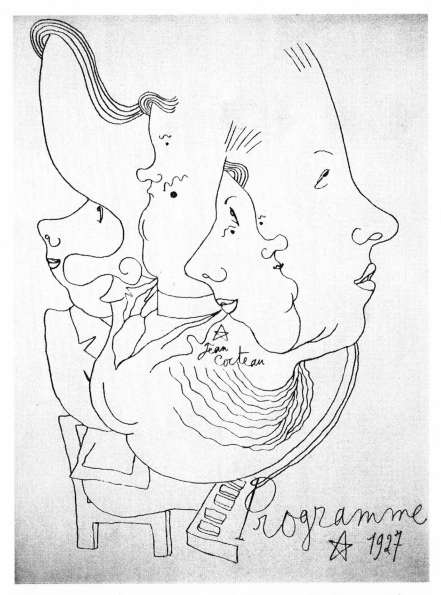

FIGURE 5.7. Cocteau, program cover, 1927. In this image of Les Six, one can discern not only the various members of the group but also the group as a whole in the shape of a large ear.

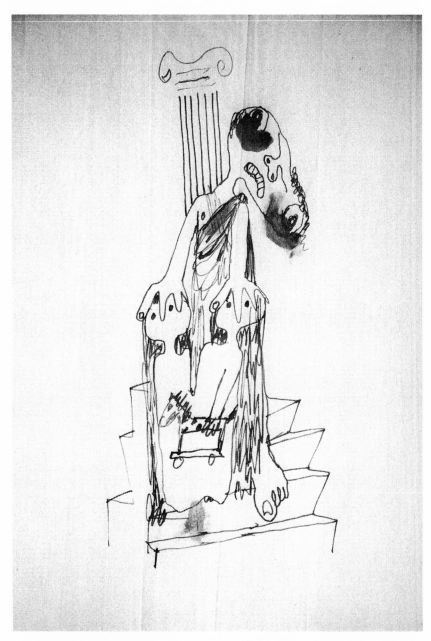

FIGURE 5.8. Cocteau, Oedipus Rex, c. 1937, pen and ink on tracing paper. Oedipus stands in front of an ionic column, his eyes disfigured with splotches of ink. According to Tony Clark, the two children represent Cocteau and Stravinsky, who, having differed about the production of the opera-oratorio, realize that it is more important than the two of them.

film had been made. The only mark Cocteau seems to have made on the music used in his films is his occasional determination of the order in which its parts would be played, as was the case for *Les Parents terribles* (1948).

"It is not easy to form oneself. To reform oneself is harder still," Cocteau recounts in his journal.[68] What makes Cocteau's musical tastes so illuminating, why they help him build his own distinct yet still socially bounded identity, and the reason that the change in these tastes is so revealing is that they reflect and express the paradoxes of the artist in the social world in which Cocteau moved. Even as the poet surprises, stuns, or insults, he appeals to what his audiences seek from him. The notion of originality—first downplayed in his association with Reynaldo Hahn and then defined as contradiction and glorified in his cult of Stravinsky—almost had to go both ways, as the old debate between *les anciens et les modernes* was being rekindled at the same time that "the new" was becoming increasingly successful as a marketing tool. The juxtaposition of the external and the internal, of what the public sees and what the poet wants it to see, the replacement of the highly refined with the simple, the serious with the humorous, literary conversation with noise, the corrupt with the pure—these paradoxical oppositions, characteristic of his life and work, still suggest an artist who wants control; a sublimated control, it is true, that is not unlike that his aristocratic audiences aspired to, even as their social and political status was increasingly negligible. Both Cocteau and his audiences were still ideologically committed to the aristocracy of the gifted. Whether art is "a kind of game and the idea of struggle" irrelevant, as in Cocteau's early career,[69] or rather is a form of insult, a passageway to the new, as it later became for him, he as an artist wants to drive that automobile, with the public following behind by bus. He still wants admiration rather than criticism.

To what extent the self-appointed avant-garde represents quasi-aristocratic values and mores is not the subject here; Poulenc's own statements about music and the subjects he chose to set to music reveal the direction this Les Six composer was moving. But one wonders about the extent to which the values that Cocteau assigned to music during this period sheltered him from the fiercely political issues of the day. Composers found ways both to confront their public yet remain accepted. Did Cocteau realize that the sanctity and "purity" of music, especially certain new music, could help him to construct an apparently apolitical identity, one that reached full bloom in his works based on classical mythologies? I would argue that the last words of his musical manifesto, *Le Coq et l'Arlequin*, address this very point: "Shelter well your gift of making miracles," because "if they know that you are a missionary, they will cut out your tongue and tear off your fingernails."[70]

68. Fowlie, *Journals*, 38.
69. Fowlie, *Journals*, 41.
70. Cocteau, *Le Coq*, 82.

6. Inventing a Tradition

John Cage's "Composition in Retrospect"

N THE OPENING SENTENCE OF A LITTLE-KNOWN TEXT, "An Autobiographical Statement," first delivered as a paper in Japan in 1989, John Cage recalls once asking Arragon, the historian, "how history was written," to which Arragon responded, "You have to invent it."[1] In the latter part of his life, Cage gave substantial attention to his own personal history. He has made numerous efforts to acknowledge his debt to others and the family of kindred spirits with whom he identified. For example, he made no secret of the fact that he wrote his *4′33″* after seeing Robert Rauschenberg's white paintings and his *Music of Changes* after hearing Morton Feldman's graphic music, that he thought of micro-macro rhythmic structure in his music as a response to Schönberg's structural harmony, and his mesostic texts as examples of Marshall McLuhan's "brushing information" against information.[2] In the Harvard lectures, *I–VI*, selections from his favorite writers, musicians, artists, and philosophers make up an entire section of the book, attesting to an interest in tradition per se, in the conscious and explicit transmission of ideas from one generation to another.

The question that interests me, however, is not which tradition, European or American, helps us to understand Cage better. That answer is surely the interplay of both, including Asian religions and philosophy. Rather, it is Cage's relationship

This essay originally appeared in *John Cage: Composed in America*, ed. Marjorie Perloff and Charles Junkerman (Chicago: University of Chicago Press, 1994), 125–43; it is included here by permission, copyright 1994 The University of Chicago. An earlier version was delivered, with John Cage in attendance, at the conference "John Cage at Stanford," Stanford Humanities Center, Stanford University, 28 January 1992.

1. John Cage, "An Autobiographical Statement," *Southwest Review* 76 (winter 1990): 59–76. This text, which Cage considered a "work in progress," he delivered first in Japan in November 1989 as a response to having received the Kyoto Prize and later at Southern Methodist University, on 17 April 1990, as part of year-long celebration of the work of Robert Rauschenberg. I am grateful to Marjorie Perloff for bringing it to my attention.

2. Cage, "An Autobiographical Statement," 66.

to the idea of tradition and how he may see himself and his work in the light of history. Cage's own tradition begins with his father, whom he describes as an inventor, and his mother, who taught him "a sense of society."[3] To what extent, then, does the composer identify the notion of tradition with that of invention and social responsibility?

Studying his 1981 mesostic text "Composition in Retrospect," among other works, has led me to thinking about Cage as consciously working to invent a tradition that reflects the way he made, discovered, invented music, that is, a tradition based on the same principles and methods he used in his music. The opening of the IMITATION mesostic in this text says as much: [4]

> the past must be Invented
> the future Must be
> revIsed
> doing boTh
> mAkes
> whaT
> the present Is
> discOvery
> Never stops

Cage does not invent without borrowing from various sources, of course, but unlike many others, he does so without the intention of elaborating on, extending, or surpassing the traditions to which he makes explicit reference in his works.

How does one produce, or invent, a tradition? In his introduction to a volume of essays on the subject, Eric Hobsbawm defines an invented tradition as

> a set of practices, normally governed by overtly or tacitly accepted rules and of a ritual or symbolic nature, which seek to inculcate certain values and norms of behavior by repetition, which automatically implies continuity with the past. In fact, where possible, they normally attempt to establish continuity with a suitable historic past. . . . In short, they are responses to novel situations which take the form of reference to old situations, or which establish their own part by quasi-obligatory repetition.[5]

For each of the elements of this definition of an invented tradition, that is, as having practices or rules often with a ritual or symbolic nature, as inculcating certain values, and as repeating suitable elements from the past, it is possible to find some-

---

3. Cage, "An Autobiographical Statement," 59.

4. John Cage, "Compositions in Retrospect," in *X, Writings '79–'82* (Middletown, Conn.: Wesleyan University Press, 1983) (hereafter *X*), 145.

5. Eric Hobsbawm, introduction to Eric Hobsbawm and Terence Ranger, *The Invention of Tradition* (Cambridge: Cambridge University Press, 1983), 1, 2, 4.

thing similar in "Composition in Retrospect." In this conscious backward glance over his years of music-making, John Cage outlines the set of practices and rules he has followed, many of which have a ritual nature; in most cases, he references the inspiring contemporaries and predecessors who, through their example, have helped him come to understand them; and he promotes a message, eventually speaking entirely in the imperative voice in the final section and concluding: "we musT do the impossible / rid the world of nAtions / briNging / the play of intelligent anarcHy / into a world Environment / that workS so well everyone lives as he needs."[6]

The process of inventing a tradition begins with Cage contemplating his own personal history, and distrusting his memory (*X*, 124):

My
mEmory
of whaT
Happened
is nOt
what happeneD

i aM struck
by thE
facT
tHat what happened
is mOre conventional
than what i remembereD

iMitations
invErsions
reTrograde forms
motives tHat are varied
Or
not varieD

once Music
bEgins
iT remains
He said the same
even variatiOn is repetition
some things changeD others not (schoenberg)

<hr />

6. John Cage, "Composition in Retrospect," in *X*, 151. Earlier in this text and elsewhere, Cage credits Buckminster Fuller with aspects of this idea. See also "John Cage. Conversation with Joan Retallack," *Aerial* 6/7 (1991): 97–98.

Cage seems to suggest that conventions are inevitably present in whatever one does, including music. Any method, especially that which begins with an exploration of memory, must begin with an awareness of them. As an example, he credits Schönberg with teaching him the preeminence of repetition in music (perhaps as in life). This passage sets the exploratory as well as didactic tone of the rest of the work, as well as the practice of citing suitable precedents for the ideas he wishes to promote. "Once Music / bEgins / iT remains / He said the same."

In the next METHOD mesostic, Cage tells the focus of his inquiry, the reason for retracing his own past (*X*, 124):

what i aM

rEmembering

incorrecTly to be sure

is wHatever

deviated frOm

orDinary practice

It is not so much the conventions encoded in memory that interest him—"iMitations / invErsions / reTrograde forms," forms and syntaxes that experienced listeners would recognize. It is the conventions of ordinary practice,[7] those that govern his compositional process.

Cage's ordinary practice begins with a method, and proceeds, as does his text, to the other aspects of his compositional process. As within the METHOD mesostic, Cage uses explicit references to ideas or actions of others to illustrate what he means by structure, intention, discipline, indeterminacy, interpenetration, imitation, and devotion in the mesostics that follow. This presentation, explanation, and citation of examples for each compositional element is characteristic of the invention of traditions, a process Hobsbawm describes as one of formalization, ritualization, and reference to the past.

In the STRUCTURE mesostic, Cage cites the example of Satie, like him a composer fascinated by numbers, symmetry, and proportion, in other words, with what Cage calls structure (*X*, 125-26):

the diviSion of a whole

inTo

paRts

dUration

not frequenCy

Taken

as the aspect of soUnd

bRinging about

a distinction bEtween

---

7. Note that this is also Hobsbawm's word.

> both phraSes
> and large secTions
> · · · · · · · · · · · · · · ·
>   thUs
>   a Canvas
>   of Time is provided hospitable to both noise
>   and mUsical tones upon which
> music may be dRawn

In the introduction to "James Joyce, Marcel Duchamp, Erik Satie: An Alphabet,"[8] Cage says that he analyzed Satie's music and found it "structured rhythmically." But it is not at all clear that Satie "divided fouR / foUrs into one two and one (four eight and four)" exactly as Cage asserts. The point is not what Satie did but how Cage uses the Satie example to help him define structure in these terms.

In the INTENTION mesostic, as in the DISCIPLINE one, Cage cites a variety of exercises others taught him. The first is a Zen exercise he uses to illustrate what he means by intention—"purposeful purposelessness," "sometImes / written Out / determiNate" (X, 128):

> sometImes
> just a suggestioN
> i found iT
> workEd
> therefor i Nap
> pounding The
> rIce
> withOut
> liftiNg my hand

The DISCIPLINE section consists not of metaphorical exercises such as this one but of practical techniques any one of which should help to do the following (X, 129):

> to sober and quiet the minD
> so that It
> iS
> in aCcord
> wIth
> what haPpens
> the worLd
> around It
> opeN
> rathEr than
> closeD

8. John Cage, "James Joyce, Marcel Duchamp, Erik Satie: An Alphabet," in X, 53.

This section is three times as long as the others, giving Cage the space to describe three exercises "of a ritual or symbolic nature," each of which leads to a similar result. The first is another Zen exercise, "sitting crosslegged." Although Cage admits he never did this,[9] he learned from Daisetz Teitaro Suzuki that the attitude underlying such a practice could help him achieve his purpose of getting away "from lIkes / aNd / dislikEs."

The second exercise is a counterpoint problem Schönberg once presented to him. In failing to solve it, Cage was forced to begin to develop his own philosophy (*X*, 132):

Devote myself

to askIng

queStions

Chance

determIned

answers'll oPen

my mind to worLd around

at the same tIme

chaNging my music

sElf-alteration not self-expression

Through discipline, Cage suggests, one can become open and prepare for change.

In the third part of the DISCIPLINE mesostic, Cage remembers an exercise the painter Mark Tobey once gave his drawing students. This suggests how altering a context through some disciplined activity can alter one's perceptions (*X*, 134).

stuDents

were In

poSitions

that disConnected

mInd and hand

the drawings were suddenly contemPorary

no Longer

fIxed

iN

tastE

As with sitting cross-legged and using chance techniques, this change of position helped put the students "out of touch" with themselves "dIscovery / suddeN / opEning // of Doors."

---

9. Cage, "Autobiographical Statement," 64.

Observing Cage build his tradition with what he learned from others, we find certain attitudes. First, his borrowing is conscious, as it has been for many modernists. As different as they were in other regards, both Schönberg and Stravinsky borrowed extensively from their teachers, friends, and predecessors. Some musicologists think of "the mainstream of musical modernism" as a preoccupation with the past.[10]

Second, Cage claims that "of the critical incidents, persons, and events that have influenced my life and work, the true answer is all of the incidents were critical, all of the people influenced me, everything that happened and that is still happening influences me."[11] The inclusion of newspaper citations in the source material of *I–VI* might reflect his desire to substantiate this position. But when it comes to citing the actual people who influenced him, Cage takes another position in "Composition in Retrospect." Here he restricts himself largely to those who have stood the test of time, "great" people, if you will. He says his memory cannot be trusted, but, except for two performers, there is a noticeable lack of reference to lesser known or unknown people. Why, for example, is Gira Sarabhai, an Indian singer and tabla player, not acknowledged as the source of the line that opens the DISCIPLINE mesostic? In his "Autobiographical Statement," Cage says he learned from her that "the purpose of music is to sober and quiet the mind, thus making it susceptible to divine influences." It is not that Cage wishes to use the phrase to promote a slightly different message, for the lines that follow, being "in aCcord / wIth / what haPpens," imply a kind of spirituality, whether this opens one to divine influences or to "whatever happens next." Does Cage think the reference would be lost on most readers, and that he does acknowledge the source, after all, in his autobiographical statement? I am not questioning Cage's judgment, for "Composition in Retrospect" is an art work; I am merely observing that, with the exception of the two performers, no one who is not already well known appears in this text.[12] Like Stravinsky's *Petrushka*, which contains traces of anonymous folk melodies and a popular tune the composer once heard someone singing in the street, Cage's work may bear the imprint of numerous sources other than those he cites, but their names will not be part of the tradition he is constructing.

10. Joseph Straus, *Remaking the Past* (Cambridge, Mass.: Harvard University Press, 1990), 2.

11. Cage, "Autobiographical Statement," 59.

12. It is also interesting to note that in his "Autobiographical Statement" Cage also tends to choose well-known people to cite or exemplify a point. In discussing his *Freeman Etudes*, for example, he refers to a 1988 performance by the leader of the Arditti Quartet, Irvine Arditti, rather than to those of other violinists, perhaps less well known to the general public, who may have played the same pieces for years and even recorded them (for example, Janos Negyesy has collaborated with the composer on numerous occasions and recorded the first set of *Freeman Etudes* in 1985).

Cage's attitude toward those who have influenced him and his way of appropriating ideas from them, however, distinguish him from many other modernist composers. He is not a Boulez, who, in works such as *Le Visage nuptial*, borrows phrases, formal ideas, and rhythmic gestures from Stravinsky and Messiaen to impose his own will on their accomplishments or, in Harold Bloom's words, "to clear imaginative space" for himself.[13] Even though Schönberg, in Cage's words, "haD always seemed to me / superIor / to other human beingS," he does not repeat what Schönberg taught him in order to reinterpret him. He does not reiterate Schönberg's notion of variation as repetition to try to assert his own version of the same, and thus his own priority, power, and strength. Cage's sense of history does not require clearing the way, surpassing what has come before in order to acknowledge that the world has progressed, that one exists.

Cage admittedly worships some of his sources. Whether those he cites were or were not, are or are not heroic in any way, he wants them to be considered examples, sources of wisdom, meriting the highest respect. His reference is almost always to the third person singular, and his tone never critical in "Composition in Retrospect." What seems important to Cage is that their ideas, with which he feels great affinity, inspire respect in his listeners and readers, the same respect and admiration they may have inspired in him.

There is at least some "creative misreading" of the sources, to be sure, in that Cage consistently emphasizes the importance of certain traits and ideas in his sources rather than others. Other aspects of Schönberg and Satie, for example, would suggest a very different portrait, as would referencing Mozart or Schubert instead of Schönberg when referring to the "micro-macrocosmic rhythmic structure" of some music. Leonard Meyer's rhythmic analyses,[14] for example, suggest that the idea of "the large parts of a composition [having] the same proportion as the phrases of a single unit"[15] is hardly a Schönbergian idea. But this matters little, as Cage is seeking not the assertion of power but, in Hobsbawm's terms, a "suitable past" from which to invent a tradition of which he is the logical heir, the next voice. A Cagean "past must be invented."

Cage's manner of inventing a tradition involves not so much extending others' ideas as re-presenting them, bringing them again to life, in part because they have become and represent aspects of Cage himself. In the introduction to "An Alphabet," Cage explains the concept behind incorporating long excerpts from the writings of Satie, Duchamp, and Joyce: "It is possible to imagine not a vocabulary but an alphabet by means of which we spell our lives." And even though he claims

13. For an analysis of Boulez's music from this perspective, see "Postmodernism, Narrativity, and the Art of Memory," chapter 2 here.

14. See Leonard Meyer, "The Rhythmic Structure of Music," and his analysis of Mozart's music, *Explaining Music* (Berkeley: University of California Press, 1973), chapter 2.

15. Cage, "Autobiographical Statement," 61.

he did not follow this idea in this text, he later admits: "The effect for me of Duchamp's work was to so change my way of seeing that I became in my way a Duchamp unto myself. I could find as he did for himself the space and time of my own experience."[16]

In "Composition in Retrospect," the first time Cage uses the first-person-singular "I" to refer to anyone other than himself is when he cites Schönberg and Thoreau in the middle of the DISCIPLINE mesostic (*X*, 131):

after eight or nine solutions i saiD
    not quIte
        Sure of myself there aren't any more
      that's Correct
      now I want you
        to Put in words
    the principLe
    that underlIes
  all of the solutioNs
      hE

In an interlocking manner, this text alternates between "i" and "he," "i" and "you," "he" and "me," "I" and again "he." At the same time the referent of the "i" goes back and forth between Cage and Schönberg, student and teacher, until Cage takes over the role of his teacher and, "Perhaps now / thirty years Later," answers his own question, "as a comPoser / i shouLd / gIve up / makiNg choicEs."

The second use of "i" to refer to someone other than himself comes in the mesostic that follows (*X*, 133):

thoreau saiD the same
    thIng
over a hundred yearS ago
i want my writing to be as Clear
    as water I can see through
  so that what I exPerienced
    is toLd
    wIthout
  my beiNg in any way
    in thE way

Here the sympathy Cage feels toward a predecessor turns into an identity. When he might like to have said something similar, Cage takes on Thoreau's voice as if it is

---

16. Cage, "James Joyce, Marcel Duchamp, Erik Satie," 53.

his own. The passage of time—"over a hundred years"—is thus irrelevant. Even though he has known personally many of the other sources mentioned in this text, Cage merges his own voice explicitly only with that of Thoreau.

Each of these citations serves not just to re-present and illustrate certain ideas dear to Cage but other purposes as well. Hobsbawm argues that "all invented traditions, as far as possible, use history as a legitimator of action and cement of group cohesion."[17] Cage, too, uses his sources to claim authority, to legitimate his concerns. But perhaps he also uses them to get people to pay attention to concepts whose importance he may feel equals if not surpasses that of his own voice. The multiple-voiced text itself exemplifies a political concept that lies at the heart of Cage's work. If he is here preaching a world where everyone should be able to find and make use of what he or she needs, perhaps this text can be read as an example of that principle in his life. But I am getting ahead of myself.

In the mesostics that follow the DISCIPLINE ones, Cage continues to refer to and cite sources to illustrate his ideas. Increasingly, however, as his message merges with theirs (and theirs with his), the first-person-plural "we" appears, and the message becomes both more pointed and more personal. Cage uses "we" briefly in reference to himself and the other students in Schönberg's counterpoint class, but it is in the opening of the INDETERMINACY mesostic that he uses it multiple times and for a certain effect (X, 138).

> you can't be serIous she said
> we were driNking
> a recorD
> was bEing played
> noT
> in thE place
> wheRe we were
> but in another rooM
> I had
> fouNd it interesting
> And had asked
> what musiC it was
> not to supplY

To explain what he means by indeterminacy, Cage makes reference to his own personal experiences and appeals to his reader's as well. From these experiences, he then rapidly begins to draw a number of insights. Using the inclusive "we," he tries to get us to accept these ideas as facts (X, 140):

17. Hobsbawm, introduction, 12.

                              musIc
                        Never stops it is we who turn away
                  again the worlD around
                        silEnce
       sounds are only bubbles on iTs
                        surfacE
                  they buRst to disappear (thoreau)
            when we Make
                        musIc
          we merely make somethiNg
                        thAt
                        Can
            more naturallY be heard than seen or touched

                  that makes It possible
            to pay atteNtion
                        to Daily work or play
                  as bEing
                  noT
            what wE think it is
            but ouR goal
       all that's needed is a fraMe
       a change of mental attItude
            amplificatioN
                        wAiting for a bus
       we're present at a Concert
                        suddenlY we stand on a work of art the pavement

Cage may nod to Thoreau in passing, but for the most part he concentrates here on expressing his own insight. After telling us what is misguided in what we may think, he tries to give us a new "frame," that which he has discovered from his own experience. He hopes this "change of mental attitude" will affect us as it did him one day while "waiting for a bus." The unspoken reference is to the early 1940s, when, as he was standing on 57th Street in New York City and thinking about the Mark Tobey paintings he'd just been looking at, he noticed "he had the same pleasure looking at the pavement."[18] By drawing the analogy, Cage suggests we might be able to have a similar experience with music.

With this new "frame" in place and the increasingly prevalent use of "we," Cage begins to define "ouR goal" more and more precisely. "We," the reader/listeners, are supposed to join in the invention of the tradition through adopting the beliefs

18. In the interview with Joan Retallack (see note 6 here), Cage explains the incident that leads him to link the "pavement" with discussions about art. See 107–8.

or doctrines Cage begins to put forth. In the INTERPRETATION mesostic, which his own work *Musicircus* illustrates, Cage gives his first dictum, again in the voice of another, Marcel Duchamp: "the resPonsibility / of Each / persoN is / marcEl duchamp said / To complete / the woRk himself" (*X*, 142). Cage makes some suggestions for how to help people accomplish this goal, both musically and politically, sometimes referring to ideas of Buckminster Fuller. But the most important point is in the recurring lines that end the section: "we need tO / chaNge."

To justify change, the "new frame" he proposes for us, and his invention of a tradition, Cage invokes the notion of "devotion." This idea describes the life of the pianist Grete Sultan, for whom he wrote "thE first of thirty-two études." Her devotion is an attitude, an acceptance, something that is not limited to the music of any one style or period. Grete "is Not as i am / just concerneD / with nEw music / she loVes the past," "she surrounDs / hErself / with mozart beethoVen bach / all Of / The best of the past." But, unlike many others, she also "loves new music / seeing nO real difference / beTween / some of It / and the classics she's sO devoted to" (*X*, 147–48). Her devotion to both old and new music thus throws into question the preeminence of old traditions. If someone can love both, then why, Cage seems to ask, should people be so reluctant to change, to accept the new? Given that this idea appears as one of the elements of the compositional process and near the end of this text, it is as if Cage believes that devotion is needed to complete a work.

In the final mesostic, CIRCUMSTANCES, Cage becomes the authority for deciding what should change. In Hobsbawm's terms, he here tries to "inculcate values and behavior," but not as he previously does by referring explicitly to someone else (although, as I wrote earlier, the final section does bear the influence of Zen and Fuller). This section consists of a series of directives concerning not only music—how to finish a composition—but also society and how to live in it. First, he addresses us in the imperative voice: "aCt / In / accoRd / with obstaCles . . . if you doN't have enough time / to aCcomplish / what you havE in mind / con / Sider the work finished . . . study beIng / inteRrupted / take telephone Calls / as Unexpected pleasures / free the Mind / from itS desire / To / concentrAte . . . if you're writing a pieCe . . . take the aMount of the money . . . and divide iT to determine / the number of pAges." Then he tells us explicitly what we must do: "aCceptance of whatever / mUst / be coMplemented / by the refuSal / of everyThing / thAt's / iNtolerable . . . we musT do the impossible / rid the world of nAtions . . . [so] everyone lives as he needs" (*X*, 149–51).

The last line is an implicit reference to the last sentence of "An Alphabet," wherein Duchamp expresses his feelings about having undergone a change, that is, having become a ghost (or, one might say, a spirit). He has no regrets: "i weLcome whatever happens next" (*X*, 101). Cage here seems to suggest that if we change as he proposes, we, like Duchamp, will not regret it either. This last line also refers to the opening mesostic of "Composition in Retrospect," wherein Cage was expressing a concern for specific elements of the past, "what happened." Here, however, the focus is on the present tense and on openness toward the future, "whatever happens next."

The tradition Cage thus invents, with its sources in both the West and East, is full of irony. He demands change—a quintessentially Western preoccupation. But unlike many of his western European contemporaries, he does not feel the pressure to change as a desire to differentiate himself from his predecessors. He does not need difference to secure his own identity. What he wishes to transmit to the next generation is what he shares with others. In some ways, his philosophy is more Eastern than Western, in that he advocates accepting the past as integral to the present, instead of relating to it as something to surpass; in other ways, it is neither, and one accepts the coexistence and interpenetration in time and place of many traditions.

This tradition resembles that advocated by Emerson in his essay "The American Scholar,"[19] in which he refers artists to "the mind of the Past," especially books, as the best kind of influence. "Instead of being its own seer," Emerson wrote, "let it receive from another mind its truth." Cage, too, turns to the spirit of his predecessors as sources of truth. His work is full of citations, as we have seen, ranging from Emerson and Thoreau to Buckminster Fuller and Marshall McLuhan. Perhaps it is fair to suggest that Cage's interest in keeping his chosen predecessors' spirits alive may be linked to his desire for his own spirit to live on and in a similar manner—through his readers/listeners.

Like Emerson, Cage believes the artist has a duty "to cheer, to raise, and to guide men." This comes from living as opposed to just thinking—"livingry" as opposed to "killingry, " when Cage uses Fuller to turn the tone political. By assimilating, in Emerson's words, "all the ability of the time, all the contributions of the past, all the hopes of the future," such an artist can be "the world's eye" and "the world's heart."

Given the importance of Emerson for Cage,[20] and what he says he learned from his mother and father, it is no surprise that two attitudes emerge as characteristic

19. These shared attitudes also include an interest in nature. To the "Man thinking" or artist, Emerson in "The American Scholar" recommends the study of nature. When Cage came to reject music's purpose as communication, he turned to similar ideas in the works of the Indian scholar Ananda Coomaraswammy, from whom he learned that "the responsibility of the artist is to imitate nature in her manner of operation." See Cage, "Autobiographical Statement," 62.

20. In the introduction to his Harvard lectures, *I–VI* (Cambridge, Mass.: Harvard University Press, 1990), 3, Cage claims he had little use for Emerson; however, it is obvious that Thoreau, whom Cage so admired, was greatly influenced by Emerson. Given this, and the points of similarity here argued, it is clear we should take Emerson more seriously in examining the sources of Cage's ideas. It is worth noting that Emerson and Thoreau were among the first Americans to take inspiration from Far-Eastern philosophies.

of the Cagean tradition: social responsibility and an inventive spirit—inspired by others. His mesostic texts present one emanation of these ideas. In the INTEN-TION mesostic of "Composition in Retrospect," Cage writes of "togetherNess" and of wanting to be "a member Of society / able to fulfill a commissioN / to satIsfy / a particular Need." (X, 127–28) Writing "globally" in these texts, "letting the words come from here and there through chance operations in a source text,"[21] Cage gives poetic form to "the sense of society" his mother inspired in him, to his understanding of the "global village" and "spaceship earth."

In his mesostic text "Overpopulation and Art," written for the Stanford Humanities Center festival (January 1992), Cage continues this tradition. Here we find the spirit of his inventive father, who "was able to find solutions for problems of various kinds" and told him "if someone says 'can't' that shows you what to do."[22] Likewise, there is Buckminster Fuller, very much like Cage's father,[23] who "is deAd / but his spirit is Now more than ever . . . Alive . . . let us nOt forget / we are now haVing to / continuE / his woRk." As his predecessors might have done, Cage puts forth a series of radical ideas for transforming contemporary life—"24 hour usE of facilities," " stOpping / the removal of fossil fuEls / fRom the earth," "the remoVal / of nations thE / Removal of schools . . . Putting / the prOcess of learning / in the hands of the Person who is doing it," "stop asking / how can i make a liVing and start asking what is it / that i lovE." Whether impractical or not, these suggestions betray hope in "the future's future" and an attempt to find "changing solutions to changing problems" in the world through the spirit of invention.[24]

Cage's music, too, reflects this inventive spirit and social responsibility. In his "Autobiographical Statement," he cites Oskar Fischinger: "Everything in the world has its own spirit which can be released by setting it into vibration." The importance Cage gives to this statement suggests that when he speaks of his music as vibrations,[25] he is perhaps referring to music's capacity to engender spirit.

21. Cage, "Autobiographical Statement," 67.

22. Cage, "Autobiographical Statement," 59.

23. Cage, "Autobiographical Statement," 65. When Cage first met Fuller at Black Mountain College, he said Fuller made him think of his father when he said, "I only learn from my mistakes."

24. John Cage, "Overpopulation and Art," in John Cage: Composed in America, 28–30, 33.

25. At the end of his "Autobiographical Statement," Cage writes: "We are living in a period in which many people have changed their minds about what the use of music is or could be for them. Something that doesn't speak or talk like a human being, that doesn't know its definition in the dictionary or its theory in the schools, that expresses itself simply by the fact of its vibrations. People paying attention to vibratory activity, not in relation to a fixed ideal performance, but each time attentively to how it happens to be this time, not necessarily two times the same. A music that transports the listener to the moment where he is" (75).

Throughout "Composition in Retrospect," Cage is careful to distinguish music from the compositional process. Music, he explains, is not a method or a set of procedures, a certain temporal structure, or approach to structure. It "is there befOre / it is writteN // compositioN / is Only making / iT / cleAr / That that / Is the case / finding Out / a simple relatioN // betweeN paper and music." What is important, he continues, is "hOw / To / reAd / iT / Independently / Of / oNe's thoughts," how to use it for "finding Out / oNe's thoughts," for changing one's "mental attitude." It requires a certain frame of mind, quiet, open, and accepting. Perhaps the word that most closely describes music is "accord." This recurring word in "Composition in Retrospect" suggests a connection, a relationship, a being-in-accord with others, with what is, with what happens.[26]

As Cage's spirit has become increasingly political, so have his works. Consider the recent explanations he gives: the *Etudes Australes* and the *Freeman Etudes* are "as difficult as possible so that a performance would show that the impossible is not impossible"; orchestral works such as *Etcetera* provide opportunities for trying out "different relations of people to people"; in *Atlas Eclipticalis* and Concert for Piano and Orchestra, the conductor is "not a governing agent but a utility, providing the time."[27]

In *I–VI*, which takes "Composition in Retrospect" as one of its sources,[28] Cage explains what he means by such statements: "the performance of a piece of music can be a metaphor of society of how we want society to be [breathe] though we are not now living in a society we consider good we could make a piece of music in which we would be willing to live."[29] The one work he discusses in "Composition in Retrospect," *Musicircus*, exemplifies this concept, as well as what he means by "interpenetration." In this work, Cage asks for no stage, no hierarchical relationship between audience and performers, no fees for performers or ticket charges, and especially "maNy / Things going on / at thE same time / a theatRe of differences together / not a single Plan / just a spacE of time / aNd / as many pEople as are willing / performing in The same place" (*X*, 141).[30]

26. I discuss this further in my "Music Is Not Music Until"—A Musicologist's Perspective," paper presented to the annual meeting of the Modern Languages Association, San Francisco, 29 December 1992.

27. Cage, "Autobiographical Statement," 68, 75.

28. Excerpts from "Composition in Retrospect" begin each of the source sections in *I–VI*, except those sections that were not a part of the 1981 text, for which Cage in 1988 wrote new entries resembling those of "Composition in Retrospect." See my "Intention and Indeterminacy in John Cage's *I–VI*," *Parnassus* 16, no. 2 (June 1991): 359–75.

29. Cage, *I–VI*, 177, 178.

30. See Charlie Junkerman's description of the Stanford performance of *Musicircus*, "'nEw / forms of living together': The Model of the Musicircus," in *John Cage: Composed in America*, 39–64.

Cage's music thus offers models of how "to build a society one by one,"[31] how to live without a conductor/president, how to be courageous, face up to difficulty, and be together while "everyone lives as he needs." His music reflects a recognition of our "need tO / chaNge," to find a new way of being, become a "society / at oNe with itself," in "accord." With these concerns in mind, Cage invents a musical tradition that will help us know how to change, because we have heard it.

Cage once said he writes "to hear the music [he] hasn't yet heard." Or in recent works like *Two*^{2} and *One*^{6}, he looks for "something [he] hasn't yet found."[32] Practicing creativity and preaching anarchy, he spent his life imagining, searching and discovering, seeking "changing solutions to changing problems." Continuing this tradition is now up to us.

31. Cage, "Autobiographical Statement," 75.
32. Cage, "Autobiographical Statement," 75.

Part III

IDENTITY AND NATION

7. Pelléas and Power

Forces behind the Reception of Debussy's Opera

*T*HE PREMIERE OF DEBUSSY'S opera *Pelléas et Melisande* in 1902 provoked a reaction comparable in historical importance to those produced by Hugo's *Hernani* in 1830, Wagner's *Lohengrin* in 1887 and 1891, and Stravinsky's *The Rite of Spring* in 1913. At the open dress rehearsal on 28 April, much of the public responded with surprise, laughter, and hostility. Ill disposed to the work by a parodying pamphlet circulated before the performance, they entered the theater resistant to the simple story; they laughed heartily at Mary Garden's English accent, when, as Mélisande, she sang "Je ne suis pas heureuse" and shouted "petit guignol [little clown]" at Yniold; and they left indignant because the opera was so different from those to which they were accustomed. Others in the audience, largely Debussysts, clapped excessively—even during the orchestral preludes—and argued vehemently during intermissions with anyone who refused to regard the work as a total triumph. For the premiere on 30 April, Debussy agreed to some prudent cuts, but both sides continued to respond to the opera with an equal lack of dignity and discrimination.

Even though these conflicts did not result in any riots or arrests—as there had been with *Lohengrin* a decade earlier—or any interruption of the music or the production, the work clearly inspired intense controversy. Every major newspaper and journal carried a review of the opera (sometimes more than one), whether the

This chapter was originally based on a paper presented to the eleventh annual conference, "Social Theory, Politics, and the Arts," Adelphi University, 27 October 1985, and first appeared in English in *19th-Century Music* 10, no. 3 (spring 1987): 243–64, and in French as "Opéra et Pouvoir: Forces à l'oeuvre derrière le scandale du *Pelléas* de Debussy," trans. Odette Filloux and Jann Pasler, in *La Musique et le pouvoir*, ed. Hugues Dufourt and Joel-Marie Fauquet (Paris: Aux Amateurs de Livres, 1987), 147–77. It is included here by permission, copyright 1987, Regents of the University of California.

I am indebted to Bennett Berger, Pierre Bourdieu, Tia DeNora, Yaffa Schlesinger, and Gaye Tuchman for valuable discussions with them concerning the sociology of the arts. I also wish to thank Ann Feldman, Joseph Kerman, and William Weber for their helpful comments.

critics were seduced by its charm or felt their values were threatened by its scorn of traditions. Moreover, the heated discussions continued well past the first two weeks of performances; they extended over ten years, through the hundredth performance of the opera on 28 January 1913. Despite (or because of) the controversy, the work made more money than established repertoire such as *Carmen* and *Manon*, and for most of its performances, significantly more than the monthly average of all performances at the Opéra-Comique (see table 7.1).

The reasons *Pelléas* triggered such a response have not been examined. Many of those who subsequently wrote about the first performances of the opera, for example, Vuillermoz, Laloy, Charles Koechlin, René Peter, and D. E. Inghelbrecht,[1] were among the original group who worked arduously to have it accepted, both through their attendance at every performance and with their pens. Because they felt that the music critics of the time were "almost unanimous in their condemnation" of the work,[2] any discussion of the criticism given to *Pelléas* by such Debussysts has been tinged with the propaganda they first used to defend the work. Two reviews of the criticism that are more objective—by Léon Vallas, in his classic monograph on Debussy and, more recently, by Christian Goubault, in his study of music criticism in the French press from 1880 to 1914—reveal that there were proponents as well as adversaries of the opera among the established critics.[3] These studies, however, do not analyze which critics had the most influence with the public, or what motivated the various critics to take the positions they did. They also fail to take into account some of the most interesting reviews in nonmusical journals.

By examining and categorizing some four dozen reviews *Pelléas* received during its first season, together with selected memoirs and novels of the period, this article will show that the controversy associated with Debussy's opera extended far beyond that of the first performances and that it was fueled more by the clash of values held by the various groups in the opera's first audiences than by the intrinsic nature of the work itself. The rich ladies who enjoyed the air of aristocracy surrounding the opera house, the professional musicians who cherished the traditions of the beloved genre, and the Wagnerian fanatics who sought quasi-religious experiences through music—each of these groups had preconceived notions of what would or could please them and came to the opera with positions fixed in

---

1. Emile Vuillermoz, *Claude Debussy* (Geneva: Kister, 1957); Louis Laloy, *La Musique retrouvée* (Paris: Desclée de Brouwer, 1974); Charles Koechlin, *Debussy* (Paris: Laurens, 1927); René Peter, *Claude Debussy* (Paris: Gallimard, 1944); Germaine and D. E. Inghelbrecht, *Claude Debussy* (Paris: Costard, 1953).

2. Laloy, *La Musique retrouvée*, 106. In his May 20 review, Pierre Lalo also argues that the work had few supporters.

3. Léon Vallas, *Claude Debussy: His Life and Works*, trans. Marie and Grace O'Brien (New York: Dover, 1973); Christian Goubault, *La Critique musicale dans la presse française de 1870 à 1914* (Geneva: Slatkine, 1984).

TABLE 7.1. Receipts for Performances at the Opéra and Opéra-Comique in 1902.

	Date	Other operas			Pelléas	
					Date	Receipt
Opéra	February	17,865[a]	*Siegfried*	18,424[b]		
			Faust	16,276		
	March	14,803	*Lohengrin*	15,825		
			Faust	18,927		
	May	16,997	*Lohengrin*	21,284		
			Faust	20,010		
	June	15,677	*Die Walküre*	18,985		
			Faust	13,445		
	September	18,401	*Lohengrin*	17,815		
			Faust	20,005		
			Samson et Dalila	18,796		
	October	17,883	*Tannhäuser*	19,637		
			Faust	17,781		
			Don Juan	17,192		
	November	15,806	*Die Walküre*	18,168		
			Lohengrin	19,451		
			Faust	17,781		
Opéra-Comique	February	6,004	*Manon*	5,801		
			Carmen	5,916		
			Louise	5,513		
			Grisélidis	6,933		
	April				**Premiere, 30**	**1,131**
	May	6,930	*Manon*	6,332	2	3,938
			Carmen	6,014	3	5,981
			Louise	6,602	8	7,364
			Mignon	8,455	10	6,819
			La Troupe Jolicoeur **Premiere**	774	15	6,517
					20	6,221
					25	6,138
					28	5,807
	June	5,632	*Manon*	6,965	1	3,815
			Carmen	5,671	6	7,395
			Louise	3,600	11	5,322
			Mignon	3,761	20	7,798
			Lakmé	7,583	26	6,699

(*continued*)

TABLE 7.1. (*continued*)

Date	Other operas			Pelléas	
				Date	Receipt
October	6,726	*Manon*	8,813	30	7,007
		Carmen	9,796		
		Louise	6,138		
		Mignon	6,100		
November	6,254	*Manon*	7,264	6	6,759
		Carmen	5,909	14	6,331
		Louise	5,698	21	4,939
		Mignon	6,991	29	7,646

[a]Average receipts for all performances, in francs. These figures come from *Le Monde musical*, April through December 1902.
[b]Average receipts per performance.

advance. Debussy's friends and supporters, who had been waiting "with curiosity and sympathy" for nine years since the composer had begun the work and had heard excerpts in salon performances, knew the work would be important,[4] and they came prepared to defend it, as their red-vested predecessors had defended *Hernani*. Up in the top gallery, the *amateurs de toute condition*—young musicians, composers, poets, and students who had never had the least contact with Debussy but who had grown to love his orchestral music—listened for what new avenues the work might suggest for the future of French music and music theater. "Licensed" critics came representing every musical persuasion, as well as much of the theatrical and literary worlds, which were intrigued by the idea of setting Maeterlinck's play to music.

In effect, the *scandale* of *Pelléas* —the shock, indignation, and outrage caused by the opera—resulted from all these writers using the work to argue for a number of opposing, even contradictory, views on the use, purpose, and nature of opera, music theater, and music in general throughout the first ten years of the century.

CHRONOLOGY OF A CRITICAL CONTROVERSY

Unlike today, artistic *scandales* occurred relatively often in Paris at the turn of the twentieth century. For one thing, theater, and particularly music, served as arenas in which the society could work out its political and social differences. In his 1902 essay "The Metropolis and Mental Life," the eminent sociologist Georg Simmel

---

4. Henri de Régnier, "Page sur Debussy," in *Vues* (Paris: Le Divan, 1926), 87.

analyzes this polemical spirit and suggests that a "latent antipathy" and "practical antagonism" were a necessary part of life in growing urban centers.[5] By effecting distances and aversions, such devaluating responses protect a person from becoming indifferent or indiscriminate in a world of unending sensual stimuli. Any new art work automatically received some hostility. Building support and understanding for a work—that is, creating a public—was a process that took time and strategy. Audiences were members of a variety of social, political, and cultural groups that could be threatened or appealed to in a number of ways.

Table 7.2 lists the reviews of *Pelléas* from May to July 1902.[6] One-half of them were collected using Claude Abravanel's bibliography on Debussy;[7] the other half were turned up by a lengthy and comprehensive search through numerous journals of the time. I have devised the categories in this table so as to identify the order the reviews appeared in, the publics they were addressed to, and the biases the critics brought to the opera. In its construction, then, the table aims to suggest in capsule form a number of forces that may have informed the critics' judgments and influenced the way they shaped public opinion.

The political orientation of the newspapers and the social class of their readers readily present two sets of potential forces that the critics must have taken into account. Table 7.2 makes it clear that, in general, the newspapers' rejection of or receptivity to *Pelléas* aligned directly with their politics.

Monarchist papers (*Le Gaulois* and *La Gazette de France*) attacked the opera viciously, while the republican ones (*Le Petit Parisien*, *Le Temps*, *Le Journal des débats*, *La République*, *La Petite République*, and *La Revue de Paris*) supported it. There were exceptions, however, depending in part on the degree of the paper's appeal to its readers' social class. The most important critical journal, the *Revue des deux mondes*, took a stance that would satisfy the haute bourgeoisie rather than other republicans among its readership; consequently, in both tone and argument, its review sounds remarkably like those published in the quasi-official papers of the aristocracy, *Le Gaulois* and *La Gazette de France*. These attacks were dangerous to the work because they addressed the very public whose subscriptions and taxes supported the Opéra. By contrast, one monarchist paper, *Le Soleil*, reviewed the opera favorably, perhaps because it had slightly different readers from the other two. Like *La Liberté* and *Le Matin*, which praised *Pelléas*, *Le Soleil* was read by businessmen, rather than the nobility, many of whom lived in the provinces.

5. *The Sociology of Georg Simmel*, trans. and ed. Kurt H. Wolff (New York: Free Press, 1950), 409–17. I am indebted to Chandra Mukerji for directing me to this book.

6. All citations from the reviews of *Pelléas* derive from the articles listed in table 7.2, and all translations from the French are my own unless otherwise indicated.

7. Claude Abravanel, *Claude Debussy: A Bibliography* (Detroit: Information Coordinators, 1974), 111.

TABLE 7.2. Critical Reviews of *Pelléas et Mélisande*, May–July 1902.

Periodical[a]	Emphasis (readers)	Critic	Critic's status, tastes	Date, evaluation[b]
Large circulation daily newspapers				
*Le Matin (200,000)↑	News, rep. all political views, not clerical (politicians)	André Corneau	Critic at the *Revue blanche*	1 May+
Le Petit Parisien (1,000,000)↑	Republican (mass market esp. in provinces)	Montcornet		1 May+
Le Petit Journal (900,000)↓	Nationalist, anti-Dreyfus (mass market esp. in provinces)	Léon Kerst	"Intellect moyen"	1 May−
Le Journal (600,000)↑	Literary, pro-Dreyfus (writers, intellectuals, mass market)	*Catulle Mendès	Writer, librettist, Wagnerian	1 May°
Other daily newspapers				
*L'Echo de Paris (80,000)↑	Nationalistic, Catholic, fearing socialism (bourgeois socialites)	*Henry Gauthier-Villars (Willy)	Novelist, Wagnerian	1 May°
L'Eclair (60,000)↓	Political, nationalist, anti-Dreyfus	Samuel Rousseau	Composer	1 May−
Le Soleil (35,000)	Defends big business, pro-Dreyfus (moderate monarchists)	O'Divy		1 May+
*Le Figaro (20,000)↑	Attempts to be apolitical, low sales but respected reviews (bourgeois, republicans)	Eugène d'Harcourt	Composer	1 May−
Le Figaro↑ (20,000)↑	*See above*	*Un monsieur d'orchestre*	Concert-goer	1 May°
*Le Gaulois (25,000)	Monarchist, Bonapartist, anti-Dreyfus (aristocracy, some haute bourgeoisie)	Louis de Fourcaud	Wagnerian, art historian, professor	1 May−

TABLE 7.2. (*continued*)

Periodical[a]	Emphasis (readers)	Critic	Critic's status, tastes	Date, evaluation[b]
Gil Blas	Short stories, gossip (socialites)	Gaston Serpette	Composer	1 May⁻
La Liberté (50,000)↑	Financial business (bourgeois)	Gaston Carraud	Composer, pro–Schola Cantorum	2 May⁺
La République (3,500)↓	(Educated republicans)	Litte (alias André Suarès)	Writer, prefers Beethoven, Wagner	2 May°
La Petite République (100,000)↓	Open to all types of socialism (less educated republicans)	Camille de Saint-Croix	Literary critic	+
La Presse (50,000)↑	Socialist, nationalist, Boulangist	Gustave Bret	Conductor	+
Gazette de France (5,000)	Monarchist (one of the oldest) (upper class, esp. in the provinces)	Henri de Curzon	Musicologist, archivist	3 May⁻
Le Figaro (20,000)↑	See above	Henry Bauër	Socialist, politically *engagé*	5 May⁺
Gazette des beaux-arts supplement	(Art lovers)	*Paul Dukas	Composer	10 May⁺
Journal des débats (15,000)↑	Old, established (moderate republicans, academic elite)	Adolphe Jullien	Pro-Wagner and Germans, musicologist, pro-Maeterlinck	11 May⁺
Le Figaro (20,000)↑	See above	Robert Flers	Interview with Debussy on his critics	16 May
*Le Temps (35,000)↑	Politically moderate, most respected (republican bourgeoisie)	*Pierre Lalo	Anti-Wagner, critic, son of the composer E. Lalo	20 May⁺

(*continued*)

TABLE 7.2. (*continued*)

Periodical[a]	Emphasis (readers)	Critic	Critic's status, tastes	Date, evaluation[b]
Journals				
*Le Ménestrel	Conservative republican, (musical public)	Arthur Pougin	Conservative republican musicologist, anti-Wagner	4 May⁻
La Revue Musicale	Music history, analysis (musicologists)	Louis Schneider	Music gossip columnist like Willy, musicologist	May⁺
Revue d'art dramatique et musical	(Writers, theater-goers)	Robert Brussel	Drama critic	May⁺
La Revue dorée	(Young writers)	Emile Vuillermoz	Young critic, Debussyst	May⁺
Revue bleue (30,000)	(Politicians, writers)	Paul Flat	Theater critic, Wagnerian	10 May°
*Revue des deux mondes (32,000)	Ideas, Catholic (haute bourgeoisie, conservative republicans)	*Camille Bellaigue	Catholic, *haut bourgeois*, prize-winning pianist	15 May⁻
*Revue de Paris (20,000)	Ideas, pro-Dreyfus (*haute bourgeoisie*, conservative republicans)	André Hallays	Ex-editor of the *Journal des débats*, music critic	15 May⁺
La Revue	Ideas (writers)	Paul Souday	Literary critic	15 May°
Le Courrier musical	(Progressive musical public)	Victor Debay	Writer, opera reviewer	15 May⁺
Le Guide musical (Brussels)	Anti-Wagner (musical public)	Hugues Imbert	Journal editor, critic, prefers chamber music (born 1842)	15 May?⁻
Le Monde musical	Instrument maker (musical public)	Auguste Mangeot	Journal publisher	15 May°
L'Art moderne (Brussels)	(Writers, artists)	M. D. Calvocoressi	Young critic	15 May°

TABLE 7.2. (*continued*)

Periodical[a]	Emphasis (readers)	Critic	Critic's status, tastes	Date, evaluation[b]
Magasin pittoresque, supplement	(Bourgeois)	Emile Fouquet		15 May⁻
L'Art moderne (Brussels)	*See above*	Octave Maus	Journal editor	25 May⁺
Mercure de France (10,000)	Ideas, some symbolist (independent writers)	Jean Marnold	Young critic, Debussyst	June⁺
Le Courrier musical	*See above*	Paul Locard	Orchestra concert reviewer	1 June⁺
Revue d'art dramatique et musical	*See above*	*Paul Dukas	Composer	June: rpt. of above
L'Occident	Anti-Dreyfus founded 1902 (artists)	*Vincent d'Indy	Composer, professor	June⁺
Le Théâtre	(Theater-goers)	Adolphe Jullien	Musicologist, *see above*	June⁺
Le Théâtre	*See above*	Louis Lastret	Theater critic	June⁺
La Renaissance latine	Interest in provincial culture	Florencio Odero	Prefers Charpentier	June°
L'Ermitage	Symbolist (writers)	Henri Ghéon	Poet, critic	July⁺
Revue universelle	Ideas (writers, intellectuals)	Camille Mauclair	Poet, novelist, aesthetician	July⁺
La Grande France	(Libertarian politicians)	Amédée Rouques	Poet	July⁺
La Grande Revue	Ideas (writers)	Alfred Bruneau	Composer, pro-Dreyfus	July⁺
Revue blanche	Ideas, pro-Dreyfus (writers)	Julien Benda	Philosopher, writer	July⁺

[a]Information on political orientation of the French press and its readership from Claude Bellander, et al., *Histoire générale de la presse française*, vol. 3 (Paris, 1972); René de Livois, *Histoire de la presse française*, vol. 2 (Lausanne, 1965); Theodore Zeldin, *France 1948–1945*, 2 vols. (Oxford, 1977); and Christian Goubault, *La Critique musical dans la presse française de 1870 à 1914* (Geneva, 1984). Information on the critics, their status, and their tastes gleaned from their own writings and from Vallas and Goubault. Here approximate circulation, rising or falling in 1902, is indicated by the arrow. The more important journals and critics are indicated with an asterisk.

[b]Positive (+), negative (−), mixed (°).

FIGURE 7.1a–d. Allegorical postcards of Parisian newspapers from the Belle Epoque, reproduced in René de Livois, *Histoire de la presse française*, vol, 2 (Lausanne: Spes, 1965). a: *Le Journal*. b: *Le Figaro*. c: *Le Temps*. d: *Le Gaulois*.

There also appears to be a correlation between the various papers' stand in the Dreyfus Affair and their disposition toward *Pelléas*. Anti-Dreyfus papers (*Le Petit Journal*, *L'Eclair*, and *Le Gaulois*) took a negative view of the opera (except for d'Indy, who, in *L'Occident*, surprisingly reversed his earlier opposition to the opera), while the pro-Dreyfus *Le Soleil*, *Revue de Paris*, and *Revue blanche* were perhaps more inclined to urge their readers to give the opera a chance. The papers' views on nationalism, however, seem not to have carried much weight, for the nationalists split over the opera, depending on whether the paper or its critic was socialist (*La Presse* and Henri Bauër came out for *Pelléas*) or antisocialist (the review in *L'Echo de Paris* was somewhat negative) and the extent to which some nationalists were also anti-Dreyfus (*Le Petit Journal* and *L'Eclair*).

The type of interest held by the readers suggests a third force to which the critics responded. To the degree that the paper addressed bourgeois socialites (*L'Echo de Paris*, *Gil Blas*, and *Magasin pittoresque*), its critics were reluctant to give much praise; but when writing for writers and art-lovers (*Le Journal*, *Gazette des Beaux-Arts*, *L'Art moderne*, *Mercure de France*, *L'Ermitage*, etc.), the reviews were mixed at worse and full of acclamation for the most part. The musical public received perhaps the most diverse response from its critics, depending, predictably, on whether it was perceived as interested in progressive new trends or conservative traditions.

A fourth consideration underlying the critics' evaluation of the opera derives from their own principal occupation and its perspectives. Most of those who wrote criticism, poetry, or novels as their main form of employment (the greatest percentage of the critics on this list) found it easy to appreciate the opera, whether they understood it or not, and none panned it outright. But the composer-critics swung both ways. The three who attacked the opera—Eugène d'Harcourt, Gaston Serpette, and Samuel Rousseau—may have felt that the little attention their music had received was called into jeopardy by the new opera, whereas those who defended it—Paul Dukas, Alfred Bruneau, and even Vincent d'Indy, all well-known composers—evidently felt secure enough to admire something that actually challenged their own compositional approaches. The greatest resistance to the opera came from the professional musicologists and historically minded music critics, for example, Camille Bellaigue and Arthur Pougin, most of whom remained committed to an earlier form of opera. Four of the six falling into this category were deeply disturbed by *Pelléas* and wrote scathing reviews.

The particular way these political, social, and cultural forces were brought into play during the first two weeks of the criticism reveals why Debussy's supporters had reason for concern about the opera's survival, let alone its success. For the first week, 30 April–5 May, the criticism was largely divided. Each of the four large-circulation daily newspapers printed reviews. The most powerful paper in town was *Le Matin*; its critic, André Corneau, who had known Debussy from the *Revue blanche*, wrote favorably, but had little influence, having worked at the paper for only a year. The two papers addressed to the working classes, *Le Petit Parisien* and

Le Petit Journal, disagreed. Montcornet, writing for the former, found that the music served its atmospheric function in the theater well, while Léon Kerst, writing for the latter, simply told people not to go hear *Pelléas* since they would not understand it.

Catulle Mendès, a much more respected writer at *Le Journal*, insisted that the collaboration had not been a fruitful one; he left the theater, he said, wanting to see the music and the play performed separately. This attack posed a real threat to the work, for even though Mendès liked the play, he found that, in the opera, the text lost its most valuable qualities—its "mystery" and the "indecisiveness of its emotions, thoughts, and language"—and even though Debussy had "never used his wonderful talents with more skill," he regretted the composer's "systematic exaggeration of monotony" in the vocal parts and his "stubborn determination to 'musicalize' even the least musical phrases." Surely some of Debussy's writer friends knew that Mendès might have a lingering resentment over Debussy's refusal to finish their mutual project, *Rodrigue et Chimènes*, when he began *Pelléas*; nonetheless, René Peter considered Mendès "the most qualified [*désigné*] of them all to penetrate this surprising work."[8] When Mendès addressed the very issues that were most dear to Debussy's symbolist supporters, such as the relationship between the music and the text, and concluded that the musico-poetic analogies were entirely superficial and "we have been deceived" in placing our hopes in Debussy, his review had the potential of scaring away Debussy's base of support.

On the next level, the twelve critics from the daily press who reviewed the work also disagreed with one another. Five who admired the work (O'Divy, Gaston Carraud, Camille de Saint-Croix, Gustave Bret, Bauër) did not pretend to understand it, but praised its novelty; some of them said that if people went without any expectations, it would delight them. André Suarès was also mystified; while he applauded Debussy's skill and originality, he also registered a few reservations concerning the excessive importance given to the text. As noted earlier, these relatively favorable reviews appeared in papers that were read by businessmen, republicans, and socialists. Four critics who condemned the work (d'Harcourt, Louis de Fourcaud, Serpette, Henri de Curzon) attacked the composer and his alleged contempt for conventions more than the opera itself. They directed their words primarily to socialites and the high society. Among those who rejected the opera, only Rousseau dismissed it after examining the music in detail.

Willy, probably the most important critic of the daily press, refused to cast his vote definitively either for or against the opera, and this was a serious impediment to its success. Not only were Willy's *Lettres de l'ouvreuse* very popular with all kinds of concert-goers and salon people but also, like Mendès, Willy knew the composer, had heard excerpts of the work as it was being composed, and was well aware of

---

8. Peter, *Claude Debussy*, 191.

how his comments would be read by the public. Remarks tinged with disapproval interrupt his otherwise sympathetic review. For example, although he scolded readers who had laughed during the opera (wondering if many of them, like Golaud, had also been cuckolded by their wives!), he made light of the story himself with a humorous plot summary. And while he called Debussy a poet and succinctly identified the opera's innovative declamation, unusual orchestration, and harmonies built of fourths, fifths, and ninth chords, he also expressed some reservation as to their aesthetic effect. Debussy's unresolved dissonances evoked his strongest objection: "My God, yes! How harsh they are! What can I say? I am without a doubt becoming a *pompier* [academic]; it's my turn, I confess that these scraping noises annoy me a little." From such a writer, these criticisms were taken to heart. (Perhaps he was the "impenitent Wagnerian" Laloy dubbed him, after all.)[9]

These equivocal, highly favorable, and downright dismissive reviews fueled the controversy surrounding the work. Some of the criticism that came out the next week began to examine the resistance to the work and defend it against specific criticisms. Dukas, who wrote perhaps the most important of these, said that the opera was just too different for anyone to think it could be understood right away. Given his position at one of the oldest papers in Paris, *Le Journal des débats*, and his longtime devotion to Wagner, Adolphe Jullien surprised his readers by placing Debussy's originality on a par with Wagner's and suggesting that if the listener allowed himself, he would find the impression often agreeable, even sometimes a bit profound.

Before this defense of *Pelléas* could win many sympathizers, the journal critics, who had not yet voiced their opinions, initiated a new series of attacks and counterattacks in the 15 May and 1 June issues of the important monthly and bimonthly journals. In the *Revue des deux mondes* and *Revue de Paris*, the most respected periodicals of Parisian high society, and in *Le Temps*, their daily equivalent, the success or failure of Debussy's opera became an issue involving some of the society's most pressing questions.

---

9. Laloy, *La Musique retrouvée*, 129. In his memoirs, *Souvenirs littéraires . . . et autres* (Paris: Montaigne, 1925), Willy mentions that he got nasty letters during the war "for having confessed to remaining an 'unchanged' partisan of Wagnerian music" (94). Even though he had moved in the same circles as Debussy, he writes: "And Debussy himself could not cure me completely of what he considered a mortal sickness. Certainly, an invincible charm emanates from the tenderness with which Pelléas showers Mélisande with her long hair; I felt it, but it does not make one forget one's old loves . . . the memory of Siegfried's horn" (95). By the turn of the century, it could not be said of Willy, Mendès, or the other Wagnerians that they "were committed to furthering the cause of forward-looking trends in French culture," as Gerald D. Turbow mistakenly concludes, "Art and Politics: Wagnerism in France," in *Wagnerism in European Culture and Politics*, ed. David C. Large and William Weber (Ithaca, N.Y.: Cornell University Press, 1984), 166, even though this may have been true in the mid–nineteenth century.

AESTHETIC RECEPTION

What kept *Pelléas et Mélisande* such a controversial topic of discussion throughout the spring and summer of 1902? From the musical perspective, the debate revolved around Debussy's approach to form, development, orchestration, and the "holy trinity"—that is, the three musical elements: harmony, melody, and rhythm. For some, the work lacked any nuance, any real "melody, motive, phrase, accent, form, and contour" (Kerst, Corneau, Pougin, Serpette, d'Harcourt, Curzon, Bellaigue); yet others heard in it an "infinity of nuances" and not a moment without all of the elements of music, only in new forms and guises (Dukas, Paul Locard, Victor Debay, Mauclair). Many objected to a total absence of development in the work, though Jean Marnold claimed that Debussy used all the resources of leitmotif, including the developmental, but in his own unusual way. As far as harmonies were concerned, those like Willy and Imbert, who found them ugly, harsh, and irritating, or like Rousseau, for whom they were too numerous, argued with André Hallays, who heard not a grating sound in the opera, and Locard, who claimed that the work's "tonal uncertainty was more apparent than real." For Mauclair, Debussy was "the most original harmonist of the times."

In addition to examining the opera's music, discussions sometimes extended to Debussy's other compositions and to his musical background. Depending on how they viewed his orchestral music, the critics at the music journals sought either to attract more concert-goers by comparing *Pelléas* favorably with this other music (Debay, Louis Schneider) or to put them off by making the same comparison (Imbert). To bolster his argument, Pougin went so far as to undermine Debussy's credibility with the conservative musical public of *Le Ménestrel* by noting how few works the composer had written and how, at forty years old, it was really too late to try to establish a reputation. (Perhaps in response to this manipulation of public opinion, Locard wrote in his 1 June review: "Let fearful souls be reassured, [Debussy] is an excellent musician," going on to explain that his musical training is solid, he cherishes Renaissance music, defends Bach, and works on his scores for many years.)

But whether the work's opponents found the music of *Pelléas* threatening or just monotonous, their criticisms were really not too original. After reading the first three weeks of criticisms heaved at Debussy's opera, Pierre Lalo writes on 20 May:

> Listen to the adversaries of *Pelléas*: you would think you were reading an article by Scudo or Oscar Comettant on *Tannhäuser*.[10] And what about this? "He abolishes melody; it's the vocal or instrumental discourse that

---

10. Lionel de la Laurencie, *Le Goût musical en France* (Paris: Joanin, 1905; rpt. Geneva: Slatkine, 1970), 327, quotes these critics as criticizing *Tannhäuser* for having a "formless melody, colorless and deafening, that condemns you to deadly boredom."

preoccupies him, not the song." Is this Debussy? No, Bizet. It's the critic of *Le Figaro* judging *Carmen* this way. And who, other than Debussy, can one reproach for his "obscure harmonies" and the "murky depths" of his inspiration? Why Mozart, in 1805.

Yet even with this defense of Debussy's musical choices, the debate continued.

Beyond the music, broader aesthetic issues and particularly the problem of music theater also created controversy. Most critics devoted the first one-third to one-half of their reviews to discussing the play. Symbolist writers applauded the work for its use of a drama based on sentiment and sensation rather than metaphysics or romance. Henri Ghéon called the opera "a dramatic event," and in the July issue of the symbolist journal *L'Ermitage* he devoted the fifth of his series on a renaissance in contemporary theater to an analysis of the work. But those devoted to Wagner or Massenet complained bitterly. Paul Souday pointed out in *La Revue* that literary decadence was dead and buried, having been killed by boredom, and that Debussy's symbolist opera—also "mortellement ennuyeux"—was behind the times rather than ahead of them.

Perhaps the greatest divergence of opinion came in discussing the relationship between Maeterlinck's play and Debussy's music. Hallays defended the few cuts Debussy made in the original text, thereby reassuring and attempting to attract Maeterlinck fans, and considered the text responsible for inspiring many qualities of the music. Ghéon, Mauclair, Auguste Mangeot, Imbert, and Bruneau, however, regretted Debussy's choice of libretto and would have wished for more cuts in the original play. The play was "too obscure, naïve, and complicated," said Mauclair, "too fragile and internal"; it is better read than staged. In general, the critics agreed that Debussy's music faithfully translated the poet's thought, but there was also considerable dissension about whether the text dominated or should dominate the music. The composer Dukas saw a perfect union between the music and words, whereas, ironically, it was such writers as Suarès and Mauclair who thought Debussy had gone too far in following the text.

One could say a great deal more about the musical and aesthetic issues at stake in this opera. Vallas and other Debussy biographers have already explained various ways the music was heard and understood. But the manner in which the opera was perceived as music theater calls for more than a study of the opera's reception, and indeed a discussion of the opera's relationship to other symbolist theater at the time.[11]

11. For an excellent in-depth analysis of Debussy's opera and symbolist thought, see Elliott Antokoletz, *Musical Symbolism in the Operas of Debussy and Bartok: Trauma, Gender, and the Unfolding of the Unconscious* (New York: Oxford University Press, 2004). See also Frantisek Deak, *Symbolist Theater: The Formation of an Avant-Garde* (Baltimore: Johns Hopkins University Press, 1993).

In this chapter, these matters will be taken up only as they play roles in the larger social-political context.

Social, Moral, and Political Impact

Behind the words used by the critics, particularly those writing for Ancien Régime or high society publications, lurk a number of social, moral, and political presuppositions. In what follows, I shall examine four such issues raised by *Pelléas et Melisande*: first, the use and purpose of opera, including the function of opera-going; second, the ability of text, music, and a composer's lifestyle to affect the morality of the audience; third, the notion of opera as a place for confronting political differences and a political tool for lauding French music over German music; and fourth, the idea of artistic innovation as a model of either individual freedom or anarchy.

Social Issues

For many, the Opéra was of course first and foremost a meeting place, a place to see and be seen, as it had been for many years. For a certain social class, indeed—the wealthy opera subscribers—such an "institution of luxury that luxury upholds, and that is made only for it,"[12] served as an important if nostalgic reminder of the days when the aristocracy flourished. By donning the right clothes and attending the opera, anyone, especially the nouveaux riches, could give the impression they belonged to the upper classes. As mentioned in chapter 5, Octave Mirbeau, a writer who frequented the same circles as Debussy, wrote in 1885:

> The Opéra is an elegant meeting place for a certain social class that can pay 34,000 francs per year for the right to show up in tuxedos and strapless gowns three times a week, from ten to midnight, in one of the boxes. It is sort of a grand banal salon, divided into an infinity of small individual salons. . . . Consequently what one asks from it is not art but elegance, and luxury, and all the conveniences for holding fashionable receptions.[13]

From this standpoint, *Pelléas* was no different from any other opera. Three of the more enlightened wealthy ladies known to have attended its premiere were the Princess de Polignac, the daughter of American inventor Isaac Singer (founder of the Singer Sewing Machine Company), who returned from Venice especially for the opening;[14] Madame de Saint-Marceaux; and the Countess Greffulhe, cousin to

---

12. Octave Mirbeau, *Des Artistes*, 2nd ser. (Paris: Flammarion, 1924), 259–60.

13. Mirbeau, *Des Artistes*, 259–60.

14. For a wonderful new biography, see Sylvia Kahan, *Music's Modern Muse: A Life of Winnaretta Singer, Princesse de Polignac* (Rochester, N.Y.: University of Rochester Press, 2003).

FIGURE 7.2. "The Snob." Figures 7.2–7.4 are caricatures of the audience from Albert Millaud, *Physiologies parisiennes* (Paris, 1887).

Robert de Montesquiou and a great patroness of the arts, who had supported the only performance of Maeterlinck's *Pelléas et Melisande* in 1893. Such listeners occupied the main floor and the principal boxes. The writer Jules Renard, attending *Pelléas* on 10 May, perceived this public as "consisting of rich ladies who go only there or to the Opéra," and he arrived at the same conclusion as Mirbeau: "It's a kind of huge café where strapless gowns and diamonds and the deaf (who want to give the impression that they can hear) hold their *rendez-vous*."[15]

At the turn of the century, the opera began to attract another type of elite, the snobs. In his *Chez les Snobs* (1896), the novelist Pierre Veber derided snobs as those "who follow the latest fashion," "who want to understand everything or at least to appear to"—"*bourgeois-gentilhommes de l'esthétique* . . . who only esteem the rare and the precious."[16] Their attraction to a personality or an artist depended not on personal taste or critical sense, but the prestige surrounding his work. For them,

15. Jules Renard, *Journal 1887–1910* (Paris: Gallimard, 1965), 751, 760. Renard found *Pelléas* "un sombre ennui [a dismal bore]" (751).

16. Pierre Veber, *Chez les Snobs* (Paris: Ollendorf, 1896), 9, 41. In her autobiography, *Earthly Paradise*, trans. from various French sources (New York: Farrar, Straus, and Giroux, 1966), Colette names Veber as one of several ghostwriters for Willy.

performances were meeting places where they hoped to be seen as associated with the avant-garde.[17]

The notorious writer Jean Lorrain called the particular snobs who attended Debussy's opera "Pelléastres," and he described them in a novel with that name. According to him and the critic Florencio Odero, many had been devotees of the Théâtre de l'Oeuvre, where Maeterlinck's play had been given its premiere. Most were quite young and dressed very elegantly. These aesthetes, dandies who "loved their mothers," "composed Greek verses," and "were good musicians," together with their mistresses—"beautiful," "useless," "concerned about intellectuality," and "scornful of the masses"—mixed with the socialites in the best seats in the house.[18] Vuillermoz notes that Lorrain painted these musical snobs with his own vices, and that their fervor exasperated Debussy.[19] Fernand Gregh says in his memoirs, however, that he and his literary friends were proud to be Pelléastres.[20]

In reality, Pelléas did attract many writers, some of whom were snobs and others who were serious intellectuals, for Debussy, ever since he had begun working on the opera in 1893, had built substantial support and interest in it among writers through frequently playing excerpts of it in various salons and literary circles—especially those of Pierre Louÿs, Madame de Saint-Marceaux, and Revue blanche. When Pelléas finally opened, Debussy put pressure on these friends to come. For example, he wrote to Louÿs, "It is necessary for our friendship that you be there," and urged him to bring along André Lebey and Valéry. Louÿs agreed to bring five friends so that the group would "fill the ground floor box with applause."[21] Writers such as Paul Valéry, Henri de Régnier, Lebey, Mirbeau, Curnonsky (Maurice Edmund Sailland), Jean-Paul Toulet, and Léon Blum were among this group.[22]

For both groups—the social and the intellectual elite, including their feigned members—the self-definition they sought in going to the opera depended on a

17. Emilien Carassus, Le Snobisme et les lettres françaises de Paul Bourget à Marcel Proust 1884–1914 (Paris: Colin, 1966), 38, 170.

18. Jean Lorrain, Pelléastres (Paris: Méricant, 1910), 24, 26, 28, excerpts first published in Le Journal (22 January 1904); Willy, Maîtresses d'esthètes (Paris: Simonis Empis, 1897), 50–54.

19. Vuillermoz, Debussy, 100. After reading the first installment of Lorrain's essay in Le Journal, Pierre Louÿs wrote Debussy that he could sue, but it would be preferable to simply ignore the writer; 23 January 1904, in Correspondence de Claude Debussy et Pierre Louÿs, ed. Henri Borgeaud (Paris, 1945), 176–77.

20. Fernand Gregh, L'Age d'or: Souvenirs d'enfance et de jeunesse (Paris: Grasset, 1947), 313.

21. Late April 1902, in Borgeaud, Correspondence de Debussy et Louÿs, 170.

22. The building of this audience was discussed in my paper, "Debussy and the Making of a Reputation," presented to the joint meeting of the Northern California and Pacific Southwest chapters of the American Musicological Society, University of California, Santa Barbara, 27 April 1985.

certain kind of art. Only that which upheld tradition could reinforce the class identification the social snobs sought. Only the new and unknown, however, could fulfill the desires of the *"chercheurs de l'inédit"* (seekers of the novel), who rapidly became the "zealots of new aesthetic enterprises."[23] And to the extent that some
zealots (like the Wagnerians) became convinced of one aesthetic direction, they
became intolerant of any other. The critics were clearly aware of these underlying motivations in their readers and appealed to them directly in their reviews.
To discourage their readers from attending, many of those who addressed high
society (such as Fourcaud and Bellaigue) placed emphasis on Debussy's rejection
of traditions, while to lure their readers to the opera, those who wrote for liber-
tarians and intellectuals (such as Bauër, Robert Brussel, Corneau, Dukas, and
Mauclair) stressed the composer's profound originality.

The kind of opera they defended also depended on what opera-goers considered
the purpose of opera to be. Mirbeau writes that opera subscribers were satisfied and
charmed with whatever was sung for them, that is, as long as they could see the latest
fashion and admire beautiful women.[24] In the journal of Edmond and Jules de
Goncourt, one gets this perspective from both the male and female points of view.
Returning from a gala at the Opéra in 1893, Edmond shares his desire to see beautiful
women there, but regrets that it was not sated: "A deception. Really this hall is not
favorable for the exhibition of a woman's beauty. Those old lights at the back of the
boxes kill everything, wipe everything out, especially the soft glow of the light-
colored outfits and strapless gowns."[25] He also reports that Countess Greffulhe,
"who was quite charming in white," was upset that evening that the large number of
military uniforms attracted too much attention away from the women. Writing of
her own experience at the opera in an essay she asks Goncourt to help her publish,
the countess describes how the "great anonymous caress" of all the eyes that admire
her there totally transforms her each night. "What a blood transfusion this communication with the eyes of the crowd gives me. How to live without it . . ."[26]

Of course, many opera-goers had more precise demands of the art form. One
group sought entertainment through the music—romance, "melodic emotions," as
Debussy called them, and charm for the ear. With their beautiful melodies, Mozart,
and more recently Massenet, pleased them the most; Wagner the least. Some critics
who stressed the sensual qualities of Debussy's music thought that *Pelléas* should
satisfy these listeners. Carraud ranked the composer with Mozart; d'Indy found the
music comparable with Rossini's, though he also primly judged it inferior for

23. André Hallays, "De la Mode en art et en littérature," *Revue de Paris* (1 May 1896):
205–24.

24. Mirbeau, *Des Artistes*, 258.

25. Edmond and Jules de Goncourt, *Journal: Mémoires de la vie littéraire, 1891–1896*, vol.
4, ed. Robert Ricatte (Paris: Fasquelle, 1956), 473.

26. Goncourt, *Journal*, 4:611.

seeking the "damnable pleasures" of sensualism.[27] The majority of those, however, who advocated this kind of opera—conservative musicians and many who favored the Ancien Régime—were quick to denounce *Pelléas* when it did not fulfill their fixed expectations. Corneau addressed them immediately in his review on 1 May:

> You will look in vain in the 283 pages of this score for a piece to detach, a melody to extract. Well-loved romance flourishes nowhere. Characters do not declaim, and avoid singing. . . . It is uniquely the orchestra that has the task of expressing everything, or better, of making one feel everything.

In *Le Ménestrel*—a journal owned by the music publisher Heugel, a firm anti-Wagnerian—the conservative republican critic Pougin told his readers that *Pelléas* would leave them cold with boredom and, at most, would give them only "mediocre pleasure."

A second group argued that entertaining, often anecdotal music like Massenet's only existed for the purposes of the theater for which it was written, and that, like the stage itself, the seductions of this kind of music were momentary and were incapable of penetrating the depths of one's soul.[28] This faction of the public came to the opera for a quasi-religious experience. In what some called "this century without faith," music had become the new religion and the opera house the temple of high art. The eminent Wagnerian Fourcaud explains: "What we aspire to is a really deep, human art, not continual effects of titillation which are fundamentally morbid."[29] After calling *Pelléas* "nihilist art," unable "to rouse any deep emotion in our hearts," he continues: "one cannot serve ideals without ideas, one cannot quench the thirst of souls with questionable pharmaceutical beverages."

In spite of this criticism, many *Pelléas* enthusiasts sought the same experience from listening to Debussy's opera as the Wagnerians sought from Wagner's. Lorrain, a staunch anti-Wagnerian, makes fun of how the snobs turned Debussy into the head of another religion. According to him, at each performance of *Pelléas* the Salle Favart took on the atmosphere of a sanctuary:

> One only went there with solemn expressions on one's face. . . . After the preludes were listened to in a religious silence, in the corridors there were the initiates' greetings, the finger on their lips, the strange handshakes hastily exchanged in the dim light of the boxes, the faces of the crucified, and the eyes lost in another world.[30]

---

27. Emile Vuillermoz, *Gabriel Fauré*, trans. Kenneth Schapin (Philadelphia: Chilton, 1969), 34–35.

28. Robert Burnand, *Paris 1900* (Paris: Hachette, 1951), 181.

29. Vallas, *Debussy*, 126–27.

30. Lorrain, *Pelléastres*, 25. In his second, preseason review of the opera in the *Revue dorée* (August 1902), Vuillermoz directly contradicts Lorrain's description of audience

Lorrain goes on to point out, however, that while the Wagnerians came from all social classes and thus occupied seats throughout the theater, the Pelléastres were more elegant and sat principally in seats on the main floor and in the lower boxes.

A third group of opera-goers looked to Debussy's opera as a means of escaping their daily routines and of being transported into an enchanted world. For them, the opera was a stimulus for dreaming. More than orchestral music, which, for the symbolist poets, offered a similar experience—opening them to inner experiences they had heretofore never known and inspiring in them a sense of communion, a oneness in feeling—*Pelléas* attracted many young writers. As Jacques Rivière put it in 1911, "*Pelléas* was for us a certain forest and a certain region and a terrace overlooking a certain sea. There we escaped, knowing the secret door, and the world no longer meant anything to us."[31] The young musicians Vuillermoz and Koechlin also considered the opera "an enchanted garden";[32] but, as their contemporary, the critic Marnold, made clear, they did not feel that the opera transported them "into an unreal sphere, into an external invented world, but rather into [their] own most profound depths." By attracting the young as well as the middle class, the opera thereby was expanding its appeal beyond the elite to new audiences during this period.

Moral Questions

Underlying these social issues were also a number of moral questions, raised particularly by the critics who wrote for the haute bourgeoisie, those who still believed in the Ancien Régime, and the conservative musicians. These critics included Bellaigue, Curzon, d'Harcourt, Fourcaud, and Imbert.

At the dress rehearsal, the story and text itself presented problems, even though the story was a classic; many compared it to the love affair of Paolo Malatesta and Francesca da Rimini in Dante's *Divine Comedy*. The play *Francesca da Rimini* had been done recently at the Sarah Bernhardt Theater.[33] Nonetheless, some were unwilling to drop the scurrilous title *Pédéraste et Médisante* (Pederast and slanderer) that had been coined at the dress rehearsal,[34] and others were so upset about the scene during which the little Yniold spies on the couple for the jealous husband that the undersecretary of state for fine arts forced Debussy to cut four measures

---

response to *Pelléas*: "Debussy's music does not encourage foolish swooning, empty looks of ecstasy, and plaintive mutterings as easily as Wagner's . . . the musical thought is too simple, too pure."

31. Jacques Rivière, *Études* (Paris: Gallimard, 1944), 127.

32. Vuillermoz, *Debussy*, 105; Koechlin, *Debussy*, 86.

33. This story clearly was quite popular that year, for in the 15 April 1902 issue of the *Revue des deux mondes*, Téodor de Wyzewa reviews two other plays with the same subject: Stephen Phillip's *Paolo and Francesca*, which was playing in London at the time, and Gabriel d'Annunzio's *Francesca da Rimini*, which was playing in Milan.

34. Pierre Lalo, *De Rameau à Ravel: Portraits et souvenirs* (Paris: Michel, 1947), 368.

FIGURE 7.3. "The Decadent."

before the opera opened, so as to expunge any reference to Pelleas's and Mélisande's proximity to the bed. Given the period, this cut must have seemed pretty silly, but the producer, Albert Carré, himself blamed the poor initial reception of the work on the text, and he, too, advised modifying several scenes.[35]

More important were the critics' attacks on Debussy himself and his way of life. He was classed with the "decadents," a name once invented by journalists to describe adherents of a literary movement—precursor to the symbolists—that flourished in the mid-1880s and is best represented by J. K. Huysmans's *A Rebours*. Known for their invented words and concentration on ornamental detail at the expense of the shape of a whole work, the group was criticized for their extravagant

35. Henri Busser, *De Pelléas aux Indes Galantes* (Paris: Fayard, 1955), 114.

writing style as well as their lifestyle—dressing in the latest fashions, always lost in the clouds (or seemingly dugged), and smelling of perfumes. The press loved to caricature them. In his *Physiologies parisiennes*, Albert Millaud gives an amusing portrait of the decadent:

> Son of the modernist, grandson of the idealist, nephew of the impassible, great nephew of the Parnassian . . . the decadent is a young man, very pale, skinny, and respected in certain literary brasseries. . . . He doesn't have any ideas; he doesn't want any. He likes words better. . . . When a word does not come to him, he invents it. It's up to the reader to understand and to put ideas under his words. The reader refuses to do so generally. From that comes the decadent's scorn for the reader.[36]

In his review of *Pelléas* in one of the oldest newspapers in Paris, *La Gazette de France*, the archivist and musicologist Curzon cites Imbert's recent description of Debussy as "enigmatic and sensual, indolent and living his life as if in a kind of dream, attracted only by poets and prose writers of the avant-garde whose troubled and trembling works he uses for his musical creations." Curzon implies a connection between the apparent formlessness of Debussy's music and a life filled with smoke, if not drugs, when he compares it with the formlessness of contemporary painting and blames that on painters who "see through a fog, a smoke, and who ignore precise lines and colors." Bruneau, too, links Debussy's music with the decadent movement and finds the play's "fatality," "disinterested approach to life," and other decadent notions as "suiting [Debussy's] temperament in the most exact way." Perhaps, as Lalo points out in a later review, this "suspicion of defects" in Debussy's character developed from the displeasure that "people of taste" experienced at having to sit beside "certain degenerate aesthetes" during performances of *Pelléas!*[37] Not everyone, however, felt this way.[38]

The ultimate attack on *Pelléas* was the claim that the music, if listened to, would ruin one's character. Although he avoids almost all discussion of the music, Curzon reaches this conclusion first by noting that the characters in *Pelléas*, like Debussy, also "act as if in a vague stupor" and then by suggesting a connection between the listener's experience and that of the characters on stage. "As if moved by some external and supernatural forces, they live, and we live with them, in the unconscious and the mysterious depths," he remarks, bemoaning the repulsive "nihilism and negation of all faith, of all guide," that informs their actions. For

---

36. Albert Millaud, *Physiologies parisiennes* (Paris: Librairie illustrée, 1887), 201–3.

37. Cited in Vuillermoz, *Debussy*, 104. According to Vuillermoz, Debussy took offense at this statement because he thought it implied that *Pelléas* was "music for riffraff."

38. In his review of *Pelléas* in the *Revue d'art dramatique et musical*, addressed to the theatrical world, Robert Brussel leapt to Debussy's defense. To him, Debussy appeared to live a "modest life"—that of an "upright artist"—"far from newspapers and salons."

Curzon, as well as d'Harcourt, Fourcaud, and Bellaigue, *Pelléas* was essentially *maladive* or unhealthy music, music "without life." Bellaigue claims that "after listening to it, one feels sick" and not unlike Pelléas, who sighs, "Nothing is left for me, if I continue in this way."

The powerful music critic Bellaigue goes perhaps the furthest in condemning the work on moral grounds. Writing for the *Revue des deux mondes*, perhaps the most important journal of the haute bourgeoisie and one that was known for having a moral authority, Bellaigue was himself from a family of the haute bourgeoisie and wielded considerable influence. He had won a first prize in piano at the Conservatoire in 1878. In reviewing *Pelléas*, he builds credibility with the reader by referring to an episode from his youth when he knew Debussy as a fellow student in the piano class of Marmontel. The story is quite a nasty one: he says that the class laughed at Debussy while he played piano because he breathed heavily on every strong beat, but now he clearly has been cured of this bad habit—all the beats in this music are weak ones. Then, after attacking the work on every possible musical ground and accusing Debussy of presiding over the "decomposition of our art," he addresses his readers—"distinguished, even superior men"—and concludes: "We are dissolved by this music because it is in itself a form of dissolution. Existing as it does with the minimum of vitality, it tends to impair and destroy our existence. The germs it contains are not those of life and progress, but of decadence and death."[39] In a November 1901 article in the same journal, Bellaigue reveals what he would prefer to have in its place: "melodic opera," especially that of Mozart, for his operas "express or realize an ideal of life itself." He gives the characteristics of this ideal as simplicity, even familiarity, and then peace, joy, and love, without violence or excess.[40] Sure enough, a lighthearted opera first performed only weeks after *Pelléas*, Arthur Coquard's *La Troupe Jolicoeur*, ironically met with Bellaigue's approval, even though he admitted it could have been "a little more profound and original."[41]

One of *Pelléas*'s staunchest supporters, Laloy, also raises the issue of morals. In his memoirs, he recalls a conversation he had with Lorrain concerning the opera. Lorrain's first words were "I don't like the subject," to which Laloy responded

39. "Pelléas et Mélisande," *Revue des deux mondes* (15 May 1902): 455; cited in Vallas, *Debussy*, 128.

40. Camille Bellaigue, "Les Epoques de la musique: L'Opéra mélodique, Mozart," *Revue des deux mondes* (15 November 1901): 904.

41. In reviewing the opera for the *Revue des deux mondes* (1 June 1902): 920–21, Bellaigue praises *La Troupe Jolicoeur*'s lack of excess together with the sincerity and delicacy of its expression. He finds many "excellent things" in it and considers it "worthy of esteem and sympathy." Bruneau, by contrast (in the same article as his review of *Pelléas*), found the comedy flawed by "inconsistent and insufficiently drawn characters, predictable *péripéties*, and easy sentimentality." The public seems to have concurred with the latter, for the work was performed only once.

"Protestant!" According to Laloy, Lorrain's biting parody of *Pelléas* supporters in his novel *Pelléastres* was due to Lorrain's Protestant education, which prevented him from understanding the moral import of the story:

I don't want to imply that a Protestant is incapable of appreciating *Pelléas*. But all moral codes that treat human nature harshly and that, considering it evil by nature or since original sin, correct it only to constrict it to the commandments and to make it do penance, will necessarily be leery about an art work so completely emancipated from any constraint and repentance.

After reminding the reader that Catholics, on the contrary, "do not believe in predestination and, through the help of grace, can always hope for forgiveness for any sin," Laloy goes on to explain that the moral message he finds in *Pelléas* is not that men and women should abandon themselves to their instincts but that they should try to preserve the state of innocence into which they were born. For him, "*Pelléas* teaches pardon."[42]

Political Implications

In addition to these social and moral issues, many critics upheld or opposed the work for political reasons, some almost entirely so. Since some considered the Opéra to be an extension of the state—a meeting place for government officials and a salon for entertaining visiting dignitaries—this intermingling of music and politics was to be expected.[43]

The most obvious and clear-cut of the political issues touching opera at the turn of the century was the question of nationalism—French music versus German music (i.e. Wagner). Nationalism was a wild card that cut across other basic issues and caused unexpected realignments. The conflict began in the 1880s, as the French concert halls and eventually the opera houses opened their doors to the German master, despite the fact that the Germans had recently taken Alsace and there was increasing resentment in the French public over embracing foreign music in their state-supported theaters. Violent riots protesting the performances of *Lohengrin* in Paris at the Eden-Théâtre on 3 May 1887 and in front of the Opéra throughout the month of September 1891 were followed by numerous anti-Wagnerian manifestoes and parodies in the press.[44] The caricatures in such books as *Physiologies parisiennes* depict "the man who listens to Wagner" as not only serious but also stark.

42. Laloy, *La Musique retrouvée*, 110, 112–13.

43. Mirbeau, *Des Artistes*, 259–61. Paul Morand, *1900* (Paris: Les Editions de France, 1931), also calls the Opéra "a combination of government office, brothel, and political club" (223). For a recent perspective on opera and politics, see James Ross, *Crisis and Transformation: French Opera, Politics and the Press, 1897–1903*, D.Phil. thesis, Oxford University, 1998.

44. See especially the exhibition catalogue, *Wagner et la France*, ed. Martine Kahane and Nicole Wild (Paris: Bibliothèque Nationale, 1983).

FIGURE 7.4. "The Man Who Listens to Wagner."

TABLE 7.3. Opéra Performances of Wagner Operas, 1890s–1902.

Opera	Year	Number of performances
Lohengrin	1891–1902	201 times
Die Meistersinger	1897–1902	65 times
Tannhäuser	1861, 1895–1902	116 times
Die Walküre	1893–96; 1898–1902	132 times
Das Rheingold	1893 [two pianos]	1 time
Siegfried	1901–2	20 times

Albert Millaud calls him generally "preoccupied and unhappy. One knows he is prey to a continual overexcitement. . . . He both delights and suffers at the same time—a blessing normally given to *morphinisme.*"[45]

But these efforts to do away with Wagner had little long-lasting effect in face of the Wagnerians' campaigns. Mendès, for example, lectured on *Lohengrin* in all the provincial cites where it was performed—together with Raoul Pugno, Debussy even accompanied a lecture he gave at the Opéra in 1893 by playing excerpts from *Das Rheingold* (see table 7.3), and Fourcaud busily translated as many of the operas as possible into French.[46] The number of concert performances of Wagner's music in Paris grew steadily throughout the 1880s and 1890s, climaxing in the period 1897 to 1900. A decrease in their number in 1900 and 1901 only reflects the fact that entire Wagnerian operas began to be produced regularly in the opera houses. (Table 7.3 shows how many times various Wagner operas were performed at the Opéra in Paris from the 1890s through 1902; compare table 7.1.)[47]

Even the Goncourts, who rarely concerned themselves about music, objected to the Opéra playing Wagner four times a week in 1895. "And there are sixty-five operas that await performances and will perhaps never be put on!" they point out in their journal.[48] On 31 December 1901, the heated confrontation between those advocating Wagner's music and those crying for more French music became lively again at the dress rehearsal for the first production of *Siegfried* and remained an undercurrent in critical writing throughout the spring of 1902, in preparation for the French premiere of *Götterdämmerung* on 17 May 1902.

45. Millaud, *Physiologies parisiennes*, 267–68.
46. Kahane and Wild, *Wagner et la France*, 165; the intellectual journal *L'Ermitage*, however, harshly criticized Fourcaud's translations of Wagner's libretti in its May 1902 issue (190).
47. The information in table 7.3 was culled from Kahane and Wild, *Wagner et la France*, 158–73.
48. Goncourt, *Journal*, 4:837.

To exacerbate the political situation, Wagnerism at the turn of the century became linked with the Dreyfus Affair and with anti-Semitism. Although Debussy claimed neutrality in the Dreyfus Affair, Debussy's supporters and friends were mostly pro-Dreyfus, which did not help the conflict with the Wagnerians; only Louÿs was passionately anti-Dreyfus, according to René Peter.[49] Lorrain recognized many in the audience for *Pelléas* from productions at the Théâtre de L'Oeuvre, which, according to its director Lugné-Poë, was a favored rendezvous of the Dreyfusards.[50] The *Revue blanche*, for which Debussy and many of his friends wrote, including Régnier, Mirbeau, and Valéry, was another important center for Dreyfusard activity and in 1898 published an article protesting Dreyfus's imprisonment.[51]

Critics who embraced *Pelléas* as an alternative to Wagner's music did not hide their motivation. Bauër, a politically committed writer who was forced to leave the newspaper *L'Echo de Paris* because he supported the First International (an international socialist organization), backed Debussy in *Le Figaro*, even if d'Harcourt, the newspaper's principal critic, had panned the work only four days earlier. While at the time of *Lohengrin* Bauër had defended Wagner from the "absurd chauvinism" of many French, in 1902 he objected to Wagnerians gaining control of the Opéra and impinging on other composers' freedom to have their works performed. "Finally someone who will liberate French music from Wagnerian oppression!" he exclaimed. In a letter of 8 May 1902, Debussy thanked him for his strong words of support.[52]

Pierre Lalo, the well-respected son of the composer Edouard Lalo and the critic for the most important paper in town, *Le Temps*, also saw *Pelléas* as strong encouragement for young composers "to emancipate themselves from the tyranny of the Wagnerian formula and to conceive and create with more freedom." Lalo goes so far as to say "There is nothing or almost nothing of Wagner in *Pelléas*" and backs up this statement with a long list of elements that the work does not share with Wagner's music.[53] Lalo's blatantly polemical essay reflects, in part, his personal feelings of gratitude toward Debussy and Carré. Debussy had expressed so much enthusiasm for Edouard Lalo's ballet *Namouna*, which flopped in 1882, that

49. Note 1 to the letter of 23 March 1898, in Borgeaud, *Correspondence de Debussy et Louÿs*, 108.

50. Lugné-Poë, *La Parade; Le Sot du tremplin: Souvenirs et impressions de théâtre* (Paris: Gallimard, 1930), 18.

51. See A. B. Jackson, *La Revue blanche, 1889–1903* (Paris: Minard, 1960).

52. *Claude Debussy: Lettres 1864–1981*, ed. Francois Lesure (Paris: Hermann, 1980), 114.

53. Scholars now know of course that, though few of Debussy's contemporaries would admit it, the opera borrows many things from Wagner, and not just the music of the interludes. See Robin Holloway, *Debussy and Wagner* (London: Eulenberg, 1979), and Carolyn Abbate, "Tristan in the Composition of *Pelléas*," *19th-Century Music* 5 (1981): 117–41.

Debussy was almost thrown out of the Conservatoire, and in 1902 Carré had put on a totally new production of Edouard's opera *Le Roi d'Ys,* which Pierre and his mother had found enchanting.[54] But Lalo's polemics also stem from the strongly nationalist feeling that pervaded his life. Throughout his memoirs, Lalo boasts of his French heritage, the fact that five generations of Lalos had been military officers and the family still possessed a commission appointing one of them captain, signed in 1709 by Louis XIV. The only music he praises, such as that of Fauré and Charpentier, is music that is "entirely our own." With *Pelléas,* Lalo felt Debussy "was serving in his own way the cause of France in the world."[55] The French composers Dukas and Koechlin also voiced nationalist feelings at the time, complaining that little French music was being played in Paris;[56] and, together with Bruneau, they hoped that Debussy's opera would "push the official Wagner imitators into the tomb."

The boldness of Debussy's innovations likewise provoked a more general, but also latently political, discussion between those who advocated following rules and those who valued freedom and individuality. Critics of the first persuasion included not only the traditionalists but also the Wagnerians, for whom Wagner had become *the* formula for music drama. D'Harcourt, Fourcaud, Bellaigue, and Pougin were convinced that Debussy followed no logic or reason and ignored the laws of the "holy trinity" (the musical elements). While harmony, by definition, involves both "order" and "hierarchy," Bellaigue found it in Debussy's music to be synonymous with "anarchy," "disorder," and "confusion": "chance seems to direct all movement"; "the notes only repel and detest each other." Odero referred to the opera as "musical anarchy," and Pougin deemed Debussy the "head of the anarchists in music." To such accusations Vuillermoz had a direct response: "So it is anarchy, is it? Maybe, but how beneficial, since [the music] attains a beauty right off the bat that the thick web of rules had never allowed it to achieve."

In calling Debussy's music anarchy, these critics were not far from wrong, given the broad definition of the term during this period. The anarchist movement preached not only political but also artistic freedom for the individual, questioned accepted institutions of all kinds, and criticized bourgeois hypocrisy. Its followers hoped that, through a series of cataclysmic changes, life would evolve to a more perfect state, and believed that art should show the possibility for change and create new ideals. Debussy was certainly receptive to these ideas. In the late 1890s, he even formalized such thoughts in a collaborative project with René Peter; their play *Les Frères en art* concerned a group of artists who sought to educate the public about the necessity of overthrowing bourgeois standards. In aesthetic terms, this meant

54. Busser, *De Pelléas aux Indes Galantes,* 108.

55. References in this paragraph to Lalo's memoirs come from his *De Rameau à Ravel,* 73, 365, and 371.

56. Koechlin, *Debussy,* 58.

rejecting rules and insisting on the sole authority of the creative mind—ideas remarkably close to those of the anarchists.[57]

In imputing to Debussy an association with the anarchists, the critics were correct, but this had been true only before the turn of the century, when he had frequented certain literary circles—not later, when, as Michel Faure points out, Debussy's political orientation turned markedly to the right.[58] In the 1890s, many of Debussy's friends and supporters were active in the anarchist movement, mostly the same group who defended Dreyfus and whom I have already named in this connection. Régnier collaborated on the anarchist literary magazine L'Endehors and was considered one of its editors. He also edited Entretiens politiques et littéraires, a symbolist review open to anarchist ideas. Mauclair, though he was more concerned with the unhampered freedom of the artistic elite than the welfare of the masses, chose to end his novel about Mallarmé's circle, Le Soleil des morts, with an anarchist revolution that included the participation of the poets. Mirbeau's involvement with the anarchists is the topic of an entire book by Reg Carr.[59] Three of the journals that were most supportive of Pelléas—Revue blanche, Mercure de France, and L'Ermitage—also sympathized with the anarchists and often reviewed articles from the anarchist and socialist press.[60] Bauër's defense of Pelléas for the sake of freedom of expression, and Brussel's point that Debussy represented no school and was the perfect example of a "personal composer," certainly must have attracted anarchist support to the opera.

Audience response to criticism of Pelléas also took on a political air. Debussy's supporters, up in the top gallery, called themselves a "sacred battalion."[61] Some of these included the composers Maurice Ravel, Paul Ladmirault, and Koechlin; the future conductor Inghelbrecht; the poet Léon-Paul Fargue; the pianist Ricardo Viñes; the music critics Laloy, Vuillermoz, and M. D. Calvocoressi; and the Abbé

57. For more on what anarchy meant to Vuillermoz and others during this period, see my "La Schola Cantorum et les Apaches: L'Enjeu du pouvoir artistique ou Séverac médiateur et critique," in La Musique: Du Théorique au politique, ed. Hugues Du towet and Joel-Marie Fauquet (Paris: Klincksieck, 1990), 313–43.

58. Michel Faure, Musique et Société du Second Empire au Années Vingt (Paris: Flammarion, 1985), 75–82.

59. Anarchism in France: The Case of Octave Mirbeau (Manchester: Manchester University Press, 1977).

60. Eugenia W. Herbert, The Artist and Social Reform: France and Belgium 1895–1898 (New Haven, Conn: Yale University Press, 1961), 96–100, 128.

61. The development of this audience is the subject of my "A Sociology of the Apaches, 'Sacred Battalion' for Pelléas," paper presented to the annual meeting of the American Musicological Society, Philadelphia, 27 October 1984. An expanded version of this is in Berlioz and Debussy: Sources, Contexts and Legacies, ed. Barbara Kelly and Kerry Murphy (London: Ashgate, 2007). For a discussion of the political vocabulary used in conjunction with music and musical alliances, see also my "La Schola Cantorum et les Apaches."

Léonce Petit. According to Vuillermoz, their principal organizer, these "mobilized troops" were needed "to assure the presence of police in the hall." But long after their demonstrations were said to have "frozen the opposition,"[62] this group continued to attend the opera for every one of the first thirty performances, almost as a political act, as each of them attests in his memoirs. A young musician and friend of Vuillermoz, Edmond Maurat, went only three times and was snubbed thereafter.[63] Political vocabulary permeates the supporters' descriptions of the resistance given to this *oeuvre de combat*.[64]

This massive attention from the press eventually succeeded in elevating Debussy to the status of a new god of music, a "French" music. But the continued controversy also turned Debussysme into music's "Dreyfus Affair," as Vuillermoz attests in a later article that points to the similar initials of their names (Achille *D*ebussy, Alfred *D*reyfus).[65] Different factions developed even among the Debussysts (Laloy, Mauclair, Vuillermoz). As one of them admitted, "the struggle became so bitter that the object was forgotten."[66]

In turn-of-the-century Paris, a scandal inevitably awaited any new masterpiece that demanded extensive public attention. "Toute vibration inconnue scandalise," as O'Divy wrote in his review of *Pelléas*. The complexity of values at the time made confrontation certain, and the number of critics on hand to represent each possible combination of social class, political preference, and musical and aesthetic taste resulted in fierce competition. Because the critics for the most part either attacked *Pelléas* or embraced it depending on what they and their subscribers valued, the opera was seen to fulfill mutually exclusive purposes. It attracted both snobs who came to the Opéra to be seen and artists who wanted to escape the world; it was held up as an example of the lowest morality, leading to one's dissolution, and the highest, teaching one pardon; it was praised by both nationalists, who aimed to preserve tradition, and anarchists, who sought renewal. Likewise, it was panned for the same contradictory set of reasons, argued by members of the same groups. Even reviews addressed to similar readers, such as those by Bellaigue and Hallays, sometimes reached diametrically opposed conclusions.

What made the critics and their public sway one way or the other was often a complex issue. As discussed earlier (and shown in table 7.2), the political orientation of the paper or journal, the social status of its readers, the perspective

62. Paul Locard, "La Quinzaine," *Courrier musical* (1 June 1902): 167.
63. Edmond Maurat, *Souvenirs musicaux et littéraires*, ed. Louis Roux (Saint-Etienne: Centre interdisciplinaire d'études et de recherches sur l'expression contemporaine, 1977), 21.
64. Critics and writers who used this expression include Paul Flat, Odero, Réné Peter, Inghelbrecht (in his *Mouvement Contraire* [Paris: Domat, 1947], 275), Rivière, and Laloy.
65. Emile Vuillermoz, "Une Tasse de thé," *Mercure musical* (15 November 1905): 505.
66. Vuillermoz, "Une Tasse de thé," 509. For more on this, see chapter 4 here, n. 5.

guiding the readers' interest in opera, and the critics' own principal professions all played important roles in predisposing both the critics and segments of the public toward either categorical opposition or an openness to the work. Monarchists, aristocrats, haute bourgeoisie, anti-Dreyfusards, socialites, and the conservative musical public tended to feel threatened by or antagonistic toward the opera; republicans, businessmen, socialists, Dreyfusards, professional writers, art-lovers, and the progressive musical public tended to give it a chance.

Any paper, reader, or critic, however, could belong to both a resistant group and a more receptive group. This explains why a republican journal such as the *Revue des deux mondes*—otherwise sympathetic to new ideas—could publish a bitter attack of the opera, as its critic, Bellaigue, came from a high social class and had very conservative musical taste. Fervent devotion to other composers also kept some avant-garde enthusiasts, who otherwise should have needed no convincing, from fully embracing Debussy's opera. Whether they were Wagnerians or ferocious anti-Wagnerians—and the discussions invariably involved Wagner—a critic's attitude toward Wagner did not automatically imply either support or rejection of Debussy. Even though Jullien was among the inner circle who helped introduce Wagner to the French public, he had to admit that *Pelléas* pleased him. Others, such as Mendès and Willy, allowed their love of Wagner to color what they otherwise admired in Debussy's opera. Of the anti-Wagnerians, only Lalo embraced *Pelléas* as a work that might lead French musicians out of Wagner's grasp, while Pougin, Imbert, and their public placed Debussy and Wagner in the same camp— neither satisfied their passion for traditional form and virtuoso singing.

One should not exaggerate the role social and political issues played, for some critics were clearly charmed or put off by the work for inherently musical reasons. But the number of extramusical issues capable of affecting how a critic formulated his message was enormous; and that formulation, then and now, might well determine whether a work failed or succeeded. It is no wonder that Debussy's supporters felt they had to organize.

8. The Ironies of Gender, or Virility and Politics in the Music of Augusta Holmès

> Women are curious when they seriously attend to art. Above all
> they seem preoccupied with making us forget they are women, of
> showing an overwhelming virility, without dreaming an instant that
> it is just this preoccupation that reveals the woman.
>
> Saint-Saëns, review of *Les Argonautes*
> in *Le Voltaire*, 26 March 1881

THE MALE-DOMINATED MUSICAL WORLD often wants women composers to act like men and write music like men. But when they do, they are "accused" of virility. This situation raises a number of questions for women in music. Is it wise to resist writing as a woman? What are the advantages and the pitfalls? Can a woman maintain a reputation based on the gains achieved in this way? What implications do such choices have for one's personal identity?

The case of Augusta Holmès (1846–1903) raises issues as vital today as they were a hundred years ago, those that come up whenever a woman takes chances, "thinks big," or addresses topics of social relevance in her music. Holmès negotiated the complexities and ironies of gender and achieved remarkable success. She used her music both to engage and to escape the social and musical stereotypes of her day. In her youth, her long blond hair helped her to get attention. Later, through her own gender-bending manipulation of ambiguities, she encouraged a different identity. She was able to convince reviewers that despite its excesses, her music's "shocking

This chapter originally appeared in *Women & Music* 2 (fall 1998): 1–25; it is included here by permission, copyright 1998, International Alliance for Women in Music. A shorter version was presented at the conference "Feminist Theory and Music 4," Charlottesville, Virginia, 6 June 1997. I am grateful to Annegret Fauser for helpful comments on an earlier draft.

Many of the articles without titles or exact dates cited in this chapter come from *Recueil d'articles de journaux sur Augusta Holmès, 1866–1888*, 4 B 391, F-Pn, Musique. Unless otherwise noted, all translations from the French, whether reviews or texts from the scores, are mine.

boldness" reflected "originality" and "courage"—words rarely used in nineteenth-century Paris to describe the work of a woman. Critics in the mid-1880s considered the adjective "feminine" "beneath her talent" and referred to her as "no longer a Venus" but a "young Apollo descended from Olympus," someone still beautiful but grand and idealistic as opposed to seductive.[1] She knew then she could succeed, as a man might. Yet could she succeed as a woman and what would this mean?

This is a story about the meaning of virility in late nineteenth-century France, how it was understood in music, and what purposes it served. The first wave of feminist achievements in the 1870s sets the context. Some women wanted to act like men, that is, to have the same rights. The Association for the Rights of Women, founded in 1870, set an ambitious agenda for the Third Republic. New journals such as *Le Droit des femmes* and *La Femme* advanced these ideas. The adoption of a new constitution in 1875, a new republican majority in 1876, and a new president in 1879 raised women's hopes of finally attaining some of these rights. A few minor successes followed. In summer 1878, nine deputies and two senators attended the First International Congress for Women's Rights in Paris, and in 1879 the First Worker's Congress in Marseilles voted for sexual equality. The Union of Feminist Socialists was subsequently formed, and under their name a number of women ran for public office, albeit as long shots (*candidates mortes*). These were largely symbolic advances. However, in 1880 the National Assembly passed a law giving women secondary education. The young deputy for whom the bill was named, Camille Sée, convinced anticlerical republicans that educating women in their own *lycées* (college prep high schools) would decrease the influence of the church. The first women's *lycée* opened in 1882. By the following year there were 29 such schools. This gave just under 3,000 young women the possibility of preparing for college, as opposed to the somewhat more than 90,000 young men enrolled in the 352 male *lycées*.[2]

Despite these advances, strict limitations on women's development continued. For years, women could not study the same subjects as men—no *matières nobles*, meaning Greek, Latin, and philosophy; nor could they study math and natural sciences to advanced levels.[3] *Lycée* graduates received only a diploma, not the *baccalauréat*. Throughout the 1880s, "feminine" education was distinguished from "virile" education, since it was commonly agreed that men and women serve different social functions. Because most republicans thought women belonged in the home, the ultimate reason for educating them, as Camille Sée put it, was to "be the

---

1. Ryno, "Augusta Holmès, Profil," *Gil Blas* (22 October 1885).

2. Maïté Albistur and Daniel Armogathe, *Histoire du féminisme français* (Paris: Des femmes, 1977), 353, 368–69, 394.

3. Karen Offen, "The Second Sex and the Baccalauréat in Republican France, 1880–1924," *French Historical Studies* 13 (fall 1983): 252–86, explains the complexities of how slowly Latin and science were introduced into women's secondary education.

mothers of men" or, as more recent scholars have concluded, "agents of republican propaganda."[4]

In the musical world, women also attempted to win new rights. On 7 May 1874, Maria Isambert petitioned the minister of public instruction and the director of the Académie des Beaux-Arts to compete for the Prix de Rome. She had the necessary diploma, albeit not from the Paris Conservatoire. The request was denied, apparently without an explanation.[5] However, women did increasingly begin to enter competitions and get more public recognition. In the 1870s, they also began to appear more frequently on prestigious concert series, such as the Société Nationale and the Concerts Colonne.

The increased presence of women composers caused both admiration and consternation. Whereas in the late 1860s, critics thought that women could write only "elegant and gracious" music, by 1880 they began to use the word "virile" to describe an occasional piece by a woman. This term was synonymous with qualities attributed to men. Yet, consistent with mixed views about the value of women during this period, "virile" does not always mean the same thing. It reflects a wide range of attitudes, some pejorative, others complimentary. Some who wrote about Holmès's music associated her music's virility with its excessiveness in expression, especially its boldness, strength, and grandeur. This meaning underlies reviews to this day that attack women's compositions that are perceived as big, loud, and (therefore) pretentious.[6] The term could imply the reviewer's surprise or envy, but usually it means that the woman has gone too far. Other critics used "virile" to describe Holmès's personality and training. This included recognizing other equally masculine but more positive values in her work, for example, tenacity and individuality, energy and vitality, skillfulness and even innovation.

4. Laurence Klejman and Florence Rochefort, *L'Égalité en marche* (Paris: Des femmes, 1989), 58.

5. Minutes of the meetings of the Académie des Beaux-Arts, 9 May 1874, Archives of the Institut de France, Paris. Isambert's two letters are attached to the minutes of these meetings. Isambert, from Metz, had a chamber music course there beginning in 1873. For a discussion of the problems women faced in trying to compete for the Prix de Rome, see Annegret Fauser, "*La Guerre en dentelles*: Four Women, the Prix de Rome and French Cultural Politics," *Journal of the American Musicological Society* 51 (1998): 83–129, especially 90–91, and "Lili Boulanger's *La Princesse Maleine*: A Composer and Her Heroine as Literary Icons, *Journal of the Royal Musical Association* 122 (1997): 68–108.

6. In discussing women's music, contemporary reviewers continue to use gender stereotypes. In the *New York Times* (15 April 1997), for example, Anthony Tommasini pans Tina Davidson's toccata "They Come Dancing" for being demure but predictable and criticizes Sheila Silver for, in her fifty-minute piano concerto, "thinking big," making "pompous" claims to the Romantic Russian tradition, and asserting "unabashedly pretentious" philosophical ideas ("struggle and transcendence"). Meanwhile, he recognizes Charles Griffes's work for having a "distinctive voice" and Karel Husa's for engaging "his intellect."

In this chapter, I propose that the discourse surrounding virility implies political meanings as well, and I suggest that these are the key to why Holmès's work was accepted and widely acclaimed. Her ability to understand and express both what the republican mainstream wanted to hear—love of country and other patriotic ideals—as well as the bold individuality dear to Wagnerians (some of whom espoused other political ideals) underlies many of her successes. It may also help explain her eventual loss of reputation. I propose that the use to which Holmès put female stereotypes in her music cast her work as more than just virile, indeed "like a man's." She, a woman, like a man, could express both virile power and feminine charm. Far more than serving as a muse,[7] I see her politics and this combination of skills as the reason her work became a symbol of the ideals of the French Republic.

THINKING LIKE A MAN

In his book *La Femme compositeur* (1895), Eugène de Solenière singles out Augusta Holmès as "the most successful, the most inspired, and the most original" woman composer of her generation.[8] Like many of her peers, she made much of her living by giving private lessons and performing in private salons as a pianist and singer. However, unlike the Viscountess de Grandval and Cécile Chaminade, Holmès tended not to perform in public venues.[9] She preferred to be known more as a composer than a performer, though late in life she occasionally conducted—an activity restricted almost entirely to men at the time.[10] Early publication of her works (by Hartmann, Flaxland, and Leduc) established her, especially the publication of her first major work, *Lutèce* (1878), by Choudens, who published

7. Although it is true that Holmès became an "icon of nation" around the time of her *Ode triomphale*, as Karen Henson claims, "In the House of Disillusion: Augusta Holmès and *La Montagne noire*," *Cambridge Opera Journal* 9 (November 1997): 233–62, I do not agree that this entailed losing her "identity as author."

8. Eugène de Solenière, *La Femme compositeur* (Paris: La Critique, 1895), 14. Moreover, of the twenty-eight composers Adolphe Jullien writes about in his *Musiciens d'aujourd'hui*, 2 vols. (Paris: Librairie de l'art, 1894), she is the only woman.

9. The Viscountess de Grandval, Chaminade, and Marie Jaëll had important careers as performers. For a study of Chaminade's performances in France and abroad, see Marcia Citron, *Cécile Chaminade: A Bio-Bibliography* (New York: Greenwood, 1988). Some women opted to limit their performances to salons to keep their reputations as good bourgeoises. For more on this idea, see Fauser, "*La Guerre en dentelles.*"

10. Holmès conducted her works in Tours in June 1899 on a concert series that regularly featured composers as conductors of their music. Later, in 1900 at the Concerts Colonne she conducted rehearsals of her *Andromède,* like other composers, who from the 1870s led rehearsals of their new works there. In this she was a predecessor to Nadia Boulanger. See Jeanice Brooks, "Noble et grande servante de la musique: Telling the Story of Nadia Boulanger's Conducting Career," *Journal of Musicology* 14, no. 1 (winter 1996): 92–116.

Gounod's *Faust*, Bizet's *Carmen*, and Berlioz's *Les Troyens*. Regular performance in important venues—a rare phenomenon, perhaps helped by her close links to Saint-Saëns and Gounod—assured her a career.

Unlike many other women composers of her time, when it came to public performances, Holmès always thought big. Her three premieres at the composer-run Société Nationale were not melodies or piano pieces but a psalm, *In exitu* (1872), for soloists, chorus, cello and organ, and orchestral excerpts from two operas, the overture to *Astarté* (1875) and the prelude to *Héro et Léandre* (1879), both conducted by Edouard Colonne.[11] This choice of works makes one wonder whether she used these occasions to announce that she was writing operas—something quite unusual for a composer of her age. Holmès then abandoned the Société Nationale, perhaps because of its emphasis on chamber music or limited public.

Holmès was also quite the strategist. For her first performance in a major public venue, she set her sights on Pasdeloup's Cirque d'Hiver, as she considered it more central and more popular than Colonne's Théâtre du Châtelet. Then, to encourage Pasdeloup to program her *Argonautes*—which took up an entire concert—she turned to the government for support, attaching letters of support from many of the major composers of the day.[12] The performances in spring 1881 and 1882 received over twenty-four reviews, most of them enthusiastic. After this success, she then turned to the most prestigious Parisian orchestra, the Société des Concerts du Conservatoire. Although they performed at most only one or two new works by living composers per year, Holmès persuaded them to do *Argonautes* and later two others, each of them substantial works, involving soloists, choruses, and orchestra.[13] The Société's premiere of her *Ludus pro patria* in 1888 was the first such honor given to a woman. In their enthusiastic reviews, both Gramont and Oscar Commettant

11. Music by the Viscountess de Grandval, Chaminade, and Marie Jaëll appeared on far more concerts at the Société Nationale than that of Holmès, but the vast majority of their works were in small genres.

12. Pleading that "all my career depends on the performance of *Argonautes*," Holmès wrote directly to the president of the Budget Commission when it was clear that Pasdeloup was willing to give her first important orchestral performanc, but needed extra funds. Attached to her letter are short notes of support from Gounod (who expresses his "liveliest and most sincere interest"), Saint-Saëns (who "recommends" it), Franck (who has "the highest esteem for the score"), Godard (who thinks "no work better deserves State protection"), and signatures by Charles Lamoureux, the Viscountess de Grandval, Massenet, and Joncières, among others. See Papers of Augusta Holmès, letter 189, n.a.fr. 16260, F-Pn, Manuscripts.

13. In a letter of 12 January 1884 to the Société des Concerts, Holmès pleads by way of flattery: "Don't ignore the great importance that I attach to a performance by the Société des Concerts. The great desire that I have for this immense honor will hopefully excuse my entreaty in your eyes." She then notes that even if they can't do the whole thing, parts 2 or 3 would do, and she'd take care of getting the soloists; Papers of Augusta Holmès.

predicted that this success and "a temperament that predisposes her to the theater" will soon "open the doors of the Great Opéra" to her.[14]

Holmès's career took off in the 1890s. She proposed writing music for the opening ceremony of the 1889 Universal Exhibition, and the organizers, convinced by her petition (and her musical record), agreed. To cover expenses, the government entrusted her with an enormous sum, 300,000 francs.[15] In the Exhibition's five official concerts, she was the only woman represented. At the Concerts Colonne, which eventually became her preferred venue, she became the most frequently performed female composer in the last quarter of the century. They performed nine of her pieces, some of them five times, and gave twenty performances of her music that decade (see appendix 2). In 1895, the Paris Opéra finally put on one of her operas, *La Montagne Noire*. She was the only woman so honored for decades. And although it was criticized for being old-fashioned, they did this opera thirteen times that season—more performances than they typically gave for most new works, and more that year than *Lohengrin, Samson et Dalila, Othello*, and *Die Walküre*. By the turn of the century, Holmès's popularity was so widespread that she (or her music) appeared regularly in family magazines. She penetrated the world of military music, appearing on the cover of its main journal, *Le Petit Poucet*, on 15 June 1897.[16] After 1900, her *Irlande* and *Sérénade printanière* became favorites at classical music concerts in *brasseries*, such as those of the Concerts Touche and the Concerts Rouge.[17]

In the musical world, such a figure exemplified the *femme nouvelle*—the independent "new" woman with priorities other than those of the home. Like other such women—sometimes considered *hommesses* or "female-men," "rigid, austere, and riddled with the appetitive combativeness of professional mobility"[18]—

14. Oscar Comettant, in *Le Siècle* (12 March 1888) and Gramont, in *L'Intransigeant* (15 March 1888).

15. The organizers of the Exhibition accepted Holmès's piece after a musical competition to set a text chosen in an earlier competition brought no suitable result. Hugues Imbert describes the context of the piece and its performance in *La Musique des familles* (21 September 1889): 386–89. Jullien gives a slightly different story in his review that month, reprinted in his *Musiciens d'aujourd'hui*, 2:417–26. Furthermore, he suggests that the work was well funded because, after paying for other necessities such as fireworks, the government had a large surplus in its budget for the opening ceremonies.

16. See fig. 13.1.

17. The reduced-size orchestras that played in these two *brasseries* should not be underestimated in their importance. They played a wide variety of classical repertoire nightly, ten months a year. The Concerts Rouge began in 1889, the Concerts Touche in 1906. Their orchestras featured mostly performers with first prizes from the Conservatoire, who were often paid up to double what they would have made at the major orchestras such as Colonne's. For more information, see chapter 12 here.

18. Debora Silverman devotes chapter 4 of *Art Nouveau in Fin-de-Siècle France* (Berkeley: University of California Press, 1989) to this idea. Her notes give an excellent bibliography.

Holmès was known for her "vigorous temperament" and will. She was evidently accustomed to getting whatever she wanted, as her career suggests. What is not so obvious is that she was also hard-working, dedicated, and full of ideas.

In her person as well as her music, Holmès exploited both feminine and masculine values. Because of her physical beauty in her youth, she is known to have had a series of love relationships before age twenty. Some thought, probably erroneously, that this included one with César Franck, with whom she studied composition.[19] Saint-Saëns once admitted, "We were all in love with her." At concerts in the 1870s, people remembered her as "remarkably beautiful," her blond hair contrasting with her dark eyes. Critics admitted to staring at her.[20] Of course, knowing how to seduce, she made a hit in salons with her songs (eventually there were over 130 of them). And in her larger works, too, she always saved a place for expressing her tender, sensual side, the antidramatic "caresses" expected of all woman's music (though also characteristic of much men's music of the time).

But Holmès was also a bit of a crossdresser. In the late 1860s, like many women composers of her time, she published her first songs under the name of a man, Hermann Zenta. And possibly because she reminded him of the Ovidian character with whom Hercules switched roles, she was the person to whom Saint-Saëns dedicated his symphonic poem Le Rouet d'Omphale (1872). But more than this, around 1885, she cut her hair and changed her appearance radically. Later she appeared in public dressed similarly to a man.

The ambiguity inherent in figure 8.1 raises questions about her desired public image. In his Nouveaux profils de musiciens (1892), Hugues Imbert surrounded an image of her with etchings of five male composers in similar poses. He thought nature had erred in making her female. In an earlier, manuscript draft of his essay in this book, Imbert points to her blouses and "famous white waistcoats in the form of breastplates [plastrons]" as a way of "masculinizing her clothes." He also notes that her handwriting is not feminine. With its "vigorously noted letters, slanted from left to right, and stressed gestures at the end of each word," he sees it as indicating someone with "great will and imperturbable decisiveness."[21]

Elaine Showalter, Sexual Anarchy: Gender and Culture at the Fin de Siècle (New York: Viking, 1990), chap. 3, also discusses such a woman, though mostly those in the English-speaking world.

19. According to Joël-Marie Fauquet, César Franck (Paris: Fayard, 1999), 518, Holmès probably met Franck before 1870 through the help of Antonin Guillot de Sainbris, a member of the grande bourgeoisie in Versailles and director of a well-respected amateur choral society.

20. Ryno, "Augusta Holmès."

21. Hugues Imbert, manuscript notes in Fonds Montpensier, Augusta Holmès, F-Pn, Musique. See also the way she dressed at a rehearsal of her opera in 1895: "her bust strapped into a masculine jacket and a quilted white waistcoat"; cited in Henson, "In the House of Disillusion," 258, n. 61.

FIGURE 8.1. Augusta Holmès in Hugues Imbert's *Nouveaux Profils de musiciens* (1892). Cliché Bibliothèque Nationale.

He even describes her in her youth as having the allure "of a very frank and natural *bon garçon* who would tell you everything on his mind." These statements contrast strikingly with what Imbert finally published. In the later, printed version, he begins by swooning over the thirteen-year-old's "striking beauty" and "marvelous blond hair . . . whose profile reflected the liveliest intelligence"—the mythology that still continues about her. There is no mention of her masculine traits, only her "virile talent," noticed by Villiers de l'Isle-Adam when she was fifteen or sixteen. This raises some interesting questions: Did Holmès consider herself masculine in some sense? Did she eventually feel she needed a masculine appearance to complement her so-called virile talent? Did she play any role in maintaining her reputation for being beautiful in her youth, despite her decision to look more masculine as her career took off, or was it the critics who preferred this image of her to the reality of her increasingly masculine self-identity?

Other ironies also permeate her life. Even though she had children, Augusta Holmès was *not* the typical bourgeoise. Virtually all printed accounts of her childhood refer to her father at her side—her mother died in 1858 when Augusta was ten. (She was born in Paris on 16 December 1847.) This may explain why she admired masculine values so much. In an interview from the 1890s, she says as much: "In fact, I have the soul of a man in the body of a woman. How could it be otherwise? It was my father who raised me: a rough old soldier."[22] Major Charles Dalkeith Holmes was a former British military officer, a Protestant landowner from Ireland who settled definitively in Versailles after 1855. Even though some think she was an illegitimate daughter of the poet Alfred de Vigny, who lived near the Holmeses' *pied-à-terre* in Paris and was close to the family, her father was clearly the major influence on her upbringing. He was a man who loved knowledge, included his daughter in his frequent discussions about philosophy and ethics with his friends, and regularly accompanied her to salon gatherings. Their house was austere and dark, with old stained-glass windows, ancient arms, knights in armor holding torches, and a huge library. Such a context offered Augusta a very different education from that of most young girls, certainly one that lacked banality and sentimentality.

It appears that from early on, Augusta's career was the most important part of her life—achievement, not marriage. For an ambitious woman, marriage could be an impediment to professional development. The law treated married women as dependents of their husbands. Until 1907, the fruits (and income) of wives' work belonged to their husbands. And until the late 1890s, arguments in favor of extending women's civic rights tended to focus on those of nonmarried women—

22. Cited in Nancy Sarah Theeman, *The Life and Songs of Augusta Holmès* (Ph.D. diss., University of Maryland, 1983), 16.

filles majeures and widows. Maintaining male authority within the family was seen as integral to the interests of the state.[23]

Holmès had reservations about a traditional bourgeois marriage. She had her children secretly and out of wedlock. The children's father was Catulle Mendès, an ambitious Parnassian poet whom she met around 1865; he was married to Judith Gautier in 1866 (they separated in 1874). Raphael, their first child, was born in May 1870. Three girls followed: Hughette on 1 March 1872, Claudine in June 1876, and Hélyonne in September 1879. Another boy, Marthian, was born around 1881. According to a recent biographer, Mendès and his sister played a greater role in raising them than Holmès did. When the oldest died at an early age and the couple split up around 1885, it appears that Mendès got custody. This, together with the fact that he promised to support Holmès for the rest of his life, allowed her to concentrate on her career, at least until he changed his mind.[24] It is possible that this rejection by her ex-mate and separation from her children contributed to the masculine identity she began to project around the same time. Certainly she had a different body after giving birth five times. Moreover, earlier descriptions of her as *opulent* (buxom) may have been when she was pregnant.[25] It is also possible she was depressed after the death of her last child and wished to have no more children. But a question remains: did the masculine projections placed on her and her music by the critics take a toll on her personal identity as a woman? I have never seen her marital status or her children mentioned in any reviews or essays about her.

It is ironic to compare Holmès's life choices with her political beliefs. She agreed with many feminists that society's future depended on women's contribution. But rather than tying this to women's rights, as socialists did, or to their selflessness, as Catholics sneered, she looked to motherhood as a form of patriotism. Women

23. Klejman and Rochefort, *L'Égalité en marche*, 58.

24. Gérard Gefen, *Augusta Holmès l'outrancière* (Paris: Pierre Belfond, 1987), 173–81, 210. In her well-researched *Judith Gautier: A Biography* (New York: Franklin Watts, 1987), Joanna Richardson tells the story somewhat differently. She suggests that Mendès was attracted to Holmès for not only her beauty but also perhaps her connections in the literary world (i.e. Mallarmé) and her "fortune," which he "ran through" before he left her. Richardson also notes that Mendès separated because he may have found it "hard to accept" her increasingly "brusque and mannish ways." In any case, this left her "reduced her to giving piano lessons for a living." When he married Jane Boussac in 1897, he stopped Holmès's allowance, and she gradually fell into debt and died poor. When it came to their children, Mendès evidently recognized them, "to spare Augusta, who was anxious to preserve her reputation as an untouchable goddess." Holmès, by contrast, never publicly admitted to their existence, "saw them only in secret, and forbade them to call her 'mother'" (35–36, 44, 76, 92, 109, 165). Some of this information comes from Cecily Mackworth, *Stéphane Mallarmé et Augusta Holmès: Une amitié de jeunesse. Documents Stéphane Mallarmé*, vol. 6 (Paris: Nizet, 1980).

25. Ryno, "Augusta Holmès."

must have children and raise them to love their country. Belief in the family as the basic social and political unit of the nation was central to the republican mainstream at the time,[26] but Holmès went further. She sympathized with the far Right. She admired Paul Déroulède, a deputy and the founder of the Ligue des Patriotes and French fascism. He considered women not just potential mothers but "mothers who make sons" for the French army.[27] Not only did Holmès have five children, she supported such an idea in the texts she set to music. Such beliefs stem from her response to the Franco-Prussian War of 1870. One critic called her "the most ardent, the most impassioned, and the most enthusiastic of French women" touched by that war.[28]

VIRILE PATRIOTISM AND MUSICAL BOLDNESS

After Prussia defeated France and took two of its provinces, Holmès was preoccupied with the idea of revenge (*la revanche*). She was intent on inspiring patriotism and a return to war. Unlike Joan of Arc, Judith, and other patriotic women admired during this period, however, she did not look to other voices for her inspiration or strength. Like Wagner, Berlioz, and some of her contemporaries, she wrote most of her song texts and all her libretti, many of which concern oppressed countries. She also designed the costumes and sets for her major staged works, *Ode triomphale* and the opera *La Montagne noire*, and expressed clear preferences about casting. Throughout her career, she won respect as a composer-poet who was both courageous and hardworking.

Holmès's first composition was a military march for piano, the "Marche des Zouaves" (c. 1861), which she evidently taught the old soldiers in the garrison.[29] Even at age fourteen, when she wrote it, she understood the basics of the genre— the ABA form and the expansion of register, dynamics, and rhythmic density that listeners might expect. Other early works also show sophistication: several large works for chorus and orchestra, the beginnings of three operas, four Latin settings, some chamber pieces, and eighteen songs. "Vengeance," a song written amid the war in December 1870 and published by Leduc in 1872, was stunningly virile. Holmès's text is full of assertive exclamations, exploring a theme that would preoccupy her and others for years. The music exemplifies a style she would embrace for most of her life (see fig. 8.2 and ex. 8.1).

26. For more on French republican feminists' emphasis on mothers-as-citizens, see Karen Offen, "Depopulation, Nationalism, and Feminism in *Fin-de-Siècle* France," *American Historical Review* 89, no. 3 (June 1984): 648–76.

27. Paul Déroulède, *Le Livre de la Ligue des patriotes* (Paris: Bureau de La ligue et du drapeau, 1887).

28. Ryno, "Augusta Holmès."

29. Paul Roquère, in *L'Évenement* (8 February 1895).

FIGURE 8.2. "Vengeance" (1872). Cliché Bibliothèque Nationale.

The extreme registral juxtapositions with which "Vengeance" begins grab the listener's attention and set a tone of urgency. *Fortissimo* chords in the middle range alternate with rising and descending chromatic octaves in the low bass. The piano doubles the baritone as he sings "French! enough embarrassment! Soldiers whom nothing subdues . . . Let's march." With fast repeated chords accompanying, the

EXAMPLE 8.1. Augusta Holmès, "Vengeance" (1872). Musical examples typeset by John Fleming.

effect is rousing, breathless. In the second half of the stanza the tone changes, as the baritone sings with resignation of the "ravaged fields" and the "insulted flags." The musical momentum turns downward. As the baritone refers to the "mothers in sorrow" and "the sons in tombs," each of the descending lines returns to C-sharp, as if the note, or the need for "vengeance" for which he eventually cries on this note, will not go away. The song that begins so passionately then ends resolutely, underlining the work's message—the French should go back to war.

Her earliest works to receive prestigious public performances, *In Exitu* at the Société Nationale in 1872 and *Andante pastorale* at the Concerts Colonne in 1877, reveal the beginnings of her musical identity. The former impressed by its "powerful inspiration" and "knowledge of modern musical resources." The latter reflected an aesthetic orientation, the result of studying with Franck and admiring Wagner. Some found her music a flagrant imitation of Wagner, whose work she heard in Germany in 1869, and, as such, offensive. Others pointed out that like the "German colossus," she knew how to write "original sonorities" and "powerful harmonies." Everyone was amazed at her *science musicale*, as rare for a woman as it was enviable for any composer at her age.[30] Critics' recurring use of "power" to describe her music says even more. Holmès understood that the French associated power, strength, and originality with Germany. If she wanted serious critical attention, tapping into German musical resources was a way to get it, even if she risked being derided as an imitator.

Lutèce, her first major work, was explicitly patriotic. Composed in the hope of winning the City of Paris prize in 1878, it came in second in the competition.[31] A "dramatic symphony" in three parts, for which she wrote text and music, the work features a Gaulois, Gauloise, messenger of war, old man, and narrator, as well as choruses and orchestra.[32] It begins with "The Departure," a four-measure call to arms by the trombones, bassoons, and piano. In five stanzas, the narrator proclaims, "Remember your ancestors," "Live and die like them," and "Wake up, for the day has come." Then the horns begin a musical metaphor for dawn. Quietly repeated octaves are followed by series of rising fifths, flute tremoli, and a thin orchestra accompanying the chorus. Reiterating the same rising fifth motive on D–E–F-sharp–G and then A, they sing "It's the dawn." When the ophicleide joins the orchestral celebration, we hear "Adore the sun and its glory. It is the day for conquering."

---

30. Octave Mirbeau, "A bas Wagner," *L'Ordre* (16 January 1877), and an anonymous reviewer, "Au rideau," *Les Droits de l'homme* (17 January 1877).

31. Godard's *Le Tasse* and Dubois's *Le Paradis perdu* shared first prize. Holmès's work was "classed in the second rank."

32. The orchestration for *Lutèce* is three flutes, two oboes, two clarinets, English horn, two bassoons, six horns, four trumpets, three trombones, ophicleide, two harps, two timpani, strings, and piano.

The Gauloise then declares her devotion to her fiancé, emphasizing each reference to strength with *forte* leaps up to f-sharp′ or g′:

> O my master, I will love you,
> Harsh or tender, your voice enchains me,
> To your strength I will unite myself
> Like a clematis [vine] to an oak tree.
> Always attentive at home,
> Your faithful wife will wait for you,
> Her fingers reddened by work,
> But singing like a swallow.
> And we'll see our sons grow up
> White and strong with blond beards,
> Those who will hurl happy challenges
> And conquer the conquerors of the world.

The man and woman then sing of their love as in a typical late nineteenth-century opera duet. The man's upwardly arching melody "Oh woman, you are my preferred one" is echoed by the woman an octave higher, "Oh man whom I have preferred." Together *forte*, an octave apart, they both sing "Yes we have joy." Soon a messenger of war calls everyone "To Arms," and a male chorus responds. Bassoons and lower strings accompany them in waves of chromatic oscillations spanning an augmented second, interrupted every other measure by startling augmented fifth chords played by the woodwinds *fortissimo*. This section and its juxtapositions move up gradually by semitones from G to E-flat before a wild series of alternating soprano and bass octaves descend by semitones from G/g and g′g″ down to G_1/G and g/g′. Holmès treats this and the opening trumpet call as leitmotifs for the army. They return to punctuate the messenger of war's narrative about the country being "under the heavy foot of the foreigner," as if to suggest what should be done. The Gauloise answers the messenger's call to arms, telling her fiancé "Go, that your first wound [might] replace my first kiss. . . . Be happy, country. Your sons give their blood. I give my husband."

These bold musical gestures mirror bold attitudes: Holmès's feelings of how women should understand war. The love between a man and wife, in such a context, has no power. The Gauloise does not try to seduce or entreat, as in most works by Holmès's male contemporaries, in which the interests of love and duty collide. On the contrary, the Gauloise happily gives up her sons and husband (ex. 8.2). The Gaulois thanks his wife and, accompanied by menacing diminished seventh chords and drum rolls in the orchestra, tells her to "be faithful and hide your fear and your heart . . . for death calls me." The music turns sentimental and heartfelt, then full of agitated brass patterns that resemble sword attacks, as he explains, "I loved you, the most courageous and the most beautiful. But Lutèce is wounded, and I [now] love only her. I'll only return if a conqueror." A children's

EXAMPLE 8.2. Holmès, *Lutèce*, pt. 1, the Gauloise and male chorus, page 39.

chorus and a women's chorus follow with an Allegro feroce. It builds to a large tutti as if in collusion with this idea. With short breath groups of two or three notes (a sixteenth or thirty-second, then eighth or quarter note), everyone drives home the message *fortissimo*: "Go brother, go son, go brother. . . . To arms! to arms! To arms! Death, death, death to the Romans. . . . Don't come back until you are wounded. . . . Kill, kill, kill."

Part 2 takes place on the battlefield, after the narrator, in three stanzas addressed to mothers, tells them to be proud of their sons because they consent to die. Four trumpets and the piano make the battle call on upper D octaves, while four trombones, an ophicleide, the bassoons, and lower strings answer with lower oscillating E-flat and C-flat octaves. This recurs over and over and in other keys throughout the movement. The critics called these "hard dissonances," "a sort of cruelty," albeit one suggesting the brutal juxtapositions of battle (ex. 8.3). Musical metaphors for sword attacks follow every other measure. These crescendo up to

EXAMPLE 8.3. Holmès, *Lutèce*, pt. 2, prelude.

loud chords that in nine measures chromatically rise from A to D. Chromatic sixteenth notes accompanying these chords keep the tension high by hovering within a narrow range. Later the woodwinds expand on these passages and, accompanied by low tremoli, drive the energy forward. Throughout this section, juxtaposed sound masses, increasing in volume, stand in the place of any melodic development.

The battle music ends with a march in a "pompous tempo." It begins in the whole orchestra, *fortissimo*, but after a very short lyrical interlude, the same material returns softly, gradually reducing to *pianissimo (ppp)*—a most unusual march ending! Over its last notes, followed by low string tremoli and eventually a minor second between the horns and double basses, the narrator explains, "In vain they fought 100 against 1000." The Gaulois moans, "Oh country, oh my mother, I've left you in the impure arms of the foreigner." A male chorus echoes these words, the tenors emphasizing their phrases with yearning octave leaps up to g′ before a dramatic descent down to C_4, where the section cadences.

With the reference to country as mother, we revisit Holmès's thoughts on patriotism. She believes a Frenchman's sense of duty should be as son to mother. The Gaulois's words express his frustration: "I've seen your bitter embarrassment without being able to avenge you." In his final words, however, it is not as mother that he refers to his country but as mistress: "I've given everything for my mistress, the country is no longer." For Holmès then, country should ideally represent two kinds of love and duty, one you are born with and one you freely choose.

Another related metaphor running throughout the work is the comparison Holmès makes between French wine and the blood of French heroes—"fertilizer for devastated fields." In part 1, the Gauloise sings, in large sweeping phrases, "Pour out all the blood from your veins while laughing / So that heroes are reborn from the fertile soil" (ex. 8.4). Part 3, "After the Defeat," returns to this theme, beginning in C minor. Although the narrator begins by calling mothers to "pour out your tears," the work doesn't dwell on grief for long. Accompanied by rolled chords in the harps and strings, the Gauloise sings exuberantly and with dotted rhythms, as if she can imagine the future glory of Paris: "The blood of heroes rejuvenates . . . saves cities . . . fertilizes devastated fields. . . . From the blood of heroes and the mothers of even more audacious sons the most beautiful country [*cité*] will be

EXAMPLE 8.4. Holmès, *Lutèce*, pt. 1, the Gauloise, page 43.

born." The chorus forthrightly sings a homophonic hymn of glory, ending in a grandiose tone backed up by the full orchestra. Whether this change of feeling at the end was convincing or not—and some critics found it was not, after the disaster depicted[33]—it is a blatant attempt to revive the French. The work suggests that, as the country gives birth to grapes each season, mothers must give birth to heroes so that the country can be "reborn powerful and prolific [*féconde*]." In this sense, it is women's fertility as mothers on which the country's salvation depends.

When Choudens published the score in 1880, two important music critics wrote about it. Both concentrated on what made it sound virile and how unusual this kind of music was for a woman. Victorin Joncières, a composer/critic with Wagnerian sympathies, wrote:

> Most women who make music only produce works that, in general, are mediocre; the most talented write what society calls "very pretty things." It's graceful, elegant, of a sufficiently poetic bourgeois ideal to merit praise from the well-raised people around them; however, from the perspective of great lyric art, it absolutely lacks any significance [*portée*]. . . .
>
> Mlle Augusta Holmès is an exception to the rule. Her music has a vigor, a virility, an enthusiasm that deserve better than the banal praise that is ordinarily given to most women composers. *Lutèce* [is] full of momentum [*élan*], strength, grandeur. There is sometimes a shocking boldness but there is also an inspiration [*souffle*], an ardor, a passion that pulls one forward. . . .
>
> Like the Gauloise whom she has made the heroine, she sings of war with the ferocious power of a *Velléda* [warrior]. Whereas in her first works this exaltation sometimes led Mlle Holmès to excessive violence, we would say almost to extravagances, today it does not at all damage the clarity of her thought and the intelligence of her developments. . . .
>
> Beginning today, this courageous artist should take her place among the *most* distinguished of the Modern School.[34]

Another critic wrote similarly:

> Ordinarily, I must admit, I am on my guard with feminine music. The extreme sensibility of women, that which makes them so good at performing great works, perhaps prevents them from creating such works. Whatever

33. Victorin Joncières, writing in *La Liberté* (8 November 1880), was not happy with such an ending.

34. Joncières, in *La Liberté* (8 November 1880). When the feminist newspaper *Le Droit des femmes* wanted to hold up a woman who "affirms her intellectual strength" and "attains all the heights," they reprinted this entire review in Georges Bath, "Les Femmes artistes," c. 1880 or 1881.

the reason, the musical baggage of the most remarkable among them reduces very often to a few sentimental and banal romances, a few compositions without color and without character. . . .

Mlle Holmès is an exception to the rule. This artist resolutely puts herself among the first ranks of the most bold of the modern school, she counts among those who believe in music and in its future and fight valiantly for it. Her score for *Lutèce* . . . full of patriotic enthusiasm and for which she wrote the words, is altogether virile. . . . The development, made in the modern style, is clear and nervous, the style is neither banal nor difficult [*cherché*] . . . her talent powerful, virile, and poetic.[35]

When the work was finally performed in Angers in 1884, the Wagnerian writer Edouard Dujardin traveled from Paris to hear it:

Finally here is a sincere, lively, strong work, a real work of art [*oeuvre véritable*]. . . . All the ardor of the beautiful poem is infused into the music. One after another, there are tender and voluptuous scenes, savage, harsh, poignant, delicious, and sublime ones. . . . The orchestra, conceived more or less in the spirit of Wagner [*wagnériquement*], overflows with caresses and fury. The theme of the country runs throughout the work, simple and superb. The love motives at the beginning tend toward the desired sensuality that is in fashion. But as soon as they mix in with the patriotism, the music gets virile, showing intense passion. . . .

The success was complete, decisive, without precedent. They almost had to interrupt the piece several times because of applause during the drama. After each part, there was enthusiastic cheering . . . at the end the cheering erupted three times. . . .

Mlle Holmès is bold and sincere. . . . Frankly it's beautiful, it's terrific, that in the middle of all the intrigues, fears, and compromises made by composers who are known and talented, a woman represents honesty, loyalty, courage, and proud boldness. . . . [She] is an admirer of Wagner and doesn't hide it. Too bad if some mock and others whistle, she is not among those who renounce their gods. . . . What an example and what a lesson . . . that a woman calmly follows her own inspiration![36]

These critics' vocabulary is very telling. Women's music, they tell us, is elegant and graceful, pleasing in domestic circles. Great art, in contrast, is virile, vital, strong, and grand (that is, like Wagner's). Joncières, in particular, expands on these and other masculine values to argue for five sources of credibility in her work.

---

35. Henri LaVoix fils, "Bibliographie musicale: Lutèce," *Le Globe* (20 January 1881).
36. Edouard Dujardin, "Lutèce," *Le Progrès artistique* (December 1884?).

- First, unlike the stereotype of women artists not thought to be able to endure the struggles great artists must go through to achieve success, Holmès has already shown "great tenacity" and "invincible energy." She returned to work after losing her first major competition. She has the perseverance and will necessary to pursue a serious career.
- Second, one can hear this "courageous character" in her music. Like the Gauloise, she "sings of war with the ferocious power of a *Velléda*" (warrior). She is bold in both action and music. Her music is energetic and seeks to infuse energy in its listeners.
- Third, though this "exaltation" may sometimes lead her music to "excessive violence," it never "damages the clarity of her thought and the intelligence of her developments." She is smart and esteems French clarity.
- Fourth, Holmès knows how to balance peaceful charming scenes and phrases "full of tenderness" with those of "movement and action," though sometimes there are "harsh dissonances."
- Fifth, she uses vocal and instrumental masses to create "brilliant sonorities" and "very grandiose" effects. That is, she commands a rich array of musical resources and can manipulate them skillfully.

In other words, she is not afraid to write big pieces, set heroic tales of war and patriotism next to her "ravishing duets" about love, explore loud, full sonorities and energetic movements—all of which begin to *define virility* in music at the time. Reviewers would return to these five attributes throughout her career.

Critics also praised Holmès for pushing audiences beyond what they were used to, for being "modern" or "advanced"—another implicitly masculine value. More than a decade before the Wagner craze hit France, her music was called Wagnerian, a code word not only for power but also the new. This meant not only the "original sonorities and harmonic power resembling those of the colossal German"[37] but also the widespread use of chromaticism, heavy brass parts, and difficult vocal writing. Critics were divided over whether the effects she was seeking were "exaggerated." Dujardin found little to fault, in part because of her "loyalty" to Wagnerian principles. Joncières, however, felt she "abused" augmented fifths in the call "To Arms" and in dissonances in the battle music. Moreover, the Romans' triumphant march seemed to him "pompously flat," possibly because of the extended repetition of the same chordal melody. Structurally, Holmès may have felt this stasis was necessary after the melody in the preceding battle section that spans three octaves and then a staggering five (page 73 in the piano-vocal score). She was willing to suffer criticism for being excessively bold, or writing beyond singers'

37. *Les Droits de l'homme* (17 January 1877).

FIGURE 8.3. "Ogier le Danois" (1900). Cliché Bibliothèque Nationale.

natural limits, as the cost of penetrating an arena from which women were normally kept out.

Another source of virility in Holmès's music, referred to only tangentially by the critics, contributed to perceptions of her music as bold (in the sense of going against what was expected from a woman) yet effective in winning audience approval. Dujardin asserts this explicitly: "When the love motives are joined by patriotic accents, the music becomes virile." He hears virility when the passion in the couple changes after the messenger's call to arms. After leaps to their upper registers, dramatic descents follow in both singers' lines, suggesting an acceptance of their fate. Meanwhile, trumpet calls direct their passion to the country. Virility here refers to putting duty to country over personal desires and going to war as the essence of that duty.

Holmès's ideas about women as mothers of soldiers recall Etienne-Nicolas Méhul's "Chant du départ," composed after the backlash against women's rights in 1793 and embraced as one of the most popular hymns of the revolution. More immediately, however, her text and music echo attitudes Déroulède expresses in his first manifesto, *De l'Education militaire* (1882). In it, the future deputy worries that France is losing the "courageous qualities of its race" while, on the other side of the Rhine, schools teach warrior songs and patriotism. To address this problem, Déroulède discusses the need to instill "male feelings and virile habits" in children, the country's future soldiers. Music and poetry are ideal for this. He says they should play an important role in helping people remember the "bitterness" of defeat. Although Holmès had a different attitude toward their German neighbors, it is not hard to see how her works could serve the same purpose. She, too, sought to recall defeat, infuse vigor, instill love of country, and promote the idea of sacrifice and duty. When Déroulède began to lose credibility with the French public, Holmès dedicated two songs to him, "Le Chevalier au lion" (1898) and "Ogier le Danois" (1900). (fig. 8.3). Both concern heroes who desire revenge, salvation for their country, and glory. These themes recur in many other songs, particularly from the 1890s, including "La Guerrière," "Ne Nous oubliez pas" (sung as if from the dead), "Marche gauloise," "La Prière au drapeau," and "Dans les Vosges."

STRIKING THE RIGHT BALANCE

In *Les Argonautes*, her second major work and a "dramatic symphony" written for the 1880 City of Paris prize competition, Holmès explores an essentialist struggle between masculine and feminine forces as represented by male and female characters (male and female choruses, a tenor and a mezzo). Holmès's biographer Gérard Gefen suggests a similarity with the musical oppositions in Franck's *Quintet* (1879), but as a genre the work follows in the tradition of Félicien David's ode-symphony *Le Désert* and Berlioz's *Roméo et Juliette*. Unlike in *Lutèce*, the women of *Argonautes* are not supportive wives; they are seducers of men or objects of men's love, while men are depicted as conquerors. As in operas of the time, *Samson et Dalila*, *Judith*, and *Salammbô*, love renders the hero and the heroine temporarily submissive. But the story does not end there.

Les Argonautes, in four parts, is about the hero Jason's search for the Golden Fleece (a reference to Wagner's holy grail). In part 1, both text and music speak of heroism and Jason's desire for renown, a kind of immortal life earned by finding the fleece. Accompanied by long chromatic waves in the lower strings and later march rhythms, his men urge him to go to sea: "Leave and come back conqueror." In part 2, they struggle with a "furious" storm at sea—an opportunity for the composer to flaunt her orchestral skill as she refers to Wagner's *Flying Dutchman*. Then they encounter the Sirens, who, in a change from 4/4 to 12/8, urge them to "forget." Holmès uses these ancient Greek charmers to write quintessentially charming music—slithering chromatic melismas and carefully articulated semitones on "ou-bli-ez." The Sirens question the pursuit of gold, which "flees," love, which "betrays," and glory, which is "ephemeral." Interrupting in another key and meter, Jason takes and transforms the chromatic material associated with the Sirens, finishing his phrases with dotted rhythms and rising triadic arpeggios. Vigorously "masculine" music accompanies—loud octaves that crescendo—in addition to some of the same registral juxtapositions that characterized the beginning of "Vengeance." At daybreak, as the men reach "clarity" and the shore, the music (now in 4/4) settles squarely on A major.

In part 3, "Médée," Holmès musically and poetically constructs a portrait of an equally strong and heroic woman, the daughter of a king. As in part 2, the challenge is one of balance between masculine and feminine forces. Set at night, it begins with a "magical dance" in E minor for women's chorus and orchestra. Low tremolos accompany Medea as she sings an invocation to Hecate in A minor,[38] using dotted rhythms and sweeping melodies to ask for her favor (ex. 8.5). Here we see not feminine grace but a powerful woman possessed and demanding "blood," as if she represents Hecate herself. Like Jason's music, Medea's proceeds in aggressive octaves and arpeggiated triads, perhaps suggesting that her nature is similar to his. When the Argonauts return and Medea first notices Jason, her music slowly modulates from aggression to wonder, accompanied by tremolos and a motive signifying love. (Critics here pointed to the influence of *Lohengrin*). Under the "conquering charm" of Eros, Medea succumbs, telling him she would betray her people, her gods, and even her father for his love. Jason tries to resist but falls for her. Well matched in both their strength and their weakness, they begin a typical imitative duet about "conquering love."

In part 4, set in the sacred forest of the Golden Fleece, Jason must confront his dilemma—to pursue gold and renown or his love for Medea. Again the music turns ferocious as Jason recounts his conquering exploits. At that point, however, Holmès alters the myth. Jason's arrogance reminds him of his goal. Medea pro-

---

38. In classical mythology, Hecate was "a goddess of the moon, earth, and Hades, later regarded as the goddess of sorcery and witchcraft" (*Webster's Dictionary*, 2nd College Ed.).

EXAMPLE 8.5. Holmès, *Les Argonautes*, pt. 3, Medea's invocation.

tests with fury and pleads him to stay. He retorts, calling on his heroic courage to overcome love itself: "I will conquer the love of a woman. . . . I don't love you. I love only glory." As in eighteenth-century operas by Gluck and others wherein this tonality signifies a peaceful resolution of a dilemma, C major returns when Jason realizes that he has "conquered clarity, the knowledge of truth, and beauty."

Whereas love triumphs in most works of the period, albeit often leading to the woman's death, few critics objected to this modification of the classical story. Saint-Saëns bemoaned the "cruel dénouement" and seemed flabbergasted that a woman should so invert the norm. Nonetheless, he pointed out, "It's a lesson."[39] Others found it "the most beautiful moment" in the piece. They understood its message: to achieve a very high ideal, one must renounce everything that makes ordinary people happy.

39. Saint-Saëns, "Les Argonautes."

The work impressed everyone on the jury. But, to the surprise of many, it took only second prize.[40] This "scandal" resulted in extensive and overtly generous critical attention, especially when the work was subsequently performed twice by Pasdeloup in 1881 and three times at the Société des Concerts du Conservatoire in 1885. Those reviewing it raised the same issues as with *Lutèce*: Holmès's vigorous temperament, energy, will, perseverance in work, creative talent, and forceful ideas.[41] They found Jason's music so "virile" that in classifying female and male geniuses, they didn't know where to place Holmès.[42] For some, the composer "revealed herself" in Medea's ferocious incantation to Hecate, whereas for others this recalled the anarchist Louise Michel! They also praised the work for combining "German knowledge/skill [*science*] and French clarity."[43]

Ironically, Saint-Saëns, her friend, wrote the most ambivalent review, envious perhaps of her courage yet disturbed by her independence.

> She has a powerful originality, too powerful maybe, because this quality in the extreme pushes her to go beyond conventional paths where she ends up alone, without a guide or help. . . .
>
> Like children, women know no obstacles; their will smashes everything, ignoring miserable material obstacles. . . . The brass explodes in her music like boxes of fireworks; tonalities collide, modulations bang together with the noise of a storm; the voices, terrified, lose all sense of their natural register and plunge from the highest notes to the lowest ones at the risk of breaking. . . . She wills it![44]

While he liked the male chorus at the end of part 2 and the "simple and grand" moment when Jason and Medea first meet, aesthetically he found much of the work overdone and some of it "not exactly comprehensible." Such a judgment is

---

40. Of the eighteen scores examined during the competitions, Duvernoy's *Tempête* received eleven votes, Holmès *Argonautes* nine votes. In his review, reprinted in his *Musiciens d'aujourd'hui*, 2:408, Jullien notes that most of the musicians on the jury voted for Holmès, which is why they were probably willing to sign the letter requesting performance funds from the Budget Commission (see note 12).

41. Jacques Hermann, "Musique: Les Argonautes," *Constitutionnel* (26 March 1881).

42. M. Crespel, "Musique," *Le Clairon* (23 April 1881).

43. Henri LaVoix fils, "Musique," *Le Globe* (25 April 1881); Charles Friedlander, "Concerts populaires," *l'Opinion* (24 April 1881). The public of 1881 was fascinated with the revolutionary activist Louise Michel (1830–1905). An instructor of drawing, she was exiled in 1873 for her Communard activities and returned to France after being pardoned in 1880. Although she expressed desire for "universal happiness," she led demonstrations during the international anarchist congress in London in 1881 and was feared for her willingness to use guns to advance her goals.

44. Saint-Saëns, "Les Argonautes."

undoubtedly tinged with disdain for Wagner, whose influences on French music Saint-Saëns rejected.

Although some critics agreed that she sometimes went too far, displayed too much vigor, and used too many trumpets, tremolos, and chromatic scales—all faults also associated with Wagner—many found reason to compare Holmès with the great composers. Several, including Henri LaVoix fils in *Le Globe*, appreciated Gluck's influence on Medea's passages. Charles Darcours in *Le Figaro* remarked that one section was as good as the "Ride to the Abyss" in Berlioz's *Damnation de Faust*.[45] The first performance received "unanimous bravos." In this context, Saint-Saëns's last words in his review—please, "fewer trumpets"— seem a futile attempt to regain his role of "guide or help" to the now-recognized genius.

DISTINCTION AS A REPUBLICAN MUSE

In her subsequent large works, *Irlande* (1882), *Pologne!* (1883), *Ludus pro patria* (1888), and *Ode triomphale* (1889), Holmès returned to patriotic subjects. Critics again focused on the coexistence of virility and feminine charm and the flaws caused by occasional excesses. The first, written during a period of political turmoil in Ireland, was "both exquisite and violent." Its call for heroism was enthusiastically applauded, but some felt its ideals "excessively elevated" and the work marred by exaggerated effects and too much percussion.[46] Fourcaud called it a "male composition, large in its layout, bold and clear in its development, full of curious rhythms, expressive harmonies, and above all an energetic sonority."[47] *Pologne!*—a symphonic poem without words—was also judged as both "virile in style and conception" and "feminine by its feelings and pity," though criticized for a "slight abuse of sonorities." Martial rhythms alternate with languorous andantes expressing the anguish of wives, lovers, and mothers. The love of country again clashes with maternal and conjugal love, only to bring, in the end, hope for revenge. The similarity of these themes to those in *Lutèce* and her other patriotic works suggests that one is meant to hear them as metaphors for France.[48]

---

45. Holmès herself begged the comparison by subtitling the work a "dramatic symphony" in the tradition of Berlioz's *Roméo et Juliette*.

46. A. B., "Concerts," *La Musique des familles* (30 December 1886): 85. In his *Augusta Holmès*, Gefen suggests that Holmès may well have written this work out of sympathy for Charles Parnell, the leader of Ireland's Home Rule movement, who was arrested in October 1881 and liberated in May 1882 (169).

47. Louis Fourcaud, "Les Concerts symphoniques," *Le Gaulois* (22 December 1885).

48. In her song "Marche gauloise," she writes of the Celts as descendants of the Gauls and thus belonging to the same race.

The subject of *Ludus pro patria*, a symphonic ode for chorus and orchestra, is again the love that produces soldiers, both literally and figuratively. The work is in five parts. It was inspired by Puvis de Chavannes' triptych that represents old men, women, and adolescents taking part in games or exercises for the glorification or defense of the country. After an orchestral Largo maestoso, a narrator invites the French: "Sing, love, wait, pray." In part 2, night falls, and love—"generator of worlds," "instigator of fertile ecstasies," and "conqueror of conquerors"—joins the couples as they "repopulate" the earth. When someone cries "treason," the men prepare to go off to war.

Critics praised the work for its patriotism as well as its synthesis of feminine and masculine elements. They appreciated the combination of martial style and profound tenderness in the verses and clarity, despite the luxurious orchestration in the music. Even Arthur Pougin, the tough and typically misogynist critic writing for one of the most important music magazines, *Le Ménestrel*, had nothing but praise for Holmès: "She is the most talented of all [our] women composers, the one who best knows all the secrets and resources of her art. And in addition to being able to express grace and feminine tenderness, she joins to them an energy of which musically women are always deprived." He liked the "Chorus of Night and Love," with its "charm and sweetness . . . grace, delicacy, exquisite poetry, and enchanting rhythm," as well as sections with "vigor, power, and male energy, inspired by Gluck," such as the chorus of the blacksmiths. He acknowledged that the public asked for encores and was never bored.[49]

Others used the occasion to reorient discussion of the work's virility. As if to counter Saint-Saëns's earlier criticism, Joncières points out that it is not the result of merely a strong will. *Ludus* is "grand and strong by the vigor of its ideas and the nobility of its feelings, *not* by its means of execution."[50] Like other Wagnerians, Adolphe Jullien uses the word "virile" to refer to the work's originality: "The most surprising thing is that it is a woman who could imagine and realize such a new format, and how often haven't we already said that Mlle Holmès has talent as virile as many musicians of the strong sex?"[51] But he goes further. Jullien worried that as she learns her profession better, her music might start to resemble what they were used to hearing and thereby lose "this strange flavor, this impulsive boldness that is so alluring in her music." He hopes that she will never compromise, that she will continue to "look up" and avoid anything that might make her "effeminate" or soft—a subtle reference perhaps to the new aesthetic currents represented by Debussy.

Such commentary suggests that while her music may seem virile because of its choice and use of instruments, its marches, ideas, style, and originality, it is something of the woman in Holmès that also attracted male admiration. She

49. A. P., "Concerts et soirées," *Le Ménestrel* (11 March 1888): 87.
50. Victorin Joncières, "Revue musicale," *La Liberté* (12 March 1888).
51. Adolphe Jullien, in *Le Moniteur universel* (12 March 1888).

represented the appeal of the unknown and the allure of the strange (a curiosity that also led to innumerable operas about exotic women).[52] While she may not have been totally at ease in the role of mother and wife, Holmès was someone who represented ideals—boldness, patriotism, glory—for a public that looked to music as a means of escaping ordinary life. In this, she was like the allegorical image of the Republic, Marianne. Women may have a tendency to be too banal, too enmeshed in sentimentality, but, as these critics imply, men can too easily fall prey to the mundane, making too many compromises to please society. Whether as a *Velléda* (woman warrior) or someone who stood for republican ideals, Augusta Holmès aspired to helping listeners imagine a world where justice and glory reign. According to her biographer, once she even proposed to Colonne that he perform her *Ludus pro patria* on the German border of Alsace-Lorraine, as if the work would empower and embolden the French living there.[53]

Her next major work, *Ode triomphale* (originally titled *Le Triomphe de la République*), concerns abstract characters who explicitly represent republican ideals. Conceived for the opening ceremonies of the 1889 Exhibition, the work was inspired by the colossal festivals of ancient Greece and the French Revolution, possibly Gossec's 1793 work of the same name.[54] It was to be performed outdoors, free, and for as many people as possible. In the tradition of Berlioz's music for the 1844 Exhibition of Industry (involving 1,022 performers) and large *orphéon* gatherings of the period, Holmès again thought big. She called for 1,200 performers— over 40 brass players (30 of them playing off stage), 4 harpists (often playing *forte*), and 900 singers. She wrote the poem and music, designed the sets and costumes, and took part in the casting; Colonne conducted. The work, transferred to the Palais de l'Industrie for fear of bad weather, lasted an hour and a half and reputedly made so much noise the hall was damaged and later had to be demolished.[55] Over 25,000 people attended its five performances.

In many ways, the work reiterates the themes and style of her previous patriotic music, including the fertility of the land and its people. It begins with four trumpets

---

52. See Susan McClary, *Georges Bizet: Carmen* (Cambridge: Cambridge University Press, 1992), and Ralph Locke, "Constructing the Oriental 'Other': Saint-Saëns's *Samson et Dalila*," *Cambridge Opera Journal* 3 (November 1991): 261–302. Both are also full of excellent bibliographies on this subject.

53. Gefen, *Augusta Holmès,* 212–13.

54. Annegret Fauser, *Musical Encounters at the 1889 Paris World's Fair* (Rochester, N.Y.: University of Rochester Press, 2005), also makes this point, adding that the text and music of *Ode triomphale* also make reference to Gossec's *Offrande à la liberté* (123–25). See her chapter 3 for a fuller analysis of this work.

55. The Palais de l'Industrie was built for the 1855 Universal Exhibition as a French equivalent to London's Crystal Palace. On that occasion, Berlioz conducted two huge concerts therein, assisted by five conductors. The building was finally torn down for the 1900 Universal Exhibition, replaced by the Grand and the Petit Palais.

sounding their calls from different points in the hall and a triumphal march. March rhythms and march structure alternate throughout the work with more lyrical sections. Most of *Ode triomphale* is a series of static choruses, each led by an allegorical figure, conceived to celebrate the grandeur of various aspects of the country, including diverse classes and ages. Dramatic juxtapositions result from the different meters and instruments associated with characters on stage. The wine growers and the harvesters, for example, alternate back and forth and finally come into unison as they sing of "the bread and wine, the flesh and blood of France." The soldiers and the sailors then do the same, followed by the workers (accompanied by percussive playing of the strings), artists (who "tell the universe of your glory"), scientists (who "help man resemble God"), lovers, youth, and children. A funeral march concludes with a figure veiled in black, carrying chains and symbolizing grief (or Alsace, as some understood her).[56] Each group bows to her as she passes. Then, the veil tears and a woman dressed in white with a red and blue belt appears, singing, "O people . . . I come to your call. . . . Come to me you who suffer for justice." The chorus responds, "Glory to you, sacred liberty, glory, the Republic!"

Throughout the manuscript, Holmès indicates the casting and costumes of the various groups. For its central figure, representing "la France blonde," she calls for a woman with long blond hair (fig. 8.4). The sailors invoke her protection by this name.[57] Except for one redhead and a dark-haired Bacchus and Minerva, she also wants all the other actors in the *Ode* to have blond hair. Amphitrite was to be "very white, and very blond, pale blond," Apollo "very tall, very young, and very blond," the Sea "a young blond woman," and the lovers "blond, white, and beautiful." The land too, full of wheat, is described as a "blond plain." Reinforcing these images, the children are to be dressed entirely in white.

This was not the first time Holmès promoted white and blond women as the ideal of French society. She, of course, was blond, but most French natives are not. In the Gauloise's first song in *Lutèce*, she sings of their "sons, white and strong, with blond beards . . . who will conquer the conquerors of the world." Indeed, in its first performance, the singer who performed the Gauloise, Marthe Duvivier, was blond. The Sirens in *Argonautes* are also blond, as is Venus, "so white and so blond," in Holmès's "Hymne à Vénus" and the woman in "Le Renouveau." The warriors, too, in "La Guerrière" and "Le Chevalier au lion,"[58] have golden helmets, meaning a head of blond hair, as does the Prince in "La Vision de la Reine." And *Andromède*, in a story set in North Africa, is white, as she was for painters, who used her as

56. According to Henson, "In the House of Disillusion," Holmès originally conceived two veiled women at the end, one representing Alsace and the other Lorraine.

57. See the libretto, referred to in Fauser, *Musical Encounters*, 119.

58. Theeman analyses these dramatic songs, *The Life and Songs of Augusta Holmès*, 179–83, 220–25.

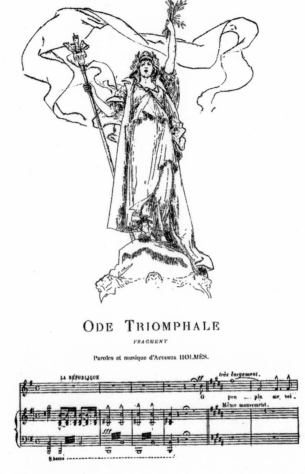

FIGURE 8.4. *Ode triomphale*, fragment, *Revue illustrée* (15 September 1889). Cliché Bibliothèque Nationale.

a metaphor for Alsace. The racism inherent in Holmès's explicit depiction of ideal people as white and blond resonates with Déroulède's *Le Livre de la Ligue des patriotes* (1887). A fervent anticolonialist, he was opposed to letting immigrants into the country and focused on who was French.

Many critics used the *Ode* as an opportunity to hold forth on their political opinions about the Republic, rejecting or embracing its poem and music for non-musical reasons.[59] It was in this context that some, such as Saint-Saëns, reflecting

59. In an interview by G. D., "Les 300,000 francs de *l'Ode triomphale*," *Le Journal* (25 December 1892), Holmès explains that although the success of her work was "enormous,"

the increasingly conservative tendencies in republicanism during this period, tried to turn Holmès into "our muse."[60] After the *Ode*, however, there are some important changes in her reception. Some grant that she now has her own style. A critic in *La Nation*, focusing on her extensive use of unisons and phrase repetition and the new-found clarity that results, reports: "It's not Gluck, nor Berlioz, nor Beethoven, nor Wagner, it's Augusta Holmès and it's really something. . . . The characteristic of this art is its absolute and magisterial simplicity, sought and found. The music of Augusta Holmès is simple, beautiful, and bare like one of the marble goddesses."[61] While Jullien found this a sellout to a far less severe and more pleasing aesthetic than that of her earlier works, Jules Ruelle, writing in *Le Progrès artistique*, concluded, "One hopes that this serenity will open a new path in our national art."[62] Undoubtedly, such recognition helped her to win her first official honor from the French government that year, the title of Chevalier of the Légion d'honneur. However, the fact that some, like Darcours, felt that its "musical value" was far beneath its "patriotic conception" introduced doubt about her talent.[63]

With the premiere of her opera *La Montagne Noire* in 1895, the reception of her music changed even more.[64] Although critics acknowledged how rare it was for a

---

Boulangist papers attacked her for glorifying the Republic and clerical (i.e. Catholic) ones for parodying the words of Christ. She also notes that the entire 300,000 francs went for the performance; "I didn't get one centime."

Some reviewers rehearsed the same comments about her "virile style" in the song of the workers and soldiers, and her "ravishing melodies" in the lovers' duo that no other woman could have written better. They also continued to see the "poignant accents she gives to the painful feelings of oppressed people" as the music least likely to come from a woman. See, for example, Horace Hennion, "Mlle Augusta Holmès," in *Conférénces diverses faites au cours de la série des Concerts de chambre* (Tours, 1899), 79.

60. *Le Rappel* (12 September 1889).

61. Minotoro, in *La Nation*, excerpted in *Fêtes du Centenaire: Ode triomphale exécuté au Palais des Champs-Elysées le 11, 12, 14, 18, 21 septembre 1889, poème et musique d'Augusta Holmès, Opinion de la presse* (Paris: Durilly, 1889).

62. Minotoro, in *La Nation*, excerpted in *Fêtes du Centenaire;* see also Jullien, *Musiciens d'aujourdhui,* 2:422–26.

63. Charles Darcours, "Les Théâtres," *Le Figaro* (9 February 1895).

64. Holmès began the opera in 1882 in a very different political and musical climate. In 1878, the Treaty of Berlin granted independence to Montenegro as part of its efforts to break up the Ottoman Empire, but problems in the region continued, and the French public followed them with great interest. Holmès finished the opera's orchestration in 1885 and then spent almost ten years trying to get it staged. According to Paul Roquère's review in *l'Evènement* (8 February 1895), the Opéra director Léon Carvalho read it, asked for a few changes, and agreed to produce it, but his successor, Auguste-Deloche Campocasso, would not admit works by women composers. Roquère notes that, as with her other works, she did everything herself, including the designs for the décor.

woman to produce an opera, and how bold, courageous, and hardworking Holmès was, few liked the story—an Orientalist tale of a soldier seduced by a Turkish slave and killed by his brother. Bauër said the "struggle between love, friendship and patriotism, the conflict of passion and duty, of femininity and brute force, of Mars and Venus" was an allegory they had simply "seen too much."[65] Moreover, when President Faure and other politicians were seen in the corridors during the performance, someone suggested that the "Orient question had been buried in 1878 and it was useless to revive it!"[66]

Besides its problems with banality and outdated politics, musical misjudgments flawed the work. Some reflected her inexperience in working with the stage and errors in the performing score. It was hard to make out the voices under the heavy orchestration and grating to hear singers attempt huge leaps and strain outside their normal registers. Those who expected a Wagnerian drama were particularly disappointed. Although critics knew she had written the opera in the early 1880s, they were shocked to hear a work more influenced by Meyerbeer, Massenet, and Gounod. In part for this reason, Imbert found much of it "very inferior" to her earlier works.[67] Jullien felt "deceived," called the opera "retrograde," and saw Holmès as pursuing public approval.[68] "Romance" dominated the work, and many considered the love duos and seduction scenes its best parts. This was enough to change the discourse. Only a few mention the virile passages (of which there were many); most underline the opera's "feminine qualities"—"sweetness, charm, and sensuality." Conservatives appreciated this preeminence of melody, finding in Holmès's intuitions a "natural clarity and healthy sharpness . . . [that] have nothing cloudy or convoluted about them."[69] But their resistance to change of all kinds was not exactly ideal support for someone like Holmès. And those looking to the future found "little modernity in her ideas."[70]

Holmès must have been shocked at being reduced to a typical "woman composer." This change in critics' perception certainly makes one reconsider her earlier achievements. Did she succeed because of the strength of her work, her universally

---

For further discussion about *La Montagne noire*, see Henson, "In the House of Disillusion," and James Parakilas, "The Soldier and the Exotic: Operatic Variations on a Theme of Racial Encounter," *Opera Quarterly* 10, no. 3 (1994): 43–69. I am grateful to the authors for providing me with advance copies of their work.

65. Henri Bauër, "Les premières Représentations," *Echo de Paris* (10 February 1895).

66. S., "La Soirée," *Le Figaro* (9 February 1895).

67. Hugues Imbert, "Revue musicale," *Le Guide musical* (17 February 1895): 153.

68. Adolphe Jullien, in *Journal des débats* (16 February 1895).

69. Henri de Curzon, in *La Gazette* (9 February 1895).

70. Charles Darcours, "Les Théâtres." This was quite a change from his review, "Notes de musique," *Le Figaro* (c. 2 May 1881), in which he wrote of *Argonautes* as "truly new" and of Holmès as an "artist of genius."

acclaimed boldness, tenacity, and courage? Or was it the vigor and energy underlying the perceived virility in those works that was socially desirable? Or that her ideology, based on women's self-sacrifice and the need to return to war, promoted widely held political ideals?

Part of her success certainly came from being a woman who could speak in the language and from the perspective of a man. She espoused beliefs and pursued professional strategies that were unusual for a woman at the time. Though she did not challenge conventional representations of women in music, neither did she embody conventional notions of what a woman could be or what kind of music she could write.[71] It is possible that excess itself—in her music, in what she required of performers, and in the scope of her works—impressed because she was a woman. That a woman would promote love of country and the desire for glory over conjugal love and personal pleasure surprised people and drew attention. That she would use political beliefs to win admirers, even if it meant betraying the needs of her gender, made her remarkably useful.

This story suggests that in the 1870s and 1880s, politics was more important than gender per se, not only to Holmès but also, arguably, to French society. What did it matter that she was a woman if she expressed views that critics and audiences wanted to hear, particularly the Wagnerians? What did it matter, ultimately, that she crossdressed with her battle music, disdaining women's traditional attitudes and subverting the norms of women's music, if her music was performed and well reviewed? Because of her achievements, people overlooked her aggressive personality, her dismissive attitude toward her own family, and her demand for overwhelmingly large forces in her major works. Her burning patriotism, together with her energy and passion, roused her listeners. Her synthesis of German musical resources and French clarity, of lofty ideals and tender feelings, were a model for the future. Using virility to focus positively on her composition and its use-value in the society, Holmès and critics colluded in the construction of a reputation that escaped stereotypes of the woman composer and helped her win remarkable success.

But this lasted only as long as she played the same game and the political climate remained relatively constant. The 1890s were a decade of flux, and virility did not continue to have the same meaning. After the first stage of the Franco-Russian alliance was signed in 1893, many French were less anxious about their own strength. At the same time, socialists were becoming powerful, and anarchist attacks proliferated. By the end of the century, the Dreyfus Affair threw into question French confidence in their military. Déroulède was cast into exile for an

---

71. In Holmès's career, one can find a "clear difference between gender of maker and strategy of representation." For more on these ideas, see Marcia Citron, *Gender and the Musical Canon* (Cambridge: Cambridge University Press, 1993), 144–57.

attempting to install a general as president.[72] The women's movement grew substantially, and men began to reconsider the enhanced role of women in the musical world.

In this context, the ideals Holmès held dear grew increasingly problematic and with them her patriotic music. In 1896 she wrote a poem, "Dans les Vosges," berating people who had forgotten the war.[73] However, she apparently never set it to music, preferring instead to write her song "A Trianon." I hear this musical *fête galante* as biting cynicism. Its classical proportions, tonal harmonies, and utterly predictable melodic lines thinly veil the hypocrisy of its eighteenth-century nostalgia. In a feature article in 1900, an anonymous reviewer advises her to "renounce any more new attempts to venture in such high places." All he can praise are her Christmas songs, which "bear the stamp of her defects" less than her other works. Gender panic underlies his tone:

> This music gives me the impression of being transvestite. She is woman and wants to wear the costume of man. . . . Oh, Ladies, be mothers, be lovers, be virgins whether it is agreeable to you or necessity requires it; but don't try to be men. . . . You will not succeed in replacing us, not entirely. Let the example of Mlle Holmès be a good lesson for you. The rare minutes when she lets her heart speak, she is no longer without talent. She should not blush to be a woman, truly and usefully [*utilement*] a woman.[74]

Holmès's reputation in elite circles did not improve. At a performance of her *Irlande* by the Concerts Lamoureux in late December 1901, audiences hissed; at the Société des Concerts Modernes the same month, her music was applauded but, the reviewer notes, "by those who like her."[75] When she died in February 1903, Debussy spoke warmly of the "beautiful sensuality and intense musicality of her innumerable melodies"—ignoring the works that had made her famous.[76]

Why then, we may ask, has she been so forgotten? Holmès's refusal to participate in the jury of a 1902 feminist art show suggests that she was not particularly involved with the movement. Yet she had no school or disciples, and without her vigorous self-promotion and demanding manner, there was no one to insist on attention. Perhaps her successors wrote her out of history because of her stylistic

72. According to Gefen, Holmès signed petitions and participated in demonstrations in defense of Déroulède. In July 1900, she wrote to the director of the Opéra-Comique asking that her song "Ogier le Danois" be performed at a concert French nationalists were giving to honor Irish nationalists. *Augusta Holmès*, 236–37.

73. Rés. Thb 56 (4), F-Pn, Musique.

74. Boîte à musique, "Mlle Augusta Holmès," *Courrier musical* (10 March 1900): 4.

75. Jean d'Udine, "Les Grands Concerts," *Courrier musical* (1 January 1902): 7, 9.

76. Claude Debussy, *Monsieur Croche et autres écrits* (Paris: Gallimard, 1971), 92.

and personal links to an earlier generation. No one in d'Indy's school, which dominated after the war, can point to Holmès as a predecessor.

After the two world wars (and until 9/11) patriotism lost its social and political significance and with it any reason for music to rekindle these feelings. If her songs have survived, perhaps it has been easier to ignore their latent values. Writing as a woman, in this sense, has its own usefulness.

With the rising popularity of Le Pen, the reactionary, antiimmigrant political leader in France in recent years, it is important to reconsider what can make virility so attractive in music. As society was struggling with change, Augusta Holmès appealed to ideals, noble feelings, and dignified subjects and, for a time, was rewarded. Her career makes a provocative commentary on what is sacrificed as well as gained when one writes politically useful music.

9. Race, Orientalism, and Distinction in the Wake of the "Yellow Peril"

*B*y 1904, the French began to understand the Orient as something other than a vague, mostly passive other, seductive as it might be, that served in the arts as the pretext for Western dreaming, escape, and an opportunity to foreground self-assertion.[1] A fear of "the yellow peril" (*le péril jaune*) set fire in French imagination when, after agreeing in 1902 to side with the Russians in their Far Eastern imperialism, the French watched in horror as the Japanese unexpectedly took on their ally, the beginning of a "war about race." "It's the yellow race threatening the white race for the first time since Genghis Khan and his band of Tartars," a French critic wrote. If the Chinese should join the Japanese, as some predicted, their power would be "colossal," a "threat to the rest of the universe."[2]

French attitudes toward the Orient were in flux. With Turkey sympathetic to Germany and the Franco-Russian alliance encouraging the French to fund Russian

A somewhat shorter version of this essay originally appeared in *Western Music and Its Others*, ed. Georgina Born and Dave Hesmondhalgh (Berkeley: University of California Press, 2000), 86–118; it is included here by permission, copyright 2000, Regents of the University of California, University of California Press.

For the interviews they granted me between 1977 and 1988, I would like to thank Georges Auric, Kaushal Bhargava, Faiyazuddin and Zahiruddin Dagar, S. A. K. Durga, Joan Erdman, Rita Ganguli, Michael Kinnear, Josef Kuckertz, T. S. Parthasarathy, V. A. K. Rango Rao, Manuel Rosenthal, T. Sankaran, Ravi Shankar, Dr. Prem Lata Sharma, and Vijay Verma.

1. From the late nineteenth century, the term "exotic" was used in France to refer to almost anything beyond French, German, Italian, and English culture.

2. "Le Péril jaune," opinions of diverse French leaders, *La Revue russe* (9 June 1904): 7. Other revolutions in Persia (1905) and later Turkey (1908), China (1912), and Mexico (1911–12) increased the ominousness of such a threat. The concurrent revolution in Russia also threatened the Franco-Russian alliance, which was based on French confidence in Russian military forces.

imperialism, France's other expanded beyond North Africa and the Middle East to encompass her ally's other, the Far East.[3] But when the Far East proved a force with military power and the capacity to defeat the West, the discourses about it became complicated. Edward Said and others have taught us to associate Orientalism with narratives of national identity as well as struggles concerning gender, class, and race, always focused on the "positional superiority" of one group vis-à-vis another.[4] But after 1905, it was no longer unambiguous who was the stronger, who the weaker in the Orientalist's conventional binary constructions. Those who stood to profit from the growing interconnectedness of the international economy found it important to diffuse these binarisms, to reinterpret them in view of coexistence, at least from a Western perspective. Those who did not responded to this threat to Western hegemony by redefining the West and what was distinctive about it in new journals like *L'Occident* and *La Renaissance latine*. French writers argued that since civilization "marched westward," they, the French, the *extrême-occidentaux*, were the ultimate representatives of the West, its "resolution," and their culture was its "harmonious or bold conclusion."[5]

French political leaders likewise began to feel that "consolidation" among European countries was necessary to match the East's potential power. In 1904, this led to the Entente Cordiale, an alliance with Britain, the other major power in the East. Struggles with Germany in North Africa in 1905–6 resulted in even closer ties and in 1907 led to the Triple Entente between France, Russia, and Britain. The politics of these agreements, an increasing fear of the Far East, and an interest in exploring the origins of Aryan Westerners may well have encouraged French artists to turn to Britain's other, India, as a safer, more neutral terrain for their Orientalist fantasies.

In this chapter, I examine two composers' responses to this Orient. Both traveled to India between 1909 and 1912—Albert Roussel (1869–1936) on his honeymoon, after visits with the French navy, and Maurice Delage (1879–1961) on tour with his parents to the family's shoe-polish factories. Both went on to the Far East, Roussel to Indochina and Delage to Japan, though what they chose to write home, keep journals, and later write music about were their experiences in India. After retracing their footsteps and locating some of their sources in the fall of 1988, I was astounded to find great variance between Roussel and Delage in the musical experiences they describe and in the influence of Indian music and culture on the music they composed after these trips, especially since they visited many of the same places. Subsequently I wrote about the relation of self and other as

---

3. D. Pistone, "Les Conditions historiques de l'exotisme musicale français," and G. Balardelle, "L'exotisme extrême-oriental en France au tournant du siècle," in "L'Exotisme musical français," special issue, *Revue internationale de musique française* 6 (November 1981): 22, 67–76, argue similarly.

4. Edward Said, *Orientalism* (New York: Vintage, 1979), 7.

5. "Déclaration," *L'Occident* (1902): 116.

represented in this music.[6] What interests me here are two other issues: first, how after 1904 India became a repository for new kinds of Orientalist projections, based on the acknowledgment of power in the other, and second, how these composers' interest in India was rooted in their own essentially Western preoccupations.

These attitudes were not so Western as to deny the influence of Indian music on their own composition,[7] but rather were shaped by these composers' contrasting backgrounds, professional situations, aesthetics, and political orientations. A heightened awareness of the world at large, with its globally interdependent concerns and highly mobile capital, and the self-critical frameworks of modernism predisposed Delage to acknowledge the value of foreign resources and to engage with the culture in its own terms more than did the royalist nationalism and the more conservative aesthetics of the Schola Cantorum, where Roussel taught. Like other modernists, Delage sought to innovate in an international context and shared with global industrialists a desire for access to ever new resources. Indian music provided him with new sounds with which to enrich a composer's palette. Scholists, by contrast, primarily landowners from the provinces, were caught up more in the debates about French music and influenced by the rhetoric of the nationalist *ligues*. The Schola's religious philosophy prepared Roussel for a spiritually enriching experience of India, though one distanced from material culture (including its music) and resulting from a projection rather than an induction of value in its culture. The range of these two composers' vastly different responses to Indian music forces us to reexamine our understanding of Orientalism during this period and to accept the plurality of its meanings and functions in French culture after 1904.

INDIAN MUSIC, UNDERSTOOD FROM AFAR

In the early nineteenth century, at a time when Paris was a "hub of Orientalist study," India was perceived as "the scene of many cultural confrontations, the ground of an East-West meeting."[8] The Belgian painter François Solvyns published

6. Jann Pasler, "Reinterpreting Indian Music: Albert Roussel and Maurice Delage," in *Music-Cultures in Contact: Convergences and Collisions*, ed. Margaret Kartomi and Stephen Blum (Sydney: Currency Press, 1994), 122–57.

7. In his "Albert Roussel et l'exotisme musical," in *Albert Roussel Musique et esthétique*, ed. Manfred Kelkel (Paris: Vrin, 1989), Kelkel speaks incorrectly of "the absence of any recourse to authentic Hindu music" (77).

8. Raymond Schwab makes this point in *The Oriental Renaissance*, trans. Gene Patterson-Black and Victor Reinking (New York: Columbia University Press, 1984; originally published as *La Renaissance orientale*, 1950), 45. For a discussion of the musical scholarship of the period and for a very extensive bibliography of Westerners who published on Indian music, see Joep Bor, "The Rise of Ethnomusicology: Sources on Indian Music c. 1780–1890," *Yearbook for Traditional Music* (1988): 51–73. I am grateful to an anonymous reviewer for leading me to this and other recent ethnomusicological work relevant to this subject.

four volumes of *Les Hindous* in Paris between 1808 and 1812,[9] and the French missionary Abbé Dubois (c. 1770–1848) left largely reliable analyses of Hindu life in his *Moeurs, Institutions, et Cérémonies des Peuples de l'Inde* (1825). Writers, too, especially Alphonse Lamartine, Victor Hugo, Alfred Vigny, and Jules Michelet, were "enchanted" by India's religion and famous epics. Until the end of the century, however, "no major French Indic scholar visited India."[10] Of course, there were the memoirs of a few French visitors, occasional articles,[11] and, throughout spring 1902, *Le Matin*'s serial publication of Kipling's novel *Kim* (based on the author's travels in India). But the country remained for most French something nebulous, largely a function of their own hunger for escape.

Music was a classic means of making this point, with vague references to India serving as ideal opportunities to coax audiences into dreaming. One has only to think of Bizet's *Les Pêcheurs des perles* (1863), a love triangle in antique Ceylon, Massenet's *Le Roi de Lahore* (1872–77), also set in ancient India, and Delibes's *Lakmé* (1883), a love story about an Indian priestess and a contemporary colonialist.[12] Each of these works explores the "enchanting Orient" as a "charming memory" or "sweet dream" of seduction, intoxication, and loss of self. Each serves as a pretext for composers to write fluid melismas, use drones, and feature delicate orchestration with harps and flutes. This suggests that, dangerous as this freedom might have been to the hegemony of late nineteenth-century musical conventions, this release from various musical constraints was as important to composers as the exotic locale.

What attracted nineteenth-century French musicians most to Indian music was the melodic character of the modes. This rendered it distinctive. The rebirth of

---

9. For an analysis of section 11 of this work on Indian music and musical instruments, see Robert Hardgrave, Jr., and Stephen Slawek, "Instruments and Music Culture in Eighteenth-Century India: The Solvyns Portraits," *Asian Music* 20, no. 1 (fall/winter 1988–89): 1–92.

10. Schwab, *The Oriental Renaissance*, 47.

11. For example, Pierre Loti, *L'Inde sans les anglais* (Paris: Calmann-Lévy, 1903), P.-J. Toulet, *Journal et voyages* (Paris: Le Divan, 1955), documenting his trip there in spring 1903, René Puaux, *Ce fut le beau voyage* [in 1911–12] (from which *Le Temps* published excerpts and Debussy was inspired to name his piano prelude "La Terrasse des audiences du clair de lune"), and Antoine Mathivet, "La Vie populaire dans l'Inde d'après les Hindous," *Revue des deux mondes* 131 (15 September 1895): 407–23.

12. Other, lesser known works from the period based on Indian subjects include Chausson's meditation on Hindu philosophy, *Hymne védique* (1886), Gabriel Pierné's incidental music for *Izeyl* (1894), what he called an "Indian drama in four acts," Florent Schmitt's *La Danse des devadasis* (1900–8), and Bertelin's *Danses hindous*. For a discussion of colonialism and the exotic woman as representing escape in *Lakmé*, see James Parakilas, "The Soldier and the Exotic: Operatic Variations on a Theme of Racial Encounter," pt. 1, *Opera Quarterly* 10, no. 2 (winter 1993–94): 33–56. For further discussion and a list of Indian-inspired French works from the period, see my "India and Its Music in the French Imagination Before 1913," *Journal of the Indian Musicological Society* 27 (1996): 27–51.

interest in modality, composers' use of scales other than the major and minor, parallels the colonial curiosity and acquisitiveness of the late nineteenth century. In France, the imperialist government of the Third Republic (1870–1940) saw music as an opportunity to expand its cultural horizons while asserting its cultural superiority.[13] In the 1870s, 1880s, and 1890s, the government gave grants to collect *chansons populaires* (indigenous folk songs), known for their modal variety, in the French provinces and abroad. Eventually this vogue extended to Indian music.[14] Some composers even borrowed Indian scales to use in their own music;[15] however, when it came to understanding the nature of these scales, their use of quarter tones, and their meaning, there was serious confusion.

Other kinds of knowledge about Indian music were even more limited. The Solvyns portraits, the first systematic study of Indian musical instruments, were virtually never cited.[16] François-Joseph Fétis, who dedicated the fifth volume of his *Histoire générale de la musique* (1869–76) to Indian music, bemoans the little he has been able to learn. Pierre Loti's description of what he heard in India and Edmond Bailly's explanation of Indian musical philosophy go into little detail.[17]

The most thorough French study of Indian music from this period is chapter 5 of Tiersot's *Notes d'ethnologie musicale* (1905). Tiersot identifies "Hindu melodies" in *Le Roi de Lahore* and *Lakmé*, though he notes they are indistinguishable from other themes in the work. But mostly he criticizes Fétis and borrows from recent English-language studies by J. Grosset (1888), C. R. Day (1891), and the Bengali musicologist S. M. Tagore (1874–96).[18] Tiersot includes musical examples and

13. So important did the government consider this project that, after a persuasive lecture on the topic by Bourgault-Ducoudray at the 1878 Exhibition, he was appointed professor of music history at the Paris Conservatoire. Bourgault-Ducoudray, *Conférence sur la modalité dans la musique grecque* (7 September 1878) (Paris: Imprimerie nationale, 1879).

14. The popular domestic publication *Figaro musical* published two "Airs indiens" transcribed by G. Pfeiffer in its March 1893 issue, including one with a "sanskrit text."

15. For example, see the use of the modes Varati and Bhairavi in Pierné's *Izeyl*, the modes Hindola and Asaveri in Déodat de Séverac's *Héliogabale* (1910), as well as those in Debussy's *La Boîte à joujoux*. In these cases, the composers explicitly notate the names of the ragas on their scores. During this period, however, because of the enormous number of pieces called "Oriental," it is impossible to determine how many compositions incorporate Indian influence, be it the use of ragas or some other attribute of this music.

16. Hardgrave and Slawek, "The Solvyns Portraits."

17. Loti describes the Indian classical music he heard at a maharajah's court in 1899–1900 in *L'Inde sans les anglais*; Bailly writes on Hindu musical philosophy in *Le Son dans la nature* (Paris, 1900). According to his article "La Musique hindoue," *Musica* (March 1909): 43–44, Bailly spent much time with the Hindu singer Nagenda Nath Roy, who spent six months in Paris in 1896.

18. Jacques Grosset, *Contributions à l'étude de la musique hindoue* (Paris: Ernest Leroux, 1888); C. R. Day, *Music and Musical Instruments of Southern India and the Deccan* (London:

describes the Indian instruments at the Conservatoire museum. Still, he, too, makes mistakes, for example, asserting that this music is "purely melodic" and that "the vīnā only doubles the voice." Tiersot concludes that "the problem of Hindu music offers [even] more uncertainty than that of Greek music . . . it remains for us, in large measure, a dead relic [lettre morte]."[19]

There is, in fact, little record of Indian musicians in Paris before 1910. Folk musicians took part in the 1900 Universal Exhibition, but Tiersot dismisses them: "We heard no song of high style or some development from their mouths . . . in general only very short rhythmic formulas." After giving musical examples, he writes, "one cannot deny that this music is simple, simple to an extreme. . . . The negroes of Africa often have richer and less elementary musical forms. Decadence, or the remnants of a primitive art from the low classes of the Hindu society?"[20] Another opportunity to hear Indian musicians apparently did not arise until Edwin Evans led "an orchestra composed of pure-blooded Indians" on a European tour in summer 1910, hailed in the Courrier musical as an "Indian invasion."[21] In 1913 and 1914, the sitar player Inayat Khan (1895–1938) visited Paris.[22]

With the growth of interest in so-called primitive or ancient societies, and the notion of India as the "cradle of civilization,"[23] came an important reason for the

---

Nocello, Ewer, 1891). Grosset's book includes discussion of Indian music theory and musical instruments. Sourindro Muhan Tagore was a wealthy intellectual dedicated to reviving interest in classical music in India and to promoting it in the West. See Bor, "The Rise of Ethnomusicology," 63. Julien Tiersot, Notes d'ethnologie musicale (Paris: Fischbacher, 1905), 62, acknowledges his use of several Tagore volumes, including Six Principal Ragas with a Brief View of Hindu Music, 2nd ed. (Calcutta, 1877), A Few Specimens of Indian Songs (Calcutta, 1879), The Musical Scales of the Hindus (Calcutta, 1884), and The Twenty-Two Musical Studies of the Hindus (Calcutta, 1886).

19. Tiersot, Notes d'ethnologie musicale, 57, 64, 73–74, 78–79.

20. Tiersot, Notes d'ethnologie musicale, 68–71.

21. According to Roussel, Lettres et écrits, ed. Nicole Labelle (Paris: Flammarion, 1987), 82–84, Evans is the same man who organized a concert of Roussel's music in London on 24 March 1909, which Roussel attended. Evans was also to do the English translation of Calvocoressi's text for his Evocations, though there is no record that he completed it. He was also a friend of Delage, possibly the person who arranged Delage's meeting with Kipling in 1913.

22. Edmond Bailly arranged his first concert; Khan later gave several lectures on music and philosophy. In 1914, he addressed the congress of the Société Internationale de Musique. These visits made a significant impact on many, including Isadora Duncan, Jules Bois, Jules Echorcheville (who organized the meeting), and Debussy, whom Khan remembers as "very much interested in our ragas." Inayat Khan, [Auto]Biography of Pir-O-Murshsid Inayat Khan (London: East-West, 1979), 129.

23. Henry Woollett, Histoire de la musique, vol. 1 (1909; 4th ed. Paris: Eschig, 1925), 37. Inayat Khan, "La Musique archaique," Revue bleue (15 November 1924): 757–60, concurs with this idea: "If anything can give an idea about the ancient music of the human race, it is oriental music, which still preserves traces of older traditions in it" (757).

French to be interested in Indian music, one that both related to their own origins and allowed them to fantasize about the Orient as separate from the colonial present. In his 1907 correspondence with the modernist writer Victor Segalen, who had served as a student interpreter in the French navy, Debussy, considering a collaboration, questions: "You must be solidly versed on Hindu music? If you so please . . . you would render a great service to musicology—so awful on these wonderful subjects." Segalen responded:

> Of course there is a lot to say about Hindu musics that has never been said. First of all, [we must] rid ourselves of all our prejudices about sound. But . . . India [is] vast and tumultuous like a continent, with two or three hundred separate dialects and different rhythms. It would be better to focus on a music assumed to be beautiful and homogeneous by reason of caste and ritual necessity: the music of the Aryans of Vedic India. . . . One would have for one's material an epoch of very noble allure, not too strange to our thinkers, because Aryan, not too familiar because distant in space and time.[24]

In the long section on Indian music in his *Histoire de la musique*, the Scholist Henry Woollett also proposed this notion of India as originally Aryan (also meaning aristocratic). Even though there has "never been any resemblance between the music of our period and that of ancient India," he reminds French readers, "don't let us forget that we [too] are Aryans."[25] By 1910 then, especially for French nationalists, Indian music came to signify the music of the distant (and aristocratic) ancestors of the French—in this context, its relative imperviousness to Western influences could appear as a strength. Confronting India in this period thus must been a complex endeavor based on little knowledge and a variety of self-serving projections.

ALBERT ROUSSEL

Albert Roussel was among the few who traveled to India. Then a professor at the Schola Cantorum, he left with his new wife on 22 September 1909. After disembarking at Bombay, the newlyweds toured the country whose shores he had often visited as a naval officer.[26] In a letter of 29 October 1909 to Henry

24. Annie Joly-Segalen and André Schaeffner, *Segalen and Debussy* (Monaco: Editions du rocher, 1961), 59–60. Roy Howat, "Debussy et les musiques de l'Inde," *Cahiers Debussy* 12–13 (1988–89): 141–52, mentions an unfinished sketch on the life of Buddha that Howat dates from 1906–9, "Siddhartha." We find the origins of this work discussed in the correspondence between Debussy and Segalen; Joly-Segalen and Schaeffner, *Segalen and Debussy*, 59–68.

25. Woollett, *Histoire de la musique*, 1:43.

26. Roussel was admitted into the naval academy in 1887 and, after many voyages abroad, resigned to concentrate on music in 1894.

Woollett—who was just finishing his music history book—he described his impressions of the country's music:

> I just traveled through Hindustan from Bombay to Calcutta and everything I saw impressed me profoundly. From the musical point of view, however, I haven't heard anything up until this moment that is really curious. The Hindu music that I have heard, stripped of harmony and very different from Javanese or Japanese music, consisted uniquely of several folk songs [*chansons populaires*] in our ordinary tonalities. Maybe there is something else that I haven't yet encountered?[27]

Such a statement suggests what predispositions Roussel brought with him and how he processed his experiences. Surprisingly, while he admits to having been visually impressed, Roussel denies finding anything particularly interesting in what he heard. He describes the music as a form of absence, "stripped of harmony." It is not even "really curious"—"curious" being a category in which music periodicals at the turn of the century published exotic music, *chansons populaires,* early music, and even some contemporary music (i.e. Satie). Roussel conceptualizes this music as if Western (calling it *chansons populaires*) but without recognizing that it has more than "our ordinary tonalities" to speak for it.

Indian music had come to signify the origins of Aryan civilization, but there was more underlying Roussel's apparent denial of exoticism and his attempt to classify Indian music as a variant of Western music—specifically the institutional politics of the Schola Cantorum, where Roussel studied beginning in 1898 and taught from 1902 to 1914, and his colleagues' conception of *chansons populaires.* Founded by a group of aristocrats, ecclesiastics, and musicians, the Schola Cantorum began in 1894 as a school to reform church music and encourage new compositions inspired by Gregorian chant and predecessors like Palestrina. Cardinal Richard, the archbishop of Paris, was its first and most important patron. In 1898 it became affiliated with the Institut Catholique and in 1900 moved to what had been a Benedictine church and became an Ecole Supérieure de Musique. As such, it became an alternative to the Paris Conservatoire, politically challenging the republican government's hegemony in the field of music education. Musically, with its emphasis on counterpoint and instrumental music, it also challenged the Conservatoire's historic emphasis on opera and virtuosity.[28]

Many of the Schola's teachers and students were from the French provinces, landowners who believed in decentralization and a return to what we might call "basic values." They were not, for the most part, part of the emerging rich industrialist class, which was centered in Paris. Many of them, after studying in Paris, returned to the provinces to start branches of the Schola there (Roussel's friend

27. Roussel, *Lettres et écrits,* 35.
28. See chapter 4 here.

Woollett founded one in Le Havre). The Schola's director after 1904, Vincent d'Indy, who came from the province of Ardèche, was staunchly Catholic and a member of the reactionary Ligue des patriotes, which espoused and promoted an antirepublican nationalism. They hoped for a return to enlightened monarchy. Some of this group started the journal *L'Occident*, which, as mentioned earlier, promoted a glorified sense of the French as the "harmonious conclusion" of the West. In one of its first issues, d'Indy articulated one of the group's main tenets: the idea of progress not as linear, as many republicans defined it, but as a "spiral," that is, one that based forward movement on incorporating the past, especially traditions that predated the French Revolution.[29] In his lectures at the Schola, *Cours de composition*, d'Indy presents a history of compositional style and method as intertwined. This *Cours* not only exemplifies his spiral notion of progress but also reflects the author's desire to codify Western syntax, defining what is Western heritage from his distinct point of view.

D'Indy and his colleagues at the Schola considered *chansons populaires*, especially those of the French provinces, to be a "collective inspiration," an important repository of their past and, as such, emblematic in some way of their character (which meant their race).[30] Like the republican scholars of this music, Bourgault-Ducoudray and Tiersot,[31] they argued that what distinguished the *chansons populaires* from modern music were its modes, remnants of Greek and old church modes. Through their modes, Scholists insisted, these songs bore some resemblance to early liturgical music, a central interest of the Schola's founders. Unlike republican scholars of the genre, however, Scholists were not drawn to this music as part of a colonialist agenda to expand the boundaries of musical expression by assimilating forgotten modes. Politically, much of the aristocracy preferred regaining Alsace and Lorraine to acquiring new land elsewhere. Neither did they wish to use it, as Prime Minister Jules Ferry did in the 1880s, to help unify the country or argue for music's universalism,[32] though they agreed that its relatively

29. For a fuller discussion of this idea, see my "Paris: Conflicting Notions of Progress," in *The Late Romantic Era*, ed. Jim Samson (London: Macmillan, 1991), 389–416.

30. In this way, they resembled the comparative musicologists of the early part of this century. As Ali Jihad Racy writes, "Historic Worldviews of Early Ethnomusicologists: An East-West Encounter in Cario, 1932," in *Ethnomusicology and Modern Music History*, ed. Stephen Blum, Philip Bohlman, and Daniel Neuman (Urbana: University of Illinois Press, 1991), these scholars considered "folk music to be the purest manifestation of history and a living embodiment of the collective 'spirit' of the people" (87).

31. See Julien Tiersot, *Histoire de la chanson populaire en France* (Paris: Plon, 1889). For more on the differences between what the genre represented to different factions of the French musical world, see my "The *Chanson Populaire* as Malleable Symbol in Turn-of-the-Century France," in *Tradition and Its Future in Music*, ed. Y. Tokumaru et al. (Tokyo: Mita Press, 1991), 203–10.

32. In his *Histoire de la chanson populaire*, Tiersot concluded: "The sum total of the *chansons populaires* is identical from one end of the country to the other." Of course, there

unchanging character over time was essential to its identity. Scholists focused on what they could learn from this music about the immutable racial qualities of the French. They also considered this genre an easy way "to inculcate a love of nature," this being another Scholist doctrine, reflecting their roots in the French provinces.[33]

Study of French *chansons populaires* was considered very important at the Schola. D'Indy collected and published a volume of such songs from the Ardèche, his *Chansons populaires de Vivarais,* and included a section about *chansons populaires* in his *Cours de composition.* Under his direction, the Schola offered an annual course on the genre. Another Schola founder, Charles Bordes, published a volume of Basque *chansons populaires,* organized a conference on the genre in 1905, and founded a journal, *Chansons de France,* to publish such songs from all over the country.

Perhaps because of their underlying political agenda and their association of *chansons populaires* with their aristocratic past, national identity, and nature, Scholists considered this music to be good, healthy "nourishment." Like Bourgault-Ducoudray, they believed certain of its modes were "full of vigor and health," "very virile," and "so masculine."[34] Scholists claimed that this music was capable of inspiring "moral renewal" in the world. But when *la musique populaire et exotique* began to appear in the same category in music journals[35]—in part because it became increasingly difficult to separate them—the Scholists became anxious. They associated exoticism with facility, impressionism, and a lack of solid construction and increasingly feared an "abuse of the picturesque"—traits they associated with "impressionist" composers trained at the Conservatoire. Scholists were reluctant to treat the *chansons populaires* of most other countries with the same respect as their own.[36]

The diary and musical sketchbook Roussel kept during his journey to India document the strength of the Schola's influence on how and what he perceived in

---

are variations, but "one always and everywhere gathers the same songs" (356–57). Moreover, in the chapter "Tonality in Popular Melody," Tiersot poses as an axiom that "whatever the tonality at hand, antique, modern, French or Chinese, all agree on one fundamental principle: the existence of a tonic and dominant in each scale" (287).

33. Charles Bordes, "Résumé des doctrines esthétiques de la Schola Cantorum," *La Tribune de Saint-Gervais* 9 (September 1903): 307.

34. Bourgault-Ducoudray, *Conférence sur la modalité dans la musique grecque,* 12.

35. For example, in the index of the 1905 issues of the *Revue musicale,* a section with this heading included *chansons populaires* from Armenia, Spain, the Arab countries, Guatemala, and Morocco, as well as sacred Brahman dances, and harmonized "Oriental" melodies.

36. For more on the meaning of this genre, see my "Race and Nation: Musical Acclimatisation and the *Chansons Populaires* in Third Republic France," in *Western Music and Race,* ed. Julie Brown (Cambridge: Cambridge University Press, 2007), 147–67.

Indian music.[37] In the forty-five-page sketchbook, the absence of complex melodic and rhythmic structures, ornaments (*gamaka*), and microtones (*śrutis*)—otherwise characterizing the ragas and talas of Indian classical music—suggests that the composer may not have gained access to the courts and temples where classical music was regularly performed. Were his musical experiences limited principally, if not exclusively, to indigenous *chansons populaires* not performed by artful singers, as Day (1891) suggested was often the case?[38] Or were the subtleties of Indian music simply unimportant to him? A. H. Fox-Strangways (1914) also kept a musical diary during his 1910–11 trip there but bemoaned his inability to record timbral and intonation variations.[39] Unlike him, Roussel does not suggest in his diary or sketchbook that the melodies he noted were only partial transcriptions of what he heard. Although they capture the two-part structure and duple meter characteristic of much folk dance music in India, Roussel's sketches do not reflect the rhythmic acceleration and excessively rapid ornamentation that he otherwise describes in his diary. Furthermore, the F-sharp at the beginning of two of the melodies suggests that Roussel heard these tunes in G major, one of the "ordinary tonalities" of which he wrote to Woollett, even though he consistently uses F-sharp or C-sharp in ascending lines and F-natural or C-natural in descending ones, which might otherwise imply the presence of ragas.

One sketch, an unmetered tune, again with a key signature of F-sharp (ex. 9.1), is Roussel's "translation" of the litany he heard sung, without stopping, by a "fakir at the edge of the Ganges [fakir au bord du Gange]" at sunset.[40] His "vision of this

37. Madame Albert Roussel gave this sketchbook to Marc Pincherle on 7 April 1951, and in 1978 its owner, André Peeters (founder and editor of *Cahiers Albert Roussel*), was kind enough to allow me to consult it. Besides Indian melodies, the sketches include three tunes described as "Thai," "Cambodge," and "Annadhapura." The diary Roussel kept from 6 October through 13 November 1909 is published in Roussel, *Lettres et écrits*, 178–202.

Daniel Kawka has written a long analysis of the notebook Roussel kept on a previous journal to Africa, the Middle East, and the Antilles in 1889–90, *Un Marin compositeur Albert Roussel "Le Carnet de bord," (1889–1890)* (Saint-Etienne: C.I.E.R.E.C., 1987), and "Le Carnet de bord d'Albert Roussel," in Kelkel, *Roussel: Musique et esthétique*, 45–61.

38. Day explained that Europeans at the time rarely had a chance to hear "the good or classical music" of India: "what is usually played for them consists . . . of modern ditties, sung by ill-instructed, screaming, dancing women at crowded native durbars, marriages, and other ceremonials" (*The Music and Musical Instruments of Southern India*, 58). In this chapter, I maintain the distinction between classical and folk music not to imply that the boundaries were clear or that folk and popular musics did not share many of the complexities of classical music—on 31 October 1988 in New Delhi, Vijay Verma pointed out to me that the "border between professional folk and classical music is quite thin"—but because composers and musicologists thought in these terms at the time.

39. A. H. Fox-Strangways, *The Music of Hindostan* (Oxford: Clarendon, 1914).

40. Fakir: a Muslim or Hindu religious ascetic, from the Arabic "faqir," meaning poor. R. V. Russell, *The Tribes and Castes of the Central Provinces of India*, vol. 3 (London: Macmillan,

Example 9.1. Albert Roussel's sketchbook, "Fakir au bord du Ganges."

half-naked young man addressing the gods and stars" greatly impressed the composer, even if the words were incomprehensible. In many ways, this tune is typical of many in his sketchbook. (Tiersot describes similar ones in Tagore's *A Few Specimens of Indian Songs*.)[41] It is in two parts, each formed of a very short period, which, according to Roussel, the singer repeated many times. Its range is a sixth and its contour that of two sine waves. This is the only tune that appears more than once in the sketchbook; in its first recurrence, it is transposed up a step, and in its fourth, it is elongated, and its highest note is reached by a fourth rather than a second.

The evolution of musical thinking in this notebook suggests that Roussel was more interested in writing a composition during his trip than in recording what Indian music he heard. From page 18 on, one finds melodies, chord structures, short passages in four-part harmony, and even those on three and four staves. From the horns, trombones, bassoons, winds, and strings indicated, it is clear that Roussel was conceiving a piece for a Western ensemble. The occasional subtitles— adagio, allegretto, and lent—suggest that he was contemplating one with three movements. "Ellora," "Udaipur," and the letter "B" (for Benares) point to the three movements of his *Evocations*, "Les Dieux dans l'ombre des cavernes" (The Gods in the Shadow of the Caves), "La Ville rose" (The Pink City), and "Au Bord du fleuve sacrée" (On the Banks of the Sacred River). He finished this on his return to France in 1910.

Of course, there was a tradition of writing music based on one's travels—his teacher d'Indy wrote a set of piano pieces, *Tableaux de voyage* (1888), as did many of those who traveled as part of their Prix de Rome. In writing his *Evocations*, Roussel was concerned to maintain the nonprogrammatic quality of much of this genre. As he began work in March 1910, he explained to the critic Georges Jean-Aubry, "This will not be Far-Eastern music, but simply the sensations I felt over

---

1916), compares the fakirs of India to the monks of the "Oriental church," who "were alike persuaded that in total abstraction of the faculties of the mind and body, the pure spirit may ascend to the enjoyment and vision of the Deity." As religious mendicants and devotees of Siva, the fakirs believe "in the power of man over nature by means of austerities and the occult influences of the will" (243–45). In vol. 2, Russell explains: "The principal religious exercise of the fakirs is known as Zikr, and consists in the continual repetition of the names of God by various methods, it being supposed that they can draw the name from different parts of the body. The exercise is so exhausting that they frequently faint under it" (537–39).

41. Tiersot, *Notes d'ethnologie*, 66.

there translated into our ordinary musical language."[42] On 21 July 1910, as he was completing its first movement, he noted d'Indy's advice:

> So write your Hindu symphony without thinking about this or that, nor even about including too much local color; believe me, a simple indication (like the discreet trumpets in the Agnus of the Mass in D) is perfectly sufficient to put us in the mood, even better than a sound photograph of "national noises." . . .
>
> Look then at your India much more for the impressions it made on the man named Albert Roussel—impressions that, taken together, are a lot more European than Hindu—instead of for the orchestral imitation you might make of observed sounds; this procedure in art, inferior as it is, is becoming so commonplace that a mind such as yours could never be satisfied with it.[43]

Two years later, in another letter to Jean-Aubry, he made it clear that "even though these *Evocations* were inspired by India, I am anxious that the country remain vague, India, Tibet, Indochina, China, Persia, it doesn't matter."[44] In a 1928 essay, he is more explicit:

> If I haven't specified these places in the titles, it's because I don't want to impose any kind of limitation on the expression of the music. However, if one absolutely must discover some bit of local color, I can point to a theme in "The Pink City" that was suggested to me by a scene I saw, the entry of the rajah into his palace, and in the third *Evocation*, the reminiscence of a melody that I heard sung on the banks of the Ganges by a young enlightened fakir.[45]

These words, even if written in retrospect, suggest how Roussel thought about his Indian experiences vis-à-vis his composition of *Evocations*. As in Lamartine's Orient, in which, as Said puts it, "the last traces of particularity have been rubbed out,"[46] they were not to "limit" his expression in any way. He might use a theme or two inspired by what he heard, but only in the tradition of "local color," that is, as a signal for Western listeners to dream. The themes used in *Evocations*, then, were not meant to appear as actual transcriptions of Indian melodies, but rather as those "suggested" by what he "saw" or by "the reminiscence of a melody" he heard in India. This would be music that respects the intervening filter of time and space and that appropriates the foreign material not to vaunt it, but for other purposes. In describing music this way, Roussel draws attention to the important role his

42. Roussel, *Lettres et écrits*, 38.

43. Arthur Hoérée, "Lettres de Vincent d'Indy à Roussel," *Cahiers Albert Roussel* 1 (1978): 46.

44. Roussel, *Lettres et écrits*, 42.

45. Arthur Hoérée, *Albert Roussel* (Paris: Rieder, 1938), 37.

46. Said, *Orientalism*, 179.

memory and creative imagination played in "translating" the Indian materials "into our ordinary musical language."

Such statements give one pause in interpreting the musical sketches Roussel made during his trip. If the tunes transcribed were meant to serve as a reminder of what he had heard, an invitation to reminiscence at some point later, Roussel might not have considered it important to try to capture the idiosyncrasies of another musical language, not even its different concepts of timbre and intonation. And there would be nothing wrong with being reductive of its aesthetic.

Examining the music of *Evocations* contributes a somewhat different sense of Roussel's perceptions of India from what his sketchbook or the letter to Woollett otherwise suggest. In many ways, the piece creates for the Western listener an evolving relationship with the differences represented by India. The first movement, virtually devoid of Indian musical influences, translates what Roussel calls his feelings of "grandeur and mystery" before the temples of Ellora. The sounds he describes in his diary—only water droplets and bird cries—may have inspired the musical opening, which resembles Debussy's and Ravel's music with its impressionist harmonies, arabesque arpeggiations, and pedal tone in the basses. In the second movement, Roussel creates a more generally Eastern sound, with his delicate instrumentation and the static, oscillating nature of his motives.[47]

The third movement shows the most Indian influence, even an engagement with Indian music. The sliding to and away from neighbor tones in the first measures recall the *gamakas* of Indian music. The rapid ornaments, syncopations, and long sweeping line of the flute melody in rehearsal number 7 show an awareness of the improvisatory qualities in Indian music not otherwise accounted for in his sketchbook. The grace notes and glissandi, played by instruments of varied timbres, reflect the composer's attempts to translate the unison sound that so impressed him, while respecting the timbral complexity that must have accompanied these unisons.

In the middle of this movement (r.nos. 31 to 36), Roussel sets verbatim his "reminiscence" of the fakir melody (ex. 9.2), using it to spin out a long ballade-like setting of six four-line stanzas written at his request by the French critic M.-D. Calvocoressi.[48] When I played a recording of this music for various Indian mu-

47. In the middle of this movement (at r.nos. 17, 20, and 21), comes a theme whose length, 6/8 meter, and descending sixth were "suggested" by those of the "Hymne du Maharana," a tune that Roussel heard when the maharana was leaving his palace in Udaipur. The quotation is far from exact, as Roussel changes its rhythmic structure, deletes the repetition in the original, and extends the consequent phrase, thus transforming it in significant ways.

48. Among his other activities as a critic, Calvocoressi lectured at the Schola and was the editor-in-chief of their biweekly publication *Les Tablettes de la Schola*, which detailed the concerts and other events at the school. He also wrote about Russian music and was an active member of Ravel's circle, the Apaches.

EXAMPLE 9.2. Roussel, *Evocations*, third movement, baritone solo.

Sous le ciel noir et sil-lon-né d'éclairs il - lu - mi- nant la nue, Plus haut que l'oeil ne peut atteindre et que l'oiseau ne peut vo-

ler, Son front ma-jes-tu- eux montant jusqu' aux palais des im - mor - tels,   Se dres____ se la mon - ta-gne sou - verai- ne.

sicians during my visit, most told me they found it totally lacking in Indian elements. In Benares, however, when I sang the tune myself after playing the recording, one of my drivers instantly recognized part of it as fakirs' devotional music, and the eminent Indian music scholar I had come to interview concurred.[49] As in Roussel's sketch, their version of the melody centered on the reiteration of one pitch surrounded by an ascending and descending pattern; but, in contrast to the Roussel version, the opening of their tune spanned a third rather than a second, did not repeat the initial pitch, and, what they found particularly significant, included an odd number of the repeated pitch in its middle section, thereby allowing the natural accent to fall on *that* pitch rather than on the next higher one, as in Roussel's version. Roussel had shifted the placement of the accent. By contrast, they found the second part of Roussel's tune totally unrecognizable: there was no consequent phrase in the music they knew. Roussel, with his classical Western training, evidently felt this tune needed one. In his sketch, he took his "reminiscence," or altered version of the Indian tune, as the antecedent of a theme and then completed it, giving it "consequence," that is, a goal, a point of arrival, as well as closure.

Repeating this theme over and over, as the fakir himself did, Roussel respects the way the original melody might be performed even today. Because this is devotional music, the fakirs may sing the same text and music for hours, stretching the tempo at will, giving it different colors and expressing different feelings through it: according to Prem Lata Sharma, they think they will derive some spiritual benefit from this singing.[50] In r.nos. 31–36, Roussel likewise sets the tune,

49. I am grateful to Dr. Prem Lata Sharma, professor emeritus of Benares Hindu University in Benares (Varanasi), Lalta Parsad, and Jay Parkash for their help in identifying this tune.

50. I had the opportunity to hear such music sung by a group of devotees at a temple in front of the train station in Benares. The "jai-lan" music goes on continuously until 4 a.m. every night, without a pause even between different singers.

with some variations, for virtually ten minutes. The only deviation in the antecedent phrase concerns whether it will begin on G (as in the first two stanzas) or
on A-flat (as in the second two). The consequent phrase, by contrast, appears in
different rhythmic and intervallic forms each time, depending on the number
of syllables in the verse and which syllable the composer wishes to stress. This
variation technique together with the timbral effects in *Evocations* suggests that
Roussel heard more than he actually noted in his sketchbook. He evidently felt
more comfortable in manipulating what he added to the music—the orchestration
and the consequent of the baritone's theme—rather than in tampering with his
transcriptions.

ROUSSEL'S CHALLENGE TO NINETEENTH-CENTURY ORIENTALISM

To explain what Roussel drew on from his Indian experiences, it is helpful to
consider *Evocations* as embodying a new kind of musical Orientalism, one that
departs from the conventions of the genre in the nineteenth century. First, it is the
male voice that represents the other, a baritone rather than a soprano or mezzo, as
had long been the norm in earlier French works like *Lakmé*. Throughout the
nineteenth century, the Republic used females as metaphors for the country, and
Conservatoire composers such as Massenet associated music with the feminine.
This shift in the gender identity of the composer's voice is consonant with the new
way the Orient was viewed after the Japanese defeat of Russia. It also signals a
change in French identity itself, at least in the identity Roussel wished to explore.

Second, Roussel sets the text of this baritone syllabically rather than melisma-
tically, that is, with one clearly articulated note per syllable rather than a string of
fluidly meandering notes on vowel sounds. As such, his text can be easily understood; indeed, the repetition of the melodic line draws attention to the changing
stanzas of text. What appears improvisatory is the text. Rational discourse draws
more attention than musical discourse; again, one might say, the conventionally
masculine is more prominent than the conventionally feminine.

The charm of such music is not erotic but almost shamanistic, for with the
magic of repetition, it lures the listener to initiate transformation. This points to
a third difference between *Evocations* and most nineteenth-century Orientalist
music. The male here is not despotic or violent but devotional.[51] He is also,
perhaps ironically, not a leader (as in works like *Samson et Dalila*) but a poor

---

51. In his monumental study of Orientalism in music, "Constructing the Oriental
'Other': Saint-Saëns' *Samson et Dalila*," *Cambridge Opera Journal* 3, no. 3 (3 November
1991), Ralph Locke describes "Orientalist stereotypes of Middle Eastern males as smug,
single-minded, intolerant, power-mad despots and fanatics, impulsive and prone to violence" (280).

beggar. His power comes from his relationship to God—a theme with which his Catholic peers at the Schola would have resonated. Already in the notebook he had kept during his first trip overseas twenty years earlier, Roussel had expressed interest in the religion of nature and in non-Christian religions as "teaching man admiration for all that is beautiful, grand, heroic." Oriental civilization, for him, was intimately connected with "the luminous environment."[52] The fakir was the embodiment of this relationship to the divine through nature.

Calvocoressi develops these themes in his lyrics for the third movement of *Evocations* in a way that draws attention to the musical structure. The movement begins with what Roussel calls "an evocation of the night." After a long choral section of homorhythmic chords followed by rich counterpoint, it ends with a contralto summing up the meaning of the musical metaphor, as one might find in a poem by Baudelaire: "more sweet than the perfumes of the night, more ardent is my love." To prepare for the dawn, to reflect on the impending, magnificent change in nature marking the end of the night, Roussel then calls on the shamanistic fakir.

Music and text play complementary roles in the fakir's section. The music's relentless thematic repetition, pulsating sixteenth notes, and gradually ascending melodic line suggest the irreversibility of change just before the sun rises. At the same time, the text unfolds visions in which the fakir focuses on his ecstasy. Each of the stanzas echoes the musical structure. Like the musical antecedent and consequent, the initial images of each stanza prepare for understanding the final ones. For example, after beginning with the line "Under the black sky cut by lightning / Higher than the eye can see and the bird can fly," the stanza culminates at "the supreme mountain," the zenith of the image. At this point, the baritone sings the longest, highest note of the musical period. The other stanzas work similarly:

> Its shade terrifies timid hearts . . .
> It's a God whose voice descends among us;
> In the thick shade of the forests . . .
> O river that reflects the luminous sky;
> Happy he whose face extinguishes on this shore . . .
> Leaving the soul free to rise towards the innumerable stars;
> Sacred river that washes the temples of the holy city . . .
> Let the sky of a new day be reborn.

After the baritone solo, the chorus returns to sing the "hymn of the sun" as if speaking directly to God. Including a chorus allowed Roussel to frame the Indian

52. See the text as analyzed in Kawka, *Un Marin compositeur*, and "Le Carnet de bord d'Albert Roussel."

material in an interesting way. While the chorus both begins and ends the piece, the baritone functions as an antecedent to the final chorus, much as the antecedent of the fakir's melody does to its consequent. That is, the Indian fakir prepares for and leads to a transformation in the chorus. This transformation takes place in the music the chorus sings; their shift from counterpoint (as in the beginning of the movement) to nonharmonized, homorhythmic singing resembles Western devotional music. Afterward, in a dynamic climax, the chorus praises God as the ultimate synthesis of masculine power and feminine beauty: "you hunt the immense army of the stars / And your passionate beauty reigns alone over the Ocean of heavens in your embrace."

This relationship of antecedent to consequent (or, preparation to arrival) in the theme, in the poetry, in the vocal forces, and in the devotion suggests a similar interpretation of how Roussel understood his Indian experiences vis-à-vis his composition. Numerous times Roussel refers to the feelings and visions he had in India, and in a letter of 20 May 1920,[53] he insists that listeners have the "text" (*argument*) before them at any concert performances of the work. The fakir and these experiences may in fact represent an India that transformed Roussel, initiating him not only into new visions of life and nature (such as those described in Calvocoressi's text) but also into a "new day" in his own spirituality, a deeper understanding of the ultimate other.

This interpretation suggests that we consider India, and not its musical exoticism, as the crucial catalyst, and transformation as the goal of each kind of antecedent in the work. Roussel later writes about both art and life as "a series of continuous transformations" and the function of a work of art as "provoking in the listener a response that if it is not identical, at least answers in some way the call of the composer."[54] From this perspective, perhaps the composer hoped his *Evocations* would likewise serve as an antecedent for his audiences, eliciting an experience of spiritual transformation that the founders of the Schola Cantorum would have enthusiastically endorsed.

MAURICE DELAGE

By contrast Maurice Delage was not yet a fully formed composer when he embarked on his voyage to India. He played the cello as an amateur and had studied composition with Ravel for about ten years. Otherwise, he was self-taught. Friends describe him as someone with a fine ear, "impatient with the weary discipline of technical training."[55] A friend of Stravinsky and host to the weekly meetings of

53. Roussel, *Lettres et écrits*, 85.

54. Roussel cited in Marc Pincherle, *Albert Roussel* (Geneva: René Kister, 1957), 53, 54.

55. Michel D. Calvocoressi, *Musicians' Gallery: Music and Ballet in Paris and London* (London: Faber and Faber, 1933), 61.

Ravel's group the Apaches,[56] Delage was an adventurer in many ways. In his first orchestral work, *Conté par la mer* (1909),[57] he wrote a note for horn outside its usual range. When, under d'Indy's leadership, the Société Nationale refused to perform it, his colleagues showed their esteem by breaking and forming a rival performance organization, the Société Musicale Indépendente (SMI).

The severity of this action suggests that by 1910 differences between Scholists and so-called impressionist composers from the Conservatoire had developed into a serious conflict, but one full of ironies, in part because some had sympathies in both directions, and the Apaches included representatives of both. Leaders at the Schola, which had been founded to allow composers more individual freedom (especially from the constraints of state competitions), were increasingly preoccupied with issues of control and structure, even in their music; those inspired by Debussy's use of unresolved, "impressionist" harmonies were intent on taking full advantage of this liberation from conventional syntax. And whereas it was d'Indy who turned to Wagner for inspiration and in 1890 argued for more inclusion of music by foreign composers at the Société Nationale, by the turn of the century, it was the young modernists trained at the Conservatoire who looked beyond national borders for new ideas. Debussy's innovations, some inspired by Javanese and Vietnamese music, were crucial to these composers, even though after 1902, like the Scholists, Debussy focused increasingly on a nationalist agenda. In their first concerts, the SMI premiered not only music by Delage but also Koechlin's transcriptions of Javanese "gamalang." In 1913 Ravel solicited Schönberg's permission to perform *Pierrot Lunaire*,[58] a work whose novel instrumentation impressed both him and Stravinsky.

Delage did not study at the Conservatoire, but he associated with those who did—though he had little interest in writing opera, took part in no competitions, and shared very little socially with the conservative republicans who ran the institution, many of whom, like Debussy, came from very modest backgrounds. Like most Apaches, he was born into a family with money that had been made in the

---

56. In my "Stravinsky and the Apaches," *Musical Times* 123 no. 1672 (June 1982): 403–07, I discuss this group and suggest that Delage was perhaps Stravinsky's closest friend in Paris before World War 1. See also my "A Sociology of les Apaches: Sacred Battalion for *Pelléas*," in *Berlioz and Debussy: Sources, Contexts and Legacies,* ed. Barbara Kelly and Kerry Murphy (London: Ashgate, 2007).

In a letter of 9 August 1905, Ravel mentions that the brother-in-law of an Apache, Bénédictus, was appointed to a judiciary position in Pondichéry, India. In *Maurice Ravel: Lettres, écrits, entretiens,* ed. Arbie Orenstein (Paris: Flammarion, 1989), 78. Around the same time, Ravel, too, hoped for a government assignment ("mission") in the East, possibly India.

57. See Ravel to Koechlin, 16 January 1909, in Ravel, *Maurice Ravel*, 101–2. The work is missing and was possibly destroyed.

58. Ravel to Mme Alfredo Casella, 2 April 1913, in Ravel, *Maurice Ravel*, 128.

industrial world of the late nineteenth century. His father owned *Lion Noir*, a shoe polish still sold today. It is difficult to say what Delage's politics were, but one thing is clear: he had a life of ease spent helping friends, especially Ravel. In the spring of 1912, his parents used their factories in India and Japan as an excuse to travel to the Far East; Maurice went along.[59] According to Léon-Paul Fargue, Delage left with the fervor of a pilgrim; he was not the kind who "brings along his slippers." Although their travels took them to many of the same places as Roussel, Delage's impressions were quite different, as was the compositional form that later emerged in his work.

In a letter from Ceylon, published in the Parisian music journal *S.I.M.*, Delage admits that he had never read anything about Indian music before his trip.[60] Yet his comments in this letter, subsequent published interviews, and a radio program on Indian music he gave in April 1948 show remarkable perceptiveness.[61] From what he writes, especially about instruments and performance practices, it is clear that Delage was exposed to Indian classical music.

Many of Delage's attitudes toward Indian music were rooted in his modernist inclinations. These differed from the concerns of Roussel and other Scholists in four ways. First, there is a tone of resistance and critique, perhaps inspired by Debussy's and Ravel's attitudes toward their Conservatoire training. Delage can't help but refer to Western musical practices and concepts; however, his focus is on their limitations. Indian improvisations, he writes, had an audacity that "escaped all organization, according to our logic, of course. . . . With my poor ear accustomed to the almost artificial subtleties of our Western polyphony,[62] I felt something that was beyond the notes." The vīnā player's use of parallel fifths led him to exclaim "severe Academy. . . . What could analysis and criticism do here, great gods! One must desire [only] to feel and love." Delage admits he "ignores what one must normally know" to speak of Indian culture. Using the other as a site for self-criticism is a typical Orientalist tactic, but he does not do this to reify the differences between the two or to demonstrate the strength and relative power of Western music. Rather, Delage hopes to set the terms for his own "naïve efforts

---

59. A close friend of Delage, the composer/conductor Manuel Rosenthal, provided this information to me in an interview in Paris in the spring of 1977. In his *Ravel: Souvenirs de Manuel Rosenthal*, ed. Marcel Marnat (Paris: Fayard, 1995), he notes that Delage's father sold this business to an Englishman who paid royalties to Delage for years (164).

60. Maurie Delage, "Lettre de l'Inde," from Kandy, 4 March 1912, *Revue musicale S.I.M.* (15 June 1912): 72–74. Except where noted, quotations in the following paragraphs come from this essay.

61. The text of Delage's radio program, "Une Géographie musicale," broadcast on channel A on 25 April 1948, Rés. Vmc. Ms. 46, is currently in F-Pn, Musique.

62. Jules Combarieu, *Histoire de la musique* (Paris: Colin, 1913), rehearses the standard view of counterpoint as the "cradle of harmony and the principle of all modern art" (350) and thus the essence of Western music, an idea shared with many Scholists.

toward novelty," his search to get beyond Western constraints, perhaps to appropriate some of the power inherent in Indian music.

Second, Delage supported Indians' resistance to foreign contamination in their musical traditions.[63] Underlying this was his respect for authenticity. Like Segalen, who proposed "salvaging the purity of the exotic by thinking it anew" for the sake of art,[64] and fantasized about India's distant past as a distraction from its colonialist present, Delage was most impressed with genres that seemed purely Hindu (performance of the vīnā and South Indian vocal music). He railed against European influences on Indian music, especially phonographs, the harmonium, and, in South India, the violin.[65] Had he had access to the sultans' or maharajahs' palaces, he might also have been shocked by the presence of pianos in their midst.[66] He worried about how the "relative perfection" of Western tuning might endanger the "purity" not so of much the syntax of Indian music as its sound.[67] This was a complicated issue for Indians, too. A writer in Modern Review, published in Calcutta, claimed in 1912 that "the greatest problem of India . . . is how we can modernize ourselves and become progressive, without losing our heritage— without losing that spiritual power and wealth which made India great in the past."[68] Delage was also bothered by other non-Hindu influences, such as the

---

63. Parakilas, "The Soldier and the Exotic," points out that musical performance can signify cultural resistance in India. In Lakmé, for example, the bell song is "a political act in the Hindus' struggle for cultural survival" (50).

64. See Chris Bongie, Exotic Memories. Literature, Colonialism, and the Fin de Siècle (Stanford: Stanford University Press, 1991), 107–18.

65. The violin became popular in South India around the time of the first Tanjore Palace Band and has remained so ever since. By the late 1880s, according to Hindu Music and the Gayan Samaj. The Gayan: Dnyan Prakesh: March 1882 (Bombay: Bombay Gazette Steam Press, 1887), "the European violin had made great encroachment on popular favor" (27–28).

The Tanjore orchestra was basically an English-style wind band formed in the late eighteenth century at the court of Tanjore. It consisted of bagpipes, flute, brass, clarinet, and drum and represented perhaps the first "recognizable impact of western music" in India; D. S. Seetha, Tanjore as a Seat of Music (Madras: University of Madras, 1981), 111. It performed its tunes in unison, accompanied by the drone and drum. Delage brought back one recording by the Tanjore band (Gramo G.C. 2 10129) and, after playing "Parathpa Varali Athi" during his 1948 radio program, called it "an experiment in harmony" that sounded like "chance counterpoint."

66. Clement Autrobus Harris, "The Bicentenary of the Pianoforte: A Link Between East and West," Calcutta Review 270 (October 1912): 425.

67. The use of the harmonium has been a subject of much debate, and was so particularly around the time that Delage visited the country. See my "Reinterpreting Indian Music," 145, n. 14.

68. If this writer is representative, their anxiety at the time seems to have been focused more on homogeneity within the country than on growing too close to the West, for he

disappearance of instruments after the Muslim invasion. But even if such criticism may have stemmed from racial prejudice, he appreciated the music of Kishori Lal, a singer from Punjab, enough to play a recording of it during his radio broadcast. Delage was especially sensitive to the importance of individual performers in maintaining musical traditions in India.[69]

With this focus on indigenous authenticity and performers, Delage differed from both Scholists (who tended to overlook the specificity of these traditions outside of France) and French republican scholars (who were more interested in the modal particularities of foreign music). In the context of the increased global contact that threatened the continuity of both Western and Eastern cultures, however, Delage and Roussel shared something crucial: both believed in preserving the "racial integrity" of musical traditions, be they Indian or French.

Delage's preoccupation with the timbral richness of Indian music is a third reflection of his modernist aesthetics. Eastern music represented for French modernists a way of validating their belief in the primacy of sound over syntax and a means of exploring the origins of music (as opposed to the origins of the French race). An interest in sound vibrations, nuance, fluidity, and spontaneity underlies the impressionist style and differs markedly from the Scholist focus on solid construction, linear clarity, and rigorous logic. Delage's attention to the immensely varied sound qualities produced on Indian instruments led him to take precise note of what he heard. Performance on the vīnā, the oldest multistringed Indian instrument used in both northern and southern India and the "most popular" one,[70] fascinated him. The slow glissandi, the striking of the strings and the case, and the staccato of the performer's left-hand fingers produced effects the composer would later attempt to imitate.[71] Likewise, he was drawn to the vocal techniques of

---

continues, "But all must admit that every race and nationality in India has an individuality which it should strive to preserve at the same time that it aspires to a closer political union with the rest of India. . . . A non-descript and amorphous cosmopolitanism which would destroy the identity and eliminate the peculiar racial characteristics of the Bengalis, Hindustanis, Punjabs, Gujaratis, and Marathis and fuse them into an incongruous whole seems equally Utopian and unwise." *Modern Review* (February 1912): 220–25.

69. R. R. Ayyangar, *Musings of a Musician* (Bombay: Wilco, n.d. [apparently after 1977]), 55, makes this point.

70. Bor, "The Rise of Ethnomusicology," 53, points out that probably the first description of the vīnā in Western sources was in Mersenne's *Harmonie universelle* (1636–37). It is possible that Delage knew the vīnā from the Musée du Conservatoire in Paris. Tiersot, *Notes d'ethnologie*, discusses one as part of the collection there (78).

71. Day was also impressed by similar techniques of vīnā-playing, notably the peculiar tuning of the instrument, the staccato sounds achieved, and the striking of the instrument by the left hand on vīnās in the North and by the right hand on the somewhat different ones in the South (*The Music and Musical Instruments of Southern India*, 110).

South Indian contraltos, especially the "voluptuous tension" of those who sang "with almost closed mouths, a high-pitched prosody involving strange nasal sonorities, cries, and breathing" and "the warm roughness of their low register where the rushed and feverish rhythms suddenly relax into a murmur full of caresses."[72] Not only in France but also in Vienna, modernists were increasingly defining research in timbre as the newest form of musical progress (for example, Schönberg in his *Harmonielehre*). Delage's desire to "discover" such riches, then, has a future-oriented, even utopian aspect.

Fourth, Delage's essays suggest that he, unlike Roussel, was more engaged by the musical traditions of India's contemporary elite—his peers—than by Indian folk or popular music. His attraction to the vīnā —what he calls the "noble instrument of modern India"—is a case in point. This instrument was associated with the upper classes.[73] Day points out that, while the playing of the vīnā—considered an "imitation of the human voice"—was restricted to professional skilled musicians in northern India, it was a favorite among amateurs of the higher classes in southern India, perhaps those with whom Delage identified.[74]

To solve the problem of access to a wide variety of Indian music, Delage resorted to buying recordings.[75] On 23 October 1912, he wrote to Stravinsky, "You will see that I have been working and I will make you listen to the Hindu records,

72. In his "Une Géographie musicale," Delage describes a singer, dressed as a tiger, who performed "vocalises produced by a staccato at the back of the throat with a whole lemon in his mouth." S. A. K. Durga and V. A. K. Ranga Rao explained to me that in the "Puli attam," a tiger's dance, performers even today place lemon wedges in each cheek so that their mouths won't get dry while they make purring/growling noises for hours.

73. As Hardgrave and Slawek point out, early nineteenth-century writers on Indian music observed that the high castes were prohibited from playing wind instruments but often sang and accompanied themselves on this instrument, "a favorite amongst the better classes" ("Instruments and Music Culture in Eighteenth-Century India," 4). This was equally true at the end of the nineteenth century, notably in the Gayan Samaj, schools that were formed in Madras and Poorna in the 1870s "to give European residents an idea of the excellence of Hindu music." (Bor points out, furthermore, that these institutions played an important role in the emancipation of classical Indian music"; "The Rise of Ethnomusicology," 63.) In this context, according to *Hindu Music and the Gayan Samaj*, the "best musician plays all but wind instruments," which were not considered appropriate for Brahmins; "wind instruments and stringed instruments are, of course, never played together" (21–28). Day echoes these observations; however, he points out that Brahmins can play a flute with their nostrils (*The Music and Musical Instruments of Southern India*, 103).

74. Day, *The Music and Musical Instruments of Southern India*, 110.

75. Recordings were introduced in India just after the turn of the century. As Pekka Gronow reports in "The Record Industry Comes to the Orient," *Ethnomusicology* 25, no. 2 (1981): 251, the Gramophone Company's representative, Fred Gaisberg, first recorded there in 1901. The first factories opened in Calcutta in 1908. See also Michael Kinnear, *The Gramophone Company's First Indian Recordings, 1899–1908* (Bombay: Popular Prakashan,

a kind of music of which you have no idea."[76] The Indian classical music preserved on these recordings, as opposed to the folk songs he might have heard or collected on records, are the key to the works Delage wrote on his return. In these compositions is a highly original approach to Indian materials, an intercultural influence that goes far beyond that of superficial impressionism, and a re-presentation of Indian music that empowers him to subvert traditional Western music practices. "Trying to find those Hindu sounds that send chills up my spine," as he explained to Stravinsky,[77] Delage experimented with unusual timbres produced by altered tunings and vocal techniques, special kinds of ornaments that modify the Western sense of interval and pitch, improvisatory rhythms, new forms, and especially novel performance techniques. The works that resulted from such exploration spanned much of his career, beginning with the *Quatre Poèmes hindous* for soprano and small chamber orchestra (written spring 1912–fall 1913) and *Ragamalika* (written 1912–22).

The most interesting of these, from the perspective of Indian influence, is the second of the *Quatre Poèmes hindous*, "Un Sapin isolé" (An Isolated Fir Tree), subtitled "Lahore." The text is a poem by Heinrich Heine. Its images invite the listener into reverie: one tree, covered with snow "on a bare mountain in the North," dreams of another, a "solitary" palm clinging to the edge of a scorched rock "in the distant East"—a metaphor for the human condition. For the opening cello solo, Delage inserted his transcription of a performance on the *surbahār* of "Jaunpuri Todika Alap" by Imdad Khan (1848–1920), probably recorded in 1905

1994) and Peter Manuel, "Popular Music in India 1901–1986," *Popular Music* 7, no. 2 (May 1988): 157–76.

In his 1948 radio program, Delage listed and described the eight recordings he played, ranging from rhythmic improvisations on the simple iron bars, called *khattali*, accompanying a wedding procession (Odeon 96. 541) and the oboe-like Nadaswaram, played in the temples of Ellora (Odeon 96. 453), to the complex singing of Kishori Lal (Gramo 12. 533) and Coimbatore Thayi (Gramo 5-013022). These were the among those he collected in India in 1912. According to my sources in India, most were extremely rare. Unfortunately, Delage's collection has apparently been lost.

What was and who were recorded in the first decade has been a subject of debate. Kay Kaufman Shelemay, "Recording Technology, the Record Industry, and Ethnomusicological Scholarship," in Blum et al., *Ethnomusicology and Modern Music History*, has found that many of these early recording efforts focused on indigenous folk music (281), whereas Delage's collection included classical music. On 15 October 1988 in New Delhi, Vijay Verma offered me a possible explanation: anyone with a patron or money, he posited, could make recordings, and so, consequently, many tended to be by popular singers, not necessarily the best performers of the day. Moreover, many musicians refused to work within the three to four minutes of the early 78 rpm disks, or to have their voices heard by "just anyone."

76. Robert Craft, ed., *Stravinsky: Selected Correspondence*, (New York: Knopf, 1982), 1:24.
77. Craft, *Stravinsky*, 1:33.

Example 9.3. Imdad Khan, "Raga Jaunpuri Todika Alap" (beginning). Transcribed by Paul Smith.

original tonic: F♯
transposed to B

TRANSCRIBER'S NOTE:
All slurred notes are played as glissandi. Portamento indicates that the marked notes are lingered on briefly in the midst of the glissando passage. A broader, more accented pause is indicated with a tenuto mark.

(see exs. 9.3 and 9.4a).[78] The performance instructions indicate that while the right hand plucks the first note, the cellist should use the same finger of the left hand to slide between the two adjacent notes. This use of ornaments and glissandi to prolong a note, stress one, or slide from one to another results in a pitch continuum, microtonal shadings, and a timbre like those produced by sitar and vīnā players.[79] After the first few bars of music, however, the transcription is no longer exact. Khan elaborates on the raga for almost three minutes, while Delage cuts some of the recurring passages and condenses the overall shape. He also alters the complex rhythms, and indicates a slower tempo—perhaps to give the cellist the time to execute the difficult techniques.

The vocal part dominates in the rest of the piece. Most of it is unequivocally Western, though conventionally Orientalist. The final solo (ex. 9.4b) recalls two

78. A *surbahār* is a bass sitar with unmovable frets and a wider range. A North Indian *ālāp* is a slow exposition without a fixed pulse. I am indebted to Vijay Verma for pointing out the *rāg jaunpuri* in the cello part and to the staff of the Music Department of Benares Hindu University for help in locating two Khan recordings, both Gramo G.C. 17364, the source of the "Lahore" opening, and Gramo G.C. 17365. Kinnear kindly provided me with the probable date of these recordings. A 1994 reissue of this by EMI is on the *Chairman's Choice: Great Gharanas: Imdadkhani* (CD CMC 1 82507-08).

79. When Khan shifts his melody to another string to move higher in pitch and weaves a duet between two strings, Delage gives the melodic line to the viola, which then enters into a duet with the cello. The subtlety of this instrumentation very much captures that of its model.

EXAMPLE 9.4a. Maurice Delage, "Un Sapin isolé," from *Quatre poèmes hindous*, opening, cello-violin solo, mm. 1–19.

EXAMPLE 9.4b. Delage, "Un Sapin isolé," from *Quatre poèmes hindous*, vocalise, mm. 10–16.

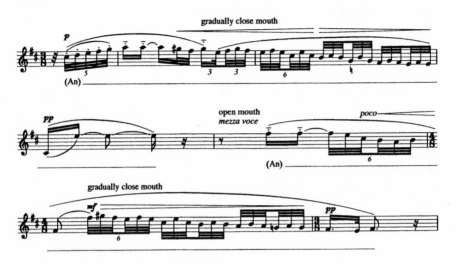

gestures from the opening of the "Bell Song" from *Lakmé*. Still, an Indian influence prevails. The Indian-type scale (built on D with three sharps), the quickly ascending scale of six notes, and the gradually descending span of a thirteenth resemble the middle of the same Khan recording. Besides the low register, the quick, delicate staccatos throughout, and the ornaments that color the descending lines, Delage also calls for an Indian-inspired closed-mouth singing in numerous places. This technique of open- and closed-mouth singing shows Delage's first attempts to forge a personal style inspired by the vocal techniques he heard in India and on his recordings yet without attempting to retrain Western singers to produce their sounds in an Indian manner.[80] It became a favorite in all his subsequent Indian-inspired pieces, especially the vocalise he wrote for a Paris Conservatoire competition in the 1920s.

In the third Hindu poem, the "Naissance de Bouddha" (Birth of Buddha), subtitled "Benares," Delage borrows much of his thematic material from the flip side of the Khan recording discussed earlier, "Sohni." Delage transcribes this raga for English horn, giving it the same rhythms as in the recording. He then repeats the exposition as on the recording, has the clarinet respond with a similar virtuoso chromatic descent, and expands on these two ideas throughout the piece. The

---

80. Delage was perhaps the first French composer to use this technique of open- and closed-mouth singing for solo singing; however, one finds this technique in choral singing in other Orientalist works such as Delibes's *Lakmé*, Pierné's *Izyel*, Schmitt's *Danse des devadasis* (1900–1908), and Lili Boulanger's *Vieille Prière bouddhique* (1917).

cello's ostinato recreates the sound of the accompanying strings on Kahn's *sur-bahār* with an accompaniment oscillating between F and repeated chords on C–A. As on the recording, they function in this piece as a drone. The text, probably written by the composer, evokes the time when the gods and all of nature rejoiced at the news of Buddha's coming.

The first and last of the *Quatre Poèmes hindous* frame the middle two and assure unity and coherence in the set. Although they set texts thought to be by Bhartrihari, an Indian king who became an ascetic, musically they express the Westerner's perspective that must frame his or her perception of Indian culture. Both have the same tempo and bear much less Indian musical influence. The first is dedicated to Ravel, the fourth to Stravinsky—composers whose approach to orchestration may have influenced Delage's chamber setting of these songs. Both songs begin with chromatic flute arabesques à la Debussy and conclude with the same gesture. The end of the first incorporates the opening motive of the last, and the closing measures of the last song incorporate the opening motive of the first one; the final measures of both pieces are the same.

These two songs are conventionally Orientalist in two ways. First, India is feminized, likened to a beautiful woman. The first depicts her wandering the forest—the object of the poet's contemplation; the last refers to her as a troubled but well-cherished memory: "If you think of her, you feel an aching torment. If you set eyes on her, your mind is troubled. If you touch her, you lose all reason. How can one call her the beloved?" Second, in setting the last two phrases, the music breaks into a Western-style climax, the apex of the song's vocal line. Outside of occasional moments in the cello solo of the second song, this is the only *forte* in the whole set. Such a moment captures the pinnacle of the composer's own emotional response to his Indian experiences, one that obviously needs Western means for its full expression.

Ragamalika, perhaps Delage's most Indian-sounding piece, is indeed his transcription of almost an entire recording, "Rāgamālika, Ramalinga swamis arulpa," sung in Tamil by Coimbatore Thayi and probably recorded in 1909 (see ex. 9.5 and fig. 9.1).[81] Thayi was a famous *devadasi* singer whom Delage had the pleasure of hearing live during a visit to the temples at Mahabalipurnam.[82] *Arulpa* are

81. Gramo G.C. 8-13793. I am grateful to S. A. K. Durga for suggesting I consult the collection of V. A. K. Ranga Rao and to Mr. Rao for allowing me to peruse his collection on the morning of Diwali in the fall of 1988.

82. Delage, "Une Géographie musicale." She is among those whom Ayyangar heard and included in his list of famous women singers before 1930, published in his *Musings of a Musician*, 40. Those interested in the *devadasis* of Tamilnadu should consult Saskia C. Kersenboom-Story, *Nityasumangali: Devadasi Tradition in South India* (Delhi: Motilal Banarsidass, 1987). I am grateful to Rita Ganguli and T. Sankaran for help in this research. When Delage met Thayi, Sankaran surmises, she must have been at Mahabalipurnam for a festival. No one seems to know to which temple she was attached.

EXAMPLE 9.5. Delage, *Ragamalika*.

devotional songs that the *devadasis* sang for the entertainment and pleasure of the gods at the temples to which they were attached. Thayi recorded many of them.[83] Her recordings are full of elaborate passages of closed- and open-mouthed singing, microtonal ornaments, and long stretches in which she might change the timbre but not the pitch of important notes.

In every way, *Ragamalika* reflects its model—in its changing modes (*rāgamālikā* means "a garland of ragas"), its recurring refrain, its multipartite form, and its tempo relationships. The piano takes the place of the tabla and the droning ac-companimental string instrument. Its ostinati octaves serve principally to support the vocal line, except in one very important instance. To articulate the system tonic, B-flat,[84] and to bring attention to the change of mode in the middle of the piece, Delage asks that one note on the *inside* of the piano be muted. This creates an unusual, otherworldly effect for the drone. It is perhaps the first ex-ample of "prepared piano" in European music. The publisher Durand was so "enchanted" by this music that on 20 June 1914 he paid Delage 500 francs to orchestrate it.

With the help of these recordings, Delage succeeded better than his con-temporaries in reproducing the spirit and the style of the music of North and South India. With its emphasis on self-criticism, sound for its own sake, and respect for traditions in their own terms, the modernist aesthetic prepared Delage to hear Indian music in its own terms. The industrialist relationship to other—based on

83. Alain Daniélou, *A Catalogue of Recorded Classical and Traditional Indian Music* (Paris: UNESCO, 1952), 160–62, is a very incomplete listing of her recordings, which are extremely rare.

84. In *The Ragas of Northern India* (London: Barrie and Rockliff, 1968), Alain Daniélou notes that the system tonic used by most singers was often B-flat (23–24).

FIGURE 9.1. Delage, *Ragamalika*.

recognizing the importance of foreign natural resources and using them for one's own purposes—inclined him to want to re-present it in his own way.

COMPOSITIONAL DISTINCTION

This chapter has looked at two French composers' relationships with India, a country that, without any French military presence, remained an "Orient of memories." Both fell under the spell of something so different from what was familiar to them and so dependent on their own consciousness that they referred to it as a dream. Both appropriated tunes and stories, but not for domination. Both became fascinated with religious characters as intermediaries with the divine. Both wrote pieces inserting French singers, French texts, and an explicit French framework to preserve their memories and, through the catalyst of their music, stimulate similar experiences in others. And both used Indian influences in their first major works to help them achieve distinction in their compositional careers.

For Scholists like Roussel, imagining another world was important. Their need to dream was a desire not for escape but for alternative power structures. The heroism and grandeur of ancient India presented these largely Catholic landowners, royalist aristocrats, and conservative traditionalists with a vision of what they sought and could not have under the anticlerical Republic. Their nationalism and fear of dealing with others, however, kept them anxious about outside influences on French culture. In response to a 1909 interview on Wagner's influence on French composers, Roussel sounds like d'Indy:

> In this question of influences, it is difficult to leave aside the question of races, and it would be very good if French music would tend to embody [*personnifier*] the genius of our race in an increasingly affirmative, vigorous way—the qualities of clarity, mind, sensibility, luminous and frank joy that form our artistic heritage.[85]

This is the context for understanding Roussel's challenge to conventional notions of the musically exotic. The Scholists could not accept any artistic limitations that might compromise their own racial "genius" and an art they increasingly defined as masculine, that is, resistant to the notion of subsuming anything external to itself.

Roussel's resistance to others' influence made sense from another perspective as well. Typically, it was important for a composer to move beyond his or her education and demonstrate a "personality." With *Evocations*, Roussel found a sly way to earn widely recognized distinction (in Bourdieu's sense). After its first performance on 18 May 1912 by the Société Nationale and on 30 March 1913 by Lamoureux's orchestra, a debate emerged. Non-Scholist critics saw Roussel breaking with Scholist principles. Some, perhaps thinking about the first movement, said he had been "contaminated by Debussysme" even before he got to the Schola and had not assimilated all their "pedagogical influences."[86] In response, Auguste Sérieyx vigorously reclaimed Roussel as a Scholist. Stressing the Western frame Roussel creates for the exotic locale, he points out specifically Scholist (and conventionally masculine) principles in the work:

85. "Wagner et nos musiciens," *Grande Revue* (10 April 1909): 562–63.

86. J. Marnold, *Mercure de France* (16 August 1912): 863, cited in Christian Goubault, "Les Premières Oeuvres de Roussel," in Kelkel, *Albert Roussel: Musique et esthétique*, 24.

What gives the magnificent triptych *Evocations* great value, above all, is the impeccable equilibrium and the strength of the thematic and tonal construction. . . . It is no longer these unhealthy and ornate visions of some Orient with opium and folding screens: instead it's the magisterial "evocation" of India, framed in the most pure form, blinding in its melodic clarity, infinitely rich in rhythm without any effort, vigorous and passionate in expression without anything disturbing the integrity of the traditional construction.[87]

Jean-Aubry, too, pointed not to the Orientalism of the music but to the suave and voluptuous "quality of the dream" and hailed Roussel as "one of the most truly French souls in music today."[88] The nationalist Lalo praised it as "one of the principal works of our time."[89] In his review of a 1919 performance at which Debussy's *Nocturnes* was also performed, Antoine Mariotte points to truth in both Scholist and non-Scholist views. He sees Roussel's music as delicate, colorful, and powerful as Debussy's but also calls it "cerebral and willful. . . . With M. Roussel, we are no longer in the clouds; we are in India." Mariotte argues that Roussel's India "impressions" are the pretext for demonstrating his ability to build and control large musical forms, to "logically order considerable developments," to express his mind and will as well as his sensibility.[90] In this sense, he is a colonialist, though his realm is music.

Taking India as his subject thus provided Roussel with a way to challenge musical impressionists on their own terrain (nature) and to demonstrate the strength of Scholist principles on new territory. This was surely the ultimate distinction for a young composer. Its success led to two of his most important commissions from the Opéra director Jacques Rouché—the ballet *Le Festin de l'araignée* and his second Indian-inspired work, the opera-ballet *Padmâvatî*.[91]

For Delage, as we have seen, India was far more than a catalyst of visions and feelings. It had what Said has called "separate sovereignty"; its natives were not

---

87. A. Sérieyx, "A propos des 'Evocations,'" *Revue musicale S.I.M.* (May 1913): 65–66; cited in Goubault, "Les Premières Oeuvres de Roussel," 25.

88. G. Jean-Aubry, *La Musique d'aujourd'hui* (Paris: Perrin, 1916), 135–36.

89. Hoérée, *Roussel*, 39.

90. A. Mariotte, *Courrier musical* (1 November 1919), cited in Goubault, "Les Premières Oeuvres," 26.

91. Roussel began this Indian-inspired work in December 1913, but it was not premiered until 1923. *Padmâvatî* has an Indian subject, the story of Padmini at Tchitor, based a novel written in 1856 that Roussel and his collaborator Louis Laloy found in the Bibliothèque des Langues Orientales in Paris; see Arthur Hoérée, "Lettres d'Albert Roussel à Louis Laloy," *Cahiers Albert Roussel* 2 (1979): 73–74. Given what he says in his diary and their absence in his sketchbook and *Evocations*, one can surmise that the numerous ragas Roussel used in *Padmâvatî* he learned after his return to Paris.

"subservient nor sullenly uncooperative" as many a colonialist or visitor imagined them but music-makers whom Delage admired, perhaps even envied.[92] As for his father, the industrialist, for Delage India was a land of natural resources. Delage's success, like his father's, was based on understanding the value of these resources, particularly their use-value in the West. Self-taught, perhaps inspired by his father's entrepreneurial spirit, and aware of the marketability of the new, the composer took what he needed from his recordings. Incorporating the sound of Indian music—new to his contemporaries—Delage built the form of capital his world traded on, distinction and prestige.[93]

One could compare Delage's works with transcriptions of Indian recordings to his father's shoe polish—something partially made in India but packaged and sold in France, something still selling today. But this would be to reduce his music to these transcriptions, to downplay his interest in Indian music as a means of criticizing Western practices, and to ignore his integration of Western and Eastern materials. Like Roussel's *Evocations*, Delage's *Quatre Poèmes hindous* is, ultimately, a hybrid form, what Said calls a "narrative of integration."[94] In this set of songs, the integration is effected not only by giving the borrowed Indian passages to Western instruments and elaborating on Indian gestures but also by juxtaposing and suggesting the interpenetration of the different materials, a device that allows each style to maintain, at least momentarily, its own integrity. In "Lahore," the text juxtaposes a fir tree on a snowy mountain with a palm on a hot rock, a vision possible only in an imaginary space. Sections of the Khan and Thayi recordings give the context for this dream, as Delage's trip helps explain his music. Placed within the same piece, these transcriptions of music of North and South India, instrumental and vocal, testify to their juxtaposition in Delage's India experience. The set as a whole also works by juxtaposition. The outer songs with their Orientalist gestures and similar structure frame the inner ones with their Indian citations. The traditional Indian music serves as the basis, even the inspiration, for the experimental use of the voice, strings, and piano. To the extent that Eastern and Western musical materials coexist and interpenetrate without conflict, this multifaceted integration of musical materials suggests the global interdependence, mobility of resources, and continued fascination with the new on which international capitalism depends.

Delage did not go unrewarded. *Quatre Poèmes hindous* was premiered at the SMI on 14 January 1914, alongside first performances of Ravel's *Trois Poèmes de Mallarmé* and Stravinsky's *Trois Lyriques japonaises*.[95] Like them, it uses a chamber

---

92. Edward Said, *Culture and Imperialism* (New York: Knopf, 1993), xxi.

93. I am using the term *capital* here in the sense of cultural capital, as coined by Pierre Bourdieu in *La Distinction: Critique sociale du jugement* (Paris: Minuit, 1979).

94. Said, *Culture and Imperialism*, xxvi.

95. The first of these is dedicated to Delage.

orchestra in part inspired by Schönberg's *Pierrot Lunaire*. Even though the audience had little idea of the work's secret—in his 1 February 1914 review in *S.I.M.*, Jean Poueigh makes reference to the "funny peculiarity" of the closed-mouth singing, which he thought Delage had borrowed from its use in choruses—they demanded an encore of "Lahore." According to Georges Auric,[96] this stole the show, upstaging Ravel and Stravinsky, and the composer knew he had found a personal voice worthy of a career.[97]

Despite their different perspectives, Roussel and Delage found in their attempts to reproduce Indian culture a means of expanding the "territory" over which they could demonstrate their compositional control. Neither created Orientalist works about their "positional superiority" or the feminine erotic in part because, for them, race was a positive attribute of a people, a key to understanding them. Still, through their integration of Western and Eastern materials—Roussel to effect spiritual transformation and argue for a certain kind of French music, Delage to introduce new musical sounds and participate in the international modernist movement—both nonetheless had Orientalist aims couched within personal hopes: to escape the constraints of their times through an exotic other, to appeal to listeners through something universal, and in doing so make a name for themselves.

96. Interview with author, 1977.

97. Delage used similar material in an orchestral work, *Les Batisseurs de ponts* [The bridge-builders], conceived as a pantomime for the Ballets Russes; the third movement of *Contrerimes* (1927–32); the Vocalise-Etude (1929); and "Themmangu," from *Chants de la Jungle* [Songs of the jungle] (1914–34).

Part IV

PATRONS AND PATRONAGE

10. Countess Greffulhe as Entrepreneur

Negotiating Class, Gender, and Nation

$\mathcal{C}$OUNTESS ELISABETH GREFFULHE, immortalized by Marcel Proust as the Duchess de Guermantes, was arguably the most important patron of modern music in the early twentieth century.[1] The principal form of her patronage, however, was not salon concerts or artistic commissions but rather entrepreneurship. Even if she was a woman of the aristocracy, born the Belgian Princess de Caraman-Chimay, she emerged from the private domain to undertake, organize, and manage public concerts. French audiences had her to thank for the Paris premieres not only of Richard Wagner's *Tristan und Isolde*,

This essay originally appeared in *The Musician as Entrepreneur, 1700–1914*, ed. William Weber (Bloomington: Indiana University Press, 2004), 221–55. It is part of a book-in-progress on the musical activities of Countess Greffulhe. Parts of it were presented in talks at the University of California, Berkeley (24 April 1992), the Musée d'Orsay (2 December 1992), and two conferences, "Concert et publics en Europe entre 1700 et 1900," sponsored by the European Science Foundation project "Musical Life in Europe 1600–1900," Göttingen, Germany, 26 March 1999; and "The Musician as Entrepreneur and Opportunist, 1600–1900," William Andrews Clark Memorial Library, University of California, Los Angeles, 2 June 2001.

I am deeply grateful to the Duchess de Gramont, granddaughter-in-law of the Countess Greffulhe, for permission to consult the archives of the Countess Greffulhe in 1988–91 and for the friendship and support she extended to me and my work until her death in 1994. I also wish to thank Joël-Marie Fauquet for a tip that led me to discover the Fondation Greffulhe, and the Duke Antoine de Gramont for permission to cite and reproduce documents in these archives.

1. The archives of the Countess Greffulhe, Archives Privés, Archives Nationales, Paris (hereafter AP), distinct from those of her husband the count, contain a diary from the beginning of her marriage, press clippings, personal correspondence to and from the countess, programs of concerts given in the Parisian salon of her in-laws, rue d'Astorg, invitation lists, and programs, correspondence, and press clippings related to the Société des Grandes Auditions Musicales de France (1890–1913). See table 10.1 for a list of royalty, politicians, and members of the press with whom she corresponded.

FIGURE 10.1. E. Hébert, Comtesse Greffulhe. *Revue de l'art ancien et moderne.*

Götterdämmerung, and staged fragments of *Parsifal* but also Edward Elgar's *Dream of Gerontius*, Richard Strauss's *Salomé*, orchestral works by Gustav Mahler and Arnold Schönberg, and the early productions of the Ballets Russes.

This essay examines how the countess negotiated the boundaries of class, gender, and politics to become one of the most powerful forces in the musical world of Paris. She identified both a body of works from which the public was being deprived and a constituency for concerts of these works. An entrepreneur motivated not by personal profit but by the desire to see ignored masterpieces performed in France, she had both the financial resources and the personal connections to act on her perceptions. Successful in attracting some supporters by her nationalist causes and others through the lure of distinction and the limelight of fashion, she created an institution to enact her ambitions, the Société des Grandes Auditions Musicales de France. With a power resembling that of the state, she used this organization not only to promote concerts as a form of international diplomacy but also to fulfill her own identity as the "Queen" of music.

PARIS AT THE *FIN DE SIÈCLE*

Certain aspects of French society set the context for such an entrepreneur. First, in the nineteenth century, nobles typically participated in the business world as investors, rather than as managers or entrepreneurs.[2] Still, as David Higgs has written, their attitude toward capitalism and the professions "was not immobile or monolithic." When they did get involved, he argues, it was their behavior and ethos that distinguished them from the untitled, in addition to concerns of collective loyalty, family status, and lineage.[3] Countess Greffulhe indeed projected a sense of "duty" and devotion to higher concerns like the nation. And to build support for her concerts, she began with her immediate family, relatives, and friends before reaching out to their social peers and other "members of the aristocracy by birth or wealth."[4] She did not assume they shared her musical tastes but rather appealed to the elitism and prestige associated with her projects. She also understood their

2. According to Jerome Blum, *The End of the Old Order in Rural Europe* (Princeton, N.J.: Princeton University Press, 1978), it was not unusual for nobles to be investors in business ventures. "In 1902 in France 30 percent of the boards of directors of railroads and 32 percent of the boards of large steel and banking firms were members of the nobility" (422–23).

3. David Higgs, *Nobles in Nineteenth-Century France* (Baltimore: Johns Hopkins University Press, 1987), 154, 129.

4. Clipping of Louis de Fourcaud, *Le Gaulois* (13 June 1891), AP. As Higgs puts it, the crucial point in any discussion about nobles in modern France is not whether someone was a true noble but whether he or she showed "the desire to appear noble" (*Nobles*, 5). Interestingly, some critics writing about Countess Greffulhe, perhaps anxious about the

attraction to good investments. Perhaps on the advice of her banker-treasurer, to pay for expensive Wagnerian productions, the countess solicited contributions not as gifts or subscriptions, like other concert societies in Paris, but as a type of stock in a company, guaranteeing it financial security. In addition to good seats at the performances, she promised a fixed rate of return on the capital invested. With her own net worth as implied collateral, she had no trouble procuring what she needed. Such private investment strategies borrowed from business and finance made possible the creation of an organization capable of acting like those subsidized by the state.

Second, the countess's public concerts coincided with the emergence of a new generation of politicians, a coalition based on broad political alliances formed to stem the rising tide of socialism and anarchist violence. Beginning with the 1893 elections, this group instigated a policy of *ralliement*, trying to incorporate first the monarchist right and the Catholic Church (whose pope finally recognized the Republic in 1891) and later a group of liberals who believed in social solidarity. The Republic's seal in the 1890s reflects this idea: on the cartouche is a ship, symbolizing the Republic, under rows of fleurs-de-lis and a crown. As Debora Silverman points out in her penetrating study of art and politics from 1889 to 1900, "the image and legend of the ship of state skillfully navigating the rough waters was appropriate for a Republic whose strength in this decade lay in its very resiliency, its capacity to chart a fluid course, shifting and gliding according to changing conditions of political winds and weather."[5] Such an ideal of political reconciliation, however, was difficult to realize. A more malleable terrain in which to seek similarities and compromise was culture. As Silverman suggests, a striking cultural analogue to political progressivism was the Union Centrale des Arts Décoratifs. Founded in 1864 as a producers' association "to industrialize art for a broad public," by 1889 its social composition, ideology, and programs had changed to reflect the confluence of politicians, cultural leaders, and educators from among the aristocracy as well as the republican administration. Its members, the antithesis of Second Empire nouveaux-riches collectors, believed in active recreation of the past rather than passive consumption. They saw art as a way to transcend political dissension and thought enlightened *amateurs* should play a leadership role in helping to educate public taste. And they looked to collaboration with the state in reconstructing the world of art patronage.[6] The Société des Grandes Auditions was a cultural analogue to this political coalition. Membership included the same mixture of bourgeois

---

claims to nobility of her husband's family, have occasionally added "de" to her name, as they have with that of the Russian impresario Serge [de] Diaghilev. For a recent example of this, see Debora Silverman, *Art Nouveau in Fin-de-Siècle France* (Berkeley: University of California Press, 1989), 191.

5. Silverman, *Art Nouveau*, 45; see also 322, n. 6.
6. Silverman, *Art Nouveau*, 110–19, 135.

republicans and titled aristocrats as that characterizing the Union Centrale after 1889, and some of the same people.

Third, Countess Greffulhe began organizing public concerts as women were becoming more attuned to feminist ideals. This was the era of the New Woman. During the 1890s, over 20,000 women joined feminist organizations in France. Some were beginning to enter professions such as law and medicine. Aristocratic women took part in this movement. In the early 1890s, the Union Centrale des Arts Décoratifs called for the country's female elites to become leaders in luxury craft production, "reclaiming the aristocratic tradition of women's central role in the decorative arts" and forming "a female aristocracy of the spirit rather than of lineage." Countess Greffulhe was among those who contributed decorative objects to the first Exhibition of the Arts of Women in 1892, as were the music patroness Madame de Saint-Marceaux and the pianist Princess Bibesco. When in 1894 the Union started a special women's committee to oversee this attempted reeducation of French taste, not only was Countess Greffulhe among its first members but also her mother-in-law, Countess Greffulhe née la Rochefoucauld. According to the committee's charter, women were expected to "involve themselves in the progress of the arts and in expressing their love of country and of solidarity." The committee proposed philanthropic programs and encouraged women to "embrace their role as patrons" as well as "instructors in refining taste."[7] In 1896, the Union president and deputy from Paris, Georges Berger, recognized women's efforts to "realize the beautiful in the useful," along with "the moral beauty represented by their charitable tendencies." He called on women to be involved in the arts as a form of patriotism.[8] Countess Greffulhe's Société des Grandes Audition is in some ways a musical response to these attitudes, and its membership undoubtedly grew because of them.

Many female music patrons in France became more ambitious at the end of the century. Some hired professional orchestras and put on Wagnerian acts, singing the principal roles themselves. For the most part, these performances took place in their private salons. Those who needed to rent halls did so only rarely. The most active women, such as the Princess Edmond de Polignac, had special rooms for music built in their homes, engaged "house musicians," sponsored performances of new works before their public premieres, and invited a regular group of friends to attend.[9] Still,

7. Silverman, *Art Nouveau*, 193–99.

8. Georges Berger, "Appel aux femmes françaises," *Revue des arts décoratifs* 16 (1896): 97–98. After successfully serving as the director of the 1889 Paris Exhibition, Berger was elected deputy from Paris, placed on the parliamentary budget committee for the fine arts, and made president of the Union Central des Arts Décoratifs. He was reelected to the Chambre des Députés in 1893, 1898, and 1902 and became known as one of the leaders of the *progressivists*.

9. For a wonderful study of Prince and Princess de Polignac's salon, see Sylvia Kahan, *Winnaretta Singer: Princess de Polignac, Intrepid Patron of Modern Music* (Rochester, N.Y.:

being a salon hostess was not an entirely private affair. The social columns of the press reported on some of these concerts, in sections called, for example, "Le Monde et la ville" (The World and the City) in *Le Figaro* and "Mondanités" (Society Life) in *Le Gaulois.*

What distinguished Countess Greffulhe was that she formalized a music society in order to realize her aspirations and conceived it to produce public concerts with hired professionals. Being a woman, an aristocrat, and an *amateur* as president of such a society was also unusual. Throughout much of the nineteenth century, women were excluded from most private clubs in Paris, except as occasional performers at their concerts, and when women were included, they were rarely involved in leadership. Moreover, aristocrats typically did not take part in public concerts other than benefits for charity.[10] Their homes and concerts sponsored by their private clubs provided ample opportunities for them to perform music and hear their compositions. Besides the Union Centrale des Arts Décoratifs, a number of clubs served as predecessors of the Société des Grandes Auditions. The Société Académique des Enfants d'Apollon and the Cercle de l'Union Artistique used their prestige to attract Parisian elites and regularly entertained them with concerts. The Enfants d'Apollon, founded in 1741, included members of the Institut de France as well as distinguished *amateurs* in all the arts. With an orchestra made up mostly of the society's members, they put on a private concert each month, sometimes featuring members' compositions. The Union Artistique, which often put local elites in touch with their foreign peers, occasionally invited well-known professional musicians from foreign countries to participate in their private concerts. Concordia, founded in 1880, perhaps most anticipated the Société des Grandes Auditions. Even if Concordia's focus was choral music and a good percentage of their members (up to two-thirds) performed in their concerts, Concordia had a similar organization, many of the same members, and a common goal: to perform little-known old masterpieces and new music.[11] Unlike the Enfants d'Apollon and the Union Artistique, Concordia admitted women as members. Madame Edmond Fuchs, a singer, was their vice-president for many years. Both Concordia and the

---

University of Rochester Press, 2003). Fauré served as "house musician" in these concerts. Works such as Debussy's *Ile Joyeuse* and *Masques* were performed there on 15 February 1905, three days before their premieres at the Société Nationale.

10. On 15 May 1894, Countess de Guerne sang for the benefit of a charity in Fauré's *Requiem* at the Salle d'Harcourt. In another such event at the Hotel Continental in 1898, Princess Bibesco performed piano concertos by Chopin and Saint-Saëns with an orchestra made up of performers from the Opéra.

11. It is possible that members of Concordia performed in the Société des Grandes Auditions productions of *Parsifal* and Beethoven's *Missa Solemnis* in 1903, for their choruses evidently included "amateurs" and "dames du monde." Concordia members had given the French premiere of the "Scenes des filles-fleurs" from *Parsifal* in Paris in 1887.

Société des Grandes Auditions were also anomalies, in that as concert societies, they were not led by professional musicians. Whereas this might have been common in Boston or New York at the end of the nineteenth century, most organizers of public concerts in Paris were conductors. Countess Greffulhe's Société was thus the only major music organization in Paris run by a woman and a titled aristocrat who organized public concerts with hired professionals.[12]

How did this come to pass? In this chapter, I examine crucial aspects of Countess Greffulhe's background that underlay her entrepreneurship and helped define it. Concerts took five forms in her life and served five related functions: patronage, entertainment, philanthropy, national pride, and international diplomacy. What made each of these succeed was not only hard work but also the way she navigated the ambiguities inherent in aristocratic identity at the time. Above all, Countess Greffulhe turned the constraints of family, gender, and class into opportunities for forging connections and alliances. With diplomatic skills learned from her father, the Belgian ambassador to France, she understood how to build networks of cooperation and collaboration. If it had not been for her personal prestige, extensive connections, and artful diplomacy, the Société des Grandes Auditions might never have lasted over twenty years.

FAMILY AND SALON CONCERTS

Through birth and later marriage, Elisabeth de Caraman-Chimay, the Countess Greffulhe, lived at the crossroads that linked nobility with the world of finance. Born in 1860, she was the eldest daughter of Joseph de Riquet, Prince de Chimay and Caraman of Belgium, and Marie de Montesquiou de Fesenzac. Her grandfather, an ambassador for the Netherlands, contributed to establishing Belgian independence and to assuring good relations with Italy and the German Confederation. He also founded one of the most important Belgian railroads, in part to provide transportation to the family chateau in Enau near the Belgian-French border. Her father, another diplomat, was governor of Hainaut from 1870 to 1878 and later minister of foreign affairs from 1884 to 1892. He also served for many years as ambassador to France. Consequently, Elisabeth grew up in Paris in the Hotel de Chimay, quai Malaquais. (When her father died in 1892, this was annexed by the Ecole des Beaux-Arts.)

Music was a family tradition. But more than merely putting on salon concerts for their own entertainment, the Chimays were patrons. Great-grandfather Chimay

12. Countess Greffulhe did hire conductors as artistic directors of individual concerts, but she remained in charge of the society as its president. The Union Centrale des Arts Décoratifs also occasionally organized public concerts. To animate their ninth exhibition at the Palais de l'Industrie, they, too, hired a conductor, Jules Danbé of the Opéra-Comique, who put on daily concerts of orchestral music there between August and December 1887.

helped to found the Brussels Conservatory. For decades, their home hosted many of the most illustrious composers in Europe—Liszt reputedly performed for the first time in public in their home and premiered works there. Every child, of course, had to play an instrument. For Elisabeth's father, it was the violin, which he studied with Charles de Bériot and later Henri Vieuxtemps, also frequent guests at the family's concerts. Her mother, too, was musical, a piano student of Chopin's last disciple and pupil of Clara Schumann.[13] Among her own siblings, Elisabeth played piano, her two brothers violin and cello. Like others of her class, she was expected to perform pretty well, but not up to professional standards.[14]

This skill came in handy, as it was meant to, in courting Henry Greffulhe, the only son of a wealthy financier. The two of them spent afternoons singing duos from *Faust* and *Don Juan*, and performed for his parents at their chateau outside Paris, Bois-Boudran.[15] This went well enough to win his hand in marriage in 1878—quite a plum. Her father had only a limited dowry to offer her, having directed most of his attention to politics. On the day they married, she received the interest on 100,000 francs (or 5,000 francs a year) while her husband received 5 percent of 8 million francs, or 400,000 year.[16] (As did many in their situation, Elisabeth's older brother Joseph, too, sought an alliance between title and money, later marrying a rich American, Clara Ward.) On Henry's, there was a tradition of using money to attract pedigree. His grandfather, the son of a Swiss banker who settled in Amsterdam, received the title of Count in 1818 for helping to fund the Bourbons.[17] In marrying Félicie de la Rochefoucauld d'Estissac, his father had succeeded in joining one of the most distinguished noble families in France. Henry's two sisters similarly married well, Jeanne Greffulhe to Prince August d'Arenberg, member of the Institut and deputy, and Louise to Count Robert de l'Aigle. The desire to appear noble, even if one had purchased or married into nobility, was crucial in a society where all Frenchmen were equal before the law. Maintaining the trappings of nobility was also important for those whose fortunes had thinned out over time and still had expensive chateaux to keep up, as was the case for the Prince de Caraman-Chimay.

13. "Notes sur les activités musicales de la Comtesse Greffulhe," AP.

14. She also studied drawing, photography (with Nadar), and literature, hoping to earn a degree that would allow her to become a teacher. See Anne de Cossé Brissac, *La Comtesse Greffulhe* (Paris: Perrin, 1991), 33, 72.

15. Brissac, *Comtesse Greffulhe*, 21, 29. Jean-Louis Greffulhe purchased the chateau in 1814.

16. To this was added Elisabeth's 15,000-franc trousseau and Henry's clothes, cars, chateau, and eighty-eight hectares of land. Brissac, *Comtesse Greffulhe*, 21. The couple also received a villa in Dieppe.

17. Louis Greffulhe was a Swiss banker who built his wealth in Amsterdam before moving to Paris in 1789.

Appearances played an important part in Elisabeth's life as the Viscountess Greffulhe.[18] First, although she was Belgian by birth, she identified and behaved as if French and was understood to be French (somewhat like César Franck). Second, Henry and his family were intent on grooming her to represent *their* social ambitions. As Higgs has pointed out,

> *titrés* sought to emulate the indefinable distinction of bearing and manners, the *je ne sais quoi* that distinguished the noblesse and the aristocracy from social inferiors. This was necessary if they were to pass into the *bonne compagnie* just as they needed wealth to enter the Parisian *haute société*. Nineteenth-century nobles and particularly aristocrats found their last redoubt of social power in control of the criteria of elegant behavior.[19]

Indeed, beginning with the journal she kept at the beginning of her marriage and throughout her correspondence with Henry, we find numerous comments about how she is to appear—at first "be pretty and "take on your grand air," later "be elegant," "don't laugh too loud," and especially "maintain a grand air and your dignity."[20] Henry and his mother wanted her to appear perfect, to please everyone— Henry consulted with all his relatives for suggestions on her education.[21] With this in mind, they employed four dressmakers and two designers. If it weren't for her beauty, her clothes alone would have been enough to attract attention and commentary at the Opéra, the Société des Concerts, and the Concerts Colonne, where they paraded her in public. In 1883, Henry commissioned a painting from Eugène Lami, Elisabeth's painting teacher. Entitled *Fête costumée chez le Duc de Sagan,* it was to represent Henry's wife as "a goddess of the night, with a scepter in her hands"—the future "Queen" of Paris.

People started to talk about Elisabeth and wanted to meet her. But while her husband wanted to show her off, like some beautiful object he'd acquired, her mother-in-law, a noblewoman, was uncomfortable with Elisabeth's name beginning to appear in the press. In her social class, it was *de rigueur not* to "get yourself talked about" (*se faire parler*) and *not* to develop a sphere of influence outside the home.[22] However, Elisabeth began to enjoy the attention, even revel in it.

The concerts she organized in the first decade of her marriage suggest some of the constraints within which she lived and the expectations her new family had of her. These took place at her in-laws' home on the rue d'Astorg, just north of the Champs-Elysées, where she and her husband occupied one wing and her

18. Before her father-in-law died in 1888, Elisabeth was known as the viscountess and her husband the viscount.

19. Higgs, *Nobles*, 181.

20. Brissac, *Comtesse Greffulhe*, 29, 48–49.

21. Brissac, *Comtesse Greffulhe*, 35.

22. Brissac, *Comtesse Greffulhe*, 84.

sister-in-law and husband, the Arenbergs, another wing. For the most part, these were closed, intimate occasions that probably took place after dinner. Besides family members, only titled monarchists and staunch Catholics were invited, unless the elder Countess Greffulhe felt someone else could be useful in her philanthropic activities.

The programs in the family archives document probably only a small subset of these concerts.[23] The first, from 8 May 1881, is one of the most ambitious. Three of the city's top opera singers—Jean-Baptiste Faure, Jean-Alexandre Talazac, and Marie-Hélène Brunet-Lafleur—were paid 5,000 francs, with 4,000 francs going to Faure. This was an enormous sum, as Faure received only 2,000 francs for each appearance at the Concerts Colonne that year, and (with Gabrielle Krauss) was their highest paid soloist for the decade. To piano accompaniment, these singers performed popular airs from Gounod, Rossini, Meyerbeer, and the Conservatoire composer Charles Lenepveu. Faure also sang his signature religious works, *Crucifix* and *Je crois*. A chorus, paid 500 francs, was hired to open both parts of the concert and end with the finale of *Lucia di Lammermoor*. An oboist, paid 200 francs, performed pieces by the prominent female composer the Viscountess Clémence de Grandval; a pianist received 200 francs and an organist 50 francs. Programs were printed, costing 42 francs. The total budget of 5,992 francs was more than half the annual salary of the director of the Conservatoire and roughly equivalent to the ticket receipts of one night at the Opéra-Comique.

After this concert, however, there is a gap, perhaps because in 1882 Elisabeth gave birth to her daughter Elaine. Then, beginning in 1884, came three years of programs with the clear sense of a "season." From 27 February to 28 May 1884, the family held fifteen concerts, one every other week, most of them on Saturday evening. The first is typical with its hand-copied program. The repertoire ranges from trios by Haydn and Beethoven to vocal works such as Massenet's *Elégie* and piano pieces like a nocturne by Chopin. Performers were mostly family members: Elisabeth played piano, Henry sang. Henry's sister, the Countess de L'Aigle, and Elisabeth's brother Pierre and his wife also performed. One professional accompanied them—Eugène Sauzay, Henry's violin teacher and professor at the Conservatoire from 1860 through 1892. For participating in nine such concerts at the Greffulhes' that year he was paid 2,000 francs, almost equal to his annual Conservatoire salary of 2,400 francs.

At other concerts that spring, the repertoire expanded to include excerpts from Beethoven symphonies transcribed for four performers, fragments from Mozart's *La Flûte enchantée* and *Don Juan*, trios by Mozart and Robert Schumann, works by Etienne-Henri Méhul, Christoph Willibald von Gluck, and French contemporaries, as well as recurring favorites like Faure's *Crucifix* and Massenet's *Elégie*, both

---

23. Soirées musicales à la rue d'Astorg, AP.

inevitably sung by Henry. Elisabeth performed in anywhere from two to four of the five works presented, for a total of thirty-two times that spring, while her husband performed three times. Other professionals also joined them, including the cellist from the Conservatoire, Richard [?] Loÿs, who received 1,800 francs for nine appearances. The total expense for these invited house musicians that season was 4,700 francs.

What is particularly interesting about these concerts is how they reflect a convergence of amateur and professional practices. On the bottom of the first program is the text: "Please do not enter or leave during the performance of the pieces"—a direct quotation of similar comments on orchestral concert programs in Paris going back to the early nineteenth century. Apparently these amateurs wanted respect from their listeners, as if they were professionals. Or perhaps Elisabeth was accustomed to professionals performing in her Belgian family's salon and had similar ambitions for that of the Greffulhes. The request may have been hard to enforce, for it did not return on subsequent Greffulhe programs. On the bottom of the programs for 12 and 19 March are two other notes: "A sudden indisposition having deprived the Société of one of its first subjects, those persons present with a particular talent are invited to put it at the disposition of the Société's members [sociétaires]"; and "One of the first subjects, who has not had an occasion to play violin for a year, asks for the public's indulgence." Regardless of their skills, the performers seem to have considered themselves as a music "society" performing for a "public."

The concert of Wednesday, 20 April 1884, resembled that of 8 May 1881, in that it offered a printed program and the opera stars Faure, Talazac, and Brunet-Lafleur, framing their solos and duets with a chorus (see fig. 10.2). In addition, the music performed was almost entirely French: instead of Italian melodies and German classics, two Charles Gounod choruses and airs from Gounod's *Mireille*, Hector Berlioz's *Damnation de Faust*, Camille Saint-Saëns's *Samson et Dalila*, and Wagner's *Tannhäuser*. With the exception of Henry's favorites that Faure performed, Massenet's *Elégie* and Faure's *Crucifix*, this suggests not only an increasing gap between what amateurs and professionals were performing at the Greffulhes but also a nod in the direction of more contemporary tastes, perhaps instigated by Elisabeth. She loved Wagner's music and was never able to hear it in her own family's home because of her father's disinterest. This concert alone cost 7,190 francs, with Talazac and Brunet-Lafleur doubling the fees they received in 1881. That so much money could be spent on *this* repertoire may reflect Elisabeth's increasing power within the family.

The 1886 season started late, on 2 April, and consisted of only five concerts, one every other week. Only professionals performed, including members of the most prestigious orchestras in Paris, the Société des Concerts du Conservatoire and the Opéra. The less expensive ones, costing 500–800 francs, took place on Friday evenings, the more expensive ones, costing over 2,000 francs, on Sunday evenings.

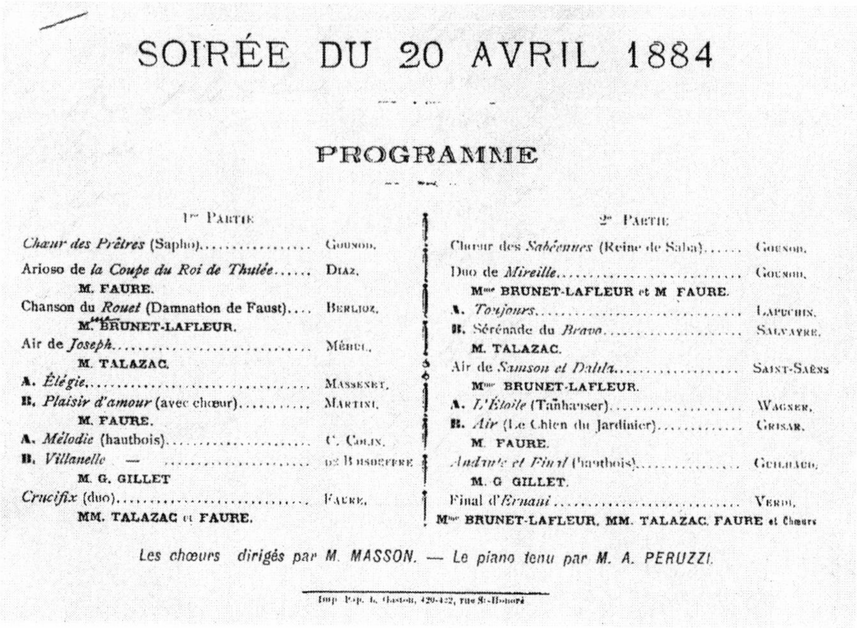

SOIRÉE DU 20 AVRIL 1884

PROGRAMME

1re PARTIE

Chœur des Prêtres (Sapho)................ GOUNOD.

Arioso de *la Coupe du Roi de Thulée*...... DIAZ.

M. FAURE.

Chanson du *Rouet* (Damnation de Faust).... BERLIOZ.

M. BRUNET-LAFLEUR.

Air de *Joseph*.............................. MÉHUL.

M. TALAZAC.

A. *Élégie*.................................. MASSENET.

B. *Plaisir d'amour* (avec chœur)........... MARTINI.

M. FAURE.

A. *Mélodie* (hautbois)...................... C. COLIN.

B. *Villanelle* — .... DE BOISDEFFRE

M. G. GILLET

Crucifix (duo)............................ FAURE.

MM. TALAZAC et FAURE.

2e PARTIE

Chœur des *Sabéennes* (Reine de Saba)...... GOUNOD.

Duo de *Mireille*........................... GOUNOD.

Mme BRUNET-LAFLEUR et M FAURE.

A. *Toujours*................................ LAPUCHIN.

B. Sérénade du *Bravo*...................... SALVAYRE.

M. TALAZAC.

Air de *Samson et Dalila*.................... SAINT-SAËNS

Mme BRUNET-LAFLEUR.

A. *L'Étoile* (Tanhauser)..................... WAGNER.

B. *Air* (Le Chien du Jardinier)............. GRISAR.

M. FAURE.

Andante et Final (hautbois)................ GUILHAUD.

M. G GILLET.

Final d'*Ernani* .... VERDI.

Mme BRUNET-LAFLEUR, MM. TALAZAC, FAURE et Chœurs

Les chœurs dirigés par M. MASSON. — Le piano tenu par M. A. PERUZZI.

FIGURE 10.2. Soirée at the home of the Greffulhes, 20 April 1884. Courtesy of Duke Antoine de Gramont.

All programs were printed, using a gothic font and a large page format. Although Elisabeth no longer performed, her signature is recognizable on them. On the top of each one she noted the cost and her evaluations—"bon," "mauvais," or "très bien." These concerts expanded the genres and kinds of performers presented at the Greffulhes' to include mandolin and lute music by performers from abroad, accompanied by the pianist-composer Ruggero Leoncavallo, music by members of the Société des Instruments à Vent, a harpist, and the organist for Queen Isabelle II, as well as monologues and one-act comedies with Ernest Coquelin, known as Coquelin Cadet (the younger Coquelin), of the Comédie-Française, and popular songs performed by the city's most famous cabaret singer, Madame Thérésa.[24] If she did not appreciate the monologues of M. Sadi-Pety from the Théâtre de l'Odéon on 2 April, noting "mauvais" next to them on her program, Elisabeth clearly enjoyed those of Coquelin Cadet. On the top of the programs with him she wrote "soirée très réussie."

24. This was not the first time Madame Thérésa appeared in a context otherwise associated with art music. In 1884–85, she also sang at the end of concerts put on by the choral society of the Bon Marché department store. It is possible that the countess heard the juxtaposition of popular and serious genres elsewhere, liked it, and wanted to introduce family members to the experience, at the very least as a curiosity. See chapter 13 here, "Material Culture and Postmodern Positivism."

What motivated these extraordinary changes? Elisabeth herself studied guitar for a year,[25] but this does not explain her interest in the wind ensemble or popular performers. In a recent biography by a distant relative, we are told that Elisabeth and Henry's marriage had more or less fallen apart by 1886 and that Henry no longer attended receptions organized by his wife.[26] Did this allow her more freedom in organizing the family concerts? Perhaps the possibility of having significant influence, even control, over these concerts ignited her entrepreneurial spirit.

Certainly in the 1886 concerts Elisabeth began experimenting with the organization, content, and form of a concert. In them she used her extensive experience in concert attendance to offer both a critique of the common practice of mixing genres and a reasoned alternative that respected audiences' desire for variety. Each of these concerts consisted of two specific genres in alternation—the first between string quartet movements and spoken monologues; the second between mandolin music and operatic song; the fourth between spoken works and music; and the fifth between humorous scenes and organ music. On 2 May, the third of these concerts, Madame Théresa's "La Tour Saint-Jacques" followed Beethoven's Quartet no. 5, and her "Vive la chanson" followed Mozart's Quartet in B-flat; other cabaret songs by her followed violin and cello solos. Each part of the concert ended with (unspecified) monologues by Coquelin Cadet (see fig. 10.3). A sense of balance and proportion pervaded, almost as if the pieces were parts of a poem—ABABC ABABC, with A the string music, B the popular songs, and C the monologues. In creating such juxtapositions, Elisabeth was clearly trying to expand her in-laws' concept of a salon concert, as well as their experience of both serious and popular genres. And she was willing to pay for it.

For 1887, only four programs remain in her archives for concerts between 17 April and 5 June, each on a Sunday evening. These show her becoming a true entrepreneur, hiring and negotiating with a wide range of professionals, the best she could find, and putting together programs that could compete with those one might find in the public marketplace. All but one were substantially longer than her previous salon concerts, and all had printed programs. Their average cost was higher as well— 3,288 francs. The first involved Talazac from the Opéra-Comique, Jean-François Delmas from the Opéra, the cellist Loÿs from the Conservatoire, and a young singer from the Opéra-Comique, Mlle Isaac, who received 2,000 francs. The second concert involved an orchestra of ten players from the Société des Concerts du Conservatoire, conducted from the piano by Emile Bourgeois and paid 1,000 francs. In addition to favorites by Gounod, Mozart, and Verdi, the repertoire in 1887 included the young French composers Paul Vidal and Gabriel Pierné and some unusual works, such as Herman Bemberg's *Chant hindou*, perhaps proposed by the performers. As in 1886,

25. Brissac, *Comtesse Greffulhe*, 72.
26. Brissac, *Comtesse Greffulhe*, 76.

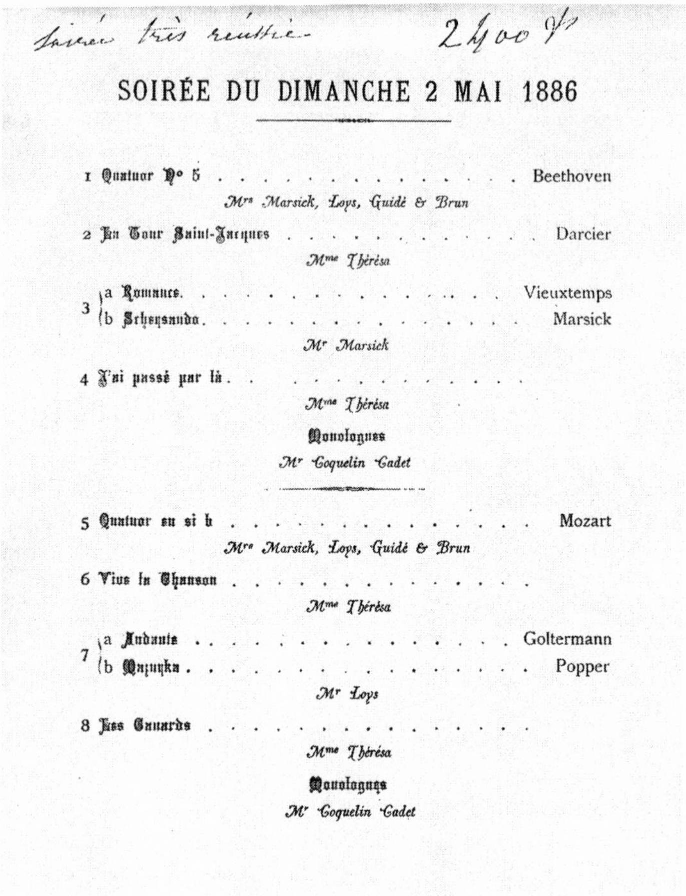

Soirée très réussie 2400 fr

SOIRÉE DU DIMANCHE 2 MAI 1886

1 Quatuor N° 5 . . . . Beethoven

Mrs Marsick, Loys, Guidé & Brun

2 La Tour Saint-Jacques . . . . Darcier

Mme Thérésa

3 a Romance. . . . . Vieuxtemps

b Scherzando. . . . . Marsick

Mr Marsick

4 J'ai passé par là . . . .

Mme Thérésa

Monologues

Mr Coquelin Cadet

5 Quatuor en si b . . . . Mozart

Mrs Marsick, Loys, Guidé & Brun

6 Vive la Chanson . . . .

Mme Thérésa

7 a Andante . . . . Goltermann

b Mazurka . . . . Popper

Mr Loys

8 Les Canards . . . .

Mme Thérésa

Monologues

Mr Coquelin Cadet

FIGURE 10.3. Soirée at the home of the Greffulhes, 2 May 1886. Courtesy of Duke Antoine de Gramont.

on two of these concerts, instrumental or vocal music alternated with poetry, as well as monologues and one-act comedies by Coquelin Cadet. This suggests that Elisabeth's family enjoyed the juxtaposition of serious with popular genres and did not consider the previous year's experience merely a curiosity. The last concert of 1887—unique in her archives—is a piano recital by a Mrs. Hoffman, possibly a soloist visiting from abroad. She received 1,600 francs for the concert, substantially more than all but the top opera singers. In a letter dated 9 July 1887, Gabriel Fauré recounts orchestra rehearsals he led of Wagner's *Siegfried-Idyl* just before performing for Elisabeth's guests later that summer.[27]

27. Gabriel Fauré to CG, 9 July 1887, AP. This relationship led him in 1888 to write a pavane for her.

These concerts probably continued each spring, although there is only one program extant from March 1889. Of particular interest is an excerpt from *Parsifal* played by the cellist Loÿs. In 1896, seven handwritten programs in the archives, costing an average of only 200 francs per concert, document important changes. First, although the performers include some of the same from the 1880s (string professors from the Conservatoire and the Société des Concerts du Conservatoire), there are more visiting artists, for example, a singer from the Imperial Theater of Saint Petersburg. Moreover, three of the concerts also include fourteen students from the Conservatoire, who, with their professors, were paid a total of 1,500 francs. Second, the repertoire reflects the *fin-de-siècle* interest in early music, some of it performed on old instruments. The countess's friend Fauré also appears regularly. Third, and most important, she engaged some administrative help. Indication of payment to musicians is signed "E. Masson."

Salon concerts continued at the Greffulhe home, although it is not clear how regularly.[28] Comprehensive guest lists suggest that the countess was meticulously careful about whom she invited, how often, and to which concert.[29] The only other program in the countess's archives documenting one of her salon concerts is that of 29 June 1900. Although the program is printed, this was clearly a private affair, involving no professional performers. The women's chorus consisted of titled aristocrats, including Countess Greffulhe, her eighteen-year-old daughter, and five of the original dames patronesses of the Société des Grandes Auditions in 1892. The guest list of thirty-eight overlaps with the chorists. Besides two Gounod fragments, the major work, *Les Adieux de Déïdamia*, was by a close friend of the countess, Prince Edmond de Polignac. The Prince also conducted, assisted by Count Henri de Ségur at the piano. All this suggests that, with the striking exception of the invited composers Massenet and d'Indy—who was a colleague of Polignac on the board of the Schola Cantorum—they were performing for and about themselves—pure entertainment.

During the first ten years of her marriage, then, like most women of her class, Elisabeth did not question "the primacy of the family realm."[30] In the context of her husband's family and their home, she learned how to appear grand and queenly while winning people's affections. Among the Parisian aristocracy, she became known for good judgment, enthusiasm for the arts, honesty, and self-respect, as well as her ability to understand a broad range of people and issues.[31] These

28. Other such concerts are occasionally mentioned in her correspondence and in the press.

29. The comprehensive guest list with addresses for her 1901 concerts has columns for six successive dates in late May and June, noting who was invited to which concert (AP).

30. Higgs, *Nobles*, 215.

31. Diary entry of 27 August 1886, in Marquis de Breteuil, *La Haute Société* (Paris: Jullian, 1979), 41–42.

contexts helped her to understand and build the kinship bonds that were so important to her class. Later she would call on those whose loyalty she had earned for their help. During this time she also learned how to accomplish things while working behind the scenes. Concerts became outlets not just for her own musical creativity and that of other family members but also her budding organizational skills. Increasingly, these gatherings developed from hodgepodges of whatever anyone felt like playing to carefully chosen, balanced programs presented by professionals—whom she chose, hired, and paid.

PREPARING FOR A NEW LIFE

When Henry's father died in 1888, the couple inherited not only his title but also his fortune. This led to many changes. First, Elisabeth, now the countess, began to open their home to other interests. Perhaps seeking to increase her sphere of influence and inspired by her own father, the diplomat, she began to invite to her receptions not only the literary friends of her cousin Robert de Montesquiou but also politicians ranging far beyond those of her mother-in-law's political orientation. Her salon quickly became known as "mixed," which, for her, meant that it had interesting people, including those who could contribute to her emerging power outside the home.[32] To set the context for receiving increasingly important people, she and her husband built a huge addition onto the family chateau.[33]

Second, she encouraged Henry to enter politics. After all, his grandfather had once been on a town council and had ended his life as a senator. Although they had many monarchist friends, the couple shared a sympathy with republican ideals.[34] Elisabeth respected the royal family but did not think they had any political future, especially under General Georges Boulanger.[35] This combination turned out to be potent in the late 1880s, with the emerging need for a coalition of old-guard monarchists and progressivist republicans. In July 1888, just before the vote, Elisabeth wrote to her husband, "It is important simply to be more shrewd than the others, to *bien jouer la comédie*, deceive with words without renouncing what one believes, never write anything compromising"—in other words, put to good use the ambiguities inherent in aristocratic identity. Running on a "conservative, independent, and liberal" platform, Henry was elected with 60 percent of the vote.

This campaign had many benefits for the countess. It taught her how to use the press as an "efficient and powerful tool for propaganda"—particularly since Henry bought a quarter and a third of the subscriptions of the two local papers to win

---

32. Brissac, *Comtesse Greffulhe*, 111.

33. Brissac, *Comtesse Greffulhe*, 198.

34. Although Elisabeth was Catholic, Henry's family historically was Protestant on his father's side.

35. Henry's mother, too, found Boulanger pitiful.

their support. And his position brought her into contact with moderate republicans such as Joseph Reinach, a leader under Léon Gambetta, and Jean Casimir-Perier, in 1894 elected president of France. She soon developed a reputation as not only a grande dame but also a "very modern" woman, one who not only read symbolist poetry, admired the impressionists, and adored Wagner but also had progressive political tastes.[36]

The countess wasted no time in putting these contacts to good use. Whereas her husband could play out his ambitions in politics, a domain gendered masculine and reserved almost entirely for men at the time, she looked to music, a realm traditionally gendered feminine. That fall she proposed to her mother-in-law that she organize a public concert to benefit the Société Philanthropique, of whose Dames Patronnesses committee the latter was president.[37] This was an extraordinary proposition, for two reasons. First, noblewomen were allowed to organize charity events but normally were proscribed from having any direct contact with theater directors, conductors, or musicians, in part because it was thought that they lived unseemly lives. Second, Charles Ephrussi had organized exhibitions for this cause, but no one had ever organized a concert. Nobles did not do this, except when it involved amateurs or private contexts. Her brother-in-law, Prince d'Arenberg, who was president of the Société Philanthropique, thoroughly approved of the countess's idea, and so she set forth on producing her first public event. She rented the Trocadéro hall, the largest in Paris, hired two singers from the Paris Opéra and the Opéra's conductor, and chose Handel's *Messiah*, a work well known in England but less so in France.[38] She paid particular attention to the press, providing them with tickets and voluminous notes. Even amid the distractions of the 1889 Exhibition, the profit from the performance in June 1889 was 25,000 francs, almost twice what the Opéra took in on a good night.[39]

This success made certain things clear. The wealthy would pay for a concert, if the proceeds went to a good cause, even those who ordinarily did not attend them. Parisians would come to hear Handel, a composer who, except for a few concerts in the 1870s, was not particularly popular.[40] And the countess had the ability to pull

36. Brissac, *Comtesse Greffulhe*, 117–26.

37. Noëlle Dedeyan, *Histoire de la Société Philharmonique de Paris* (Paris: 1983), 84. Many people among the Greffulhe extended family and friends have been and continue to be involved with this charity.

38. The *Messiah* was performed by Guillot de Sainbris's amateur choral society in 1887, and excerpts by the Société des Concerts du Conservatoire in 1886, 1887, and 1889.

39. Brissac, *Comtesse Greffulhe*, 84–85.

40. From the 1870s, complete Handel oratorios were performed only by amateur choruses in Paris. Concordia did *Ode for Saint Cecilia's Day* in 1884 and *Alexander's Feast* in 1889. His instrumental music, however, had a regular presence in various settings. For a discussion of their meaning for French audiences, see Katharine Ellis, *Interpreting the Musical Past: Early Music in Nineteenth-Century France* (New York: Oxford University Press, 2005).

these things off—to have an idea, motivate others to get involved, organize the event, publicize it, and make it succeed. Her challenge in 1890 was to find a cover for what was increasingly clear: her desire to become an entrepreneur, not just at home, but in the public sphere.

BECOMING AN ENTREPRENEUR: THE SOCIÉTÉ DES GRANDES AUDITIONS

In January 1890, Elisabeth approached members of the executive committee of the Société Nationale, the organization of composers that had been created to perform recent French works.[41] She proposed to create a joint society with the Société Philanthropique that would help both with larger, more expensive projects. What they both shared, particularly when d'Indy became president upon Franck's death that November, was an interest in performing old works and works by foreign composers. These had been ignored by the Société Nationale's previous focus on living French composers. Her friend Fauré, who was the organist at her church, La Madeleine, and the Société Nationale's secretary, thought it a great idea. If they fused, he observed, it would be "recognized as indispensable to have her as President."[42] D'Indy, too, initially thought it would not work without a "unique and personal director, you," along with a "*fantôme*-committee such as that of the Société Nationale to approve your proposals" and "a Gounod extremely honorary and completely invisible on high, near the clouds."[43] After meeting with his cohorts, however, and perhaps feeling a threat to his emerging power at the Société Nationale, on 20 February d'Indy expressed anxiety about getting the Société Nationale involved in anything that cost real money. He told her that they would be happy to help but that their statutes made such a collaboration impossible.

Not deterred, she cast off on her own, conceiving an organization that had all the appearances of being a large-scale collaboration but in effect was run by one person. Of course, she would be president. Even if not everyone liked the name, some thinking it referred to "big ears," she settled on Société des Grandes Auditions Musicales de France. Her first move was to ask a friend, a Protestant banker and a Bois-Boudran neighbor, Baron Francis Hottinguer, to serve as her treasurer.

41. The Société Nationale had a little over 250 members in the 1890s and produced eight or nine concerts per year after 1871. Composers were expected to bear the costs of concerts of their music, except when their administrative committee decided otherwise. Women were welcome in the society but could not serve on any committees.

42. Gabriel Fauré to Countess Greffulhe, 3 February 1890, AP.

43. Vincent d'Indy to Countess Greffulhe, 17 January 1890, AP. D'Indy attached the statues of the Société Nationale to this letter to serve as a model, if she wished, for the organization she was conceiving.

Upon his advice and d'Indy's, she put together an elaborate committee structure.[44] Most people would be nonactive participants—an honorary president, Gounod; an honorary committee with prestigious members of the Académie des Beaux-Arts, Conservatoire professors, and two opera singers; and a committee of eleven musical advisors from the Société Nationale. Ernest Reyer, who was among them, considered these committees a "sort of protectorate." They assured her organization of credibility in the musical world, although they had little influence on the society's programming. In effect, her archives contain no evidence of committee meetings. She also had a small administrative committee consisting of people she knew through her family—people whose loyalty and support she could count on: her brother the Prince de Caraman-Chimay, her brother-in-law the Prince Arenberg, her dear friend the Prince de Polignac, and two powerful men associated with the Union Centrale des Arts Décoratifs who had also helped with her mother-in-law's philanthropic activities. Count de Ganay, vice-president of the Union in the 1880s, had served on its administrative committee in the 1890s and on the committee that organized the first women's exhibition in 1892. Charles Ephrussi, who had helped raise money for the Société Philanthropique, was also on the 1892 women's committee.[45] And Countess Greffulhe set up an office at 8 rue Favart, shared with the *Gazette des beaux-arts,* directed by Ephrussi. She also organized a women's committee and by her second season succeeded in attracting eighty-six *dames patronnesses.*[46] Their job was mostly just to show up, as Reyer put it, to set a good example by their good behavior, or, in the countess's words, to "propagandize," that is, spread the good word. Such committees demonstrate not only the good will many people had toward her idea but also her ability to approach and convince them to support her. No one, however, was fooled about who was in charge. Even the press remarked, "the Société des Grandes Auditions, it's Countess Greffulhe!"[47]

Her intent, both patriotic and educational in nature, was to "attract all who love art and France" and "to fortify the musical education of everyone from the most

44. François Hottinguer to Countess Greffulhe, 19 February 1890, AP.

45. Silverman, *Art Nouveau,* 190. Proust, who based many of his characters on this group, met them at a reception hosted by the countess's cousin Robert de Montesquiou at Versailles in 1894. Ephrussi was one model for Charles Swann. See Jean-Yves Tadié, *Marcel Proust,* trans. Euan Cameron (New York: Viking, 2000), 183–84, for a discussion of the others.

46. This included her relatives with such names as Bibesco, Pourtalès, Montesquiou, Brancovan, Caraman-Chimay, and Ségur, five women who had been *dames patronnesses* for Concordia's production of Bach's *Saint Matthew Passion* in 1885, and most members of the Union's women's committee who were also Opéra subscribers.

47. "The Société des Grandes Auditions, it's Countess Greffulhe. She is the soul, it is she who has the idea and deserves the honor, president Greffulhe." Ernest Reyer, *Journal des débats* (7 June 1891).

humble to the most fortunate."[48] Having seen *Lohengrin* in Carlsruhe, as she recounted in one of her early fundraising brochures, she returned with a sense of what was lacking in Paris: "we still want to hear produced in our country the budding works of our own national genius." Her connections with politicians and the press helped immensely, as did her *ralliement* politics. The Société's grandiose name and her promise to perform "first and foremost great composers from yesteryear"[49]—complete works never before done in their entirety in France— appealed to titled aristocrats focused on past French glories, while the patriotic tone of her announcements and her projected French premieres of Berlioz and newer French works drew support from republicans, including President Félix Faure. *Le Figaro*, *L'Art musical*, *Le Ménestrel*, and others published her prospectus and expressed enthusiasm about her promise to do entire works rather than fragments, as most large works were performed at the time. The Société hoped to perform works six times in Paris and, if possible, twice in the provinces. By mid-April, the press understood that "this society is not a reunion of dilettantes con-fined in a corner of our divided social world" but rather an "eminently national association," one serving a "public need."[50]

Money came in, and membership grew. Countess Greffulhe and the Princess de Scey-Montbéliard (divorced in 1892 and later married to the Prince de Polignac) each gave 10,000 francs, and Baron Edmond de Rothschild gave 8,000. Founding members contributed 1,000 francs, or promised 100 francs a year, for two seats at the dress rehearsals and two at the second performance of each of the society's productions. Subscribing members gave 25 francs for one seat at each dress re-hearsal. Seats for all the first performances, except for those reserved for critics, were to be sold to the general public. Following this strategy, in only six weeks she raised 163,000 francs. This was the equivalent of 20 percent of the state's annual Opéra subsidy, and 50 percent of the state's annual Opéra-Comique subsidy.

Besides the fundraising, Countess Greffulhe was involved in every detail and decision concerning the concerts. After choosing the first work to be produced, Berlioz's two-act *opéra comique Béatrice et Bénédict*, a French premiere, she initi-ated a collaboration with one of the most prestigious conductors in Paris, Charles Lamoureux, and sought permission to use the second most important theater in the country, the state-subsidized Théâtre de l'Odéon. By 23 April, she and Lamoureux had decided on a program that would begin with an orchestral work by Berlioz, followed by a short poem, "A Berlioz," commissioned for the occasion, which would explain in verse what the society was all about. The next day she was advised on how much to charge for the tickets and what the projected revenue would be. Lamoureux, too, wrote asking for her approval in the choice of soloists

48. Cited in a review of their first concert, *La Liberté* (16 April 1890), clipping in AP.
49. Cited in *Le Figaro* (26 May 1890), clipping in AP.
50. *La Liberté* (16 April 1890); "Semaine théatrale," *Le Ménestrel* (13 April 1890): 114.

and their fees. On 28 April, the director of the theater gave the society tentative permission to borrow the theater's costumes and to rehearse in the hall for free. Deputy Georges Berger wrote to the countess on 7 May, "In reading your name as president of the Société des Grandes Auditions de France, I'm rushing to become a permanent subscriber and put myself under your orders and those of the Count,"[51] and the very next day the minister of public instruction confirmed permission to use the Théâtre de l'Odéon, its director, and its costumes. Later that month, Brandus, the publisher of the score for *Béatrice*, sent her proofs of the score to review and told her no more changes would be possible after the next draft. It seems there was no detail she did not oversee. With the final cost coming to 44,596 francs, she had over 100,000 francs left to move on to her next production.[52]

Not all of the Société's productions made a lot of money. In 1891, its production of Handel's *Israel in Egypt*, a work only known in France for a few fragments done by the Société des Concerts du Conservatoire in 1884 and 1885, more or less broke even, with 25,120 francs in expenses and 23,650 francs in donations. To fill the 5,000-seat concert hall at Trocadéro, the society had to use a huge chorus and orchestra of 300 performers, including 30 first violins. Gabriel Marie conducted, with d'Indy at the organ. Ticket prices were kept low, from 2 to 10 francs; the best seats cost half what had been charged for *Béatrice et Bénédict*. Critics praised the society's top-notch orchestra, but found the work "too sad and boring," its "constant repetition of counterpoint" "severe" and inaccessible to "the ordinary intellect." Many wondered why the countess chose an English favorite over works she was also considering, Handel's *Judas Maccabaeus* and a *Passion* by Johann Sebastian Bach, which some would have preferred.[53]

In 1892, the Société turned to living French composers, holding a competition for two one- or two-act dramatic works, one in a serious or tragic genre, the other in a lighter genre. Composers, judged anonymously, were encouraged to write their own libretti and to experiment with new forms. The Société promised to put on the winning works, due in their office that December. While the statutes for this competition exist in the Bibliothèque de l'Opéra in Paris, apparently nothing resulted from this idea, perhaps because in February 1893 d'Indy talked the countess out of it.[54] Instead, the Société concentrated on producing four works that year, Bach's *Christmas Oratorio*, a concert presenting French premieres of works by Russian composers with Alexander Siloti from Moscow, the French premiere

51. Georges Berger to Countess Greffulhe, 7 May 1890, AP.

52. Her budget for this production included 300 francs for the conductor Chévillard and 375 francs for Debussy for help in rehearsing the chorus.

53. Léon Kerst, *Le Petit Journal* (4 June 1891); Henri de Curzon, *La Gazette de France* (5 June 1891); Guy Tharres, *L'Echo du boulevard* (6 June 1891); Alphonse Duvernoy, *Le Progrès libéral* (7 June 1891).

54. Vincent d'Indy to Countess Greffulhe, 5 February 1893, AP.

of Berlioz's *Les Troyens*, and a Gounod festival. The Russian and Gounod concerts took place at Trocadéro, Bach at the Théâtre de Vaudeville, and Berlioz at the Opéra-Comique. Gabriel Marie again conducted the Bach and Russian concerts, and all involved large orchestras and opera singers. Most budgets, however, were modest. The Bach oratorio cost only 7,500 francs, the Russian concert 11,643 francs, and *Les Troyens* 16,216 francs. The Gounod festival cost 21,151 francs, but lost almost 11,000 francs. Given the range of works performed, the collaborations negotiated, and the prestigious theaters used, money continued to pour in to make up for such problems, not only from the wealthy but also those of moderate means. The number of members contributing from 100 to 1,000 francs per year that year increased to 408. This included not only titled elites but also numerous composers and music critics.[55] Subscribers who gave 25 francs numbered even more. However, as the countess's secretary pointed out that June, she also had defections from among her *dames patronnesses* and subscribers, people who left because of the "insufficiency of performances."[56]

In 1893, Countess Greffulhe set her sights again on the Opéra-Comique. As early as 1891 and after her first visit to Bayreuth that summer, d'Indy and she had been discussing the possibility of her producing Wagner. That March he sent her extensive comments on a proposal Lamoureux made to her that involved *Lohengrin*. After the Opéra produced *Lohengrin* that September, in December and January 1892 she and d'Indy began discussing the possibility of collaborating with the Opéra-Comique on the French premiere of *Tristan und Isolde*.[57] Encouraged by Léon Bourgeois, the minister of public instruction and fine arts, in December 1892 she requested and received permission to stage the production from Cosima Wagner, whom she may have met in Bayreuth. Plans had already advanced when in January she received a second letter from Cosima, withdrawing this permission. Wagner's French editor, Durand, had informed her that since the Opéra intended to put on *Die Walküre* and *Tannhäuser*, they did not want the distraction of more Wagner at the Opéra-Comique. The countess appealed to her minister friends, and by 5 May she had a proposal from Eugène Bertrand and Pierre Gailhard, directors of the Opéra. They agreed to put on *Tristan* and add it to their repertoire after three performances if she picked up all the start-up costs: costumes, décors, accessories, study and rehearsal costs, and the fees for the orchestra and chorus.[58] These

55. These included Charles Gounod, Fromenthal Halévy, André Messager, and Arthur Meyer, director of *Le Figaro*.

56. E. Ehret to Countess Greffulhe, 30 June 1892, AP.

57. D'Indy continued to advise her on how to approach Léon Carvalho, the director of the Opéra-Comique, and suggested singers for each role. See Vincent d'Indy to Countess Greffulhe, 9 March 1891, 25 December 1891, 1 January 1892, and 5 February 1893; Cosima Wagner to Countess Greffulhe, 26 December 1892, AP.

58. Bertrand and Gaillard to Countess Greffulhe, 5 May 1893, AP.

performances, however, did not come to pass, perhaps because of a misunderstanding with Madame Wagner or continuing problems between the two French institutions. The countess then proposed to Léon Carvalho, director of the Opéra-Comique, two eighteenth-century works that had been completely forgotten—Pierre Monsigny's *Le Déserteur* and André Grétry's *Les Avares*. He countered that he would agree to one performance of these works on 23 June 1893 if she not only paid for them but also helped fund a work he wished to produce that May, Gluck's *Iphigénie en Tauride*.

Part of the countess's success undoubtedly came from the allure of elitism with which these productions were surrounded, necessary—as Fourcaud, an influential monarchist critic, noted—if the Société was to "interest the upper classes in serious art for which they had rarely any concern."[59] The high quality of the musicians also helped. Having engaged distinguished soloists for concerts in her home for years, she was used to paying huge fees.[60] She also had the help of twelve personal secretaries for her voluminous correspondence.[61] These productions led people, such as the composer d'Indy, to refer to her power as "magical."

It is not clear, then, why the Société went temporarily inactive after this, except for sponsoring a Wednesday afternoon concert of contemporary French works at the Paris zoo on 29 May 1894. This concert was conducted by Edouard Colonne, involved opera singers, and featured premieres by members of the Société Nationale. In the spirit of *ralliement* politics, many suggested nostalgia for the past with old modes (Pierre de Bréville's *Hymne de Vénus* in Phrygian mode) and old dance forms (Charles Bordes's *Dansons la gigue* to a poem by Verlaine, Fauré's *Pavane*, and an orchestral suite in the old style by Albéric Magnard).[62] The bank records in July 1894 show only 40,000 francs left in the Société's account. Was it that after her father died in 1892 and when her husband retired from politics in 1893, her husband wanted her at his side in the country? Or did the experience with *Tristan* reveal difficulties resulting from her ambitions?

In the late 1890s, she dove back in. Appealing to many of her members who had been regular Bayreuth pilgrims throughout the 1890s, in 1899 she tackled the French premiere of *Tristan*, producing it at the Opéra three times that fall. Then, putting her organization on a different financial footing in 1902 to raise money for another performance of *Tristan* and the French premiere of *Götterdämmerung*, she promised a 5 percent dividend and 5 percent interest for each 500 francs donated,

59. Louis de Fourcaud, *L'Art dans les deux mondes* (13 June 1891).

60. The cost of attending the Société's concerts consequently was double that of Colonne's concerts, with tickets ranging from 10 to 12 francs.

61. Duchess de Gramont, interview with author, 8 December 1988, Paris.

62. I discussed the meaning of such juxtapositions in "Forging French Identity: The Political Significance of *la Musique ancienne et moderne*," paper presented at the annual meeting of the American Musicological Society, Washington, D.C., 28 October 2005.

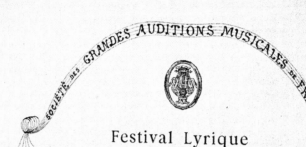

Festival Lyrique

AU

Théâtre du Château-d'Eau

Mai–Juin 1902

Le Crépuscule des Dieux

ET

Tristan et Isolde

DE

Richard Wagner

FIGURE 10.4. Société des Grandes Auditions Musicales de France, Festival lyrique, May–June 1902. Courtesy of Duke Antoine de Gramont.

calculated on ticket sales less expenses. For this, she provided two seats at the dress rehearsals. The success was enormous, and she ended up with 40,000 francs profit, after paying all expenses and stockholders (see fig. 10.4). The power she demonstrated by the successes of the 1902 and 1903 season (with fragments of *Parsifal*) led the press and others to call her, at only forty-three years of age, the "Queen of Music."

CONCERTS AS A FORM OF DIPLOMACY

In the years that followed, the countess turned increasingly to music by living foreign composers, and her concerts evolved into a means of building bridges between nations. It was common for the aristocracy to receive foreign visitors in their homes regularly, including musicians. On one occasion in 1905, she invited Alexander Scriabin, who had been introduced to her by the minister of foreign affairs, to perform at her home, with the intention of meeting the Russian ambassador to Paris. Royalty and nobility from abroad knew her well, if not from hunting at the chateau with Henry, then from her frequent Parisian receptions.[63] The list (see table 10.1) is long. Her sister was lady-in-waiting to the queen of Belgium, and the English kings and queens of the era, the Russian czar and grand dukes, Queen Elisabeth of Austria, and many others came to her chateau.[64] She made close friends particularly of diplomats, not just those from foreign countries, but especially those from France. President Faure was included on her guest list in 1896, along with Gabriel Hanotaux, the minister of foreign affairs. The latter visited their home frequently after meeting her in 1894 and developed what their correspondence suggests was a deep affection for her. Her relationship with European royalty was such that she often proposed her "diplomatic services" to him, whether it meant organizing a private hunt for the Russian czar or delivering messages to King Léopold of Belgium. It was known she could obtain a loge at the Opéra for the asking. She befriended those who were nostalgic for the Ancien Régime as well as republican ministers such as René Waldeck-Rousseau and Gaston Galliffet, who, like her, were in favor of exonerating Alfred Dreyfus of charges of treason. She also knew Théophile Delcassé, the minister of foreign affairs at the time of the Entente Cordiale, who sent her notes on foreign policy each week.[65] These friends helped

---

63. According to a handwritten note in her archives meant to serve in writing her memoirs, Elisabeth first went to Russia at age five with her mother and father, who was appointed to the Belgian embassy there (AP).

64. After a visit in 1907, she recounts that the king of England wrote to her that they had been treated as "from an equal to an equal." See Henry Greffulhe to Countess Greffulhe, 14 February 1907, and the countess's essay "Récit [d'une] visite royale anglaise," 1907, AP. The czar sent her a huge, magnificent brocaded coat in 1900 to thank her for one such visit and sent a gift when her daughter Elaine was married in 1904.

65. Tardié, *Proust*, 319,

TABLE 10.1. Countess Greffulhe's Personal and Political Connections.

Group	Group
Société des Grandes Auditions	**French royalty**
Treasurer: Baron Francis Hottinger (banker, neighbor)	Empress Eugénie
	Princess Mathilde Bonaparte
ADMINISTRATIVE COMMITTEE:	Prince Roland Bonaparte
Prince August d'Arenberg	Duchess d'Aoste, born Marie L. Bonaparte
Prince Pierre de Caraman-Chimay (Elisabeth's brother)	Henri d'Orléans, Count of Paris
Charles Ephrussi	Philippe d'Orléans, Count of Paris
Count de Ganay	Philippe d'Orléans, his son
Prince Edmond de Polignac	Jean, Duke de Guise
Relatives	**Foreign royal families**
Bibesco (cousins)	Grand Duke Alexandre of Russie
Pourtalès (cousins)	Grand Duke Nicolas Nicolaevitch
Montesquiou (cousins)	Grand Duke Vladimir
Brancovan (cousins)	Grand Duchess Vladimir
Clara Ward (sister-in-law)	Prince Henri of Bavaria
Ségur (cousins)	Princess Christophe of Greece
Prince August d'Arenberg (Henry's brother-in-law)	Ernst-Louis, Grand Duke of Hesse and the Rhine
Marquis de Voguë (Arenberg's son-in-law)	Emmanuel, prince of Naples
Marquis Robert de l'Aigle (Henri's brother-in-law)	Josephine-Charlotte, princess of Luxembourg
Duke Armand de Gramont (son-in-law, 1904)	Frederic-Francois, Grand Duke of Mecklemburg
	Prince Mohamed Ali
Orléanist/monarchist friends	**Foreign rulers**
Count Albert de Mun	Wilhelm I, emperor of Germany
Prince Edmond de Polignac	Frederic, mother of Wilhelm II
Prince de Sagan	Wilhelm II, emperor of Germany
	Edward VII, king of England
Republican friends	Mary, queen of England (wife of Georges V)
Jean Casimir-Perier, president of France, 1894–95	Edward VIII, king of England
Félix Faure, president of France, 1895–99	Elizabeth, queen of England
Armand Fallières, president of France, 1904	Léopold, king of Belgium
	Elisabeth, queen of Belgium
Antonin Proust, minister of fine arts	Elena, queen of Italy (wife of Victor Emmanuel III)

TABLE 10.1. (continued)

Group	Group
Marcellin Berthelot, minister of public instruction	Maria Jose, queen of Italy
Antonin Dubost, president of the Senate, 1907	Carlos II, king of Portugal
Joseph Reinach, deputy	Amelie, queen of Portugal
Gabriel Hanotaux, minister of foreign affairs	Carol, king of Rumania
Charles Dupuy, deputy, minister of public instruction	Oscar II, king of Sweden
	Gustave V, king of Sweden
	Albert, prince of Monaco
	Alice, princess of Monaco (second wife of Albert)
Press connections	Louis, prince of Monaco
	Negus Taffari, emperor of Ethiopia
Charles Joly (*Figaro*)	Maharajah of Kapurthala
Gaston Calmette (*Figaro*)	Maharajah of Patiala
André Meyer (*Gaulois*)	

her to navigate the complex and ever fluid political context of Paris and use her power to help those in need.[66]

Her belief in "the fraternity of nations and people" and in "all men as brothers of the same blood"[67] and her desire to enhance mutual understanding and respect resulted in concerts of music by composers her foreign peers thought were the best from their countries (see table 10.2). Some showed her support for alliances between France and her European neighbors, especially the Franco-Russian alliance cemented in 1893 and 1896, and the Triple Entente that included Great Britain in 1907. When her friend the Grand Duchess Vladimir sought help with the wounded from Russia's war with Japan, in 1904 she organized a fundraising performance of Verdi's *Rigoletto* in Paris. The editors of *Le Figaro* offered whatever they could do to help, and President Armand Fallières joined the Société in support. Then, when the Russians had trade deficit problems resulting from the war, she got her Société to sponsor Serge Diaghilev's Russian painting exhibition in Paris in 1906, as well as the five concerts of Russian music there in 1907. These actions were facilitated by her relationship with Hanotaux, a principal architect of the Franco-Russian alliance. Other performances, as well as art exhibitions, show her desire to support her English, Italian, Austrian, and American peers, even if, as in the case of *Salomé*, she was harshly criticized in the press, and subsequently by

66. It is possible that she helped Fauré to be named director of the Conservatoire in 1905. Before this time, he was little known by the *grand public*.

67. Notes for an international conference hall in Paris, 30 March 1907, AP.

TABLE 10.2. Repertoire and Other Activities of the Société des Grandes Auditions Musicales de France.

Type of work	Type of work
German classics	**French classics**
Handel, *Israel in Egypt*, 1891	Monsigny, *Le Déserteur*, 1893
Bach, *Christmas Oratorio*, 1892	Grétry, *Les Deux Avares*, 1893
Beethoven, *Missa Solemnis*, 1906	Gluck, *Iphigénie en Tauride*, 1893
Beethoven (Capet Quartet), 1912	Rameau, *Anacréon*, 1909
German/Austrian contemporaries	**French contemporaries**
Wagner, *Tristan*, 1899, 1902	Berlioz, *Béatrice et Bénédict*, 1890
Wagner, *Götterdämmerung*, 1902	Berlioz, *Les Troyens*, 1892
Wagner, *Parsifal*, fragments, 1903	Gounod Festival, 1892
Strauss, *Salomé*, 1907	New French works, 1894
Mahler, Symphony no. 2, 1910	Berlioz, *La Damnation de Faust* (staged), 1903
Russian contemporaries	Soirée à Versailles, Gala, 1908
	Bagatelle Concert, 1909
Russian Five concert, 1892	Debussy, *Le Martyre de Saint-Sebastien*, 1911
Russian art exhibition, 1906	
Five historic Russian concerts, 1907	**English contemporaries**
Boris Godunov, Opéra, 1908	
Ballets Russes, 1909, 1910, 1915	Elgar, *Dream of Gerontius*, 1906
	Exhibition of French art, London, 1912
Italian contemporaries/classics	
	American relations
Prince Caetani, Concert Lamoureux, 1903	
Rigoletto, Gala for Grand Duchess Vladimir, 1904	Organized visit of Murray Butler, president of Columbia University, May 1914
Saison Italienne, 1905	
Caruso concert, Gala, 1910	
Palestrina motets (Schola, St-Gervais), 1910	
Lorenzo Perosi, *Florence, Dies Irae*, 1910	
Lorenzo Perosi, *Le Jugement universel*, 1911	
Rossini, *Barbier de Seville*, 1911	
International concert	
Concert of new works with the Société Musicale Indépendente, 1913	

her husband, who told her that if she insisted "on being talked about, which is already a mistake," at least let it be positive words.[68]

Some of these productions were huge hits, especially the five Russian concerts and the first two seasons of the Ballet Russes. Diaghilev's programming in 1909 showed an understanding of the countess's supporters. The first Russian ballet she presented was *Le Pavillon d'Armide*, a love story about aristocrats in eighteenth-century France. Stravinsky's *Firebird* and Rimsky-Korsakov's *Shéhérazade*, in the 1910 season, appealed to the idea the Société's public held of exotic Russia. These productions implied that all periods, places, and ways of life can coexist, serving equally as stimuli for art and beauty, just as in them multiple styles, personalities, and disciplines coexist.

It didn't really matter to Countess Greffulhe that other concerts she sponsored did not break even. English music also interested her. In 1906, a year before the Entente Cordiale was signed, the Société engaged Camille Chévillard and the Lamoureux orchestra to give the first French performance of Elgar's *Dream of Gerontius*. It cost over 16,000 francs but brought in just under 11,000. The French premiere of *Le Jugement universel* by Lorenzo Perosi, who was *maître de chapelle* at the Vatican, cost almost 25,000 but earned less than 7,000 francs. The countess did her best to produce these premieres in collaboration with established groups, rather than hiring everyone herself, as was the case in all her concerts up to *Götterdämmerung*. At her expense, in 1903 she got Chévillard to do a work by Prince Roffredo Caetani, an Italian composer, and in 1910 she convinced Colonne's orchestra to program Mahler's Second Symphony on one of his regular Sunday matinées. This was the first performance of Mahler's music in France. The publicity flyer notes that Mahler was "*the* national composer"—the "direct descendent of Mozart . . . and, above all, Beethoven"—and that his Second Symphony was his best known work. Countess Greffulhe also supported many of the concerts involving foreign music that were organized by Gabriel Astruc under the aegis of his Société Musicale, including the French premiere of Strauss's *Salomé* in 1907. This interest in using diplomacy to bridge differences stands in contrast with the increasing nationalist tension in Paris in the years before World War I.

The countess's *ralliement* politics—a form of diplomacy internal to France—also informed her musical choices up through World War 1. In 1908 and 1909, she put on benefit concerts at Versailles and in the Bagatelles gardens of the Bois-de-Boulogne, bringing new life to these spaces traditionally associated with the old monarchy. In that context, old dances performed in costume by professionals from

---

68. Note from Henry without date, c. May 1907, AP. A reviewer in *La Libre Parole* (10 May 1907) lambasted the countess for supporting a concert organized by a Jew, Astruc, conducted by a Jew, Colonne, and of a work composed by a Jew, Richard Strauss. See Brissac, *Comtesse Greffulhe*, 210.

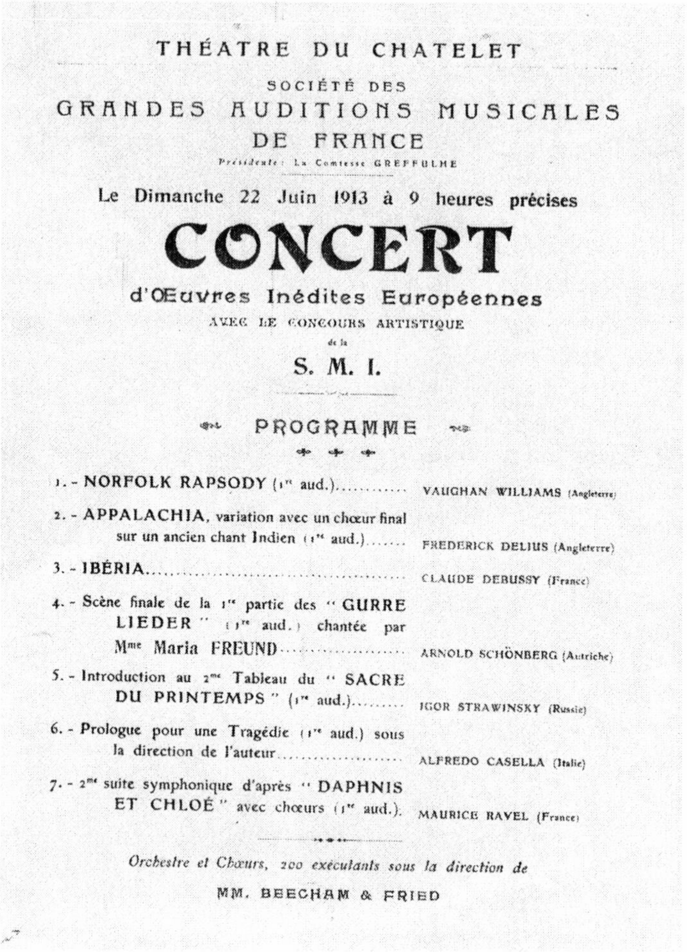

THÉÂTRE DU CHATELET

SOCIÉTÉ DES
GRANDES AUDITIONS MUSICALES
DE FRANCE
Présidente: La Comtesse GREFFULHE

Le Dimanche 22 Juin 1913 à 9 heures précises

CONCERT

d'Œuvres Inédites Européennes
AVEC LE CONCOURS ARTISTIQUE
de la

S. M. I.

PROGRAMME

1. - NORFOLK RAPSODY (1ᵉ aud.)............ VAUGHAN WILLIAMS (Angleterre)

2. - APPALACHIA, variation avec un chœur final
sur un ancien chant Indien (1ᵉ aud.)....... FREDERICK DELIUS (Angleterre)

3. - IBÉRIA................................. CLAUDE DEBUSSY (France)

4. - Scène finale de la 1ᵉ partie des " GURRE
LIEDER " (1ᵉ aud.) chantée par
Mᵐᵉ Maria FREUND.................. ARNOLD SCHÖNBERG (Autriche)

5. - Introduction au 2ᵐᵉ Tableau du " SACRE
DU PRINTEMPS " (1ᵉ aud.)........ IGOR STRAWINSKY (Russie)

6. - Prologue pour une Tragédie (1ᵉ aud.) sous
la direction de l'auteur.................. ALFREDO CASELLA (Italie)

7. - 2ᵐᵉ suite symphonique d'après " DAPHNIS
ET CHLOÉ " avec chœurs (1ᵉ aud.). MAURICE RAVEL (France)

Orchestre et Chœurs, 200 exécutants sous la direction de
MM. BEECHAM & FRIED

FIGURE 10.5. Société des Grandes Auditions Musicales de France, concert of
unpublished European music, 23 June 1913. Courtesy of Duke Antoine de Gramont.

the Opéra and old music such as Rameau's *Anacréon* could help members of her
Société indulge their nostalgia and experience what life back then might have been
like. But lest the countess's politics be confused, the evening in the Bagatelles
concluded with the Republican National Guard playing the ball scene of Berlioz's
Symphonie fantastique.

The most radical new music she supported and that which most shows the
influence of her interest in diplomacy took place on 22 June 1913 (see fig. 10.5). This
concert, cosponsored by the composer-run Société Musicale Indépendante, consisted of important works by seven composers from five countries. With the excep-

tion of Debussy's *Ibéria*, most were French premieres: Ralph Vaughan Williams's *Norfolk Rhapsody*, Frederick Delius's *Appalachia*, the final scene from part 1 of Schönberg's *Gurrelieder*, with Maria Freund, Alfredo Casella's *Prologue for a Tragedy*, the concert version of the introduction to the second tableau of Stravinsky's *Rite of Spring*, and the second symphonic suite from Ravel's *Daphnis and Chlöé*. Through an English friend, Lady Cunard, the countess was able to get Sir Thomas Beecham to conduct, among others. The performance had the benefit of 200 singers and instrumentalists as well as the comfortable Théâtre du Châtelet, even if the ticket prices were very high, between 10 and 20 francs. Throughout her career, Countess Greffulhe was interested in attracting audiences by the appeal of the new and unusual. Such concerts, I would suggest, go further, representing a conscious form of international diplomacy. They also support the notion of modernism as an international aesthetic.

The formation of new musical institutions like the Société des Grandes Auditions in 1890, together with d'Indy's transformation of the Société Nationale after 1890, set the foundation for the aristocrats to play an increasingly important role in the musical world of Paris. The countess indeed succeeded where few had before her, escaping the boundaries of her class and gender to collaborate with major partners, like the Opéra and the Opéra-Comique, the Colonne and Lamoureux orchestras, the Ballets Russes, even Versailles. Together they put on old as well as new music, French premieres of both French and foreign masterpieces, in a range of genres from oratorios and symphonies to opera and ballet.

What underlay this entrepreneurial talent and shaped it? First, people pointed to her wealth, beauty, and intelligence. Proust, on meeting her, declared her incomparable; "I have never seen a woman so beautiful."[69] Elisabeth was acutely aware of the power and the responsibility emanating from these gifts. An essay preserved in her archives—"The Action of the Woman in Humanity" (c. 1898), perhaps written by her under the pen name Anna Lampérière—summarizes her life philosophy: "every woman should be an artist." This means not only "creating the impression of beauty in life itself . . . the source of happiness" but also, in

---

69. Marcel Proust to Robert de Montesquiou, 2 July 1893, in *Correspondence de Marcel Proust*, ed. Philip Kolb, vol. 1, *1880–1895* (Paris: Plon, 1970), 217. See also "the novel of a woman of high society" she asked Edmond de Goncourt to publish. In it she describes the "wild and supernatural joy that sweeps over you when you know yourself to be beautiful" and (as already mentioned in chapter 7 here) the "great anonymous caress" of those who admired her at the Opéra: "What a blood transfusion this communication with the eyes of the crowd gives me. How to live without it. . . ." See Edmond et Jules de Goncourt, *Journal: Mémoires de la vie littéraire, 1891–1896*, vol. 4, ed. Robert Ricatte (Paris, Laffont, 1989), 473, and Tadié, *Proust*, 317.

recognition of one's power to influence others, using beauty to "elevate the modern soul." Certainly her Société des Grandes Auditions fulfilled the "social duty" expected of women of means.[70]

The second element in Elisabeth's leadership was her sense of self. A biographer in 1894 pointed to her "strong will, sure of its goal, and supreme love of independence, this a sure sign of a superior soul."[71] For Elisabeth, her power was based on her prestige. In a sketch for her "philosophical book," she wrote, "Always look at a person telling yourself: I want them to take away a memory of unmatched prestige."[72] As early as 1889 in notes on the subject, she described prestige as "an impression of superiority . . . that forces minds to transform even the most natural acts into superhuman schemes."[73] Not surprisingly, Elisabeth always signed her letters Caraman Chimay Greffulhe, reminding readers of her roots as a princess.

Third were the connections this prestige enabled with not only nobles, bankers, and politicians but also musicians, concert organizers, and the press. Extraordinary was her ability to know whom to approach, how to elicit their support, and, as might any good politician, what to give in return. D'Indy once called her "power magical."[74] By mobilizing her numerous connections and savvy use of intermediaries, she helped others as much as they helped her.

Armed with these personal, social, and political advantages, she created a concert society that blurred the lines between individual and institution, allowing her to act out her own agendas while addressing national concerns. Calling on fashion, a liminal area between private desire and public display, to broaden the range of elites attending performances, the countess attracted a new public to art music concerts. In rendering their tastes public, she gave aristocrats and other elites a sense of themselves as a group with shared values, not just a class divided by old rivalries among the legitimists and the Orléanists or monarchists and republicans. She proved that elites could become interested a wider range of genres than opera, and that they were willing to invest their own money in unknown contemporary music.

Of course, not everyone liked all that she did. Early on, her musical choices of Bach and Handel caused some disappointment about this "Société des Grandes Illusions."[75] Later on, her galas of Italian operas to make money for charity and her

70. Anna Lampérière, "L'Action de la femme dans l'humanité," *Revue pour les jeunes filles* (c. 1898): 225–36, clipping in AP.

71. In his short monograph in a series on great contemporary women, *La Comtesse Greffulhe* (Paris: Mirbeau, 1894), Hippolyte Buffenoir refers to her as an Apollo sanctifying wherever she is, a queen of Paris by birth and by conquest, the aristocratic type *par excellence*.

72. Brissac, *Comtesse Greffulhe*, 103.

73. From her diary, 1891–92, AP.

74. Vincent d'Indy to Countess Greffulhe, Wednesday (c. April 1893), AP.

75. Jules Martin, review of Handel's *Israel in Egypt*, *L'Estafette* (5 June 1891).

garden parties, albeit with Rameau, were criticized as productions of the "Société des Grandes Deceptions Musicales."[76] And not everyone bowed to Countess Greffulhe's will. Her ability to endure difficulties and failure is important in understanding the nature of her entrepreneurship. The Société Nationale de Musique refused to merge. Paris's most prestigious orchestra, the Société des Concerts du Conservatoire, would not accept proposals from her, in part because "they only did works whose composers had already established a reputation and notoriety." It took Herculean efforts to get the attention of the Opéra and a proposal that she pick up most of the costs—yet the project fell apart. Her proposal to put on Saint-Saëns's *Le Deluge* also failed. Still, through her concert society, members had a voice in the musical world that could not be ignored and a means of supporting the kind of music they wanted to hear. As these musical societies grew in strength and number, the presence of their differing agendas began to diffuse the power of the state and its traditional subsidies. Women, too, became more broadly accepted and integrated.

In 1909 Elisabeth wrote in her personal journal of the satisfaction her entrepreneurship had brought her; "At this culminating point of my life, I feel as if I possess all that I want: to have everything, to make happen what pleases me and this upon a simple desire on my part as in fairy tales."[77] Then to Henry she explained the meaning she found in this: "It's necessary to serve something well as long as one lives. I am more and more convinced of this duty. . . . One must have a useful life and in certain situations where one exercises a moral influence, one should use this to direct others towards good."[78] In the twenty-four years of the Société des Grandes Auditions, Countess Greffulhe had gone well beyond family, as conceived by most nobles: "One no longer exists in a time such as ours except by one's own personality. Our caste no longer exists." In the place of birthrights, she had come to value "the rights of intelligence"[79] and a useful life that she built beyond the borders of her class, gender, and nation.

76. *La Liberté* (10 June 1911).

77. Thoughts dated 16 July 1909, AP, cited in Brissac, *Comtesse Greffulhe*, 223–24.

78. Elisabeth Greffulhe to Henry Greffulhe, 3 September 1909, AP. Count Greffulhe, cited in Brissac, *Comtesse Greffulhe*, 222.

79. Elisabeth Greffulhe to Henry Greffulhe, 9 September 1909, AP. Count Greffulhe, cited in Brissac, *Comtesse Greffulhe*, 222.

11. The Political Economy of Composition in the American University, 1965–1985

There is no more significant determinant of the cultural musical life of our country, no more significant indication of the cultural reorientation of music in this country, and its new intellectual status, than the fact that a great majority of American composers are university-trained and are university teachers. Now this makes our life a very different life from that of our European counterparts.

> Milton Babbitt, "The University and
> the Unlikely Survival of Serious Music"
> (lecture given Melbourne, Australia, 1975)

*T*O SPEAK OF THE CULTURAL IDENTITY of American music is problematic, to say the least. The enormous size of the United States, the decentralization of music-making activities, the heterogeneity of Americans' cultural backgrounds, the continuous influx of foreign artists into the country, and its relatively short history mitigate against any single identity, that is, any identity existing at all. This fragmentation has been particularly evident in the high-art musical culture. When individual composers have attempted to create a

A previous version of this chapter, here revised and expanded, appeared in French as "Musique et Institution aux Etats-Unis" in "Musiques, identités," special issue, *Inharmoniques* (May 1987): 104–34, included here by permission.

For the interviews they granted me between March 1986 and March 1987, I would like to thank Milton Babbitt (Princeton University and the Juilliard School), Robert Erickson, Will Ogdon, and Roger Reynolds (UC San Diego), Bernard Rands (Boston University and the Juilliard School), Tod Machover (Massachusetts Institute of Technology), Pauline Oliveros (formerly of UC San Diego and, in the fall of 1986, at Mills College), Ralph Shapey (University of Chicago), Martin Bresnick (Yale University), and Joan Tower (Bard College and, at the time, composer-in-residence with the St. Louis Symphony Orchestra). I'm also grateful for conversations with music administrators Nancy Clark (American Music Center), Karen Moynihan (National Association of Schools of Music), and Fran Richard (ASCAP) concerning their various perspectives and the statistics needed for this study. Court Burns (National Endowment for the Arts), Barbara Peterson (BMI), Morris Phibbs (College Music Society), and Michael Yaffe (National Association of Schools of Music)

318

specifically American music, not only have they encountered resistance but also such styles have had short-lived, if any, appeal to the majority of American composers. Both the nostalgic, antimodernist music of the early twentieth century—nationalist by virtue of its quotation of transplanted English folk tunes, Indian melodies, or Negro spirituals—as well as the easily accessible tonal music incorporating folk melodies between the wars provided only a "content" that was American, not a style. Barbara Tischler suggests that composers even failed in that regard, as no one kind of indigenous music was recognizable by the entire population.[1] Advocating the development of an American music, in fact, has come to mean not promoting one style over any other, but rather defending American composers' right to have their music heard. In the United States, audiences, conductors, and radio stations have consistently tended to prefer the art music of foreigners. Perhaps Virgil Thomson summed up American music the best when he defined it as simply the music written by Americans.[2]

One way to go beyond such a definition is to turn to the art world in which this music is produced and to examine influences and constraints on the music emanating from it.[3] In this country, there are three socioeconomic art worlds for music. The commercial one supports music written for film, television, theater, and various popular media; academia supports music written in institutions of higher learning; and independent composers, those who work for the most part

---

provided further invaluable information. References to these interviews will be made without further explanation unless the same people are cited from another source, so indicated in a footnote. For additional information concerning the American composer, the reader is encouraged to contact the American Music Center, 250 West 54th Street, Suite 300, New York, New York 10019.

This version of the "Musique" article includes a discussion of women in the NEA study as well as stimulating and important comments on the subject from Ben Boretz's correspondence with me in February 2006.

I would like to thank Will Ogdon, Bert Turetzky, Garrett Bowles, Gordon Mumma, Jonathan Kramer, and Ben Boretz for reading earlier drafts of this article and making helpful suggestions.

1. Barbara Tischler, An American Music: The Search for an American Musical Identity (New York: Oxford University Press, 1986), 5–6.

2. Tischler, An American Music, 183. Howard Hanson, "Twenty Years Growth in America," Modern Music 20, no. 1 (January/February 1943), comes to the same conclusion: "It should be apparent that there can be no uniform "American music" short of Gestapo control. . . . Standardization in this country would be disastrous and contrary to the most fundamental doctrines of American social and political philosophy. . . . American music is the music by American composers which Americans hear and know" (96–97).

3. Howard Becker, Art Worlds (Berkeley: University of California Press, 1982), defines an art world as "the network of people whose cooperative activity, organized via their joint knowledge of conventional means of doing things, produces the kind of art the art world is noted for."

outside both of these, have their own networks, as well as associations with the commercial market and academia. Although radio has the potential to disseminate serious music widely, almost all radio broadcasting in the United States has been and still largely is commercial, despite the Public Broadcasting Act of 1967, which gave federal funds to support National Public Radio. While from time to time some public radio stations (such as KPFA in Berkeley and WNYC in New York) have devoted regular air time to contemporary music, the great majority of the so-called classical music stations across the country, commercial or not, play standard repertory, rarely contemporary music, and almost never discuss or analyze music. In recent decades, then, although it represents a relatively small and often marginalized aspect of our music culture, academia has been the largest context for serious contemporary music in the United States. Especially since World War II, writing, thinking about, and even performing new music have taken place predominantly in academia. Of course, the boundaries between the three art worlds are fluid and permeable, and academic institutions are not the only influence on a composer's status and success. Academia-based composers can have performances of their music outside academia, their scores and recordings published, and their music reviewed in the press. Such factors not only help composers promote their work and build their reputations but also can contribute to academic hires and promotions. Still, academic institutions have played a significant role in the lives of a majority of American composers in the second half of the twentieth century.

Until recently, teaching has been the most important musical profession in the United States. It was once estimated that in this century, 90–95 percent of all composers of serious music in this country have flocked to academia.[4] As is not the case in Europe, composers have had few other ways of meeting their fundamental economic needs. The kinds of economic resources available to European composers—state-supported subsidies and private patrons—have been more limited in the United States, in part because of the capitalistic and decentralized nature of our musical world. Furthermore, when government grants, like those of the National Endowment for the Arts (NEA), have been forthcoming, their modest sums have usually functioned as symbolic capital—awards signifying special honor—more than as means of support. The other professions often filled by composers in Europe—conducting, performing, writing criticism, or working in administrative positions at the radio or the Ministry of Culture—traditionally have not been open to the great majority of American composers.[5] The generation of

---

4. William Baumol and William Bowen, *Performing Arts: The Economic Dilemma* (Cambridge, Mass.: MIT Press, 1966), 108.

5. Many of our orchestras still persist in hiring foreign conductors. The highly competitive world of performance is reserved for only the most technically trained. Our music critics, with the notable exception of Virgil Thomson, have traditionally been predominantly journalists.

composers who arrived in academia midcentury considered it a composer's "last hope." "It's our only hope," Milton Babbitt explained in an interview with me in the spring of 1986, "so ergo it's our best hope." George Rochberg calls academic life "the single decent option left to the American composer where he can pursue his work according to his own inner pressures and needs."[6] Since "composers have little other source of income," Ross Lee Finney points out, "teaching, therefore, is the natural way" to make a living.[7]

Yet the university has not been merely an employer of the composer, nor has its value been entirely or primarily economic. Academic institutions have come to rival the old cultural capitals as centers of musical production and consumption in America and as power brokers. In many ways, Seymour Shifrin was right when he called them the "last open city,"[8] for by 1970 they had taken over the functions elsewhere served by various urban artistic groups. As forums for discussion, they complement the cafes that often surround them; as places to make professional contacts, they resemble publication headquarters; as patrons providing a public for composers' works, often one of peers, they have taken over the role traditionally played, particularly in Europe, by salons. Few American composers have escaped such an allure, not even Leonard Bernstein, who turned to Broadway and conducting, and Aaron Copland, who had a private patron to help him get established. Both taught at Harvard for a short time. Even when professional opportunities began to open up outside academia in the 1980s, prominent composers capable of living on grants, performances, or the earnings of their music (such as Elliott Carter and Charles Wuorinen) still chose to teach in academia.

In the first half of this chapter, I interrogate not only the consequences of such economic security but, more important, the influence of the academic institution's social environment, its aesthetic and material resources, and its function as a power base on the musical choices made by the academia-based composer. To what extent do teaching contexts affect what kind of music is written? How might working in academia, with its professors and students, its performers and other intellectuals, shape a composer's taste, particularly in one's younger years? What compromises are needed to secure and maintain an academic institution's support? And how can such institutions help build a composer's reputation? Only a book-length study of music curricula and pedagogy as it related to compositional activity across the United States could do justice to this subject. Within the limitations of one chapter, I can only begin such an inquiry. However, using material from interviews with composers many of whom began teaching midcentury, I hope to clarify why composers gravitated toward academia after its doors were

6. "The Composer in Academia: Reflections on a Theme of Stravinsky," *College Music Symposium* (1970): 90.

7. Ross Lee Finney, "Employ the Composer," *American Music Teacher* 11 (1961): 9.

8. "The Composer in Academia," 92.

opened to them and how academia became meaningful for these composers. In this context, I argue, academia has had a significant impact on American music. While this discussion of music-making within the academic art world still does not explain what makes American music recognizable, it brings to light a number of values that are encouraged by the university environment.

To determine the most influential teaching institutions where composers have been studying in the United States, the academic degrees they have been earning, and the institutions at which they have been subsequently teaching, in the chapter's second half I examine the subset of American composers receiving composer grants from the NEA from 1967 (when the competition began) until 1985. The NEA grants, of course, are not a measure of a composer's artistic value or importance, especially since more established composers have less need for them. If I wanted to study the most illustrious American composers, I might have looked instead at recipients of Guggenheim or Koussevitsky Foundation grants, MacArthur fellowships, Rome or Pulitzer prizes. But NEA grants have been by far the most numerous, allowing for consideration of a broader range of composers. Determined by large and geographically diverse advisory panels, they gave the patina of national recognition to almost 1,000 composers during this period, not only major figures such as Elliott Carter, Ernst Krenek, George Crumb, and Morton Feldman but also mid-career and younger composers, all of whose careers in the United States the grants helped to build or sustain.

My sample consists of the 125 composers who received at least $9,500 or at least three of these grants and the 79 composers who received the largest grants each year (fourteen of whom are not included in the first group). Because I am interested in the extent to which their academic institutions may have played a role in helping them win these awards, I examine these composers' educational backgrounds—that is, their highest academic degrees and the schools at which they earned them—and their institutional affiliations or teaching positions at the time they received their grants. This study brings to light the significant presence of university composers among these grant recipients and the dominant role that composers associated with certain schools, such as Eastman School of Music and Columbia University, have played in musical politics at the national level. To the extent that these schools have promoted a modernist aesthetic and their composers have been largely male, the analysis unveils the climate that has kept many women, people of color, and those embracing significantly different aesthetics in their music from receiving the support they might have hoped for from a federal agency.

Study of the NEA grants also reveals how, in the 1980s, university composers began to lose their dominant position in the world of contemporary music in the United States. Thanks largely to the accessibility of minimalist music and neo-tonality, the commercial market became increasingly receptive to serious music. The number of independent composers rose drastically, in part because of the great quantity of composers produced by academic institutions and the absence of growth in the academic market. The NEA began supporting composers in alternative art worlds. By examining NEA funding patterns in the 1980s, I reveal some of the economic, sociological, and aesthetic forces that have motivated composers like Pauline Oliveros to leave the university and seek their living outside the university, particularly in New York City. To the extent that university life became a career choice more than a necessity, it is important to rethink the privileges and opportunities, along with the constraints, that academia offers a composer.

PART 1. INTEGRATING THE MODERNIST COMPOSER

EMERGENCE OF A HOSPITABLE
ENVIRONMENT FOR NEW MUSIC

To understand the significant role academic institutions have played in the composition of serious music in the United States, we must first review the events that catapulted these institutions to the position they came to hold, that is, (1) the gradual transformation in their attitude toward music as a field of study; (2) the growth in the university system itself, the funding for it, and the number of composers produced by it; and (3) the change, since the 1960s, in the composer's relationship to the university and in the nature of the musical environment there.

The emergence of music in general and composition in particular as formal disciplines taught in academic institutions is a relatively recent phenomenon in the United States. Before 1838, when Lowell Mason convinced the Boston School Committee to include music in the curriculum of local public schools, the subject was considered inappropriate for study in tax-supported institutions. American music education, which took place largely in singing schools, was oriented toward practical and religious needs. After the Civil War, a number of conservatories sprang up to offer increasingly specialized private instruction—Oberlin (1865), New England (1867), Chicago Musical College (1867), Cincinnati (1867), and Peabody (1868)—and in 1870 Harvard University began to offer courses in music. John Knowles Paine became the first professor of music there in 1876, Horatio Parker began to teach in the School of Music at Yale University in 1894, and two years later Columbia University created a position for Edward MacDowell. Shortly thereafter, composers began to teach in most of the "Ivy League" schools, but the number of university positions remained very limited, and many young, up-and-coming composers worked for women's colleges. Roger Sessions first taught at Smith College (1917–21), Quincy Porter at Vassar (1932–38), Randall Thompson at Wellesley (1927–29, 1936–37), William Schuman at Sarah Lawrence (1935– 45), Otto Luening at Bennington (1932– 44), and Finney at Smith (1929– 48). As Babbitt relates, "that's what people always thought was appropriate. It's okay for girls, you know, to teach girls; these are just finishing schools."

When Sessions returned from Europe in 1933 after eight years there, he recalled, "If somebody had told me, just before I landed in New York, that . . . I would be teaching at a university within three years, I would have tossed him overboard or jumped overboard myself, because it was the last thing in the world that I wanted to do."[9] When he did come to Princeton University in 1935 (because he "had to earn a living"), there was not even a music department, only a "section of music under art and archaeology"—"Roger Sessions, the composer, represented art and Oliver Strunk, the historian, represented archaeology," explained Babbitt with his characteristic wit. Moreover, soon thereafter, when Babbitt graduated from college and began studying privately with Sessions, he said he had "no idea of teaching in a university. Not because I wouldn't have wanted to, but because it was one of those things that just didn't occur to me."

The situation, however, began to change rapidly. As America became conscious of itself as a world power, it gradually became "an American thing," Will Ogdon remembers, "to have our composers coming out of American universities." Eastman School of Music opened in 1921, Juilliard added a graduate school in 1923, and the number of institutions accredited by the National Association of Schools of Music grew from 23 in 1924 to 158 in 1947. Moreover, the composition programs in major academic institutions began to grow, for example, that of Walter Piston at Harvard (1926–60), as documented by Randall Thompson in his 1935 study of college music.[10] In the next two decades, the arrival of numerous émigré composers from Europe enriched academic programs while bringing a decidedly European aesthetic bias to some of them.

Then in the late 1950s and early 1960s, the attention of the country began to focus on education and, consequently, the economic support for academic institutions increased substantially, leading to the rapid growth of academia and academic positions, including those for composers. Michael Marks explained:

A climate of urgency developed, and was greatly intensified when, in October 1957, the Soviet Union launched *Sputnik* I. This was a shock for Americans because for the first time there was public revelation that the Soviet Union had pulled ahead of the United States in space technology. Thus the need for improved education was not only based on the requirements of improved living standards, but also on a struggle for national survival.[11]

---

9. Cole Gagne and Tracy Caras, *Soundpieces: Interviews with American Composers* (Metuchen, N.J.: Scarecrow Press, 1982), 357.

10. Randall Thompson, *College Music: An Investigation for the Association of American Colleges* (New York: Macmillan, 1935), 41.

11. Michael Marks, *Contemporary Music Education* (New York, 1978), 13.

In 1958, Congress passed the National Defense Education Act to encourage students to enter the teaching profession by providing inexpensive loans and agreeing to cancel 10 percent of their debt for each year after graduation that they taught in the public schools. To accomplish real educational reform in a country whose schools are controlled at the local and state level, the federal government and large private foundations concentrated their efforts on curriculum development. In 1959 the Woods Hole (Massachusetts) Conference, sponsored by the Education Committee of the National Academy of Sciences, initiated curriculum studies in all fields relating to the advancement of the postindustrial society, and the government followed suit with sizable grants for such studies. Large foundations concentrated their efforts on education, to such an extent that in 1961 more than half of all their funds went to "educational enterprises."[12] Higher education thus gained in the public's esteem and began to prosper financially.

The arts were not omitted from this support, as many understood the need for balanced curricula. In 1958 the National Society for the Study of Education devoted its yearbook to music education. And in 1959, at the suggestion of the composer Norman Dello Joio, the Ford Foundation began funding a program to place young composers in the public schools as composers-in-residence. It was felt that this would both help launch young composers' careers, giving them specific compositional and performance opportunities, and provide the schools with new music.[13] From 1959 to 1962, this program, providing $5,000 annually for each composer, placed thirty-one composers in schools (at a cost ranging from $71,000 to $94,000), and in 1962 the project's success led to it becoming one of the Ford Foundation's ten major programs. In 1963, Ford provided $1,380,000 for its six-year continuation as well as for related seminars on contemporary music. The same year the Yale Seminar on Music Education, sponsored by the federal government, further encouraged teaching by composers in the schools.[14] In 1965, these efforts culminated in the creation of the National Endowment for the Arts, the first federal agency to award grants for the creation, production, and performance of new works, as well as for other forms of aid to composers' careers.[15]

12. Marks, *Contemporary Music Education*, 15.

13. Philip Glass was one of those to profit from the support.

14. Marks, *Contemporary Music Education*, 23–25, 29–36; Baumol and Bowen, *Performing Arts*, 543–45.

15. At first the NEA awarded grants to intermediaries, such as orchestras and the Thorne Fund, who then distributed the money to composers chosen by their committees. These grants were intended to help defray the cost of copying scores and parts of works already commissioned and guaranteed a performance. From 1975 to 1981, the grants instead went directly to the composers, either for the creation of new works and research related to it or for their "professional development"/"career" (i.e. to purchase other composers' scores, copy and reproduce parts of completed works, use electronic music studios, prepare tape

By the 1960s, the presence of composers became fairly standard in most, although not all, major academic institutions, and their influence on the milieu began to be felt. As they became increasingly incorporated into the academic system, they took part more and more in curricular and admission decisions,[16] self-governance, and the distribution of funds. The latter power had far-reaching consequences for composers associated with academia, for not only could they train generations of students in certain ways of thinking about music as well as creating it, they could also form performance groups trained to play their music, give concerts of their music, and invite other composers for residencies. A university's performing groups could serve as not only a performance outlet, or even commissioner of new works from the composer, either directly or through faculty research grants; they could also influence the kind of ensembles for which a composer might write, as well as the degrees of complexity of the music written.

Even the presence of only one composer could significantly affect the music-making at a university. For example, while at Hamline University (1943–48), Ernst Krenek provided the incentive to do difficult contemporary music by composing for the women's chorus active during the war and the mixed chorus after the war.[17] The choral conductor Robert Holliday presented Krenek's *Santa Fe Timetable* there fifteen years before its first European performance. Krenek was also invited by the university to sit on degree committees of graduate musicians and such distinguished artists as Dimitri Mitropoulos; there he also hosted a meeting of the International Society for Contemporary Music. Ogdon, the "official" composer at Illinois Wesleyan University from 1956 to 1965, remembers that his contemporary music symposium committee was very happy to give him "carte blanche" to invite whomever he wished. Consequently, he was able to introduce students to the music of not only Krenek, Roy Harris, Copland, and Robert Erickson but also Salvatore Martirano, Kenneth Gaburo, Glenn Glasow, and others. As he points out, "if the composer himself is a strong stimulant, it'll change the environment; if not . . . they will at least play his music."

Indeed, the growth of the university as a performance environment accelerated rapidly under composers' influence. A 1968 study claimed that 70 percent of the

---

recordings, and travel to prepare performances). Beginning in 1982, the "career advancement" grants were merged with those supporting the creation of new works, and in 1980 the Endowment started a new category, supporting "collaborations" between composers and, for example, librettists or poets. In 1985, "research" was deleted as an activity funded by these grants. (Citations here refer to the annual reports of the NEA for the years 1965–85.)

16. Finney points out: "The contribution that the composer makes to the curriculum differs from that of the historian or the theorist. . . . The function of the composer in education [is] to *upset the apple-cart*. . . . What he will offer in all his courses . . . will be a unique and individual way of looking at music" ("Employ the Composer," 9, 28).

17. From the interview with Will Ogdon.

concert activity of professional musicians took place in universities.[18] And by the early 1970s, Leslie Bassett of the University of Michigan spoke for the great majority of university composers when he claimed that "most all performances of my music are given in some university."[19] (Here one should read "some" as indicating not merely his university but others as well.)

With composers well established in academia, a new philosophy of hiring developed. Before the 1960s, music departments were concerned that their composers be committed to teaching. In the 1960s, a few daring institutions began to look instead for professionals rather than principally teachers. Russell W. Smith explained:

> We need scholars in a university because students are given their best chance if they learn philosophy from philosophers, sociology from sociologists, and biology from biologists, not from historians and appreciators of philosophy, sociology, and biology, so they have their most real introduction to the arts from artists, not from historians or appreciators of the arts.[20]

When Rochberg came to the University of Pennsylvania in 1960, he said the institution brought writers and artists as well: "This was a movement. So it wasn't as though I were alone. They were somehow supremely conscious of the importance of the simple presence of the guy who knocks his brains out trying to make a piece of art."[21] In 1964 the University of Chicago and later in 1972 the State University of New York (SUNY) at Buffalo hired two composers *without* any university diplomas, Ralph Shapey and Morton Feldman, respectively. A few others began to accumulate a significant number of composers—Kenneth Gaburo, Ben Johnston, Salvatore Martirano, Herbert Brun, Edwin London, and Lejaren Hiller, among others, all worked at the University of Illinois in the 1960s. Then, in the mid-1960s, the University of California (UC), San Diego, and the California Institute for the Arts created two music departments consisting entirely of composers and performers. At these schools, composers determined the direction in which these schools would develop.

The possibility of having one's music played in academic institutions across the country and the exponential increase in the number of composers in academia after World War II gradually gave rise to a network permitting exchanges

18. Judith E. Adler, *Artists in Offices: An Ethnography of an Academic Art Scene* (New Brunswick, N.J.: Transaction, 1979), 4.

19. Morris Risenhoover and Robert T. Blackburn, *Artists as Professors: Conversations with Musicians, Painters, Sculptors* (Urbana: University of Illinois Press, 1976), 33.

20. "A Community of Artists and Scholars," *Arts in Society* 2, no. 3 (1963): 69, cited in Risenhoover and Blackburn, *Artists as Professors*, 9. In 1947, Edward Cone wrote similarly in "The Creative Artist in the University," *American Scholar* 16 (April 1947): 192–200.

21. Risenhoover and Blackburn, *Artists as Professors*, 130.

among such institutions and the need for formalizing this network. In 1966, a group of East Coast composers, including Benjamin Boretz, Donald Martino, and Charles Wuorinen, formed the American Society for University Composers (ASUC). As Boretz explained, their purpose was to address "the awkwardness of the university as a venue for exploratory composition" and to "refashion the structures of academe to make them more amenable to the independence and non-predeterminedness which creative thinking requires." Although the founders became frustrated with their colleagues' resistance to these ideas and quit two years later, the organization continued to meet once a year, growing to 900 members in 1984, and hosted a conference at which members presented papers and heard each other's music. Until 1977, it also published the proceedings of these conferences. With the opportunity to win the support of one's colleagues through the ASUC and with awards such as NEA grants (judged largely by university composers), composers could begin to depend on universities, rather than journalists and success in the world at large, to build their careers and reputations. The university network, or "circuit," as composers call it, rapidly ripened into a complex art world of its own, quite separate from that supported by the marketplace.

Composers in universities have been an undeniable force in the world of American contemporary music. In December 1986, 1,494 composers were listed as teaching composition in the 1,543 schools on file with the College Music Society, and this figure is far short of the actual number. Not counted are young composers and composers who teach theory and appreciation as itinerant part-time faculty in many academic institutions. Moreover, the number of composition students in these institutions is high. For each year in 1982–84, of the 550 schools accredited by the National Association of Schools of Music,[22] 23 reported around 500 students enrolled in master's programs in composition, between 128 and 167 master of music degrees in composition granted, around 230 students enrolled in doctoral programs in composition, and from 37 to 51 doctoral degrees in composition granted.[23] This means that during this three-year period, 456 master's degrees and 135 doctoral degrees in composition were earned at these schools. Furthermore, the real number of composition students and degrees earned is in all probability more than double, if not triple, these (i.e., 1,000 to 1,500 M.M. degrees

22. These include Yale University, Northwestern University, and the universities of Michigan, Illinois, Iowa, Indiana, Minnesota, Southern California, and Cincinnati.

23. Calling for an additional two years of courses, the master of music (M.M.) usually requires a composition, whereas the master of arts (M.A.) may also require a prose analysis of some aesthetic or compositional issue. The doctoral degrees usually call for an additional three to seven years of work, depending on how long it takes a student to complete additional coursework and other requirements, plus either a major composition, in the case of the doctor of musical arts (D.M.A.), or a major composition plus one large or several smaller written theses, as is sometimes in the case of the doctor of philosophy (Ph.D.).

and 300 to 400 doctoral degrees), for many of the most important composition schools are not members of the National Association of Schools of Music and therefore their students are not counted in this sample.[24] During his spring 1986 visit to the California Institute for the Arts, Babbitt found that composition majors significantly outnumbered the performers there. This produced a surfeit of composers in America, the great majority of whom were university trained. Even though he was exaggerating, Babbitt pointed to a reality when he said: "anytime you advertise a job in a university, if it's a first rate university, you get 600 to 800 applications; and if it's an absolutely undesirable job, you get about 200." The question to ask, then, is not why the university affects the life of a composer in America but how it does so.

DIVERSITY OF ENVIRONMENTS

Academic institutions in the United States are numerous and diverse, especially compared with those in Europe. They are also independent vis-à-vis the federal government as well as one another. The kind of influence these institutions have on composers depends to a significant extent on the type of institution and its size, a composer's relationship with colleagues there, the type of students he or she teaches, and his or her department's attitude toward their public and the outside world. Certain universities have been more conducive to composers' work than others.

A variety of institutions train and employ our composers. Although very few of these can be neatly categorized—most are hybrids as to type, quality, and eminence across and within their academic contexts—for the purposes of discussion I will refer to four broad contexts in which composers work: research universities (which can also be state-funded when the state's politics so permit), state universities, colleges, and conservatories. The first category includes private institutions such as Columbia University, Yale University, Princeton University, the University of Chicago, and Massachusetts Institute of Technology (MIT), and public ones such as the University of Michigan and the University of California. These treat a composer like a research scientist. Up to 50 percent of a composer's salary goes to support time for creative work. Therefore, he or she may teach only one or two courses per quarter or semester. Because composers are expected to sustain an international reputation, they may travel extensively during the school year, thereby being less available to their students and colleagues. The students at research universities generally come to pursue graduate degrees that will help them get academic jobs. Often, less attention is given to undergraduate programs.

---

24. Institutions not belonging to the National Association of Schools of Music include the Juilliard, Philadelphia, Manhattan, and Mannes conservatories, as well as Columbia, Princeton, Harvard, Stanford, Pennsylvania, and Cornell universities, all nine University of California campuses, and Mills College.

State universities, supported by state governments and open to far larger numbers of students (up to eight times the number at research universities), frequently require a composer to teach more courses, three or four per term, leaving much less time for composition. Undergraduate education is the principal focus of these institutions, and while some give doctoral degrees (especially in the Midwest), others do not (e.g., California State University, as opposed to the University of California).[25]

Colleges are generally the smallest postsecondary educational institutions in the United States, educating somewhere between five hundred and a few thousand students per college.[26] In most colleges, the music department is small and only one of many (except for conservatories that are absorbed within colleges, such as Oberlin). Usually the curriculum balances the arts with the humanities and the sciences. Most colleges are primarily undergraduate institutions, leading to the bachelor's degree, and many have special characteristics, such as religious colleges and women's colleges. Among the few that grant master's degrees, Mills College in Oakland, California (with its approximately nine hundred students) was a haven for composers during Darius Milhaud's tenure there (1940–47 and periodically until 1971), including Terry Riley, Robert Ashley, and Lou Harrison. It has continued this tradition ever since. Even after Pauline Oliveros left the University of California, San Diego, in 1981, she occasionally taught at Mills. Her reasons: "I guess in a small place if you like the people, you can work very well . . . if you're in a big place, then all that politics and sociology gets in the way."

Conservatories contrast with most colleges and universities and function somewhat like the Paris Conservatoire: their students are largely performers and preprofessionals, including some composers. Most conservatories educate between several hundred and a few thousand students, the vast majority of whom are undergraduates. A few conservatories, for example Juilliard and Peabody, also have graduate schools that give the master of music (M.M.) as well as the doctor of musical arts (D.M.A.) degrees.

Schools of music and departments of music in American universities present a confusing distinction that does not hold up in many institutions across the country. They also vary one to the next. Schools of music are often associated with state schools and emphasize practical music-making. They developed in Mid-

---

25. The nine University of California campuses (which include Berkeley, Los Angeles, and San Diego) in principle accept students from the top 10 to 12 percent of high school graduates, whereas the California state universities (such as San Diego State University or California State University, Long Beach) are intended to accept students from the top 50 percent of the state's high school graduates.

26. In size, they may be compared to the Ecole Normale de Musique in Paris, which in 1986 had around two thousand students and three composition teachers (one of whom is a film music composer); it awards approximately three *diplômes supérieurs* in composition per year.

western state universities in response to the need to provide the state with music for local bands and orchestras and with performers to play in these groups. However, state-supported research universities, such as the University of Michigan and the University of Texas, Austin, also have schools of music; these contain both scholarly divisions that resemble research universities and music-making divisions that resemble conservatories. In the middle of the twentieth century, departments of music at research universities grew under the leadership of musicologists, some of them also European émigrés, who focused on developing theory and history programs and tended to keep instruction in composition and performance to a minimum. These days, however, many departments of music teach both scholarship and music-making. Although they may be smaller than schools of music and employ fewer faculty, some departments of music are otherwise indistinguishable from the schools of music in research universities. Yale and the University of California, Los Angeles (UCLA), also stand out, in that they separate music scholarship and music-making into separate academic units. While UCLA has distinct departments of music, musicology, and ethnomusicology, musicology and theory at Yale are taught in the Department of Music and performance and composition in its School of Music, even if over the years composers at Yale have taught in both.[27]

The size of an institution may also play a role in a composer's involvement. Small universities often expect a composer to cover courses in music theory, run performing ensembles, and the like, whereas large universities can require extensive administrative and committee work. In large music departments, certain problems may develop as well. Erickson clarified:

> Probably the crucial thing is the minute your faculty gets bigger than a group that can sit around a fairly small table and shout at each other, you're going to develop stresses and strains because you're going to have little groups—what they call in France "chapels"—and you're going to have lots more pushing and shoving and eventually some large-scale dissension. As long as you have seven or eight people, these can be resolved on some informal basis, and they were in our place.

Colleagues, too, can affect a composer in academia. In most academic institutions, one's colleagues are one's academic equals, in that the institution places similar demands on them and, in principle, values them similarly, although they may be peers in no other sense. Sometimes they act like what Erickson calls "independent columns" to whom the most one says is "What are you teaching this

---

27. For a Yale faculty member, the difference is one of contract: Department of Music faculty are generally tenured or on tenure tracks (in reality, this applies only to musicologists and theorists, for no composer since Hindemith has apparently received tenure at Yale); School of Music faculty are hired for a number of years on the basis of a contract, although this may include some provision for long-range job security.

year?" Other times, like members of a family, they require difficult compromises on issues of mutual interest. Being understood, particularly by those outside the music department, is not always a given. Babbitt complained:

> My colleagues in other fields felt that music was something that provided them with entertainment, surcease from their very important activities. And what were we doing in a university anyhow? We must be failed composers. If we were successful composers, we'd be out in the great world of television and Hollywood and radio. . . . Many of them don't take us seriously.

However, if one's colleagues in academia are stimulating, understanding, and themselves exploring new perspectives, they can be valuable resources. Composers there have the opportunity to work with and get to know colleagues outside music. In recent years, important collaborations have taken place between composers and scholars in other fields, especially with newer developments in computer music and the increased interest in relationships between the music scholar/creator and those working in the other arts and disciplines such as psychology, linguistics, mathematics, cognitive science, literary criticism, and critical theory. The potential influence of American academia on music and musical composition, and vice versa, is thus becoming increasingly complex.

Composers' attitudes toward teaching vary. Some find it stimulating and tremendously useful, others a drain on their time and energy. These perspectives are often related not only to their own aesthetic proclivities and self-image but also to the kind of students they prefer to teach. Erickson, who taught at the San Francisco Conservatory before UC San Diego, preferred preprofessional conservatory students to liberal arts undergraduates:

> It is absolutely wonderful to teach a dozen kids sight-singing and dictation when half of them have perfect pitch and most of them have perfect rhythm. That's very different from the university situation where what they have is the ability to chatter about almost any topic at all, but they can't put up.

Babbitt, who has taught at both Princeton and Juilliard, sees undergraduates at research universities differently and has enjoyed the intellectual challenge and curiosity they can bring:

> You try to teach a freshman course [at Princeton] using the Piston harmony book and you'd be thrown out, you'd be run out of the school. Students are at the same time taking a philosophy of science course . . . and they would say, "You call this a theory of harmony? What is this? You've got a cookbook here that tells you what?" So a book had to be written for them, and for a long time there was no book by Peter Westergaard. . . . It's exactly the opposite from Juilliard, where the students would know a tremendous amount of music and would not have the slightest idea of how to cope with

any book—they can hardly read. I mean it's an utterly different intellectual orientation, the demands they make and the way they respond to what is either the music itself, or what they read about music is so utterly different.

Elitist dismissiveness and disdain for students by some composers has typically been aimed at undergraduates more than graduate students. Roger Reynolds has found that while some are talented and reasonably bright, teaching those who are attending the institution without any precise career goals or who are studying music only to round out their liberal education can force a composer to avoid difficult issues and "dilute the force of ideas." Graduate students, however, are "not totally naïve and not exhausting," Reynolds reports, and real research, sometimes even one's own, can at least be discussed. Depending on the kind of students a composer has, academic teaching then can be a radically different experience.

Besides students and colleagues, academia may also present the composer with the opportunity to build a relationship with the community around the school. Many universities, especially the larger ones, have developed their own publics and function like regional cultural centers. Over the years, their public relations personnel have consciously worked to build an audience from the local community by hosting all kinds of cultural and musical events, ranging from the most traditional string quartet series to contemporary dance groups and experimental performances. Some music departments have also organized concerts off campus and in coordination with local groups. Ogdon has found that the members of the community who regularly come to university concerts of contemporary music may become participatory. Because they have gotten to know the composer over a period of years, they are willing to criticize him or her on the basis of where the composer has been and is now. The academic context thus can invite and facilitate critical interaction between a composer and his or her public.

While the academic environment, particularly in remote areas, may seem to separate a composer from his or her peers, it is unlikely that a composer could feel genuinely isolated in any academic institution in recent years. The mobility that telecommunications permit and the use Americans have increasingly made of the telephone, fax, email and overnight courier in the last decades make frequent contact and interaction with colleagues all over the country the norm more than the exception. Without needing to travel very often, a composer in academia can remain in contact with the rest of the musical world and, like Bach and the Mannheim School composers, still reap the benefits of remaining in one place for a number of years.

Influences on a Composer's Music

Such an environment can readily affect the aesthetic choices a composer may make and, depending on the composer and the academic institution, may either nourish his or her composition or constrain it. Academic institutions, particularly those focused on research, usually quite adequately fill the need for time and basic resources; they also free the composer from the role of entertainer, enabling more concentration on research. Moreover, no one there questions the value of experimentation and the importance of exploring new avenues of research. Yet, as one would expect, compromises are required in return.

For some composers, one of the most important activities that has taken place in academia is what Ben Boretz has called "musical thought."[28] There, until recently, the theory, aesthetics, and philosophy of music have been studied and advocated primarily by composers. Boretz explains:

> Schenkerian theory was first promoted by Roger Sessions and elaborated by Milton Babbitt and Edward T. Cone as a matter of intellectual and musical conviction. Arthur Berger promoted the aesthetic theories of D. W. Pratt and greatly elaborated the theoretical ideas of Nadia Boulanger as well as the philosophies of people like R. G. Collingwood and T. E. Hume, not to mention Whitehead and Dewey and Bergson. If you were a music student in the 1950s, it would only have been from composers that you would have been made aware of these thinkers, of the notion of "musical thinking" as such, or of theory as an intellectual and crucial compositional issue, including the thought of people like Schönberg, Hindemith, Stravinsky, Varese, Partch, etc.; the whole "avant-garde" of both "serial" and "indeterminacy" oriented thinking was, first and foremost, a nexus and a debate of and about ideas rather than practices.

Starting in the 1960s, such interests led to intellectual forums exclusively for composers, such as the Princeton Seminar in Advanced Musical Studies, and in 1961 a new journal, *Perspectives of New Music*, conceived by Boretz while a graduate student at Brandeis and later coedited with his teacher, Arthur Berger.[29] Com-

28. For an example of what he means by this concept, see Benjamin Boretz, *Talk: If I Am a Musical Thinker* (Barrytown, N.Y.: Station Hill, 1985).

29. Boretz relates that one of his main projects at *Perspectives of New Music*, the "Younger American Composers" series, "was designed to promote the notion of 'colleagueship' as against 'celebrity-hood' so that everyone who participated had to be interested in writing about a colleague as well as being written about." The list was intended to welcome a broad range of composers—Pauline Oliveros was one of the original participants. That *Perspectives* became "a tool in the 'publish or perish' academic business," Boretz confesses, "was a torment to us as editors." Their intention had been that it "serve as a forum for whatever intellectual urgencies were of concern to composers, whether in writings by them, or by anyone else, whether about 'contemporary music' or anything else that might have been particularly compelling to them." Boretz retired from the position as editor of *Perspectives* in 1983 because of his perception that his conception of the journal was no longer relevant to its constituency at that time.

posers also began to introduce high-level theory into the university music curriculum. This gave rise to the profession of "music theorist"—a discipline sometimes taught and practiced by composers but eventually embraced by those "no
longer professing musical thought as a single occupation whose branches might be
composing, performing, writing (i.e. theorizing/analyzing/criticizing including
historically)." From Boretz's perspective, it was composers' function as the "principal purveyors of theoretical knowledge" about music before the advent of theorists that made their presence viable in academia.

A composer's immediate peers present another potent force in academia that
is capable of affecting his or her work. Having performers and composers on
the same faculty over a long period of time can lead to very productive working
relationships. Erickson wrote pieces for a number of university colleagues over the
years (including the trumpeter Ed Harkins, the trombonist Stuart Dempster, the
soprano Carol Plantamura, the violinist Janos Negyesy, and the bass player Bert
Turetzky). He described the benefits of composing for his performer colleagues:

> If I am trying to get something a little different out of an instrument, I can't
> go to a performer and say, "Show me your bag of tricks." (I can, but it's a
> self-defeating request. He'll show me his bag of tricks and sometimes I get a
> notion from that . . . but then, in a very important sense, it becomes his
> piece rather than my piece.) What I have to do is live around him for a long
> enough time that I get beyond the bag of tricks and make suggestions like
> "Can you do this? Can you do that?" Suggestions have to be done very
> carefully too, so I got in the habit of writing little exercises and telling him
> not "Can you do this?" but "Play this, play it faster, play it slower, can you
> play it a third higher?" . . . I simply recorded hours and hours of these
> people doing this stuff—"Can you do this? And try it a little faster?—and
> then I studied the results, listening for the kinds of mistakes that might be
> converted into something useful. If a player made some mistakes, I'd in-
> terrupt, "Hey, How did you do that?" and he would say, "I just goofed."
> "Well, goof again," I'd say, and pretty soon you'd have your hands on a new
> way of doing something. A lot of trust gets built up over time and then the
> player will get into the game and say, "Hey! I just discovered something that
> I didn't think I could do." And you play with it from there. At some point
> then, you write your piece.

Of course, not all university composers work with their colleagues. Some, like
Reynolds, think that a work of art should not be based on "social or intellectual
contrivance" but rather on "personal conviction." Still, colleagues can become
important collaborators. Over the years a composer can learn "how to think like
a performer thinks . . . how his hands move, and how he works his instrument";
a composer can develop instincts for what is difficult or easy for the player. At
institutions where the split between performance and composition is not severe,

a composer may be more apt to find performer colleagues willing to collaborate than in institutions where, as Erickson observed, performer teachers tell their students, "I don't want you playing that stuff: it'll ruin you ears."

To varying degrees, teaching may also influence a composer's work, and whether one's students are essentially preprofessionals or amateurs can influence the kind of music one writes. Much of the chamber music written for unusual groups of instruments in America has its origins in academic situations. Furthermore, for some composers, such as Ogdon and Oliveros, the composition is a direct response to their teaching.[30] Oliveros's *Sonic Meditations* arose "out of [her] desire to make pieces available to non-musicians." Many composers, however, keep composition a private activity, separate from their teaching, and claim that it has little if any effect on their music.

Whether teaching constitutes an appropriate complementary activity to composing has long been a subject of heated debate. Two famous nonteachers in America, Igor Stravinsky and Virgil Thomson, have urged composers to stay away from universities. In 1959, Stravinsky warned them that "teaching is academic"[31]—it orients a composer toward conventionality and categorization. Thomson elaborated:

> Teachers tend to form opinions about music, and these are always getting in the way of creation. The teacher, like the parent, must always have an answer for everything. If he doesn't he loses prestige. He must make up a story about music and stick to it. Nothing is more sterilizing. . . . One ends by being full of definite ideas about music; and one's mind, which for creative purposes should remain as vague and unprejudiced as possible, is corseted with opinions and *partis pris*.[32]

Many may well find such a stereotype of teachers offensive as well as inaccurate. However, some composers in academia have agreed. Oliveros complained about the codification and constant proving that the University of California requires, and even though she admitted "it was a challenge to my intellectual growth and development," teaching ended up requiring too much creative energy for her to continue it full-time. Rather than faulting teaching, however, Erickson blamed institutions for "this tendency to formalize their operations, get organized, highly organized, super organized because it's far more efficient," although "every time something like this happens, there is real art that drops by the wayside." His solution: "be in it, but not of it." Other composers have relentlessly rejected the notion that teaching has to be "academic," and the wide range of teaching methods now

30. In the late 1980s, Will Ogdon wrote tonal songs for one of his classes, and these have turned out to be among his finest works.

31. Igor Stravinsky and Robert Craft, *Conversations with Igor Stravinsky* (Garden City, N.Y.: Doubleday, 1959), 153–54.

32. Virgil Thomson, *A Virgil Thomson Reader* (Boston: Houghton Mifflin, 1981), 134.

used by composers in American academic institutions, to be discussed shortly, tends to support their objection to Stravinsky's dismissal.

The debate also revolves around whether teaching ultimately has a deadening or a stimulating effect on one's composition. Pointing to "the constant association with dead men's music" that teachers have, Thomson wrote: "Daily dealing with the music of the past is probably all right after fifty," but "it never fails to produce in a younger man a derivative manner of writing that no amount of surface complexity can conceal."[33] Babbitt and many others, by contrast, considered it a fruitful opportunity "to be confronted with and learn a tremendous amount of music" and "to listen to things that you never would have otherwise," for it obliges them to study closely issues they might otherwise ignore or avoid. Moreover, some have felt as Leslie Bassett, who claimed: "If I were never challenged as somebody who is not progressing—the way young people challenge you—I think it would be the professional death of me."[34] In 1970, twenty-three major composers in academia vigorously defended their occupation in response to Stravinsky's dictum of eleven years earlier. Their essays give clear evidence that, at least from their perspectives, Stravinsky's fears were not well founded—a real composer does not necessarily become dull from studying or teaching counterpoint—and the advantages of working at universities outweigh any disadvantages.[35]

The stance of the university toward a composer's freedom of expression and the ability to experiment can also influence one's work. Universities normally will support what might not necessarily survive in the marketplace. Babbitt pointed out that one of the reasons composers moved into universities was that "music itself changed and changed in fundamental ways, which made difficulties for the public as well as for the composer as well as for the performer." (One can also argue that some universities fostered the new complexity in the music.) Composers in universities such as Erickson and Babbitt have had the luxury of working to please themselves. Babbitt noted:

> A lot of us write the music we most want to hear and never think about the audience. We think about performers, we think about what can be heard, we think about what we're hearing. . . . As for the audience, it's very, very hard to even talk about it because we know how often the audience response is based upon totally irrelevant considerations.

Erickson agreed:

> When I write a piece. . . . I don't think anybody's going to like it except me. . . . It would be nice, you know, to write for a public, but then you'd

---

33. Thomson, *A Virgil Thomson Reader.*
34. Risenhoover and Blackburn, *Artists as Professors*, 32.
35. "The Composer in Academia," 77.

get into problems. You'd have to do some market research and it might be wrong, it might be right, and I think it's too tricky to do that.

Such comments ignore the fact that their peers constitute an audience and a public for their music. Even if younger composers have not always shared this attitude toward writing for the public at large, still composers in academia do have the choice to write for whomever they wish.

Academic institutions may also be supportive of experimentation and innovation, whether it is because administrators do not know or care, because "research" in music is considered comparable to scientific research, or because composers in academia are able to secure outside grants to support their work. In research universities, ironically, it is often the university's research committee rather than a composer's peers in the music department who offer the most support. But the reality of working in a university is complex. Some composers feel their work there is constrained. As Oliveros observed, "what the standard bearers are pushing is academic excellence and when you use that term, then you're meaning something that is known, and that doesn't leave room for the edge where you might do something wrong." Erickson concurred:

> Unless you fit things into a University style, you cannot proceed. There isn't really room for lively, individual endeavor in a strange direction. . . . You have to tread a well-worn path because the university administration doesn't know whether the stuff's any good, they just call up all your colleagues and ask them. Well, I think that's, first of all, demeaning. . . . We're processing human beings into educational sausage and it's sort of crushing to anybody who has ideas, but you can see their point of view. They can say they have no way of telling whether this is worthwhile.

Composers also have complained that the language universities understand is verbal. Unless they can translate their work into verbal explanations, they fear having trouble being understood and adequately supported. However, some composers have appropriated elements of positivism from their colleagues in philosophy and the language of science to explain their experimentalism in a way that has allowed them to justify their existence to university administrators and to be rewarded for their music as a form of research. It would be interesting to examine the extent to which these tactics for seeking legitimacy have affected a composer's work over time.

Many composers consider the idea of "academic music" a misunderstood one. As in any other discipline, Babbitt pointed out, "it's assumed that the most informedly problematical, that the most responsibly advanced work takes place in the academy, and it does in music too. Not all of it, but most of it and a lot of it." In the 1960s, university campuses (thanks in part to Rockefeller Foundation support) began to support performance groups with whom composers could work and who might play their music. In 1966, Wuorinen cited ten academia-based ensembles devoted to performing new music, all of which were directed or substantially influenced by academia-based composers.[36] Besides serving as a tool for local composers and enabling them to exert direct control over the performance of their music, these groups have helped to build an audience in academia for contemporary music. They have raised the performance standard for new works through long and thorough concert preparations,[37] and they have engaged composers in playing and conducting their own music as well as that of their colleagues. Such ensembles have also played a crucial role in the dissemination of contemporary music *outside* academia. The Group for Contemporary Music, for example—originally a nonunion group of graduate students at Columbia University devoted to performances of contemporary music and adequate rehearsal time—gave rise to many spin-off contemporary music groups in New York City—"in some cases, the exact players, and sometimes the students of the players, people who were associated with them," explained Babbitt. "It's impossible to find a group of that kind in New York which did not originally have some kind of a really close relationship with the Group for Contemporary Music."

Likewise, the presence of numerous material resources at universities (such as good libraries, electronic music studios, and even computer music research centers) has encouraged composers to explore new ideas, new languages, even new approaches to music-making. Three university composers—Luening, Vladimir Ussachevsky, and Babbitt—made use of the first important electronic music synthesizer in this country at the Columbia University studio. Before the advent of personal computers, composers from throughout the country traveled to use the technical resources at Stanford University, MIT, Mills, North Texas State University, and the Center for Music Experiment at UC San Diego, among others. As technology came to play an increasing role in new music, composers in academia for a time had an important advantage over those not affiliated with institutions. Academic institutions had computers for sound production, for the printing of music, for the analysis of music. As small home computers increasingly served

36. In his "Performance of New Music in American Universities," *Proceedings of the American Society of University Composers* 1(1966): 20–21, Charles Wuorinen mentions performing groups at "the Universities of Illinois and Iowa; Yale, Columbia, and Brandeis Universities; the State Universities of New Jersey and New York—Rutgers and Buffalo, respectively; the Universities of Chicago and Colorado, and others." Among these, Ralph Shapey's Contemporary Chamber Players at the University of Chicago presented me with my first encounters with new music.

37. As an example of how these ensembles worked, David Burge, then the director of the contemporary ensembles at the University of Colorado, explains that "rehearsals began in October for concerts in February or March" and were "held at least once per week during the entire time"; moreover, when possible, each piece was given "several informal performances or at least open rehearsals prior to the more formal concert or concerts"; "Toward a Higher Standard of Performance," *Proceedings of the American Society of University Composers* 3 (1968): 70.

a composer's needs, academic research facilities in the 1980s still helped produce large-scale works and those of unusual complexity.

From a Student's Perspective

Learning to compose in an American academic institution—probably the most important influence on one's musical development—has changed significantly over the past few decades. First, beginning in the 1960s, composers in some academic settings incorporated the spirit and liveliness of the private studio into their teaching by working with their students on a one-to-one basis whenever possible. Certain institutions offered both composition master classes and regular private lessons. And while some composers assume a student has come to learn how *they* compose and thus teach the student to do that (as Hindemith and Wuorinen have), the variety of teaching philosophies is probably as great as the number of composers teaching. Some, for example, Leon Kirchner, Andrew Imbrie, Carter, Krenek, and Erickson, have focused on seeing what a student is attempting to do and trying to assist rather than dictate. Such composers, for example, direct the student to scores that seem to be along the lines of what the student is thinking about, instead of giving certain exercises to complete. This approach to teaching may be more idealistic than realistic—in fact, few, especially in the 1960s–1980s, supported students writing tonal, postmodern, or commercial music.[38] Still, to the extent that a nonprescriptive, nonacademic approach is practiced, it can lead to a collegial relationship developing between teacher and student. "As we've been together for a long time," Erickson commented, "I can be more forthcoming with my notions if something's right or wrong because they know . . . it's not an order."

Second, the presence of more than one composer in many academic institutions has made studying there sometimes more than a mere apprenticeship, especially if young composers work with more than one teacher. Erickson explained this philosophy:

> There has to be a critical mass of composers, not just one. The old "I am the chief" kind of composition teaching (that held during the forties, fifties, sixties) is bad news because then you have some dictator running everything and it's not good for the students because what they have to do is to be thrown into despair and confusion, and have a place where they can work their way out. And they have to have colleagues their own age who they can talk to and they have to have professors with opposing views so they can see there's room for lots of argument.

---

38. When increasing numbers of students in the 1980s wanted to have lessons to learn to write popular music in otherwise "serious" or "concert" music–oriented departments, they presented a challenge to the older generation of composers, as few felt qualified to teach them or were even interested in such an endeavor.

Even two composers can be enough to create an aesthetic conflict. At Duke University in the late 1960s, for example, Paul Earls and Iain Hamilton "used themselves as two paddles, bouncing students back and forth" for just such a purpose. "He will take a stance," Earls remembers, "and I'll take another stance. We set up a polarity between ourselves."[39] Of course, there can be a downside to polarization, whether deliberate or not, if students and junior faculty get caught up in vicious disputes between senior composers.

Third, academic institutions can serve as laboratories for young composers. They can provide performers with whom to try out their new works, other departments (such as drama and visual arts) that may encourage mixed-media projects, and even campus radio stations that can get their work to a larger audience. The university thus functions as an important proving ground for young composers, both helping them to sort through their ideas about music, especially their own music, and giving them a sense of how the world of music works.

Where young American composers have chosen to study has also changed with each successive generation. Before and after World War I, serious composers often went to Europe for their training—Paine, Parker, and MacDowell to Germany, and many of the Copland generation (including Berger, Carter, Copland, David Diamond, Finney, Imbrie, Piston, and Thomson) to France. But gradually American academic institutions began to attract students by virtue of their aesthetic orientation and their own strong musical figures, such as Piston at Harvard from 1926 to 1961. This was especially the case for the Eastman School of Music at the University of Rochester. From the 1920s through the 1960s, Howard Hanson worked aggressively at Eastman to build their program and to develop a specifically American music. In 1934, Hanson served as chair of the Committee on Graduate Study in Music for the National Association of Schools of Music. Through his efforts (and because many of the other conservatories were forced to close down during the depression and the women's colleges graduated very few future professionals), Eastman became the most popular school at which to study composition between the wars. From 1934 to 1944, it granted 274 master of music degrees in theory and composition, that is, 57 percent of all such degrees granted during that period by the forty-three schools surveyed.[40] These students, later called the "Eastman group," became known for a style based on tonality, diatonic melodies, and traditional forms. H. Wiley Hitchcock described them as follows.

39. "Should Composition Be Taught in Universities, and If So, How?" *Proceedings of the American Society of University Composers* 4 (1969): 85.

40. During the same period, the University of Michigan gave the second largest number of master of arts degrees in composition, that is, 62, and the forty-one other schools gave only a total of 143 similar degrees. See Paul S. Carpenter, *Music: An Art and a Business* (Norman: University of Oklahoma Press, 1950), 181.

All shared the relatively conservative, evolutionary attitudes of their mentors; all seemed to share an aim to write the Great American Symphony by way of the Depression-era Overture, a one-movement piece ten minutes in length or less, usually titled something like *Jubilation* ([Robert] Ward, 1946), *Poem* ([Robert] Palmer, 1938), *Psalm* or *Elegy* (Diamond, 1936 and 1938 respectively), with at least one section of broadly arching, wide-intervalled, mostly diatonic melody supported by slow-moving, rich harmony.[41]

In the succeeding years, Eastman spread its power and influence by helping its students get jobs in music departments across the country, especially in state universities. Eventually these Eastman graduates became chairmen of their departments. They controlled hiring and promoting, and in the late 1940s and 1950s (according to Ogdon) made it very difficult for anyone not from the Eastman–Northwestern University–University of Michigan bloc to get a university job. Over the years, Eastman also built an important alliance with Juilliard. Of the original Eastman group, Ward taught there from 1946 to 1956, Diamond taught there from 1973 on, and in 1962 Peter Mennin became its president.

When the émigrés arrived from Europe just before World War II, their complex music posed a threat to that of the Eastman group, and their presence challenged the Hanson hegemony. Attaching themselves to colleges and universities throughout the United States—Krenek at Vassar College from 1938 to 1942 and then at Hamline University in Minnesota for five years, Milhaud at Mills College from 1940 to 1971, Schönberg at the University of Southern California in 1935–36 and UCLA in 1936–51, Hindemith at Yale from 1940 to 1953, Ernest Bloch at the UC Berkeley, beginning in 1940, and Stefan Wolpe at various schools on the East Coast from 1939 to 1972—they soon produced a large number of students with a heightened awareness of international musical currents. Such students also often embraced a more revolutionary approach to composition. At Princeton in particular, Sessions and Babbitt built a very important following of composers who extended Schönberg's serial techniques. Yet, according to Erickson, it still took until the late 1950s for Schönberg's music to be accepted in most academic institutions and for their music libraries to purchase his scores in any quantity.

Since the 1960s, the conflict between the nationalists and the émigré-inspired composers has been less of an issue as a wider variety of composers have been invited to join faculties. These include those Randall Thompson once called the eclectics, esoterics, eccentrics, and innovators.[42] Boretz describes what led universities to find a place for radicals like himself, Jim Randall, Gaburo, Brun,

---

41. H. Wiley Hitchcock, *Music in the United States: A Historical Introduction* (Englewood Cliffs, N.J.: Prentice Hall, 1969), 213.

42. Randall Thompson, "The Contemporary Scene in American Music," *Musical Quarterly* 18, no. 1 (January 1932): 9–17.

Johnston, Hiller, Oliveros, Martirano, and Alvin Lucier as the "pseudo-adventurous spirit which infected academe (thinking it was an institutional/sur-survival issue) in the 1960s." Certain schools became known in the 1960s and 1970s for experimental approaches to composition. Composers on their faculties embraced aesthetics ranging from, for example, meditation music to serialism. The Tape Music Center at Mills, the Center for Music Experiment at UC San Diego, California Institute of the Arts (Cal Arts), Stanford, SUNY Buffalo, North Texas State, Brooklyn College, and MIT were among those institutions that supported considerable research into new musical languages, performance techniques, and technologies. By the mid-1980s, composition and composers were fully integrated into academic institutions of all kinds and were obtaining there much of what they needed in terms of support and recognition.

As Babbitt put it in 1986, "the total range of musical activity is to be found not by moving from inside the university to outside the university, but from university to university and within any music department of any university." If this statement tempts one to try to categorize universities, or at least to think in terms of regional or coastal differences, one should keep in mind that composers, like other Americans, enjoy living in different parts of the country. Sessions, for example, moved back and forth between Berkeley and Princeton for years; Cage and Oliveros, who developed their styles in the West, moved to New York; Bernard Rands taught or was otherwise in residence at Princeton, the University of Illinois, Cal Arts, UC San Diego, Yale, Boston University, Juilliard, and finally Harvard. Likewise, important computer music centers eventually sprang up all over the country. Any adequate discussion of the differences between specific American universities, other than what I have already implied, merits a full-length study. In the second part of this chapter, I turn to one of the important ways to understand these differences, differences that reflect or result from the political connections of a small number of determined, mostly East Coast composers who used academic institutions to promote their careers. Through their significant influence over government grants as well as fellowships and other awards available to young composers, they not only assured the continued power and status of certain educational institutions but also propagated and maintained a modernist aesthetic.

PART 2. PATRONAGE, POWER, AND NEA FUNDING

The University as Patron

The advantages of working for a university extend well beyond the social, the intellectual, and the musical, especially if one is inclined to pursue them. First, they are economic. Most American composers, when asked why they first joined academic faculties or why they moved from one academic institution to another, mention the money. Although the situation outside academia was improving in the 1980s, of the 430 composers who responded to a 1961 American Music Center survey, only 16 claimed they had earned $5,000 or more from serious composition that year, half had earned less than $100, and 145 reported no income at all from their music.[43] A 1970 study showed that 92 percent of American composers could earn a living from their composition alone.[44] Yet, as Finney put it, there is something in the American temperament that makes the composer feel he or she has a right to be employed rather than supported through subsidies.[45] Many composers of art music, especially those who grew up in the depression, took jobs in academia because at these institutions (particularly research universities) they could earn more than elsewhere in the American economy.

The economic benefits of academic jobs do not stop with the income they provide. Bernard Rands pointed out that the security of such a job might protect a composer from the pressure to accept unwanted commissions, thereby allowing him or her to maintain independence. In reality, the academic institution is as much a patron of the composer as an employer. Research universities, in particular, provide sabbaticals, and large, research-oriented libraries purchase costly scores and records so that composers may keep abreast of musical developments globally. As already mentioned, institutions with electronic music and computer music studios provide expensive equipment to which composers might otherwise not have had access. Academic institutions of all kinds also furnish concert halls for performances, sponsor festivals of new music, and advertise to attract an audience. Research grants may even defray the cost of copying parts and publishing music, paying musicians to rehearse, making recordings, attending conferences, and traveling to hear one's music performed out of town or attending conferences.

Working for a university, moreover, can significantly help a composer to secure other forms of funding, particularly government grants. The composers at several colleges in Vermont, including Bennington, for example, relied on the NEA in its early years to support them in bringing young composers to Vermont from throughout the country each summer for a two-week festival.[46] In addition, NEA grants have been used to add composers-in-residence to a faculty (as at SUNY Albany in 1978 and 1979) and to support contemporary music performance in academia (i.e., at Columbia and Hunter College in 1969, Peabody and Eastman in 1971, SUNY Buffalo and Albany in 1972 and 1973, and Northern Illinois University in 1974 and 1976). Many more academic institutions throughout the country have

---

43. Baumol and Bowen, *Performing Arts*, 107–8. See the last part of this chapter for what changed in the 1980s.

44. *Saturday Review* (28 February 1970), cited in "The Composer in Academia," 81.

45. Finney, "Employ the Composer," 8.

46. In the mid-1970s, the composers' conference moved to Johnson State College and later to Wellesley in Massachusetts.

been able to put on contemporary music series since 1976, thanks to the NEA's establishment of new music performance as an independent grant category (see table 11.1, col. 6).

Beginning in 1979, another new category of NEA grants, "Centers for New Music Resources" (see table 11.1, col. 5), has been particularly useful to university composers by helping them build and develop computer and electronic music studios.[47] Such schools as Princeton, Stanford, UC San Diego, Colgate University, Mills, Columbia, Dartmouth College, Brooklyn College, MIT, Michigan, and North Texas State have taken advantage of this support to purchase equipment, upgrade their facilities, invite visiting composers, and host computer music symposiums.

Of course, even with government help, an academic institution's ability to support a composer's needs is not complete. A composer must still deal with journalists, even if the school may employ publicists; she or he must still go to publishers and recording companies. The University of California Press at one time contemplated publishing music and chose three works to issue;[48] however, as Andrew Imbrie explains, the problems of promotion, distribution, and royalties proved too cumbersome for the academic book publisher, and the project was dropped. American recording companies usually require subsidies, sometimes up to $10,000, to record contemporary music. Some academic research committees are willing to underwrite part or all of the expense of producing a record, especially if a composer wins a major prize. However, such support is not available everywhere. To cover such expenses, a composer must turn to personal grants, for which an academic affiliation may again prove quite useful.

THE POLITICS OF GETTING, KEEPING, AND USING ONE'S UNIVERSITY AFFILIATION

In 1981, the *College Music Symposium* published a letter from an anonymous music department chairman to an anonymous dean entitled "Why Mozart Lost the Job."[49] Although it exaggerates every point, this humorous letter does reveal what many, although not all, American academic institutions look for in their composer-professors.

---

47. In 1979, six of the seven centers funded were at universities; in 1980, it was sixteen of the twenty funded; in 1981, twelve of the fourteen; in 1982, fourteen of the seventeen; in 1983, nine of the twelve; in 1984, fourteen of the eighteen; and in 1985, six of the nine.

48. The press planned to issue one work each by Arnold Elston, Seymour Shifrin, and David Lewin. See Andrew Imbrie, "The University of California Series in Contemporary Music," *Proceedings of the American Society of University Composers* 1 (1966): 7–13.

49. "Why Mozart Lost the Job," *College Music Symposium* 21, no. 2 (fall 1981): 158–59.

TABLE 11.1. NEA Financial Report, 1967–85: Budget Breakdown of Selected Grant Categories of the Music Division, Opera-Theater Division, and Inter-Arts Division.

		Music division					Opera/theatre division	Inter-arts division
Year	Total NEA budget	Total budget	Composer grants: new works, career devlpt.	Consortium commissions[a]	Center for New Music Resources	Contemporary music performance	New American works	Total budget
1967	$7,632,021	$653,858 (8.6%)	$68,458[b] (10.5%)					
68	10,670,004	1,154,969 (10.8%)	58,485 (5.1%)					
69	6,370,639	861,620 (13.5%)	19,355 (2.2%)					
70	12,982,667	2,525,195 (19.5%)	4,870 (0.2%)					
71	13,271,679	5,188,383 (39.1%)	6,888 (0.13%)					
72	33,113,035	9,745,797 (29.4%)	38,825[b] (0.4%)					
73	42,030,998	10,382,210 (24.7%)	69,611 (0.7%)					
74	67,616,003	16,116,310 (23.8%)	320,975 (2.0%)					
75	81,665,448	14,894,833 (18.2%)	384,665 (2.6%)					

Year							
76	92,646,702	17,249,296 (18.6%)	363,150 (2.1%)		$55,520		
77	94,644,284	17,332,202 (18.3%)	392,700 (2.3%)		222,725		
78	105,576,817	19,457,000 (18.4%)	431,315 (2.2%)		352,500		
79	118,528,887	16,375,408 (13.8%)	387,220 (2.4%)	89,000	441,500		
80	115,612,558	13,572,300 (11.7%)	323,685 (2.4%)	223,000	571,800	$377,000	$4.2 million
81	135,742,256	16,183,266 (11.9%)	209,920 +132,800 / 342,720 (2.1%)	107,760	442,500	402,700	4.2
82	117,358,179	14,094,201 (12.0%)	229,000 +30,000 / 259,000 (1.8%)	118,900	357,650	262,500	4.2
83	112,920,653	12,940,169 (11.5%)	298,200 +160,000 / 458,200 (3.5%)	71,000	401,000	355,500	4.4
84	128,675,151	15,218,925 (11.8%)	285,000 (1.9%)	100,450	387,400	518,000	3.4
85	128,661,797	15,311,968 (11.9%)	164,500 +312,000 / 476,500 (3.1%)	52,000	374,760	512,000	4.3

[a]Consortium commissions are grants to consortia of three or more music organizations to support commissioning works by a number of composers which they will eventually perform.

[b]These sums include grants to the Thorne Music Fund, an organization whose advisory council subsequently awarded the money to a selection of composers.

While the list of works and performances that the candidate submitted is undoubtedly a full one . . . it reflects activity *outside* education. Mr. Mozart does not have an earned doctorate; indeed very little in the way of formal training or teaching experience. There is a good deal of instability too evidenced in the resume. Would he really settle down in a large state university? And while we have no church connections, as chairman I must voice a concern over the incidents with the Archbishop of Salzburg. They hardly confirm his abilities to be a good team man.

A list of Mozart's shortcomings then follows: he does not know enough music before Bach and Handel to teach a large undergraduate survey in music history; his playing of the violin, viola, and piano "stretches versatility dangerously thin"; and the fact that no major foundation has yet given him a grant makes one question the quality of his music.

The situation of the composer in American academic institutions is not nearly so bleak. Of course, there is a price to pay for the advantages the occupation offers, and certain expectations are associated with it. First, a composer must have a strong education and, by the 1980s, preferably a doctorate. Winning an academic job also depends on where a composer went to school. All admission to American academic institutions is highly competitive, particularly for graduate schools, and the more prestigious the school, the more difficult it is to enter and the more symbolic capital the degree carries.[50] Those who complete a degree and get an academic job must then worry about earning tenure, the school's commitment to a permanent job for them. Although the process is never an easy one, given the difficulty of evaluating a composer's work, it is a necessary rite of passage at virtually all academic institutions. Yale is an exception, to the extent that historically it has not given tenure to composers. As Erickson described the review process, "they go by reputation, they go by his past—is he a hard worker and things like that—and they go by politics—the department pushes or somebody else pushes." He pointed out that "it is by no means perfect, but it does something to hold the really dead heads back and reward hard work." The procedure of peer review may also continue at periodic points throughout one's academic career, thereby giving some the feeling that they are, in Oliveros's words, "constantly on the ladder" and have to "climb it." It may also encourage them to undertake projects that can be finished in a few years rather than those requiring a long gestation period. But for as many of those who dislike the system, one can probably find an equal number who favor it and think it keeps a composer producing.

---

50. Whereas in France the Conservatoire is the most important institution teaching music, the hierarchy among American universities is one of plateaus (with a number of schools on each plateau). One should also note that a university's reputation can change, depending on who is teaching there at any one time.

Erickson commented, "It was security to be myself. . . . On my own time, I could do what I wanted to do, so it gave me a lot of freedom."

Given the world of contemporary music in America, there has been no better place for a composer to become known. School friends and colleagues can help immensely in building one's reputation and career. Through a study of the educational background and university affiliation of the composers who won the largest or most frequent NEA grants given between 1969 and 1985 (shown in table 11.2, appendices 3–6, and the conclusions at the ends of them), I will point out the extent to which academic institutions, and some more than others, have indeed functioned as political entities. Academic associates, I show, tend to protect and promote each other. While close examination of other major grants, such as the Guggenheim, may lead to somewhat different results,[51] one should keep in mind that the NEA grants come from the federal government, which intends their distribution to be as regionally and aesthetically equitable as possible. Obviously, this study can make no comment on composers who did not apply for such grants, or did not win them, or did not win enough to become part of the sample studied— some of whom are major figures. But, for those in the sample, the study raises a number of thought-provoking issues, discussed below.

Table 11.2 provides some background information: grant minimum and maximums, number of grants awarded, and how the money was distributed. Note that the number of grants and the spread of money jumped in 1973, then rose with each successive year until 1976, and changed radically in 1981 as endowment polices evolved. Whereas 98 percent of the 110 awards in 1980 were less than $7,000 and 75 percent of them less than $3,000, in 1981 it was decided to decrease the number of awards by almost a third, raise the amount of most awards, and reduce the spread, so that over 90 percent of them were between $7,000 and $10,000. Appendices 3 and 4 start out with Earl Kim and Barbara Kolb, both winners of six NEA composer grants between 1973 and 1985, that is, almost every other year—which, as the grants were construed as for two-year periods, was the maximum allowed under NEA rules. However, table 11.2 shows that the Endowment's concept of diversity, in general, did not mandate gender equity. Between 1969 and 1985, only 10 percent of NEA composers' grants went to women; only 8 percent of the highest funded grantees listed in appendices 3 and 4 went to women (conclusions 3a, 3e, and 4d).[52]

51. With a few notable exceptions (such as Bernard Rands, who received a major NEA grant as well as a Guggenheim in 1982), there was little overlap between the eight to eleven Guggenheim winners and the highest NEA winners in the early 1980s and no overlap with the MacArthur fellows.

52. This was similar to the percentage of Guggenheim fellowships that went to women during the same period (10.7 percent), but considerably more than the 3 percent of grants from the Koussevitzky Foundation, 4 percent from the Fromm Foundation, and the 5 percent of Pulitzer prizes that went to female composers before 1986.

TABLE 11.2. Breakdown of NEA Composers' Grants, 1969–85.

	1969	1970	1971	1972	1973	1974	1975	1976	1977	1978	1979	1980	1981	1982	1983	1984	1985
Smallest	$350	1,100	900	1,285	331	1,280	625	800	1,000	1,000	500	1,100	7,680	5,000	5,000	5,000	4,000
Largest	$2,000	1,700	4,000	6,000	10,000	10,000	10,000	10,000	10,000	10,000	7,000	8,250	9,600	11,000	12,000	12,000	12,000
Number of grants	14	3	3	2	21	90	120	137	110	89	127	110	36	34	42	39	23
1000																	
Grants to women	1 (7.1%)				2 (9.5%)	9 (10%)	6 (5%)	13 (9.5%)	8 (7.3%)	13 (14.6%)	16 (12.6%)	12 (10.9%)	7 (19.4%)	2 (5.9%)	2 (4.8%)	5 (12.8%)	3 (13%)
99 (9.9%)																	
Distribution of money																	
$0–999	5* (35.7%)		1 (33.3%)		1 (4.8%)	2* (2.2%)	6 (5.0%)	1 (0.7%)			3 (2.4%)						
1,000–1,999	5 (35.7%)	3 (100%)	1 (33.3)	1 (50%)	6* (28.6%)	10 (11.1%)	25 (20.8%)	53 (6*) (38.7%)	18* (16.4%)	8* (9%)	5 (3.9%)	15 (2*) (13.6%)					
2,000–2,999	4 (28.6%)				3* (14.3%)	25(5*) (27.8%)	42* (35.0%)	44 (6*) (32.1%)	40 (4*)% (36.4)%	16 (2*) (18%)	45 (6*) (35.4%)	68 (9*) (61.8%)	2 (1*) (5.5%)				
3,000–3,999					4 (19.0%)	23(2*) (25.6%)	13 (3*) (10.8%)	11 (8.0%)	10 (9.1%)	17 (2*) (19.1%)	51 (8*) (40.2%)	2 (1.8%)					
4,000–4,999			1 (33.3%)		2 (9.5%)	6 (6.7%)	2 (1.7%)	12* (15.3%)	8* (7.3%)	8 (4*) (9%)	7* (5.5%)	13 (11.8%)					2 (8.7%)

350

5,000–5,999	3 (14.3%)	13 (14.4%)	22 (2*) (18.3%)	28 (2*) (25.4%)	21 (2*) (23.6%)	13 (10.2%)	8* (7.3%)	1* (2.8%)	11* (32.3%)	12* (28.6%)	10* (25.6%)	1 (4.3%)
6,000–6,999	3 (3.3%)	1 (0.8%)	2 (1.5%)	2 (1.8%)	9 (10.1%)	9	2 (1.8%)		6 (17.6%)	8 (23.8%)	5* (12.8%)	8 (2*) (34.8%)
7,000–7,999	1 (50%)	5 (5.6%)	6 (5.0%)	1 (0.9%)	9 (2*) (10.1%)	3* (2.4%)	1 (0.9%)	13 (4*) (36.1%)	5 (14.7%)	6* (14.3%)	3 (7.7%)	5 (21.7%)
8,000–8,999		2* (2.2%)	3	1 (0.9%)	1 (0.9%)		1 (0.9%)	11* (30.6%)	3* (8.8%)	1 (2.9%)	8* (20.5%)	2 (8.7%)
9,000–9,999			1 (0.8%)					9 (25%)	3 (8.8%)	2 (4.8%)	3* (7.7%)	3* (13.0%)
10,000–10,999	2 (9.5%)	1 (1.1%)	2 (1.7%)	2 (1.8%)	1 (1%)				1 (2.9%)	3 (7.1%)	3 (7.7%)	1 (4.3%)
11,000–11,999									3 (8.8%)		4* (10.3%)	
12,000–12,999									1 (2.9%)	1 (2.6%)	1	1 (4.3%)

*Includes one or more grants to women composers.

Furthermore, before 1975, no women served on the NEA's music advisory panel. As appendix 5 outlines, beginning in 1975, six women, five of them either college or university professors, were included on multiple granting panels: in 1975–79 Vivian Fine and Pauline Oliveros, in 1980–82 Tania Léon, Shulamit Ran, and Joan Tower, and in 1983–85 Daria Semegen. With other women also serving, albeit less often, women made up 20–33 percent of these panels. Still, their presence did not lead to any substantial support for women. The spike to almost 20 percent in 1981 was counterbalanced in 1982 by a drop to 6 percent.[53]

As appendix 3 suggests, a composer's educational background may play an important role in his or her ability to win NEA grants. Although it appears at first glance that the most frequent winners graduated from quite a variety of schools, a closer look at the list as a whole, as summarized in the conclusions at the end of the appendix, reveals a number of recurrences and trends. For example, whether a composer has a master's degree or a doctorate clearly has not mattered in winning these grants, for there are almost equal numbers of those holding the master of music, doctor of musical arts, and doctor of philosophy here represented, and only slightly more holding the master of arts. However (according to conclusion 3a), female grantees were much more likely to have only a master of music degree (six of the ten in the sample), and this included Barbara Kolb; only two women had doctoral degrees. Conclusion 3b shows that some degree holders won more money than others. During the period studied, those with the master of music degree won almost twice as many of the awards totaling over $20,000 and less than half as many of the awards totaling $10,000 or less, as compared with those holding other degrees. Probably because doctorates were rare in composition until the 1970s and 1980s, those holding the doctorate, by contrast, won none of the awards totaling over $20,000, and instead won 45 percent of the smaller grants totaling $10,000 or less. Still, conclusion 3c suggests that this trend may reverse in future years, for although applicants born before the 1940s have tended to prefer to earn

53. As table 11.1 shows, this pattern continued through the late 1980s, with the total NEA budget rising gradually to $133,113,529, the music budget remaining flat at $15 million, and composer and consortium commission funding rising slightly to $500,000 in 1989. Only opera/theater funds grew substantially, rising 59 percent from 1985 to 1989. Composers' grants also remained about the same, with twenty-one grants given in 1986, seventeen in 1987, twenty-eight in 1988, and seventeen in 1989, and the grant spread ranging from $5,000 to $25,000. These continued to be very competitive, with 416 applications reviewed by the composer's panel in 1987 and only 5 percent of these funded. Moreover, women continued to be disadvantaged. Only one woman won such a grant in 1986 (4.8 percent of those awarded) and in 1987 (6 percent). Seven women won in 1988 (25 percent)—all but two of them freelancers or students—but the next year, even with the nine-person panel in 1989 that included an unprecedented four women (44 percent), two of them freelancers (Larsen and Zwilich), only two women won grants (12 percent). Earlier favorites continued their successes: Earl Kim won again in 1987 and Barbara Kolb in 1992.

master's degrees, those born after 1940 were increasingly preferring to earn doctoral degrees.

The most startling conclusion of appendix 3 (conclusion 3d) is the dominance of certain schools. Half the winners graduated from one of eight institutions on the East Coast—Columbia, Yale, Juilliard, Princeton, Eastman, the University of Pennsylvania, Brandeis University, and Harvard—34 percent from one of the first four, and 20 percent from one of first two, which is even more than all those who graduated in the western states. Equally startling is (conclusion 3e) that although the women who won these awards resided in twenty states and abroad and 69 percent of them were on the East Coast—not much more than the percentage of grantees who went to East Coast schools—50 percent of them were living in New York at the time they received their grants, most of them in the city, and a good number were not affiliated with academic institutions. This suggests that having a career in New York afforded these women the recognition that women elsewhere may have had a difficult time attaining.

Appendix 4 reveals that 74 percent of these composers had academic jobs when they received their grants. Among the types of schools at which composers were working, those at universities, particularly research universities, fared much better, both in terms of the numbers of grants and the total amounts (as conclusions 4a and 4b demonstrate)—than composers at colleges and conservatories: 70 percent of those winning over $10,000 and over $20,000 were teaching at universities, whereas no one winning over $20,000 was teaching in a college. The appendix also demonstrates how much more money, 68 to 70 percent of the total, was distributed to composers working on the East Coast, as opposed to anywhere else in the country, and how (as conclusion 4b shows) certain schools—especially Juilliard, Eastman, Columbia, Harvard, and the University of Pennsylvania—are much more frequently represented than any of the others. Yet (if one compares conclusions 4b and 3d) it is clear that the winning composers were teaching at a greater number and wider variety of institutions than those at which they had studied, and that a more significant number of these composers were teaching in the West (22 percent), as opposed to those who had graduated there (15 percent).

Female composers (according to conclusion 4d) received only 4.9 percent of these grants, and far fewer of them were in academic positions than their male counterparts: 50 percent, as opposed to 75 percent. Whereas both men and women were similar in the likelihood of their teaching at conservatories and colleges, there was an inverse relationship between the men and the women when it came to positions at universities or no educational affiliation at all. Moreover, the most successful of these women, in terms of total grants and amounts received—Kolb, Priscilla McLean, Doris Hays, Margaret Garwood, and Lucia Dlugoszewski—were *not*, for the most part, in teaching positions when they received the grants. This suggests that the network linking universities to NEA grants before 1985 for the most part did not benefit women.

Appendix 5, a brief examination of the educational background and institutional affiliation of the most frequent NEA panelists (responsible for choosing the grant winners) may provide one reason why three schools appear more often than the others in the conclusions of appendices 3 and 4. Even though in 1978 Livingston Biddle, the Endowment's chairman, instituted a rotation policy for program directors, thereby limiting the tenure of panelists as well as directors, conclusion 5a demonstrates that more panelists studied at Eastman, Columbia, and Juilliard than at any other school. Only one of the women in this group, Joan Tower, studied at one of these institutions. Furthermore, a majority of frequent panelists, 50 percent of both men and women, were teaching at universities, as opposed to 25 percent in administrative positions and 25 percent at colleges and conservatories. However, whereas only one female panelist had a doctoral degree (Joan Tower), 63 percent of male panelists had doctoral degrees. In terms of serving on the composer panels, women seem also to have been at a disadvantage because of not having higher degrees and an education at one of the powerful institutions.[54]

The preferential treatment which composers associated with Eastman, Columbia, and Juilliard have received is explicitly demonstrated in appendix 6, which examines annually and on an individual basis various relationships between the panelists and the seventy-nine composers who won the highest grants each year (according to the annual breakdown in table 11.2). Twice as many of these winners got their degrees from Eastman (as conclusion 6b shows). In 1974, for example, three winners in the top 9 percent—Alec Wilder, Dominick Argento, and Ussachevsky—studied at Eastman and with the same teacher, Howard Hanson, as did two of the panelists, Jacob Avshalomov and Ward. From 1975 to 1979, five more graduates from Eastman and two composers teaching there were awarded high grants, while four panelists from the same alma mater served on planning and composer panels: the composers listed on this appendix, as well as the voice professor Jan DeGaetani, who served on the composer panel in 1978 and 1979.[55] And in 1983 and 1984, when two others from Eastman, Samuel Adler and Joseph Schwantner, were on the panel, two of their colleagues, Sydney Hodkinson and Christopher Rouse, also received grants. While this does not prove that panelists from Eastman deliberately intended to help their friends or successors at the same school, it does suggest that panelists tended to value the education they received or about which they were most fully aware.

Columbia—where the chairman of the NEA composer-librettist panel, Ezra Laderman, got his master's degree, and where the cochairman of the NEA planning

---

54. In 1981, the composers Margaret Garwood and Ursula Mamlok were on the composer panels. Throughout the early 1980s, Libby Larsen, while not a professor, served on other NEA music panels that helped composers, in the categories "New Music Performances," "Music Recording," and "Festivals."

55. In 1974–76, Bethany Beardsley, voice professor at Harvard, also served on this panel.

panel, Jacob Avshalomov, was a professor from 1946 to 1954—also attracted a large number of the most important grants for its graduates and professors, perhaps for the same reasons already mentioned. When Davidovsky, for example, was on the panel, his colleagues Ussachevsky and Chou Wen-Chung received major grants. Columbia graduates Wuorinen and David Hykes, as well as a professor at Columbia, Fred Lerdahl, also won grants when, from 1980 to 1982, two fellow graduates of the same generation, Charles Dodge and Joan Tower, served on the panel.

Juilliard's graduates and professors occasionally also did well. In 1976, for example, four composers—Elliott Carter, Vincent Persichetti, and Burrill Phillips, who were teaching or had taught at Juilliard, and Henry Brant, who had studied there—each received one of the highest grants, while Norman Lloyd, a professor there from 1946 to 1963, was on the panel. The first year Persichetti was a panelist in 1977, two Juilliard colleagues from his generation, David Diamond and Hugo Weisgall, were also awarded significant grants.

Some years the graduates of other universities received a significant number of the highest grants. Again, that a composer studied at an institution may have had no bearing on other generations of graduates' ability to win grants. There are other friendships and alliances beyond old school ties. Nonetheless, this appendix is suggestive. In 1981, for example, three of the five top winners had studied at Princeton (perhaps supported by the two panelists from Columbia, traditionally an ally of Princeton). In 1984, two of the top eight winners had studied at Yale, where the panelist Daria Semegen had studied, albeit at a different time. Colleagues and students at the same school as the panelists also did well, even though, according to Oliveros, it was common for a panelist to leave the room during the vote on the application of someone from the same institution as that panelist. The committee on which Richard Felciano and Pauline Oliveros served awarded high grants to their University of California colleagues in 1975, 1977, and 1979. Perhaps due to their support, composers teaching at the UC San Diego (according to conclusion 4b) received more of the highest grants than those teaching anywhere else. The appendix suggests other connections as well. In 1978, a student from Stanford received a grant when a Stanford professor, Loren Rush, was on the panel, and a colleague of Vivian Fine got one when Fine was on it. In 1980, students at schools where Jacob Druckman and Morton Subotnick taught also won grants when these composers served on the panel. And in one case, that of Carlisle Floyd, a composer received a grant the same year, 1975, during which he served on another NEA panel. With a full study of all the panelists, not merely those who served three or more times, it might be possible to trace still more links between panelists and grant winners, as well as other links besides those of the university, although to prove any real correlation, one would have to examine NEA archives.

Three more conclusions remain to be drawn from appendix 6. First, as shown in the other appendices, women were at a disadvantage. On only four occasions did women receive among the highest grants—5 percent of those in appendix 6—and their academic affiliation could not have helped them. None of them worked at the major academic institutions: three were freelance musicians, and two were from out-of-way institutions in Vermont and Hawaii. By contrast, of the 95 percent male grant winners in appendix 6, the percentage with university jobs is very high, particularly between 1973 and 1979. In 1974 and 1975, for example, seven of the top eight and nine of the top nine winners, respectively, worked for academic institutions. Second, beginning in 1980, when both the panel changed entirely and the applications began to be judged blind, that is, without names attached to them, this dominance by academia-based composers is no longer necessarily true. In 1980, only two of the top seven winners had academic positions. In addition, from 1980 to 1985, increasing numbers of students and lesser known composers received these grants. Third, one will note (in comparing conclusions 6b and 6c) that after 1979, when grants began to be judged blind, no Eastman graduates received grants and no composers teaching at Juilliard or a number of other schools received grants either.[56] These facts seem to suggest, though by no means do they prove, that an association with Eastman, Juilliard, or some other prominent university can help a composer more when such an association is known. In 1986 the panel, not completely happy with the results of blind judging of its grant applications, decided to limit blind judging to the final stage in their review only, after all the initial eliminations had been effected with full knowledge of who the applicants were. After 1987, according to the panelist Bernard Rands, the NEA decided to eliminate blind judging and return to its earlier procedures. Another study will be needed to examine whether a composer's university association continued to play an important role in the ability to win such a grant.

It is difficult, of course, if not impossible, to ascertain whether the schools receiving favor from the NEA were producing students whose music had a style that the panelists preferred—be it the conservatism at Eastman, the electronics at Columbia, the experimentation at UC San Diego, or similar aesthetics associated with one of their allies. In addition, we can never know if the panelists at times voted in expression of certain loyalties or if the awards only coincidentally ended up going to colleagues and fellow graduates of the same universities. It is, furthermore, not clear whether some institutions advise composers better on the preparation of grant applications than others and what role this help might play in their ability to win grants. Nonetheless, clearly the NEA and male composers in academic institutions have had a symbiotic relationship for almost twenty years. A composer's academic credentials, if known to the panelists, would seem to provide the NEA with a guarantee of credibility; NEA grants, in turn, have helped academic institutions to evaluate composers other than by examining press criticism. To

---

56. Reynolds, for example, received three grants while Oliveros was on the granting panel (in 1975, 1977, and 1979) but none in the early 1980s after Oliveros stepped down.

reap the benefits of working in an American academic institution, a composer need not win such grants or use an academic affiliation to enhance his or her reputation. Other grants and prizes can also contribute. But this study demonstrates that academic institutions have the potential to help a composer in political as well as economic, social, and musical ways, and some such institutions more than others.

THE NEA AND TRENDS IN THE 1980S

In the 1980s, the situation of the American composer began to change. Whether fluctuations in NEA policy effected some of these changes or merely responded to them, an examination of NEA funding patterns provides a way to trace and articulate new support that was subsequently given to composers outside universities.

Four aspects of NEA funding typically varied: who was funded, how many received grants, in what amounts, and how the money was distributed among the grant winners. As tables 11.1 and 11.2 show, funding for composers increased dramatically in 1974, when the NEA instituted the composer-librettist category, for before that time, most of the grants had gone to organizations such as orchestras. Between 1974 and 1980, when the total composer budget was increased to over $320,000, composer grants constituted a little over 2 percent of the total annual budget for music, the exact amount following fluctuations in the total budget, except in 1983 and 1985, when, with the consortium commissions included, it rose to over 3 percent. In this category, the NEA awarded between 90 and 137 grants each year; the vast majority of these grants were small sums of less than $3,000.[57] (Such grants could cover expenses in writing or copying a piece of music, or a composer's time. In effect, however, most functioned as awards of distinction.) When in 1981 the composer-librettist budget was reduced by more than a third, the number of composers funded was cut to twenty-five: the grants increased to between $7,000 and $10,000, and the distribution thus narrowed significantly. Although the budget was subsequently increased somewhat and the grants distributed in a wider variety of amounts, the number of composers funded continued to remain between twenty-three and thirty-seven through 1985.

Around the same time as these changes in the composer-librettist grants, the NEA instigated a number of new programs. While they were perhaps not specifically created to help the freelance composer, they nevertheless had that effect. Some of them supported composers indirectly by underwriting performances. The "Contemporary Music Performance" category (table 11.1, col. 6), started in 1976, rapidly grew in importance. Beginning in 1979, it had more money to give than the composers program, and regularly funded a number of groups with whom

57. As table 11.2 shows, the grants of less than $3,000 made up 60 percent of the total number awarded in 1975, 70 percent in 1976, 53 percent in 1977, 75 percent in 1979, and 73 percent in 1980.

composers have worked, such as the Glass and Reich ensembles. The next year, the new Inter-Arts Division of the NEA (col. 8) and the "New American Works" category of the Opera-Theater Division (col. 7) started pouring an enormous amount of money into the support of mixed media, much of which is done by those working outside academia. In 1980, for example, the New American Works category funded the American premiere of Glass's *Satyagraha* with $25,000; Inter-Arts funded the same opera's Brooklyn performance with $17,500 in 1981 and the New York premiere of Robert Ashley's *Private Lives* with $20,000 in 1982. Many of these grants also went directly to composers who collaborate with other kinds of artists. In this category, women outside academia, for example, Meredith Monk, Pauline Oliveros, Libby Larsen, and Laurie Anderson, found an important source of support. Inter-Arts, furthermore, supported composer residencies at artist colonies such as the MacDowell Colony and the Virginia Center for the Creative Arts. In 1981, the "Consortium Commissions" category of the NEA's Music Division (col. 4) began to support consortia of three of more music organizations to commission works they would eventually perform. This involvement by performers in the choice of where the money goes took much of the power out of the hands of academia-based composers and marked a return to procedures used by the NEA in the late 1960s and early 1970s. In addition, the fact that in 1985 this budget was twice that of the composer-librettist category raised the question of the extent to which the NEA would fund composers directly in the future.

Three kinds of composers outside academia could take particular advantage of these NEA grants and others like them. First, composers who could perform and incorporated themselves into nonprofit foundations could apply for grants in many categories simultaneously. From 1972 to 1985, for example, the Reich Music Foundation received $5,000 to $7,000 from the NEA virtually every year, whereas Steve Reich himself received a composer fellowship only in 1974 and 1976 for a total of $3,950. Thanks to her performances, consultations, grants, and the help of her foundation's employees, for a time Pauline Oliveros was able to make as much money as she did when working as a full professor at the University of California. Although she was not able to depend on NEA composer-librettist grants, despite serving on the panel for five years,[58] other NEA sources supported her in 1983, 1984, and three times in 1985, especially the Contemporary Music Performance category and the Inter-Arts Division.

Second, those associated with local composers' groups that emerged all over the country in the 1980s could solicit grants as part of a performing organization and a center for new music resources, while still applying for composers' fellowships. For those who did not want to teach or could not find good teaching positions, such

58. The NEA composer-librettist panelists rejected Oliveros's application for several years before she received a moderate grant in 1984. She believes this piece won because it used conventional notation and the applications were judged blind.

groups in Louisiana, the Dakotas, Washington state, south Florida, Atlanta, New Jersey, Cincinnati, Minnesota, and elsewhere provided alternative support groups outside academia. Functioning as mini–art worlds, these groups set up their own centers of information; they shared knowledge, presented concerts of their music, and otherwise filled advocacy and networking roles. With such groups active and thriving throughout the country in the 1980s, Fran Richard of ASCAP remarked that New York was no longer necessarily the most important place for a composer to live nor where most of the innovation was taking place.

Third, after the early 1980s a small number of composers were able to make a living as composers-in-residence with major orchestras, thanks to the joint support of the NEA, corporations such as Exxon, and the Meet the Composer Foundation. Composers in these positions, for example, Stephen Paulus, Joan Tower, John Harbison, and Bernard Rands, were paid to write an orchestra piece during their two-year residency, organize contemporary chamber music concerts, host visiting composers, and advise conductors on what new music to perform. If they could also conduct their music, they had the opportunity to earn even more in such positions.

As fewer and fewer academic jobs became available and salaries went down in real terms after peaking in 1972, it became important for young composers to consider these options. As Oliveros pointed out, "There is a billion dollar music industry going on that doesn't have anything to do with the universities." While major foundations like Rockefeller and Ford no longer supported composers to the extent that they had previously, the NEA provided grants in many categories. As more and more professional situations for music-making developed outside academia, the American composer could turn increasingly to the marketplace, regardless of the advantages of an academic affiliation.

IS THERE AN AMERICAN MUSICAL AESTHETIC? A PERSPECTIVE FROM THE 1980S

The development of serious music in the American academic institution, particularly since World War II, brings to light three characteristics of American music. Most obviously, it is pluralist, although this does not necessarily mean that diversity of all kinds is as supported as one might wish. The existence of many academic institutions, both public and private and in every state of the union, together with the lack of both federal control over their funding and outside interference in their operation, has encouraged the blossoming of music. The composers interviewed for this study, whose music ranges from the most intellectually conceived and structured to the most improvisatory and undetermined, represent only a fraction of the many compositional approaches developed in American academic institutions. Two fundamentally opposed aesthetics, associated with the nationalists or the followers of European émigré composers, came into conflict within the academic environment in the 1940s and 1950s. They struggled for preeminence but ultimately became coexisting alternatives, along with other aesthetic positions. With no national radio station devoted to culture and the arts, the United States has never had any means of introducing a centralized distribution of contemporary music. Consequently, despite the modernist bias in NEA grants for two decades, pluralism will probably continue, especially as jazz, improvisation, and popular musics play an increasing role in academic curricula and influence composers of art music.

A second fundamental quality of American music is its propensity for change and synthesis. In part, this arises from American composers' attitude toward history and its traditions, as can be seen particularly in academia. Since little American music from the eighteenth, nineteenth, and early twentieth centuries is known widely—even that of Charles Ives was not widely celebrated until his 100th birthday in 1974—Americans cannot have the same relationship to their predecessors that Europeans have. Unlike Schönberg, who consciously built on the musical developments of Bach, Beethoven, and Brahms, or Debussy, who saw himself as working in the tradition of Rameau and Couperin, the American composer feels less burdened with a responsibility to continue a tradition, even that of his or her own teacher. For example, Erickson's most important teacher was Krenek, and his first preoccupations were with counterpoint. But he later turned his attention to musical timbre and made his own instruments.[59] The American composer is also more apt to pick and choose ideas from all kinds of cultures and all types of music—popular and elite, Western and Eastern, European and American—many of which are increasingly taught in American academic institutions. Inspiration for Erickson's music came from not only the American Harry Partch and the sounds and shapes of the California countryside but also Europeans such as Debussy, Stravinsky, and Mahler, as well as gypsy, Balinese, and contemporary popular music, including new age. Moreover, American composers may use these traditions in ways that differ from or even conflict with their original uses. Babbitt, for example, invented his own form of serialism, going beyond that of Schönberg and in quite a different direction from his European contemporaries. Erickson expressed such an attitude well when he said, "What we really do is compose our environment." By this, I think he meant that he felt free to pick and choose among all available musical traditions to make a language that was uniquely his own.

Because composers in academia are more or less sheltered from fluctuations in the country's economy and its politics, as well as from the necessity of pleasing the

---

59. The evolution in Erickson's thinking is reflected in two books, *The Structure of Music: A Listener's Guide to Melody and Counterpoint* (New York: Noonday, 1955) and *Sound Structure in Music* (Berkeley: University of California Press, 1972).

public at large, their music is often free of stylistic constraints, a third character-istic. In an academic institution, no one dictates musical style, although the culture of academia might encourage one kind of music over another. Review committees are often made up of nonmusicians who are not in a position to evaluate a com-poser's music in aesthetic terms. And even if certain values have been deeply felt at certain times and in certain places (as, say, Eastman), there have been no national norms that have led to their imposition on others, only occasional "fads" that come and go, as in much of American culture. Because American composers, unlike their European contemporaries in this century, have not had to live up to or break down preestablished norms, only rid themselves of domination by European cultures and develop a sense of accomplishment about their own music, they make style a matter of personal choice. If someone wants to write the most adventurous music he or she can imagine or tread a well-worn path, the choice is his or hers alone. In being pluralist, synthetic, and free from any one kind of stylistic constraint, American music is quintessentially of the twentieth century.

In the 1980s, the concerns of American composers began to shift. A new open-ness and mutual willingness to adapt emerged in both composers and art worlds beyond academia. Audiences were becoming better musically educated, thanks in part to the enormous number of performances in academic settings in the 1960s and 1970s, when the institutions were expanding considerably. Such composers as John Cage and Philip Glass achieved enormous popularity in part because of this change. In addition, since 1976, when the copyright laws changed, composers had more reason to be attentive to audiences, both within academia and outside it, because they began to receive more income for performances of their music than they had in previous decades. Academic institutions began to pay royalties, whereas before 1976 they had not had to do so. Local orchestras began to employ composers as consultants for new music and to perform their music. When a contemporary work played by a major orchestra is broadcast over national radio, a composer can receive a substantial sum. Moreover, as contemporary theater and dance compa-nies have begun to use more and more contemporary music in their performan-ces, composers have found an additional source of revenue. According to Barbara Peterson of BMI, in the 1980s a composer received $17,000 for the performance of a five-minute piece when it was broadcast over national television during a pro-gram about contemporary dance.

While the academic institution was still central in the world of contemporary music in the mid-1980s, it was an open question whether its relative role had peaked, at least as a power broker. As funding became increasingly available to composers outside academia, the importance of NEA grants to composers was diffused. Blind judging at the NEA led to support for a wider range of composers, some without close ties to academia. Certainly a teaching position and an academic affiliation continue to be important influences on a composer's career. But as the boundaries become blurred between art music and other musical genres (whether jazz, improvisation, popular musics, or non-Western traditions), so, too, are those that have otherwise differentiated academia from both the commercial market and the concerns of independent composers. It is gradually becoming no longer possible to think of any one institution or art world as the most "significant determinant of the cultural musical life of our country."

Part V

THE EVERYDAY LIFE OF THE PAST

12. Concert Programs and Their Narratives as Emblems of Ideology

ℋOW DID THE FRENCH at the end of the nineteenth century understand their music? What did it represent for them? What did they do to construct and manipulate its meaning? Concert programs from the period give some fascinating answers to these questions. French critics commonly referred to concerts as *consommation musicale,* a form of musical consumption. Along with the other food metaphors they used, this image refers not so much to the public's participation in the emerging market for music as to their concern that music *nourish* the population. Many composers, patrons, and even state officials, too, believed that "concerts have a mission to accomplish . . . they are educators and it is they who have the honor of forming *musical taste.*"[1] "Music is not only an art, it is a means of education . . . a discipline, a way to cultivate feeling, in any case healthy recreation when physical play is impossible."[2]

Linked as it was with education, music easily became associated with whatever values different social groups wished to promote. From this perspective, I examine the concert programs of various musical groups. Important and provocative sources of reception history that have been virtually ignored by scholars, these programs tell a story about musical taste and the society's values. Studying them, year by year from the 1890s to 1914, we can trace the gradual repudiation of one form of modernism, commonly associated with feminine imagery, art nouveau design, and Beauty with a capital B, for another that was more male-oriented, abstract, and valued for embodying the new. The story is not without its surprises.

This essay originally appeared in the *International Journal of Musicology* 2 (Frankfurt: Peter Lang, 1993): 249–308; it is included here by permission, copyright 1994 Peter Lang GmbH. A shorter version was presented at the annual meeting of the American Musicological Society, Chicago, 8 November 1991, and at the Music Department, Brandeis University, Waltham, Massachusetts, March 1992.

1. "Lettre de Marseilles," *Courrier musical* (26 November 1899): 7.
2. Paul Landormy, "L'Enseignement de la musique," *Courrier musical* (1 February 1908): 78.

MUSICAL ASSOCIATIONS, THEIR REPERTOIRES, AND THEIR PUBLICS

After 1884 and 1901, when new laws overturned the Napoleonic Code, which forbade meetings of over twenty people without explicit police permission,[3] numerous associations of all kinds formed in France. With the growing interest in music, increasing numbers of concert-giving organizations arose. In addition to the opera companies in Paris at the turn of the century, there were five full-time professional orchestras (two of which performed seven days a week), other amateur and part-time orchestras, and innumerable music societies satisfying amateurs of religious music, Bach's and Handel's music, old music, music on only old instruments, only new music, and only French music. There were quartets and choruses, those serving the mandolinists and guitarists, and all sorts of contexts in which to perform.

Because my intention here is to examine changing conditions not motivated principally by state intervention, I focus this study on a selection of the major private musical organizations of the period, leaving aside the heavily subsidized opera companies and the Société des Concerts du Conservatoire because of the significant role state employees played in their musical decisions.[4] Three types of private organizations concern me here—the large orchestras, the music societies, and the musical salons.

The Concerts Lamoureux and the Concerts Colonne were associations of orchestra players that were both started by violinists who became conductors.[5] Both advocated for the recognition of performers as artists.[6] Although each received a small state subsidy (15,000 francs a year) their support came largely from subscriptions and a few donations.[7] Ticket prices were relatively low, 2–6 and later 10 francs, and program booklets were normally small, free, and on inexpensive paper.

---

3. Theodore Zeldin, *France 1848–1945* (Oxford: Clarendon Press, 1977), 573.

4. For an excellent study of this organization, see D. Kern Holoman, *The Société des Concerts du Conservatoire, 1828–1967* (Berkeley: University of California Press, 2004).

5. Both Lamoureux and Colonne studied in Bordeaux with the same violin teacher, M. Baudoin.

6. It is interesting to note that in a letter of 29 October 1904 to Gabriel Astruc, Chévillard refers to the musicians in the Association Lamoureux as "artistes" rather than as "interprètes." Gabriel Astruc papers, Archives Nationales, Paris, 409 AP 29.

7. To qualify for the state stipend, the orchestra had to perform a certain number of new works by French composers. The association's correspondence with the minister concerning which works counted as "new" and would thereby qualify it for its annual subsidy is a fascinating footnote to French music history. In a letter of 12 August 1897 to the minister of fine arts, Lamoureux explains his perspective on the arrangement as he complains of losing more money on the performance of new works that year than was received in state subsidy (28,000 francs lost compared to the 15,000 received). "Isn't there anything interesting in music other than the composers? And the performers who make sacrifices to give their

Their repertoire reflected not only public taste but also performers' preferences. Sometimes they were criticized for predictable programming, especially Lamoureux's orchestra, but both accomplished their most important goal, consistently excellent performances.

Lamoureux, who had conducted at the Opéra, the Opéra-Comique, and the prestigious Société des Concerts du Conservatoire, founded the Concerts Lamoureux in 1881 (it became an officially recognized association in 1897). After hearing *Tristan* in Munich, he decided he needed his own organization to bring Wagner to the French, because the Conservatoire's concerts were too "invariable" to accommodate this music.[8] From the beginning, the Concerts Lamoureux almost always had Wagner on their programs, sometimes several Wagnerian fragments. This presence characterized their concerts even after Lamoureux's son-in-law, Camille Chévillard, took over after Lamoureux's death in 1899. Perhaps to defend their support of German music, in the program notes—which remained virtually the same from year to year—the annotators made every effort to appropriate Wagner as one of their own. From the 1880s through the 1910s, program notes about *Tristan*, for example, begin with the sentences "The Tristan legend, so famous in the Middle Ages, is by origin Celtic and by consequence essentially French"; "Tristan is borrowed from a cycle of French myths"; or "Tristan is the son of Brittany." *Parsifal*, they write, "is borrowed from the Christian legends of France."[9] As for Wagner's other works, such as the *Faust overture* and *Rienzi*, they cite the composer's various stays in France, meticulously describing which parts he composed in Paris. When it comes to other composers, the program notes likewise point out any association the composers might have had with France. For example, we're reminded Gluck wrote his masterpieces for the French, Tchaikovsky had a French mother (or at least a mother with French blood), and so on. This kind of information invariably comes in the first sentence of the notes.

The Concerts Colonne began in 1873. Georges Hartmann, a wealthy music publisher, hired Colonne to conduct a concert series called "Concert National," intended to promote works Hartmann published. When this venture did not make

---

country beautiful performances that do honor to Paris, don't they too deserve some support?" Archives Nationales, F^{21} 4626 (28). I am grateful to Annegret Fauser for bringing my attention to this archive.

When he retired, Lamoureux wrote to the minister that, in good times, he passed on all the profits of their concerts directly to the musicians, never taking a centime for himself; in difficult times, he carried the group at his own expense.

8. Victor Debay, "Charles Lamoureux," *Courrier musical* (31 December 1899): 1.

9. The same sentence also introduces *Parsifal* in the programs of the Société des Concerts du Conservatoire. See the program of 10 January 1897, Edouard Risler Collection, Neuilly, France. I am grateful to Madame Risler for granting me permission to study the extensive archives of her grandfather.

enough money, he abandoned Colonne, but Colonne kept the orchestra together as an "association artistique" with the goal of "popularizing French and foreign music." As Wagner became associated with Lamoureux's concerts, Berlioz became linked with Colonne's concerts. Colonne, a disciple of Berlioz and Franck (with whom he studied organ), performed Berlioz's music 448 times during the first thirty years of the orchestra, that is, more than Beethoven, his second choice (374 times), Wagner (366 times), and Saint-Saëns (338 times). Berlioz's *Damnation of Faust* appeared on the Concerts Colonne every year an average of four to six times, normally on the first several concerts of the fall season, before and after Christmas, and several times each April. By 11 December 1898, the Concerts Colonne had performed it 100 times![10]

The success of such a work is difficult to explain. For each of these performances, the program annotator Charles Malherbe never fails to explain in detail how Berlioz was shunned during his lifetime and, in spite of having won the Prix de Rome, was ignored by critics and most of the French public, and that he had to fight for whatever support he received and pay for many of his own performances. (Malherbe was inclined to defend works that initially were not well received. In other notes, he makes a similar argument for Gluck's *Alceste*, Bruneau's *Messidor*, and Wagner's *Meistersinger*.) Perhaps Malherbe felt people should measure a composer's heroism by the extent of his struggle. Or perhaps Malherbe, like many others, thought the French had a patriotic duty to reappropriate a composer who had had more success in Germany than in his own country. Only after their 1870 defeat, when the French began to search for models of national genius, did the republicans reevaluate his importance, like that of Victor Hugo. By 1890, Berlioz had become a republican hero, with statues erected to his memory.

There were other differences between the Concerts Lamoureux and the Concerts Colonne. In 1903, when asked which series he preferred, Saint-Saëns responded, "Oh these gods! One is more precise and more cold; the other is more free and inspired."[11] A critic predisposed to Colonne wrote similarly:

> At the Lamoureux concerts (where the programs change so rarely!) you will often encounter more meticulous, careful, and precise performances; sometimes they achieve perfection. But this perfection is not without some coldness and some dryness. Their beauty is academic. . . . At the Concerts Colonne, the marble becomes flesh.[12]

10. For a close study of this organization and its repertoire, see my "Building a public for orchestral music: Les Concerts Colonne," in *Le Concert et son public: Mutations de la vie musicale en Europe de 1780 à 1914*, ed. Hans Erich Bödeker, Patrice Veit, and Michael Werner (Paris: Edition de la Maison des Sciences de l'homme, 2002), 209–240.

11. Balsan de la Rouvière, "Edouard Colonne," *Musica* (November 1903): 216.

12. Julien Torchet, excerpt from his article in *Semaine française* (March 1903), cited in Charles Malherbe, *Trente Ans de concerts 1873–1903* (Paris: Kugelman, 1903), 17.

Their repertoires, however, share notable similarities—after all, they were competing for some of the same audiences. Both performed long programs on Sunday afternoons to large crowds. (The Théâtre de Châtelet had 3,000 seats, the Château d'Eau at the Place de la République about the same number.) Until around 1905, both series normally consisted of an overture, a symphonic work, a vocal work, sometimes by a French contemporary, and some fragments of Wagner. (Sometimes one can find the same fragments performed on a given day by both organizations, as if in competition for the Wagnerians.)[13] The Lamoureux programs also typically included a concerto and some nineteenth-century program music (see fig. 12.1). When there were new works, they normally came in the middle of concerts in both series. The organizing principle, in both cases, was to include as many genres as possible. This preoccupation reflects both the late nineteenth-century French desire to democratize as much of the society as possible and the widespread belief in progress as boundless expansion.[14]

The repertoire of these concerts also reflects another notion of progress that was slowly gaining proponents. This is particularly evident in a second series of the Concerts Colonne that took place on Thursday afternoons in the Nouveau Théâtre (see fig. 12.2). Like the Sunday series in the Théâtre du Châtelet, the Thursday one presented as many genres as possible at each concert; unlike them, however, the Thursday concerts concentrated on chamber music. From 1897 through 1901, each of the programs on this series had two parts, the first called *musique ancienne,* the second *musique moderne.* Among the music considered *ancienne* were not only transcriptions of sixteenth-century *chansons populaires,* Schütz, Lully, Rameau, Bach, Handel, and Mozart but also Beethoven, Rossini, and Glinka. Their definition of "old music" thus extended from the sixteenth century through the mid-nineteenth century (Glinka died in 1857). Recurring *moderne* composers on the list included Chopin, Schumann, Brahms, Grieg, and their French contemporaries, some of whose works were here given first performances. This conscious juxtaposition of *ancienne* and *moderne,* each given equal place, implies a similar valuing of the old and the new.[15] Such coexistence also suggests an emerging notion

13. For example, on 31 March 1899, both associations performed excerpts from *Parsifal* and *Götterdämmerung,* in addition to other Wagnerian fragments. On 30 November 1913, the Concerts Lamoureux did *Parsifal,* while on 14 December 1913, the Concerts Colonne performed it. On the thirtieth anniversary of the Concerts Colonne in March 1903, possibly so as not to lose their audience, Chévillard invited Siegfried Wagner to conduct the Concerts Lamoureux.

14. I discuss this idea at length in "France: Conflicting Notions of Progress," in *Man and Music: The Late-Romantic Era,* ed. Jim Samson (London: Macmillan, 1991), 389– 416.

15. I examine the precedents and the larger context for this juxtaposition in my "Forging French Identity: The Political Significance of *la Musique ancienne et moderne,*" paper presented at the annual meeting of the American Musicological Society, Washington, D.C., 28 October 2005.

CONCERT - LAMOUREUX
du 30 Octobre 1898

PROGRAMME

1. **Symphonie** en *ut* (n° 36) . . . . Mozart.
   Allegro — Adagio — Minuetto — Finale.

2. **Penthésilée** (Reine des Amazones).
   Poème de M. Catulle Mendès.
   Musique de M . . . . A. Bruneau.
   (2° Audition aux Concerts Lamoureux).
   Chanté par Mlle Lina Pacary.

3. **La Procession** . . . . C. Franck.
   Chantée par M. J. Gogny.

4. **Concerto** en *sol* majeur (n° 4) . . . . Beethoven.
   Cadences de Saint-Saens
   M. Louis Diémer.

5. **Grand Duo du Crépuscule des Dieux.** R. Wagner.
   Traduction Française de Alfred Ernst
   Brunehilde : Mlle Lina Pacary.
   Siegfried : M. J. Gogny.

6. **Ouverture du Freischütz** . . . . Weber.

PIANO DE LA MAISON ERARD

FIGURE 12.1. Courtesy of the Bibliothèque Nationale.

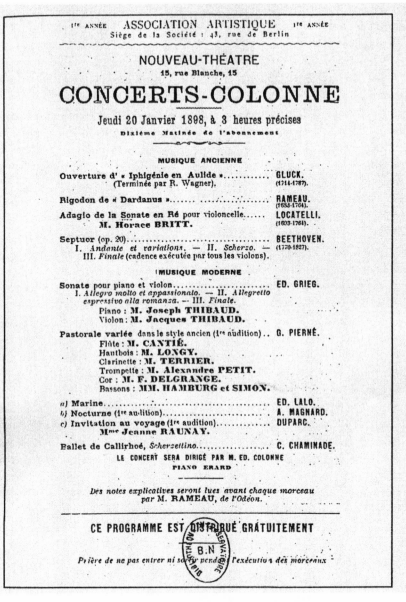

FIGURE 12.2. Courtesy of the Bibliothèque Nationale.

of progress as a spiral. In 1901, the aristocratic composer d'Indy began to promote an image of art as a spiral that must turn back to propel itself forward. He sought to draw on traditions predating the nineteenth century, the French Revolution, and the French Republic. Such a notion of progress became increasingly important in the new century. Gluck, Rameau, and their predecessors had been performed in these series since the 1880s, but, as we shall see, they played an increasingly prominent role in the concert programs of the first decade of the new century.

Two other orchestras, the Concerts Rouge and the Concerts Touche, attracted a somewhat different public from the Concerts Lamoureux and the Concerts Colonne.[16] Their ticket prices were all less than 2 francs and their venue the backs of brasseries. The atmosphere here was much more relaxed—concert admission entitled everyone to one drink (coffee, beer, liqueur, or, for an extra 50 centimes, champagne). Both series presented concerts every evening of the week, sometimes twice a day, and by 1907 were highly praised for their excellent performances.

The Concerts Rouge began in 1889 at the Café Rouge, a left-bank café, frequented by students at 6 rue de Tournon. The café was owned by Monsieur Rouge, who was considered a sort of Napoléon III, with a long beard. While playing in the small orchestra of five musicians at one of these concerts in 1897, the not-yet-famous violinist Jacques Thibaud met the conductor Colonne. In his memoirs, Thibaud notes that even though the Concerts Colonne paid less than the Concerts Rouge (who offered about double, i.e., 10 francs per concert), he left to join the Concerts Colonne because of their "enriching" repertoire—Berlioz, Franck, Saint-Saëns, and Lalo.[17] At the time that of the Concerts Rouge was certainly more limited; later, however, this series presented all kinds of music and a different genre every night. In 1908, for example, concerts on Tuesday and Friday were billed as "classical music," which could include Wagner and Debussy; on Monday, Wednesday, and Saturday, it was symphonic music, on Thursday chamber music. Once a month the Concerts Rouge devoted a concert to foreign music. By 1910, they were putting on entire Wagner operas after having performed major works like *La Damnation de Faust* the night before and difficult chamber music such as Franck's the same afternoon. With the "moral support" and financial help of a patronage committee formed in 1912,[18] the repertoire of the Concerts Rouge in any one week could extend from Gluck's *Armide* to Beethoven symphonies and operas by Debussy and Wagner. (see fig. 12. 3). The music journal *Courrier musical*, whose director took over the administration of Concerts Rouge in 1907–8, reviewed their concerts regularly and in 1913 praised them not only for having

16. I have not yet located their archives—only a few programs in the Bibliothèque Nationale, the Bibliothèque historique de la ville de Paris, and some reviews in *Courrier musical*. My perspective is limited to what I have learned from these sources.

17. Jean-Pierre Dorian, ed., *Un Violin parle: Souvenirs de Jacques Thibaud* (Paris: Editions Du blé qui lève, 1947), 270–82.

18. Among those asked to serve on this committee was Gabriel Astruc. See his secretary M. Masselay's letter of 9 January 1912 to him, Gabriel Astruc papers, 409 AP 29.

FIGURE 12.3. Courtesy of the Bibliothèque Nationale.

performed all of Beethoven, Mozart, Wagner, and Debussy and all the great works of Russian music (for orchestra and chamber groups) but also for not allowing their eclecticism to overshadow their consistently excellent performances.[19]

The Concerts Touche was started by Francis Touche, a virtuoso cellist and *premier prix* from the Paris Conservatoire, like most of the players in these two

19. "Salles diverses," *Courrier musical* (1 March 1913): 139–40.

brasserie orchestras. Touche began his career as a cellist-conductor at the Concerts Rouge.[20] When he was twenty-three, audience enthusiasm encouraged him one day to do an entire Beethoven symphony with only eight musicians! His success there from 1894 to 1906 led him to found his own concert series in back of another brasserie, this time on the right bank, at 25 boulevard de Strasbourg. The rectangular hall had the orchestra at its center, sixteen musicians or more as the occasion required. It also contained a Cavaillé-Coll-Mutin organ and held 394 seats. Like the Concerts Rouge, the Concerts Touche played every day, ten months a year. Unlike them, however, the Concerts Touche apparently did not have separate chamber music concerts, preferring instead to intersperse chamber works with orchestral ones.

The program booklets of the Concerts Touche, like the Concerts Rouge, consisted of an entire week's program. The format, too, was similar. Rarely were there explanatory notes, unless the work was an opera, although sometimes the Concerts Touche, more often than the Concerts Rouge, provided a sentence or two about first performance dates or the like. One of the few exceptions is a paragraph on Debussy's *Prélude à l'aprés-midi d'un faune,* performed at the Concerts Touche on 11 November 1909—exactly the same paragraph that appears in the notes accompanying the piece in the Concerts Lamoureux programs around the same time!

The Concerts Touche used a number of innovative techniques to attract audiences. In December 1907 they inaugurated a series in which composers (such as Camille Erlanger and Henri Rabaud) conducted their own work. They also initiated various marketing endeavors—listing the three metro stations nearby and their telephone number on the programs, allowing people to receive the weekly programs through the mail for 1 franc a week or 5 francs a season, and selling reduced-price ticket coupons (fifteen at a time) that could be used at the same concert, for the same seat at fifteen concerts, or for concerts later that year or the following year. Like the other orchestral organizations of the time, they helped enhance their listeners' experience of the music by occasionally selling miniature scores of the works performed (usually at a cost of only 1–3 francs).

Of the private music societies in Paris, the most well known to scholars are the Société Nationale and, to a lesser extent, the Société Musicale Indépendente. Composers formed these to present first performances of their works—the Société

---

20. Born the son of a highly respected piano maker in Avignon, Francis Touche was destined for commerce. However, he so excelled in his studies of piano and cello at the Marseilles Conservatoire that his family sent him to the Paris Conservatoire, where in 1892 he received his *premier prix.* Later that year, he was offered a job as professor of cello at the Nîmes Conservatoire. But after eighteen months, unhappy with provincial life, he quit to return to Paris, where he took the job at the Café Rouge. "Francis Touche," *Courrier musical* (1–15 September 1910): 604–5.

Nationale in 1871, the Société Musicale Indépendente in 1909. After 1890, when d'Indy became president of the Société Nationale, their membership eventually included composers both at the Conservatoire and the Schola Cantorum, Debussy, Ravel, and most of their contemporaries. Ravel and his friends broke off to form the Société Musicale Indépendente when d'Indy's control of the Société Nationale became intolerable. Composers in these groups were expected to pay for their own production expenses, but could call on performing members to participate. Although each society might hire an orchestra once or twice a year, most of what they performed at their fewer than a dozen concerts per year was chamber music.[21]

Much less well known are the societies started by nonmusicians, which depended for their existence on issuing stock and paying interest on investments to stockholders. The most important of these was the Société des Grandes Auditions Musicales de France, which has been very little known to scholars because until very recently the archives remained in a private collection.[22] This society was started by a coalition of republicans and aristocratic elites for the purpose of performing "first and foremost great composers from yesteryear whose masterpieces, too often expatriated, are unknown to thousands of French." The overtly patriotic tone of the initial announcements and the projected premieres of important French works brought in republican support; the older works attracted the wealthy aristocrats. The Conservatoire composers Ambroise Thomas, Ernest Reyer, and Jules Massenet served on its honorary committee, while d'Indy, Pierre de Bréville, and Fauré advised the president, the Countess Greffulhe, on which works to perform. The choice of Berlioz's *Béatrice et Bénédict* as the first production of the society in June 1890 reflects the politics of *ralliement* that motivated the group's existence. By that time, Berlioz had become a symbol of French greatness on which republicans and aristocrats could agree.[23]

As nationalism grew throughout the first decade of the new century, there also appeared in this society's programs an increasing interest in foreign music per se and in its national identity. When it comes to which foreign music to perform and which visiting composers to invite, the program notes make it clear that the organizers chose what their peers in Russia, Germany, Austria, England, and Italy

---

21. For two excellent studies of these organizations, see Michael Strasser, "Ars Gallica: The Société Nationale de Musique and Its Role in French Musical life, 1871–1891" (Ph.D. diss., University of Illinois, 1998), and Michel Duchesneau, *L'Avant-garde musicale à Paris de 1871 à 1939* (Sprimont, Belgium: Mardaga, 1997).

22. See chapter 10 here.

23. The closing scene of the opera may have been heard as a metaphor of this emerging political coalition. After years of fighting, Beatrice and Benedict are tricked into thinking the one loves the other, and they join in marriage. Their final duet, however, betrays the irony of the situation: "Better be mad than foolish. / So let's fall in love. . . . For today we'll sign a truce / And be enemies again tomorrow!"

considered their countries' best work. In this spirit, the society produced the Paris premieres of *Götterdämmerung* and *Tristan und Isolde*, sponsored various Diaghilev productions of Russian art and music, brought Mahler for the first time to France, and introduced the music of Vaughan Williams and Schönberg. As such, their concert programming functions as subtle flattery of their peers in other countries and an expression of support for nationalist energies.

The Société Musicale, founded in 1905 by Gabriel Astruc, is an example of a profit-oriented, market-driven organization whose purpose was to present concerts and theater in France, the French colonies, and abroad. Founded with 500,000 francs, against which stock was issued and a 6 percent return promised, this society was an outgrowth of Astruc's earlier musical activities, notably the journal *Musica*, which he founded in 1902, and the publishing house he started in 1904. Through the Société Musicale, Astruc sought to attract and respond to the desires of a wealthy public. On his patronage committee were not only French aristocratic names like Uzès, Murat, Ganay, Broglie, and Polignac but also the Americans Vanderbilt, Whitney, Gould, Hyde, and Kahn, as well as a number of Italians. The society's ticket prices ranged up to 20 francs, double those of the Concerts Lamoureux and Colonne, and often went even higher in the case of galas. Astruc printed his own programs, using expensive paper and many full-page photographs. They were among the most luxurious in Paris.

Like those of the Société des Grandes Auditions, sometimes a coproducer of their events, many of the concerts of the Société Musicale were devoted to foreign music and foreign musicians. Their first season in 1905 included an impressive four-day Beethoven festival, with Felix Weingartner conducting the Colonne orchestra, an English festival with the London Symphony, an Italian opera season, a Mozart festival, and prestigious recitals by Wanda Landowska and Ricardo Viñes. Over the years Astruc also brought such visitors as Strauss, the New York Metropolitan Opera, and the Ballets Russes.[24]

Musical salons, sometimes in homes and other times in public venues, are the most difficult to study, for in general most did not keep good records of their concerts. Music magazines and the newspaper *Le Figaro* are the best source of their activities. Those few programs that remain range from handwritten ones to, more

---

24. In addition, Astruc managed Saint-Saëns's American tour in 1906 and presented Parisians with English musical comedy. The next year, with the help of the Société des Grandes Auditions, he produced Strauss's *Salomé* and "Five Historic Russian Concerts." In 1908, he brought to Paris the Berlin Philharmonic, in 1909 a French-English festival, and in 1910 the New York Opera and a series with music organized by nationality at the Théâtre Fémina. From 1907 to 1913 he managed seven Russian seasons (Russian opera and the business affairs of the Ballets Russes), and in 1911 the Debussy-d'Annunzio collaboration *Le Martyre de Saint-Sebastien*. Astruc opened the Théâtre des Champs-Elysées in 1912, and there began four seasons of music, ranging from opera to ballet to operettas.

rarely, full-scale printed ones with notes. Some musical salons, such as that of Countess Greffulhe, were musical evenings organized for friends to perform for one another at home. Their programs tended to be mere lists of works and performers.[25] Other salons occasionally went public, renting public halls in which to perform. Jean Girette, the architect who designed a sunken orchestra pit for the Château d'Eau theater so that the Société des Grandes Auditions might give the Paris premiere of *Götterdämmerung* there, was a very capable amateur singer who, with his cousin, the pianist Edouard Risler, performed entire Wagner operas together. On 30 March 1895, Girette, Risler, Alfred Cortot, and their friends put on Wagner's *Das Rheingold*, according to their program notes "for the first time in Paris in private performance in its absolute entirety from the first to the last measure."[26] This concert performance with four-hand piano accompaniment was evidently also the first time the new prose translation by Alfred Ernst was used (it later became the standard). The program booklet for this concert, eight printed pages, provided extensive notes and excerpts from the libretto.

Among the most long-lasting, strictly organized, and well-documented private concert series is, ironically, one of the least well known. Founded in 1861 by the engineer Emile Lemoine, who enjoyed playing quartets with three fellow polytechnic students, the soirées of "la Trompette" began as an amateur quartet series for entertaining friends.[27] When increasing numbers wished to hear this music, it became a weekly private concert series, and the organizers began to hire young artists and rent halls. In 1878, finding other spaces too small, they moved into that of the Société d'Horticulture, at 84 rue de Grenelle, on the left bank. It had 850 seats. There, from late December to early May, they gave seventeen to eighteen concerts a year. Lemoine's wife continued the series even after he died in February 1913.

The audience, most of whom Lemoine knew, came to these concerts by invitation only. Lemoine considered them "very musical and ultra-select, with distinction and intellectual value but without snobbery."[28] To attend these "sophisticated, almost intimate" concerts, guests paid 50 francs a year. No children were allowed, except at Carnival. Concerts began at 9 p.m., often with a quartet. They

25. See the discussion of the society's programs in chapter 10.

26. The same group, including Thérèse Roger, Mlle Lundh, Maurice Bagès, Jean Girette, Georges Humbert, and Edouard Risler, also performed other Wagner operas, sometimes in public venues that charged admission. For example, they did *Die Meistersinger* at the Hotel des Sociétés Savantes, with the director of fine arts, Henry Roujon, present on 5 January 1897 and in a private salon on 7 April 1897; on 27 March and 26 April 1897 at the Salle Pleyel, audiences could pay 3–10 francs to hear Bagès, Girette, and Emile Engel sing the first act of *Siegfried* with Risler and Alfred Cortot accompanying on the "piano-double Pleyel, système G. Lyon."

27. The name "la Trompette" was adopted from a nonsympathetic remark a teacher once made to try to quiet the quartet.

28. Program of 26 March 1909. These programs are in F-Pn, Musique.

lasted around two hours—reputedly among the shortest in Paris in the 1880s.[29] Performers ranged from Conservatoire professors (Louis Diémer, Jules Delsart, and Paul Taffanel) to the Chanteurs de Saint-Gervais to visiting foreigners such as Weingartner in 1902, Serge Koussevitzky in 1907 and 1908, and Maria Freund in 1911, 1912, and 1914. Local virtuosi such as Risler, Landowska, Viñes, Jane Bathori, Rose Féart, and, in 1901, Francis Touche performed there as well. The series presented chamber works ranging from old music, sometimes on old instruments and usually by French composers, to the classics, to new works by contemporary French composers,[30] Scholists, and foreign composers such as Strauss, Hugo Wolf, Grieg, and Mahler. Most concerts combined a variety of styles, periods, and genres—songs, quartets, and other mixed ensembles. In the late 1880s, Lemoine was conscious of placing both *la musique ancienne* (or in 1896 *la musique archaïque*) and *la musique moderne* on the same programs, as was the case ten years later at the Concerts Colonne. During Carnival each year, the audience was encouraged to come dressed up and, along with "serious" chamber music, they were treated to "light fare" and chansons *populaires* from various countries.

The printed programs of "la Trompette," mailed to patrons a few days before the concerts, are a treasure for what they reveal about private music-making. Rather than giving notes about the pieces performed, these programs contain personal messages from Lemoine and responses to letters from guests (sometimes there were also translations of sung texts on separate pink sheets). Lemoine considered the concerts his "daughter," and his tone shows it. Sometimes he makes announcements, for example, informing guests of the building of a Beethoven monument in the spring of 1905. More often than not, however, and especially after 1900, he scolds people for misbehaving during concerts and reminds them of his explicit rules: absolute silence during performances, no saving seats for one's friends, no moving around during the performances, and no leaving early.[31] "La Trompette," he insisted, "is a salon where courtesy is necessary among the guests."[32]

---

29. In the program of the 12 January 1895 concert, Lemoine apologizes for the concert having to go past 11 p.m., "which is the extreme limit that experience has taught me for 'la Trompette.'"

30. The program of 3 January 1891 notes that at Lemoine's request, Saint-Saëns wrote his Septet, op. 65, for "la Trompette." Also written for Lemoine's series was a Sonata for trumpet by Frédéric Lentz "dans le stile ancien," performed there on 25 April 1896.

31. In the note of 22 March 1881, for example, he recounts how angry he was when, after Brahms's Sextet in B-flat was announced at 10:40 p.m. the previous week, half the audience stood up to leave and another third of the room left after the first movement. They should realize, he writes, that performers are paid for only one rehearsal and that, despite how busy they are, this group had rehearsed the work three times. If such things continue, as they do in other concerts, he says, he will be forced to discontinue the concerts, for no one would want to play at the end of one of them.

32. Program of 28 February 1908.

Such instructions to the audience concerning their behavior at concerts appeared as well on the programs of the orchestral series and public recitals throughout the 1890s and first decade of the new century. In the middle of the first page of most Lamoureux and Colonne programs, one finds something to the effect that no one will be allowed to enter or leave during the performances (Concerts Colonne, 31 March 1898) or "the public is informed that moving around in the hall during the performances is strictly forbidden" (Concerts Lamoureux, 1899–1906). At the Concerts Lamoureux, people are told in 1885 not to clap until the end of each act of *Tristan* and in 1901 and 1909 that no one will be allowed to leave the hall during *Das Rheingold*. Likewise, on many of the recital programs at the Salle Pleyel during this period, one finds the request "Please do not enter nor leave during the performance of the pieces." These ever-present statements suggest that, in spite of the difficulty of training the public to act in certain ways, a specific kind of comportment was increasingly expected at concerts. It not only helped turn concert attendance into a ritual, especially for the Wagnerians, but also would become crucial in the reception of complex, abstract music in later years.

CONCERT PROGRAMS: CHANGING REPRESENTATIONS OF MUSIC

From the 1890s to World War I, concert programs document a series of radical transformations in how concert organizers represented music to the public and, analogously, how the French thought of music. Malherbe once commented on these changes in his notes for Strauss's *Don Juan*, a work initially criticized for having "color" but "few ideas." Comparing this response to its Paris premiere in 1891 with its enthusiastic reception a decade later, he writes:

> Since 1891 the public brings to concerts a different spirit and some other perspectives. Without daring to say that their taste has been perfected, at least it has become more refined. They ask of music something more than pleasure for the ear. Their eyes are opening to new beauties. There where obscurity used to reign, clarity is now emerging.[33]

Exploring what concert programs of the time reveal about fluctuations in French musical taste leads us to Malherbe's perceptions, to question our eyes as well as our ears, to take note of new musical and cultural priorities as they emerge in these programs, as well as to reflect on the conventional practices of the time. Our focus, then, will be (1) the visual design of these programs, especially that

---

33. These notes for *Don Juan* appear in all Concerts Colonne programs that feature the work from the turn of the century until World War I.

of the covers, as well as the typefaces used for works', composers', and performers' names; (2) the order of works at the concerts, the genres preferred, the composers played, and the size of the orchestra; (3) the descriptive notes; (4) the extent and nature of the advertising in the programs; and (5) what changes in these visual, musical, and marketing choices might mean in terms of taste and ideology.

In the 1890s, the programs of the large orchestral series as well as the salon concerts shared important similarities (see figs. 12.1 and 12.2). Besides mixing many composers, genres, and styles at each concert, the most common attribute was a certain visual design. For the most part during this period, this design expresses little hierarchy of importance among the works performed. Compositions tend to be numbered in a vertical list and their titles printed in the same typeface and size, whether they are popular excerpts—like the Overture to *Freischütz*, Berlioz's *Marche héroique*, or opera arias such as the "Grand Duo" from *Götterdämmerung*— or symphonies, concertos, and program music. There is also little hierarchy implied in the typefaces that might rank some works, composers, or performers as more important than others. Typefaces are few in number and almost the same size, although music titles are normally somewhat larger and in bolder print than the names of the composers and performers, and performers' names are often the smallest during this period.

The exception to this nonhierarchical arrangement is in certain programs of the Concerts Colonne. Unlike other concert programs during the 1890s, those of the Concerts Colonne use a wider variety of type sizes and type styles, perhaps to draw attention to well-known favorites on the program. On that of 16 January 1898, for example, large thin type spells out Beethoven's Ninth Symphony and wide bold type Wagner's *Rheingold*, while a contemporary work given its first performance, d'Indy's *Istar*, appears in much smaller print between them (fig. 12.4). Still, d'Indy must have had some importance, for his name appears in bold and somewhat taller type than that used for Beethoven and Wagner's names.

The female figures that appear on many of these programs is their most striking aspect. In the late 1890s, on the covers of the Concerts Lamoureux, for example, there are proud women with long hair, enormous wings, flowing gowns, a laurel wreath, and sometimes one breast bared.[34] Each holds an ancient lyre. For the season programs of 1898–99, the winged woman is a barely clothed blonde playing the lyre (fig. 12.5). Over her head a star shines down on her closed eyes, as if to

34. Charles Lamoureux probably took an active interest in the design of these programs, for he himself was an amateur painter. In a letter to d'Indy of 17 June 1893, he writes, "I have thrown myself into my oil painting. I'm making wonderful countrysides, I've found some very unusual greens and I promise to decorate your study in Paris with one of my Dauphinois products. If you will, please make some room next to the impressionist masters that I admire for my next visit"; l.a. Lamoureux 9, F-Pn, Musique.

24ᵉ ANNÉE ASSOCIATION ARTISTIQUE 24ᵉ ANNÉE
Siège de la Société : 43, rue de Berlin

CONCERTS-COLONNE
THÉATRE DU CHATELET

Dimanche 16 Janvier 1898, à 2 h. 1/4 précises
Treizième Concert de l'abonnement

PREMIÈRE PARTIE

SYMPHONIE AVEC CHŒURS
Nº 9
BEETHOVEN
Traduction de l'ode de SCHILLER, par M. Alfred ERNST

I. *Allegro maestoso.* — II. *Scherzo.* — III. *Adagio.* — IV. *Finale avec soli et chœurs.*

Soprano	Mᵐᵉ LEROUX-RIBEYRE.
Contralto	Mˡˡᵉ Louise PLANÈS.
Ténor	M. CAZENEUVE.
Basse	M. AUGUEZ.

DEUXIÈME PARTIE

ISTAR, variations symphoniques (1ʳᵉ audition). V. D'INDY.

L'OR DU RHIN
(LE RHEINGOLD)
De Richard WAGNER
Traduction de M. Alfred ERNST

1ᵉʳ Tableau. — *Alberich et les trois Filles du Rhin.*
2ᵉ Tableau. — *Wotan et Fricka.*
3ᵉ Tableau. — *Scène finale : Entrée des Dieux aux Walhall.*

Alberich	M. AUGUEZ.	Fricka	Mˡˡᵉ QUIRIN.
Loge	M. CAZENEUVE.	Woglinde	Mᵐᵉ AUGUEZ DE MONTALANT
Froh	M. CAZENEUVE.	Wellgunde	Mᵐᵉ DE RUNA.
Donner	M. BALLARD.	Flosshilde	Mˡˡᵉ LOUISE PLANÈS.
Wotan	M. CHALLET.		

LE CONCERT SERA DIRIGÉ PAR M. ED. COLONNE

Orchestre et chœurs : 250 *exécutants.*

CE PROGRAMME EST DISTRIBUÉ GRATUITEMENT

Prière de ne pas entrer ni sortir pendant l'exécution des morceaux

FIGURE 12.4. Courtesy of the Bibliothèque Nationale.

suggest inspiration. The next year, the woman on the cover has dark hair, open eyes, and the lyre hanging from her arm (fig. 12.6). The curves of her hair and her gown imitate those of the incense smoke rising beside her and out of which she herself seems to emerge. Above her the smoke clears to reveal a halo full of other symbols—stars, small harps and lyres, hearts, and sun/moon circles.

FIGURE 12.5. Courtesy of the Bibliothèque Nationale.

These images suggest that woman was an allegorical representation of music during this period. The program of a private soirée on 23 May 1891 makes this perfectly clear, as the female depicted next to the numbered list of works is covered with musical notes and G clefs. Female figures frequently served as allegories during this period. They were linked with the idea of beauty per se, at a time when Beauty with a capital B was perhaps the primary aesthetic criteria in the arts.[35] Women, particularly their hair, were also typical symbolist and art nouveau icons signifying mystery and seduction. And, as represented in Emile Zola's novel *Fécondité*, written in 1899, they stood for fertility, so important to the Republic,

---

35. Throughout journals such as *Courrier musical* in the late 1890s, many critics used Beauty as their buzzword for judging favorably or discrediting entirely all kinds of music.

FIGURE 12.6. Courtesy of the Bibliothèque Nationale.

undergoing a population crisis.[36] But it is not beauty in general, physical eroticism, or maternal fertility that the women on these programs conjure. They, after all, are not real—they have wings—and they are surrounded with incense, a symbol of inspiration and the transformation of the physical into the spiritual. In such a context, their exposed breasts refer to music's capacity for spiritual nourishment and its power to seduce the imagination more than to arouse the body.[37] The long

36. Karen Offen, "Depopulation, Nationalism, and Feminism in *Fin-de-Siècle* France," *American Historical Review* 89, no. 3 (June 1984): 663–64, explains the numerous organic metaphors in Zola's *Fécondité* as part of his vision for a new republic, one based on defining women as "goddesses of fertility."

37. In reviewing Armand Dayot's *L'Image de la femme* (1900), the theater critic Paul Flat points out that woman's ideal function is to "incite the desire to paint not only with lines and colors, but also with words and sounds." Dayot's book, Flat explains, gives many examples of "the dream that this beauty brings to life in the most impressionable, the most sensitive of men." "Notes d'Art," *Revue bleue* (13 January 1900): 56–57.

and flowing hair likewise signifies vitality more than seduction, especially given that it is crowned with laurel, an ancient Greek symbol of inspiration, physical and moral cleansing, artistic achievement, and immortality. On the 1899–1900 covers, the images emanating from the woman's halo suggest that the program designer associated music with its roots in ancient Greece, with spiritual light penetrating the darkness, and with love itself.[38]

Interpreted in this way, such women, like the music they stand for, are spiritual sources. In the words of symbolist scholar Robert Goldwater, they serve as a "gateway to the imagination," an image of the "tension between representation and idea," and a "symbolic expression of the moral force which, for good or evil, woman exercises over the will and psyche of man."[39]

During this same period, the Concerts Colonne also put female figures on the covers of their programs, but not exactly the same kinds. At the Nouveau Théâtre chamber music series, the covers show simple line drawings of female performers. In 1897–98, these are two women in simple dresses playing small portable harps (fig. 12.7). Three birds in flight and some trees in the distance, together with a flowering plant in the foreground, place them in nature, where they seem to be wandering in no specific time or place. Unlike the allegorical figures on the Concerts Lamoureux program covers of the time, these have their hair tied up, perhaps signifying the disciplined restraint that music requires of performers.[40]

On the 1898–99 covers of the Concerts Colonne, four women are standing in a courtyard, the same women as on the 1897–98 program covers but here in unisex tunics and their bound hair now covered with laurel wreaths. Two carry small lyres and one a rolled-up page of music. The woman in the foreground is waving to

38. Three good sources that can be used to interpret the symbolic meaning of the imagery on these program covers are Boris Matthews, *The Herder Symbol Dictionary* (Wilmette, Ill.: Chiron, 1986); Steven Olderr, *Symbolism: A Comprehensive Dictionary* (Jefferson, N.C.: McFarland, 1986); and Barbara Walker, *The Woman's Dictionary of Symbols and Sacred Objects* (San Francisco: Harper and Row, 1988). In her study on the allegory of the female form, *Monuments and Maidens* (London: Weidenfeld and Nicolson, 1985), Marina Warner discusses the symbolism of breasts, particularly in sculpture on public architecture. Her discussion of Jules Dalou's "The Triumph of the Republic" (1899) and the female imagery on the Grand Palais (1900) and the Pont Alexandre III (1896) echoes some of my own points on the program covers of the period.

39. Robert Goldwater, *Symbolism* (New York: Harper and Row, 1979), 67.

40. While it is not entirely clear why some of these women have long, flowing hair and others bound, tied-up hair, the difference is significant. In *The Woman's Dictionary*, 313–14, Walker interprets Saint Paul's insistence that women cover their hair at religious services "because of the angels" to mean that "the spirits were supposed to be attracted or controlled by unbound hair." In Eastern religions, she explains, tantric sages have associated the binding of women's hair with cosmic powers of creation and its unbinding with destruction.

FIGURE 12.7. Courtesy of the Bibliothèque Nationale.

the others, as if bidding adieu to the end of the nineteenth century. The following year, by contrast, the image on the program covers is completely different, an anomaly, in that it is very localized in time and place with little left to the imagination (fig. 12.8). The woman is a buxom lute-player in eighteenth-century attire, with long curly locks under a flamboyant plumed hat. She is performing for a male listener of noble allure. They are outside in the grass under a tree that encircles them, and she is smiling as she reads the musical score before her. The specificity of this reference to the eighteenth century—a Watteau-like *fête galante*—suggests that perhaps with the advent of the new century, concert organizers were eager to remind audiences of how music connects them to the past. The reference also underlines the organization of this concert series, wherein *la musique*

FIGURE 12.8. Courtesy of the Bibliothèque Nationale.

ancienne—largely from the eighteenth century—takes up half of every program from 1897 to 1901.

In 1900–1901, the Nouveau Théâtre programs return to depicting a female figure in a generalized way (fig. 12.9). This time she is a winged conductor, her hair tied up, an angel in a night sky full of stars under a crescent moon. She is directing a little angelic singer, who faces her, reading from a score. In 1901–2, the covers show two more female performers, a violinist and cellist this time, in modern gowns and playing in duet—an especially appropriate image, as there were sometimes concerts of duos on this series (fig. 12.10). On the score next to these women (who have flowers in their bound hair), two small birds are singing simultaneously. The cellist looks up at the violinist as she plays, just as the birds face each other. Behind them are some

FIGURE 12.9. Courtesy of the Bibliothèque Nationale.

green branches—a symbol of honor, fame, and immortality—and a lyre that is somewhat larger than the performers and serves as a framework for their music-making. Like most images from these chamber music programs of the Concerts Colonne, this one suggests that music is something human-sized, a context for collaborative human expressive activity. It is not just an abstract art of symbols, represented by the lyre and the illegible score. The performers embody the music and give it life. Such an image suggests that chamber music at the time conjured a very different notion of music than did orchestral music. According to these program designs, the former was generally associated with actual performers, usually more than one; the latter, with its often undifferentiated sounds, more easily served as a "gateway to the imagination."

FIGURE 12.10. Courtesy of the Bibliothèque Nationale.

The program covers for the orchestral series of the Concerts Colonne (performed at the Théâtre du Châtelet) also feature images of women musicians. But unlike those on the covers of the Colonne chamber series, these women are not just performers. The 1897–98 covers show a prim and proper woman in contemporary dress, her long hair tied on top of her head, playing the full-size modern harp with pedals. Her face betrays no emotion, while her hands on the strings suggest grace and sensitivity. The imagery on the 1898–99 covers, however, is more timeless and allegorical, like that of the Concerts Lamoureux program covers of the time (fig. 12.11). Here, with a lyre at her side, is a Grecian-dressed woman again with flowers in her bound-up hair and breasts partially exposed. With quill in hand and a score on her lap, she is composing music. At her feet is flowing water that might symbolize the music she is imagining, abundant with possibilities and the power to

Figure 12.11. Courtesy of the Bibliothèque Nationale.

renew and transport elsewhere. A star hovers over her forehead, guiding her struggling spirit, and behind her are tree branches and a full moon, whose light, symbolizing intuition and imagination, is permitting her to write.[41] The city, with its bridges and churches, is far away in the distance. She seems oblivious to it, enraptured as she is, with her arms outstretched and a contemplative smile on her face.

41. Walker points out two additional meanings associated with the moon that bear consideration here: first, that the Greek name Europa (the mythological mother of continental Europe) means "full moon" and, second, that in Central Asia the moon has been seen as a mirror reflecting everything in the world. *The Woman's Dictionary*, 344–45.

FIGURE 12.12. Courtesy of the Bibliothèque Nationale.

On the 1899–1900 covers, the female figure is both a performer in modern dress, a violinist, and an imaginary character with those immortalizing laurel leaves atop her long hair. A lyre crowns the scene (fig. 12.12). Like the 1898–99 figure, the 1899–1900 one is standing on water, this time a quiet pond. She appears to be emerging from the water itself, like the lily pods and grass that encircle her and that the bottom of her dress resembles. In back of her is the outline of a large moon, in which are reflected a forest (symbolizing the unconscious, fertility, and enchantment), three listeners (two females and one male), three swans (symbolizing the ancient Muses), and a small edifice with columns resembling a Grecian temple. Such an image suggests that music is a beautiful flower of nature, an emanation of life's source (represented by the water), as well as a mirror of the unconscious and the spirit of ancient Greece. As in the 1898–99 image, the trees provide a backdrop to the metaphorical light of the music, and their shade also serves as a place of refuge and seclusion from the world.

On the 1900–1901 covers, the forest and pond reappear, but there are only two women, each dressed in the unisex tunics, as on the covers of the Colonne chamber music programs the year before (fig. 12.13). One is standing and has her hair down; the other is seated with her hair up. Since they are at the edge of the water, staring off, apparently caught up in their own musings, they recall the listeners in the background of the previous year's design. There are other reminiscences as well in this otherwise very stylized art nouveau drawing. One of the trees has arched around the women, as the moon shape did on the 1898–99 and 1899–1900 covers. The only musical image on this cover is a tiny *flûte de pan* (panpipes) lying silent and hidden among the grass in the lower right corner.

FIGURE 12.13. Courtesy of the Bibliothèque Nationale.

FIGURE 12.14. Courtesy of the Bibliothèque Nationale.

When an institution of high art turns to folk instruments to represent music in general, it is worth pondering the possible reasons, especially when the reference continues the next season. On the 1901–2 covers, the forest and pond are still there, the birds are now in flight, perhaps alluding to the movement of the music, and the idealized female figure, with hair up and one breast exposed, returns as a performer (fig. 12.14). This time, however, she is playing the panpipes. Did the Colonne program designers feel that depicting music in such a humble way was the most appropriate response to the beginning of the new century—after all, who could imagine what music might become? Or, more likely, was it that their replacement of the lyre of classical Greek society by the panpipes associated with the Greek god of the forests, Pan, followed a corresponding aesthetic change in their concept of music?

FIGURE 12.15. Courtesy of the Bibliothèque Nationale.

Both the design with the panpipes as well as the chamber music program covers showing the eighteenth-century couple put music in a pastoral context. This suggests that around 1900 the Colonne program designers came to associate music with nature more than with the imagination in general or performance in particular.[42]

The advertisements in the Concerts Colonne programs also depict females and in similar ways. On the back of the 1900–1901 covers is an advertisement for Pianos A. Bord (fig. 12.15), in which a contemporary woman muses in the lower right, across from a scene depicting Paris, and perhaps dreams of feeling like

42. See Brooks Toliver, "Debussy After Symbolism: The Formation of a Nature Aesthetic, 1901–1913" (Ph.D. diss., University of California, Los Angeles, 1994).

FIGURE 12.16. Courtesy of the Bibliothèque Nationale.

a queen, represented in front of her by the image of "la Parisienne," the statue of the quintessential modern woman built for the 1900 Exhibition atop the Porte Binet.[43] She not only reigns over all Paris but also has the entire globe at her feet when she imagines movers carrying an upright piano toward her. The ad for Pianos A. Bord the following year is completely different (fig. 12.16). Like the image on the program cover that year, it shows a female figure with her hair tied up and one breast exposed, surrounded by green branches and stars, suggesting inspiration and immortality. Smiling, she plays the lyre. At her feet is little Pan, a

43. Compare this image with a drawing of "la Parisienne," reproduced in Debora Silverman, *Art Nouveau in Fin-de-Siècle France* (Berkeley: University of California Press, 1989), 292.

mythological faun with goat ears and feet, who accompanies her on the panpipes. Even though this is an ad for new and used pianos, the only modern instrument represented is the cello at their side, shown from behind. The point is that one can sell pianos by selling music itself, whether represented by performing females, ancient instruments, or modern ones—all shown here simultaneously.

Around 1900, concert programs began to change in many ways. The covers of the Concerts Lamoureux programs in 1900–1901 and 1901–2, which are identical, no longer present female figures but are plain, sober designs showing a lyre over an open score. At the same time, there many more typefaces are used—fifteen in 1900–1901, as opposed to six in 1898–99. And, although the relative size of the names of works, composers, and performers is the same as on the preceding years' programs, one or two works are sometimes singled out with larger type than that used for the other works, especially in the middle of concert programs. For example, Liszt's *Faust* Symphony, fourth on the program of 3 March 1901, stands out in larger type, as does Beethoven's Ninth Symphony, likewise fourth on 27 October 1901, Lalo's Symphony in G minor, on 16 February 1902, Schumann's Fourth Symphony and Beethoven's Seventh on 13 April 1902, the first performance in this series of Guy Ropartz's *Symphony on a Breton Chorale* on 22 February 1903, Mozart's Symphony no. 38 on 8 November 1903, and Borodin's Symphony in B Minor on 16 December 1906.[44] It is interesting that in each case the program designers have used a larger size type for symphonies, whether classical or contemporary, in repertory or in first performances. Even though this differentiation does not hold for all symphonies performed during this period at the Concerts Lamoureux, it does argue for the increasing importance of the genre during this period,[45] and suggests that, in spite of the staggering variety performed on each concert, it is the symphony that the Association des Concerts Lamoureux saw as its most important genre.[46]

The year 1900 also marks a remarkable change in the size of the program books, especially those of the Concerts Lamoureux. Whereas previously they were no

44. The 3 March 1901 concert also included Weber's Overture to *Freischütz*, a Saint-Saëns work for violin, songs by Lalo and Saint-Saëns for voice and orchestra, an aria from Berlioz's *Les Troyens*, and a Wagner march; on 27 October 1901, the Beethoven was preceded by the Overture to Wagner's *Meistersinger*, an excerpt from Borodin's *Polovtsian Dances*, and the first performance of Debussy's complete *Nocturnes*; the concert on 13 April 1902 started with Berlioz's Overture to *Benvenuto-Cellini* and later included a Saint-Saëns violin solo, Emmanuel Chabrier's *España*, a minuet from Gluck's *Orfeo*, and an excerpt from Wagner's *Tannhäuser*.

45. For an analysis of this genre at the time, see Brian Hart, "The Symphony in Theory and Practice in France, 1900–1914" (Ph.D. diss., Indiana University, 1994).

46. This singling out of one or two works is rare in the programs of the Concerts Lamoureux in later years, whereas at the Concerts Colonne, different sizes of type were common both before and after this period.

more than four to six pages, after 1900 they expanded dramatically, often including up to thirteen pages of advertising—for pianos, organs, perfumes, train travel, and clothes. Over the next few years, the number of advertisements in these programs increased even more, as various concert organizations and music publishers inserted flyers announcing special events and newly published scores.

The most significant change in concert programs after 1902 is again on the covers. At both the Concerts Lamoureux and the Concerts Colonne, as well as at some salon concerts, male figures gradually replace female ones on the covers. The gender of the lutenist pictured on Louis Diémer's private program of 12 May 1902, for example, is androgynous, for the shapely legs and delicate fingers suggest a woman, while the short pants and medium-length hair a man (fig. 12.17). Perhaps she is Lady Music masquerading as a male bard, but gone are her traditional lyre and laurel wreath. On the cover of the Concerts Lamoureux programs for 1903–4, however, the figure is unmistakably male (fig. 12.18). Head in hand, possibly relaxing in a corridor outside a concert hall, he seems lost in a dream. The smoke rising over him contains an image of that dream, its sinuous lines recalling the incense encircling the female figure on the 1899–1900 programs. Out of the smoke, and functioning visually and symbolically as an intermediary between the male figure's thoughts and the dream itself, is a female figure with flowers in her hair and breasts exposed—Lady Music. From her arm, extended behind her, women warriors on horses emerge. With wing-shaped helmets, breasts exposed, and their hair flowing behind them, they are Lady Music given an explicit form, an obvious reference to the Walkyries. For the first time, then, the reference here is not music in general but Wagner's music, with which the Concerts Lamoureux had been associated since the 1880s.

The Concerts Colonne introduces male figures on their program covers beginning in 1902–3. Gone are the references to ancient Greek instruments and nature. In their place are a cherubic girl playing the violin on the upper half of the cover and a photograph of the conductor Edouard Colonne on the lower half. This is the first time I know of that an actual performer appears on a program cover of the time, and the first time there is a photograph instead of a line drawing. Probably responsible for this change was the manager of *Musica*, Gabriel Astruc, who began publishing the Colonne programs that year, along with the first issues of his monthly music magazine. In taking on the Colonne programs, perhaps he hoped to enhance the magazine's visibility and readership. Astruc was a promoter of performers and someone intent on capitalizing on modern life; he understood the market perhaps better than anyone else in the musical world. To distinguish his magazine from others, he used photographs on virtually every page. For the next three years, the covers of *Musica*, as well as the Colonne programs, present the same image—the idealized young violinist above a photograph of some eminent performer: Edouard Colonne on the Colonne programs and a different performer each month on the cover of *Musica* (fig. 12.19). Woven into the lines encircling

FIGURE 12.17. Courtesy of the Edouard Risler Collection.

these images on both covers are two excerpts of a musical score, and written overhead on both is "La Musique et les musiciens." This text suggests that while the young female violinist still represents music in general, the scores and the actual performers, be they men or women, begin to represent themselves.[47]

47. Women as well as men appear on the covers of *Musica* during this period. On that of the December 1902 issue, for example, there is a photograph of the Swedish opera singer Aïno Ackté.

FIGURE 12.18. Courtesy of the Bibliothèque Nationale.

The following year a more scholarly journal, the *Revue musicale*, took over publication of the Colonne programs, and all generalized references to music disappear, including the idealized violinist and the scores. Over the same photograph of Colonne and in the place of the violinist is a drawing of a smiling angel holding a plaque, on which the names of one or two composers appear. This drawing is identical to the one that appears with the magazine's table of contents and announces one of the subjects to be discussed in each issue. It is as if the music critics and historians who directed the *Revue musicale* thought of the composers performed at the concerts as they did the topics addressed in their journal. That is, the composers' names cited on the program cover point to specific music, as the image of the Walkyries suggests Wagner the same year on the Lamoureux programs. But because, as with the Lamoureux design, the references remain unchanged for the whole season, regardless of which music is performed at the concerts, the composers' names here function as examples of music in general rather than as signifiers of particular music.

When *Musica* resumed publication of the Colonne programs in 1904–5, the cover imagery reverts to that of 1902–3, though with some variation (fig. 12.19). Here we again have the entwining scores, as well as the little violinist; however, whereas she took up half the page on the 1902–3 design, on the 1904–5 one she is much smaller and is relegated to the upper right corner. The size of Colonne's photograph also increases to take up almost the entire page.

What led to this change on the program covers between 1902 and 1904—from females to males, from generalized images of music to scores, photographs of illustrious performers, even references to popular composers? In this limited context, we can only begin to suggest some answers. Feminism was on the rise, especially after the international women's congresses in 1889, 1896, and 1900 and with the formation of the Conseil National des Femmes Françaises in 1901. By 1900

FIGURE 12.19. Courtesy of the Bibliothèque Nationale.

there were seven women's organizations in France and twenty-one feminist periodicals.[48] Political writers who considered "the feminist movement a historical necessity" pushed women to consider themselves "a class."[49] Still, even though there were numerous changes in women's social, civil, and economic rights, most laws remained rigorously male oriented.[50] In 1903, husbands continued to own everything connected with their wives, including whatever art they might produce.[51] The music critic Willy's treatment of his wife, Colette, exemplifies the problem and points to the legal battles yet to be fought. (For years Willy published and advertised Colette's works under his own name.)

In the musical world, two significant changes may have contributed to the transformation of the program designs. Beginning in 1902, women were allowed to compete in the prestigious Prix de Rome competitions in the arts. And in 1904, with much public debate, the minister of fine arts opened the string classes at the Conservatoire to women for the first time. Perhaps as feminism became an increasingly important force and female musicians were more broadly accepted, everyone was less likely to idealize women, to use them to represent something other than themselves.

The design decisions made about the insides of the programs between 1900 and 1904 reveal important changes in values as well, especially the rising status of performers. The names of important soloists systematically appear in larger and larger type on the programs of both Colonne series—a tactic Colonne used only occasionally in the 1880s and 1890s.[52] Sometimes they are in big, bold type above the list of works performed, where they can take up one-third of the page, as was the norm in recitalists' programs. By 1903, a soloist's relative renown begins to determine the size of type used for his or her name. For example, on the orchestral program of 22 March 1903, the typeface used for the name of the famous opera singer Ernest van Dyck is even larger and bolder than that giving the name of the Concerts Colonne. Next on this program, in decreasing size, come two female opera singers' names, followed by those of two additional male soloists (fig. 12.20).

48. La Société pour l'Amélioration du Sort de la Femme et pour la Revendication de ses Droits, la Solidarité, la Ligue pour le Droit des Femmes, l'Union Universelle des Femmes, l'Avant-Courrière, l'Egalité, and le Féminisme Chrétien. See Gaston Choisy, "Le Féminisme en Europe," *Revue bleue* (January/June 1900): 271, 273. For a list of some of the feminist journals, see Offen, "Depopulation, Nationalism, and Feminism," 655.

49. Léon Parsons, "Les Congrès de l'Exposition," *Revue bleue* (July/December 1900): 59.

50. For a list of laws enacted between 1880 and 1914 that increased women's rights, see Jean Rabaut, *Histoire des féminismes français* (Paris: Stock, 1978), 240–42.

51. Louil Delzons, "Le Féminisme et la loi," *Revue bleue* (1 August 1903): 137–44.

52. In the 1880s, Colonne occasionally used very large bold type for major works, such as Berlioz's *Roméo et Juliette* and Wagner's *Tannhäuser* on 27 November 1881, and for singers' names, such as that of Jean-Baptiste Faure, whose type size is even thicker than that used for Massenet's *Hérodiade* and Reyer's *Sigurd* on their program of 17 February 1884.

CONCERTS-COLONNE
THEATRE DU CHATELET

Dimanche 22 Mars 1903, à 2 h. 1/4
(Vingtième Concert de l'abonnement)
AVEC LE CONCOURS DE M.

ERNEST VAN DYCK
DE Mmes

ADINY, DE L'OPÉRA
KORSOFF, DE L'OPÉRA-COMIQUE
ET DE MM.

CLAUDE JEAN ET GUILLAMAT

OUVERTURE D'EGMONT.................... BEETHOVEN.

PARYSATIS, Drame de Mme J. DIEULAFOY (2e Audition) C. SAINT-SAENS.
PROLOGUE. — *a)* PRÉLUDE — *b)* MUSIQUE DE SCÈNE.
  1er ACTE. — *a)* CHŒUR — *b)* DUO ET CHŒUR. — *c)* ENTRÉE DE PARYSATIS.
  d) MARCHE ET CHŒUR. — *e)* ENTRÉE D'ASPASIE — *f)* FINAL AVEC CHŒUR.

  2e ACTE. — *a)* CHANSON AVEC CHŒUR.
   b) SCÈNE ET BALLET (Entrée du Ballet). — A. *Allegro non troppo.*
    B. *Le Rossignol et la Rose.* — C. *Moderato.*

  3e ACTE. — CHŒUR FINAL (*O soleil de justice*).
    Soprano solo : **Mlle KORSOFF.**
    Ténor solo : **M. CLAUDE JEAN.**
    Baryton solo : **M. GUILLAMAT.**

LA DAMNATION DE FAUST............. H. BERLIOZ.
  Invocation à la Nature.
    M. VAN DYCK.

ADONIS, Poème symphonique (2e Audition)...... TH. DUBOIS.
  I. *Mort d'Adonis* (Douleur d'Aphrodite).
  II. *Déploration des Nymphes.*
  III. *Réveil d'Adonis* (Renouveau de la vie. — Le Printemps).
Sous la direction de l'AUTEUR.

a) **L'OR DU RHIN.** — Récit de Loge.......... R. WAGNER.
    M. VAN DYCK.

b) **LA WALKYRIE.** — Chant d'amour......... R. WAGNER.
    M. VAN DYCK.

c) **SIEGFRIED.** — Chant de la Forge.......... R. WAGNER.
    M. VAN DYCK.

d) **LE CRÉPUSCULE DES DIEUX**......... R. WAGNER.
  Duo du 1er Acte.
    Brunnhilde : **Mme ADINY.**
    Siegfried : **M. VAN DYCK.**

Orchestre, soli et chœurs, *250 exécutants dirigés par*

M. ED. COLONNE

CE PROGRAMME EST DISTRIBUÉ GRATUITEMENT

Prière de ne pas entrer ni sortir pendant l'exécution des morceaux.

FIGURE 12.20. Courtesy of the Bibliothèque Nationale.

At the same time, less and less space was devoted to the composers' names on these programs. For example, on that of 24 January 1901, the name of the director of the Conservatoire, Théodore Dubois, appears in the list in large type at the top of the page, directly under the names of Aïno Ackté and the other singers, whereas on the program of 22 March 1903, his name is noticeably missing from an analogous list and appears only in small type next to the works performed.

During this period, the Colonne program designers also begin to use typeface size to indicate the relative importance of the conductor and the number of performers. In 1901, Colonne's name appears in very small type at the bottom of each program; on 22 March 1903, however, it is equal in size to some of the performers' names at the top of the page. The Concerts Colonne also give increasing attention to the number of performers on stage when that number is larger than normal. On 22 March 1903, for example, they note 250 performers under Colonne's direction. Two years later, the typeface used to indicate the number of performers at a concert grows so large and bold that it begins to dwarf all other type on the page. When it comes to the participation of 200 children and 500 other performers on 22 January 1905, for example, the program uses print for these numbers that exceeds the size of everything but the typefaces of the work, Gabriel Pierné's *The Crusade of the Children*, and the name of Colonne himself.

The Concerts Lamoureux programs also increasingly draw attention to performers after 1900. Whereas the conductor's name is absent from their 1898 programs (fig. 12.1), it is in bold face on the bottom of the 1900–1901 programs. The name of the concert organization also increases in size and importance. By 1903–4, it takes up one-fifth of the page, significantly more than any other element of the design. For most of the first decade, that name, the place, and the date occupy one-half of the page, crowding the list of works on the other half.[53] This is quite different from the programs of the Concerts Colonne, where the list of works takes up far more space than the name, date, and location. Nonetheless, the Lamoureux programs, like the Colonne programs, begin to feature well-known performers, placing their names in large bold type above the list of works.[54] It is also significant that the Concerts Lamoureux, for the first time in the fall of 1903, and the Concerts Colonne, somewhat later, begin to list the names of the orchestra members and their instruments. In their notes, they also start listing previous performers of

53. The name of the Société des Concerts du Conservatoire, Lamoureux's previous employer, together with the date and location of their concerts, could also take up to two-thirds of the page on their programs in 1902, leaving only one-third to the list of works.

54. Other concert series—for example, those of the Société Nationale, the Schola Cantorum, and the Concerts Le Rey—treat major participating artists' names similiarly just after the turn of the century.

noted roles, such as the four or five best known singers who sang in Gluck's *Armide* between 1777 and the revivals of 1905 and 1906.

This is not the advent of star performers or virtuosi, of course, but it does document the increasing use of performers' names as a marketing tool. Without changing the basic concert formula of multiple composers, genres, and styles, organizers apparently believed that performers would attract audiences more than works or composers.[55] It should be no surprise, then, that just as Colonne's photograph remains on the covers of his orchestral concert programs until the war, Francis Touche put a drawing of himself on the programs of his orchestral series from its inception in 1907, and eventually even the Concerts Lamoureux used this design tactic. On their 1912–13 program covers, they placed a photograph of Lamoureux, the association's founder, next to that of Chévillard, its conductor since 1899. Concurrently throughout this period, organizations such as Gabriel Astruc's Société Musicale sponsored increasing numbers of solo recitals.

Keyboard manufacturers also began to use performers rather than allegorical females to sell their merchandise. In the fall 1902 programs of the Concerts Lamoureux, the ad for Steinway pianos, for example, consists of a list of performers who have played or intend to play Steinways—Ferruccio Busoni, Leopold Godowski, and Ignacy Paderewski, among others. Their 1903 ads reproduce letters from various performers praising the beauty, power, and solidity of the instruments. In 1904–5, their ads feature not only laudatory citations from Berlioz, Paderewski, and Liszt but also their photographs; in 1907 only photographs of famous pianists appear in these ads in the Concerts Colonne programs. Estey Organ ads during this period consist of a similar list of praising remarks, as do the Bechstein piano ads, which reproduce endorsements from Liszt, Saint-Saëns, and Pablo de Sarasate.[56]

The enormous variety at most of the concerts eventually began to wear on listeners, and complaints from critics, together with the example of a few performers, gradually stimulated programming that diverged somewhat from the traditional fare. In the 5 January 1901 issue of the influential political and literary journal the *Revue bleue*, the music critic Adolphe Boschot rails: "The big concerts have stopped adapting to the tastes of true music-lovers. . . . At least half the room already knows by heart the music it will hear." The overabundance of variety at concerts, he argues, makes them more exhausting than pleasurable. And it encourages composers to use the "most regrettable spices" to get attention. To counterbalance this, he suggests "composing" programs "as a poet composes a stanza, or as a woman puts together her apartment," that is, presenting works that

---

55. Performers' salaries also rose significantly during this period, especially for those who traveled abroad.

56. Unlike those of their competitors during this period, the ads for Pianos Alphonse Blondel keep the image of the idealized woman playing a lyre next to water.

bear some relationship to one another, whether all by the same composer or all written during the same period.[57] The success of Risler's six piano recitals "in historical form" in 1900 and 1901 encouraged this new approach to programming, as did Colonne's concerts that were dedicated entirely to Massenet on 6 November 1898, to Saint-Saëns on 4 November 1900, and to a Berlioz cycle in 1900.[58]

Between 1901 and 1905, Chévillard infused slightly more coherence into the Concerts Lamoureux by performing some composers' symphonies in chronological order. In November 1901, December 1902, and May 1905, he conducted the symphonies of Beethoven, in November 1902 those of Schumann, and in November 1903 a set of five Mozart symphonies. In 1902, Colonne presented all four Brahms symphonies. These symphonies continued to share the concerts with other composers' music; however, there were more and more exceptions. Compare, for example, the experience of two visiting composer-conductors: at the Concerts Colonne on 25 March 1900, Siegfried Wagner conducted works not only by himself and his father but also by Liszt, whereas when Richard Strauss came in March 1903, he conducted a concert of his own works exclusively. Whereas orchestras in the 1890s on occasion devoted an entire concert to Berlioz or Wagner, on 21 April, the Schola Cantorum presented an all-Debussy concert. The Concerts Lamoureux presented all Beethoven on 1 January 1905 as well as all Wagner on 24 December 1905 (still in the conventional assortment of an overture, three vocal excerpts, and six orchestral ones). During the first season of his Société Musicale that same year, Astruc sponsored an all-Mozart festival and an all-Beethoven one.

Arguably the most unusual development in 1905 were two concerts that focused on a single genre. On 19 November the Concerts Lamoureux presented only program music. And in February Wanda Landowska offered a concert entitled "Voltes et valses," in which she performed seventeenth-century *voltes* (a dance form originally from southwest France) on the harpsichord and nineteenth-century waltzes on the piano.[59] In the notes, Landowska explained the history of this genre. That

---

57. Adolphe Boschot, "Quinzaine Musicale: L'Art des programmes," *Revue bleue* (5 January 1901): 29–30. This notion ignores other more subtle relationship among works.

58. Although the Saint-Saëns concert focused entirely on that composer, it included all the genres one might expect on a typical mixed program, beginning with a march, followed by a piano concerto, a symphony, a vocal work in first performance, a violin concerto, and a symphonic poem. In his notes for this concert, Malherbe praises Saint-Saëns for having written for all genres and thus knowing "everything that one can know."

The Société Nationale put on two such concerts as commemorative gestures, the first one of all Franck on 24 March 1900 and the second of all Chausson on 9 April 1900. These, however, were rare exceptions and the only concerts they presented between 1890 and 1910 that included no premieres of new works.

59. This concert, which included Schubert's noble and sentimental waltzes (opus 50 and 77), perhaps inspired Ravel to write his own set.

year, she and the pianist Ricardo Viñes also gave concerts in the tradition started by Risler, that is, organized by historical period. Viñes did four spanning the history of music, organized by nationality and style, and Landowska did one called "J. S. Bach and His Contemporaries."

In 1904–5 and 1905–6, the covers of the Concerts Lamoureux changed again, this time totally eschewing allegorical imagery in favor of an increasing simplicity or abstraction (fig. 12.21). The covers for both years, as well as 1907–8, have a very plain border edged with stylized identical flowers that change slightly each year. Absent is any reference to music. The program booklets are smaller than before and on less expensive matte paper, although they are still published by the concert organization, unlike those of the Concerts Colonne during this period.

Some of the program notes also depart from conventional formulas during this period, changing their focus at times to argue similar points. On 8 January 1905, for example, instead of giving the usual biographical and performance history of the works performed, which had been the norm at the Concerts Lamoureux and Colonne, the annotator uses Beethoven's Sixth Symphony, Florent Schmitt's *Etude symphonique pour le "Palais hanté" d'Edgar Poe*, and Richard Strauss's *Tod und Verklärung* to question the genre of program music. For the Beethoven, he cites Victor Wilder, who, in a book on the composer, asserts that Beethoven was averse to programmatic music and believed more in "the expression of feeling than in musical painting." Then, just as the covers of these concerts had abolished references to women and music, he cites Wilder as promoting a similar tactic: "Abolish the program and the musical framework of the symphony is not less clear." The notes for the Schmitt work also diverge from conventional practice and seem intended to rebut anyone who might be tempted to assume a program in it. Before giving the text the work is based on, the notes say (perhaps in the words of the composer), "This music makes no attempt to follow the poem literally. It only wants to give an impression of the fantastic and imprecise vision that the Mallarmé translation suggests." After such an introduction, it is hard to read both the Poe text that follows and the argument given for the Strauss work without reconsidering the relationship between the music and its program.

The notes accompanying the 1906–7 Concerts Lamoureux also signal an increasing interest in the eighteenth century and a sympathetic nod to aristocratic preoccupations. The covers, printed on pale green shiny paper, are a complete departure from those of the two previous years (fig. 12.22). Like the Concerts Colonne programs with the eighteenth-century lutenist in 1899–1900, they are a complete anomaly. On the top is a drawing of a man in eighteenth-century dress and a wig playing the violin. A neoclassical garden design surrounds the image. The notes, introducing a new perspective, underline not the performance history of the works but the international experience of the composers performed. In the six lines given to Florent Schmitt for the first performance of his *Musiques de plein air* on 16 December 1906, for example, we learn of his travels to Spain, Germany, and

FIGURE 12.21. Courtesy of the Bibliothèque Nationale.

FIGURE 12.22. Courtesy of the Bibliothèque Nationale.

Turkey; and of Edward Elgar, whose Serenade was given its first performance at the same concert, we're told only that he is the most well known of the modern English school and that his works are often performed in England and Germany. This concert began with Gluck's overture to *Iphigénie en Aulide*, a work often performed with a coda written by Wagner in 1854.

In 1907–8, the covers return to the abstract designs of 1904–6, but the interest in eighteenth-century music and in the juxtaposition of eighteenth-century music with late nineteenth-/early twentieth-century music becomes even more prevalent.[60] On 19 January 1908, for example, the Concerts Lamoureux began with the popular Gluck overture to *Iphigénie en Aulide* and presented the predictable array

60. This juxtaposition builds on the tradition articulated by the chamber music series of the Concerts Colonne in 1898–1900 and discussed in my "Forging French Identity."

Association
DES
Concerts Lamoureux

QUATORZIÈME CONCERT
(Série B)

Dimanche 19 Janvier 1908

PROGRAMME

1. *OUVERTURE D'«IPHIGÉNIE EN AULIDE».*   GLUCK
2. *LES EOLIDES.* Poème symphonique...... César FRANCK
3. *DARDANUS (Fragments)*........... RAMEAU
   I. Troisième acte : *Scène 1re et Air.*
   Mme Marthe PHILIPP.
   II. Quatrième acte : *Scène III et Air.*
   M. Louis BOURGEOIS.
   III. Airs de Ballet : A. *Menuet.* — B. *Rondeau du sommeil.* — C. *Rigaudon.*
4. *SAUGEFLEURIE,* Légende pr Orchestre... Vincent D'INDY
5. *DEUXIÈME SYMPHONIE* en *si bémol*
   (en quatre parties)................... Vincent D'INDY
   I. *Introduction et premier mouvement* (très vif).
   II. *Modérément lent.*
   III. *Intermède* (modéré et très animé).
   IV. *Introduction, Fugue et Finale* (assez vif).

Le CONCERT sera dirigé par M. Vincent d'INDY

PARFUM ULTRA PERSISTANT
La Corrida
ED. PINAUD
18, PLACE VENDOME. PARIS

FIGURE 12.23. Courtesy of the Bibliothèque Nationale.

of genres—an overture, two tone poems, some vocal excerpts, short dances, and a symphony. The music, however, is limited to Gluck and Rameau representing the eighteenth century and Franck and d'Indy the late nineteenth/early twentieth century (compare figs. 12.2 and 12.23).[61]

61. D'Indy conducted this concert, as he did several of the Concerts Lamoureux during this period, juxtaposing his music with that of Gluck, Rameau, and his own contemporaries. He had just conducted *Dardonus* in Dijon in December 1907.

The extensive notes for Rameau's *Dardanus* on this program provide a provocative window on the contemporary fascination with eighteenth-century music. In them, ideology takes precedence over the works' performance and reception history. Excerpted from Laloy's analysis of the work in the *Tablettes de la Schola*, the notes present *Dardanus* as an example of music that turns its back on "the modern musical drama since Wagner, full of symbols and moral or social ideas." Laloy remarks:

> The opera of the eighteenth century is a festival [or feast, *fête*], not an instructive lesson [*enseignement*]. Everything here breathes of joy, magnificence; everything is more beautiful than nature; everything happens in a happy dream and perpetual enchantment. If the plots seem conventional to us, the episodes predictable . . . the feelings expressed in too florid a language to be sincere, let us not forget that these heroes . . . these gods . . . these temples . . . gave the public of the period what the dry literature denied them, that is, the emotions of tenderness and heroism . . . in a word, poetry. . . . There is no music that feels like his great lord more than that of Rameau, none that approaches this elegant liberated pride, none that gives the idea of a man so sure of himself and his thought, so perfectly born for leadership [*commandement*]. The entrance of the warriors in the first act of *Dardanus* is of a heroism without equal. . . .
>
> With time, Rameau's music has lost the harmonic and tonal obscurities that so shocked the large public of the time; it has become entirely clear and luminous. In this way, with unerring certainty, the genius of Rameau has revealed the path in which our music should proceed if it is to satisfy the new demands of our own sensibility.

Laloy was not alone in thinking of Rameau as a model from which his culture could learn, even if this music did recall the old world of "great lords," that is, aristocrats.[62] He and another respected critic, Lionel de la Laurencie, both published books about Rameau in 1908, and in May 1908 the music journal *Courrier musical* devoted an entire issue to Rameau. After hearing *Hippolyte et Aricie* at the Opéra on 14 July 1908, the music critic Pierre Lalo wrote to the minister of fine arts on January 1909: "There is a lot more novelty in such a work than in the combined operas of most of the musicians of our time."

---

62. Michel Faure, *Musique et société du second empire aux années vingt* (Paris: Flammarion, 1985), argues that Rameau's music was an emblem of the Right (280–85). He cites Wanda Landowska as among those who pushed for aristocratic art through Rameau. For recent studies of Laloy's and Debussy's attitudes toward Rameau, see Anya Suschitzky, "Debussy's Rameau: French Music and Its Others," *Musical Quarterly* 86, no. 3 (2002): 398–448, and Jane Fulcher, *French Cultural Politics and Music* (New York: Oxford University Press, 1999), 183–86.

Program annotators of this period also give increasing attention to Gluck's music, and gradually its novelty for them takes precedence over classical beauty or universal appeal. In 1899, for example, the Concerts Colonne programs describe this music the way the cover designers depict their female figures, that is, "as a pure and beneficial source in which the dramatic art of all times and all countries can drench itself." In 1900, the programs speak of this music as "full of unending beauty." In 1906, however, the notes detail a performance history of Gluck's works—*Armide*, they say, has been performed 382 times since its premiere in 1776. And in the 20 October 1912 program of the Concerts Colonne (when three of Gluck's works were interspersed with Debussy, d'Indy, Moussorgsky, and Wagner), the annotator goes even further, explaining the differences between the Italian and French versions of Gluck's music, summarizing Berlioz's appreciation of it and describing the revolutionary nature of its innovations, especially in the overtures.

Whether this eighteenth-century music was actually "novel" to twentieth-century ears or part of a ploy to reinvigorate eighteenth-century values at the expense of nineteenth-century ones, interest in novelty per se rose steadily after 1905 and eventually became an important marketing tool. On 13 August 1906, J. Guyot, director of the Société Moderne des Instruments à Vent, wrote to Gabriel Astruc, who was fast becoming an expert in music marketing, "We have done a lot of premieres and have the merit of being innovative. Don't you think this is a genre to exploit in our time?"[63]

Concert organizations, too, began to focus on the new, or the pretense of the new. The first "Concerts d'Avant-garde," produced by Astruc for *Musica* on 9 December 1907, presented five premieres—of works by Schmitt, Casella, Martin Marsick, and Philippe Gaubert—and recent works by Bruneau, Pierné, and Ravel, along with d'Indy's *Symphony on a Mountain Air* (1886). Although the title might imply otherwise, however, this concert was no more adventurous than the typical programs of the Société Nationale, none of the music being particularly "avant-garde" for the time. The orchestral series, too, occasionally departed from their normal fare around this time. On 26 January 1908, the Concerts Colonne performed a concert of entirely late nineteenth-century and early twentieth-century music. Debussy's *La Mer* was given its second Colonne performance at this concert. In the notes, Malherbe presents these works as exploring new territory. On *La Mer* he writes, "fantasy takes precedence over rules"; in Franck's symphonic poem *Psyche*, "the ideal dream of the soul reaches for the unknown."

Public taste was changing. Even the advertisements in the programs followed this increased interest in the new. In the program of 26 January 1908 described earlier, there is an ad for pearls showing a half-naked female inside half an oyster

63. Gabriel Astruc papers, 409 AP 29.

shell, under which is written "Novelty" [*sic*]. Likewise an ad for Belgian furs in a May 1909 program features in large type the words "To Innovation." At the same time, the number and variety of ads published in concert programs, especially those sponsored by Astruc, grew dramatically, sometimes at the expense of space for program notes—ads not only for clothes, pianos, train travel, and music, as before, but also for furniture and food. The quality of these ads demanded that they often take up full pages. Photographs in ads became equal in size or larger and certainly as good in quality as those of star performers or composers. This was especially true in the programs of the expensive series to which Astruc wished to attract high-class audiences. A 1908 concert organized by Astruc and called "Performance of Modern Works" features full-page ads for hats by Amicy and something else new—ads for banks, such as the Société Générale.

The taste for luxury and luxurious programs grew as aristocratic audiences increased, drawn by the increasing amount of music composed during the Ancien Régime. With its "Evening at Versailles" on 11 July 1908 and its "Evening at the Bagatelle Gardens" on 20 June 1909, the Société des Grandes Auditions sought to attract those with family dating back to the Ancien Régime as well as contemporaries with aristocratic pretensions. The entertainment consisted of musical and literary analogues to this audience. At Versailles, music by Gluck and Rameau was interspersed with *danses anciennes* by Fauré; excerpts from Moliére were followed by poems of Robert de Montesquiou and Henri de Régnier. At the Bagatelle gardens, Charles Bordes conducted Rameau's *Anacréon*. The programs and invitations consisted of very elaborate lithographs on thick textured paper. The cover of the Versailles program was printed in color.

Concert organizers conceived of luxury in specifically musical terms, too. Note the number of performers listed on the cover of the program for the Festival Franco-Anglais in May 1909. At this concert, organized by aristocrats and those in power for the purpose of increasing communication between the English and the French and acknowledging their political and social alliances, a thousand performers from the two countries participated. The year before, at a concert called "La France héroique" and organized by Astruc for a countess, there had been 2,000 performers, many of them children from schools in Paris.

By 1910, the number of ads in concert programs grew to overwhelm whatever musical information they contained. Even the most modest concert series such as the Concerts Rouge featured fashion ads in their programs. Moreover, critics, marketing managers, and the public began to think of music increasingly in terms of ever-changing fashion and fashion in terms of trends in music. That year, the music journal *Courrier musical* published a regular column among the advertisements at the back of each issue entitled "La Mode à travers les arts" (Fashion by way of the arts). In it, Jan de la Tour rails against the constantly new and ever more bizarre fashions, which he blames on certain women's taste for avant-garde music:

This title, chosen to flatter feminists, ambitious for the right to vote [*ambitieux de suffrages, même universels*], would become even more true with the variant, "Fashion by way of the artists." Three-fourths of all women have become worshippers of Debussy under pressure from fashion, which has made a god of this musician of troubling and perverse harmonies. Proud of their solid majority, the clothes of these devotees boldly celebrate the new cult.

In the May issue, he writes more of the same about Ravel and his admirers, "whose hats have the characteristics of his music. . . . When searching for new sensations and rare invention, when declaring Wagner 'finished' and Franck 'without any skill,' one does well to affirm a personal aesthetic even in one's coiffure."

Just as a woman's taste in hats and dresses might reflect her musical tastes, marketing managers sometimes borrowed names from successful musical works to use with their newest products. Writing of the spring 1911 performances of the Ballets Russes in *Comoedia illustré*, a critic takes particular notice of certain perfumes he smelled there to explain the extent of their beauty, elegance, and luxury: "Exquisite emanations of the perfume *Mary Garden* by Rigaud mixed in with those of *Prince Igor* and the hall [smelled like] a veritable bouquet of the most rich colors and rare perfumes."

Increasingly, certain concerts demonstrate not only an alliance between fashion and the new in music but also shared concerns and even collaborative relationships between aristocrats and avant-garde musicians. On 17 April 1910, the Société des Grandes Auditions, headed by Countess Greffulhe, sponsored the first French performance of Mahler's Second Symphony by the Concerts Colonne. (Among the many fashion ads in their program, one finds an unusual one for American shoes!) Among the first concerts given by the newly formed Société Musicale Indépendente was one on 4 May 1910 in which John Bull's seventeenth-century harpsichord pieces were performed alongside transcriptions of Javanese music, Manuel De Falla's music, and seven premieres of works by other Western composers. And then on 22 June 1913, the Société des Grandes Auditions joined forces with the Société Musicale Indépendente to present a concert that was not only international in flavor but also dedicated to the newest trends in contemporary music (see fig. 10.5). Beecham conducted first French performances of works from five countries, including Maria Freund singing the final scene of the first part of Schönberg's *Gurrelieder*, the final chorus, based on an Indian chant, of Delius's *Appalachia*, excerpts from the symphonic suite of Ravel's *Daphnis et Chloé*, and a work by Casella. This concert was also the occasion of the first concert performance of an excerpt from Stravinsky's *Rite of Spring*.

Concert programs help us to trace the history of musical taste and the changing values embedded in musical reception. Physical documents handled by many,

many people, they are important links between on the one hand, concert organizers and their musicians and on the other marketing managers and their designers. They reflect the decisions and compromises made by these groups, their
competing practical concerns and shared need for a public, the confluence of taste
and ideology.

This study suggests numerous conclusions. The most obvious and perhaps most
revealing is what the program covers intimate about what music meant to French
audiences and how this meaning changed over time. In the late 1890s, as I have
shown, music was associated with allegorical female figures and other images that
suggested fertility, spirituality, and the imagination. In the first decade of the new
century, however, images of male figures and of performers and musical scores
together with specific male composers' names replaced this allegorical and feminine imagery. This transformation not only offers documentary substantiation of
the notion that high modernism increasingly repudiated femininity in preference
for a male orientation;[64] it also helps us to date this change and to expand the
context for such a conclusion.

Program covers document a variety of other cultural and ideological fluctuations. While at the end of the nineteenth century imaginary imagery and the cosmos
permeated these designs, after 1900 nature begins to prevail. This shift, however
short-lived, parallels an emerging fascination with nature at the time. The *Revue
naturiste*, founded in 1897—as well as Debussy's articles on music in the "plein air"
in 1901 and 1903 issues of the *Revue Blanche*[65]—links a concern for nature with an
increasing nationalism in the culture. These authors refer to nature, for example, as
"le culte du sol,"[66] and discuss it alongside old French traditions, be they, for
Debussy, the "old masters of the French Renaissance" or, as suggested on the covers
of the programs for the large orchestral series, the wigged musicians of the classical
era. The arabesque lines of nature also draw attention to the merits of abstract
formal beauty, devoid of iconic value, especially as Debussy understands it. By the
middle of the first decade of the twentieth century, then, images characterized by
abstract designs and neoclassical references gradually replace nature imagery on

64. Andreas Huyssen makes such an argument in *After the Great Divide: Modernism,
Mass Culture, Postmodernism* (Bloomington: Indiana University Press, 1986), especially
chapter 3.

65. In "Debussy After Symbolism," Toliver suggests that Debussy considered nature "a
source of artistic renewal." At the same time that we find changes from allegorical to
natural imagery on the concert program covers, Toliver shows that critics of the time found
a similar change in Debussy's own aesthetics, one that evolved from presenting "idealized
images" of nature (in such works as "Sirènes" from *Nocturnes* [1900]) to translating nature's "shivering totality, [her] multiple life in all of its complexity" (in later works such as
La Mer). See Daniel Chennevière, *Claude Debussy et son oeuvre* (Paris: Durand, 1913), 37.

66. Bouhélier, "Manifeste," *La Revue naturiste* (March 1897): 1.

concert program covers, as well as those signifying ancient Greece (laurel wreaths, lyres and panpipes, Greek temples and swans) and the implication that Greece is the source of Western culture. Many of these changes, I suggest, coincide with the increasing role aristocrats and would-be aristocrats played in the musical world of the period.

Changes in concert programming between the late 1890s and 1914 and in the manner in which works were presented also reflects the flux in cultural values. As critics began to complain and audiences to tire of an overwhelming number of genres and types of music at each concert, many began to reject the notion of progress, especially progress as boundless expansion and its equivalent in the arts.[67] Around 1905, just before Georges Sorel published the articles that became *Les Illusions du progrès* and Wanda Landowska published her book *Musique ancienne*, arguing against the idea of musical progress, we find increasing numbers of concerts that are more obviously "composed," whether they are more limited in scope or more focused on an individual composer or genre. Throughout this period, we also find increasingly the juxtaposition of *ancienne* (pre-nineteenth-century) and *moderne* works in the same programs, particularly those of the chamber music concerts of "la Trompette" and the Concerts Colonne. And we find an increasing assertion of the value of the old even as the very new attracted more and more support, especially among the wealthy class. D'Indy argued for this coexistence by proposing a notion of progress as a spiral that, in life as well as art, must return to the past to propel itself toward the future. With some common goals, then, eventually the old-world aristocracy and the avant-garde began to collaborate: Charles Bordes from the Schola Cantorum helped to produce operas by Rameau at aristocratic garden parties, and composers of the Société Musicale Indépendente cosponsored premieres of contemporary works by the composers whom the aristocrats thought their peers in other countries most esteemed.

These concert programs reveal how the market system came to influence the presentation of music; how, after 1900, concert organizations increasingly used star performers and secondary material—especially fashion—to attract their public, and how the worlds of fashion and music became more and more responsive to and reflective of one another.[68] At the same time, these programs also intimate that the public had a deep appreciation for music, although it might have needed constant reminders about what would come to be considered proper concert behavior. The fact that miniature scores of the works performed were sold both at large orchestral concerts and at brasserie concerts suggests that much of the public

67. For further discussion of this idea, see my "France: Conflicting Notions of Progress."

68. For a recent study that builds on this idea, see Mary Davis, *Classic Chic: Music, Fashion, and Modernism* (Berkeley: University of California Press, 2006).

could read music and approached it seriously, no matter what the setting. That the program notes of many of the concerts take great pains to recount the performance history of each of the works presented implies that the public also took seriously their own critical responses to the music and were interested in comparing their perceptions with their predecessors' judgments, especially when a work had previously been ignored or critically rejected.[69]

Because this chapter attempts to offer a picture of those aspects of concert life that could adapt to shifting cultural values, I have chosen to leave aside concert organizations directly tied to the state and decisions that may have resulted from public policy. I have also underemphasized music societies run by composers, such as the Société Nationale, because in the past scholars have tended to overrate their importance in the French musical scene. It is true that such organizations presented many important premieres, but the state considered these premieres private— perhaps because of the limited size of their audiences (i.e., works premiered at the Société Nationale could be performed again in one of the state-supported orchestral series, and these performances "count" as among the new works the state required in return for its subvention). Composer-run concert organizations also presented a very limited number of concerts and tended not to be able to afford orchestral concerts, except perhaps once a year.

If more materials had been available, it would have been useful to have studied in much more in detail the programs of brasserie orchestras. The Concerts Rouge and the Concerts Touche presented far more concerts in Paris than the composer-run organizations, and certainly as much contemporary music as the large orchestral series. They performed chamber, orchestral, and operatic literature almost daily, despite the often limited number of musicians. They also presented repertory in ways that reveal what were the "greatest hits" and who were the favorite composers. (By 1908, for example, Concerts Rouge administrators had already categorized Debussy as a "classical" composer.)

More systematic study of individual salon concerts than has here been possible would also be very helpful. The salon concert programs I was able to consult suggest that many reinforce patterns we find in the larger public series. In the 1890s, for example, we find the same motley variety of genres and works listed without any hierarchical importance implied in the programs' layout or use of typestyles. Imagery of women and/or flowers decorate the few that use visual imagery, but most are mere lists of works. After 1902 (as fig. 12.17 shows), male imagery appears on occasional salon programs around the same time that Colonne's photograph appears on his concert programs. And by 1908, the programs for concerts given by aristocrats become increasingly luxurious, just as advertisements, especially for

---

69. Program notes during this period offer excellent performance and reception histories.

fashion, grow increasingly numerous in the various orchestral concert programs. Those for concerts organized by Countess Greffulhe and the Princess de Polignac, for example, are often printed on expensive oversize paper and exude opulence.[70] At the same time, their design, like that of the covers of the orchestral concert programs, embodies a classical restraint.

The setting these salon concerts give to works, however, is obviously quite different from that of the orchestral series. Because of the possible influence of a patron, salon concerts can sometimes shed light on the context of a composition's creation or its intended audience. In 1914, for example, Debussy's song cycle *Trois Chansons de Charles d'Orléans* was performed at the Princess de Polignac's home after *chansons* by Josquin des Pres, Orlando de Lassus, Claude LeJeune, and Clément Jannequin, "Chansons et Madrigaux" by Reynaldo Hahn, and two madrigals by Palestrina and Monteverdi. Both the forms used and the language of the texts here link the twentieth century with the sixteenth—they also foreshadow the Domaine Musical concerts of the 1950s.

Such a study can never be exhaustive or complete, or its conclusions true without exception. Of those concert programs from the period that still exist, rarely is there a complete set; even the Bibliothèque Nationale does not own copies of all the programs of the most important orchestral organizations of the time, the Concerts Lamoureux and the Concerts Colonne. Moreover, their collection of other programs as well as the private collections I have consulted are also incomplete, reflecting the interests and idiosyncrasies of the original collectors. Still, especially as a group, concert programs are precious documents. When read carefully, they provide a wealth of information about the contexts for music-making at the time, what music signified to the French, how that understanding changed, and how modernism became embedded in and accepted as integral to French culture.

---

70. While she does not reproduce these programs, Sylvia Kahan summarizes the contents of programs sponsored by the Princess de Polignac in *Music's Modern Muse* (Rochester, N.Y.: University of Rochester Press, 2003), app. A.

13. MATERIAL CULTURE AND POSTMODERN POSITIVISM

RETHINKING THE "POPULAR" IN LATE NINETEENTH-CENTURY FRENCH MUSIC

ECENTLY WE HAVE COME to think of the proliferation of "pop music" and its implications as products of the twentieth century. But a preoccupation with "popular" culture also drove much of the musical world of late nineteenth-century Paris. This period saw the rise of music-hall entertainment and big exotic spectacles, as well as more intimate café-concerts and cabaret. The former dazzled audiences with their endless variety; the latter offered simpler escapism and sometimes social critique. In part to combat their influence, those committed to serious art music—composers and performers, publishers and concert organizers,

This essay was published in *Historical Musicology: Sources, Methods, Interpretations*, ed. Roberta Marvin, Michael Marissen, and Stephen Crist (Rochester, N.Y.: University of Rochester Press, 2004), 356–87. Portions have appeared previously: in "Music in Service of Public Utility in Four Late Nineteenth-Century French Concert Societies," paper presented at the conference "Concert et publics en Europe entre 1700 et 1900," Göttingen, Germany, 26 March 1999; in "Popularizing Classical Music in Paris, 1870–1913: The Contribution of Popular Venues," paper presented at the annual meeting of the American Musicological Society, Kansas City, 4 November 1999; in "Ideologies of the Popular: Morality and Ethics in the Music Culture of Late Nineteenth-Century Paris," paper presented at the Music Department, University of California, Santa Barbara, 3 February 2000 and the Music Department, University of California, Los Angeles, 29 February 2000; and in "Democracy, Ethics, and Commerce: The *Concerts Populaires* in late Nineteenth-Century France," at the conference "Les Sociétés de musique en Europe, 1700–1920: Structures, practiques musicales et sociabilités," Zurich, 7 October 2000. I devote fuller discussion to these organizations and their concert repertoire in my *Useful Music, or Why Music Mattered in Third Republic France*, vol. 3: *Useful Performance*, in preparation.

This chapter entailed research in private archives as well as participation in conferences. I am very grateful to the following individuals for permission to consult their materials: Lt-Col. François Boulanger, conductor of the Orchestra of the Garde Républicaine, and Lt-Col. Verdy of their public relations division; Guy François, sécrétaire général of the Bon Marché department store, and its archivist, Elizabeth Russo; and Valérie Magnier of the Jardin Zoologique d'Acclimatation.

private patrons as well as state officials—were driven by the desire to reach large audiences. They wished to popularize music that would elevate public taste. This meant finding a balance between pleasing listeners by catering to what they liked—thereby seeing their numbers grow—and educating them while shaping their taste.

This story about the popularization of art music has many surprises. These come to light only in rethinking our assumptions and scholarly methodologies. First, we know that people at the time looked to opera and opera singers to confer distinction on their consumption, in part because of opera's traditional association with elites. Workers rarely had the chance to see an opera staged, even if the government periodically attempted to provide cheap seats. Contrary to what this may imply, not only did the lower classes have access to art music, including operatic music (albeit in transcriptions), they also participated in the supply as well as the demand. Moreover, performing and listening to this music provided new opportunities for self-expression and self-development, in addition to the possibility of imitating the upper classes. Elites were not alone, therefore, in determining the evolution of musical tastes.

Second, as we shall see, boundaries were fluid in this musical world, throwing into question our concepts of not only center and periphery but also the serious and the popular. Musicians and repertoire migrated from venue to venue. For example, concerts at the Bon Marché department store often presented performers and music from the Opéra. And instead of taking years, their organizers chose some excerpts only months after their Opéra premieres, and other works even before these premieres. Such practices force us to reconsider "trickle-down" theories about cultural hegemony.[1] A close look at concert life of the time also reveals how heterogeneous musical experiences often were. At the Bon Marché, as well as in prestigious private salons, audiences could hear humorous monologues and comic scenes by star cabaret performers interspersed with the art music. Moreover, the heterogeneity of Bon Marché concerts extended to a public that included employees as well as potential customers. These juxtapositions of musicians, repertoire, and publics suggest that, despite what some elites may have preferred, in some contexts music helped mediate class and cultural differences.

Third, the struggle over what would become "popular" in France after 1871 did not concern principally the emergence of a canon of Western musical classics as we conceive of it today. Rather, it supported and perhaps even fueled a renaissance in French contemporary music. The example of France is important. It forces us to reexamine our presumption that dead composers dominated concert life in the late nineteenth century and that music's domestication necessarily implied learning the German canon. French audiences of all types were strikingly tolerant of the unfamiliar, even drawn to it, and this included new music. Moreover, many

---

1. Georg Simmel, "Fashion," *International Quarterly* 10 (1904): 130–55.

composers, including the most illustrious, were committed to helping amateurs perform and understand their music.

Such conclusions come from studying a wider array of primary sources than those related to scores, composers' manuscripts, letters, and first editions. Of course, critical reviews and other print journalism of the time are a good place to start. Lesser known sources, however, can also be immensely helpful, even those usually dismissed as of transient value. This essay seeks to expand our notion of archival research by suggesting how useful popular music magazines, sheet music reproduced in newspapers, military band transcriptions, and especially concert programs can be in investigating the growing taste for art music in the French populace.

To understand concert life in Paris—the best evidence of what was popular—it is also important not to focus exclusively on elite cultural organizations, as many scholars have done in studying cities. Of course, the two Opéras and the Société des Concerts (the professional orchestra of the Conservatoire) maintained a certain prestige with the social status of their publics and the quality of their performances. The government expected as much in return for generous subsidies. But when other institutions, such as the Concerts Colonne, were praised as equally good, competition sometimes forced the former into following rather than leading, especially when it came to presenting new French compositions. In the 1890s, when elite institutions were museums more than trend-setters, even concerts at the zoo had more music by living composers than did the Conservatoire. Concerts in a wide range of venues—from public spaces like the zoo and city gardens to private ones such as department stores and salons—tell us much about what became "popular." Investigating the network of relationships connecting them, as I shall do through a discussion of *Samson et Dalila*, sheds important light on the process of popularization at the time.

DEFINITIONS OF THE POPULAR

What gave rise to a pronounced interest in the popular in late nineteenth-century Paris and what attracted large, diverse audiences to music? To answer these questions, we must understand that the *populaire* was neither a single nor a reified concept. When it came to music, there were three categorical definitions. The first comes from the Latin *populus*: the inhabitants of a state, as distinct from its rulers.[2] *Populaire* was sometimes associated with large numbers of people. In music this was significant, for with the population of Paris rising 50 percent between 1860 and 1896, audiences for music were bound to grow. Generally speaking, then, *populaire*

---

2. The word *populaire* does not translate well into English, in part because of differences between French and Anglo-American sociopolitical cultures. For an excellent discussion of the etymological origins and use of *populaire* and *le peuple*, see Geneviève Bollème, *Le Peuple par écrit* (Paris: Seuil, 1986), chap. 1.

could mean having broad appeal, something that could be understood or at least appreciated by many people, or else representing, being associated with, or standing as an emblem for many people.

The genre *chanson populaire* (indigenous folk song) points to the inherent complexity of this concept. Throughout Europe in the late nineteenth century, musicians and scholars combed the countryside seeking to find and write down such music. Many associated it with what was meaningful and authentic in culture, what persevered beyond politics—not as during the French Revolution, when popular songs often concerned social critique or resistance. Beginning in the 1880s, French republicans advocated teaching *chansons populaires* in the primary schools as a way to inculcate a shared sense of identity. Because children in the various provinces spoke different languages and had somewhat different cultures, *chansons populaires* could serve as a common language, especially to the extent that they were transcribed into French. That people of different social and political orientations used this genre at the end of the century to argue for mutually contradictory social goals—including the perpetuation of differences in regional identity—suggests that intense controversy surrounded this meaning of the word and that the term "the people" could be used to refer to various interests.

For most republicans, *populaire* referred to a utopian sense of the lower classes that had developed during the Revolution. In their attempts to address the enormous divisions and inequalities within the nation, it came to imply a kind of righteousness associated with the lower classes and a debt elites owed to them because they had a special place in God's eyes (according to Catholic tradition) or had been victimized, exploited, or alienated (according to socialist tradition).[3] *Populaire* also referred to the need in a democracy to assimilate these classes through education in order to produce informed citizens who would support the political order. In the nineteenth century, then, *populaire* could mean not so much what was produced by the lower classes as what was given to them for their consumption to bring their ideals into conformity with those of their leaders. Education of the lower classes thus was a crucial element of the concept of the *populaire*. The historian Jules Michelet saw politics and education as synonymous: to make a democracy was to educate its people, and that education should last a lifetime. Educating social sentiments, in particular, would allow identification with the general interest of the country. This meant domesticating passions and elevating desires.[4]

This "top-down" aspect of the *populaire* was especially important when it came to music. Many believed in the ancient Greek practice of education through music. This art was thought to be the "direct translation of moral feelings," capable of teaching feelings as well as of "softening one's manners, raising man to the level of

3. For this insight, I am grateful to my research assistant Jean-Louis Morhange.
4. Jules Michelet, *Le Peuple* (Paris: Hachette, Paulin, 1846).

his intelligence . . . [and] making him understand the precious resources that nature has given him." Participation in choral singing was believed to help people "control their passions themselves" while serving as a "respite from their problems, a relaxation from their work, and a remedy to all their suffering." Municipal music societies, made up of workers, were called "conservatories of the people" because they not only taught them singing "within the limits of their hearts and purses" but also "habituated them to loving, or at least respecting, social institutions." In this context, music was considered the "most human, the most social" art because it often needs groups and depends on collaboration.[5] By 1876, François-Auguste Gevaert claimed that "no art plays a more important role in modern life, none fascinates [*passionne*] the public and the masses more than music, this art which is democratic by its very nature." He believed music would help lead to the "moral and ideal perfection of humanity."[6]

Still, the concept of the popular did not always refer just to workers or peasants, even if it was rural culture that maintained the tradition of the *chansons populaires*. In his influential text *Le Peuple* (1846; 4th ed. 1866), Michelet described suffering in all classes of society: peasants, machine workers, manufacturers, bureaucrats, even the rich. The term *populaire* sometimes referred to all classes, or their coexistence, though this usually meant a conscious attempt to include the lower ranks. Those in government trying to make a democratic society out of disenchanted monarchists, religious conservatives, provincial traditionalists, and hopeful socialists valued music for its capacity to cross class lines and bridge political differences, even within the various classes and specially within the elites who attended the Opéra or the Société des Concerts. Republican politicians supported music generously for this reason, linking their subsidies to the requirement that certain concerts and low-cost tickets be made available to those who could not otherwise attend. As might be expected, "the people" who actually benefited were less often the urban poor than the bourgeois middle class.

The second category of the *populaire* extends this notion of something shared to a public. Building a public meant turning the contagious emotions of a crowd into a sense of solidarity through shared experiences. This implied getting people to develop tastes, have opinions, and participate as the early revolutionaries dreamed they might—a collective body acting in the interests of the whole. This definition points to the culture of sociability at the heart of the concept of *populaire* in France. It suggests that people in groups affect one another reciprocally. The late nineteenth-century sociologist Gabriel Tarde considered the public the social group of

5. Marcel de Ris, *L'Orphéon* (1 October 1855); J. F. Vaudin, "Les Orphéons devant l'histoire," *L'Orphéon* (1 January 1859 and 1 September 1865). All translations from the French are my own unless otherwise indicated.

6. François-Auguste Gevaert, "De l'Enseignement public de l'art musical à l'époque moderne," *Le Ménestrel* (8 October 1876): 356–59 and (15 October 1876): 364–65.

the future and defined it not as the people or classes that made it up but rather as "a purely spiritual collectivity, of which the cohesion is entirely mental." He felt that "social evolution begins and ends in games and *fêtes*" and that "the communion of ideas" shared by a public would form "the basis for a new social morality," similar to what Emile Durkheim called *conscience collective*. Tarde explained the process of becoming a public, of forming opinions, as "assimilation by collective contagion." For him, the purpose of public opinion is "to turn the reason of today into the tradition of tomorrow."[7]

The composer Louis Bourgault-Ducoudray alluded to this function in his first lecture as historian at the Conservatoire. After preaching that instruction turns people into "real men" by "rendering their judgment free," he concluded:

> The public is the majority, and the majority rules. If public taste is raised, if it has noble aspirations, art rises. If public taste is lowered, the level of art goes down. One can say that public taste is a touchstone that makes it possible to asses the value and strength of production of an age.
>
> The public makes art and the artists what they are.
>
> Therefore, nothing is more useful in the interest of art than for public taste to rise and its aspirations to grow.[8]

To the extent that this public embraced, appreciated, and came to respect French music, they attached prestige to it. This prestige—an important element of the *populaire*—carried its own self-generating authority, the first stage of becoming a tradition. A tradition represents the transformation of public opinion into belief, or what Michelet called faith. These beliefs, once formed, determine the trend of ideas. As such, Gustave Le Bon considered them "the indispensable pillars of civilizations."[9] When French music became increasingly *populaire*, it had the capacity to become a tradition, not only to represent the nation but also to influence the future in part by feeding nationalist pride.

7. Gabriel Tarde, *La Psychologie économique*, vol. 1 (Paris: Alcan, 1902), and *L'Opinion et la foule* (Paris: Alcan, 1901), quoted in Rosalind Williams, *Dream Worlds: Mass Consumption in Late-Nineteenth-Century France* (Berkeley: University of California Press, 1982), 374–77, 425, n. 82. Durkheim developed the idea of *conscience collective* in several books, including *The Division of Labor in Society*, trans. George Simpson (New York: Free Press, 1965); *The Elementary Forms of Religious Life*, trans. Joseph Ward Swain (New York: Free Press, 1965); and *Suicide: A Study in Sociology*, trans. John Spaulding and George Simpson (New York: Free Press, 1951).

8. Louis Bourgault-Ducoudray, "Cours d'histoire générale de la musique, séance d'ouverture," *Le Ménestrel* (1 December 1878): 3.

9. Although his study is highly critical and focused on crowds, a fear of rising socialism, and a belief that the opinion of crowds was becoming "the supreme guiding principle in politics," some of the conservative Le Bon's work *The Crowd: A Study of the Popular Mind* (London: Ernest Benn, 1896; originally published as *La Psychologie des foules, 1895*), is

The third definition of *populaire*, associated with the growing commodification of music as a consumer product, refers to both generating and responding to a demand. Composers and music publishers popularized a work by making it as accessible as possible, that is, by producing transcriptions of it for diverse instrumental combinations and getting it reproduced in multiple print sources. Conductors and performers popularized music by repeating it immediately as a *bis*, at the end of a concert, or on later concerts. Any *première audition* audiences liked might reappear as a *deuxième audition*, noted on the subsequent program. To hear a work performed twice not only signaled some success for a composer; it also informed listeners of others' approval or at least desire to hear it again—indicated by the expression *redemandé*. To give a *troisième audition* carried the hope of general acceptance. Colonne's orchestra made Berlioz's *La Damnation de Faust* popular by performing it on successive Sundays, threatening that each would be the last, until they no longer had a sold-out hall. In the late 1870s, this meant seven or eight times in a row. By the late 1890s, they had done it one hundred times. This tactic allowed the orchestra to stay solvent while assuming the financial risk of performing new works. It also helped Colonne build a loyal following and encourage a taste for Berlioz.

The power of repetition was well recognized. As Le Bon pointed out, "The thing affirmed comes by repetition to fix itself in the mind in such a way that it is accepted in the end as a demonstrated truth."[10] Extensive repetition plants the work in the unconscious, making possible subsequent reflection. Multiple performances of works such as *La Damnation de Faust*, especially in the context of competition with other orchestras doing the same work, sometimes the same day, pushed musicians to play it better, both technically and musically. The saturation of repeated performances allowed assimilation into the general music culture, where a work could become "popular" in the American sense.

RETHINKING LEISURE

New attitudes toward leisure contributed significantly to music's appeal. The pressures and pace of life under industrialization brought a need for the renewal and recreation associated with leisure activities. According to the urban historian

---

helpful in reflecting on the nature of musical publics in the late nineteenth century, including Bourgault-Ducoudray's notion of opinion as "free judgment." Le Bon defined prestige as "a sort of domination exercised on our mind by an individual, work, or idea. This domination entirely paralyses our critical faculty, and fills our soul with astonishment and respect. . . . It is easy to imbue the mind of crowds with a passing opinion, but very difficult to implant therein a lasting belief. However, a belief of this latter description once established, it is equally difficult to uproot it" (130, 142).

10. Le Bon, *The Crowd*, 125.

Peter Bailey, in the Victorian era, "men were encouraged to seek recreations that provided the greatest contrast to their normal occupation." As he has pointed out, however, work and play in this period were "antithetical in form only. . . . Play was change *of* work, as much as change *from* work."[11] This attitude had several implications.

First, and crucial when it came to the marketing of music, was the association of "amusement" with "instruction," as if they should go hand in hand. "To amuse, to interest, and to instruct" was the emblem of not only numerous family magazines of the 1880s and 1890s but also Colonne's orchestral concerts when the magazine *La Vie de famille* was publishing his programs. To say that a leisure activity could address these simultaneously was the ultimate draw for consumers.

The development of program notes during this period reflects this increasing preoccupation. Programs of Pasdeloup's orchestral Concerts Populaires in the 1860s—famed for successfully attracting "all classes" of society—usually consisted of a single page. Beyond giving the list of works, composers, and performers, they tended to include more information only for multimovement works or instrumental excerpts from dramatic works (e.g. overtures drawn from those by Wagner, Schumann, Beethoven). In the 1870s, with the increased prevalence of French music on concert programs, these often increased to two pages to reproduce the long descriptive programs of Saint-Saëns's symphonic poems or the extended texts of Berlioz's dramatic symphonies, as well as *drames lyriques* by various French contemporaries. Program notes presenting historical details about composers and short analyses of their works did not appear until the 1880s. At the Concerts Colonne, these increased to twelve pages in the late 1890s, as education became an explicit reason to attend concerts and orchestral concerts took to presenting chronological successions of works as a "history of music."[12] Programs provide a fascinating record of not only what audiences heard but also what they were supposed to listen for, especially when notes evolved over time or differed from venue to venue. They also give remarkable and, for the most part, accurate performance and reception histories of the works, presented in part to offer audiences a basis of comparison.

11. Peter Bailey, *Popular Culture and Performance in the Victorian City* (Cambridge: Cambridge University Press, 1998), 24–25. In her *Music in Everyday Life* (Cambridge: Cambridge University Press, 2000), Tia DeNora also describes music as a "place or space for 'work,' " which she defines as "meaning or lifeworld making" (40). See also her "How Is Extra-musical Meaning Possible? Music as a Place and Space for Work," *Sociological Theory* 4 (1986): 84–94.

12. For more on this, see my "Building a Public for Orchestral Music: Les Concerts Colonne," in *Concert et public: Mutation de la vie musicale en Europe de 1780 à 1914*, ed. Hans-Erich Bödeker, Patrice Veit, and Michael Werner (Paris: Editions de la Maison des sciences de l'homme, 2002), 209–40.

In general, there is little evidence that nonorchestral music societies provided such notes, although both amateurs and professionals distributed free programs listing works and performers. One exception is significant: *Le Petit Poucet*, a pocket-sized military music magazine (see fig. 13.1). Its purpose was to announce the programs for the military-band concerts in Paris. After its first season in 1895, it, too, entered the business of education. Each issue thereafter began with a three-page biographical essay about a French musician. Composers varied in age, professional stature, occupation, and gender, ranging from Thomas, Bizet, and Charpentier to Charles Bordes, Cécile Chaminade, and Holmès. Conductors included Lamoureux, Gabriel Marie, and those leading the major military bands. Biographies of lesser known musicians often provide information that would be difficult to learn elsewhere. To accompany one military band concert each week, the magazine added analytical program notes especially written for them. Typically three to four pages in length, these are every bit as informative as those for the Concerts Colonne. They discuss previous performances and reception, often citing what the composer or major critics had written. They also explain the original source of any excerpts as well as the dramatic context or texts underlying the music. When a cover was added in 1899, *Le Petit Poucet* became a veritable music journal, with occasional concert reviews by major critics, such as Bruneau on Charpentier's *Louise* and Dukas on Richard Strauss. These suggest that by 1900, popular audiences were keen to follow the latest developments in avant-garde art music.

After 1870 and the frivolous abuses of the Second Empire, those espousing republican ideals also wished to redefine the function of leisure, conceiving it as a fundamental component of the "good life" for all classes. Even aristocrats such as Georges d'Avenel endorsed "the idea of equalizing enjoyments rather than money," thereby "approving a vast delusion whereby human inequalities are masked by material appearances."[13] The unprecedented abundance of leisure activities expanded occasions for the exercise of free will among the lower and middle classes, with all that this meant in terms of taking responsibility for one's choices. This gave them a "mobility and anonymity that removed them from supervision by their fellows."[14] However, this abundance also raised new issues: how to educate people's desire; how to seduce them away from the dangerous frontier zones of certain kinds of entertainment and provide them with "healthy" alternatives. As Bailey puts it, "leisure constituted a threat to the discipline and cohesion of the bourgeois world," even as it "tested the elasticity of class mores."[15]

Many looked to music for help in negotiating these challenges. Like other consumer goods, music helped people "contemplate the possession of an emotional

13. Williams, *Dream Worlds*, 5.
14. Bailey, *Popular Culture*, 20.
15. Bailey, *Popular Culture*, 21, 29.

3 Année   Dimanche 13 Juin 1897   Numéro 11

Le Petit Poucet

JOURNAL DES CONCERTS MILITAIRES

ADMINISTRATION — 63, Avenue du Roule, 63 — NEUILLY-s/-SEINE

Augusta HOLMÈS

Augusta - Mary - Anne Holmès est née à Paris de parents irlandais résidant en France. Elle fut élevée à Versailles dans un milieu artistique : son père, après avoir été un brillant officier, était devenu un savant distingué, et sa mère cultivait avec passion la peinture et la littérature.

Dès l'enfance, ses dispositions musi-

cales s'éveillèrent, et, à l'âge où les fillettes ne songent qu'à la poupée, elle se serait adonnée au piano si on lui en avait laissé la liberté.

Mais sa mère, qui détestait la musique et déplorait que sa fille consacrât à cet art une ardeur qu'elle eût souhaité voir s'appliquer à la peinture, l'arrachait à son instrument et l'installait devant un chevalet. Poussée par la force

LE PORTRAIT DE LA SEMAINE

---

13 Juin 1897   ## Place de la Nation   De 4 à 5 h.

89e D'INFANTERIE — Chef : M. SUZANNE

1. **Isabelle-Marsch** (pas redoublé)............... Pétrowski

2. **Les Noces de Figaro** (ouverture .... Mozart

3. **Coppélia** (valse lente)........................ L. Delibes

4. **Lakmé** (fantaisie).. .. .. L. Delibes

     Basse, M. July ; bugle, M. Déparday ; cornet, M. Blanchetière.

5. **Polka du Cheval** .... Lecocq

FIGURE 13.1. An example of *Le Petit Poucet*, a journal of military music featuring biographies of musicians, concert programs for performances in Parisian gardens, and extensive program notes. Courtesy of the Bibliothèque Nationale.

condition, a social circumstance, even an entire style of life."[16] To the extent that all classes developed similar tastes, as Tarde put it, ideally they would come to resemble one another internally, for tastes express one's inner desires. In his analysis of the fashion world, Georg Simmel saw this process as unidirectional, with "subordinate social groups" seeking new status claims by imitating the tastes of "superordinate groups." He called this "trickle-down."[17] From this perspective, the dominant classes could use the dissemination of taste (and moral values) through art music to expand their influence over the lower classes. To the extent that the appropriation of certain musical practices and tastes resulted from envy, however, this imitation by the lower classes could involve a kind of interaction with their social superiors rather than passive receptivity. For Tarde, this was the symptom of a "social transformation." If he was right in believing, as Williams put it, that "unseen and mental imitation lessens the psychological distance between superior and inferior," then shared musical experiences could, ideally, constitute "a form of democratization."[18] Exploring the meaning of shared musical experiences in more recent years, Christopher Small also made the analogy to play as a model for social transformation.[19]

Workers' musical societies, of which there were hundreds, illustrate well the domestication and democratization of art music in Paris at the time. Learning to sing or play an instrument demonstrated to the world liberation from the assumptions one might make about workers. The acquisition of musical skills suggested certain virtues—evidence of devotion, study, self-discipline, and interest in "the finer things in life," including charm and grace. Knowledge of art music also allowed for performance of another kind of social identity, something workers could use to trade up socially, possibly to marry better, or at the least to command respect from superiors and coworkers. The allure of respectability, considered by many "a principal prerequisite for true citizenship,"[20] was central to the appeal of performing art music. It not only encouraged the lower classes to feel part of

16. Grant McCracken, *Culture and Consumption: New Approaches to the Symbolic Character of Consumer Goods and Activities* (Bloomington: Indiana University Press, 1990), 110.

17. In his *Culture and Consumption*, McCracken explained that this theory puts fashion diffusion in a social context, which helps determine fashion's "direction, tempo, and dynamics" (93).

18. Williams, *Dream Worlds*, 356. Underlying this ideal is Tarde's belief that there was no line between society and the individual, between internal feelings and external constraints. He conceived the two as in a dynamic relation of role-setting and role-following. See Gabriel Tarde, *Les Lois de l'imitation, étude sociologique*, 3rd ed. (Paris: Alcan, 1900).

19. Christopher Small, *Musicking: The Meanings of Performing and Listening* (Hanover, N.H.: Wesleyan University Press, 1998), 63.

20. Bailey, *Popular Culture*, 32. For an illuminating summary of the latest thinking on working-class respectability, see his chap. 2.

bourgeois society but also provided for differentiation, or distinction, within these classes.

Membership in these societies served other, more tangible functions as well. Not just a medium for social imitation, they also constituted a form of fraternity. Although some societies bemoaned frequent turnover in their membership, those who stayed were known for their esprit de corps. (This may have contributed to the emerging class consciousness underlying the rise of trade-unionism.) Workers joined for other reasons, too. Besides serving as outlets for their creativity, participation in these societies held the promise of release from the grind of daily life. All organizations held annual banquets and offered the possibility of travel to the provinces. Moreover, performing as a soloist, with one's name in concert programs, or winning prizes in city or national competitions brought public recognition, something otherwise utterly lacking in workers' lives. Competitions also brought workers into contact with a wide range of their peers across the country. And because the competitions often involved commissions from contemporary composers, they ensured that workers learned to perform new music and had opportunities to compare their performances with those of others. Such personal, social, and musical benefits were undoubtedly unobtainable outside such contexts.

THE USEFULNESS OF TRANSCRIPTIONS

Except for those who could afford a subscription to the Opéra or Opéra-Comique or who produced operas in their own homes—the musical manifestation of luxury for its producers and consumers—most people got to know art music through some virtual representative, whether an excerpt or, more often, a transcription. Transcriptions, in particular, blurred the boundaries between classes, as did consumer goods at department stores, which likewise helped domesticate luxury products and encourage desire for them. Most Parisians could afford to purchase only cheap imitations of the real thing, be it furs, jewelry, or music. Transcriptions allowed for performances by and for people from a wide range of classes and orientations and in a diversity of venues.[21]

Two forms of transcription dominated in the late nineteenth century: piano and wind band. Since increasing numbers of people had pianos in their homes—rentals were only 10 francs per month—piano transcriptions were by far the most numerous. Whether for piano solo, piano four-hands, two pianos four-hands, two pianos eight-hands, or piano and voice, they ranged in difficulty from those for "easy piano" to those requiring pianistic virtuosity. Such scores could be purchased directly from the publisher or acquired through music magazines for sale

21. See also Thomas Christensen, "Four-Hand Piano Transcription and Geographies of Nineteenth-Century Musical Reception," *Journal of the American Musicological Society* 52, no. 2 (summer 1999): 255–98.

at newspaper kiosks, train stations, and bookstores.[22] They also could be borrowed from one of the many municipal lending libraries, located in both wealthy and poor neighborhoods.

Professionally oriented journals, produced by music publishers, regularly included a piano or piano-vocal score with each bimonthly issue. These reflect what publishers wished to promote. To coincide with important premieres of works they published, their magazines often reproduced several excerpts. For example, in 1882 *Le Ménestrel*, published by Heugel, printed nine transcriptions from Ambroise Thomas's *Francoise da Rimini* and in 1883 six from Léo Delibes's *Lakmé*. That Massenet's music appeared disproportionately—in ten out of twenty-four issues in 1892, 1894, and 1899—suggests his popularity with the public as well as his status with the publisher.

Despite the relatively high level of its reporting and the musical training expected of its readers, *Le Ménestrel* also published light works. These included polkas by Philippe Fahrbach and Joseph Gung'l, quadrilles and cornet solos by Jean-Baptiste Arban, waltzes by Johann Strauss, and sentimental religious works by the composer/Opéra singer Jean-Baptiste Faure. This suggests that at least some of *Ménestrel*'s readers had enough interest in this repertoire to want to perform it themselves. Some of these composers and works also turned up on concerts in popular venues. Heinrich Strobl's polka "The Sewing Machine" appeared in *Le Ménestrel* (17 December 1876) and was performed at the Bon Marché department store (7 July 1877). Such juxtapositions defy any strict separation between the serious and the popular, even in one of the period's most prestigious publications.

Other music magazines (less cited by scholars) tell us more about the emerging taste for art music.[23] The weekly *Journal de musique* (1876–82) was one of the most sophisticated and varied in terms of its repertoire. Each issue featured three to five works for piano or piano and voice. As in *Le Ménestrel*, the scores signaled the latest developments in concert life. In addition to including not only opera premieres but also "fragments of almost all lyric works, whether important or light, that had success on Parisian stages," they consciously varied "genres" and "degrees of force" (i.e., difficulty?) to satisfy "all whims, all levels of knowledge . . . all ages and all tastes."[24] In 1877–78, this meant transcriptions of orchestral music at the Concerts Populaires, an oratorio at the Société des Concerts, military marches of the Garde Républicaine, a chorus written for an *orphéon* competition, polkas in the ball repertoire, *chansons populaires* from other countries, and exotic music at the 1878

22. Magazines also occasionally rented their issues. In 1895, *La Quinzaine musicale*, which published the music of many women composers, lent their scores for three days in Paris, or eight days in the provinces.

23. Some, such as *La Musique des familles*, began earlier in the century and were explicitly oriented toward families.

24. "A nos lecteurs," *Le Journal de musique* (19 May 1877): 1.

Exposition. Besides giving access to a full range of what Parisians might be hearing, these transcriptions provided a broader context for understanding works gaining popularity. For example, just as *La Damnation de Faust* was taking orchestral audiences by storm and its Hungarian march was being encored at virtually every performance, in the spring of 1877 and throughout 1878 *Le Journal de musique* published numerous Hungarian marches and songs, including other versions of the Rakoczy tune (the Hungarian national anthem) that Berlioz borrowed, sometimes accompanied by explanatory articles. One was from a gypsy performance at the 1878 Exposition. For this service, readers paid only 40 centimes per issue, or 18 francs per year.

Another, even cheaper bimonthly music magazine from the 1870s and 1880s, *Le Mélomane*, is a good source for studying the tastes of a less musically cultured audience, or those who could afford only 10–25 centimes per issue (a penny in England). Some works reproduced in *Mélomane* also appeared in *Journal de musique*—evidence of their broad appeal. Some, such as Rameau's "Le Tambourin," were published in *Mélomane* (1877) before *Journal de musique* (1879). The magazine offered its subscribers not only classics—by Beethoven, Bach, Gluck, Donizetti, Rossini, and others—but also music performed in popular venues (such as skating rinks). Beginning in 1885, "unpublished music" became *Mélomane*'s explicit focus (as indicated at the top of each cover). This magazine offers a context for studying what new music meant in such a setting at this point. Some pieces derived from *Mélomane*'s annual "International Composition Competition" for the best (1) prelude, fugue, or minuet, (2) romance without words, and (3) dance music, all for piano. Contestants were exhorted to seek "grace, elegance and originality, but not difficulty." The winners—including little-known women, Conservatoire instructors, and the future director of the Garde Républicaine, Gabriel Parès—were awarded medals and publication of their winning composition in the magazine. These works reveal which aspects of art music—genres, styles, and aesthetics—were increasingly appreciated.

Newspapers (and illustrated Sunday supplements, very popular in the 1890s) also reproduced piano or piano-vocal transcriptions. In terms of amusing, interesting, and instructing their publics, these were like reproductions of paintings or short stories. They are also important records of taste and concert life. *Le Figaro*, one of the most respected Parisian dailies, reproduced two to four pages of scores each Wednesday from the 1870s through the 1890s. In many ways, the paper tried to be balanced and thoughtful about its choices by not giving undue advertising advantage to any one music publisher, theater, style, composer, or performer. Piano-vocal scores dominated (sometimes almost two to one over piano scores), with songs often outnumbering opera excerpts. Orchestral works occasionally appeared in transcriptions for two pianos. Light genres such as polkas and other dances were rare because, more than any other collection of scores from the time, *Le Figaro*'s transcriptions documented important performances or musical events.

These included premieres in Paris, the French provinces, and abroad; cantatas winning the annual Prix de Rome; and piano pieces written for the Conservatoire's annual sight-reading exam (perhaps included to inform future potential candidates of the level required for admission to the Conservatoire's piano class). Short explanatory notes sometimes indicated what to expect in performing this music. This suggests that the scores were not just news items but also part of the popularization of serious music. Through them, readers could participate vicariously in the music world.

Another medium through which the French got to know art music was the wind-band transcription. Whereas some were for small groups called *fanfares*, most called for around thirty woodwinds and brass instruments. Some of the best transcribers, like Louis Mayeur and Gabriel Parès, were conductors as well as authors of orchestration treatises and instrumental method books. These men helped liberate wind-band transcriptions from being restricted to martial-type music or certain tonalities. Increasingly, thanks to their treatises, transcribers were able to reproduce the effects of orchestral music and present works in their original keys. Parès wanted to make wind bands the equal of symphonic orchestras, especially in "translating a composer's inspiration." In his volume, dedicated to his composition teacher Théodore Dubois, Parès explained that he wished to "charm the listener and [sometimes] give the illusion of a string orchestra (the most perfect creation of the musical art)." To translate a full range of sentiment, he advocated learning to produce not only power and brilliant sonorities but also variety and sweetness.[25] Such language and the intentions underlying it most likely were meant to bring wind-band transcriptions closer to the original music and to the composer's intended expression. However, ironically, they also upset the gender stereotypes associated with band music, and, by emphasizing feminine as well as masculine sentiments, suggested the kind of bimusicality that is inherent in larger forms such as the symphony and opera.

Indeed, during this period, military bands as well as amateur wind bands (*harmonies*) performed not only marches and polkas but also transcriptions of overtures, symphonic poems, and opera—music that called for a wide range of expressivity. Opera transcriptions were called "fantasies" and "mosaics." They resemble piano fantasies, in that both string together a selection of excerpts, most with a strong melodic or rhythmic allure, not necessarily in the original order. As in Walt Disney's film *Fantasia*, material could also return (possibly for the sake of musical closure) even if this did not take place in the original. In its program notes, *Le Petit Poucet* increasingly indicated where the opera's excerpts were in the piano-vocal scores, implying that some military-band fans might own these scores.

25. Gabriel Parès, *Traité d'instrumentation et d'orchestration à l'usage des musiques militaires, d'harmonies, et de fanfares* (Paris: Lemoine, 1898), 111.

The typical transcription, in full score for the conductor, is over thirty pages long. Individual instruments—such as the bugle, cornet, and trombone—perform singers' arias. Lyrics are sometimes printed below the notes. Parès's mosaic for Bruneau's *Messidor* (Opéra, 1897) was performed by the Garde Républicaine in 1899. The story of overt class conflict between a peasant family and a factory owner is resolved by the love between the peasant hero, Guillaume, and the industrialist's daughter, Hélène. Their dialogue appears in the score and *Le Petit Poucet*:

> TROMBONE: But I love you! I want you today as I wanted you yesterday. And aren't you mine, since here you are poor?

> CORNET: O how wonderful to be loved! I have always loved you, dear spouse, I have never loved anyone but you.

> TROMBONE AND CORNET: Like two flames that come together, let our hearts burn all our lives.[26]

Such works, especially newer works with more complicated rhythms and timbral interrelationships, served as occasions for performers to practice expressivity as well as coordination.[27] They also suggest that military-band audiences may have been open to newer French works because of the ideologically subversive content some promoted.

This repertoire reached diverse audiences and made works accessible to the public sometimes years before they were heard on the stage. Often it was the only form in which audiences in the provinces or colonies could hear certain music. As *Le Petit Poucet* pointed out (14 June 1899), it was in the provinces that Parès first popularized his fantasies based on music by Wagner, Reyer, Saint-Saëns, Massenet, and others. Because the journal saw popularizing art music as the role of wind bands, *Le Petit Poucet* wished that more contemporary composers would write for them.

How to explain the success of such replicas? One should remember this was the era of reproduction—the early years of the phonograph, the wax museum (founded

---

26. "Programme analytique du concert de la Garde," *Le Petit Poucet* (19 September 1899): 4. Among other descriptive passages and scenes presented by various instruments, this one ends:

> TROMBONE: Mais je t'aime! je te veux aujourd'hui comme je te voulais hier. Et n'es-tu pas à moi, puisque te voilà pauvre?

> CORNET: O délices d'être aimée! je t'ai toujours aimé, cher époux, je n'ai jamais aimé que toi.

> TROMBONE ET CORNET: Comme deux flammes qui se rejoignent, que nos coeurs brûlent pour la vie entière!

27. A mosaic of Berlioz's *La Damnation de Faust*, performed in 1898, is evidence of the degree of difficulty that ensembles and their public could handle by the end of the century.

in 1882), and the craze for panoramas representing current events, modern life, and imaginary tours of the world. Parisians were used to blurred lines between fantasy and reality. In *Spectacular Realities*, the historian Vanessa Schwarz has argued that illusion itself was a source of consumer pleasure, especially the illusion of voyage.[28] The sociologist Rosalind Williams has concurred. In *Dreamworlds*, she points out that the character Des Esseintes in Joris-Karl Huysmans's novel *A Rebours* is someone who consciously pursues the "pleasure of self-deception." For him, inner vision is what counts, not the thing itself, and one achieves visions through self-deception. Des Esseintes believes that, as in religious practice, the validity of an experience depends on the "quality of faith in the consumer, not on the quality of the product used to stimulate the experience."[29] Agreeing with him, I would go further and suggest that the object, or signified of musical transcriptions, was not necessarily the thing itself, the original form of a work—I do not think transcriptions always functioned as iconic signs. Rather, their object may have been what they evoked in the listener, whether this meant, for Parès, the wind band as string orchestra, or, for others, feelings or ideas they linked to the music. Grant McCracken has called this their displaced meaning, often "an idealized version of life as it should be lived."[30] To the extent this was true, success—or popularity—may have depended on what people associated with certain music as much as the music itself.[31]

CONCERTS, POPULAR VENUES, AND THEIR PUBLICS

Interesting and informative documents, concert programs have also been too long ignored by scholars. As shown in chapter 12, these provide a treasure of information about repertoire, premieres, performers, and concert venues, as well as the nature of musical production and consumption at the end of the nineteenth century. Their first function was to attract as well as to inform audiences. Programs were sent through the mail, published widely in the press, and distributed free at virtually all public concerts, regardless of venue. For concert societies, they were

28. Vanessa Schwarz, *Spectacular Realities: Early Mass Culture in Fin-de-Siècle Paris* (Berkeley: University of California Press, 1998).

29. Williams, *Dream Worlds*, 142–45.

30. McCracken, *Culture and Consumption*, 104–17. I agree with McCracken's critique of Williams, who assumes that people consume only out of superficial motives, and I also think we should consider other cultural meanings in consumption.

31. André Michael Spies, *Opera, State, and Society in the Third Republic, 1875–1914* (New York: Peter Lang, 1998), makes this point about Opéra audiences as well, arguing that aristocratic subscribers embraced Wagner when they began "to identify with the heroic outsider as a symbol of opposition to the corrupt, vacillating—in short, bourgeois—Third Republic" (86).

evidence of the organization's performance history—a form of collective memory, and of particular value to concert organizers and program annotators.[32]

Some programs preserved at the Bibliothèque Nationale and elsewhere contain handwritten notations. Comments may refer to works a listener liked or disliked—those he or she found "pretty," "charming," "mediocre," or "too long." Other indications point to how the general public responded. An 11 February 1866 program of the Concerts Populaires, for example, tells us that at the orchestra's first performances of these works, audiences demanded encores of the minuet from Haydn's Symphony in C minor and the prelude from Wagner's *Lohengrin* and that, after his performance of Mendelssohn's Violin Concerto, Joseph Joachim gave four curtain calls. This suggests that listening was often accompanied by the recording of aesthetic judgments from the individual as well as public perspective. Concert programs are thus important records of audience reception and demonstrate that the French were self-conscious about their musical tastes.

Military bands concerts reached the largest audiences. Each summer in the gardens and squares of the city, Parisians could hear twenty to thirty such concerts per week. In provincial villages and colonies, military bands were the mainstay of musical life. Demand was such that in 1899 the Ministry of War increased the number of military bands from 177 to 195. Military band programs, often printed in local newspapers, allow us to study the works the masses had easy access to and help us trace the evolution of public taste.

The most prestigious military band was the Garde Républicaine. Many of its seventy-nine members had earned first prizes from the Paris Conservatoire. Unlike other military band performers who were soldiers, Garde musicians were hired as professionals with civil contracts. Most of the Garde also played with the principal Parisian theater orchestras or those of Colonne or Lamoureux.[33] Between 1855 and 1873, Georges Paulus turned the Garde into a prestigious institution of excellent musicians who in their wildly successful ninety-three-day tour of the United States in 1872 were hailed as the best of their kind in the world. His standards of performance were quite high, helping to inspire the notion that this band could help restore French pride and glory. Adolphe Sellenick, assistant conductor under Paulus, took over when Paulus reached retirement, and Gustave Wettge followed when Sellenick retired in 1884. Several concurrent developments helped their successor, Gabriel Parès, a saxophonist and member of the Garde, turn the organization into one even more valued for its seriousness of purpose and musical achievements. In 1893 when Parès took over, the Garde got a new building conceived specifically for

32. Using the press, the industrious scholar can reconstruct programs that are no longer extant. The process is valuable, for which newspaper or magazine published an organization's programs tells us about their public, their relative reputation, and their peer groups.

33. "Historique de la musique de la Garde républicaine," *Le Petit Poucet* (25 July 1897): 7.

music, where they could rehearse three times a week. Parès put this to good use in expanding their repertoire. He, together with Emile Leblan, conductor of the Twenty-eighth Regiment, considered it their duty to promote modern music.

Upon their retirement, two of the Garde's conductors, Paulus and Wettge, took positions conducting the wind band of the Bon Marché, one of the city's most important department stores. It was the creation of Aristide Boucicaut, who took over a small drapery and notions store in 1853 and began to transform it immediately. When the store expanded into a whole city block in 1872, including dormitories, a dining hall, and recreation areas for his employees, Boucicaut began to offer them free music lessons (voice as well as wind instruments) along with free courses in English and fencing. With an explicitly educational purpose in mind, he hoped to "encourage a taste for study" and wanted to do everything he could to help his male as well as female employees "use their evenings in an instructive and attractive manner." Besides conceiving of the store and its employees as a "big family," he hoped to produce a new kind of employee. Music lessons taught discipline and personal competitiveness, useful attributes in an effective sales force. After passing solfège classes, employees were allowed to join the choral society, or in the case of men only, the Harmonie, the wind band. All employees of the store could become members of the society, either as performers or as honorary members.[34] The former, of which there were about sixty at any one time, rehearsed two evenings per week; the latter were given a special concert each spring. Each paid 1 franc per month in dues, the standard for workers' societies. Both groups encouraged loyalty, commitment, and a sense of community—virtues Boucicaut needed when training employees for long careers. Although the choral society and the wind band remained strictly amateur ensembles, their concerts—whether within the store itself in winter, outside in the square in summer, or in competitions in Paris and the provinces— gave the store a way to advertise its efforts and largesse, build good will, and attract customers. The programs of these concerts, bearing the stamps of police approval and now in the store's private archives, offer the modern scholar a window on the participation of workers in the concert life of the city.[35] They also provide an

34. Michael B. Miller, *The Bon Marché: Bourgeois Culture and the Department Store, 1869–1920* (Princeton, N.J.: Princeton University Press, 1981), argued that department stores did much to give "shape and definition to the very meaning of a bourgeois way of life" (182). It is not clear, however, that they did much for workers (*ouvriers*). Employees, many of whom were from the lower middle class in the provinces, received fixed salaries and could earn additional commissions on sales in the store. *Ouvriers*—those in the workshops and the women who cut catalogue samples—were paid hourly or daily wages. As part of "the family," employees could receive music lessons; workers, excluded, could not.

35. I am grateful to Miller, *The Bon Marché*, app., 241 n., for indicating the existence of a "trunk containing concert documents," and to the Bon Marché for permitting me to consult and organize its contents.

TABLE 13.1. Conductors

La Garde Républicaine	Société chorale and Harmonie du Bon Marché	Concerts at the Jardin zoologique d'acclimatation
G. Paulus (1855–73)	L. Mayeur (1872–77)	L. Mayeur (1872–93)
A. Sellenick (1874–84)	G. Paulus (1877–94)	L. Pister (1893–96)
G. Wettge (1884–93)	G. Wettge (1895–1900+)	J. Lafitte (1896–1900+)
G. Parès (1893–1910)		

important basis for comparison with other groups their conductors directed and with amateur groups from the upper classes (see table 13.1).

The first conductor of the Bon Marché concerts, Louis Mayeur, a clarinetist and saxophonist at the Opéra, also directed a new concert series at a city zoo.[36] The Jardin Zoologique d'Acclimatation opened in 1855 as a place to introduce, domesticate, and reproduce animals and plants from foreign lands. Administrators sought to understand their use-value in the West and render them popular by exhibitions and sale. After the Franco-Prussian War, when people were tired and needed places of leisure, the Jardin continued to encourage the study of natural history but added recreation and amusement. To attract people to the park on days of low attendance, in 1872 they began to give concerts on Thursday afternoons. The idea was to excite the interest of a broader public than would otherwise visit the Jardin. The success of these concerts financially, as demonstrated by an increase in admissions on Thursdays, led in 1873 to giving two concerts per week and to constructing a kiosk for music. In 1893, so performances could be given all year long, they built the Palais d'Hiver, an immense structure containing a large concert hall, and a palm-tree-lined "Palmarium," 50 meters long and 25 meters wide, to which chairs could be brought. The administration also hired Louis Pister, who had worked under Pasdeloup at the Concerts Populaires, and asked him to recruit their musicians from the most prestigious institutions in town—the Société des Concerts du Conservatoire, the Opéra, and the Opéra-Comique. As the level of performance rose, the music grew more serious, and the Sunday concerts began to be listed in Le Ménestrel, as if an alternative to those of Colonne and Lamoureux.

Each of these societies contributed significantly to the expansion of the public for art music, and all relied on their venue to facilitate this. Military bands played all over the city for an hour a day on five days per week, beginning at 4 or 5 p.m. They could be heard in poor neighborhoods in eastern Paris, such as the Buttes

36. Mayeur brought both organizations the prestige of the Opéra as well as practical understanding of musical life as author of saxophone method books and opera transcriptions.

Chaumont in the nineteenth *arrondissement* and the Place des Nations in the twelfth, and in wealthy ones in the west, such as the Place du Ranelagh in the sixteenth and the Parc Monceau in the seventeenth. Such concerts were occasions for people from different classes and backgrounds to mix. As a critic recounted in 1898, one such concert in Montmartre "overflowed with women and children and on the sidewalks, a crowd of men, both bourgeois and workers, sales people [*calicots*] and artists, all of whom stood to hear the music."[37] Whereas in the 1880s, the Garde Républicaine performed at up to seven venues all over town, in the late 1890s they restricted themselves to twice a week at the city's central, prestigious gardens—those of the Tuileries, the Palais du Luxembourg, and the Palais Royal. These attracted foreign visitors, students, and occasionally aristocrats. On 21 July 1899, *Le Petit Poucet* noted that, while visiting their favorite shops in the Palais Royal, elegant female Opéra subscribers mixed in with "humble music-lovers." The press often reported 5,000 to 6,000 people at military band concerts, regardless of the weather, and sometimes up to 15,000 for the Garde Républicaine. In 1905, one publisher bragged that they printed 150,000 programs for military band concerts that season. Audience behavior at these concerts was not necessarily what one might expect. As the end of the century neared, critics praised Parès for getting his listeners to pay attention silently, although many still liked to beat the measure with their bodies.

The ten to thirteen summer concerts of the Bon Marché wind band, occasionally accompanied by the choral society, resembled those of military bands, except that they took place on Saturdays at 8:30 p.m. only, in the square beside the store. Typically, 1,000 programs were printed for each concert. The press, however, reported that sometimes 6,000 people attended. Interestingly, the name of the store is always set in the largest type on these programs, as if the Bon Marché itself was the main attraction (see fig. 13.2).

The indoor concerts of the Bon Marché, which began three years earlier in January 1873, were quite different. In the beginning, they were called "musical meetings" (*réunions musicales*), as if they were intimate gatherings. By 1880, however, the store began to take them seriously. For the two or three choral concerts that took place within the main hall of the store each winter, the merchandise was cleared out, Oriental rugs, curtains, exotic plants, and lighting were brought in, and the space was turned into a huge, luxurious salon. Six thousand invitations were sent for one concert in 1881. This included 300 pink ones for female employees, 2,000 green ones for male employees, and the balance presumably for customers and invited guests. Four thousand free programs were printed. After 1881, it was decided that the first concert should take place between the exhibition of new coats and the end of the fall season, and the second should coincide

37. "Musiques militaires," *Le Monde musical* (15 July 1898): 102.

FIGURE 13.2. The program of a concert given by the wind band (l'Harmonie) of the Bon Marché department store in the square outside the store on Saturday evening, 21 July 1894. Courtesy of the Bon Marché department store.

with the January white sale, a marketing device Boucicault invented. Ads for the white sale were occasionally inserted in the programs. To attract a sophisticated audience, in January 1883 Opéra stars began to be invited, for example, Jules Bosquin and Marie-Hélène Brunet-Lafleur, as well as Comédie-Française actors like Ernest Coquelin, known as Coquelin Cadet (see fig. 13.3). At this point, "CONCERT," in capital letters, began to appear at the top of the programs, perhaps to imply the increasingly public nature of these events or the credibility to which they aspired. In 1885 the invitation list included the Baroness de Rothschild and in 1887 Colonne and Gounod.

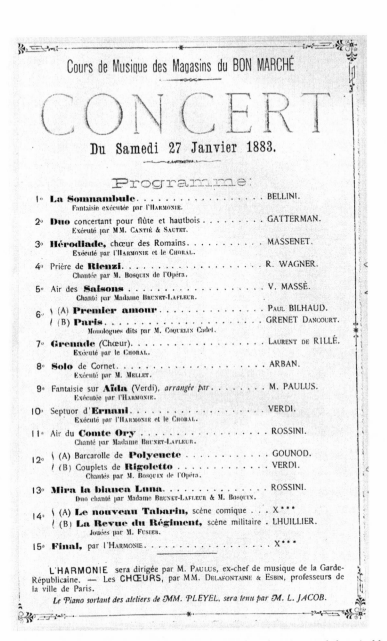

Of the various concert societies in Paris, the Jardin became the most conscious of the diversity of its potential publics and the need to serve each of them. Each summer in the 1870s and 1880s, fifty concerts were held in the outdoor kiosk. A subscription cost 25 francs for men but only 10 francs for women and children, perhaps to make it easier for the latter to attend. In 1893, however, as the construction of the Palais d'Hiver led the organizers to reconceive their musical activities, a decision was made to provide concerts for three types of public. The Sunday concerts, performed in the main hall, continued, with works by the "best-known masters" or what the organizers considered "easy and likeable music"—overtures, fantasies, genre pieces. Besides the price of entry to the zoo (1 franc), concert admission cost only 20 centimes to 1.5 francs. The Jardin also initiated concerts in the Palmarium—"promenade concerts"—for 20 centimes, from 3 to 5 p.m., four days a week. Listeners were invited to relax and converse with friends under the shade of the palm trees while their children played. With the warm temperature, evergreen trees, and fresh flowers, the space was conceived as a big salon giving the illusion of eternal spring. On Wednesdays in 1893 the Jardin began a third concert series, one with advanced music, which the promotional materials noted would be addressed to a "more initiated" public, those interested in the "progress of art." The organizers hoped the public would enjoy the historical part of the programs and the works by young composers. For these concerts, the size of the orchestra was increased from sixty to ninety musicians, they occasionally invited guest soloists—pianists, organists, and opera singers—and, to cover the higher expenses, they had higher ticket prices of 1–4 francs. In 1896, the organizers bragged they had been able to attract the high society of Paris as well as the middle class, businessmen, and government employees—though not yet the working class.

These examples suggest that several strategies helped to make music available and appealing to a wide range of people. First, it was brought to their neighborhoods. Second, it was performed in familiar settings, not only local squares and gardens but also indoor spaces transformed into salons. This made the bourgeoisie feel comfortable, as if at home, while offering those of lesser means access to an aristocratic model of consumption. Third, concerts were accompanied by programs, turning the listening experience into more than entertainment.

Repertoire

Given the huge number of people listening to concerts in popular venues, we should take seriously what was performed. The extent to which repertoire was shared or overlapping in diverse venues suggests the emergence of both a "popular culture" that included art music and a national culture that transcended the crude, divisive nationalisms troubling France at the end of the century.

Most concerts, of any type, embodied an aesthetic of variety. This underlies the almost obligatory alternation of genres, the often eclectic juxtaposition of styles, periods, and composers, and the variation in a group's programs from week to week. As they hoped to "amuse, interest, and instruct," most concert organizers were mindful not to tire listeners. Concerts were to provide a succession of experiences, like parts of a meal. Lighter works, such as marches or polkas, came at the end, as if "desserts," with the middle reserved for more difficult music, "main courses."

The formula for military band concerts was four or five pieces, starting with a march or military music, followed by an overture, dance, opera fantasy, or mosaic, and then a polka or other dance (see fig. 13.1). What filled this formula, however, changed over the years. Although Paulus popularized his transcription of the prelude from *Lohengrin*, in the early 1870s under Sellenick and in the 1880s under Wettge, the works the Garde Républicaine most frequently performed were Sellenick's marches, fantasies from Gounod's *Faust*, and Auber's overtures, followed by fantasies on operas by Thomas, Meyerbeer, Verdi, and Adolphe Adam. Wettge gradually added more works by French contemporaries, especially Delibes and Saint-Saëns. In the summer of 1896, Massenet joined Gounod and Thomas as the favorites, followed by Verdi, Meyerbeer, Messager, Auber, Delibes, and Wagner. Increasingly, there were also fantasies on French operas recently premiered in Paris, such as Massenet's *Navarraise, Esclarmonde,* and *Le Cid*; Bruneau's *Attaque du Moulin* and *Messidor*; Saint-Saëns's *Ascanio* and *Samson et Dalila*; and Vidal's *Maladetta*. The 1890s also show more and more French symphonic music in transcription, for example, the tone poems of Saint-Saëns and Massenet, Bourgault-Ducoudray's *Rapsodie Cambodgienne*, and Grieg's *Peer Gynt*. Excerpts from Wagner's *Ring* and *Parsifal* could also be heard here in transcription, especially in the 1890s. In August 1898, Parès even added opera singers to a concert, and in 1899 the Eighty-second Régiment de ligne performed a complete transcription of Massenet's *Eve*, one of the only long, complex works in their repertoire not consisting of excerpts. In the provinces and colonies, military bands often performed more recent French music than local orchestras or theaters did. This should give us pause and encourage us not to underestimate the level of popular interest in art music, the capacity of the general public to appreciate it, and the ability of amateurs to perform it.

Beginning in January 1873, Bon Marché concerts within the store consisted of fourteen or fifteen short pieces, typically ten to fifteen minutes long, with alternating solos and chorus (see fig. 13.3). These lasted two hours and twenty minutes— the same as a typical concert by Colonne's orchestra. From the beginning, the programs juxtaposed art music (mostly opera overtures, choruses, and solo excerpts) with popular genres (*chansonnettes*, monologues, and comic scenes). Occasionally these included recent works, such as excerpts from Charles Lecocq's

Kosiki performed by the wind band on 10 February 1877, only four months after its premiere at the Théâtre de la Renaissance. That concert ended with a spoof entitled "Titi at a Performance of *Robert-le-diable*," suggesting that at least some of their public could identify with the experience of attending the Opéra. These concerts are a fascinating example of concerts shared by professionals and amateurs, for even with the addition of stars from the Opéra, the Comédie-Française, and the most famous Parisian cabarets, employees performed in at least half of the works presented.

The summer concerts of the Bon Marché resembled military band concerts in length and repertoire. Most presented six works and included an overture, an air, an instrumental solo, and one to three opera fantasies (increasing to three to five in 1887; see fig. 13.2). Marches began many concerts; polkas ended them, as in military band concerts. The conductor and an elected committee of four to eight member-performers chose the repertoire. Beethoven, Mozart, and Berlioz are absent from the programs until 1896. Wagner first appears on them in 1879, coinciding with the return of his music to the Concerts Pasdeloup after a two-year hiatus. Like military bands, the Bon Marché wind band programs included recently composed French work, as well as old music by Méhul, Grétry, and Rameau. From the 1870s through the 1890s, eighteen opera fantasies the band performed were based on new works. For example, they did Saint-Saëns's *Henry VIII* in July 1883 after its premiere at the Opéra that March and his *Phryné* a year after its Opéra-Comique premiere in May 1893. They played a fantasy of Massenet's *Hérodiade* the summer after its premiere in Brussels, almost two years before its Paris premiere. Only months after premieres or recent revivals at various Paris theaters, they also performed fantasies on Gounod's *Roméo et Juliette*, Victor Massé's *Paul et Virginie*, Offenbach's *La Fille du tambour major* and *Belle Lurette*, Emile Paladilhe's *Patrie*, Robert Planquette's *Les Voltigueurs* and *Rip*, Gaston Serpette's *Madame le Diable*, and, two years after their premieres, Reyer's *Sigurd* together with Massenet's *Le Cid* and *Esclarmonde*. Most of these remained in their repertoire, suggesting wide-ranging aesthetic tastes. Perhaps a product of the store's interest in fashion, Bon Marché concert organizers were astutely aware of what elite institutions were performing and were intent on keeping their audiences abreast of the newest developments.

Bon Marché concerts allow us to examine changes in audiences' tastes from the 1870s through the 1890s (see table 13.2). Early on, Italian opera fantasies dominated the programs. Other works (e.g. by Meyerbeer and Auber) coincided with what was being performed in theaters and by military bands. In the 1880s, under Paulus and Wettge, however, this focus of the repertoire shifted. Music by living French composers (e.g. Gounod, Massenet, Paladilhe, Delibes, Reyer, and Chabrier) rose to 40 percent, with Italian opera fantasies dropping to 25 percent. As elsewhere, music by living French composers grew still more prevalent in the 1890s, rising to 47 percent. Gounod's presence also increased over this decade, as did Wagner's. Perhaps reflecting a more general decline in their popularity, performances of

TABLE 13.2. Concerts in the Square, Repertoire of the Bon Marché Wind Band

1870s	1880s	1890s
Donizetti (9)	Verdi (17)	Gounod (27)
Verdi (9)	Rossini (16)	Wagner (25)
Lecocq (6)	Donizetti (14)	Meyerbeer (13)
Meyerbeer (4)	Gounod (14)	Verdi (12)
Rossini (3)	Offenbach (12)	Thomas (11)
Auber (3)	Meyerbeer (11)	Delibes (11)
von Suppé (3)	Planquette (10)	Saint-Saëns (10)
Guiraud (3)	Auber (9)	Donizetti (10)
Bellini (2)	Joncières (9)	Rossini (8)
Rameau (2)	Wagner (9)	Massenet (8)
Wagner (2)	Massenet (7)	Bizet (8)
Miscellaneous solos,	Paladilhe (7)	Auber (6)
polkas, waltzes, etc.	Lecocq (5)	Chabrier (6)
	Halévy (5)	Bellini (5)
	Delibes (5)	Offenbach (4)
	Bizet (5)	Hérold (4)
	Hérold (5)	Paladilhe (4)
	Reyer (5)	
	Chabrier (5)	
	Thomas (4)	
	Liszt (4)	
Italian opera (23 of 59 on this list), 39%	Italian opera (53 of 209), 25%	Italian opera (34 of 213), 16%
	Gounod, 7%	Gounod, 13%
	Wagner, 4%	Wagner, 12%
Living French composers (14), 24%	Living French composers (83 of 209), 40%	Living French composers (98 of 213), 47%

Italian operas dropped to 16 percent.[38] Further study of the precise repertoire shared with Paris theaters will shed light on the meaning of this evolution in musical tastes.

38. As with premieres of new French works, Bon Marché performances of Italian opera sometimes followed premieres and revivals in various Parisian theaters. For example, they did fantasies from *Aida* only months after the Opéra premiere in 1880, *Rigoletto* soon after performances there in 1885, and *La Traviata* after those of 1886. In *Le Ménestrel* (10 January 1892), a critic points to declining taste for Italian opera in Europe, noting that the number of troupes performing it in Italy as well as elsewhere decreased from twenty-eight in 1883 to nineteen in 1892 (14).

In the 1870s and 1880s, the Sunday concerts at the Jardin Zoologique d'Acclimatation had a similar formula, only the programs were twice as long. Most, presenting eight to ten works, started with a march, ended with a light work such as a
dance, and included opera fantasies and overtures. This was the case without exception during the 1881 season:

Part 1	Part 2
March	Potpourri opera/march/other
Overture	Polka/solo
Opera fantasy	Opera fantasy
Waltz (Mayeur)	Dance/march

That summer, the most frequently performed composers were Mayeur himself,
followed by Auber, Sellenick, Rossini, Meyerbeer, Donizetti, Verdi, and Strauss. Massenet, Gung'l, and Fahrbach also appeared. In the 1890s, after the construction of
the Palais d'Hiver, the zoo's concerts became a home for more serious music. The
Wednesday concerts presented symphonies and Opéra singers for the first time. On
5 April 1893, audiences heard Saint-Saëns's Symphony no. 3 (C Minor, op. 78), and
on 17 May Beethoven's Symphony no. 1 (C major, op. 21). Pister also began promoting more French music, especially by his contemporaries, at all of his concerts.
The press followed his Wednesday series with particular excitement. In addition to
Saint-Saëns, Massenet, and Widor, lesser known composers Paul and Lucien Hillemacher and a young Prix de Rome winner, Pierre Letorey, appeared there to conduct
their own music. In 1895, Pister fashioned their Sunday concerts to compete with the
contemporary music series at the Opéra, offering some of the same repertoire. Later
in the century, Jacques Lafitte initiated one-composer festivals with large choruses
and opera singers, a formula popularized by Colonne and Lamoureux.

Thus, to understand how music was used to mediate differences of class and
culture, we need to understand how those contexts overlapped, which works appeared in elite, bourgeois, and working-class venues, and what those works meant
to multiple publics (a study beyond the scope of this essay). This entails examining
a broad range of data, much of it derived from transient material culture, and
interrogating its social as well as musical significance. We also need to see that
women, through their magazine consumption, use of piano transcriptions, and
choral societies, were not the only ones domesticating art music. Men, too, especially through wind bands, contributed to blurring the boundaries of art and
consumer society. And, to the extent that Parès got his way, men explored feminine
as well a masculine forms of expressivity in their performances. We need to admit
further that using music for commercial ends had some benefits. Concerts attracting people to commercial venues made art music—even operas and symphonic poems by living French composers—available to the masses as well as
the elites. Just as consumer goods in department stores became "instruments of

instruction and politics," so, too, could concerts play an important role in pro-moting social change.[39]

Perhaps the most striking conclusion of this study is the dramatic increase of new music on concert programs in the 1890s. We know that in 1891 the government, through its Cahier de Charges, forced the Opéra to perform more new works. Despite this, elites increasingly gravitated to music representing the distant past, seeking to shelter their hopes and ideals from the realities of the bourgeois Republic. Those hoping to improve their lot in life, by contrast, remained focused on the present. Whether they were roused by Auber's, Meyerbeer's, and Rossini's overtures to operas about great men or they preferred *Patrie, Henry VIII*, and *Messidor*, which were about the social and political aspirations of common people, we cannot know how the lower classes understood this music. Still, this study has shown that they willingly performed and listened to new works as well as traditional favorites. We should not then assume that ordinary people liked only what they already knew, or that the march of progress meant the march of the classical German canon. The ideal of using music and musical tastes as a form of democratization had some success, especially in disseminating modern French music to the general public. Perhaps just as important as elites' increasing embrace of museum culture, this fusion of art and consumer culture set the stage for modernist reaction.

SAMSON AND DALILA: BECOMING POPULAR

Saint-Saëns's opera *Samson et Dalila* offers a good example of how a work became popular and raises important questions about the process of popularization. The Opéra did not lead the way, yet by the time it finally produced the work in 1892, *Samson et Dalila* was already hailed as the composer's most popular. The story of how this paradox emerged leads us to examine other aspects of the musical world—performers, transcriptions, and popular venues. These initiated the public to the work and kept it before them. Without pressure from them, the Opéra might never have performed *Samson et Dalila*.

The first performance consisted of excerpts—a piano transcription of act 2, with the composer accompanying Pauline Viardot in her salon, purportedly in 1868 and 1874. The Opéra's director may have heard one of these, but he refused to stage the work, finding it more oratorio than opera. Colonne gave the first orchestral performance of act 1 on Good Friday in March 1875. Clearly he meant to do the composer a favor, scheduling it with Beethoven's ever popular Ninth Symphony on a day when everyone went to concerts. The concert was indeed well attended—

39. McCracken, *Culture and Consumption*, 28.

ticket sales at the door were the highest for the season. This success led Colonne to program "Dance of the Priestesses" the following January and may have convinced Durand to publish Saint-Saëns's piano transcription of it later that year. When Weimar agreed to produce the opera in 1877, with the composer conducting, Durand published a piano-vocal score of the entire opera in French and German for 15 francs and an eleven-page piano fantasy based on the work, called "Reminiscences," by Henri Cramer.[40]

The story of why Weimar took on the opera goes beyond the well-known story of Liszt's intervention and is worthy of closer examination. In brief: Saint-Saëns had enjoyed a good career in Germany as a respected performer of Austro-German music, especially the works of Mozart. Although Frenchmen disagreed, some Germans considered him an alternative to Wagner, "one of the few not taken in" by him.[41] *Le Journal de musique* contextualized this premiere abroad by comparing it to the performance of Delibes's *Sylvia* in Vienna and by finding glory in the export of French music. In part to draw attention to it, in August 1877 the journal reproduced a piano transcription of the "Dance of the Priestesses." Colonne repeated this with his orchestra in November, while Pasdeloup did the "Bacchanale." The following year, Ernest Guiraud made a version of both excerpts for piano four-hands. Already by 1877, then, both publishers and performers had perceived these two excerpts as capable of achieving popularity, despite the absence of dancers.

Thus, before its theatrical premiere in France in 1890, French audiences got to know *Samson et Dalila* through multiple performances of orchestral excerpts as well as piano transcriptions and airs. In the 1880s, Colonne performed fragments of the work at eight concerts, with Saint-Saëns conducting selections from act 3 on Good Friday in 1880. Lamoureux, too, performed excerpts in 1884, 1885, and 1889. And Opéra singers, such as Gabrielle Krauss and Marie-Hélène Brunet-Lafleur, sang airs in private homes, for example, at that of Countess Greffulhe in April 1884.

On 3 March 1890, the Rouen premiere at the Théâtre des Arts, known for supporting new works, stimulated a new wave of interest, as did the Paris premiere that October at the Eden Théâtre, famous for its exotic spectacles but not opera. Both settings attracted the musical cognoscenti, but few others. Thankfully, critics

---

40. In my "Contingencies of Meaning in Transcriptions and Excerpts: Popularizing *Samson et Dalila*," in *Approaches to Meaning in Music*, ed. Byron Almén and Edward Pearsall (Bloomington: Indiana University Press, 2007), 170–213, I discuss the important role played by orchestral excerpts and transcriptions for piano or wind band not just in popularizing *Samson et Dalila*, but especially in shaping public perception of its meaning over time.

41. Hans von Bülow, "Samson et Dalila," *La Renaissance musicale* (7 May 1882): 145. This was written after the Hamburg premiere and originally published in *Allgemeine deutsche Musik-Zeitung*.

embraced the work immediately, calling it Saint-Saëns's best for the theater. Others helped draw attention to it as well: *Le Figaro* published "Dalila's song" on 19 March 1890 (see fig. 13.4), and fantasies for easy piano, for piano and violin, and for wind band followed.Colonne opened his concert season the following fall again with the "Bacchanale" and the "Dance of the Priestesses," repeating the "Bacchanale" a month later. Amateurs also began to perform the work widely. The piano students of Mme Bosquet-Luigini, for example, played piano four-hand versions in their recital that May. Military bands performed excerpts in September and October 1890, and the Bon Marché wind band opened its 1891 season that June with the wind-band transcription.

FIGURE 13.4. "Chant de Dalila," from Saint-Saëns's *Samson et Dalila,* reproduced in the newspaper *Le Figaro* (19 March 1890). Courtesy of the Bibliothèque Nationale.

Still, the Paris Opéra did not produce the opera until 1892, and then only because of pressure from previous productions in the provinces (Bordeaux, Toulouse, Nantes, Dijon, and Montpellier) and abroad (Geneva, Monte Carlo, Algiers, New York, and Florence). At the Opéra's first performance, beginning on 23 November, although Colonne conducted it from memory, Blanche Deschamps-Jehin was unconvincing as Dalila, her talents being perceived as "a little too bourgeoise."[42] Moreover, throughout that December, another new work of far less significance, Alix Fournier's one-act opera *Stratonice* (1892), was performed before it.[43] For reasons I explain elsewhere, however, the work caught on. Sixty-one performances followed in two years, as did transcriptions for other instrumental combinations. Interestingly, after being produced as an opera, *Samson and Dalila* left the repertoire of major orchestras, but joined that of military and wind bands (see fig. 13.2). From July 1892 through 1894, there were over sixty-one military band performances in more than a dozen Paris gardens. No one in Paris was deprived of hearing the work. Indeed, it would be hard to imagine anyone not being familiar with some aspect of it by the time the Opéra gave its hundredth performance in 1897.

This example suggests that theaters did not always determine which operas the public heard and came to appreciate. Even after *Samson et Dalila* entered the Opéra's repertoire, other musical organizations, especially military bands, may have done more to popularize it. Such circumstances challenge the direction, tempo, and dynamics of Simmel's trickle-down theory, together with any notions we may have about the Opéra's hegemony or its mechanisms of control. Repertoire moved in multiple directions, both up and down as well as across organizational categories, defying differences not only in musical genre but also in listeners' class, education, politics, and location. To understand this, one must acknowledge connections and dialectical relationships within the music world and ask a broader range of questions than modernists have been willing to consider. When works like *Samson et Dalila* were performed by and for amateurs as well as professionals, provincials as well as Parisians, and in a wide diversity of venues, both private and public, they lived up to the three definitions of the popular discussed here. We may not know exactly how such music was understood, but we know how, when, and where it was performed—in other words, how it was used.

What is a work in the context of so many diverse uses? This chapter proposes that not only do discourses help to articulate the musical object; so do its mediators—performances in whatever form or format, venues, and publics. The

42. F. Régnier,"Premières Représentations. Opéra. *Samson et Dalila*," *Le Journal* (24 November 1892).

43. Emile Eugène Alix Fournier (1864–1897), a pupil of Delibes, won a Deuxième Second Grand Prix de Rome in 1889. Louis Gallet wrote the libretto of his one-act opera, *Stratonice*, published by Paul Dupont in 1892. Interestingly, the reviews of *Samson of Dalila* I've consulted do not even mention this work on the same program.

identity of the work, then, together with its intertextual meanings, is not just musical but also social, and like all social identities, as Tia DeNora has pointed out, "emerges from its interaction and juxtaposition to others, people and things."[44] From this perspective, *Samson et Dalila* was part of a shared tradition and, because French, one associated with the nation.

44. DeNora, *Music in Everyday Life*, 31.

Appendix 1 DEFINITIONS OF TERMINOLOGY USED IN CHAPTER 1

DISCOURSE

"[Discourse] is language being performed." (Christian Metz, *Film Language*, trans. M. Taylor [New York: Oxford University Press, 1974; originally published as *Essais sur la signification au cinema*, 1967], 25.)

Discourse is "the means by which the content is communicated"; its manifestation in a medium, involving order and selection. (Seymour Chatman, *Story and Discourse* [Ithaca, N.Y.: Cornell University Press, 1978], 19.)

NARRATABLE

Means "worthy of telling." (Jonathan Culler, *The Pursuit of Signs* [Ithaca, N.Y.: Cornell University Press, 1981], 184.)

"The narratable: the instances of disequilibrium, suspense, and general insufficiency from which a narrative appears to arise. This term is meant to cover the various incitements to narrative, as well as the dynamic ensuing from such incitements." (D. A. Miller, *Narrative and Its Discontents* [Princeton, N.J.: Princeton University Press, 1981] ix.)

NARRATIVE (RÉCIT)

"Narrative is a closed discourse of unclosed events that proceeds by unrealizing a temporal sequence of events." (Metz, *Film Language*, 28.)

Narrative is a "discourse that undertakes to tell of an event or series of events." (Gérard Genette, *Narrative Discourse*, trans. J. E. Lewin [Ithaca, N.Y.: Cornell University Press, 1980; originally published as *Discours du récit*, 1972], 25.)

"Narrative discourse consists of a connected sequence of narrative statements" (i.e., expression of events or existents). (Chatman, *Story and Discourse*, 31.)

Narrative discourse is "a locus of the figurative representations of different forms of human communication produced from tension and of returns to equilibrium." A narrative schema is "the narrative organization of discourses," the series of establishments, breaks, reestablishments of contractual obligations between sender and receiver. A narrative strategy orders the arrangements and intertwinings of narrative trajectories, or the series of simple or complex narrative programs (i.e. the elements of narrative syntax "composed of an utterance of doing governing an utterance of state"). (A. J. Greimas and J. Courtés, *Semiotics and Language*, trans. L. Crist et al. [Bloomington: Indiana University Press, 1982; originally published as *Sémiotique*, 1979], 203–8, 245.)

Narrative is "a way of interpreting, valuing, and presenting" in a certain order a series of events chosen for their "appropriateness to a thematic structure." (Culler, *The Pursuit of Signs*, 171–72, 178.)

Narrative is "one method of recapitulating past experiences by matching a verbal sequence of clauses to the sequence of events which (it is inferred) actually occurred." (William Labov, *Language in the Inner City* [Philadelphia: University of Pennsylvania Press, 1972], 359–60.)

Narrative time "mediates" between two dimensions. "The episodic dimension of a narrative draws narrative time in the direction of the linear representation of time," "an open series of events" which "follow upon one another in accord with the irreversible order of time"; the configurational dimension "transforms the succession of events into one meaningful whole" and, through this reflective act, translates the plot into one "thought," which is its "point" or "theme." To make a narrative, that is, concretely to lead a situation and characters from some beginning to some end, requires the mediation of recognized cultural configurations; that is, plot-types handed down by tradition. (Paul Ricoeur, "Narrative Time," *Critical Inquiry* 1, no. 7 [1980]: 178–79; *Time and Narrative*, vol. 1, trans. K. McLaughlin and D. Pellauer [Chicago: University of Chicago Press, 1984; originally published as *Temps et récit*, vol. 1, 1984], 66–67.)

NARRATIVITY

"The organizing principle of all discourse, whether narrative or non-narrative"; narrativity governs the production and reading of this kind of discourse and depends on the perceiver's narrative competence (i.e., syntagmatic intelligence). (Greimas and Courtes, *Semiotics and Language*, 209.)

"The narrativity of a text is the manner by which a text is decoded as narrative." (Mieke Bal, *Narratologie* [Paris: Klincksieck, 1977], 5.)

One law of narrativity is "the ability or rather the necessity of proceeding like a series of options directed by the narrator." (Claude Bremond, *Logique du récit* [Paris: Seuil, 1973], 99.)

Narrativity is "the language structure that has temporality as its ultimate reference." (Ricoeur, "Narrative Time," 169.)

SIGNIFICATION

A process "the act which binds the signifier and the signified, an act whose product is the sign." (Roland Barthes, *Elements of Semiology*, trans. A. Lavers and C. Smith [Boston: Beacon Press, 1967; originally published as *Eléments de sémiologie*, 1964], 48.)

"The minimum structure any signification requires is the presence of two terms and a relationship linking them." (Greimas, cited by Metz, *Film Language*, 16.)

"Signification presupposes perception (of the terms and their relation)." (Greimas, cited by Metz, *Film Language*, 16.)

Signified

The succession of events that are subjects of this discourse and its series of internal relations. (Genette, *Narrative Discourse.*)

The signified is the narrative content, or story (*histoire*). (Genette, *Narrative Discourse;* Bal, *Narratologie.*)

Signifier

The material mediator of the signified. (Barthes, *Elements of Semiology*, 47.)

The signifier signifies the signified by means of connotation (i.e., using style, genre, symbol, poetic atmosphere) or denotation (i.e., by diegesis, or reciting of the facts). (Metz, *Film Language.*)

Story (Histoire)

"A series of events" (the passage from one state to another) "which are logically related" (i.e., ordered in time and space) "and caused or undergone by actors" (something that acts). (Bal, *Narratologie*, 4.)

A story is "the content of the narrative expression," a chain of events (actions and happenings) and existents (characters and setting). (Chatman, *Story and Discourse*, 19, 23.)

Appendix 2 Public Performances and Publications of Music by Augusta Holmès

Opera

Opéra de Paris

La Montagne noire (13 times in 1895)

Orchestral Concerts in Paris

Société Philharmonique de Paris

In exitu (1873)

Société Nationale

In exitu (7 December 1872)
Overture to the opera *Astarté* (15 May 1875)
Prelude to *Héro et Léandre* (20 April 1879)

Société des Concerts du Conservatoire

Les Argonautes, part 3 (4, 11 January 1885)
Ludus pro patria (4, 11 March 1888)
Hymne à Apollon (22, 29 January 1899)

Concerts Pasdeloup[1]

Les Argonautes (26 March and 24 April 1881, 26 February 1882)
Irlande (26 March 1882, 26 November 1882)

1. According to Elizabeth Bernard in "La Vie symphonique à Paris entre 1861 et 1914" (thesis, Doctorate, 3rd cycle, in history, University of Paris 1, 1976), the Concerts Pasdeloup performed Holmès's music thirteen times between 1879 and 1887. In Holmès's archives at

Pologne! (9 December [played twice], 16 December 1883, 25 April 1884 at Trocadéro, 27 March 1887)

Concerts Lamoureux[2]

Irlande (21 October 1885, 5 December 1886, 27 November 1887, 22 December 1901)

Sociéte d'Auditions Emile Pichoz

Pologne! (17 May 1888 at the Opéra-Comique)

Concerts Colonne

Andante pastorale (14 January 1877)
Une Vision de Sainte-Thérèse (17 March 1889)
Ludus pro patria, "La Nuit et l'amour" (6 June 1889, for the Universal Exhibition at Trocadéro, 25 October 1891, 19 February 1893, and 24 February 1894)
Ode triomphale (11, 12, 14, 18, 21 September 1889)
Contes mystiques—a collaborative work to which she contributed a movement along with Paladilhe, Widor, Fauré, and others (28 December 1890, 11 January 1891, 27 March 1891)
Au Pays bleu (8, 15, 22 March 1891, 21 February and 6 March 1892)
Irlande (2 February 1890, 3 November 1890, 22 March 1896, 16 April 1899)
Kypris (1897)
Andromède (14 January 1900)
(her image appeared on the cover of their concert program, 14 February 1892)
Holmès read her poem "A César Franck" after intermission during the third performance of Franck's *Béatitudes* (9 April 1893)

Salle Erard

Hymne à la paix and various songs (7 March 1891)[3]

Théâtre d'Application, La Bodinière

"Noël" (19 December 1891)
"Le Retour du paladin" (22 February 1892)
"Fleurs des champs" (5, 9 June 1894)
"Les Griffes d'or" (22 December 1894)
"Hymne à Eros" (25 December 1894)
"Contes Mystiques" (5, 12 December 1896)

---

the Bibliothèque Nationale, Paris, a press clipping suggests that he also conducted her "Chanson de la Caravane" in 1867.

2. Bernard has found only four performances of Holmès's music at the Concerts Lamoureux ("La Vie symphonique").

3. Edouard Colonne conducted the chorus, accompanied at the piano by Holmès and M. Maton. Mme. Colonne sang her songs during the first half of this concert.

Jardin Zoologique d'Acclimatation

Irlande (28 April 1895)

Bon Marché, Société chorale

"Noël" (30 January 1886)

Société chorale d'Amateurs (Guillot de Sainbris)

Ludus pro patria (March 1892)
Lutèce (28 February 1897)

Théâtre de l'Ambigu

"Les Griffes d'or" (26 May 1898)

Salle d'Horticulture

"Le Chevalier Belle-étoile" (February 1901)

Société des Matinées Artistiques Populaires, Théâtre de la Renaissance

"Le Chevalier Belle-étoile" (13 March 1901)

Le Salon du *Figaro*

"L'Heure d'azur" (6 April 1904)
"Le Chevalier Belle-etoile" (6 April 1904)

Concerts Rouge (surveying only 1903–4)

Sérénade printanière (25 Oct 1903)
Irlande (22 November 1903, 9 January 1904, 3, 22 April 1904, 6 November 1904, 15 December 1904)

Concerts Touche

Sérénade printanière (17 February 1907)
Irlande (17 March 1907)

Féte nationale (the military bands of the first Régiment du génie and the first Brigade d'artillerie de Vincennes with the Galin-Paris-Chevé chorus)

"Triomphe de la République," from *Ode triomphale* (22 September 1892)

PROVINCIAL CONCERTS

Association Artistique d'Angers

Pologne! (11 November 1883)
Lutèce (30 November, 1 December 1884)

Aix-les-Bains (Colonne conducting)

Ludus pro patria (July 1888)

Nancy

Ludus pro patria (13, 14 May 1893)

Concerts populaires de Nantes (January 1891)

"La Nuit et l'amour" from *Ludus pro patria*
Sérénade printanière
"Les Griffes d'or"

Festival Augusta Holmès, Tours (conducted by Holmès, 4 June 1899)

Ludus pro patria
Au Pays bleu, "En mer"
Eight melodies

Festival Augusta Holmès, Société Philharmonique de Bourges (May 1901)

"Belle du roi"
"Noël d'Irlande"
Au Pays bleu

Association symphonique de l'Ecole nationale du Conservatoire de musique, Roubaix (31 January 1904)

Florence, Italy

Hymne à la paix (May 1890)

SELECTED PUBLICATIONS IN NEWSPAPERS AND MAGAZINES

Le Figaro

"Noël," *chanson populaire* (23 December 1885)
"Le Clairon fleurie," *chanson populaire* (20 July 1887)
"Les Griffes d'or" (29 May 1889)

Ode triomphale (3 October 1889)
La Montagne noire (13 February 1895)
"A Trianon" (11 July 1896)

L'Illustration

"C'est ici le jardin du rève," from *La Montagne noire*, act 4 (9 February 1895)

La Vie de famille

"Serenade de toujours" (13 September 1891)
(her image appeared on the cover of the 13 March 1892 issue)

La Famille

"Noël" (27 December 1891)

Figaro Musical

"L'Hymne des prêtresses de Vénus," from *Héro et Léandre* (November 1891)

Le Ménestrel

"La Barque des amours" (3 April 1892)
"L'Oiseau bleu" (13 November 1892)
"La Belle du roi" (26 November 1893)
"La Chatte blanche" (11 February 1894)
"L'Eternelle idole" (6 May 1894)
"La Guerrière" (15 July 1894)
"Les Trois Serpentes" (10 March 1895)
"Les Voix du rève" (17 October 1897)
"Noël d'Irlande" (14 November 1897)
"L'Heure d'azur" (16 December 1900)

La Quinzaine musicale

Kypris (15 April 1895)

Appendix 3 RELATIONSHIP BETWEEN NEA SUPPORT AND COMPOSERS' EDUCATIONAL BACKGROUND

Number of NEA grants[a]	Degrees unknown	Highest degree:[b] M.M./M.S.	M.A./M.F.A.	D.M.A.	Ph.D./Ed.D.
Six			Kim (UC Berkeley) $41,190		
		*Kolb (Hartt) $32,350			
Five			Rorem (Juilliard) 34,750		
				Walker (Eastman) $27,750	
			McKinley (Yale U) 23,500		
Four		Rands (U Wales) 29,150			
				Hodkinson (U Michigan) 25,800	
		Ashley (Manhattan) 21,280		Schwantner (Northwestern U) 21,450	
		Burton (Peabody) 20,350		Bolcom (Stanford U) 20,250	

Number of NEA grants[a]	Degrees unknown	Highest degree:[b] M.M./M.S.	M.A./M.F.A.	D.M.A.	Ph.D./Ed.D.
			Stock (Brandeis U) 18,200		
			Wuorinen (Columbia U) 15,200)		
		Glass (Juilliard) 14,200		Milburn (CCM) 14,150	
				Smart (Yale U) 13,700	
			W. Kraft (Columbia U) 13,150		
			Lentz (Ohio U) 11,950		
		*Semegen (Yale U) 8,400			
Three		Reynolds (U Michigan) 21,200			
		*P. McLean (Indiana U) 21,120			
			Lucier (Brandeis U) 20,320		Fetler (U Minnesota) 19,950
		Zupko (Juilliard) 18,700			
		Asia (Yale U) 18,625			
	Calabro (Juilliard) 17,280			Rodriguez (USC) 17,150	
				Fox (Indiana U) 16,950	

Number of NEA grants[a]	Degrees unknown	Highest degree:[b] M.M./M.S.	M.A./M.F.A.	D.M.A.	Ph.D./Ed.D.
			Del Tredici (Princeton U) 15,250		
	Baur (CCM) 14,200	Wernick (Mills) 14,140	Lieberson (Columbia U) 13,800	Rouse (Cornell U) 14,000	
		*Hays (U Wisconsin) 12,750		Chihara (Cornell U) 12,950	
		Parris (U Penn) 12,700		Consoli (Yale) 12,000	Logan (U Iowa) 12,000
		*Garwood (Philadelphia) 11,630			Fennelly (Yale U) 11,750
	Helps (UC Berkeley) 10,250	Koblitz (U Michigan) 10,200	Trimble (Carnegie-Mellon U) 10,000	Dodge (Columbia U) 10,300	
			Kohn (Harvard U) 10,000		Stokes (U Minnesota) 10,150
			Martino (Princeton U) 9,800		Reale (U Penn) 9,850
		Rhodes (Yale U) 9,225	Lazarof (Brandeis U) 9,150	R. Nelson (Eastman) 8,900	
				*Tower (Columbia U) 8,750	
	R. Hoffman (UCLA) 8,450				
	F. Thorne (Yale) 7,650	Curtis-Smith (Northwestern U) 7,625	Heiss (Princeton U) 7,700		Moss (USC) 7,650
			Adler (Harvard U) 6,300		London (U Iowa) 6,250
					Julian (UCSD) 6,150

461

Number of NEA grants[a]	Degrees unknown	Highest degree:[b] M.M./M.S.	M.A./M.F.A.	D.M.A.	Ph.D./Ed.D.
					*Barkin (Brandeis U) 5,250
		Ballard (U of Tulsa) 4,825	Pleskow (Columbia U) 4,800		Schwartz (Columbia U) 4,850
					Penn (Michigan S U) 4,500
Two				Erb (Indiana U) 17,250	
		Curran (Yale U) 16,200	R. Berger (Columbia U) 16,000		
	W. Hendricks 15,600		Harbison (Berlin) 15,000	McNabb (Stanford U) 15,000	
			Hykes (Columbia U) 14,700	M. Harris (Juilliard) 14,700	Perle (NYU) 14,450
					Karchin (Harvard U) 14,000
					Weisgall (Johns Hopkins U) 13,500
		Bubalo (Chicago Mus) 13,450	Lerdahl (Princeton U) 13,100		D. Jones (UCSD) 13,300
	Antoniou (Greece) 12,950	Snow (Yale U) 12,920	Subotnik (U Penn) 13,000		
	Kupferman (Queens Col) 12,950				
	*Dlugoszewski (Mannes) 12,500	Rochberg (U Penn) 12,500		Rush (Stanford U) 12,660	
					Ussachevski (Eastman) 12,500

Number of NEA grants[a]	Degrees unknown	Highest degree:[b] M.M./M.S.	M.A./M.F.A.	D.M.A.	Ph.D./Ed.D.
					Dembski (Princeton U) 12,420
	Krenek (Austria) 12,000		S. Silverman (Mills) 12,000		
					Argento (Eastman) 11,700
		Nurock (Juilliard) 11,500			Sur (Harvard U) 11,600
			Wright (Columbia U) 11,000		Downey (Sorbonne) 11,100
	Mayer (Mannes) 10,750	Stalvey (CCM) 10,700	M. Levy (Columbia U) 10,700		
	*Chance (Columbia U) 10,500	Korte (Juilliard) 10,450	Hoiby (Mills) 10,650		
		*Mamlock (Manhattan) 10,420	Moran (Mills) 10,450		
	Heinke (Stanford U) 10,100	Picker (Juilliard) 10,400			
	Feldman 10,000				
	Balada (Juilliard) 9,750				Duckworth (U Illinois) 9,800
					D. Riley (U Iowa) 9,600
					Suderburg (U Penn) 9,500

Number of NEA grants[a]	Degrees unknown	Highest degree:[b] M.M./M.S.	M.A./M.F.A.	D.M.A.	Ph.D./Ed.D.
One			Lindroth (Yale U) 11,000	S. Smith (U Illinois) 11,000	
				Brooks (U Illinois) 11,000	
	Schurmann (Royal College) 10,000			Hackbarth (U Illinois) 10,800	
	Diamond (Eastman) 10,000		Chou Wen-Chung (Columbia U) 10,000	Carter (ENM, Paris) 10,000	
	Myrow (USC) 10,000		Dempster (San Fran SC) 10,000	Crumb (U Michigan) 10,000	
				Persichetti (Philadelphia) 10,000	
			Babbitt (Princeton U) 9,500	Clayton (U Michigan) 9,500	Lansky (Princeton U) 9,600
	Tudor 9,600				
Total	20 unknown degrees	27 M.M./M.S.	31 M.A./M.F.A.	25 D.M.A.	24 Ph.D./Ed.D.

[a]Composers were not allowed to apply for a composer-librettist grant in consecutive years.
[b]Master of Music (M.M.), Master of Science (M.S.), Master of Arts (M.A.), Master of Fine Arts (M.F.A.), Doctor of Musical Arts (D.M.A.), Doctor of Philosophy (Ph.D.), and Doctor of Education (Ed.D.). See note 24 for an explanation of what earning the M.M., M.A., D.M.A., and Ph.D. degrees entail. The M.S. and the M.F.A. are roughly the equivalent of the M.M., while the Ed.D. is a degree in the field of education, with music as a specially rather than as a primary focus.
*Woman composer.

Conclusions of Appendix 3

3a. Women in this sample receiving NEA support (noted above with *), their degrees, and the percentage of female degrees vs. male degrees:

Total	2	6	0	1	1
10	unknown	M.M./M.S.	M.A./M.F.A.	D.M.A.	Ph.D./Ed.D.
(8%)	degrees	(22%)		(4%)	(4%)
	(10%)				

3b. Distribution of total amount of awards to composers receiving at least $9,500 or at least three grants:

11%	over $20,000
58%	10,100–20,000
31%	4,500–10,000

Distribution by educational level

Unknown degrees	0%	Over $20,000
	57%	10,100–20,000
	43%	4,500–10,000
M.M./M.S.	**23%	Over $20,000
	62%	10,100–20,000
	**15%	4,500–10,000
M.A./M.F.A.	13%	Over $20,000
	55%	10,100–20,000
	32%	4,500–10,000
D.M.A.	16%	Over $20,000
	60%	10,100–20,000
	24%	4,500–10,000
Ph.D./Ed.D.	**0%	Over $20,000
	54%	10,100–20,000
	**46%	4,500–10,000

**Significant deviation from the mean

3c. Comparison of highest degree with the age of the composer:

Birth date	M.M./M.S.	M.A./M.F.A.	D.M.A.	Ph.D./Ed.D.
1900–09	0%	0%	4%	0%
1910–19	4%	3%	4%	13%
1920–29	21%	26%	13%	22%
1930–39	42%	48%	31%	26%
1940–49	29%	13%	44%	30% + 1
1950–59	4%	10%	4%	9%

3d. Distribution of institutions from which grantees graduated by region:

Most highly represented institutions (all East Coast)	*40 = 34%*
Columbia University	13
Yale University	11
Juilliard School	9
Princeton University	7

Other institutions on the East Coast	*33 = 28%*
Eastman (University of Rochester)	5
University of Pennsylvania	5
Brandeis University	5
Harvard University	4
Cornell University	2
Philadelphia Conservatory	2
Manhattan School	2
Mannes School	2
Carnegie-Mellon University	1
New York University	1
Johns Hopkins University	1
Queens College (CUNY)	1
Hartt School	1
Peabody School	1

Total East Coast institutions	*73 = 62%*

Midwest institutions	*27 = 23%*
University of Michigan	5
University of Illinois	4
University of Iowa	3
University of Indiana	3
C.C.M. (University of Cincinnati)	3
University of Minnesota	2

Northwestern University	2
University of Wisconsin	1
Ohio University	1
Michigan State University	1
Chicago Musical College	1
University of Tulsa	1

West Coast institutions	*17 = 15%*
Mills College	4
Stanford University	4
University of Southern California	3
University of California, Berkeley	2
University of California, San Diego	2
San Francisco State College	1
University of California, Los Angeles	1

3e. Women in this sample receiving NEA support (noted above with *), by region:

Total	East Coast (w/o NY)	New York	Midwest	West	California	Abroad
10 (8%)	20	49	3	7	13	3

The information in appendices 3 through 6 has been obtained from ten major sources, plus the various editions of each source: *Contemporary American Composers: A Biographical Dictionary*, first edition, compiled by E. Ruth Anderson (Boston, 1976) and second edition (Boston, 1982); *Contemporary American Composers based or affiliated with American Colleges and Universities*, compiled by Hugh Wm. Jacobi(y) (Paradise, California, 1975); Neil Butterworth, *A Dictionary of American Composers* (New York, 1984); *Dictionary of Contemporary Music*, edited by John Vinton (New York, 1974); *Directory of Music Faculties in American Colleges and Universities, 1968–1970*, compiled and edited by Harry B. Lincoln (College Music Society, 1968); *Directory of Music Faculties in Colleges and Universities, U.S. and Canada, 1970–1972*, compiled and edited by Harry B. Lincoln (College Music Society, 1970), plus the 1974–76 edition, compiled and edited by Craig R. Short (College Music Society, 1974), the 1978–80 edition (College Music Society, 1979), the 1980–82 edition (College Music Society, 1980), the 1982–84 edition (College Music Society, 1983), and the 1984–86 edition, compiled and edited by Robby Gunstream (College Music Society, 1985); *Directory of New Music*, 1979 edition, edited by Carol Cunning (Los Angeles, 1979) plus the 1980 edition, the 1981 edition, and the 1982–83 edition; *The New Grove Dictionary of Music and Musicians*, edited by Stanley Sadie (London, 1980); *The New Grove Dictionary of American Music*, edited by H. Wiley Hitchcock and Stanley Sadie (London, 1986); *Who's Who in American Music: Classical*, first edition, edited by Jaques Cattell Press (New York, 1983) and second edition (New York, 1985). I wish to thank my two research assistants Toshie Kakinuma and Eduardo Larin for help in compiling the information needed to make these tables.

Number of grants (total award)	University (department of music or school of music)[a]	Conservatory	College	Non-teaching position (or job unknown)
Six ($30,000– 42,000)	Kim (Harvard U, 1975, 1977, 1979, 1981, 1983, 1985)			
	*Kolb (Brooklyn, CUNY, 1975; Temple U, 1979)			*Kolb (1973, 1977, 1981, 1984)
Five ($23,000– 35,000)		Rorem (Curtis, 1980, 1983, 1985)		Rorem (1975, 1978)
	Walker (Rutgers U, 1973, 1979, 1982; U Delaware 1977)	Walker (Peabody, 1975)		
		McKinley (New England, 1976, 1977, 1979, 1981, 1983)		
Four ($20,100– 23,000)	Rands (UCSD, 1977, 1978, 1982, 1984)			

Number of grants (total award)	University (department of music or school of music)[a]	Conservatory	College	Non-teaching position (or job unknown)
($10,100–20,000)	Hodkinson (Eastman, 1975, 1977, 1979, 1983)			
	Schwantner (Eastman, 1974, 1975, 1977, 1979)		Ashley (Mills, 1976, 1978, 1981, 1984)	
	Burton (George Mason U, 1974, 1977, 1980, 1983)			
	Bolcom (U Michigan, 1974, 1975, 1979, 1982)			
	Stock (U Pittsburgh, 1978, 1983)		Stock (Antioch, 1974)	Stock (1976)
	Milburn (Rice U, 1974, 1975, 1977, 1983)	Wuorinen (Manhattan, 1974, 1976, 1978)		Wuorinen (1980)
	Smart (U Alaska, 1974; Wykeham Sch, 1975; U Wyoming 1978, 1980)			Glass (1974, 1975, 1978, 1980)
	W. Kraft (Queens, CUNY, 1975; USC, 1977)			Kraft (1969, 1979)
			Lentz (Antioch, 1973)	Lentz (1975, 1977, 1980)

Number of grants (total award)	University (department of music or school of music)[a]	Conservatory	College	Non-teaching position (or job unknown)
($4,500–10,000)	*Semegen (SUNY, Stony Br, 1974, 1976, 1979, 1980)			
Three ($20,100–22,000)	Reynolds (UCSD, 1975, 1977, 1979)			
	*P. McLean (U Hawaii, 1985)			*P. McLean (1979, 1981)
			Lucier (Wesleyan, 1977, 1981, 1984)	
($10,100–20,000)	Fetler (U Minnesota, 1975, 1977, 1982)			
	Zupko (Western Mich U, 1978, 1980, 1985)		Asia (Oberlin, 1985)	Asia (1978, 1980)
	Rodriguez (USC, 1975; U Texas, 1980, 1983)		Calabro (Bennington 1973, 1976, 1980)	
	Fox (Indiana U, 1976, 1979, 1982)			
	Del Tredeci (Boston U, 1974, 1975; CUNY 1984)			
	Baur (Tulane, 1978; Memphis S U, 1982)	Baur (Shenandoah Cons, 1974)		

Number of grants (total award)	University (department of music or school of music)[a]	Conservatory	College	Non-teaching position (or job unknown)
	Wernick (U Penn, 1975, 1979, 1981)			
	Lieberson (Harvard U, 1985)			Lieberson (1975, 1980)
	Rouse (U Michigan, 1980; Eastman, 1984)			Rouse (1976)
	Chihara (UCLA, 1977)	Chihara (Cal Arts, 1975)		Chihara (1980)
				*Hays (1977, 1979, 1982)
	Parris (George Wash U, 1974, 1976, 1983)		Logan (Oberlin, 1974, 1978, 1984)	Consoli (1979, 1980, 1984)
	Fennelly (NYU, 1977, 1979, 1984)		*Garwood (Mulenburg, 1977, 1981)	*Garwood (1973)
		Helps (Manhattan, 1974, 1975)		Helps (1977)
	Koblitz (Pace U, 1975, 1979)			Koblitz (1983)
	Dodge (Columbia U, 1974, 1975; CUNY 1979)	Trimble (Juilliard, 1975, 1979, 1984)		
	Stokes (U Minnesota, 1974, 1975, 1977)		Kohn (Pomona, 1975, 1976, 1979)	
($4,500– 10,000)	Martino (Brandeis U, 1979)	Martino (New England, 1974, 1976)		

Number of grants (total award)	University (department of music or school of music)[a]	Conservatory	College	Non-teaching position (or job unknown)
	Reale (UCLA, 1976, 1978, 1980)		Rhodes (Carleton, 1974, 1975, 1976)	
	Lazarof (UCLA, 1975, 1977, 1979)			
	R. Nelson (Brown U, 1974)			R. Nelson (1969, 1977)
			*Tower (Bard, 1974, 1975, 1979)	
			R. Hoffman (Oberlin, 1976, 1977, 1979)	
		F. Thorne (Juilliard, 1973)		F. Thorne (1976, 1979)
	Curtis-Smith (Western Mich U, 1975, 1980; U Michigan, 1977)	Heiss (New England, 1973, 1975, 1980)		
	Moss (U Maryland, 1975, 1977, 1980)			
	Adler (Eastman, 1974, 1978, 1980)			
	London (U Illinois, 1973, 1975; Cleveland S U, 1979)			Julian (1974, 1975, 1976)
	*Barkin (UCLA, 1974, 1976, 1978)			Ballard (1971, 1975, 1977)

Number of grants (total award)	University (department of music or school of music)[a]	Conservatory	College	Non-teaching position (or job unknown)
	Pleskow (Long Island U, 1974, 1975, 1977)			
	Schwartz (UCSB, 1974)		Schwartz (Bowdoin, 1976, 1980)	
	Penn (Eastman, 1974, 1975; Howard U, 1979)			
Two ($10,100–20,000)	Erb (Southern Meth U, 1984)	Erb (Cleveland Inst, 1980)		R. Berger (1983, 1985)
	Curran (Italy, 1978)			Curran (1984)
	Harbison (MIT, 1974, 1977)			W. Hendricks (1983, 1985)
	M. Harris (Fordham U, 1983, 1985)			McNabb (1979, 1984)
	Perle (Queens, CUNY, 1977, 1983)			Hykes (1978, 1982)
	Karchin (NYU, 1982, 1983)	Weisgall (Peabody, 1975; Juilliard, 1977)		
	Bubalo (Cleveland S U, 1977, 1984)			
	Lerdahl (Harvard U, 1977; Columbia U, 1981)			
	D. Jones (UCSC, 1982)			D. Jones (1978)

Number of grants (total award)	University (department of music or school of music)[a]	Conservatory	College	Non-teaching position (or job unknown)
		Antoniou (Philadelphia, 1975, 1977)		Snow (1981, 1984)
		Subotnick (Cal Arts, 1974, 1978)	Kupferman (Sarah Lawrence, 1974, 1977)	
	Rochberg (U Penn, 1973, 1975)			*Dlugoszewski (1975, 1979)
	Rush (Stanford U, 1975, 1981)			
	Ussachevski (Columbia U, 1974, 1975)		Dembski (Dartmouth, 1979, 1981)	S. Silverman (1976, 1979)
	Argento (U Minnesota, 1974, 1977)			Krenek (1977, 1980)
	Sur (MIT, 1976, 1978)			Nurock (1978, 1984)
	Wright (Boston U, 1979; Temple U, 1982)			
	Downey (U Wisconsin, Milwaukee, 1977, 1982)		Stalvey (Immaculate Heart, 1975, 1978)	Mayer (1976, 1984)
	M. Levy (Brooklyn, CUNY, 1974)			Levy (1978)
	Korte (U Texas, 1975, 1977)			*Chance (1980, 1982)
				Hoiby (1975, 1980)

Number of grants (total award)	University (Department of music or school of music)[a]	Conservatory	College	Non-teaching position (or job unknown)
	*Mamlock (CUNY, 1974)	*Mamlock (Manhattan, 1981)		Picker (1979, 1981)
	Moran (Northwestern U, 1977)			Moran (1979)
				Heinke (1975, 1978)
($4,500–10,000)	Feldman (SUNY, Buffalo, 1974, 1977)			
	Balada (Carnegie-Mellon U, 1977, 1980)			
	Duckworth (Bucknell U, 1977, 1983)			D. Riley (1980, 1983)
	Suderburg (U Washington, 1974)	Suderberg (North Carolina, 1984)		
One ($10,100–11,000	S. Smith (U Maryland, 1984)			Lindroth (1984)
				Brooks (1982)
	Hackbarth (Arizona S U, 1983)			
	Chou Wen-Chung (Columbia U, 1975)	Diamond (Juilliard, 1977)		Schurmann (1984)
		Carter (Juilliard, 1976)		

Number of grants (total award)	University (Department of music or school of music)[a]	Conservatory	College	Non-teaching position (or job unknown)
	Dempster (U Washington, 1978)			Myrow (1985)
	Crumb (U Penn, 1977)	Persichetti (Juilliard, 1976)		
	Lansky (Princeton U, 1981)			Tudor (1981)
	Babbitt (Princeton U, 1975)	Babbitt (Juilliard, 1975)		Clayton (1984)
Total 329	168 grants to university professors (51%)	38 grants to conservatory teachers (11.5%)	38 grants to college professors (11.5%)	85 grants to others (26%)

Total to professors: 74%

This table complements appendix 3 in giving the university, conservatory, or college for which the NEA winner was working at the time the grant(s) were received, or the composer's independent status. The dates in parentheses are those of the grants. The vertical order of the names follows exactly that of appendix 3.

Conclusions of Appendix 4

4a. Among those with teaching positions, the distribution of the total amount of awards to composers receiving at least $9,500 or at least 3 grants was as follows:

A.	At universities	70%	of those winning over $20,000
		70%	10,100–20,000
		62%	4,500–10,000
	At conservatories	30%	of those winning over $20,000
		11%	10,100–20,000
		27%	4,500–10,000
	At colleges	0%	of those winning over $20,000
		19%	10,100–20,000
		11%	4,500–10,000
B.	East Coast institutions	70%	of those winning over $20,000
		57%	10,100–20,000
		68%	4,500–10,000
	Midwest institutions	12%	of those winning over $20,000
		25%	10,100–20,000
		16%	4,500–10,000
	Western institutions	18%	of those winning over $20,000
		18%	10,100–20,000
		16%	4,500–10,000

4b. Distribution of institutions at which the grantees were teaching:

	Number of grantees per institution
41 East Coast institutions	
27 universities	
Eastman University of Rochester	4
Columbia University	3
Harvard University	3
University of Pennsylvania	3
Princeton University	2
Boston University	2
New York University	2
Brooklyn, CUNY	2
Queens, CUNY	2
MIT	2
University of Maryland	2
16 others	1

	Number of grantees per institution
7 conservatories	
Juilliard	7
Manhattan	3
New England	3
Peabody	2
3 others	1
7 colleges	1

Total East Coast: 55%

17 Midwest institutions

13 universities	
University of Michigan	3
University of Minnesota	3
Western Michigan University	2
Cleveland State University	2
9 others	1
1 conservatory	
Cleveland Institute	1
3 colleges	
Oberlin	3
Antioch	2
Carleton	1

Total Midwest: 23%

16 Western institutions

12 Universities	
University of California, LA	4
University of California, SD	2
University of Southern Califorina	2
University of Washington	2
8 others	1
1 conservatory	
Cal Arts	2
3 colleges	1

Total Western: 22%

4c. Distribution of the ages of composers not in teaching positions when they received one or more NEA grants:

Birth date: 1900–1909	1910–1919	1920–1929	1930–1939	1940–1949	1950–1959
2%	0%	24%	27%	31%	16%

4d. Grants to women in this sample receiving NEA support (noted above with *), their institutional affiliations, and percentage of women vs. men with these affiliations:

Total women 16	5 grants to university professors	1 grant to conservatory teachers	2 grants to college professors	8 grants to others
(4.9% of all grantees) % to women	(3%) 31%	(2.7%) 6%	(5.3%) 12%	(9.4%) 50%
Total men 313	163 grants to university professors	37 grants to conservatory teachers	36 grants to college professors	77 grants to others
(95.1% of all grantees) % to men	(97%) 52%	(97.3%) 12%	(94.7%) 11.5%	(90.6%) 24.5%

Appendix 5 EDUCATIONAL BACKGROUND AND INSTITUTIONAL AFFILIATION OF MOST FREQUENT NEA PANELISTS

Number of times on NEA panel	Name (years on panel)[a]	Educational background (highest degree)	Institutional affiliation
Seven	Laderman (1973–1979; P,C)	Columbia U (M.A.)	State University of New York, Binghamton
Six	Avshalomov (1974–1979; P)	Eastman (M.M.)	Nat. Council of Hum, (ex-prof, Columbia U)
Five	Erb (1975–1979; P,C)	Indiana U (D.M.A.)	Cleveland Inst Music
	*V. Fine (1975–1979; C)		Bennington College
	*Oliveros (1975–1979; C)	San Francisco S C (B.A.)	U California, San Diego
	Ruggeri (1975–1979; P)	Eastman (B.M.)	U Wisconsin (bass, Milwaukee Symphony)
	Ward (1974–1978; C)	Eastman (B.M.)	North Carolina Sch for the Arts, president; Duke U
Four	Felciano (1974–1977; C)	U Iowa (Ph.D.)	U California, Berkeley
	Husa (1977–1980; C)	Prague (D.M.A.)	Cornell U

Number of times on NEA panel	Name (years on panel)[a]	Educational background (highest degree)	Institutional affiliation
	Schuller (1969, 1974, 1977, 1979; P)	Manhattan Sch	New England Cons, president; Nat Council for the Arts
	Subotnik (1973, 1980–82; C)	Mills (M.F.A.)	Calif Inst for the Arts
	Suderburg (1976–1979; C)	U Penn (Ph.D.)	North Carolina Sch for the Arts, president
Three	Adler (1982–1985; C)	Southern Meth U (D.M.A.)	Eastman
	Argento (1978, 1979, 1981; C)	Eastman (Ph.D.)	U Minnesota
	Campos-Parsi (1980–1982; C)		Arts Administrator, Puerto Rico
	Dodge (1980–1982; C)	Columbia U (D.M.A.)	Brooklyn, CUNY
	Druckman (1980–1982; P,C)	Juilliard (M.S.)	Yale U
	Gould (1973–1975; P)	Juilliard	Conductor, New York
	Kay (1981–1983; C)	Eastman (M.M.)	CUNY, Lehman, BMI
	*Leon (1980–1982; C)	New York U (M.S.)	Music dir, Dance Theater of Harlem
	Lloyd (1974–1976; C)	New York U (M.A.)	Ex-dir, Rockefeller Fd; ex-prof, Juilliard, Oberlin
	London (1983–1985; C)	U Iowa (Ph.D.)	Cleveland S U
	Mann (1972–1974; P)	Juilliard (diploma)	Juilliard; violin, Juilliard Quartet
	Persichetti (1977–1979; C)	Philadelphia Cons (D.M.A.)	Juilliard

Number of times on NEA panel	Name (years on panel)[a]	Educational background (highest degree)	Institutional affiliation
	*Ran (1980–1982; C)	Mannes	University of Chicago
	*Semegen (1983–1985; C)	Yale U (M.M.)	SUNY, Stony Brook
	Smith (1978–1980; C,P)	Cleveland Inst (M.M.)	U Connecticut
	W. Thompson (1972–1974; P)	Indiana U (Ph.D.)	Cleveland Inst, U Arizona
	*Tower (1980–1982; C)	Columbia U (D.M.A.)	Bard College, Da Capo Chamber Players
	Weisgall (1978–1980; C)	Johns Hopkins U (Ph.D.)	Juilliard

[a]This table lists only those composers who served on NEA planning panels (P) or on composer/composer-librettist panels (C) at least three times; it specifically excludes participation on other NEA panels.
*Woman panelist.

Conclusions of Appendix 5

5a. Distribution of schools from which panelists received their highest degree:

Eastman	5
Columbia University	3
Juilliard	3
New York University	2
Indiana University	2
University of Iowa	2
10 others	1

5b. Distribution of their degrees:

Unknown	2 (2 women)
B.A., B.M.	3 (1 woman)
M.M.	6 (2 women)
M.A.	2
D.M.A.	6 (1 woman)
Ph.D.	7

5c. Distribution of institutional affiliation:

7 administrative/other	1 (2 women)
15 universities	1 (3 women)
5 conservatories	
Juilliard	3
Cleveland Institute	2
North Carolina	2
2 others	1
2 colleges	1 (2 women)

Principal grant recipient[a]	Date, amount	University affiliation	Links to panelists
Rochberg	1973 $10,000	U Pennsylvania	
Calabro	1973 10,000	Bennington College	

Total 1973 recipients in universities: 2/2

Harbison	1974 10,000	MIT	
*V. Fine	1974 8,000	Bennington College	
Wilder	1974 8,000	Free-lance study at Eastman	Panelists Avshalomov, Ward studied at Eastman
Burton	1974 7,500	George Mason U	
Argento	1974 7,500	U Minnesota, Ph.D. Eastman	Panelists Avshalomov, Ward studied at Eastman
Ussachevski	1974 7,500	Columbia U, Ph.D. Eastman	Panelist Davidovsky, Columbia U; Panelists Avshalomov, Ward studied at Eastman
Kupferman	1974 7,500	Sarah Lawrence College	

Principal grant recipient[a]	Date, amount	University affiliation	Links to panelists
Subotnick	1974 7,000	Cal Institute of the Arts	

Total 1974 recipients in universities: 7/8

Principal grant recipient[a]	Date, amount	University affiliation	Links to panelists
Chou Wen-Chung	1975 10,000	Columbia U	Panelist Davidovsky, Columbia U
Hodkinson	1975 10,000	Eastman	Panelists Avshalomov, Ruggeri, Ward studied at Eastman
Babbit	1975 9,500	Princeton U, Juilliard	
Floyd	1975 7,500	Fla State U	Panelist for Opera grants, 1975
Imbrie	1975 7,500	U California, Berkeley	Panelist Felciano, U California, Berkeley
Reynolds	1975 7,500	U California, San Diego	Panelist Oliveros, U California, San Diego
Fetler	1975 7,500	U Minnesota	
Walker	1975 7,500	Peabody, D.M.A Eastman	Panelists Avshalomov, Ruggeri, Ward studied at Eastman
Antoniou	1975 7,500	Philadelphia Conservatory	

Total 1975 recipients in universities: 9/9

Principal grant recipient[a]	Date, amount	University affiliation	Links to panelists
Carter	1976 10,000	Juilliard	Panelist Lloyd, ex-prof Juilliard, 1946–63
Persichetti	1976 10,000	Juilliard	Panelist Lloyd, ex-prof Juilliard, 1946–63
Brant	1976 8,000	Free-lance, study at Juilliard	Panelist Lloyd, ex-prof Juilliard, 1946–63

Principal grant recipient[a]	Date, amount	University affiliation	Links to panelists
Phillips	1976 8,000	Retired, ex-prof Eastman, 1933–49; Juilliard 1968–69; M.M. Eastman	Panelists Avshalomov, Ruggeri, Ward studied at Eastman
Silverman	1976 8,000	Free-lance	
Lewis	1976 6,650	Peabody; Ph.D. Eastman	Panelists Avshalomov, Ruggeri, Ward studied at Eastman
Shifrin	1976 6,450	Brandeis U, M.A. Columbia U	Panelist Laderman studied at Columbia U

Total 1976 recipients in universities: 4/7

Crumb	1977 10,000	U Pennsylvania	Panelist Suderburg, Ph.D., U Pennsylvania
Diamond	1977 10,000	Juilliard, studied at Eastman	Panelist Persichetti, Juilliard
Weisgall	1977 8,500	CUNY, Queens, part time Juilliard	Panelist Persichetti, Julliard
Feldman	1977 7,000	SUNY, Buffalo	Panelist Laderman, SUNY Binghamton
Nolte	1977 6,250	Free-lance?	
Reynolds	1977 6,200	U California, San Diego	Panelist Oliveros, U California, San Diego

Total 1977 recipients in universities: 5/6

Dempster	1978 10,000	U Washington (M.A. San Francisco State Coll)	Panelist Oliveros studied at San Francisco State Coll
Heinke	1978 7,600	Free-lance, studied at Stanford U	Panelist Rush, Stanford U
*Amacher	1978 7,600	Free-lance	
Levine	1978 7,400	Bennington College	Panelist Fine, Bennington College
Sur	1978 7,100	MIT	

Total 1978 recipients in universities: 3/5

Principal grant recipient[a]	Date, amount	University affiliation	Links to panelists
*Dlugoszewski	1979 7,500	Free-lance	
Reynolds	1979 7,500	U California, San Diego	Panelist Oliveros, U California, San Diego
Schwantner	1979 7,500	Eastman	Panelists Avshalomov, Ruggeri, Argento studied at Eastman
Walker	1979 5,500	Peabody, D.M.A. Eastman	Panelists Avshalomov, Ruggeri, Argento studied at Eastman

Total 1979 recipients in universities: 3/4

Erb	1980 8,250	Cleveland Inst	Ex-panelist, 1975–79
Krenek	1980 7,500	Free-lance	
Rorem	1980 6,750	Curtis, M.A. Juilliard	Panelist Weisgall, Juilliard
Wuorinen	1980 6,300	Free-lance, M.A. Columbia U	Panelists Dodge, Tower studied at Columbia U
Schiff	1980 5,700	Free-lance	
Asia	1980 5,625	Free-lance, studied at Yale U	Panelist Druckman, Yale
Kievman	1980 5,550	Free-lance, M.F.A. Cal Arts	Panelist Subotnik, Cal Arts

Total 1980 recipients in universities: 2/7

Lansky	1981 9,600	Princeton U, studied at Princeton U	
Lerdahl	1981 9,600	Columbia U M.F.A. Princeton U	Panelists Dodge, Tower studied at Columbia
Tudor	1981 9,600	Free-lance	
Jenni	1981 9,120	U Iowa	
Dembski	1981 9,120	Dartmouth, Ph.D. Princeton U	

Principal grant recipient[a]	Date, amount	University affiliation	Links to panelists
Total 1981 recipients in universities: 4/5			
Bolcom	1982 11,000	U Michigan	
Brooks	1982 11,000	Free-lance	
Rands	1982 11,000	U California, San Diego	
Fox	1982 10,000	Indiana U	
Downey	1982 9,000	U Wisconsin	
Hykes	1982 9,000	Free-lance, Studied at Columbia U	Panelists Dodge, Tower studied at Columbia U
Schoenfield	1982 9,000	U Toledo	
Total 1982 recipients in universities: 5/7			
R. Berger	1983 12,000	Free-lance, Studied at Columbia U	
Hackbarth	1983 10,800	Free-lance	
Kim	1983 10,800	Harvard U	
Rorem	1983 10,800	Curtis	
Hodkinson	1983 9,000	Eastman	Panelist Adler, Eastman
Perle	1983 9,000	CUNY, Queens	Panelist Kay, CUNY, Lehman
Total 1983 recipients in universities: 4/6			
Rands	1984 12,000	U California, San Diego	
*Kolb	1984 11,500	Free-lance	
Lindroth	1984 11,000	Free-lance, studied at Eastman, Yale U	Panelist Semegen studied at Yale U; panelist Adler taught at Eastman

Principal grant recipient[a]	Date, amount	University affiliation	Links to panelists
S. Smith	1984 11,000	U Maryland	
Rouse	1984 11,000	Eastman	Panelist Schwantner, Eastman
Curran	1984 10,000	Free-lance, studied at Yale U	Panelist Semegen, studied at Yale U
Schurmann	1984 10,000	Free-lance	
McNabb	1984 10,000	Free-lance	

Total 1984 recipients in universities: 3/8

Kim	1985 12,000	Harvard U	
Myrow	1985 10,000	Free-lance	
Lieberson	1985 9,500	Harvard U	
*P. McLean	1985 9,500	U Hawaii	
G. Smith	1985 9,000	Free-lance	

Total 1985 recipients in universities: 3/5

[a]Recipients listed here are those who received the highest grants each year, as determined by the distribution breakdown outlined in table 11.2. This table demonstrates the flux in NEA policy from year to year with regard to grants to university-affiliated or free-lance composers and, in conjunction with appendix 5, permits examination of any preferential treatment that may have resulted, coincidentally or not, from common educational background or institutional affiliation.

* Woman composer.

6a. Women among the Highest Annual Grant Winners:

4 of 79 = 5%

Their associations at the time of their grants:

Free-lance	3
Bennington College	1
Hawaii	1

6b. Preferred educational background for highest annual grant winners:

Eastman	8	3 in 1974, 1975, 2 in 1976, 1977, 1979 (0 after 1979)
Columbia University	4	1976, 1980, 1982, 1983
Yale University	3	1980; 2 in 1984
Princeton University	3	3 in 1981
Juilliard	2	1976, 1980

6c. Preferred institutional affiliation for highest annual grant winners:

UC San Diego	5	1975, 1977, 1979, 1982, 1984
Eastman	4	1975, 1979, 1983, 1984
Columbia University	3	1974, 1975, 1981
Harvard University	3	1983; 2 in 1985
CUNY Queens	2	1977, 1983

Institutions with composers winning grants up to 1979, but none from 1979 to 1985:

Juilliard	4	1975; 2 in 1976, 1977
Bennington	3	1973, 1974, 1978
Peabody	3	1975, 1976, 1979
MIT	2	1974, 1978
University of Minnesota	2	1974, 1975
University of Pennsylvania	2	1973, 1977

Index

Note: Page numbers in *italics* refer to illustrations or musical examples; a *t* following a page number indicates a table.